Also by Geoffrey Nelson and Isaac Prilleltensky:

Doing Psychology Critically: Making a Difference in Diverse Settings (2002)*
Promoting Family Wellness and Preventing Child Maltreatment: Fundamentals for Thinking and Action (2001) (with L. Peirson)

Also by Geoffrey Nelson:

Shifting the Paradigm in Community Mental Health Towards Empowerment and Community (2001) (with J. Lord & J. Ochocka)

Also by Isaac Prilleltensky:

Critical Psychology: An Introduction (1997) (with D. Fox)
The Morals and Politics of Psychology: Psychological Discourse and the Status Quo (1994)

* Also by Palgrave Macmillan

This book is dedicated to all our community partners and our students, graduate and undergraduate, who have taught us so much about community psychology.

Contents

About the Authors

Geoffrey Nelson is Professor of Psychology at Wilfrid Laurier University and a member of the MA and PhD programs in community psychology. Geoff was senior editor of the *Canadian Journal of Community Mental Health*, and he is a fellow of the Society for Community Research and Action (Division 27, Community Psychology, of the American Psychological Association). He is co-editor of *Promoting Family Wellness and Preventing Child Maltreatment: Fundamentals for Thinking and Action* (University of Toronto Press, 2001), senior author of *Shifting the Paradigm in Community Mental Health: Towards Empowerment and Community* (University of Toronto Press, 2001), and second author of *Doing Psychology Critically: Making a Difference in Diverse Settings* (Palgrave Macmillan, 2002). Together with the Canadian Mental Health Association/Waterloo Region Branch, he was the recipient of the McNeill Award for Innovation in Community Mental Health from the American Psychological Foundation and the Society for Research and Action of the American Psychological Association in 1999.

Isaac Prilleltensky is Professor and Director of Graduate Studies in the Department of Human and Organizational Development at Vanderbilt University in Nashville, Tennessee, where he also directs the PhD program in community research and action. He is the author of *The Morals and Politics of Psychology: Psychological Discourse and the Status Quo* (State University of New York, 1994), co-editor of *Critical Psychology: An Introduction* (Sage, 1997), senior editor of *Promoting Family Wellness and Preventing Child Maltreatment: Fundamentals for Thinking and Action* (University of Toronto Press, 2001), and senior author of *Doing Psychology Critically: Making a Difference in Diverse Settings* (Palgrave Macmillan, 2002). Isaac is also a fellow of the Society for Community Research and Action (Division 27, Community Psychology, of the American Psychological Association). He was formerly the director of the MA program in community psychology at Wilfrid Laurier University in Canada and Professor of Psychology and Director of the Wellness Promotion Unit at Victoria University in Australia.

Chapter Authors

Ed Bennett is Professor of Psychology, Wilfrid Laurier University, (WLU), Waterloo, Ontario, Canada. Ed has served as a social justice worker in the classroom and in the community for over 35 years. He initiated the first community psychology courses and field placement experiences at WLU in 1971 and the community psychology MA program at WLU in 1976. He served as the program's director for many years. In the 1970s, Ed played a provincial and national leadership role in advocating for many community-based prevention and health promotion policy initiatives. During the 1980s he served as the co-founder and co-editor of the *Canadian Journal of Community Mental Health* and edited three books including, *Social Intervention: Theory and Practice* (1987). During the past 15 years Ed has focused on community-based economic development as a form of primary prevention. He co-founded Sand Hills Co-operative Homes Inc. (a multicultural housing cooperative) in 1989 and a non-profit community economic development corporation in 1999, in the rural area where he lives. Since 1992, he has worked with the Old Order Amish of Ontario on land use planning challenges, sustainable agricultural practices and strategies to adapt to global economic restructuring. He has helped to initiate several community-based economic development ventures including the Mornington Heritage Cheese and Dairy Co-operative Inc., which now has sales across Canada. Most recently he provided the leadership for the community to buy back a century-old cheese plant in his area – the Millbank Cheese and Butter Factory, from a transnational corporation.

Mark Burton works on service development and quality in a large public sector service for people disabled through intellectual difference. His work uses ideas from community psychology and other disciplines. His more than 20 years of work have seen a major change in the location of, opportunities for, and perceptions about severely disabled people, but nevertheless there is still much to do, particularly to facilitate real inclusion and meaningful community life. Mark is Head of Development and Clinical Services, Manchester Learning Disability Partnership, Visiting Professor of Disability Service Development and Evaluation, University of Northumbria at Newcastle, and Honorary Lecturer at Manchester Metropolitan University. Outside paid work Mark is active in international solidarity work with progressive social movements.

Pat Dudgeon was born in Darwin, Northern Territory. Her people are Bardi, from Kimberley on the north-west coast of Australia. She is a psychologist and current head of the Centre for Aboriginal Studies at Curtin University. For several years she has been active in the discipline of psychology, particularly with the Australian Psychological Society, serving as convenor of the interest group Aboriginal Issues, Aboriginal People and Psychology.

Associate Professor **Adrian Fisher** was born in Perth, Australia. Aside from some time travelling overseas, he lived and worked in Perth for most of his young life. When he was about 24, he worked with community health in the remote Kimberley Region of Western Australia, where the main client group was Australian Aborigines. Following this, he returned to Perth to study psychology. He then became a sojourner, travelling to the United States as a graduate student, where he remained for more than five years and earned his PhD at the University of Illinois at Urbana-Champaign. Adrian returned to Australia, taking up a university post developing and teaching community psychology programs in Melbourne. His main interests are psychological sense of community and its impact on social identity, particularly in relation to inclusion and exclusion processes.

Dr Marewa Glover is a Maori woman of Nga Puhi, Irish and English descent. She has majored in psychology from her undergraduate years at the University of New South Wales in Sydney, Australia, through to masters at the University of Waikato, where she concurrently studied for a diploma in community psychology. Since 1995, she has worked as a Maori health consultant/contract researcher undertaking a range of evaluation research, advisory roles and training jobs, particularly in public health and more specifically in the area of tobacco control. Her doctoral research was on Maori smoking cessation behaviour. She is currently a *Hohua Tutengaehe* Postdoctoral Research Fellow in Applied Behavioural Science at the University of Auckland.

Heather Gridley coordinates one of Australia's two postgraduate programs in community psychology at Victoria University in Melbourne. Her interest in community psychology stemmed from her work in community health, where she became aware of the limitations of interventions directed solely at individuals. Heather's teaching, research and practice are based on feminist principles, and in 1995 she received the Australian Psychological Society's (APS) Elaine Dignan Award for significant contributions concerning women and psychology. She has held national positions in both the APS College of Community Psychologists and Women and Psychology interest group, and has served two terms on the APS board of directors. Her career history as a humanities-based psychologist with a passionate commitment to social justice bridges the practitioner–academic divide.

Gary W. Harper joined the faculty in the Department of Psychology at DePaul University in Chicago during the 1995–96 academic year, where he is currently an Associate Professor. Gary is the Program Director of DePaul University's clinical-community doctoral training program, Co-Director of the university's Center for Community and Organization Development, and Co-Chair of the university's HIV/AIDS task force. He recently served as chair of the American Psychological Association's Committee on Psychology and AIDS and is currently a member of the American Psychological Association's Committee on Lesbian, Gay, and Bisexual Concerns. The focus of Gary's research and community work is on improving the psychological and physical well-being of various groups of adolescents and young adults who are marginalized in society, including lesbian/gay/bisexual/transgender (LGBT) young people, urban ethnic-minority young people, and young people living with HIV. Gary was the founding chair of the LGBT interest group within the Society for Community Research and Action and is the co-editor of a column on LGBT issues in *The Community Psychologist*. He co-edited a special issue of *The Community Psychologist* on LGBT community interventions, as well as a special issue of the *American Journal of Community Psychology* on linking theory, research, and action related to LGBT people and communities.

Ingrid Huygens was born in Auckland, New Zealand, to Dutch immigrants. Her master's thesis concerned attitudes by New Zealanders to the accents of Dutch, English and Maori speakers. She has been working as a community psychologist since 1983 and as a pakeha (white) anti-racism educator and decolonization worker since 1989. She is currently undertaking doctoral research at the University of Waikato into processes of conscientization for the pakeha dominant culture about Maori self-determination.

Carolyn Kagan is Professor of Community Social Psychology, Manchester Metropolitan University, and runs the first UK masters course in community psychology. She has worked in the main in the north west of England with people who are marginalized through poverty or disability. Much of her work has been in the collaborative development and evaluation of community projects and in facilitating system change in health and social care. She has developed a community psychological praxis that is critical, has social justice at its core, and combines social action with community and organizational development. With Mark Burton she is active in local and international solidarity work with progressive movements.

Bret Kloos is a faculty member in the clinical-community psychology program at the University of South Carolina. His work has been strongly influenced by the concepts of social ecology, dissatisfaction with the shortcomings of our mental health and social service systems, and a sense of social justice rooted in his faith tradition. Along with students and community colleagues, his work has focused on housing issues, promoting mutual help, and fostering community development to create structures that sustain people's well-being and that allow for liberation from oppressive conditions. Bret was encouraged to 'discover' community psychology during doctoral studies at the University of Illinois, Urbana Champaign because it has allowed him to pursue work that is consistent with his values. He has conducted research funded by the US National Institute of Mental Health, Center for Mental Health Services, and Department of Housing and Urban Development. He has also held positions as director of a supportive housing program and the Connecticut Self-help Network. In all of these activities, his community psychology training has provided the tools to make a difference in communities where he lives and in broader global contexts.

Maritza Montero is Professor of Social Psychology and Community Social Psychology at Universidad Central de Venezuela. Maritza has a PhD in sociology from Paris University. Since the late 1970s, her working, teaching, and writing has been in the field of community psychology. She has published several books and papers, both in Spanish and English, including *Psicología Social Comunitaria: Teoría, Método y Experiencia* (1994/2002, México, EUdG) and *La Tensión entre Comunidad y Sociedad* (2003, Buenos Aires, Argentina: Paidós). She has been visiting professor in several universities in Latin American countries and in Spain, France and England.

Leslea Peirson holds an MA degree in community psychology from Wilfrid Laurier University in Waterloo, Ontario and is currently a PhD candidate in the Department of Public Health Sciences at the University of Toronto. She has worked primarily in applied research settings and was the project manager and a co-investigator for the Family Wellness Project, a national study of best practices for the promotion of family well-being and the prevention of child maltreatment. In her home community, Leslea is a volunteer board member for a newly created organization that facilitates access to the system of ministry funded children's and developmental services.

Tod Sloan completed his doctoral work in personality psychology at the University of Michigan. He was a Professor of Psychology at the University of Tulsa (Oklahoma) from 1982–2001. He is the author of *Life Choices: Understanding Dilemmas and Decisions* (Westview, 1996) and *Damaged Life: The Crisis of the Modern Psyche* (Routledge, 1997). He also edited *Critical Psychology: Voices for Change* (Macmillan, 2000). Tod has also served as a Fulbright visiting professor in

Venezuela and Nicaragua. He is Professor and Chair in the Department of Counseling Psychology in the Graduate School of Education at Lewis and Clark College in Portland, Oregon.

Christopher Sonn was born in South Africa. At the age of 18, he emigrated to Australia with his parents and younger brothers. He faced numerous settlement challenges in the first few years including language issues, isolation, lack of familiarity with social systems and prejudice. One of the major challenges revolved around ethnic and cultural identity. In South Africa, identity was tied to the apartheid structure – it was imposed. In Australia a different set of historical and contemporary discourses inform race relations. Christopher started his studies in Melbourne soon after arriving. Ten years later, after completing his PhD, he relocated to Perth with his wife and two children to take up a position at Curtin University Technology before moving to Edith Cowan University. Christopher teaches and researches topics in cultural and community psychology, with a specific focus on community responses to intergroup contact and adversity, sense of community, and cultural competence. He is currently at Victoria University in Melbourne.

Colleen Turner's career journey spans more than a decade in applied research and community-based practice. Her work in aged and disability services in local government, migrant women's health, the Victorian AIDS Council, and earlier, within the trade union sector, together indicate the breadth and grounded nature of her experience. Colleen served on the APS Board as Director of Social Issues, bringing to the role a strong personal background and work record of achievement in real-world social issues. She is currently working as a senior researcher at the Australian Institute for Family Studies, working in the Stronger Families project using participatory action research to work collaboratively with community-based projects around Australia to enhance family and community resilience. Colleen is a doting sole parent of Jessie who provides a reality check vis-à-vis the life experiences of Australian families.

Glen W. White, PhD, has been involved in the rehabilitation and independent living field for over 30 years. He is currently Director of the Research and Training Center on Independent Living at the University of Kansas. He serves as Principal Investigator of the Research and Training Center on Full Participation in Independent Living. Dr White has had numerous opportunities to work with consumers with disabilities in identifying, developing and shaping on-going disability research. He has conducted research in the areas of housing, advocacy and developing community support for Independent Living centers, and for several years he has been developing a systematic line of research in the area of prevention of secondary conditions. He is past president of the National Association of Rehabilitation Research and Training Centers, and chair of the American Public Health Association's DisAbility Forum, and serves as an advisor and consultant to many national organizations. Dr White is currently a professor in the Department of Human Development and Family Life and directs the Research Group on Rehabilitation and Independent Living at the University of Kansas, where he teaches in the area of behavioural and community psychology, and disability studies.

Commentators

Charity S. Akotia is a Senior Lecturer in the Department of Psychology at the University of Ghana. She received her BA (Honours) from the University of Ghana and an MA from Wilfrid Laurier University, Waterloo, Ontario, Canada. She is currently a faculty member at the University of Ghana, where she teaches both undergraduate and postgraduate courses in community and social psychology respectively. Charity has performed several studies among refugees and their adjustment in Ghana. She has also conducted research on stress and coping. Currently, she is a part-time doctoral student at the University of Ghana working on obstacles that women face on their jobs. Charity is married with three children, Steven, Nigel and Michael.

George W. Albee is Professor Emeritus at the University of Vermont and Courtesy Professor at the Mental Health Research Institute, University of South Florida. He is past president of the American Psychological Association. Dr Albee was chair of the Task Panel on Manpower for President Eisenhower's Joint Commission on Mental Illness and Health, chair of the Panel on Prevention for President Carter's Commission on Mental Health and 2003 guest fellow of the British Psychological Society. He established the Vermont Conference on the Primary Prevention of Psychopathology and has co-edited (with Justin Joffe) 17 volumes on prevention.

Meg A. Bond is a professor of psychology and Director of the Center for Women and Work at the University of Massachusetts Lowell. She is a community psychologist whose work focuses on the interrelationships among issues of diversity, empowerment, and organizational processes. Meg has published and conducted research on dynamics of gender and race in the workplace, sexual harassment, and collaboration among diverse constituencies in community settings. She is particularly interested in the articulation of a feminist community psychology. Meg is an active member and former president of the Society for Community Research and Action, past chair of the APA Committee on Women, and a national board member of the Society for the Psychological Study of Social Issues. Meg is a fellow of SCRA and the American Psychological Association, as well as a member of the Senior Editorial Board for the *American Journal of Community Psychology*. Meg lives in Cambridge, Massachusetts and has two incredible and lively children, Arlyn and Erik.

Camil Bouchard, PhD, is professor at the Université du Québec à Montréal (UQAM, Department of Psychology). He has been researching and teaching family psychology and community psychology for the past 17 years of his academic career. His main research interests are: poverty and child development, poverty and child maltreatment and community-based prevention. In 1990, he was mandated by the Minister of Health and Social Services of Quebec to chair a task force on Quebec children and youth. One year later, he published a report entitled *Un Québec fou de ses enfants (Quebec crazy about its kids)* which proposed a governmental and societal agenda of actions to prevent major psychological distress and adaptation problems to children and young people. The report has been largely disseminated and has influenced government and community agencies in the adoption of several social and family policies or the pursuit of preventive approaches to childhood problems. Dr Bouchard has also been heavily involved in implementing a community-based project for children called 1, 2, 3 GO! in the area of Greater Montreal as a United Way (Centraide) volunteer. In June 1995, he was appointed as co-chair of the Quebec Commission on Welfare Reform still under discussion. From 1997 to 2001, he chaired the Conseil Québecois de la Récherche Sociale (CQRS: Quebec Social Research Council), responsible for allocating grants to social researchers and for promoting the development of social research in Quebec. Dr Bouchard is a member of the Society for Community Research and Action. He is also member of Centraide du Grand Montréal board and of the Fonds de récherche en santé du Québec board.

Rebecca Campbell, PhD, is an Associate Professor of Community/Quantitative Psychology at Michigan State University. Her current research includes studies on the community response to rape, vicarious trauma among violence against women researchers and service providers, and the evaluation of rape crisis centre services. She is the author of *Emotionally Involved: The Impact of Researching Rape* (2002, Routledge), which won the 2002 Distinguished Publication Award from the Association for Women in Psychology. Dr Campbell received the 2000 Louise Kidder Early Career Award from the Society for the Psychological Study of Social Issues (Division 9) of the American Psychological Association and the 2002 Emerging Leader Award from the Committee on Women in Psychology of the American Psychological Association.

Dennis Fox is Associate Professor of Legal Studies and Psychology at the University of Illinois at Springfield. With Isaac Prilleltensky, he co-founded RadPsyNet (radpsynet.org) and co-edited *Critical Psychology: An Introduction* (1997, Sage). His early efforts to merge communalist/anarchist/environmentalist politics – seeking the difficult goal of maximizing both individual autonomy and community well-being – with social psychology's focus on the individual–society relationship led to a series of academic essays critical of psychology's role in maintaining the legal, political and socioeconomic status quo. Fox's political commentaries and personal/political essays have been published in a variety of forums, including *Radical Teacher*, *Salon*, *Tikkun*, *Education Week*, the *Boston Globe*, *Social Anarchism*, and the *Progressive Populist*.

Suzanne Galloway is a graduate of Wilfrid Laurier's MA program in community psychology. She has been involved in creating positive alternatives at the community level (such as a car co-operative, a food co-operative, a community bike center and a local trading network) and has also been a radical cheerleader, puppeteer, and general rabble-rouser at protests against globalization in Washington, Windsor and Quebec City. She is currently interested in despair and empowerment work.

Lesley Hoatson teaches community development at Victoria University, Melbourne, Australia. She has been active in low-income communities as a community developer and social worker for such a long time that you may think she is ancient! She has also worked in community development policy, practice and training roles in federal, state and local government and in a central Australian Pitjantjatjara community. Lesley regularly provides support, supervision and training to community development practitioners around community building strategy, problem solving and conflict management. She recently co-edited a new community development text *Community Practices in Australia* (the editors are Wendy Weeks, Lesley Hoatson and Jane Dixon), that was published by Pearsons.

Adeline Levine earned a doctorate in sociology from Yale University in 1968. She was a faculty member in the Department of Sociology at SUNY/Buffalo, from 1968 to 1990. From 1972 to 1976 she chaired the Sociology Department. Her research and teaching interests include environmental issues, women and work, and race and ethnic relations. She is best known for her 1982 book *Love Canal: Science, Politics and People*. She has been a director of the Love Canal Medical Trust fund since its inception in 1984. In 1990, she became a professor emeritus.

Murray Levine, JD, PhD is Distinguished Service Professor emeritus of Psychology at SUNY Buffalo, Adjunct Professor of Law and editor of the journal *Law and Policy*. He is co-author with David Perkins of *Principles of Community Psychology* (Oxford University Press; 1st and 2nd editions) and with Leah Wallach of *Psychological Problems, Social Issues and Law* (Allyn and Bacon, 2002). For many years he directed the clinical-community psychology program at the State University of New York at Buffalo. He worked with Lois Gibbs on the first edition of *Love Canal: My Story*. He has been chairperson of the Center for Health Environment and Justice, an organization Lois Gibbs started, since its inception 20 years ago.

Colleen Loomis is Assistant Professor of Psychology at Wilfrid Laurier University in Ontario, Canada. She received her PhD in community–social psychology from the University of Maryland Baltimore County in May 2001 and was a postdoctoral scholar at Stanford University Medical Center for two years. Her research examines the meaning of sense of community and its relation to preventing alienation and promoting social responsibility. She also investigates how sense of community relates to positive and negative educational (for example literacy and numeracy) and health consequences for young people in the US, Canada and Cameroon. She has published on these and related subjects, including self-help groups, gender and power, socioeconomic class, mentoring, and bilingual education in the US. Currently, Dr Loomis is writing a manuscript exploring the conceptual boundaries and overlap between self-help, support groups, social networks, and psychological sense of community, as well as investigating the psychometric properties of the Sense of Community Index. She also serves as a consultant to the US Centers for Disease Control for the Legacy for Children project and collaborates in psychosocial research on HIV prevention and AIDS care in Cameroon.

M. Brinton Lykes is a community psychologist, activist and Professor of Community/Social Psychology at the Lynch School of Education at Boston College. She has lived and worked among women and child survivors of state-sponsored violence and war in rural Guatemala, Northern Ireland and South Africa. Her research focuses on indigenous cultural beliefs and practices and western psychology, towards creating community-based psychosocial and educational development programs. She teaches courses in participatory action research and on psychosocial perspectives on children, family and society, focusing on the USA, Latin America and South Africa. Her recent books include, *Myths about the Powerless: Contesting Social Inequalities* (1996) and a co-authored photo essay with the Association of Maya Ixil Women – *New Dawn, Voces e imágenes: Mujeres Mayas Ixiles de Chajul/ Voices and images: Maya Ixil women of Chajul* (2000).

Elba Martell, MSc, MA, received her MA in community psychology from Wilfrid Laurier University, Waterloo, Canada in 2002. Her thesis project explored the perceptions and experiences of immigrant youth involved with the Canadian justice system. Elba's interests are immigrant and refugee issues, the study of their interaction and integration to the host society and how the community responds to integration and access to services by diverse communities. Elba works currently as Health Promotion Officer with the Region of Waterloo Public Health, in Ontario, Canada, where she is involved with projects related to access and equity, food security and the development of healthy public policies that increase community capacity, participation and access to supports and services by diverse communities.

Eliseo Martell, a physician from El Salvador, holds a masters degree in public health and a master of science in public administration. Eliseo has been involved in different initiatives such as neighbourhood health committees in urban and rural communities and projects addressing health and refugee issues in Ontario, Canada. As a former president of the Ontario Public Health Association, Eliseo also has been involved in provincial and national initiatives. Some of his areas of interest are violence prevention, urban health and access of disenfranchised communities to health services with emphasis on prevention. He is currently manager of the Youth Health Program with the Region of Waterloo Public Health in Ontario, Canada.

Michael Murray is Associate Dean of Community Health and Professor of Social and Health Psychology at Memorial University of Newfoundland, St. John's, Newfoundland and Labrador, Canada. His research interests are narrative and social representation theory, qualitative research, community health action, literacy and occupational health. He is the co-author (with David Marks, Brian Evans and Carla Willig) of *Health Psychology: Theory, Research and Practice* (London: Sage, 1999), co-editor (with Kerry Chamberlain) of *Qualitative Health Psychology: Theories and Methods* (London: Sage, 1999) and editor of *Critical Health Psychology* (London: Palgrave, 2004). He has also edited three special issues of the *Journal of Health Psychology* on Qualitative Research (1998, **3**(3) with Kerry Chamberlain) on Reconstructing Health Psychology (2000) **59**(3) and on Community Health Psychology (2004) **5**(2) with Catherine Campbell).

John Robert ('Bob') Newbrough is Professor Emeritus (2001) in Peabody College of Vanderbilt University, where he continues to be very active in the life of the PhD program in community research and action, which he co-founded with Paul Dokecki. Bob is a former editor of the *Journal of Community Psychology* (1974–1989), former president of the Division of Community Psychology of the American Psychological Association (1979), past recipient of the Award for Distinguished Contribution for Research and Theory of that division (1994) and recipient of the Interamerican Psychology Award (1989). He is a board member of the Rosalyn Carter Institute for Human Development (1988–2002) and is currently on emeritus status. He has been a proponent of a 'third position' in community psychology; a perspective that moves beyond dualism and is based primarily on. John Dewey's 'transaction'. His work has been recently directed to the establishment, under the auspices of the Community Psychology Division (SCRA), of a 'Woods Hole' for community psychology through a network of local community action-research centres.

Blanca Ortiz-Torres is a professor at the University of Puerto Rico. She teaches in the graduate social/community psychology program and conducts research at the

University Center for Psychological Services and Studies. She earned a doctoral degree in community psychology at New York University and a Juris Doctor at the University of Puerto Rico. In the past 12 years she has been doing research on normative beliefs on gender, sexuality and the prevention of HIV/AIDS in New York, Puerto Rico, the Dominican Republic and Haiti. She is also involved in community development and mobilization and the study of social movements.

Randolph Potts is a member of the Association of Black Psychologists and the Society for Community Research and Action. The focus of his work has been on emancipatory education, and the relationships between spirituality and health in communities of people of African descent. For the past few years, while on the psychology faculty at Holy Cross College in Massachusetts, he facilitated a rites of passage program within a medium-security prison and worked with an African-centered academy within a public middle-school. Randolph now lives in Memphis, Tennessee, and works with LeBonheur Children's Medical Center and the Memphis City Schools.

Ora Prilleltensky earned her doctorate in counselling psychology from the Ontario Institute of Studies in Education at the University of Toronto. From 2000 to 2002 Ora taught in the counselling program at Victoria University in Melbourne, Australia. Ora is now teaching counselling in the Department of Human and Organizational Development in Peabody College at Vanderbilt University. Ora is a mother with a physical disability and the author of the forthcoming book *Motherhood and Disability: Children and Choices* (Palgrave Macmillan).

Julian Rappaport is Professor of Psychology at the University of Illinois where he has been since receiving his PhD from the University of Rochester in 1968. Rappaport is a recipient of the American Psychological Association's Division of Community Psychology Distinguished Career Award for Theory and Research in Community Psychology and Community Mental Health, and of the Seymour B. Sarason Award for 'novel and critical rethinking of basic assumptions and approaches to human services, education and other areas of community research and action'. He is a past president of the Society for Community Research and Action and editor emeritus of the *American Journal of Community Psychology*. Julian was awarded the psychology department's Graduate Student Organization Teaching/Advising Award three times, and he was the 1999 recipient of the department's Hohenboken Teaching Award for contributions to teaching and curriculum. He recently edited the first *Handbook of Community Psychology*. Julian's past research has been concerned with empowerment theory and alternatives to professional services for people who are typically labelled as dependent or disordered, and his current interests are in the relationship between community narratives and personal stories in the construction of identity and social change.

Janice L. Ristock is Professor of Women's Studies at the University of Manitoba. She is the author of *No More Secrets: Violence in Lesbian Relationships* (New York: Routledge); is the co-author of *Community Research as Empowerment: Feminist Links, Postmodern Interruptions* (Toronto: Oxford University Press); and is the co-editor of *Inside the Academy and Out: Lesbian, Gay, Queer Studies and Social Action* (Toronto: University of Toronto Press) and *Women and Social Change* (Halifax: James Lorimer Press). She works closely with many community groups on research projects that address issues of violence against women and/or anti-homophobia initiatives. She is currently guest editing a special issue of the *Canadian Journal of Community Mental Health* entitled 'Disrupting normalcy: Lesbian, gay, queer issues and mental health' which was published in the fall of 2003.

Alipio Sánchez Vidal is professor of Community Psychology and Ethics at the University of Barcelona. He is author of several books (in Spanish): two on community psychology (3rd edition to appear soon), one on the ethics of social intervention, and one on applied social psychology; editor of one on community and prevention programs and co-editor of another on community intervention. Alipio is a member of SCRA and the European Network of Community Psychologists (soon to be called the European Community Psychology Association); he conducts (empirical) research on sense of community and (theoretical-applied) research on the ethics of social intervention.

Paul Speer, PhD, is an Associate Professor in the Department of Human and Organizational Development, Peabody College at Vanderbilt University. His research interests are in community organizing, empowerment and community change. Currently he is conducting a five-year evaluation of community organizing in Brooklyn and Rochester, New York, Kansas City and northern Colorado.

Allan Strong has been employed in the social service sector for close to 20 years. He has had a variety of employment experiences, particularly in mental health. Mr. Strong is currently employed as Self-help Resource Coordinator for the Self-help Alliance in Waterloo and Wellington-Dufferin regions of Ontario.

Mary Watkins, PhD, is the Coordinator of Community and Ecological Fieldwork and Research in the depth psychology MA/PhD program at Pacifica Graduate Institute. She is the author of *Waking Dreams, Invisible Guests: The Development of Imaginal Dialogues*, the co-author of *Talking With Young Children About Adoption*, a co-editor of 'Psychology and the Promotion of Peace' (a special issue of the *Journal of Social Issues*, **44**(2)), and essays on the confluence of liberation psychologies and depth psychology. She has worked as a clinical psychologist with adults and children, and has also worked with small and large groups around issues of peace, envisioning the future, diversity, vocation, and social justice.

Note to Instructors

Instructors can obtain a sample of multiple-choice, short-answer and essay questions for each of the chapters in this text by contacting the website for Palgrave Macmillan, http://www.palgrave.com/psychology. We have also prepared exercises for students that can be used in class. Some of the exercises can be used in a small-group or class-wide discussion format, while others are meant to be personal reflections that can subsequently feed a class discussion. Most of the chapters contain these exercises.

Note to Instructors and Students

Additional resources for this text can be obtained from the website for Palgrave Macmillan: http://www.palgrave.com/psychology.

Preface

Many of you reading this book are students in a course in community psychology for which this book is the assigned text. Welcome to community psychology! We hope you find not just information and wisdom from what you read, but also inspiration and maybe even personal transformation. As a colleague of ours, Don Morgenson, once remarked, it is important for students not just to learn *about* psychology, but also *from* psychology.

Community psychology (CP) has sometimes been referred to as the social conscience of psychology. As such, we believe that CP should be on the cutting edge of social change. Throughout the book, you will be exposed to a variety of social issues and problems, equipped with analytic and research tools to help you understand and interpret those issues/problems and introduced to action tools that can be used to address them. The ways that community psychology frames and understands social issues and intervenes to create social change are often at odds with mainstream societal views about social problems and how they should be addressed. We hope that this book opens your eyes to different ways of thinking about social issues and motivates you to become active agents of social change.

Others of you reading the book are experienced community psychologists who are contemplating whether or not to adopt this book as a text for a course in CP. We hope this book suits your needs. As you will see, we are introducing some topics and perspectives that are a little different from other CP texts. Yet we have tried to balance these new topics and perspectives with a faithful adherence to the roots and core concepts that have guided the field. We hope you find our perspective and the topics covered to be valuable and re-invigorating.

We want to draw your attention to some of the features of the book. First, each chapter begins with an overview of the organization of the chapter and a warm up exercise that we encourage you to use to start thinking about the issues covered in the chapter. Second, each chapter is followed by a commentary by another community psychologist or community activist. These commentaries are designed to provide different perspectives on the material that was presented. Finally, at the end of each chapter, there is a glossary of terms and a list of various resources that you may wish to consult. Additional resources can be found at the following website: http://www.palgrave.com/psychology. We hope you find these features of the book useful.

Let us tell you now about some of the goals that we had in mind in constructing this book. First, we want to emphasize the values, social ethics and politics of CP as much as the research and scientific base of the field. Since its inception, CP has, unlike other sub-disciplines of psychology, been motivated by a set of values (Rappaport, 1977) and scientific evidence. Yet, there is a tremendous pull from mainstream psychology on CP to be scientifically respectable. As such, concerns about the trust-worthiness of research evidence and the empirical grounding of scientific theories take precedence over discourses about values and social ethics in psychology, CP, and all the social and health sciences.

Values and scientific research are not mutually exclusive. Rather, they are in a dialectical tension with one another. Just as there is no such thing as a 'value-free' science, values are not independent of evidence. Values are concerned with what *should be*, while science is concerned with what *is*. One cannot be derived from the other. Community psychologists pay attention to both values and evidence in their theory, research and action. In this text, we wanted to elevate conversations about values, value dilemmas, and how values are implemented or constrained in the work of CP. Moreover, we want a balanced and integrated discussion of the values and science of CP.

We have also been concerned that CP has focused more on personal and rela-tional values, such as well-being and collaboration, than on collective values, such as social justice. This is reflected in the theory, research and action base of CP. Thus, a second goal of the book is to re-invigorate the discussion of social injustice and the need for social action and social change. We want to inject critical, liberation and human rights perspectives into CP, perspectives that have recently coalesced into critical and liberation psychology (Fox & Prilleltensky, 1997; Prilleltensky & Nelson, 2002; Watts & Serrano-García, 2003). More explicitly, we want to advance a CP that is critical of the status quo and that actively pursues social justice and the reduction of inequities in power and resources in its theory, research and action. Part and parcel of this social justice agenda is situating CP, the problems it studies and the interventions it pursues, in the larger context of global capitalism and the increased power of transnational corporations.

A third goal of the book is to provide a text with an international perspective, drawing upon the work of community psychologists, allied professionals and community activists, from around the world. We have experience as CP academics inside and outside the US. We have constructed a book that can be used as a text, not just in the US, but in Canada, the UK, Australia and New Zealand, and perhaps even in other parts of the world. We have done this by including examples of work done in many different countries and by including chapter authors and commenta-tors from countries around the world. The chapter authors, except for one, are all from English-speaking countries (Australia, Canada, New Zealand, the UK and the US), but the commentators span most of the continents and include people from non-English-speaking countries. One limitation of the book is that there is limited coverage of Africa and Asia, where much of the world lives. This reflects the state of the field, as CP as a formal field of study is only in its formative stages of develop-ment in these continents. We believe that the diversity of contexts, viewpoints and experiences of community psychologists from around the world provides a rich base from which to learn.

A fourth goal of the book is to emphasize the reflexive and subjective nature of the field. There is a danger when well-respected authors write a book, that students and others will take what is written as gospel, when in fact the views of authors are shaped by their location and historical context and should be open to scrutiny, critique and alternative viewpoints. Towards this end, each chapter includes a commentary written by other people. These commentators include other community psychologists, activists and people who have experienced significant disadvantages in their lives. Our intention with these commentaries is to incorporate diverse voices and viewpoints into the book. Also, the construction of the book was designed to include many voices. We wrote the first half of the book (Chapters 1–13) to provide the reader with a common framework regarding the foundations of CP, while the second half of the book (Chapters 14–24) was written by contributing authors.

Finally, since CP is quite a broad field and draws from the knowledge and perspective of other disciplines, we have strived to bring an interdisciplinary emphasis to the book. While most of the authors of the chapters are community psychologists, all the authors draw their sources from many different disciplines. You will also hear from people who may not have an identification with an academic institution or discipline but who have been active in the community or society and who have much practice wisdom and experiential knowledge to share. We believe that the inclusion of different perspectives and experiences expands the boundaries of CP and increases its ability to understand and solve social problems.

We can think of CP as a journey and we use this metaphor throughout the book. In putting this together, we have strived not only to tell the story of where CP comes from and where it is now, but also where we believe it should be headed. Thus, we think of this book as a 'work in progress', rather than a definitive statement.

GEOFFREY NELSON
and ISAAC PRILLELTENSKY

Acknowledgements

We are appreciative of the encouragement, enthusiasm and guidance of Frances Arnold and Andrew McAleer, our editors for this project. We want to thank Meghan Kenny for compiling the list of references for the book. Thanks to David Fryer's undergraduate CP students at the University of Stirling and Geoff's students in the undergraduate seminar in CP at Wilfrid Laurier University who provided many valuable comments on draft chapters for the book. The Laurier students are: Tania Anderson, Sarah Cady, Frances Choi, Bob Davis, Deanne Larsen, Gillian Hubbick, Stacey McCormick, Jen McKercher, Dana Sproule, Tasha Stoodley, Micha Tsarfati and Nicholle Webber. Special thanks to Micha for his help in putting the final draft together. Warm thanks to Ingrid Huygens, our colleague in New Zealand, who early on in the process of conceiving this book encouraged us to broaden the scope of the book and to make it more inclusive of other voices. Thanks also to Nicole, Laura and Daniel Nelson, who completed the index for the book.

The publisher and authors would like to thank the organizations and people listed below for permission to reproduce material from their publications:

Sage Publications for Table 1.1. Original source is Prilleltensky, I. & Nelson, G. (1997) *Community Psychology: Reclaiming Social Justice*. In D. Fox and I. Prilleltensky (eds) *Critical Psychology: An Introduction* (pp. 166–84). London: Sage.

Kluwer Academic/Plenum Publishers for Table 3.1. Original source is Prilleltensky, I. (2001) 'Value-based Praxis in Community Psychology: Moving Toward Social Justice and Social Action', *American Journal of Community Psychology*, 29, 747–78.

Palgrave Macmillan for Table 3.2. Original source is Prilleltensky, I. & Nelson, G. (2002) *Doing Psychology Critically: Making a Difference in Diverse Settings*. New York: Palgrave Macmillan.

University of Toronto Press for Figures 4.1 and 4.2 from Prilleltensky, I., Nelson, G. & Peirson, L. (eds) (2001a) *Promoting Family Wellness and Preventing Child Maltreatment: Fundamentals for Thinking and Action*.

The Australian Institute of Family Studies for Figure 5.1 from Wendy Stone and Jody Huges (2002).

The Journal of Community Psychology for Tables 6.1 and 6.2 from Prilleltensky, I. 'The Role of Power in Wellness, Oppression and Liberation' (in press).

Kluwer Academic/Plenum Publishers for Table 6.3 from Prilleltensky, I. (2001), 'Value-Based Praxis in Community Psychology', from the *American Journal of Community Psychology*, 29, 747–77.

Palgrave Macmillan for Figure 7.1 and Table 7.3 from Prilleltensky, I. & Nelson, G. (2002) *Doing Psychology Critically, Making a Difference in Diverse Settings.*

Douglass St.Christian, University of Western Ontario for Box 7.3.

Michael McCubbin, PhD for Figure 9.1 from McCubbin, M. & Dalgard, O.S. (2002) *Le Pouvoir Comme Determinant de la Sante Publique* (Power as Determinant of Population Health), Presentation to Faculty of Nursing Sciences, Laval University.

Lawrence Erlbaum Associates, Inc. for Table 9.5. Original source is Nelson, G., Amio, J., Prilleltensky, I. & Nickels, P. (2000) 'Partnerships for Implementing School and Community Prevention Programs'. *Journal of Educational and Psychological Consultation*, **11**, 121–45.

John Lord for Table 12.3 from Lord, J. & Hutchison, P. (1993) 'The Process of Personal Empowerment', from the *Canadian Journal of Community Mental Health*, **12**(1): 55–70.

Ian Thomson for Figure 15.1, the 'Students Against Sweatshops' logos.

Elena Johnson for Box 15.3, reprinted courtesy of *Alternatives Journal: Canadian Environmental Ideas and Action*; www.alternativesjournal.ca.

Rod Watts for Table 17.2 from Watts, R. J. (1994a) 'Oppression and Sociopolitical Development'. *The Community Psychologist*, **12**(2): 24–6.

Judy Horacek for cartoons in Chapter 18.

Glen White for Box 20.1, from the Research and Training Center on Independent Living.

Every effort has been made to obtain necessary permission with reference to copyright material. The publisher and authors apologize if, inadvertently, any sources remain unacknowledged and will be glad to make the necessary arrangements at the earliest opportunity.

Part I

Context and Overview

In the first part of this book, we set the field of community psychology (CP) in context and provide an overview of CP. The goal of the first part of the book is to answer the following questions: What is CP? Where does it come from? Where is it now? And where should it be going? In order to look forward to the future of CP, it is important first to look back at the historical roots of the field and to observe contemporary trends. There are two chapters in this part of the book; the first of which looks at the history of CP and contemporary trends, while the second provides the conceptual framework for the book.

In the first chapter, we begin with a discussion of the value of metaphors as a way of guiding thinking and action. We use the metaphor of a journey as way of understanding the context and history of CP. We then describe three types of journeys in CP:

1. the journey of the field of CP
2. the journeys of the two authors/editors of the book, Geoff and Isaac, and
3. the journey of the reader of this book.

We note that these journeys intersect in many different ways. The fate of CP and community psychologists, like ourselves and the authors who contribute chapters to this book, is tied to that of disadvantaged people. The wellness and liberation of those of us working in the field of CP cannot be complete until those disadvantaged people we work with experience wellness and liberation. We invite the readers to join us in this journey.

In Chapter 2, we introduce the conceptual framework underlying the book. The framework consists of four main components:

1. issues and problems
2. values
3. principles and conceptual tools, and
4. the science of CP.

Using this framework, we discuss the 'problems' that have been the focus of the field of CP. CP is an action-oriented field that strives to address problems and create change. This is why values are so important for CP. Science can tell us what *is*, but not what *should be*. We need values to guide us to what *should be*. We examine the values that underlie CP and discuss which values have received the most emphasis and which values require more attention.

The way that problems are framed depends on one's values and principles. We note that the ways that CP frames problems have changed over time, and we clarify the principles and conceptual tools that are used to frame problems. For example, the problems experienced by people with serious mental illness have traditionally been viewed from a medical viewpoint, but CP helped shift the frame to one emphasizing competence, health and community support. More recently, there has been a further shift to viewing the plight of people with serious mental illness in terms of power and social justice. These different principles and concepts reflect different values. Finally, the science of CP helps us to understand how wellness and liberation can be promoted.

1

Community Psychology:
Journeys in the Global Context

Warm-up Exercise

Please reflect on the following questions as you begin your journey in CP:

1. What drew you to the course that you are taking in CP? Describe some of your motivations for pursuing CP.
2. What particular issues or topics would you like to learn more about in CP?
3. Where do you see yourself headed in the future in terms of work, further education and participation in the community?

In this chapter, you will learn about:

- the defining features of CP
- the roots of CP in the US
- factors leading to the emergence of CP
- how CP has developed around the world
- a bit about the two authors of this book.

We begin this book with a brief history of the field of CP. History is about the roots of a subject, where it comes from and why. As Rappaport and Seidman (2000) stated in the introduction to their *Handbook of Community Psychology*, 'every field requires a narrative about itself – a vision of its possibilities, a story that explains why it studies what it deems to be important' (p. 1). In the case of CP, a historical review provides an analysis of the development of the identity of the field. In order to look forward to the future of CP, we need first to look backwards to our history and the lessons that we have learnt from the past.

Throughout this book, we use metaphors as a way of understanding the field of

CP, its phenomena of interest, key concepts and methods. In this chapter on the history of CP, we use the metaphor of a journey as way of understanding the context of CP. Journeys have personal, community and historical dimensions; journeys are about individuals and communities and how their stories unfold over time. Journeys are also stories or narrative accounts that describe important milestones and turning points, highlight the contributions of key players and settings, note main themes and trends and different points in the journey, and provide coherence and meaning about the journey. Are you ready to travel with us? Then let us begin the journey.

The Journey of Community Psychology

The first journey that we describe is that of CP. CP is a sub-discipline of the larger discipline of psychology. While the roots of psychology were in Europe, the field of psychology expanded at a rapid rate in the US during the 20th century. CP was a part of this growth. The specific historical context of the US in the 1960s played an important role in shaping the field of CP. At the same time, however, CP has grown and developed in other countries around the world as well. In this section, we trace the roots of CP in the US and in other countries. Before we consider where CP comes from, we first consider what it is.

What Is Community Psychology?

CP is hard to define in a sentence or even in a paragraph. As the authors of a recent CP text book stated: 'No single definition can accurately capture the complexities inherent in its theory and praxis' (Seedat, Duncan & Lazarus, 2001, p. 19). In one of the first textbooks on the subject, one which played a major role in defining the field, Julian Rappaport (1977) noted the problem of defining CP. He argued that it is difficult to define precisely, because it is more of a new paradigm, perspective, or way of thinking whose contours are constantly emerging, than a distinct and fixed entity. Similarly, the authors of another recent text note that CP entails a 'shift in perspective' (Dalton, Elias & Wandersman, 2001, p. 6). In discussing what CP is, Rappaport (1977) wrote about the following themes: its ecological nature (the fit between people and their environments), the importance of cultural relativity and diversity so that people are not judged against one single standard or value ('an attempt to support every person's right to be different without risk of suffering material and psychological sanctions', p. 1), and a focus on social change ('toward a maximally equitable distribution of psychological as well as material resources', p. 3). Moreover, Rappaport (1977) argued that CP is concerned with human resource development, political activity and scientific inquiry, three elements that are often in conflict with one another. As the subtitle of his book *Community Psychology: Values, Research and Action*, suggests, CP is a balancing act between values, research and action.

Like others who have tried to define the field, we believe that what CP has been in the past is different from what it is now, and that the field will continue to change. Nevertheless, there are some themes that have been consistent over time in its short history. Because we believe that CP represents a different paradigm or world view of psychology, we find it useful to describe how it is different from the more traditional fields of applied psychology (for example clinical, educational, industrial/organizational, see Table 1.1).

Psychology has traditionally focused on the individual level of analysis. While applied psychology sometimes pays attention to micro-systems, such as the family or peer group, most of the major theories of personality and clinical psychology emphasize individualistic explanations of behaviour and individual strategies of change such as psychotherapy. This is a very western view that puts the individual in the foreground over the collective, whereas other parts of the world do the opposite. In contrast, CP is the study of people in context. There is a more holistic, ecological analysis of the person within multiple social systems, ranging from micro-systems (for example the family) to macro-sociopolitical structures. There is a strong belief that people cannot be understood apart from their context. When problems are defined in terms of individualistic conceptions of human nature, this can lead to a stance of 'blaming the victim' (Ryan, 1971), which is common in the social sciences. Whether intentional or not, victim-blaming holds individuals responsible for the causes of and solutions to their problems. However, when problems are reframed in terms of their social context and seen as arising from degrading social conditions, this tendency of blaming the victim is reduced. Moreover, CP tends to focus on the strengths of people living in adverse conditions as well as the strengths of communities, rather than focusing on individual or community 'deficits' or problems

Table 1.1 Assumptions and practices of traditional applied psychology and community psychology

Assumptions and Practices	Traditional Applied Psychology	Community Psychology
Levels of analysis	Intrapersonal or micro-systems	Ecological (micro, meso, macro)
Problem definition	Based on individualist philosophies that blame the victim	Problems are reframed in terms of social context and cultural diversity
Focus of intervention	Deficits/problems	Competence/strengths
Timing of intervention	Remedial (late)	Prevention (early)
Goals of intervention	Reduction of 'maladaptive' behaviours	Promotion of competence and wellness
Type of intervention	Treatment-rehabilitation	Self-help/community development/social action
Role of 'client'	Compliance with professional treatment regimes	Active participant who exercises choice and self-direction
Role of professional	Expert (scientist–practitioner)	Resource collaborator (scholar–activist)
Type of research	Applied research based on positivistic assumptions	Participatory action research based on alternative assumptions
Ethics	Emphasis on individual ethics, value neutrality and tacit acceptance of status quo	Emphasis on social ethics, emancipatory values and social change
Interdisciplinary ties	Psychiatry, clinical social work	Critical sociology, health sciences, philosophy, law, social work (community development and social policy), political science, planning and geography

Adapted from Prilleltensky and Nelson (1997)

(Rappaport, 1977). Focusing on problems puts people in a subordinate position to whoever is making such a categorization or diagnosis and suggests that they need monitoring and correction, whereas focusing on strengths enables people to build upon their pre-existing resources, capacities and talents.

In terms of intervention, traditional applied psychology intervenes late after problems have already developed, whereas CP emphasizes the importance of prevention and early intervention. While traditional applied psychology interventions have a goal of reducing 'maladaptive' behaviours or overcoming deficits through treatment and rehabilitation, CP has a goal of promoting competence and well-being through self-help, community development, and social and political action. From a CP perspective, behaviour is not viewed as maladaptive. People are viewed as adapting in the best ways they can to oppressive and stressful conditions. In traditional psychology, the role of the client is a passive one, with compliance and deference to the professional helper as the norm. CP emphasizes active participation, choice, and self-determination of the participants in any intervention, assuming that people know best what they need and that active participation in individual and collective change is healthy and desirable. Community psychologists eschew the traditional role of the helper as the 'expert' who knows best and who is well versed in the science and practice of assessment, diagnosis and treatment. Instead, community psychologists typically function as resource-collaborators, who bring both science and social activism to their community work.

Research in applied psychology is typically guided by a philosophy of science known as logical positivism/empiricism, or what we more commonly know as the scientific method. Community psychologists believe that there is no one scientific method, but many, and their research is often very participatory, action-oriented, and guided by assumptions of alternative philosophies of science. Research is not conducted just for the sake of developing new knowledge; research is conducted to create knowledge and change social conditions. Since community psychologists do not believe in the 'expert' approach of traditional applied psychology, community stakeholders participate in the creation of knowledge. The question of 'whose knowledge?' is one that concerns community psychologists. The ethics of traditional applied psychology are focused on the individual client or research participant and emphasize values such as informed consent and confidentiality. CP also abides by such individual ethics, but it goes further to consider social ethics and values that promote social change. Traditional psychology often claims to be 'value-neutral' when it comes to social ethics, but such a position often provides tacit acceptance of unjust social conditions.

Finally, traditional applied psychology has interdisciplinary ties with other helping professions, such as psychiatry and clinical social work, while CP allies itself with critical perspectives in a range of social and health science and humanities disciplines that focus on the interface between people and social environments. The question of how CP differs from social work often arises. Like psychology, social work is a broad field; unlike psychology, social work has more of a professional practice orientation and less of a research orientation. As in applied psychology, the dominant approach to social work training focuses on clinical intervention with individuals, families and groups. CP has much more in common with that part of social work which emphasizes community development and social policy. In CP, research is emphasized much more than social work and is seen as inseparable from practice.

Finally, while there is diversity within CP, the field is based on a fairly coherent set of values and concepts. In contrast, social work is a broader field with more diverse strands and less of a uniform ideology.

The Emergence of Community Psychology in the US

Having provided a brief sketch of CP, we now turn to an examination of the roots of CP. We begin with a focus on the US scene, because much of the early history of CP has been centred there. We want to examine the context from which these emphases and themes emerged.

The Foreshadowing of Community Psychology

While the field of CP did not formally coalesce until the 1960s, the work of CP was foreshadowed as early as the turn of the last century. From 1890 to 1914 was a time of considerable social unrest in the US, with social institutions being plagued with problems related to immigration, industrialization, urbanization and poverty. Community psychologist Murray Levine and sociologist Adeline Levine wrote an important book about this time period, entitled *Helping Children: A Social History*. In their book, Levine and Levine (1992) described how many social programs that are common today throughout North America had their roots during this time period, including mental health associations, the YWCA and YMCA, scout groups, juvenile courts and psychological clinics. While these activities were not typically tied to the field of psychology, in many ways they were the beginning of the journey of CP.

Box 1.1   Jane Addams and Hull-House

One important setting during the time period between 1890 and 1914 was the settlement house, which provided support to immigrants to the US who were living in large cities. But settlement houses dealt with much more than immigration issues; they served as a base for community organization, social action, education, the labour movement and the peace movement. In her book *Twenty Years at Hull-House*, community developer and social activist Jane Addams (1910) describes Hull-House, a settlement house on the west side of Chicago which consisted of several different ethnic enclaves (Italians, Polish and Russian Jews, Irish). All these groups lived in slum conditions. The description of Hull-House is strikingly similar to contemporary community-driven prevention projects or neighbour-

hood organizations with a community development, prevention and social change focus. Hull-House operated a coffee house, a gymnasium, a coal cooperative, cooperative housing, a day nursery and much more. When workers at Hull-House learnt that women and children were working from dawn until late in the evening in sweatshops, they advocated successfully for labour legislation that included an eight-hour day and a minimum age limit of 14 for young people to work. For people like Jane Addams, social issues of women, children, poverty, education, health and social justice were interrelated and thus action was called for on several fronts and at several different levels. Addams went on to found the Women's International League for Peace and Freedom and she won the Nobel Peace Prize in 1931.

Returning to Levine and Levine's (1992) historical study of children's services, they found that the progressive era at the turn of the century was followed by a conservative era in the aftermath of World War I during the 1920s. With this shift in political climate, there was also a shift in the ideology of social services from one of social change to one emphasizing individual change and blaming the victims for not 'adjusting' to degrading social conditions. As an example, the field of psychology had created intelligence testing in the UK (Francis Galton) and France (Alfred Binet) and

IQ tests were imported to and refined in the US during this period. Galton and other psychologists in the area of intelligence testing were proponents of Social Darwinism (Albee, 1996a), which took Darwin's concepts of natural selection and survival of the fittest and applied them to human beings and intelligence. IQ was viewed as an innate quality of individuals, and people with low IQ scores were seen as inferior and unworthy, people who should be 'weeded out' of society because they weakened the genetic stock. The eugenics movement, which was prominent in the 1920s, used the philosophy of Social Darwinism to advocate for the separation of the 'feeble-minded' from the rest of society into institutions, sterilization of people with low IQ, and restrictions on the immigration of people deemed to be inferior (those from eastern and southern Europe, Africa and Asia). Consider the following chilling quotes that Albee (1981) has gathered from advocates of the eugenics movement.

> We face the possibility of racial admixture here that is infinitely worse than that favoured by any European country today, for we are incorporating the Negro into our racial stock, while all of Europe is comparatively free from this taint ... the decline of American intelligence will be more rapid ... owing to the presence of the Negro. (Brigham [Princeton psychologist], 1923)

> [Massive sterilization] is a practical, merciful and inevitable solution of the whole problem and can be applied to an ever widening circle of social discards, beginning always with the criminal, the diseased, and the insane and extending gradually to types which may be called weaklings rather than defectives and perhaps ultimately to worthless race types. (Grant [New York Zoological Society], 1919)

Grant's quote foreshadowed the Nazi holocaust against Jewish people, gypsies, homosexuals and other supposedly 'inferior', non-Aryan ethnoracial groups.

Based on their historical review, Levine and Levine (1992) advanced the following thesis:

> Social and economic conditions and the intellectual and political spirit of the times greatly influence the mental health problems that concern us and forms of help that flourish ... More specifically our thesis states that there are essentially two modes of help, the situational and the intrapsychic ... We believe that the situational modes of help, which demand that we question the social environment – and change the social environment – flourish during periods of political or social reform ... Intrapsychic modes of help ... are prominent during periods of political or social conservatism. (p. 8)

This thesis provides an interesting perspective on the emergence of activities and settings at the turn of the century that bear a striking resemblance to contemporary CP in terms of the values and strategies employed by people working within this Zeitgeist. Psychology was still in its infancy during this period, and thus the role for psychology in community action was not yet evident. However, by the 1960s much had changed.

The Roots of Community Psychology in the US

There are three important aspects of the social context to be aware of in understanding the beginning journey of CP in the US: (a) the growth of mental health services, (b) the rapid expansion of clinical psychology and (c) the social–political context of the 1960s.

The mental health connection. In the aftermath of World War II, the US government devoted considerable attention to mental health issues. Many veterans of the war returned home with mental health problems, variously labelled as 'shell shock' or 'combat neurosis'. Veteran's Administration (VA) hospitals were established to attend to these problems, as well as other problems of health and disability. A Joint Commission on Mental Health and Illness was formed, and this Commission released its final report, *Action for Mental Health*, in 1961, along with several other reports. Two years later in 1963, the federal government enacted legislation establishing a nationwide program of Community Mental Health Centers (CMHCs). While proclaimed as a 'bold, new approach' to mental health, the CMHCs retained a strong medical model and clinical approach to mental health problems. The intrapsychic approach elaborated by Levine and Levine (1992) in the previous section continued to dominate mental health services.

The shift away from clinical psychology. Clinical psychology grew rapidly at this time. The National Institute of Mental Health (NIMH) was established at the end of World War II, and it provided funding for training in the mental health professions and for research in mental health. Clinical psychology emerged as a major subdiscipline of psychology during this time, and the Boulder 'scientist–practitioner' model of training in clinical psychology (named after a training conference held in Boulder, Colorado in 1949) became the dominant approach to training in clinical psychology. Clinical psychologists were to have a Ph.D. degree, with emphasis on both research and practice. While clinical psychology was expanding, psychiatry continued to be the most powerful player in mental health. Clinical psychology and social work clearly played secondary roles in many hospital and clinic settings, functioning as 'handmaidens' to psychiatry (Rappaport, 1977). Clinical psychologists were often relegated to diagnostic testing and did not play much of a role in treatment, in spite of their training in psychotherapy.

The 1960s and social reform. CP was born in the 1960s, a time of social and political change in the US. Bob Dylan, an American folk musician who emerged during this time, sang 'we'll soon shake your windows and rattle your walls, for the times they are a changin'. The 1960s was much like the turn of the century; it was an era of social reform which saw the emergence of several different social movements in the US, including the civil rights movement, the women's movement, the peace movement in the context of the Vietnam war, and later the disability rights movement and gay, lesbian and bisexual movements. Clinical psychologists who began to create the field of CP were aware of how sociopolitical conditions impact on the competence and well-being of individuals. Many became active in the so-called 'Great Society' programs of the 1960s, including preschool education programs (for example Head Start), community mental health centres, and community action centres. The 1960s was certainly not a radical or revolutionary time period in the US, but it was a progressive era, much like the period at the turn of the century that Levine and Levine (1992) have written about. It was a time of change, hope and acknowledgment of the important role of the state in addressing social issues.

Summary. CP in the US grew out of this context and has roots in mental health, clinical psychology, and the time of change in the 1960s. Originally, CP was quite strongly tied to the mental health field. In its developing discourse, CP and community mental health were often mentioned in the same breath. A pivotal moment in the journey of CP was the Swampscott conference, named after the Boston suburb in which it was held in 1965. The focus of this conference was on the training of psychologists in community mental health, but those present were dissatisfied with the individually centred approaches of clinical psychology that emphasized the roles of testing and psychotherapy. Conference participants were searching for conceptual and practical alternatives. They were interested in applying public health concepts of prevention and promotion to mental health, in the creation of innovative program approaches, and in social action regarding broader issues of social injustice. The notion of a 'participant–conceptualizer' role was advanced as an alternative to the scientist–practitioner role (Bennett, Anderson, Cooper, Hassol, Klein & Rosenblum, 1966). This role is quite similar to the resource–collaborator role that we described earlier.

In 1967, following the Swampscott conference, CP became a Division (27) of the American Psychological Association (it is now called the Society for Community Research and Action) and, in 1973, Division 27 started its own journal, the *American Journal of Community Psychology*. Another US-based journal, the *Journal of Community Psychology*, was also developed at this time to provide another outlet for the research of community psychologists. Until the 1990s, these journals published mostly quantitative research based on the traditional scientific method, with few examples of qualitative and participatory studies. Thus, in its early history, CP in the US tended to adopt traditional research methods, such as those used in clinical research. Since 1987, the Society for Community Research and Action has held a popular and well-attended biennial conference.

Factors Leading to the Emergence of Community Psychology in the US

In this section, we consider the question of why CP emerged in the US during the 1960s.

The gap between the scope of mental health problems and available resources. First, there was, and there remains today, a large gap between the scope of human problems and professional psychological resources to deal with such problems. For example, studies of the prevalence of mental health problems have revealed very high rates for both adults and children. The Ontario Health Supplement conducted in 1991 found that in a representative sample of adults in Ontario (close to 10,000 respondents) the one-year prevalence rate for any disorder was 19%, and the lifetime prevalence rate for any mental disorder was 48% (Offord et al., 1994). In the Ontario Child Health study of a representative sample of children and young people (3,000 children) in Ontario, Offord et al. (1987) found a one-year prevalence rate of 18% for any disorder.

What is most disturbing about these findings is that the majority of adults and children with mental disorders were not receiving any mental health intervention for their problems (Offord et al., 1987; Offord et al., 1994). Based on his report on human resources in mental health, George Albee (1959) concluded that there were not, and never could be, enough trained mental health professionals to provide treatment services to everyone with a mental health problem. Even if therapy were 100% effective, mental health problems could not be eliminated, because the need for services far outstrips their supply. As Albee (1996a) has reminded us, 'no mass disease (disorder) in human history has ever been eliminated or significantly controlled by attempts at treating the affected individual, nor by training large numbers of individual treatment personnel' (pp. 4–5).

Dissatisfaction with the medical model of mental health. A second reason for the development of CP in the US is a dissatisfaction with traditional modes of service delivery in mental health. As we just noted, most people who need help do not receive it. In fact, there appears to be a middle-class bias in the provision of psychotherapy. Schofield (1964) argued that psychotherapy tends to be geared to clients who are young, attractive, verbal, intelligent and successful. To this list we can add that psychotherapy clients are those who have health insurance or can afford this treatment. In their famous study of social class and mental illness, Hollingshead and Redlich (1958) found a two-tiered system of treatment, one for the affluent and one for the poor. Affluent people with less serious mental health problems tended to receive psychotherapy, while poor people with more serious mental health problems tended to be 'treated' in mental hospitals with drug therapy and custodial care.

As Offord et al. (1994) reported, nearly half (42%) of those respondents who do not have a diagnosable mental disorder receive some form of mental health intervention. Beiser, Gill and Edwards (1993) reviewed factors that influence people's utilization of mental health services and they argued that treatment approaches typically reflect Euro-North American values, which may contradict the beliefs of people from different cultures. Language is another barrier for some cultural and ethnic groups to receiving mental health intervention. As a result, many ethnic minority consumers either do not access services or they drop out of programs after their initial contacts. Moreover, while there is a growing trend for people who experience personal problems to use the services of non-medical mental health professionals (Gurin, Veroff & Feld, 1960; Kulka, Veroff & Douvan, 1979; Swindle, Heller, Pescosolido & Kikuzawa, 2000), a large number of people tend to seek more informal sources of support, including family, friends, clergy, hairdressers, lawyers, job supervisors, bartenders, and self-help groups (Cowen, 1982; Gurin et al., 1960; Kulka et al., 1979; Swindle et al., 2000). These findings call into question the way treatment services in mental health are organized (Swindle et al., 2000).

Recognition of the importance of the social environment. A third reason for the shift to CP was the recognition of the importance of social environment for the development of competence and well-being. Mental health research had shown that the prevalence of many mental health problems was inversely related to one's social class position (Dohrenwend & Dohrenwend, 1969; Hollingshead & Redlich, 1958). Later community psychologist Barbara Dohrenwend (1978) formulated a social stress theory to demonstrate and explain the ways that poverty and low social status could cause mental health problems. Also, research from several different strands of psychology (for example behaviourism, group and organizational dynamics, family systems) was beginning to indicate the powerful role that social environments play in human welfare. For these reasons, CP recognized the need to consider social and community-level interventions over individually focused approaches to change.

The Emergence of Community Psychology Around the World

While CP became a distinct sub-discipline of psychology in the US context, it was also developing in many other countries as well. The stories of how CP developed in other parts of the world bear many similarities to those of CP in the US. However, the particular contexts of other countries also uniquely shaped the form that CP has taken in those countries.

Community Psychology in English-speaking Countries

Overall, CP as a sub-discipline of psychology has been more organized in English-speaking countries in the so-called 'developed' world.

Canada. In Canada, the roots of CP can be traced back to the University of Toronto. Professor Edward A. Bott was the first chair of the Psychology Department at Toronto and served from 1926 to 1956 (Pols, 2000). Bott and his colleagues were concerned with human development and had strong ties to the Canadian National Committee for Mental Hygiene (now the Canadian Mental Health Association). There is a story that Yale University tried to hire the entire Psychology Department from the University of Toronto, offering to double their pay (Babarik, 1979), but Clarence Hincks, the founder of the Canadian National Committee for Mental Hygiene, was able to come up with money from this new organization to keep these faculty members in Canada. This is quite an interesting element in the journey of CP, because when Seymour Sarason was later hired as a psychology professor at Yale University, he established the Psychoeducational Clinic, which became a major training ground for CP in the US.

While psychology at the University of Toronto was definitely applied in nature before World War II, it was not until after the war that a CP orientation became clearly evident through the leadership of William Line. It was Line who first coined the term 'CP' (Babarik, 1979), and as President of the Canadian Psychological Association (CPA) in 1945, Line exhorted his colleagues to resist the status quo and work for social responsibility (Pols, 2000). Line had an international influence through his involvement as President of the World Federation for Mental Health from 1951–52.

In spite of these early roots, the CP Section of the CPA was not formed until 1982. There was an influx of US-trained community psychologists during the 1970s that began to mobilize CP in Canada (Davidson, 1981; Walsh, 1988). Also, in 1982, the first issues of a bilingual (French and English) Canadian CP journal with an inter-disciplinary emphasis, the *Canadian Journal of Community Mental Health* (*CJCMH*), were published, with the second issue devoted to CP in Canada (Tefft, 1982). Both francophone and anglophone community psychologists have been strongly influenced by US CP. While CP is practised today in both French-speaking and English-speaking Canada, there are relatively few graduate-level training programs and the sub-discipline is marginalized in the broader field of psychology in Canada (Walsh-Bowers, 1998). The programs at the Université du Québec à Montréal (UQAM), Université Laval and Wilfrid Laurier University are the only free-standing training programs in Canadian CP.

While CP in Canada has been influenced by US-trained community psychologists and, like the US, has deep roots in the mental health field, there are some interesting differences. First, the particular faculty members at Wilfrid Laurier University espouse a critical, value-based approach to CP with a strong emphasis on social intervention and social justice (Bennett, 1987). Second, Canadian CP has a longstanding tradition of participatory, action-oriented and qualitative approaches to research, as is evident in the research published in the CJCMH.

Australia and New Zealand. In Australia and New Zealand, CP has roots in mental health, but it has also been influenced by other applied areas of psychology (Bishop & D'Rozario, 2002; Bishop, Sonn, Fisher & Drew, 2001; Wingenfeld & Newbrough, 2000). As in Canada, CP formally emerged in these two countries in the early 1980s. The National Board of Community Psychologists was founded in Australia in 1981, and now the College of Community Psychologists of the Australian Psychological Society (APS) plays an important role in enhancing the profile of the profession. In recent years, most of the Chairs of the Social Issues Directorate of the APS have been community psychologists. A Vice-President of the APS (2003 – present), Heather Gridley, is one of the main CP figures in the country. Recently, CP has developed a more prominent profile in Australia, particularly in Victoria and Western Australia (Bishop et al., 2001).

New Zealand community psychologists have played an active role in the New Zealand Mental Health Foundation and contributed to the journal *Community Mental Health in New Zealand*. There is a graduate training program at the University of Waikato, in which there is a major focus on feminist issues, diversity, and social justice (Thomas, Neill & Robertson, 1997). New Zealand and Australian community psychologists have close ties and hold joint CP conferences. Within New Zealand and Australian CP, there is an emphasis on issues of social justice, with a particular focus on colonization of aboriginal people and the need for reconciliation through healing and depowerment of the dominant white majority (for example Bishop, Higgins, Casella & Contos, 2002; Huygens & Sonn, 2000).

Another influence on CP in New Zealand and Australia is that of critical psychology. Critical psychology is not so much a sub-discipline of psychology as it is a perspective or alternative view of all of psychology, or at least applied psychology. Moreover, critical psychology is not a single, unified perspective, but rather a focal point for a number of diverse critiques of psychology and society from feminist, anti-racist and other radical psychologists (Prilleltensky & Fox, 1997). The University of Western Sydney has become a focal point for critical psychology with the development of a program in critical psychology, the birth of a journal, the *International Journal of Critical Psychology*, and an international conference on critical psychology, under the leadership of Valerie Walkerdine. While critical psychology has thus far been more of a critique than an action-oriented approach, this is changing (Prilleltensky & Nelson, 2002).

The United Kingdom. In the UK, CP has been growing for more than a decade. CP also has roots in both clinical psychology and mental health and in applied social psychology. Jim Orford of the University of Birmingham has written a CP textbook (Orford, 1992) and co-edited the *Journal of Community and Applied Social Psychology,* launched in 1991. Critical psychology is another influence on UK CP. Ian Parker and Erica Burman of Manchester Metropolitan University have developed a program in critical psychology, a new journal, the *Annual Review of Critical Psychology*, and a network called 'Psychology Politics Resistance'. Moreover, programs at the University of Stirling in Scotland (David Fryer and Steve McKenna) and Manchester Metropolitan University (Carolyn Kagan and Mark Burton) strive to integrate critical and CP. Several CP conferences have been organized in the UK beginning in the 1990s. Interest groups also hold several meetings during the year. Many of the people who identify with CP in the UK work in traditional clinical settings but have an affiliation with the field. Another emerging trend in the UK is the association between health psychologists and CP. At London's City University, for instance, David Marks and Carla Willig engage in health psychology research and action that is very much in line with the vision and values of CP.

South Africa. The legacy of colonization, oppression and segregation of black people under the system of apartheid is the backdrop against which CP has developed in South Africa (Pretorius-Heuchert & Ahmed, 2001). CP emerged as part of a critique of the individual-centred approach of mainstream psychology in South Africa, which did not challenge the status quo of racism in the state. Thus, it is not surprising that CP in South Africa has a more radical and political edge than CP in other English-speaking countries. In fact, one of the chapters in a recent South African CP text is entitled 'Towards a Marxist CP: Radical Tools to Community Psychological Analysis and Practice' (Seedat et al., 2001). The journal *Psychology in Society* has provided an outlet for the work of critical and community psychologists in South Africa. In addition to focusing on social change, South African CP has also been concerned with mental health issues (Pretorius-Heuchert & Ahmed, 2001). Training in community and critical psychology is offered at several South African universities.

Community Psychology in Continental Europe

CP has also developed in some countries on the European continent, including Italy, Germany and Poland (Wingenfeld & Newbrough, 2000). In Italy, the Division of CP of the Italian Psychological Association was created in 1980. As was the case in the US, CP grew out of social protest movements and government legislation in human services and mental health (Francescato & Ghirelli, 1992). There have been major reforms in the mental health system in Italy, and there has been training in CP for over 20 years. CP in Germany has been influenced by European critical theory perspectives, which have been used to analyse and critique the mental health system in particular (Keupp & Stark, 1992). A European Network of CP, including the UK, was formed in 1996 and meetings and conferences have been held. While there are pockets of CP in continental Europe, the field is very much in its developmental stages.

Francescato and Tomai (2001) assert that European CP differs from US CP in at least three ways. First, there is less emphasis on the individual and more emphasis on the collective. Moreover, the individual and the collective are considered within the broader trends of globalization and free trade. Second, following from the first point, western and northern European countries have stronger social policies than those in the US, particularly those that emphasize income redistribution.

> Most European community psychologists have underlined the importance of not importing acritically values from the US and of preserving as a precious resource the European tradition of valuing social capital and welfare policies that mitigate economic inequalities (Francescato & Tomai, 2001, p. 374).

Third, they argue that European CP emphasizes theory (theory that strives to integrate traditional, postmodern and critical approaches) more than US CP, which tends to be more pragmatic.

Latin American Community Psychology

Through their publications in US CP journals, some of the work of Latin American community psychologists has come to the attention of English-speaking community psychologists (for example Bernal & Enchautegui-de-Jesús, 1994; Bernal & Marín, 1985; Montero, 1998a; Serrano-García, 1984). According to Montero (1996b), the origins of Latin American CP are more diverse than those in other countries, because Latin America constitutes a large area, composed of many different states. CP is practised in many different Latin American countries (Wiesenfeld, 1998; Wingenfeld & Newbrough, 2000), some of which have training programs in community and social psychology, and there is a Community Psychology Task Force of the Interamerican Society of Psychology (Wingenfeld & Newbrough, 2000). While there are parallels with the US field of practice, Latin American CP has had many unique influences and emphases (Montero, 1996b).

In the 1950s and 60s, the popular education approach developed by Brazilian Paulo Freire (1970) was very influential in social intervention throughout Latin America. Freire's work with illiterate, poor people linked education with emancipation from oppression through a highly participatory and action-oriented process. He introduced the concepts of conscientization – the process whereby students develop awareness of the psychological and sociopolitical circumstances oppressing them – and praxis, which refers to critical 'reflection and action upon the world to transform it' (1970, p. 33). This cycle of reflection and action in social intervention has been a model for Latin American CP.

Within the Latin American academic community, CP is closely related to Latin American sociology, social psychology, critical theory and other social science disciplines (Montero, 1996b). Columbian sociologist Fals Borda emphasized the need for social scientists to be engaged in social and community intervention with disadvantaged people. Community and social psychology are much more strongly linked in Latin America than in North America and have a strong social activist and community development orientation (Wiesenfeld, 1998). The social and political engagement of El Salvadoran social psychologist Ignacio Martín-Baró is an example of this emphasis. For Latin American community and social psychologists who live under repressive dictatorships, their political engagement is very risky. Martín-Baró, who argued for a psychology of liberation, was assassinated by death squads for his beliefs and actions in 1989. Montero (1996b) has asserted that while the development of CP was impeded in Latin American countries in which there were or are repressive dictatorships, such conditions also 'forged a powerful and lasting link between CP and political causes related to the development of social consciousness' (p. 593). Latin American community and social psychologists have been practising research that is participatory and action-oriented for many years, and they have been influenced by critical, alternative philosophies of science (Montero, 1996b).

CP in Latin America is distinctly political. Unlike North America, where there is more of a pull towards mainstream psychology, in Latin America the political and the professional are closely intertwined. This is why there is a close affinity between community and political psychologists in that continent. The political overtures of CP in Latin America have much to offer to the practice of the field in other areas of the world.

> **Box 1.2   Community Psychology in Cuba**
>
> Of particular interest is community psychology in Cuba, which, as a communist country, has a strong ideological commitment to economic equality and collective well-being (see Bernal & Marín, 1985). Cuba's social policies emphasize full employment, universal health care and education, and housing, with the goal of promoting quality of life and preventing social problems (Nikelly, 1987). In spite of material deprivation resulting from the embargo by the US and the loss of support of the former Soviet Union, Cuba boasts high rates of literacy and few problems related to malnutrition, homelessness, anti-social behaviour or alcoholism. What role has psychology played in Cuba? It is interesting to note that some more traditional clinical practices have been retained in Cuban psychology, such as the emphasis on psychological testing (Bernal, 1985). At the same time, however, Cuban psychology is guided by a 'pragmatic,
>
> action-oriented model focused on resolving social and community needs in areas such as health and education' (p. 234). When psychologists graduate they find work immediately and are incorporated in practically all sectors of society: industry, education, health, human services, and corrections among others (Ardila, 1986). At present the work of psychologists is focused on helping citizens face the difficult economic situation. Research is directed at the effects of the 'special period' on the Cuban family, formation and strengthening of values, and the impact of tourism on society (Torre & Calviño, 1996). Psychologists are aware of the impact of the 'special period' on their own subjectivity and professional behaviour, as they are not immune to the adverse effects of the social and economic crisis (Sánchez Valdés, Prilleltensky, Walsh Bowers & Rossiter, 2002).

Community Psychology in Other Developing Nations

While there is not a formal 'CP' in many developing countries, particularly in Africa and Asia, we believe that the defining characteristics of CP are compatible with the values and needs of collectivist societies. The emphasis on extended family, community and collective well-being that is more characteristic of Africa and Asia than English-speaking countries and continental Europe is a natural fit with CP. Moreover, there is a clear need for prevention and health-promotion interventions in Africa and Asia. Consider the widespread poverty and alarmingly high rates of malnutrition and various diseases, such as the AIDS epidemic, found in many developing countries (Prilleltensky, 2003a; UNICEF, 2001). Community approaches to the prevention of disease and death and the development of individual, family, community, and economic well-being are sorely needed.

There is currently a trend to 'internationalize' psychology in such developing countries (see the American Psychological Association's Office of International Affairs and their newsletter *Psychology International*). However, community psychologists who are interested in working with developing countries or preparing students to work in such countries need to be careful not to engage in paternalistic 'helping' responses. Just as trade agreements between industrial powers of the world and developing nations have led to exploitation of people in developing nations, a growing division between 'have' and 'have not' nations (the north–south divide), and 'third world debt' (Korten, 1995), 'exporting' western CP to developing nations might unintentionally serve to colonize psychology in developing nations.

A better stance for community psychologists might be to work with psychologists and disadvantaged people in developing nations to help them construct their own indigenous forms of CP, as community social psychologists have done in Latin America (Montero, 1996b). Working in partnerships with disadvantaged people in developing countries requires a mindset of humility, a desire to hear people's stories and learn about their strengths, and a willingness to share power. Consider the following quote from a Canadian psychologist who speaks of her experiences in preparing students to work in developing countries.

> There is nothing like hands-on applications to alert one to the relevant elements of one's knowledge and skills. I learned this humbling lesson when a former student spoke to my current class about her summer experience with a Ghanaian local NGO (non-government organization). She spent two months solving daily survival issues and learning from her Ghanaian colleagues, before even thinking to unpack her text and lecture notes on delivering health promotion messages and constructing latrines and safe water sites. (Aboud, 2001, p. 4)

The work of community psychologist Brinton Lykes (2001a, 2001b, 2001c) with Mayan women in Guatemala stands out as an example of how to work in solidarity with disadvantaged people in developing countries. (For more information, see the Commentary at the end of Chapter 7 by Brinton Lykes.)

The Journeys of the Authors/Editors

In this section we discuss our journeys – those of the two authors/editors, Geoff and Isaac. We think that it is important that you know something about who we are and where we are coming from. This will help you, the reader, to understand our construction of this book and the field about which it is written. As feminist writers have argued, it is important for researchers and writers to own their location and position in their field and the larger social order. In the social sciences, it is the norm for researchers and writers to be objective and dispassionate. We do not believe it is possible to be completely objective, because all of us have values and biases. Objectivity is important, but so is subjectivity. Moreover, we think that it is sad if people are not passionate about their field of work. For us, CP theory, research and practice are passionate and engaging – a major part of our personal and professional lives; and it is often impossible to draw a boundary between the personal and professional. In fact, we have learnt that it is important for our identities to connect the personal, professional and political parts of ourselves, as feminists have argued. In what follows, we provide a brief biographical sketch of ourselves and our involvement in the field of CP.

Geoff

I grew up on the south side of Chicago in the 1950s, back when the Prudential building was the tallest skyscraper in the city. My family moved 'downstate' to central Illinois in the 1960s. My concern with social issues came at an early age from my mother and father, and I became active in social issues when I attended the University of Illinois as an undergraduate from 1968 to 1972. This was the era of the Vietnam War and my friends and I were involved in anti-war protests. I was in the first class of students to take a new course in CP introduced by Julian Rappaport. There wasn't even a textbook in CP then (and if someone had told me at the time that I would someday be the author of a CP text, I am sure I would have seen this as ludicrous). Sometimes people take a university course that makes a lifelong impression and serves as a turning point in their life journey. That's what happened to me. I resonated to the readings, the lectures, and my field placement experience working in a Head Start program for disadvantaged preschool children. This course brought together my interests in psychology, mental health and working with people and my views about politics and the need for social change.

In 1972, my wife Judy and I moved to Canada where I attended graduate school in psychology at the University of Manitoba. I pursued my interest in CP through coursework; pushing my program to offer more community-oriented courses; through employment and practicum placements, including conducting research and doing front-line work with a storefront community health clinic and crisis intervention centre; consulting with resident advisory groups to promote citizen participation in city government; helping to create community mental health programs in rural areas in southern Manitoba; and through a one-year internship at the Mendota Mental Health Institute, which was a very progressive, community-oriented setting in Madison, Wisconsin.

I moved to Kitchener-Waterloo, Ontario in 1979 to take a faculty position in a CP program at Wilfrid Laurier University. This position has been a very good 'fit' for me. I have had the good fortune to work with colleagues and graduate students in CP and community members, with whom I share many values, experiences and interests. I have been able to pursue my research and action interests in community mental health, community development, and prevention – some of the main themes of CP. Over the past decade, I have become increasingly concerned about the growing power of transnational corporations and the impacts that this trend is having on global economic inequality, democracy, the environment, and the diminishing role of the state in providing social policies that promote human welfare. These larger global issues are having an enormous impact on the issues, people and interventions that are the concern of CP. I believe that education about these issues, civic participation and political action must become part of the mainstream of CP.

I am well aware that I lead a very privileged life. As a white, male, well-paid full professor, I am often in a position of power in relation to other people. I enjoy a wonderful family; Judy and I have three youngsters, all in university at the time of writing of this book. The eldest, Nicole, is working on a PhD on the social, ethical and legal aspects of genetics at Cornell University. Imagine that, a scientist, who is also a feminist social activist! Then there are our twins, Laura and Dan. Laura is a psychology and English major who is taking courses in CP and who completed a field placement looking after the children of single women while they attend a mutual support group in a church basement; Dan is a kinesiology major who is definitely a 'people person', having what we call a high level of 'emotional intelligence' (an understanding of and deep compassion for people). I also have cherished friends, colleagues, and community partners, and I live in a safe and prosperous community. I lead a comfortable life. I also spend much of my time working with people who have only dreamed of having all the advantages that I have. These experiences, my values about social justice, and the vast gaps between what the world *is* like and what I believe it *should* be like are constant sources of discomfort which motivate me in my personal and professional life to work with disadvantaged people and like-minded individuals for social change.

Isaac

I was born in Argentina and grew up during turbulent times. There was constant and consistent persecution of social and political activists and there was marked anti-Semitism. As a young Jewish boy I remember going to school and reading graffiti on walls imploring fellow Argentinians to 'be a patriot, kill a Jew'. I joined a Zionist Socialist youth movement at a young age. We were taught how to decipher the news and the media and to become political actors in a highly charged environment. My sister was one of the people who were made to 'disappear' by the dictatorial government. She was one of the very few people who ended up in exile, who was not killed or thrown from an aeroplane in chains into the freezing waters of the Atlantic.

My parents died when I was young and I spent a lot of my time with friends in the youth movement, talking and discussing politics, injustice, and the fate of some of our friends and relatives who were 'disappeared'. I emigrated to Israel in 1976 with a group of friends. Paradoxically, I had a couple of very quiet years while I was finishing high school there. Compared to Argentina, Israel was a calm place. I met Ora, my wife, during my MA studies and we moved together to Canada. In Winnipeg, our port of landing, I completed a Ph.D. at the University of Manitoba and worked for the Child Guidance Clinic of Winnipeg for six years. Upon completion of my PhD, I joined the faculty of the CP program at Wilfrid Laurier University, where I worked for nine years. I moved with my family to Melbourne, Australia in 1999, and then to Nashville, Tennessee in 2003.

My affiliation to CP is no doubt connected to my early political experiences and family circumstances. In my present family we experience a physical disability which reminds me of how little attention societies pay to the needs of people with different abilities and disabilities. Ora and I talk a lot about social and psychological issues. Matan, our son, who is also a very good conversationalist, keeps me honest in terms of my espoused values and is quick to point to incongruence between espoused and lived principles. Thanks Matan.

Throughout my adult life I've been involved with various child advocacy and community groups trying to promote the well-being of children and families. I struggle to contribute to community wellness in ways that are not just ameliorative but transformative as well. This is my biggest personal and professional challenge; a challenge that is only matched by my arduous attempts to live the values that I write about.

Like Geoff, I consider myself privileged. Although I grew up very poor, I belong now to a privileged class of academics. Sometimes I find myself having more privileges than I ever thought I could. Some of my efforts to contribute back to the community involve volunteer work in social change and mental health organizations. Together with Dennis Fox, I co-founded the Radical Psychology Network (www.radpsynet.org), and with Scot Evans, a PhD student, PsyACT (www.psyact. org) – Psychologists Acting with Conscience Together: A Global Coalition for Justice and Well-Being. The latter is a coalition dedicated to concrete actions to promote social justice.

The Journey of the Reader

We want to briefly consider the journey of you, the reader. We invite you to join us in the journey of this book, which is your introduction to CP. You will learn about the story of CP, its mission, its founders, key ideas and applications. This journey may be bumpy, jarring and upsetting, both emotionally and intellectually, as we consider the gaps between our own privilege and the disenfranchisement and pain of those with whom we work. In this book we challenge the field of CP to expand its boundaries and to consider new ways of thinking and acting. Many of you who read this book will be students taking your first course in CP. You may have a field placement experience as part of your course, in which you will come face-to-face with the issues that we discuss and the disadvantaged people with whom we work.

We encourage you to go gently into these uncharted waters, listening respectfully to disadvantaged people, suspending judgement and constantly reflecting on your thoughts, actions and experiences. Don't take everything that we or the other authors or commentators say as 'gospel'. The ability to think critically, challenge ideas, question assumptions and develop alternative arguments based on experiences, values and evidence is fundamental to CP. Remember that social change movements have often started with student activism. What follows in the book and in your journey may be very sobering, disturbing, or eye-opening for those of you who are new to the field of CP. At the same time, however, we want to convey a message of hope and inspiration that change is possible and suggest ways that you can contribute to personal and collective change.

Chapter Summary

In this chapter, we used the metaphor of a journey to introduce the field of CP. We began by outlining the contours of CP and differentiating it from mainstream applied psychology. We then traced the origins of the journey of CP in the US and other parts of the world to put CP in its global context. We then introduced you to ourselves, the authors/editors, and told you a bit about our journeys.

COMMENTARY: Values and Principles of Community Psychology: Views from Ghana
Charity Akotia

I grew up in several towns and villages in Ghana as both my parents were teachers and were frequently transferred from one community to another. During this period, I learnt of the many struggles that people go through to make life a little more comfortable. Everywhere my parents stayed, they played key roles in the community. They served as church leaders and 'counsellors' in the community as a whole. They joined the community in initiating and executing projects and also advised on healthy practices. I followed their lead and also got involved in community work. I became convinced about the need to do something to improve people's quality of life.

On moving to the city, the contrast between life in the rural areas and the city became obvious to me. Many people, especially those in the rural areas, were struggling to make ends meet. Many of them, particularly women, were living in very challenging environments compared with residents in the cities, who were better off economically and had better access to social services.

In 1991, I started my journey to Waterloo, Ontario, Canada as a graduate student at Wilfrid Laurier University (WLU). This was a turning point in my life, not only because I was leaving my country for another, but also because the program reinforced my desire and determination to be involved in the community, giving a hand to improve the quality of life. The practical experiences shared with my colleagues in the program, the approach to teaching, and so on, all served different purposes in my life. CP actually provided a fit between my goals and how to put these into practice.

On my completion of the program in 1992, I joined the faculty at the University of Ghana and introduced CP into the existing psychology programs. As the sole community psychologist at the university, I have taught several undergraduate students over the years. CP always serves as an eye-opener to my students. Often they wonder why this field of psychology is late in arriving in Ghana, considering its values and their relevance in solving the multifaceted problems in the country. Currently, past students of CP are all over the country (and abroad) serving in various positions and helping to develop the various communities. I am learning a lot from teaching and working with students and other community members. In the past years, I have worked with refugees. I have also been involved in community health-related issues in some rural communities. Currently, my research focus has been on obstacles faced by professional women in Ghana. I am collaborating with some colleagues in one of the universities in Norway on this project. I also involve myself in debates and discussions on social and community issues on radio and in newspapers.

Are the concepts, ideals and values of CP applicable in the Ghanaian society? As the authors point out, although the field of CP did not formally coalesce until the 1960s, its work was foreshadowed as early as the turn of the century. In the same way, in Ghana, many people have been practising the values and principles of CP without its being officially referred to as such. The ideals, concepts and values of CP are very much applicable in Ghana. In the following paragraphs, I shall highlight some values and concepts and indicate how applicable and relevant they are in our society.

The shift from treatment to prevention is also an ideal option in Ghanaian society. Just as there were too few mental health professionals in the US to handle the throngs of patients in the hospitals at the time of the birth of CP, so there are even fewer in Ghana in relation to the number of patients needing professional attention. Additionally, social conditions in the country are very challenging. Many citizens live in poverty. Diseases such as malaria, tuberculosis, diarrhoea and HIV/AIDS abound, and yet the few medical professionals we have often leave the country in search of greener pastures in the developed countries. Those who stay seem to be overconcentrated in the cities to the neglect of the rural areas. Furthermore, there are no major health insurance schemes in the country, making it difficult for the poor to attend hospital when they fall ill. This makes prevention very applicable and relevant in the country.

Understanding and enhancing community and individual life, rather than the individual, is crucial to community psychologists. Our culture is based on collectivism, rather than the individualism which characterizes many western cultures. Thus, Ghana is already a natural fit for this value. The happiness of community members depends on the happiness of each individual within the community. Consequently, the quality of life of both individuals and the community are intertwined (Prilleltensky, 1999).

Sadly, however, the communal system that has held the communities together for centuries is being lost gradually to western individualism without the benefit of western intervention programs and social policies. For example, there is a break in our external family system (Nukunya, 1992; Asenso-Okyere, 1993), as many families, especially those in the urban areas, now focus on the nuclear family system. Thus the emphasis on community well-being rather than individual well-being helps bring back the original Ghanaian value.

Unlike mainstream psychology, which uses person-centred approaches in studying behaviour, CP advocates the use of a wider framework in understanding behaviour. According to Orford (1992), behaviour is a function of the person, his or her environment and the interaction of the two (that is, $B = f(P, E)$. Studying people out of their social context only leads to 'blaming the victim', as indicated by the authors in this chapter. In Ghana, for example, many people hold strong beliefs and taboos about eating certain types of food. Avoiding these foods may pose health problems. To change the beliefs of this group of people, one needs to go beyond the individual and look at the wider cultural context. In a study, Ofori Atta (2001) suggested that in dealing with problems, therapists must go beyond the person and look at the wider environment. The identified patient, according to her, may not be the one who bears the symptoms, but rather the system within which the individual operates.

Serving as 'resource collaborators' rather than 'experts' is also a laudable and feasible idea in Ghana. People generally want to feel respected and recognized by others. Indeed, it is more enjoyable working with others in this type of role than in the role of an 'expert'. Personal experiences with the rural folks in Ghana, who comprise most of the country's poor, clearly show how ready these people are to share information and give out ideas if they are treated with respect. CP's value of active participation of citizens in any planned change is therefore healthy for Ghanaian society.

I personally think the ideals of social change advocated by CP are the ultimate desire of every Ghanaian. According to the authors of this chapter, mainstream research is usually basic in nature (that is, done for the sake of knowledge). However, CP believes research should go beyond this and bring about change in the lives of people and their communities. Considering the poverty in which people live and the feeling of helplessness among many of them, particularly in the rural areas, one can think only of helping to plan change in their lives. Furthermore, it is uncommon to get the government's support for change in many communities. Thus, social change as a value is also very helpful and feasible in our communities.

In recent years, Ghana has seen the emergence of many non-governmental organizations that are helping in various ways to bring change in the lives of individuals. They help build community clinics, school and roads and also provide drinking water to many communities. From experience, it works better when people are involved in defining their own problems and in finding solutions to the problems. The best sustainable projects in the country are those that involve the community in identifying needs, and planning and implementing change in the community. Thus, citizen participation as a value of CP, though time consuming, is also very relevant and applicable in our communities.

In conclusion, personal experiences with some people living in rural Ghana clearly show how applicable the values of CP discussed above are in Ghana. Even though the authors advocate that the field should be left to develop within the socio-cultural context of each country, I believe the multi-faceted problems faced by many developing countries make the values adopted by the field already a natural fit in these countries.

Chapter glossary

community psychology the sub-discipline of psychology that is concerned with understanding people in the context of their communities, the prevention of problems in living, the celebration of human diversity, and the pursuit of social justice through social action

conscientization the process by which individuals become aware of the sociopolitical and psychological conditions that oppress disadvantaged people

eugenics movement guided by the philosophy of Social Darwinism, this movement asserted that certain groups of people were of inferior genetic stock and advocated restrictive immigration policies to keep some people (for example African Americans) out of the US, as well as institutionalization and sterilization to prevent people with intellectual and mental health challenges from procreating

informal support social and emotional support that comes from one's informal network (for example family, friends, spiritual advisors, mentors) rather than formal sources (that is, professionals)

logical positivism/empiricism the scientific method as we understand it traditionally, including a focus on describing, explaining and predicting reality through objective research and hypothesis-testing, that aims to discover natural laws

participatory action research collaborative research between professionals and disadvantaged community members towards the goals of knowledge creation and social change

resource-collaborator in contrast to the 'expert' role of diagnostician or therapist, this is a role taken by the community psychologist to offer resources and collaborate with community groups

social stress theory a theory that emphasizes the role that social stress plays in the causation of psychological problems

strengths orientation an emphasis on the strengths and capacities of individuals and communities, rather than a focus on deficits

victim-blaming holding individuals responsible for problems that they experience without acknowledging the role that various ecological contexts may play in contributing to such problems

RESOURCES

Websites in Community Psychology

Community Psychology Network, http://www.cmmtypsych.net.

Community Psychology UK, http://homepages.poptel.org.uk/mark.burton/index.htm.

Council of Community Psychology Program Directors, http://www.msu.edu/user/lounsbu1/cpdcra.html.

European Network of Community Psychologists, http://userpage.fu-berlin.de/~cpbergol/.

Society for Community Research and Action, http://www.apa.org/divisions/div27/.

Videos relevant to community psychology, http://www.msu.edu/user/lounsbu1/clearfilms.html.

2

The Project of Community Psychology:
Issues, Values and Tools for
Liberation and Well-being

Chapter Organization

Oppression, Liberation and Well-being: The 'Big Picture' of Community Psychology	◆ Oppression: Silence and Invisibility ◆ Resistance and Liberation: Framing Problems, Listening to the Voices and Making the Invisible Visible ◆ Towards Well-being
Issues and Problems	◆ Problems ◆ The Global Context
Values of Community Psychology	
Principles and Conceptual Tools of Community Psychology	◆ Ecology ◆ Prevention and Promotion ◆ Community ◆ Power ◆ Inclusion ◆ Commitment and Depowerment

The Science of Community Psychology	**Chapter Summary**

COMMENTARY: Why Community Psychology? A Personal Story	**Glossary**	**Resources**

Warm-up Exercise

Please reflect on the following questions as you think about yourself in relation to community psychology:

1. What are some of the values that are personally important to you and how you want to live your life? How did you come to these values?
2. Describe one social issue about which you are concerned. How did you come to be concerned about this issue? How have you been involved in dealing with this issue? How could you become more involved in this issue?
3. Community psychologists are particularly concerned with power relationships. Think of a situation in which you have been involved or which you know about where one person (or group) has less power than another person (or group)? What kinds of problems result for the party with less power? the party with more power? Think about how CP concepts could be helpful in equalizing power between the two parties.

In this chapter, you will learn about:

■ the 'big picture' of community psychology (CP) (oppression, liberation and well-being)
■ the four main components of the conceptual framework of CP that is used in this book (issues and problems, values, principles and conceptual tools, and the science of CP).

We begin by presenting the 'big picture' of what CP is all about. We argue that the central problem with which CP is concerned is that of oppression, and that the central goals of CP are to work in solidarity with disadvantaged people and to accompany them in their quest for liberation and well-being. While oppression, liberation, and well-being are the overarching concepts of CP, more specific principles and conceptual tools are needed to address the many different manifestations of oppression. The conceptual framework that we propose consists of four main components:

- issues and problems
- values
- principles and conceptual tools, and
- the science of CP.

In subsequent chapters, we expand on the values, principles, and concepts and describe how they can be used to address the issues and problems that are of concern to CP. The issues and problems are those with which CP has been concerned; the vision and values are the ideals towards which CP strives; and the principles and conceptual tools are what are used by CP to address problems and issues in pursuit of its vision and values.

Oppression, Liberation and Well-Being: The 'Big Picture' of Community Psychology

In this section we provide an overview of the project of CP. We believe that it is important to start with a focus on the people and communities with whom community psychologists work, the way community psychologists think about the problems those communities and people face, and the goals towards which CP works.

Oppression: Silence and Invisibility

As we argued in Chapter 1, community psychologists are concerned with the issues and problems facing disadvantaged people, problems that have deep historical roots. The journeys of disadvantaged people have been ones of pain and suffering, dislocation and colonization, oppression, and marginalization. Society has constructed stories about disadvantaged people, making them into something different from you and me. These stories, which Rappaport (2000) calls dominant cultural narratives, are often of the victim-blaming variety and help members of dominant groups to rationalize their role in contributing to and perpetuating the oppression of disadvantaged people. They also serve to disconnect disadvantaged people from the journey of their people and themselves. Listening to the stories of disadvantaged people is a first step in undoing the damaging stories that society has constructed about 'those people'.

When we listen to stories, the pain and suffering of disadvantaged people become more real and apparent, and they have an impact on us. We often feel shocked, hurt, angry, guilty and/or defensive, and many of us want to do something to correct the injustices that people have suffered. Telling stories is also empowering for people and helps to create and inspire a vision of a better future. It helps individuals and collectives to reclaim their history, to understand and appreciate their strengths, resilience and resistance, to overcome their silence and shame, and to build community. We see part of the mission of CP as helping disadvantaged people to tell their stories so that dominant cultural narratives that have been imposed on them can be challenged and alternative stories can be promoted. It is also important for those of us who come from privileged backgrounds to be aware of where we stand and where our predecessors have stood historically vis-à-vis oppressed groups (McIntosh, 1990). Such reflexive awareness is necessary for dominant groups to embark on their own journeys of change in order to create more just and equitable relationships.

Throughout this book, we will hear stories of people who have experienced disadvantage. Disadvantaged people have often been forced to move to physically segregated environments or they have had to flee oppressive conditions. Many of the original settlers of North America came to the New World to escape religious persecution and economic deprivation. At the same time, the 'founding fathers' of the New World inflicted subjugation and oppression on the aboriginal people of North America, black people from Africa and women. When a society is hierarchically constructed with vast disparities in power between different groups, it is possible that a previously disenfranchised group can become the oppressors of less powerful others.

Using the ecological metaphor, the issues and problems with which CP is concerned can be conceptualized as occurring at different levels of analysis (see Table 2.1). Different social issues and problems that occur at different levels of analysis are not isolated; they are interrelated. We argue that the common thread that links together the different problems and issues that we touch upon here and throughout the book is that of oppression. Elsewhere, we have defined oppression as follows:

> Oppression is described as a state of domination where the oppressed suffer the consequences of deprivation, exclusion, discrimination, exploitation, control of culture, and sometimes even violence. (Prilleltensky & Nelson, 2002, p. 12)

The core of oppression is power inequality. Oppression is a relational concept that implies asymmetric power relations between individuals, groups, communities or societies (Prilleltensky & Gonick, 1996; Watts & Serrano-García, 2003). Moreover, oppression is experienced at multiple levels of analysis: personal, relational and collective (see Table 2.1). At the level of the individual, disadvantaged people often internalize the dominant cultural narratives about themselves, which is psychologically damaging. This internal psychological oppression includes self-blame and feelings of personal worthlessness (Moane, 2003). In relationships with others, disadvantaged people are often seen as inferior and are treated as such by people who have more power. These dominant–subordinate relationships are characterized by an inequality in power, and they are embedded in larger structural arrangements that are manifested in social policies and community settings.

There are many different stories of oppression (see Box 2.1). Consider how African people came to the new world. Alex Haley's (1977) *Roots* tells the story of

Table 2.1 A journey of personal and political change

Ecological Level	Oppression →	Resistance and Liberation (processes to overcome oppression and achieve well-being) →	Well-being (a state of personal, relational and collective well-being)
Personal	Internalized, psychological oppression	Conscientization situates personal struggles in the context of larger political and structural forces	Control, choice, self-esteem, competence, independence, political rights and a positive identity
Relational	'Power over', domination of or by others	'Power with', power sharing, egalitarian relationships, solidarity	Positive and supportive relationships, participation in social, community and political life
Collective	Oppressive social practices manifested in policies and community settings	Resistance, social action	Acquisition of valued resources such as employment, income, education and housing

the roots of an African-American man and his family. Nearly two million Africans were taken from their homelands and packed on slave ships bound for the new world, where those who survived the journey were bought and sold as slaves. African-Americans have had to overcome slavery, segregation, racism, the Ku Klux Klan, brutal repression and violence, and economic disenfranchisement. The journeys of other marginalized groups have been characterized by social exclusion and segregation. People with disabilities (physical, developmental, mental health) have been excluded from mainstream community life and settings and sent off to special buildings, schools or institutions and had their power and civil rights stripped away. Women have experienced barriers to their participation in civic life. Gay, lesbian, and bisexual people have been forced into the 'closet' because of the tremendous social stigma that they experience.

Box 2.1   **Manifest Destiny and the Colonization of Native People in North America**

In his book, *Bury My Heart at Wounded Knee: An Indian History of the American West,* historian Dee Brown (1971) tells the story of 'how the west was won' in the late 19th century. Guided by a belief in 'manifest destiny', which upheld the innate superiority of white people, the US government and military embarked on a campaign of systematic destruction of aboriginal people to pave the way for settlers of European ancestry. This is a hard book to read. Each chapter tells a story of aggression against and conquest of a different nation of people. 'The Long Walk of the Navahos' is a story about the journey of these people on foot, in frigid weather, from their homeland into an internment camp. In Canada, aboriginal children were sent to residential schools run by missionaries to sever them from their families, communities, language and culture. Much the same happened in Australia with the stolen generation. The legacy of these schools is one of physical and sexual abuse and cultural genocide, whose impacts are still felt today. Brown's book, which was based to a large extent on oral history of aboriginal people, also demonstrates the resistance of aboriginal people who were vastly outnumbered and lacking in resources to combat the powerful US government. The stories in the book, and Brown's conclusion that aboriginal people stand among the most courageous of North Americans, present a compelling alternative to the 'cowboys and Indians' narrative promoted in popular culture.

Resistance and Liberation: Framing Problems, Listening to the Voices and Making the Invisible Visible

While part of the stories of disadvantaged people is about injustice and oppression, there are also hopeful and inspirational parts as well. There are many examples of resistance and heroic people who have fought bravely for social change against insurmountable odds. From the underground railroad and activists such as Sojourner Truth during the time of slavery, to the more recent civil rights and black power movements and leaders such as Martin Luther King Jr. and Malcolm X, and 'ordinary' citizens like Rosa Parks who refused to give up her seat and move to the back of the bus in the segregated southern US, African-Americans have resisted slavery and racism. The first wave of feminism focused on women's right to vote, while the second wave has striven to liberate women from the home and create opportunities for them to participate in, and contribute to, work, education and politics, and to have control over their bodies and reproduction. Different oppressed groups all have their stories of resistance.

In the third column of Table 2.1, we highlight the importance of disadvantaged people reclaiming power in their struggle to liberate themselves from oppression. Social change often begins with disadvantaged people's awareness and understanding of the unjust psychological and sociopolitical circumstances oppressing them. As we noted in Chapter 1, Brazilian educator and activist Paulo Freire (1970) referred to this as a process of 'conscientization'. In a study of the process of personal empowerment, Lord and Hutchison (1993) found that 'gaining awareness' was often a beginning point in people's journeys of empowerment. At the relational level, connecting with others in mutually supportive relationships in which power is shared is also important for regaining power (Moane, 2003). Solidarity with others can be found in self-help groups and social movement organizations, which can serve as vehicles for collective resistance and social action (Moane, 2003).

Along their journeys, many disadvantaged people have encountered psychologists. Sometimes the response of psychology has been to further perpetuate oppression, as the quotes from the eugenics movement in Chapter 1 illustrate. Today the more typical response of psychology is to offer 'help'. But the help is typically in the form of some type of therapy or intervention that strives to change disadvantaged individuals so that they can better adjust to unjust social conditions. We believe that the response of CP should be one that recognizes the injustices that disadvantaged people have experienced and that involves a partnership to work in solidarity with disadvantaged people towards social change. In this regard, consider the following statement from Australian Aboriginal social worker Lilla Watson: 'If you've come to help me you're wasting your time. But if you've come because your liberation is bound up with mine, then let us work together' (cited in Stringer, 1996, p. 148). To help create social change, community psychologists must reframe problems, listen to the voices of disadvantaged people, and make the invisible visible. This involves challenging commonly held assumptions and consciousness-raising about the sources of problems.

In many respects, CP appears to have suffered from the same historical blinders as the rest of psychology and the 'helping' professions. The problems facing people with serious mental health problems were framed in terms of deinstitutionalization and the need for community services, rather than in terms of larger social processes of social exclusion. While community psychologists played a leadership role in the development of preschool and school-based prevention programs for African-American children and families, the problems that they faced were not typically framed in terms of racism and economic disenfranchisement. Other issues and problems with structural roots have been ignored by CP. For example, in the early days of CP, the field was dominated by men and the issues facing women were invisible to the field (Bond & Mulvey, 2000). In spite of the commonalities between CP and feminism explicated by Anne Mulvey (1988) more than a decade ago, it is only recently that the value of feminist perspectives in CP has been recognized (Bond, Hill & Terenzio, 2000a, 2000b).

More recently there has been an increase in voices within the field of CP that have pushed for the inclusion of diverse groups and issues, with a focus on issues of power, oppression and liberation (Serrano-García & Bond, 1994; Watts & Serrano-García, 2003). Today, CP is broadly concerned with the issues and problems facing disadvantaged people, including minorities, women, children and adults living in poverty, people who are homeless, people with serious mental health problems, people with disabilities, gay, lesbian, and bisexual people, and many more. We believe that these voices have been helping the field to reframe problems so that there is more of a structural analysis of the causes of individual problems.

Towards Well-being

In earlier work, we have defined well-being as occurring at multiple levels of analysis (Nelson, Lord & Ochocka, 2001a; Prilleltensky, Nelson & Peirson, 2001b). At the individual level, well-being is manifested in terms of personal control, choice, self-esteem, competence, independence, political rights and a positive identity (see Table 2.1). At the relational level, the individual is embedded in a network of positive and supportive relationships and can participate freely in social, community and political life. The person is an active member of community. At the community and societal level, the individual is able to acquire such basic resources as employment, income, education and housing. Thus, well-being is not a matter of individual health, but rather a state of affairs that involves a transaction between individuals and supportive relationships and environments (Stokols, 2003). In its work with disadvantaged people, CP is not just concerned with liberation from oppression, but also with the achievement of a state of personal, relational and collective well-being.

Having provided the 'big picture' of CP, we now turn to an overview of the four main components of our conceptual framework for CP: (a) issues and problems, (b) values, (c) principles and conceptual tools, and (d) the science of CP. We begin by considering some of the dimensions of the issues and problems experienced by disadvantaged people.

Issues and Problems

Problems

It is important to make a distinction between the surface manifestations of problems, such as mental health problems, school underachievement, and crime, and the root causes of those surface manifestations. Joffe (1996) refers to these root causes as the 'causes of the causes'. These historical and structural problems are all characterized by oppression and power inequality between groups of people.

There are many dimensions of the issues and problems that can be traced to root causes of oppression and loss of power. First, as we noted in the previous section, society tends to engage in 'victim-blaming' of disadvantaged people (Ryan, 1971). The social context in which the problems facing disadvantaged people arise is ignored, and individuals are expected to 'pull themselves up by their bootstraps'. Framing problems in terms of individual-level difficulties leads to fragmented services for individuals, rather than efforts at collective or social change. An example of victim-blaming is blaming women who have been sexually assaulted by challenging them in terms of the clothing they were wearing when assaulted, suggesting that they did not try to fight off their assailant, or refusing to believe those who have been assaulted. Widespread victim-blaming tends to lead individuals to self-blame and internalized oppression. Second, disadvantaged people experience a multitude of health issues and psychosocial problems in living. For example, there is abundant research showing that children who have been maltreated live in families that are often stress-plagued and chaotic, and that these children manifest a variety of health and psychosocial problems (Peirson, Laurendeau & Chamberland, 2001).

Third, disadvantaged people are often isolated from networks of support. People with mental health problems, parents who maltreat their children, and many others tend to be socially isolated. Fourth, disadvantaged people experience powerlessness. Moreover, powerlessness is not just a personal quality (for example feelings of helplessness and lack of control), but rather something that is experienced in the context of asymmetric relationships with other people and systems (Prilleltensky & Gonick, 1996). Fifth, powerlessness is related to the discrimination that is experienced by groups and individuals who are held to single standards (that is, those that assert the superiority of male, white, heterosexual able-bodied people). Long-standing patterns of sexism, racism, heterosexism, ableism and stigma serve to rationalize and perpetuate power inequalities at multiple levels of analysis. Moreover, disadvantaged people have been and continue to be subjected to exclusion and segregation from a range of social and community settings. Women who experience the 'glass ceiling' in career advancement and who are confined to low-paid 'pink collar' jobs or social assistance are but one example of how existing social conditions maintain inequality and social exclusion.

However, perhaps the largest social problem today is the complacency of people who enjoy many social and economic privileges. Many people have little awareness of the problems facing disadvantaged people, ignore these issues, or construct the problems in terms of 'victim-blaming'. As a consequence, advantaged people tend go blithely along in their lives, without much concern about these issues. But this is not just about 'other people'; it is about all of us. In the 1950s, there was a cartoon strip called Pogo that often included political satire. In one sketch, Pogo said 'I have met the enemy and (s)he is us'. This statement captures the complicity and complacency of the dominant culture and CP regarding the problems facing disadvantaged people. Consciousness-raising, anger about social injustice and a passion for social change are antidotes to this complacency.

The Global Context

Society is also becoming more global with technology, communication, travel, trade and capital. One of the consequences of globalization is the increasing gap between the 'haves' and 'have nots', both within societies and between countries. Economic exploitation and disenfranchisement of disadvantaged people are widespread in both developed and developing countries. More and more low-income people in western countries are being forced into 'McJobs' (that is, low-paying jobs in the service sector), while individuals in developing countries, particularly women and young people, are paid a pittance in wages to make the athletic shoes, clothing and other commercial products that are widely advertised and marketed in western countries.

Corporate power and global capitalism are also bringing about sweeping changes in the natural environment (environmental degradation), working condi-tions (loss of power and rights of working people and unions), culture (a rapidly developing 'monoculture'), and government policy (tax cuts and a diminished role for the state in addressing social inequalities, preserving the environment and ensuring the health of the population) (Korten, 1995). With government cutbacks at national and state levels, infrastructures (schools, housing, social programs) at the community level are being diminished, and communities are increasingly being asked to 'do more with less' and to develop plans for 'sustainability' (that is, find ways of maintaining services and supports in the absence of government funding) (Barlow & Campbell, 1995).

We want to acknowledge that 'globalization' is a contested term. It means differ-ent things to different people. It has economic, cultural, social and health connota-tions. Joseph Stiglitz (2002) knows both the cold and the human faces of globalization only too well. As chief economist and vice-president of the World Bank from 1997 until January 2000, he knew the cold face of globalization: the numbers, the trade statistics, the graphs and the deficits on pieces of paper. But he also got to know the human face of globalization: the people affected by unfair trade policies and the poor children going hungry because of the Washington consensus that imposed severe austerity measures on many developing countries.

Stiglitz is well positioned to document the positive and negative effects of glob-alization in the economic, social, cultural and health domains. He admits that glob-alization brought medicines to developing nations, and attention to human rights violations, and made people worldwide more aware of our interdependence. Stiglitz, winner of the Nobel Prize in Economics in 2001, points out that:

> Opening up to international trade has helped many countries grow far more quickly than they would otherwise have done. International trade helps economic develop-ment when a country's exports drive its economic growth. Export led growth was the centrepiece of the industrial policy that enriched much of Asia and left millions of people there far better off. Because of globalization many people in the world now live longer than before and their standard of living is far better. People in the West may regard low-paying jobs at Nike as exploitation, but for many people in the developing world, working in a factory is a far better option than staying down on the farm and growing rice ... Globalization has reduced the sense of isolation felt in much of the developing world and has given many people in the developing countries access to knowledge well beyond the reach of even the wealthiest in any country a century ago.

The anti-globalization protests themselves are a result of this connectedness. Links between activists in different parts of the world, particularly those links forged through the Internet communication, brought about the pressure that resulted in the international landmines treaty – despite the opposition of many powerful governments. (Stiglitz, 2002, pp. 4–5).

Stiglitz (2002) goes on to document in his *Globalization and its Discontents* the many benefits derived from open communications between developed and developing nations. In some poor countries irrigation projects doubled the incomes of farmers, HIV/AIDS projects prevented the spread of the disease, and literacy initiatives enhanced the education of children and women. When Jamaica opened the market to the import of US milk, local producers suffered, but many more children had access to cheaper milk. Of course, these are not ideal solutions. But in every calculus of globalization, children's access to milk has to count for something, as do literacy and the prevention of infectious diseases. Imperfect as they may be, Stiglitz could live with these solutions, were it not for the fact that the World Bank and the International Monetary Fund (IMF) began pushing for an agenda that did not take into account the needs of the people in developing nations. Governed by the mantra that market liberalization should cure all countries of their economic woes, they proceeded to impose measures that were inadequate for the realities of many countries, because of either timing, pace and culture or lack of infrastructure. The cure turned out to be worse than the disease in many cases. Stiglitz recounts the growing gap between poor and rich countries, the devastation of some local industries due to unfair competition with subsidized products in the US, and the lack of investments in unstable economies. In essence, Stiglitz contends that the interests of developed nations superseded the concern for poor nations. While poor countries were expected to open their markets in return for financial aid, the rich nations continued to subsidize products, creating an unfair advantage in their favour. The narrow focus on monetary policies superseded concerns for safety nets. The obsession with economic growth superseded concerns for human development. Imposed solutions were no solutions at all.

For Stiglitz, democracy is part of the cure. When China and other countries in East Asia designed their own economic path, the results were favourable. When other countries relied primarily on the IMF, the results were disastrous. In 1990 China's gross domestic product was only 60 per cent that of Russia. In only 10 years the numbers had been reversed. While China reduced poverty greatly, Russia increased it. China was in charge of its reform, Russia was led by international financial institutions.

> Globalization itself is neither good nor bad. It has the *power* to do enormous good, and for the countries of East Asia, who have embraced globalization *under their own terms*, at their own pace, it has been an enormous benefit, is spite of the setback of the 1997 crisis. But in much of the world it has not brought comparable benefits. For many, it seems closer to an unmitigated disaster. (Stiglitz, 2002, p. 20)

CP, which is concerned with social context, needs to be cognizant of these larger global changes because they are having enormous impacts on the mission of the field. CP, like much of the dominant culture, has acquiesced to and been complacent with some of the damaging aspects of globalization. As the saying goes, 'if you are not part of the solution, you are part of the problem'. In Chapter 15, Tod Sloan provides a more in-depth look at globalization, poverty and social justice in relation to CP.

Values of Community Psychology

Against this background of historically and structurally rooted problems, community psychologists have been concerned with creating social change. But social change towards what ends? We argue that the vision for the work of CP should be guided by a set of values. Values alone inform a vision closer to an ideal or utopian future or a good society, because values are concerned with *what should be*, not what *is*. Science and conceptual tools can help us to realize the utopian future, but they cannot inform us what that future should look like. The problems tell us where we are coming from and what we are trying to change, the vision and values tell us the direction in which we should be headed. One's values and the values of a field such as CP come from several sources. Values derive from one's personal experiences and moral philosophy (Prilleltensky, 2001), and one's spiritual and religious beliefs (Mankowski & Rappaport, 2000; Mustakova-Possardt, 2003).

In striving to become a science, psychology, particularly applied psychology, has ignored the moral, ethical and value dimensions of its work. Failure to attend to value issues has led to psychology upholding the societal status quo (Prilleltensky, 1994b) and to the continued oppression of marginalized people. For example, while the field of behaviour modification has led to the development of many powerful and helpful therapeutic tools, its lack of attention to value issues has been a recurring problem. Behaviour modification has used aversive 'treatment' (that is, physical punishment); it has restricted the civil liberties of captive and dependent people in institutions; it has been used to try to 'convert' individuals' sexual orientation from gay to straight; and its applications in educational settings have emphasized compliance and docility of children. While CP has had its blind spots, as we noted earlier, it has paid attention to value issues since the inception of the field (Rappaport, 1977).

Elsewhere, Isaac Prilleltensky and colleagues (Prilleltensky, Laurendeau, Chamberland & Peirson, 2001) have offered a template of values which we argue should guide the work of CP. These values are: (a) holism, (b) health, (c) caring, compassion, and support for community structures, (d) self-determination, participation and social justice, (e) respect for diversity and (f) accountability to oppressed groups. While we elaborate on these values in the next chapter, here we briefly define them.

The first value of *holism* reminds us of the importance of focusing on the whole person, including his or her strengths, in the context of the many relationships, settings and environments in which the person is embedded. Second, *health* can be defined as a state of physical, psychological, social and material well-being. Health is more than the absence of illness; it is a positive state that includes personal, relational and collective dimensions. Third, the value of *caring, compassion, and support for community structures* involves empathy and concern for the welfare of others.

Moreover, this value emphasizes the importance of settings and community structures that facilitate the pursuit of personal and communal goals.

Fourth, *self-determination* can be described as having the opportunity and power to direct one's life as one wishes; *participation* entails individuals playing an active role in decisions that affect their lives, and meaningfully contributing to their communities; and *social justice* is concerned with the fair and equitable allocations of resources and obligations in society. Fifth, the value of *diversity* asserts that the unique social identities of individuals need to be respected and accepted. Finally, *accountability to oppressed groups* refers to the responsibility of dominant groups and individuals, including community psychologists, to work with disadvantaged people towards social change.

These values have been expressed, either implicitly or explicitly, in the principles and concepts of CP, to which we now turn.

Principles and Conceptual Tools of Community Psychology

In this section, we briefly note the key principles of CP: (a) ecology, (b) prevention and promotion, (c) community, (d) power, (e) inclusion, and (f) commitment and depowerment. Moreover, each of these principles can be applied to promote liberation and well-being at different levels of analysis: (a) personal, (b) relational, and (c) collective. To date, CP has focused much of its energy on the personal and relational levels of analysis. We agree with a tenet of the feminist movement that 'the personal is political' (for example Moane, 2003), which suggests to us that CP needs to push its boundaries to the collective level of analysis. We briefly identify the conceptual tools that flow from the core principles to these specific levels of analysis. We elaborate more fully on these principles and conceptual tools in Chapters 4–6.

Ecology

Community psychologists James Kelly, Ed Trickett and colleagues (Kelly, 1966; Trickett, Kelly & Todd, 1972) introduced the metaphor of ecology to CP. Kelly argued that in studying the transactions between people and their environments the metaphor of an eco-system is more appropriate than the dominant mechanistic, reductionistic metaphor used in individual psychology to study basic human processes of learning, cognition, perception and brain–behaviour relations. The ecological metaphor, which flows from the value of holism, suggests that communities are open systems with many different levels and connections. The value of the ecological metaphor for CP lies in its ability to contextualize the issues and problems that face disadvantaged people over time and across multiple levels of analysis, and to embrace the value of holism over reductionism. The ecological metaphor views human problems and competencies within the context of characteristics of the individual (for example coping skills), micro-level analysis (for example family, peer group), meso-level analysis, settings that mediate between smaller systems and the larger society (for example work settings, schools, neighbourhood organizations), and macro-level analysis (for example social policies, social class, social norms). The smaller systems are nested within the larger systems, and the various levels are interdependent (Bronfenbrenner, 1979). Failure to think and practice ecologically reproduces the dominant culture's emphasis on individualism and encourages the tendency to engage in 'victim-blaming'.

Prevention and Promotion

Prevention and health promotion are also founding concepts that have guided the work of CP. The concepts of prevention and promotion reflect the value of health and are used to promote well-being and prevent psychosocial problems. Community psychologists adapted the concept of prevention from the field of public health, which has emphasized population health and the prevention of physical diseases. Gerald Caplan (1964), a community psychiatrist, applied the concept of prevention to mental health problems and introduced a threefold typology of prevention: primary (reduction of the rates of a mental health problem in the community), secondary (early detection and treatment), and tertiary (treatment and rehabilitation to reduce disability resulting from problems). Several community psychologists studied public health or were strongly influenced by public health and began the work of translating prevention concepts into workable program models to promote competence, mental health and well-being and to prevent various psychosocial problems in living.

In his review of the literature on mental health promotion and primary prevention 20 years ago, community psychologist Emory Cowen (1977) referred to progress as being made in 'baby steps'. In a review 20 years later, Cowen (1996) spoke of the 'lengthy strides' that had been made in the field. Clearly the past three decades have seen tremendous growth in the research and practice bases of prevention and promotion. Recent reviews of the literature have demonstrated the effectiveness of prevention programs. For example, on the basis of a review of 177 evaluations of prevention programs for children and adolescents, Durlak and Wells (1997) reported that a number of different types of intervention have proved to be effective in preventing emotional and behavioural problems in children. Moreover, prevention programs have been applied in a wide variety of settings to address many different problems, including violence against women, criminal behaviour and conduct disorder, the mental health of school-aged children (Greenberg, Domitrovich & Bumbarger, 2001), and child maltreatment and family well-being (Nelson, Laurendeau, Chamberland & Peirson, 2001; MacLeod & Nelson, 2000).

The principle of prevention and promotion can be applied at different ecological levels. Much of the early work of community psychologists in prevention was person-centred in its focus on promoting the well-being and enhancing the competence of individuals (Cowen, 1985). An example of a person-centred approach to prevention is teaching young children social problem-solving skills. Prevention can also be practised on a community-wide basis to change the social environment (Cowen, 1994). Prevention programs of this sort typically target meso-level settings, such as schools, to promote relational well-being. An example of this type of prevention is changing the high school environment to ensure a better transition of students from middle school to high school. Finally, prevention and promotion can also be applied at the macro level. Macro-level prevention and promotion seek to promote collective well-being through changes in public policy (Albee, 1986).

Community

The concept of a psychological sense of community was introduced by community psychologist Seymour Sarason (1974). Sarason astutely observed a decline in support in traditional communities and an increased alienation on the part of people in western countries. Communities help to fill human needs for support and connection, and isolation and psychosocial problems in living are likely to follow when these needs are not met. He argued that the overarching mission of CP should be to create a psychological sense of community. Sarason's concept of a psychological sense of community has generated a great deal of research (Chavis & Pretty, 1999; Fisher, Sonn & Bishop, 2002; McMillan & Chavis, 1986).

Various conceptions of community and psychological sense of community are related to the values of caring, compassion and support for community infrastructures. Moreover, community and sense of community can be conceptualized at multiple levels of analysis. In shifting away from clinical psychology, early community psychologists recognized that distressed individuals need more than caring and compassionate therapists; they need caring and compassionate relationships and communities. At the level of the individual, the concept of social support highlights the importance of relationships and the different types of support that stem from supportive relationships, including emotional support, guidance, tangible and financial support and socialization. Many community psychologists, like Canadian community psychologist Ben Gottlieb, have contributed greatly to the development of the concept of social support, research on social support, and the development of social support interventions (Gottlieb, 1981; Cohen, Underwood & Gottlieb, 2000). As an alternative or complement to professional treatment, community psychologists have helped to conceptualize, design and evaluate individual-level support interventions, using non-professional and volunteer helpers. Meso-level interventions to promote relational well-being include professionally led support groups and self-help/mutual aid groups and organizations that are formed by and for people who share a common problem or concern (Cohen et al., 2000; Humphreys, 1997).

Community capacity and social capital are relatively new terms that have yet to receive much attention in CP, but which have potential for addressing collective well-being at the macro level. Community capacity and social capital refer broadly to the qualities of communities that are related to the well-being of individuals. While capital is usually thought of in terms of economic assets, Putnam (2000) argued that communities can also have social capital, including a range of community organizations and networks, civic participation, community identity, and norms of trust and mutual support. The development of community capacity and social capital through community development and social policy formulation is important for the promotion of collective well-being.

Power

In the 1980s, community psychologist Julian Rappaport introduced the concept of empowerment (Rappaport, 1981, 1984, 1987) to the field. He challenged the dominance of the concept of prevention in CP, arguing that prevention ignored the critical issue of power. Like clinical psychologists, community psychologists with a prevention orientation could work from an 'expert' model in which they developed interventions *for* other people. Alternatively, he argued for an empowerment approach in which community psychologists work *with* disadvantaged people to promote their self-determination and control. The concept of empowerment has had a tremendous impact on the field and has generated a great deal of theory, research and practice within CP (Swift & Levin, 1987; Zimmerman, 2000; Zimmerman & Perkins, 1995), as well as in other disciplines.

Rappaport (1981, 1987) argued further that empowerment is ecological in nature and can be conceptualized at multiple levels of analysis. We believe that power is an overarching concept for CP. At the individual level, people who have typically experienced a lack of control in their lives not only need a change in their thinking about power but experiences of actually having authority over events in their lives (Riger, 1993). Personal empowerment is the process of reclaiming power in one's life (Lord & Hutchison, 1993). An important component of empowerment is active participation in the life of the community (Zimmerman, 2000).

It is also important to conceptualize power at the relational or meso-level of analysis. Elsewhere, we have introduced the concept of 'partnership' to address power at the this level. We defined partnerships as:

> relationships between community psychologists, oppressed groups, and other stakeholders that strive to advance the values of caring, compassion, community, health, self-determination, participation, power-sharing, human diversity, and social justice for oppressed groups. These values drive both the processes and the outcomes of partnerships that focus on services and supports, coalitions and social action, and research and evaluation. (Nelson, Prilleltensky & Gillivary, 2001, p. 651)

For us, the concept of partnership provides community psychologists with a way of thinking about how they work with disadvantaged groups. While CP has been concerned with citizen participation for some time (Wandersman & Florin, 2000), the concept of partnership that we are promoting highlights the importance of the participation of disadvantaged groups in community research and action and suggests that community psychologists should work in solidarity with disadvantaged people towards the goals of liberation and well-being (Lykes, 2001a).

At the macro level, social change is needed to promote collective well-being. As we stated earlier, social change is not a new idea in CP. During the 1960s, a time of social change in the US, many of the founders of CP argued for the need to change oppressive social conditions in pursuit of social justice (Albee, 1986; Goldenberg, 1978; Rappaport, 1987). Social change emphasizes the importance of a vision and values of a more just and caring society (Prilleltensky, 2001) and recognizes the fact that many social problems, including health and mental health problems, are strongly related to socioeconomic inequalities (Dohrenwend & Dohrenwend, 1969). But social change is very difficult to achieve because it threatens the power of dominant groups within society.

Community psychologists have contributed to the development of social intervention strategies and concepts that we discuss in more detail in Part III of this book (Bennett, 1987; Seidman, 1983a, 1983b). However, the field of CP has not yet fully embraced the need for social change in its research and practice. To do so, CP needs to adopt the value of social justice as a major principle, become more political, engage in solidarity with oppressed groups and social change movements, and utilize alternative research methods that are suited to the study of social change.

Inclusion

The value of cultural relativity and diversity occupied a prominent position in Rappaport's (1977) early textbook in CP. He argued that people, particularly disadvantaged people, should have the right to be different and not to be judged against one single standard. In spite of this early focus on diversity, the concept of diversity and equity promotion did not develop more fully until the 1990s. As Trickett (1994) stated, 'the diversity concept has been ideologically central but relatively neglected in the field of CP over time' (p. 584).

As western societies have become more culturally diverse and CP has become a more diverse body of people, there has been greater attention to diversity and the promotion of inclusion in CP theory, research, practice and training. In the 1990s and early 2000s, feminist, critical and community psychologists, such as Ingrid Huygens, Irma Serrano-García, Meg Bond and Rod Watts, have shown how racism, sexism, classism, ableism and heterosexism are forms of sociopolitical oppression and have elaborated on interventions that strive to eliminate such oppression and to promote inclusion (Huygens, 1996a, 1996b; Serrano-García & Bond, 1994; Trickett et al., 1994; Watts, 1992; Watts & Serrano-García, 2003).

To overcome discrimination and to promote inclusion, interventions need to occur at multiple levels of analysis. At the individual level, the recovery of a positive identity and the development of an awareness of sociopolitical conditions that create shame and stigma are important parts of the journey of disadvantaged people (Watts, Williams & Jagers, 2003). For example, in the mental health field, the current emphasis on empowerment and recovery narratives (for example Deegan, 1988; Nelson, Lord & Ochocka, 2001a; Rappaport, 1993) underscores the importance of mental health consumer/survivors striving to overcome the damaging impacts of stigma, labelling, powerlessness and segregation that they have experienced.

But processes of recovery do not occur in isolation; rather they occur in supportive contexts. At the relational level, settings that are run by and for people with disabilities, such as self-help/mutual aid organizations and Independent Living Centres (Deegan, 1988; Rappaport, 1993), appear to provide many of the favourable qualities that researchers and individuals who experienced serious mental illness have suggested facilitate the process of recovery. The qualities include the opportunity to share stories, the promotion of a positive alternative community narrative from which people can draw and incorporate into their personal stories, peer and natural support, and opportunities to contribute to the group, organization or community. At the macro level, policies that strive to enhance the equity of disadvantaged groups are needed to promote an inclusive society. Continuing with the example of mental health consumer/survivors, such policies would address structural problems facing consumer/survivors, including lack of affordable housing, unemployment and poverty (Nelson, Lord & Ochocka, 2001b).

Commitment and Depowerment

Partnerships with oppressed groups require accountability on the part of professionals to the oppressed group (Nelson, Prilleltensky et al., 2001). This involves both a commitment to social change and working in solidarity with members of the oppressed group and a conscious effort on behalf of professionals to 'depower' themselves in these relationships. Sharing power and knowledge is vital to the development of more equal working relationships (Ochocka, Janzen & Nelson, 2002). To overcome complacency, professionals must raise their consciousness about oppression. Critical psychologists and feminist psychologists have introduced the concept of reflexivity to highlight the fact that the subjectivities of community researchers and interventionists are an important part of any research or intervention process (Wilkinson, 1988). According to conventional wisdom, the researcher or professional is assumed to be a detached, objective expert. One unfortunate consequence of this position for CP is that it treats disadvantaged people as objects to be studied or helped, rather than as whole people with strengths, who actively resist the unjust social conditions in which they live. This process of objectifying or 'othering' people who are different or disadvantaged maintains the power imbalance between professionals and disadvantaged citizens. Detached objectivity emphasizes surveillance, control and compliance with authority.

While there is value in objectivity, there is also value in subjectivity. Subjectivity introduces the human dimensions (personal, interpersonal and political) of the researcher and professional and draws attention to the relationship between the researcher–professional and disadvantaged people. For the community psychologist who is guided by the values that we outlined earlier in the chapter, community research and action are a passionate undertaking. But we need to be critically aware that in our desire to help and change the world, we can cause harm through our blind spots. For this reason, it is important to be self-critical and reflexive about one's research and action. Reflexivity suggests that we acknowledge our subjectivity, share the interpretation of research findings with disadvantaged people, be aware of the political and ideological character of our research and action, and reflect on the problem of representation and authority in the construction of knowledge and social change (Alvesson & Sköldberg, 2000).

At the relational level, there must be mechanisms set in place for mutual accountability in value-based partnerships. In their work with mental health consumer/survivors, Geoff Nelson and his colleagues (Nelson, Ochocka, Griffin & Lord, 1998; Ochocka et al., 2002) found several useful mechanisms for the promotion of accountability, including having a steering committee composed of all partners and a research team with researchers from the disadvantaged group working as paid employees within the project. New Zealand community psychologist Ingrid Huygens (1997) has argued that disadvantaged groups do not want professionals or dominant social groups to empower them, rather they want these dominant groups to 'depower' themselves. To promote collective well-being, structural depower-ment of dominant groups and institutionalized processes of accountability to disad-vantaged groups are needed.

The Science of Community Psychology

While values, principles and concepts are of central concern to CP, so too is the scientific base of CP. In fact, it is the scientific base that distinguishes CP from social and political movements and community action groups (Dalton et al., 2001). Like CP, such movements and groups are value-driven, but they lack a scientific base that creates new knowledge towards the goal of social change. One of the founders of CP, Seymour Sarason, makes the following point about the science of CP:

> I have long believed that among the major contributions a CP can make are demon-strations that theory and research provide a basis for interventions that make a positive difference in community living and activities. Without such demonstrations, CP lacks persuasive justification. (2003, p. 209)

Without a sound scientific base, CP would lack credibility as a social and human science or as a sub-discipline of psychology.

While the necessity of a scientific basis for CP is not in dispute, the nature of what counts as 'science' is very much contested in CP and psychology (Kelly, 2003). While CP is meant to be an action science that creates social change, community psychologists experience considerable pressure from their mainstream psychology colleagues (who judge their research for tenure and promotion decisions) to conform to more conventional, quantitative, hypothesis-testing research that usually has nothing to do with social change. Moreover, the relationship between citizens and community psychologists is of vital importance for collaborative participatory research (Chavis, Stucky & Wandersman, 1983), but the only model that main-stream psychology has to offer is that of 'experimenter' and 'subject'. Consequently, very few of the reports of CP research published up until the mid-1980s described the types of partnerships between community psychologists and citizens that we alluded to earlier (Walsh, 1987).

Since the mid-1980s, the field of CP has held two conferences on CP research, one in 1988 (Tolan, Keys, Chertock & Jason, 1990) and one in 2003 (Jason, Keys, Suarez-Balcazar, Taylor, Davis, Durlak & Isenberg, 2004). The books on the proceedings of these two conferences and recent papers on the science of CP (Wandersman, 2003) have articulated different approaches to community science that strive to link the goals of understanding and action, as well as emphasizing the importance of participatory and collaborative processes between CP researchers and community groups and citizens. Also, these publications and others have broad-ened the range of research paradigms (assumptions about the nature of the world and how it can be understood) and legitimate research approaches, including qual-itative methods, in which the 'data' are people's words rather than numbers (for example focus group interviews, in-depth, open-ended interviews). In fact, the nature of CP research has changed so much since the mid-1980s that there are now several competing ways of doing community research. In Part IV of the book, we explore in more detail various approaches to CP research.

Chapter Summary

In this chapter, we provided an overview of the conceptual framework for the entire book. We began with the 'big picture' of CP, including the central problem with which CP is concerned – oppression – and the central goals of CP – liberation and well-being. In so doing, we argued that CP is primarily concerned with disadvantaged populations, such as children and families living in poverty, people of colour, immigrants, refugees, women, people with disabilities, and gay, lesbian and bisexual people. These groups have been historically subject to oppression by virtue of having considerably less power than dominant groups in a society.

We further argued that it is easy to lose sight of the people community interventions are designed to 'help'. This is because western science and professionalism have historically emphasized distance, objectivity and expertise when it comes to 'helping'. The intervention and the research are typically at the forefront of professionals' consciousness, while those they 'serve' are often more distant objects of their good intentions. For this reason, we believe that community psychologists need to be more self-reflexive about both themselves and the people with whom they are working. They need to start listening to the stories of disadvantaged people, rather than constructing solutions for them, and to make visible the invisible issue of power inequality that characterizes oppression.

We then provided an overview of the main dimensions of the conceptual framework underlying this book:

■ issues and problems
■ values
■ principles and conceptual tools, and
■ the science of CP.

We pointed out some of the different facets of the issues and problems that face disadvantaged people. The overarching concept which links the different issues and problems is that of oppression or power-inequality.

Next, we argued that CP, like all of the social sciences and helping professions, is a value-laden field. While science and professionalism have been dominant in the training of applied psychologists, values and social ethics have been neglected. But it is not possible to adopt a scientific and professional position that is 'value free'. Moreover, we argued that it is dangerous to proclaim such a position, because failing to acknowledge one's values often leads, whether intentionally or not, to upholding the societal status quo. There are many examples of how scientific psychology has been used to rationalize racism and sexism for instance (Teo, 1999). Alternatively, we proposed a set of values that we claim can help to guide a CP that promotes liberation and well-being. Finally, we provided a brief overview of key CP principles: ecology, prevention and promotion, community, power, inclusion, and commitment and depowerment. For each of these principles, we highlighted conceptual tools that can be used at the personal, relational and collective levels of analysis.

We ended by discussing briefly CP as a science. We noted that unlike the mainstream of psychology, CP is concerned not just with the creation of new knowledge but with how knowledge can create social change. We also observed that CP has had a difficult time breaking away from the traditions of mainstream psychological research, but that since the early 1990s there has been an expansion of approaches to doing CP research.

COMMENTARY: Why Community Psychology? A Personal Story
Julian Rappaport

The offer to comment on this chapter included an invitation to write in the first person. I am grateful for both the offer and the invitation. My own journey as a student of psychology has been going on for more than 40 years, and perhaps that story can help make explicit some of the ideas presented in this book as they have played themselves out in the professional life of one psychologist.

As a high school student growing up in Philadelphia in the late 1950s I had been too young to appreciate the importance of the US Supreme Court's 1954 ruling that ended legally sanctioned intentional segregation in public schools. However, between 1954 and 1964 (the year I graduated from college) I learned a great deal about social justice from the collective struggles of African-American people for desegregation, jobs and voting rights. Although I was interested in these social issues I did not connect that interest to my own educational goals until I saw the *connections between social, political, economic and psychological well-being*. But this is a connection that took me a long time to make. Nowadays community psychologists, thanks to books like this one, help to make these connections more obvious.

When I was in high school, the mid-20th century African-American civil rights movement had already begun to build momentum, but the war in Vietnam was yet to emerge in US politics. These two forces would prove to be important in the formation of CP. By the time I entered graduate school both forces were fully entering my consciousness, competing for space with traditional psychology. Fortunately for me, while I was a graduate student (1964–68) this new field emerged as a professional identity. CP offered me a way to reconcile my personal values and my vocational interests.

Ultimately, I came to understand that the struggles of African-Americans in the 1950s and 1960s were only grudgingly supported by many key legislators because at that time they saw our country to be in a worldwide conflict with Communism. It was impossible to assert (to countries we were asking to join us in a struggle against Communism) that American democracy stood for freedom when African-Americans were intentionally subjected to legalized segregation and deprived of access to the very human rights wo argued for elsewhere. This was my first glimpse of the fact that US foreign policy is intimately tied to domestic policy. At the present time this connection, thanks to many changes in the world's communication systems, economic policies and balance of power, is far more obvious. It is also more obvious that psychologists have a contribution to make by collaborating with citizens who are concerned about social justice. For example, my colleagues and I currently work with local leaders and citizens concerned with making our public schools more responsive to the needs of families of colour, and people who are not economically privileged. Our work revolves around finding ways to break down the barriers between community and school, especially in neighbourhoods where there has been a history of alienation from the school (Good et al., 1997; Kloos et al., 1997).

When I entered college I thought I would become a history teacher. I soon found that emotionally I wanted to study psychology in order to be able to 'help people'. However, intellectually I was struck by two things: (a) how broad the study of psychology can be, and (b) how narrow its practitioners (scholars and researchers, as well as human service workers) want to make it. It was the first observation, its breadth, that intellectually attracted me to psychology. It has been the second observation, encountered over and over again, that has driven my career towards CP's attempts to resist a narrowing of the field. *The need for a wider, rather than a narrower vision for psychology is an underlying theme in CP*. It leads us to consider both the content and the methods of social history, economics, political science and anthropology, as well as social work, community development, education, medicine and law. Work for social justice in the community uses every tool we can find. Disciplinary boundaries are of less concern than crossing boundaries. We seek to collaborate both with other scholars and with ordinary citizens.

Eventually I began to see that efforts to organize for social justice both had a positive psychological effect on the people who participated, and enabled many who had been shut out from the benefits of prosperity to join in the fruits of democracy. Yet many others remained outsiders, and those outsiders generally suffered higher rates of the various problems in living that psychologists want to reduce. Although my own grandparents had immigrated from Eastern Europe early in the 20th century, and my family had many experiences as the objects of discrimination, both in Europe and in the US, growing up I did not connect these experiences with the struggles of 'Negroes' (as they were then called in polite conversation) or with the tramps (as homeless men were then referred to) I often saw on the city streets. I did not connect the anti-Semitism my family experienced with religious or ethnic prejudice and discrimination more generally. Nor did I wonder why, despite the high rates of white collar crime, most prisons are filled with poor people, or why some problems are considered social issues and others are not (Humphreys & Rappaport, 1993).

Although I knew of people called seriously mentally ill who were confined in squalid and punitive mental institutions (they were often the subject of journalistic exposé) I never connected their placement with social, economic or professional decisions about their care. I assumed that their situation was just the result of an unfortunate 'disease'. I assumed the same thing about people referred to at that time as 'retarded', who were also living in large state institutions.

I thought that people who were referred to as 'homosexuals' suffered from an illness. I did not understand the ways that professional helpers (psychiatrists, psychologists, social workers) had combined a bio-medical framework with a moralistic version of character and individual responsibility so as to blame many of the victims of social practices, economic decisions, cultural biases and historical inequities for all of their own problems in living. I had no idea that lay people could form their own organizations for assisting one another, or that every problem encountered did not require a highly paid professional to provide expert advice. I did not realize that personal responsibility can be expressed in opposition to, as well as in congruence with, status quo power relationships among people, or that gay people could live healthy and productive lives. I took it for granted that women stayed at home to raise children and men worked outside the home. Men 'helped out' with housework and child rearing, but these jobs were clearly women's work. At that time I had only a faint understanding that the Native people, who had lived in North America before Europeans 'discovered' it, had complex and well-organized civilizations, and that the Europeans had actually stolen their land, their children, their culture and their way of life. Nor did I realize that there were many Native people alive today, not as romanticized historical curiosities, but as citizens with both needs and rights. There was, when I entered psychology, no systematic study of domestic violence, no serious recognition of gender, ethnic and cultural differences in psychology, no understanding and no notion of prevention of problems in living outside the field of public health, and no sense in which the psychology of helpers was about more than mental health or adjustment to the world as it is.

As a graduate student I learned to do psychological assessment and psychotherapy. However, I soon discovered that those who needed help the most were least likely to get it. Many people in need had no medical insurance, others were unlikely to come to mental health clinics or to benefit from talk therapies, even if they did show up. When insurance payments ran out people were often discharged or sent to long-term institutional care, where they became lost for years in a poorly run system. Social class and race were the best predictors of diagnosis and treatment. Often the job of the therapist was to help people fit into the world around them, no matter how unjust. Something was wrong. Later I realized that the mental health system, including its venues for service delivery and the style of that delivery, was a reflection of the larger society's (lack of) regard for people of colour or for the economically poor.

I first encountered, in a direct way, the effects of oppression on mental health when I began to work with the seriously mentally ill. This happened for me in two very different settings – first, at a university-run medical centre, and later at a state hospital. The medical centre operated a large general hospital that included a psychiatric unit. Many psychologists, psychiatrists, social workers and nurses staffed the unit as a teaching hospital for medical students, residents and interns, as well as psychology students and post doctoral appointees. I discovered that we spent a great deal of time diagnosing people and that the diagnosis, except for purposes of medication, had little to do with the treatment and nothing to do with the patient's actual life circumstances. The best predictor of how long a person would be hospitalized was the number of days their medical insurance covered. Power relations between staff and patients were very clear. The model of care was an expert providing advice and medication to people in need who could afford their services. Unfortunately, for many people such help was either not available, or insufficient. It seemed to me that how people were treated depended on who they were and how much money they had, not on their particular problems in living. In the state hospitals of that time I found literally thousands of patients. Such large settings are rare today, although many seriously ill mental patients continue to be treated in ways that condemn them to inadequate care. This problem is still frequently reported in the *New York Times*, as a search of that newspaper for stories appearing in the last five years concerning the inadequate care provided for mental patients will quickly reveal. *CP is one effort to identify and support alternative care, including prevention, mobilization of citizen volunteers, mutual help organizations, advocacy and other empowering social policies.*

My experiences directly observing the oppression of people identified as 'seriously mentally ill' led me into the field of community mental health in an effort to liberate people from the confines of mental hospitals. I conducted a variety of studies looking for alternatives, including one that led to a book describing how my colleagues (Jack Chinsky and Emory Cowen) and I brought college undergraduates into a large state hospital in order to serve as discussion group leaders with the patients (Rappaport, Chinsky & Cowen, 1971). Our work was based on studies by other investigators who had found that undergraduates and other citizen volunteers can have as much, or more, of a positive impact on people with problems in living as do professional mental health workers. We also extended this kind of work into the field of delinquency prevention (Rappaport, Seidman & Davidson, 1979). It eventually led me to go a step further. I began to collaborate with a mutual-help organization entirely run by former

mental patients, without any professional control. They ran their own groups, and even established group homes for their members. They developed their own methods of care. My job was to help document what they did. My research group, including my colleague Edward Seidman and a large number of graduate students, tried to detail, in both formal research and writing, the story of this patient-run organization, showing how they took control of their own lives (Rappaport et al., 1985). Our aim was not to tell people what to do, but to provide resources, and social and scientific support. This required us to listen to the people of concern, to hear and to help them tell their story (Rappaport, 1993, 2000). *This orientation, which rejects the usual power arrangement of expert/helper relationships, guides much of CP.* It directly confronts the contradiction of telling people to be responsible for their own lives without providing access to necessary resources.

In one form or another, the things I took for granted in the 1950s began to be challenged in the 1960s. In the 1970s new ideas exploded into the practice of psychology as a discipline and a profession. In the 1980s and 90s some of these ideas challenged the received wisdom and won dominance, others have retreated; but psychology in the 21st century is very different from what it was when I started paying attention to it in the middle of the 20th century. *One lesson to learn is that psychology is very much a product of its times and the values and interests of its practitioners.* Many of the new ideas that challenged old ways of thinking in psychology had their origins in the social and political struggles of oppressed people. Awareness of this connection is an important aspect of CP. One would do well to ask, 'Who are the oppressed people of this time and place, and what do I have to learn from them? How can I collaborate rather than dominate? How does oppression express itself in today's world?' Asking such questions is central to the project of CP.

Chapter glossary	**commitment and depowerment** the conscious decision of people who are privileged to share power and work with disadvantaged people towards their goals of liberation **community** the interrelationships and connections of people and	settings, including the concepts of sense of community, social support, community capacity, and social capital **community science** the community psychology approach to research that links understanding and action and strives to create participatory	and collaborative relationships with community members **complacency** lack of understanding or concern on the part of members of the dominant culture regarding their role and that of society in the oppression of disadvantaged groups

Chapter glossary continued

dominant cultural narratives socially constructed stories about disadvantaged people, often of the victim-blaming variety that help members of dominant groups to rationalize their role in contributing to and perpetuating the oppression of disadvantaged people

ecology a metaphor used in community psychology to understand the interrelationships of people with various eco-systems (from small systems to large social systems)

global capitalism concentration of wealth and power in the hands of a small number of individuals and corporations at the expense of the majority of citizens and nations of the world and the natural environment

inclusion embracing and integrating people from diverse backgrounds into community

liberation freedom from oppressive life circumstances

oppression a state of domination where the oppressed suffer the consequences of deprivation, exclusion, discrimination, exploitation, control of culture, and sometimes even violence; while the sources of oppression are external, oppression can also be internalized into negative beliefs about oneself

power and empowerment a relational concept that emphasizes choice, control and the ability to influence

prevention/promotion a concept that emphasizes the promotion of

well-being and competence and the prevention of psychosocial problems

resistance the struggle of disadvantaged people to resist and overcome oppression

reframing a tool used by community psychologists to shift the analysis of social problems from one of dominant victim-blaming narratives to alternative accounts that consider the sociopolitical context and power inequalities

well-being a positive state of affairs that involves a transaction between individuals and supportive relationships and environments that results in meeting the needs of individuals

RESOURCES

Journals in Community Psychology
American Journal of Community Psychology, http://www.wkap.nl/journalhome.htm/0091-0562.
Canadian Journal of Community Mental Health, http://www.wlu.ca/cjcmh/.
Journal of Community Psychology, http://www3.interscience.wiley.com/cgi-bin/jhome/32213.
Journal of Community and Applied Social Psychology, http://www.wiley.com/WileyCDA/WileyTitle/productCd-CASP.html.
Community Psychology Net: Campus Library – a website with links to community psychology-oriented journals, http://www.communitypsychology.net/library/journals.shtml.

Part II

Values, Principles and Conceptual Tools

The goal of the second part of the book is to answer the question: Why does CP want to promote liberation and well-being and what principles and conceptual tools should guide the work of CP? In each of the four chapters in this section, we elaborate on key principles and conceptual tools and show how they can address important social issues and problems.

In Chapter 3, we argue that CP is, by its very nature, a value-laden field of action and research. We define values and offer a template of three different types of values that we argue should guide the work of CP: personal values, relational values, and collective values. Personal values include caring, compassion, health and self-determination; relational values include participation/collaboration and diversity; while collective values are those which focus on support for community structures, social justice and accountability. We argue that the different values we have identified are important for meeting different human needs. Moreover, we assert that personal, relational, and collective values must be enacted in a balanced way to move us nearer to an ideal society. Values ground the work of CP, be it action, research or training, by providing a guiding vision and reminder of what we are working towards. The values of CP provide a utopian vision of the 'good society' towards which the field can strive.

Chapter 4 describes two of the key principles on which CP was founded: ecology, and prevention and promotion. CP utilizes an ecological metaphor in its emphasis on people in the context of social systems. We outline the principles of ecology and draw attention to three interdependent levels of analysis: individual and small group (micro), organizations and social settings (meso) and community and society (macro). Each smaller level is nested within a larger level. We argue that CP has tended to focus on micro and meso levels, and that greater attention needs to be paid to macro level structures and interventions. Also in this chapter, we provide a historical perspective on prevention and promotion, present a typology of prevention programs (universal, high-risk, indicated), provide examples of each approach, and review literature on the effectiveness of prevention approaches. We conclude this chapter by noting that these founding concepts tend to focus on personal and relational values, to the neglect of collective values; on ameliorative rather than

45

transformative change; to surface manifestations of larger social problems rather than unequal power relations; and to a focus on wellness rather than liberation. As such, these founding concepts can inadvertently lend support to the existing societal status quo.

In Chapter 5, we introduce the principles of power and community. CP has been concerned with empowerment, a multi-level ecological concept that focuses on both perceptions of control and actual control over life circumstances. However, CP has tended to treat empowerment as a commodity and psychological construct that can be measured. We argue that CP needs to embrace power as an overarching sociopolitical concept that suffuses all the issues of concern to CP. The language of oppression and liberation gives the concept of power more of an 'edge' than is currently the case in CP. In particular, attention is paid to the current context of globalization and corporate rule and the need for political resistance and solidarity partnerships with disadvantaged people to promote social justice around the world.

In this chapter, we also discuss various concepts of community. Community psychologists have argued that a psychological sense of community is an antidote to an increasingly individualistic lifestyle, fragmented life experiences, and experiences of isolation and loneliness. In addition to discussing social support and self-help/mutual aid, we also discuss recent work on the emerging concepts of community capacity and social capital.

Chapter 6 examines accountability, commitment and inclusion. In this chapter, we discuss subjectivity and reflexivity. In particular, we argue that whereas modernist schools of thought have been concerned with objectivity and truth, critical and postmodern schools have shifted the focus towards multiple voices, particularly those who are disadvantaged, a focus on subjectivity, location, and agency of community activists and researchers, and the need for dialogue and reflexivity. We, as community psychologists, need to be open and aware of our privileged position and potential blind spots in our quest for understanding and change. While we strive to 'do the right thing', there are slippages and it is easy for us to become complacent and to have biases that limit our ability to understand phenomena and create social change. We are urging ourselves and others to take a risk and overcome complacency and collusion with unjust social structures and processes by working in solidarity with, and being accountable to, disadvantaged people. More than anything else, the concepts of subjectivity and reflexivity remind us that we have to 'walk the talk' every day, and that every day we face numerous challenges, big and small. In this chapter, we also discuss the concept of inclusion. The need for individuals and groups to define their unique identities without censure or denial of access to social resources is fundamental to CP. In particular, CP has been concerned with individuals and groups who are subject to discrimination based on their gender, race, culture or sexual orientation. Sexism, racism and homophobia are all manifestations of the oppression of people who differ from the mainstream. In this chapter, we describe theory and research regarding these problems and how CP can strive to create inclusive communities.

3
Values for
Community Psychology

Warm-up Exercise

You can do this exercise by yourself at home or in class with other students. Your instructor may assign it as homework so that you're better prepared for class.

1. Think of the values of the French Revolution: liberty, equality and fraternity. Which one of these values is more prevalent in your society?
2. If you could change something about the way these values are played out in your community, how would you change them?
3. Try to identify a group of people with values different from yours. What are the reasons for the differences? Would these differences prevent you from living in harmony in the same community?

The goals of this chapter are for you to:

- identify the sources of values for community psychology (CP)
- consider ways of promoting a balance of values for personal, relational and collective well-being
- explore ways of implementing CP values in practice
- take into account threats to value-based practice.

Introduction

Think again of the values of the French Revolution: liberty, equality and fraternity. Although these values should exist in inseparable form, in fact most societies prefer one over others. In our society, the supremacy of liberty over equality and solidarity is costing us dearly. Not because liberty is an unworthy value, but because liberty in the absence of equality and solidarity degenerates into selfishness and greed.

All over the world, values are out of balance, out of context and out of control. Values are out of balance because self-interest takes primacy over all other values. Values are out of context because many people want more solidarity and sense of community, but popular culture continues to produce images of personal success as the ultimate goal in life. Finally, values are out of control because individualism is rampant and nearly uncontrollable, with greed and competition at an all-time high in many countries. In many societies, collective values such as social justice and solidarity are given minimal attention. Even in countries with customs of mutual support, globalization is eroding the sense of community and the health of the poor (Aristide, 2000; Kim, Millen, Irwin & Gersham, 2000; Korten, 1995). Even strong collectivist societies such as kibbutzim in Israel, have experienced demoralization. In Box 3.1 you can see the dilemmas of a former kibbutz member, Isaac's sister.

Box 3.1   **Life on a Kibbutz**

After nearly 20 years, I left the kibbutz a year ago. When I reminisce about my life there, I feel a combination of pride and sadness. I feel pride in having been part of a social experiment to put personal interests aside and strive towards a new form of life; a life in which people contribute according to their abilities and receive according to their needs. But I also feel sadness because we didn't adjust our ideals to the context of our lives, and because we gradually broke the very norms of sharing and cooperation we created. Today, the norm is 'save your own skin'.

Today I can see more clearly the circumstances that shaped our life on the kibbutz. At the beginning, the socialist ideals and the need to build a country from scratch enabled people to put their personal and family interests aside. The family disappeared and children were not their parents' – they were the kibbutz's. Collective responsibility fostered the loss of personal responsibility.

Although the kibbutz became an oasis of communitarian life, over the years the vision proved somewhat unsustainable. Consumerism and the erosion of ideals gave way to a wave of personal and material interests. Given that economic conditions didn't allow many kibbutzim to fulfill the material (new fridge, an air conditioner) and individual (personal development, studies) expectations of their members, pessimism and discontent replaced idealism. Some kibbutz members began to earn money from outside sources without contributing to the central fund. While still living in it, they abandoned the spirit of the kibbutz. Others, who didn't want to deceive themselves and could afford to leave, just left. Fewer and fewer struggled to reinvent the kibbutz into a place where personal and collective needs could be fostered at the same time.

I belong to the group who left the kibbutz. For my family, the price of living in the kibbutz was too high. We became part of a demoralized community where private interests overshadowed the collective vision.

After a year, the nagging question remains: Did I do enough to save our unique form of life? Did we do enough to build a new vision?

Source: Myriam Prilleltensky, February 9, 2002

To fulfil our needs and obligations we require three sets of linked values. We require personal, relational and collective values. Personal and collective values go hand in hand. But in order to avoid potential conflict between private and social interests we need a third set of values: relational values. Values such as collaboration and participation are essential for respectful relationships. In Myriam's kibbutz, relational values suffered because people began to concentrate on their material well-being and the collective ideals pretty much collapsed. In the absence of relational values, you can't really promote personal or collective well-being.

The urgent and constant need to attend to the three types of values at the same time is noted by the overall value of holism. By holism we mean the complementary attention to personal, relational and collective values. Unless we espouse holism, we are bound to abdicate responsibility for one or more of the three domains of well-being. Holism is complemented by the value of accountability, according to which we commit ourselves to answer to oppressed groups. Research and action about the poor and the disempowered must take place with the poor and the disempowered. In the previous chapter we linked the value of accountability to the issue of complacency and to the principle of commitment and depowerment. For us, this is a new dimension in the values of CP. It impels us to evaluate our work in the light of its potential contribution to people who suffer oppression and marginality.

The values of holism and accountability are conceptually distinct from the values of health, caring, compassion, support for community structures, empowerment, social justice and respect for diversity. Holism and accountability are meta-values that apply to the implementation of all the other values. Holism is precisely about the inclusion of personal, relational and collective values in our work, whereas accountability is about the beneficial effects of all these values for the oppressed.

In this chapter we present a framework for choosing and implementing different values in CP. We discuss the sources of values as well as the criteria we need to select them. We then offer a set of values for CP and discuss its application in practice, programs and policies. We include a critique of the field and suggestions for improvement.

Our approach to values integrates considerations that are usually fragmented. When thinking about values, community psychologists typically pay attention to needs, philosophers to moral theory, sociologists to norms and activists to social change. The chapter offers a way of integrating complementary deliberations of values. In CP we have often invoked one set of considerations at a time and have rarely seen how the various parameters come together. The framework we suggest incorporates multiple voices, combines research and action, draws on various disciplines, pays attention to power and context and can be applied to CP practice.

Sources of Values

We shouldn't take any set of values for granted, nor should we believe in any of them just because they are endorsed by authority figures. We should question where values come from, what the rationale is for choosing them and what contradictions are present within any set of values. Take the French Revolution again as an example. Although the values of liberty, equality and fraternity have been espoused since at least 1789, women were not allowed to vote or hold public office in France until 1944. In the case of the kibbutz, the proclaimed ideology is one of sharing, but more and more people are doing the opposite. Because of contradictions everywhere, we recommend scepticism before adopting or believing in any set of values. In order to make sound decisions regarding values we recommend taking into account a variety of sources (Flyvbjerg, 2001). Table 3.1 shows diverse and complementary sources of values. We will consider each one of these sources, but first, let's define what we mean by values.

Kekes (1993) defines values as 'humanly caused benefits that human beings provide to others ... By way of illustration, we may say that love and justice are moral

Table 3.1 Sources of values for holistic and accountable practice in community psychology

Sources	Key Question	Situation Explored	Tools for Developing Values	Contribution to Community Psychology
Vision	What should be?	Ideal vision	Moral, spiritual and political thinking	Vision of well-being and liberation
Context	What is?	Actual state	Social science studies of individuals and communities	Understanding of social conditions
Needs	What is missing?	Desirable state	Experiences of community members	Identification of human needs
Action	What can be done?	Feasible change	Theories of change	Strategies for change

From: Prilleltensky (2001)

goods' (p. 44). Values guide the process of working towards a desired state of affairs. These are principles that inform our personal, professional and political behaviour. But values are not only beneficial in that they guide behaviour towards a future outcome, for they also have intrinsic merit. We espouse values such as empowerment and caring, not just because they lead towards a good or better society, but also because they have merit on their own (Hill Collins, 1993; Kane, 1994; Kekes, 1993). Indeed, according to Mayton, Ball-Rokeach and Loges (1994), 'values may be defined as enduring prescriptive or proscriptive beliefs that a specific mode of conduct (instrumental value) or end state of existence (terminal value) is preferred to another mode of conduct or end state' (p. 3). Schwartz (1994) points out that values 'serve as guiding principles in the life of a person or other social entity' (p. 21). Values, then, are principles to guide action. We invoke them when we have a conflict with a friend or when we take a stand on a political issue. Are you in favour of insurance benefits for same sex partners? What is your position regarding the US embargo on Cuba? Would you boycott a movie theatre because there is no access there for your physically disabled friends? Each time you take a stand you're invoking a value. When Myriam left the kibbutz, she took a stand, not without hesitation, to protect her family from the deterioration of the quality of life in the kibbutz. Now the question is, how do we choose values? We suggest basing our values on vision, context, needs and action.

Vision

Moral and political philosophers debate visions of the best possible society. They use the terms 'good life' and 'good society' to refer to visions of the best possible situation. They explain the merits and shortcomings of different values, the conditions under which one value may supersede another and potential contradictions between competing orientations. These considerations answer the question: What should be? Philosophers contribute to the discussion on values by portraying an *ideal vision* of what we should strive for. They can provide a blueprint of a better society in which values of autonomy and community will be mutually enhanced (Etzioni, 1996).

Liberal philosophers, for example, emphasize autonomy, self-determination and the rights of the individual. They are reluctant to promote too much state intervention because they are afraid that governments will end up dictating to private citizens how to run their lives. They may point to countries like the former Soviet Union where citizens did not have much personal freedom. Today, they may even point to the declining kibbutz movement.

Communitarian thinkers, on the other hand, claim that we have gone too far in meeting the needs of individuals and that we have sacrificed our social obligations in the pursuit of private satisfaction (Etzioni, 1993, 1996; Lerner, 1996; Sandel, 1996). They may point to countries like the US where there is no national health care system and where people live in gated communities (ghettos?) to protect themselves. What type of communities are those?

Each position poses risks as well as benefits (Mulhall & Swift, 1996). Liberals deserve recognition for promoting liberation from oppressive social norms and regulations (citizens of the former Soviet Union did not appreciate the KGB compiling files on them, nor did citizens of the Victorian era appreciate the repressive sexual norms of the time). But these worthy ideals notwithstanding, liberal philosophy is not without problems. In excess, the pursuit of private goals can lead to unmitigated individualism, selfishness and materialism (Etzioni, 1996). 'When people pursue private goals, the risk is that they may never acquire an ennobling sense of a purpose beyond the self' (Damon, 1995, p. 66). This risk is very apparent in market societies where state intervention is minimal and the powerful are free to seek pleasure at the expense of others (Sen, 1999a, 1999b). Indeed, we hear that to climb the corporate ladder you may need to trample on a few people. Not everyone in society has the same amount of power and those with less power have fewer opportunities to advocate for themselves (O'Neill, 1994).

Communitarian thinking, on the other hand, is based on the assumption that without cooperation individuals cannot achieve their personal goals. Like liberals, they endorse the fulfilment of personal goals and liberation from oppressive social forces; but unlike liberals, they think that we should strengthen social and communal institutions because personal happiness is not possible without them (Etzioni, 1993, 1996). Liberals freed us from coercive institutions, but along the way they also weakened those institutions we need to promote not only the good of the collective, but also the good of the individual (O'Neill, 1994; Sandel, 1996). We know that strong communities provide a better environment for well-being than weak communities (Putnam, 2000). Essential public programs, sufficiently funded and effectively managed can have long-lasting and beneficial effects on all children (Schorr, 1997).

But communitarian thinking is not without risks either. Collectivist societies are known for expecting great sacrifices from their members for the benefit of the public good. Citizens feel coerced to do things they don't like and they experience state intervention as oppressive (Melnyk, 1985). In addition to political philosophies, visions are also informed by webs of meaning, religion and spirituality. As Maton and colleagues recently observed, 'one major way in which religion has the potential to influence the common good is by providing meaning to individuals, groups, and societies, thereby influencing values, attitudes, affect, and behavior' (Maton, Dodgen, Sto Domingo & Larsen, 2003, pp. 3–4). In some cases spirituality and meaning are equated with religious affiliations, but in other cases they represent beliefs in transcendental beings, or in transcendental roles. Some religions, like the Baha'i faith, are very explicit about the role of spirituality in reaching transcendence. According to Mustakova-Possardt (2003):

> Baha'i understanding helps demystify the notion of spiritual potential and links it in clearer terms with overall psychological functioning and moral motivation ... every living thing on the material plane reflects some of the qualities of infinite divine potentiality, and that represents its particular beauty, dignity, and purpose. Human beings are endowed with a unique potentiality, which it is the purpose of their lives to manifest more fully – the human spirit ... Baha'i psychology recognizes at the heart of human motivation the desire for transcendence, an attraction to and a desire to know truth, beauty, and goodness. (pp. 16–17)

Often, although not necessarily, these reflections derive from religious affiliations. People's spiritualities and pursuit of meaning are as varied as the range of religious and political persuasions. People can exercise their spiritual potential with or without a formal religious affiliation. In either case, historians have persuasively argued that spiritual beliefs inform vision, values and devotion to causes. An example from psychology that merges spirituality with social justice is liberation psychology, a movement pioneered in Latin America and closely associated with liberation theology (Martín-Baró, 1986, 1994).

Convincing philosophical and religious positions notwithstanding, they are insufficient to mount social policies that meet the needs of minorities, women, families, children and the disadvantaged. An ever-present danger in philosophical discourse is its detachment from the social conditions in which people live. To counteract this risk we need to explore the contextual circumstances that complement philosophical considerations.

Context

This set of considerations explores *the actual state of affairs* in which people live. Community psychologists and social scientists strive to understand the social, economic, cultural and political conditions of a specific community. This line of inquiry helps us to determine social norms and cultural trends influencing people's choices and behaviour (Trickett, 1996).

A contextual assessment is necessary to understand the subjective experience of the residents of a particular community. Individualist and collectivist societies differ with respect to socialization, customs and visions. Poor and rich communities ascribe different values to basic necessities. An analysis of culture and context draws on resources from history, anthropology, sociology, communications, politics, economics and cultural studies. These sources combine to provide a picture of the context in which we want to intervene. Knowing the context will help to determine the most appropriate values for a particular situation (O'Neill, 1998).

The meaning of self-determination in an individualist society is vastly different from its meaning in a collectivist environment. In a totally collectivist society, citizens yearn for more autonomy and resent state and communal intrusion. Examples include 'curtailing individual rights in the name of community needs; suppressing creativity in the name of conformity; and even suppressing a sense of self, losing individuality in a mesh of familial or communal relations' (Etzioni, 1996, p. 26). In an individualist environment, on the other hand, citizens want more sense of community and less selfishness. Unless we know the context, we cannot really know what values to promote.

Needs

It is not enough for philosophers to ponder what the rest of us need, or for social scientists to recommend what will make our communities better places. Visions of the good society have to be validated with the lived experience and the needs of community members (Kane, 1998, Montero, 2000a). The story of Myriam Prillel-tensky (see Box 3.1) shows that for any vision to succeed, people's changing needs must be taken into account.

Needs are an important source for considering values. Needs address key questions: What is missing? and What is a desirable state of affairs? This source of values pays explicit attention to the voice of the people with whom we partner to improve community well-being. CP is uniquely placed to elicit the needs of people in positions of disadvantage.

Qualitative studies of people's struggles, aspirations, conflicts, frustrations and joys provide a picture of what people regard worthwhile in life. Parents disclose their doubts about how to raise children, children share their fears and pleasures and minorities relate experiences of discrimination. These accounts reveal their needs and aspirations.

By asking people what they want, need and consider meaningful in life, we learn about the ingredients of an appealing vision (Fals Borda, 2001). This does not mean that whatever people say should be acceptable. For it is quite conceivable that the majority of people in a society may be wrong or malicious. History shows that majorities can endorse vicious attitudes. Just as philosophical arguments have to be as checked against human needs, human wishes have to be subjected to ethical scrutiny. This ensures that the needs and desires expressed by people are not immoral or unethical.

Action

Whereas the previous sources examined actual, ideal and desirable states of affairs in society, action concerns *feasible change*. Unlike previous deliberations, which asked what is, what is missing, or what should be, the main question answered by this set of considerations is: What could be done? This question is meant to bridge the gap between the actual and the ideal states of affairs. Feasible change draws our attention to what social improvements can be realistically achieved – a distinct political goal (Fals Borda, 2001).

Agents of change translate values and community input into action. These are the professionals, para-professionals, politicians, volunteers and activists who combine values with human experience to improve the welfare of a particular population. Agents of change strive to promote well-being by combining values with knowledge of what people want, need and regard important in life (O'Neill, 1989, 1998). Agents of change bridge between the abstract notions of philosophers and the lived experience of community members. They try to adapt ideals of the good society to specific contexts. In that sense, all of us who work in communities are agents of change.

The complementary nature of the four sources of values now becomes apparent. Without a philosophical analysis we lack a vision; without a contextual analysis we lack an understanding of social forces; without a needs assessment we lack an idea of what people want; and finally, without a strategy we lack action. The interdependence of these sources makes it clear that we cannot rely on single sources of values (Montero, 1994a, 2000a).

Criteria for Choosing Values

Now that we know what sources should contribute to our menu of values, we need criteria to choose from the menu. From all the potential values suggested by philosophers, community members, psychologists and social activists, how do we know which ones are congruent with the mission of CP? We recommend four criteria that try to balance complementary considerations.

Balance Between Theoretical and Grounded Input

A balance between theoretical and grounded input is needed to complement analytical with experiential approaches to knowledge. Philosophical analyses of what values can lead to a good life and a good society are useful but limited. What is the use of a philosophical framework that does not reflect the living realities of people? The corollary of this question is that *moral philosophy is not enough*. On the other hand, we can ask what is the point of knowing people's needs and aspirations if that knowledge is not translated into action? The corollary of this question is that *grounded input is not enough* (Kane, 1998). Theories of values have to be validated with lived experience and lived experience has to be interpreted meaningfully and converted into action.

Balance Between Understanding and Action

A balance between *understanding* and *action* is needed to ensure that knowledge does not end up on a shelf. The ultimate purpose of values is to enjoy a fuller life. To make an impact in the world, our theoretical sophistication has to be followed by action, a principle inscribed in the very name of the Division of CP (Division 27) of the American Psychological Association: The Society for Community Research and Action.

Imagine what an incredible waste of resources it would be to generate a lot of knowledge about a social issue and not implement any of it in action. Pairing research and action ensures that knowledge generation is tied to program or policy implementation.

But the urge to act should not come at the expense of reflection. We need to reflect on the risks and benefits of pursuing one course of action over another (Sánchez Vidal, 1999). Whereas one set of values may be appropriate to one social context, it may be inappropriate in another. Thus, while we promote more autonomy and control for disadvantaged people in oppressively controlling environments, we don't want to push for more self-determination of violent people. Blind adherence to any value, from personal empowerment to sense of community, is risky.

Balance Between Processes and Outcomes

A balance between *processes* and *outcomes* is needed to ensure that dialogue is not an end in itself. By the same token, we need to assert that ends do not automatically justify any means. If the object of an intervention is to uphold the rights of a minority group, do we justify any means, including terrorism? On the other hand, can we justify endless talk when the lives of vulnerable children and families in conflict zones are at risk? These tensions between valid processes and just outcomes should be reflected in any framework of values.

When Isaac was director of the CP program in Wilfrid Laurier University, staff and students embarked on a curriculum revision. People were so focused on reaching consensus and having a good process that we nearly forgot the main reason for the whole exercise. Students and staff became disenchanted with the process because nothing much was being accomplished. Once we realized as a group that process is not an end in itself we made progress on the curriculum revision. Too much process at the expense of outcomes is not a good process.

Balance Between Differing and Unequal Voices

A balance between *differing* and *unequal voices* is the fourth criteria for choosing values. Social policies and programs are typically formulated by powerful politicians, educated government officials and privileged academics. Efforts by community psychologists to work in partnership with disadvantaged members of society are not typical of social policy formation (Nelson, Prilleltensky et al., 2001). On the contrary, most social policies are conceived in the absence of meaningful input from those most affected by them (Taylor, 1996). Hence, a framework of values should be attentive to differing voices and in particular to those who are often rendered invisible by the political process. Unequal power and unequal representation must be considered in proposing values. Values that are based on the voice of the powerful will usually perpetuate the status quo, whereas values that are based on the voice of the powerless have a better chance of promoting change (Jaggar, 1994; Sánchez Vidal, 1999).

Assume for a moment that you want to establish a prevention program and you want to work with a community on a vision of physical and mental health. You invite to the table professionals, hospital administrators, city officials and some community members. If the vision and values of the program do not reflect the voice of the community members themselves, it is likely that the new initiatives will represent the voice of the powerful professionals and not of the community. These two groups have unequal power in articulating their views. Values and vision need to reflect the various perspectives and interests involved in the matter. Otherwise, chances are the powerful will impose their views, however well-intentioned they might be.

Values for Community Psychology

Based on the sources and criteria presented above, we are now in a position to suggest some core values for CP. We classify core values into three groups:

- values for personal well-being
- values for relational well-being
- values for collective well-being.

Well-being is a positive state of affairs, brought about by the satisfaction of personal, relational and collective needs (Prilleltensky, Nelson & Peirson, 2001a). As a vision, well-being is an ideal state of affairs for individuals and communities. To achieve it, we have to know the context, the needs of people and groups and the best available strategies. Well-being consists of individual components (personal, relational and collective needs) and of the synergy created by all of them together. In the absence of any one component, well-being cannot really be achieved. To make this dictum an integral part of our values we invoke the meta-value of holism. As Cowen (1996) observed, 'optimal development of well-being ... requires integrated sets of operations involving individuals, families, settings, community contexts and macro-level societal structures and policies' (p. 246). Table 3.2 shows the diverse needs and values required to achieve well-being at different levels. We examine next each category of values on its own. Later we consider the holistic synergy created by combining them.

Values for Personal Well-being

These are values that serve the needs of the person. Self-determination, caring and compassion and personal health advance the well-being of individual community members. Self-determination or autonomy refers to the ability of the individual to pursue chosen goals in life without excessive frustration. This is akin to the concept of empowerment, according to which individuals and groups strive to gain control over their lives (Zimmerman, 2000). Personal health, in turn, is a state of physical and emotional well-being that is intrinsically beneficial and extrinsically instrumental in pursuing self-determination. The values of caring and compassion meet the need for empathy, understanding and solidarity. When people are the beneficiaries of these values their personal well-being is enhanced. But for them to enjoy these values, they have to engage in relationships that support them and they have to live in communities that care about these values (Ornish, 1997). Caring and compassion are based on sensitive relationships and self-determination is based on resources and opportunities. Without caring relationships there is no mutual understanding and without public resources there is little chance of fulfilling personal goals, especially for the poor and disadvantaged (Narayan, Chambers et al., 2000; Narayan, Patel et al., 2000).

Values for Relational Well-being

Neither philosophers nor social scientists can tell community members what they need. They can offer ideas, but they cannot replace the voice of the people themselves. People have to participate in decisions affecting their lives and they need to

Table 3.2 Selected values for personal, relational and collective well-being

Domains	Personal Well-being		Relational Well-being		Collective Well-being	
	Well-being is achieved by holistic practice that attends to the following domains:					
Values	Self-determination	Caring and compassion	Respect for diversity	Participation and collaboration	Support for community structures	Social justice and accountability
Objective	Creation of opportunities in self and others to pursue chosen goals in life without excessive frustration	Expression of care and concern for the physical and emotional well-being of self and others	Promotion of respect and appreciation for diverse social identities and for people's ability to define themselves	Promotion of fair processes whereby children and adults can have meaningful input into decisions affecting their lives	Promotion of vital community structures that facilitate the pursuit of personal and communal goals	Promotion of fair and equitable allocation of bargaining powers, obligations and resources for the oppressed
Needs Addressed	Mastery, control, self-efficacy, voice, choice, skills, growth and autonomy	Love, attention, empathy, attachment, acceptance, positive regard	Identity, dignity, self-respect, self-esteem, acceptance	Participation, involvement and mutual responsibility	Sense of community, cohesion, formal support	Economic security, shelter, clothing, nutrition, access to vital health and social services

From: Prilleltensky and Nelson (2002)

collaborate with others in achieving their goals (Montero, 2000a; Sánchez, 1999). When conflicts between individuals or groups arise, it is crucial to have collaborative processes to resolve them. Otherwise, it is just a matter of the powerful imposing their will on others. Relational values remind us that self-determination must have limits. My wishes and desires have to take into account your wishes and desires. If they conflict, we have to have a process to resolve our differences. We have to be able to appreciate diversity and to respect it and we should not romanticize communities and expect everyone to show caring and compassion for others.

Respect for a person's identity is, according to Canadian philosopher Charles Taylor (1992), 'not just a courtesy we owe people. It is a vital human need' (p. 26). When we affirm people's identities, we help them affirm themselves. When we respect their defining human qualities, we help them respect themselves. Conversely, 'a person or group of people can suffer real damage' Taylor says, 'if the people or society around them mirror back to them a confining or demeaning or contemptible picture of themselves. Nonrecognition or misrecognition can inflict harm, can be a form of oppression' (p. 25).

From a mental health perspective, studies have shown the beneficial effects of granting children and adults an opportunity to define their own personal identity, without fearing oppression or discrimination. On the other hand, when people's identities are disparaged or diminished, there are negative effects on their self-esteem and overall mental health (for reviews of research see Dudgeon, Garvey & Pickett, 2000; Moane, 1999; Prilleltensky & Gonick, 1996; Trickett et al., 1994). Appreciation for diverse social identities serves as a protective factor, whereas lack of respect constitutes a definite risk factor. In Canada and Australia, aboriginal peoples have been subjected to demeaning and racist treatment that has led to serious emotional and community problems (Dudgeon et al., 2000).

Values for Collective Well-being

Collective values complement individual aims, for the attainment of personal objectives requires the presence of social resources. Distributive justice, or the fair and equitable allocation of bargaining powers, resources and obligations in society, is a prime example of a collective value. Support for societal structures and for the environment is another key value. Both of these values enable the achievement of personal and communal well-being.

Community psychologists have long recognized that people need resources to enjoy good health, to reach their potential and to nurture their identity (Dalton et al., 2001). This is why the pursuit of social justice is so decisive. Without it, the prospects of personal and relational well-being remain elusive. To place social justice at the forefront of our priorities, we link it to the meta-value of accountability. Together, social justice and accountability to the oppressed mark the top priority for CP.

The United Nations Convention on the Rights of the Child (UNCRC) recognizes the need for strong community structures in the development of children around the world (United Nations, 1991). 'States Parties recognize the right of *every* child to a standard of living adequate for the child's physical, mental, spiritual, moral and social development' (UNCRC, Article 27.1, emphasis added). The same

Article insists that countries 'shall take appropriate measures to assist parents and others responsible for the child to implement this right and shall in case of need provide material assistance and support programs, particularly with regard to nutrition, clothing and housing' (Article 29.3).

How could we pursue well-being in the absence of institutions such as public health, schools or transportation systems? Can you think of healthy development in a toxic environment? What about poor children and single parents without government supports? Societal structures that look after people and the environment are essential for the promotion of health and well-being. Research on social determinants of health provides convincing evidence that environmental factors, broadly defined, influence our level of well-being in multiple ways. Physical, cultural, political, economic and psychological factors combine to promote or decrease personal and collective health. There is a great deal of research showing that inequality and lack of control are conducive to poor outcomes, not only for the poor, but also for middle-class people (Keating & Hertzman, 1999a; Marmot & Wilkinson, 1999; Wilkinson, 1996). This is why we need to uphold the values of social justice and support for public institutions.

Publicly funded institutions perform a critical role in preventing disempowering chain reactions for people at risk. But their virtue goes beyond supporting the needy, for these organizations enhance the health and welfare of the population at large. Strong community structures afford us clean water, sewage systems, child-care (in countries where it is publicly funded), recreational opportunities, libraries, unemployment insurance, pension plans, free primary and secondary education, access to health care and many other social goods (Prilleltensky, Laurendeau, et al., 2001).

The Synergy of Values

Well-being comes about in the combination of personal, relational and collective values. The net effect of all the values combined is called synergy. This is reflected in our meta-value of holism. What is unique about CP is that it seeks to integrate the three sets of values. As we can see in Figure 3.1, well-being is at the intersection of the three domains. Traditional approaches to psychology have concentrated on the personal and relational domains, to the exclusion of the collective. As a result, psychologists neglected to consider the powerful impact of the psychosocial environment; not only on physical, but also on emotional health.

Consider for example the impact of inequality. Societies with higher levels of inequality have poorer outcomes for the entire population, not just for the poor and disadvantaged:

Figure 3.1 Values for holistic well-being

Differences in equity of income distribution is one of the principal determinants of differing health status among wealthy societies. Countries with highly unequal income distributions have poorer health status than those with more equitable income distributions ... This pattern suggests that health status (as a measure of human well-being) may be embedded in collective factors in society, not just in individual factors ... These findings led us to the conclusion that the underlying factors that determine health and well-being must be deeply embedded in social circumstances. (Keating & Hertzman, 1999b, pp. 6–7)

Given this evidence, we cannot accept definitions of well-being that are based exclusively on individual factors. The problem is that these definitions are psychocentric – they concentrate on the cognitive and emotional sources and consequences of suffering and well-being, to the exclusion of the political roots of power and well-being. While beliefs and perceptions are important, they cannot be treated in isolation from the cultural, political and economic environment (Eckersley, 2000, 2001).

We require 'well-enough' social and political conditions, free of economic exploitation and human rights abuses, to experience quality of life (Eckersley, Dixon & Douglas, 2001). Similarly, we need nurturing and respectful relationships to experience well-being. Eckersley (2000) has shown that subjective experiences of well-being are heavily dictated by cultural trends such as individualism and consumerism; whereas Narayan and colleagues have claimed that the psychological experience of poverty is directly related to political structures of oppression (Narayan, Chambers, et al., 2000; Narayan, Patel, et al., 2000).

Amartya Sen, the Nobel Laureate economist, describes well-being in terms of capabilities and entitlements (1999a, 1999b). Without the latter the former cannot thrive. Entitlements such as preventive health care and educational opportunities are not only means to human development but also ends in their own right. Well-being at the collective level is not measured only by the health and educational outcomes of a group of individuals, but also by the presence of enabling institutions and societal infrastructures. Hence, we define well-being in broad terms that encompass social progress and human development. We cannot talk about psychological well-being in the absence of interpersonal and collective well-being. The three kinds are mutually reinforcing and interdependent.

Sen (1999a, 1999b) articulates the complementarity or holism of diverse social structures in fostering what we call 'well-being' and what he calls 'human development'. Sen invokes the interaction of five types of freedoms in the pursuit of human development: (a) political freedoms, (b) economic facilities, (c) social opportunities, (d) transparency and honesty, and (e) protective security.

> Each of these distinct types of rights and opportunities helps to advance the general capability of a person. They may also serve to complement each other ... Freedoms are not only the primary ends of development, they are also among its principal means. In addition to acknowledging, foundationally, the evaluative importance of freedom, we also have to understand the remarkable empirical connection that links freedoms of different kinds with one another. Political freedoms (in the form of free speeches and elections) help to promote economic security. Social opportunities (in the form of education and health facilities) facilitate economic participation. Economic facilities (in the form of opportunities for participation in trade and production) can help to generate personal abundance as well as public resources for social facilities. Freedoms of different kinds can strengthen one another. (Sen, 1999b, pp. 10–11)

The presence or absence of health-promoting factors at all levels can have positive or negative synergistic effects. When collective factors such as social justice and access to valued resources combine with a sense of community and personal empowerment, chances are that psychological and political well-being will ensue. When, on the other hand, injustice and exploitation reign, the result is suffering and oppression (Moane, 1999).

Principles for Action

We have reviewed so far the sources and criteria for choosing values. Based on that we then selected a set of values (see Table 3.2). The challenge now is to actualize them; to put them into practice. The meta-value that reminds us to put values into action is the value of accountability. In an earlier publication (Prilleltensky & Nelson, 1997) we suggested a few principles to guide the implementation of CP's values. The following is an updated and expanded list of key principles:

Principle 1

Advancing the well-being of disadvantaged communities requires actualizing all values in a balanced and holistic way.

Table 3.3 shows our assessment of the current prominence of CP values. As can be seen, not all values are equally prominent. Some are given more attention than others. According to our assessment, collective values are somewhat neglected, if not in theory, certainly in practice (Ahmed & Pretorius-Heuchert, 2001; Prilleltensky & Nelson, 1997).

As each value by itself is insufficient, problems arise when we adhere too closely to one principle but neglect another equally important one. A typical case is the extolment of autonomy and self-determination at the expense of distributive justice or sense of community (Riger, 1993). There cannot be justice in the absence of care, and there cannot be care without justice.

Table 3.3 Prominence and potential for social change of community psychology values

Values	Current Level of Prominence Background------------Foreground	Potential for Social Change Ameliorative----------Transformative
Caring and compassion	-------------------------------------X	X--
Health	-------------------------------------X	X--
Self-determination	------------------ X-----------------	------------------ X--------------------
Participation and collaboration	------------------ X-----------------	------------------ X--------------------
Respect for diversity	------------------ X-----------------	------------------ X--------------------
Support for community structures	------ X----------------------------	---------------------------------------X-------
Social justice	---X----------------------------------	--------------------------------------- X ---
Holism	---X----------------------------------	--------------------------------------- X ---
Accountability	---X----------------------------------	--------------------------------------- X ---

Principle 2

Within a given social ecology, some values appear at the foreground of our consciousness while others remain in the background. We must move the neglected values to the foreground to attain the necessary balance.

The social ecology influences the particular configuration of values at a certain time and place. As a result, some values are more prominent than others. In western societies, for example, the values of social justice, support for community structures and environmental protection are currently in the background. In contrast, caring, compassion and health are in the forefront. In this type of context it is necessary to accentuate the background values. In another place or in another historical moment, the values might be configured differently. This may occur under regimes that want to advance social ideals, however just in the end, without caring and concern for the individuality of its members. If that were the case, we would have to restore the suppressed values of compassion and health to ensure that citizens enjoy the full range of values.

The saliency and effects of values vary not only across time and place, but also across communities of peoples. Different groups may share a temporal and geographical location, but their needs may be vastly distinct. Women and people of colour may need more self-determination, participation and human diversity; while people who experience sudden illness may have a greater need for health and compassion (Trickett et al., 1994).

Principle 3

Within the present social context, the value of social justice remains in the background. By neglecting this value, we reinforce the same unjust state of affairs that disadvantaged many communities in the first place.

Neglecting social justice reinforces an unjust state of affairs (Prilleltensky, 1994b). But our historical analysis suggests that most of our work as community psychologists tries to ameliorate – not transform – living conditions within the existing distribution of resources. Herein lies the main barrier for the fulfilment of our mission (see Table 3.3). For as long as we try to address only the consequences of uneven allocation of resources, without looking at the problem's root cause, we confront only the surface of the issues. Most of the issues we deal with in our preventive and community interventions are symptoms of profound social injustice (Martín-Baró, 1994).

Principle 4

We must distinguish between ameliorating living conditions within the present social structure and transforming the conditions that create disadvantage.

We need to ask ourselves whether our persistent efforts to organize communities are directed at amelioration or transformation. *Amelioration* means change within a system, or what has been termed 'first-order change', while *transformation* means changing the basic premises of a system or 'second-order change' (Rappaport, 1977). To be sure, ameliorative work is important and needed. However, without larger transformative efforts these gains may be undermined in the long term.

The irony is that social justice, one of the neglected values in the practice of CP, holds the most promise to deliver long and lasting social change (see Table 3.3). Once structures of inequality are changed, it is likely that many of the current social ills will be alleviated (Marmot & Wilkinson, 1999; Wilkinson, 1996).

Principle 5

We must expand the implementation of values from micro and meso contexts to macro social ecologies. This is part of our accountability.

Applied psychologists usually implement values at the micro level (for example family and interpersonal relationships) or, at best, at the meso or middle level (for example workplace, schools). Many psychologists try to enhance the self-determination of clients or small groups. Furthermore, they show empathy and concern for people suffering from life stressors. But these micro and meso interventions are embedded within a larger social context of inequality, oppression and discrimination. Hence, efforts to promote collaboration and respect for diversity at the micro level are undermined at the macro level by social structures of inequality.

Principle 6

Vested interests and social power interfere with the promotion of values. We need to monitor how subjective, interpersonal and political processes facilitate or inhibit the enactment of values for well-being.

The promotion of values is threatened by personal interests. Values exist in a context of wishes, desires, insecurities, domination and power dynamics (Prilleltensky, 2000, 2001). As such, we have to take into account how these factors may jeopardize our ability to foster value-based practice. These threatening dynamics operate within ourselves and within the people and groups we work with. There is no point in pronouncing all kinds of wonderful values if private interests and power inequalities are really against justice or fairness. Unless we pay attention to the objective and subjective dynamics of power, our chances of enacting value-based practice are greatly diminished.

Principle 7

We should strive to create a state of affairs in which personal power and self-interest do not undermine the well-being or interest of others.

We should develop an awareness of how personal power and vested interests suffuse all aspects of organizational and community work. This is an awareness that should be spread throughout the organization, project or community. Workers and leaders need to reflect how their personal lives and subjective experiences influence what they deem ethical or valuable for themselves, the organization, the project and the community (Sánchez Vidal, 1999). Awareness, however, is only the first step in keeping vested interests in check. The satisfaction of personal needs is another important requisite. Citizens are more likely to abide by collective values and norms when they feel that their personal needs are met.

The process of balancing interests with values, however, can be subverted in various ways (see Box entitled 'Ten Threats to Value-based Practice' on website). One possible subversion is the development of a discourse on values that legitimizes self-interests. For example, the notion of a 'self-made person', which is quite prevalent in North America, can justify privilege on the basis of merit (Prilleltensky, 1994b). The value of personal merit can be distorted into a pretext for not sharing power or resources.

Another potential subversion is the creation of a safe space for discussion of values that doesn't challenge participants to change but, rather, appeases their conscience. A final subversion is sharing token power to prevent sharing of actual power. There are many ways to protect power structures and, ironically, sharing power is one of them. Giving a little power can prevent the demand for a lot of power (Bradshaw, 1998).

Principle 8

We should strive to enhance value-congruence within ourselves and between groups and communities.

First, we should try to establish concordance among our own personal values, interests and power. Then, we should try to spread this process throughout organizations and communities. The next step is to enhance the zone of congruence among citizens, workers and leaders. Community psychologists should try to create partnerships among the different stakeholder groups to achieve concordance of values and objectives. The primary task in the creation of partnerships is the establishment of trust. This is achieved by meaningful and collaborative participation of workers and communities in decision-making processes. There are many examples and guidelines for the successful and meaningful engagement of communities in organizations (Nelson, Prilleltensky et al., 2001). Token consultative processes subvert the intent of true partnerships. When consumers realize that their voice is only minimally respected but maximally exploited for public relations purposes, a great deal of damage can ensue. Worst of all, we allow the value of accountability to be violated.

Principle 9

There is a need to confront people and groups subverting values, abusing power or allowing self-interest to undermine the well-being of others in the organization or in the community.

Efforts to promote value-based practice notwithstanding, chances are that some people will behave in ways that contradict the vision and values of a project or organization. This is when we need to engage in conflict resolution with the person or group undermining organizational values. This is part of the value of accountability. A culture of openness and critique facilitates the resolution of conflict. In a climate of respectful debate the opposing parties can come to an agreement that is in line with the vision of the organization. But there are times when such a healthy climate cannot prevent serious conflict. If the conflict is about ideas and differing interpretations of values, it is likely that a resolution may be easily reached. But if the conflict is about personal interests or power, chances are that differences may be irreconcilable.

Confrontation may be used for the good of the organization and the public, but it may also be used to suppress legitimate voices of discontent. In the latter case, leaders can exercise their power to silence opposing views. This is an example of how conflict resolution can be subverted in the interest of enhancing the power of leaders. But confrontations can also be used by workers and community members to undermine legitimate leadership.

Principle 10

Community psychologists and community leaders need to be accountable to the stakeholder groups.

Community workers need to be accountable to stakeholder groups about their efforts to promote value congruence and to confront people abusing power. In an effort to avoid conflict, some people sweep the unacceptable behaviour of colleagues under the carpet. In an effort to find conflict, others seek fault in their peers. Community psychologists need to be wary of these hyper- or hypo-confrontational styles. Whereas the former may be just an expression of anger and aggression, the latter may be a manifestation of fear.

Chapter Summary

Values are guidelines for promoting a better state of affairs for ourselves and others (Kekes, 1993). Table 3.4 provides a checklist to ensure that we strive to achieve all values in our practice, programs and policies. This table can be used as a template in

Table 3.4 Questions for assessing the values of programs, practices and policies in community psychology

Values	Questions
Self-determination	Do they promote the ability of children, adults and communities to pursue their chosen goals without excessive frustration and in consideration of other people's needs?
Caring and compassion	Do they promote the expression of care, empathy and concern for the physical and emotional well-being of children, adults, families and disadvantaged communities?
Health	Do they promote the health of individuals and communities?
Respect for diversity	Do they promote respect and appreciation for diverse social identities?
Participation and collaboration	Do they promote peaceful, respectful and equitable processes whereby children and adults can have meaningful input into decisions affecting their lives?
Support for community structures	Do they promote vital community structures that facilitate the pursuit of personal and communal goals?
Social justice	Do they promote the fair and equitable allocation of bargaining powers, obligations and resources in society?
Holism	Do they promote holistic reasoning and interventions at the micro, meso and macro levels of analysis?
Accountability	Do they promote accountability to oppressed groups and depowerment of the privileged?

devising value-based interventions in multiple settings (for example, schools, work-place, hospitals, communities) and with a variety of foci (for example, health promotion, drug-abuse prevention, teenage pregnancy, formal and informal support, minority rights, child abuse).

Community psychologists are interested in values that promote the well-being of disadvantaged people. However, given that people's needs vary according to their particular circumstances, it is nearly impossible to formulate a universal list of values (Giddens, 1994; Kane, 1994, 1998; Kekes, 1993). Hence, we must remember that any proposed set of values contains contextual limitations. We should also recognize that some groups may require certain values more than others. Keeping in mind that context determines the best set of values is an antidote against dogmatism – the rigid application of beliefs regardless of context. Asking people themselves what they need goes a long way to ensure that we do not impose inappropriate values on them.

We emphasized the need to distinguish between ameliorating living conditions and transforming the conditions that create and perpetuate oppression. Alleviating suffering is commendable, but there comes a point where amelioration by itself works against the eradication of oppressive conditions. This is because amelioration allows the system to keep working smoothly (Prilleltensky, 1994b).

The challenge of harmonizing personal and collective interests is not trivial. How do we promote the unique identity and rights of a certain group without sacrificing solidarity with other oppressed groups? At which point do we turn our attention to other groups suffering from discrimination? How do we balance attention to processes of dialogue with outcomes of social justice? At which point do we say that we have discussed our differences long enough and that it is now time for action? (Jaggar, 1994). All these questions involve values and cannot be answered in the abstract, for each unique constellation of factors requires a unique solution. The framework presented in this chapter is a place to start because it identifies three complementary sets of values. Giddens promotes these values because they imply a 'recognition of the sanctity of human life and the universal right to happiness and self-actualization – coupled to the obligation to promote cosmopolitan solidarity and an attitude of respect' (1994, p. 253).

COMMENTARY: Socioethical Ecology of Community Psychology: Communitarian Values in an Individualistic Era   *Alipio Sánchez Vidal*

Although CP is a value-laden field, it has always exhibited a rather ambiguous attitude towards values and ethics. While values are recognized as a central ingredient – Rappaport (1977) subtitled his book 'values, research, and action' – they remain largely hidden or implicit in theory and action. Whereas the field takes pride on its ethical position ('we are the good guys'), it has been reluctant to openly confront issues and conflicts generated in actual practice (Davidson, 1989). Nelson and Prilleltensky's exploration of CP values is then a welcome task. In this chapter they propose a

framework for selecting values. Furthermore, they put forward a set of values and action principles to translate them into reality in current social contexts. And they do so in a critical, balanced and positive way. I find especially valuable the orderly structure and clarity of the proposal, the authors' willingness to support countercurrent social values (such as social justice), and the emphasis put on the often forgotten category of relational values, so important in any psychosocial endeavour.

In this comment I will briefly elaborate on some points regarding CP and values. I will try to place

CP values into the larger social picture on the one hand, and into the ethical process of social action, on the other.

Social dynamics of values: The large picture. Agreeing with the authors that values are 'out of balance, out of context and out of control' and recognizing CP's value-activist role, I believe the level of analysis has to be elevated and widened even further if we are to understand and counteract the powerful forces moulding social values. It is not enough for community psychologists to promote collective, solidarity-fostering values such as social justice, community and empowerment of the poor and disadvantaged. We must realize that we are also confronting certain values – self-interest, individualism, competition – that are the very cultural grounds of capitalism and other modern institutions, their 'implicit program', so to speak. And what is the inexorable result of capitalism's implicit program? The systematic destruction of the very social and moral fabric (bonds, relations, trust, otherness) that CP is supposed to promote. For as long as rich societies are willing to maintain their current living standards and support the socioeconomic logic grounding it, confronting 'market values' would mean challenging the economic basis upon which the affluent world is set. While we keep wanting more and more material artifacts and services and build our well-being on consuming things, advancing adversarial values such as social justice or community appears rather difficult, but not impossible, as the emergence of ecological values has shown.

Global solutions to global problems. We also have to be aware that individualistic, 'market values' are very powerful and difficult to counter in western countries for at least three reasons:

1. They are 'executive', functionally effective values that govern a large portion of social life. Vital tasks such as looking for a job, progressing socially or getting good grades in school, are ruled by the values of autonomy, competition and self-interest, not by those of community, social justice or empowerment.
2. Those values are sustained by an impressive machinery of media and advertising which is very effective in creating artificial needs in rich countries and in supporting a wasteful, economically unequal order within and across countries (North–South dimension).
3. They are presented as the 'only' effective way to a good life and a good society ('unique way of thinking') since 'there are no alternatives' to dominant neoliberalism, individualism and utilitarian calculus. Social *conformity* to such values – and to its derived way of living – is to be expected as

a basic component of current, unilateral globalization. To manage this situation CP should, first, fight on all those fronts: social conformity and homogenization of thinking, setting forth humanizing values and alternatives and spreading them socially; unmasking media and manipulation and cooperating with allies in showing that there are alternative values and ways of organizing society. Since changing values is a first step to change social priorities, that certainly implies – I agree with Nelson and Prilleltensky – bringing forgotten values into the foreground.

We must, second, be aware that global problems require *global solutions*, not only community ones. That positions CP in a quandary typical of all psychological attempts at social action. Confronting global, multisectoral problems with psychosocial instruments we run the risk of staying within psychological limits at the cost of 'psychologizing' problems and leaving deep roots of social problems and aspirations untouched.

Solutions? Multidisciplinary approaches and partnerships with community and social groups are necessary. What else? I think that community psychologists need to be humbler about the changes that we can bring about (without being *too* humble). We must also recognize the need for convergent approaches to social change, either from the top (redefining institutions and governments so they are responsive to people's needs rather than to some elites managing the multinationals' interests), or from the bottom. Social movements that reject the view of the world as a big market, seek *actual* changes and advocate for more collective and humane values. This is parallel to advocating for 'transformative' rather than 'ameliorative' changes (a distinction so appealing in theory as it is blurred and hard to maintain in daily practice!).

Third, we must remember that, contrary to neoliberal myths, the interests of the majority are best represented by *public* institutions, while deregulation, flexibility and pure competition generally work to the benefit of the few powerful, at the expense of the (silent) majorities and, worst of all, against the needs of the weaker and unorganized sectors. Fourth, CP must sustain its 'natural' values – community, empowerment, solidarity and social justice – although they challenge established values such as individual autonomy.

Introducing an ethical perspective in the analysis of values will help, I believe, to render a more practical orientation. How? In several ways:

1. Ethics would introduce a *process* axis connecting the more abstract level (vision and core values) to the more concrete level (actual action

and behaviour) in two directions: bottom-up (behaviour and consequences to values) and top-down (values to behaviour).

2. Acknowledging the importance of holism, we need to recognize the *interrelated* nature of values (so that advancing value A – say, efficacy – we would reduce value B – say, equality) and the inevitability of *priorities* (something implied in the background–foreground distinction) as difficult but necessary steps for making decisions in practice, especially in situations of value conflict. The conflict of community and individual autonomy is a case in point. CP cannot be built on the bases of individual autonomy and self-reliance since, as argued, those values result from the dissolution of bonds and relationships that weave the very community tissue (Bellah, Madsen, Sullivan, Swidler & Tipton, 1985; Kirpatrick, 1986; Montero, 1991; Sawaia, 1995; Serrano-García & Vargas, 1992).

3. Although I agree with Nelson and Prilleltensky's call for collaborative values, I find it necessary to add *conflict models* (for example Laue & Cormick, 1978) to deal with divergent interests in cases where collaborative models will not work. Since conflict models are frequently based on power and self-interest, we need to balance them with shared conceptions of the good acceptable by all community parties (Williams, 1978). Introducing *relational* values as a bridge between personal and social values – a relevant contribution of the chapter – is a step in the same direction. The value of trust can be proposed as a core collaborative value so that we conceive the relationship with the community as a *trust building process*.

Power. I would suggest considering power both as a *value* and as a *resource*, whose equitable distribution among persons and communities is conducive to human development. Being, however, a *political* commodity as well, its use has to be ethically monitored. How? In the case of community interventions that can be done by defining a *legitimate self-benefit* that sets and limits

the rewards – usually linked to power – that the practitioner may legitimately seek for him/herself: self-esteem, security, social recognition for his/her work and so on. Besides, if power is a *resource* contributing to well-being and welfare, community psychologists should help to 'create' power in others (empowering them). How? At least in two ways. At the micro level *sharing* power with others (keeping egalitarian relationships, and 'giving away' useful psychology). At the macro level, fostering social participation and struggling for a more equitable distribution of power and resources among social groups (helping the powerless to organize, unmasking oppressive situations and so on).

... And beyond. CP requires good evaluation and intervention techniques derived from sound psychological and social science to 'produce' desired results. We need a strategy that takes into account the resources of the intervenor and the external means necessary to translate designs into actions (time, energy, social motivation and solidarity, internal and external power and so on).

Managing uncertainty and complexity. Ethical and value problems grow in conditions of social complexity and *uncertainty* (Kelman & Warwick, 1978; O'Neill, 1989) so common in CP. In such conditions the community psychologist should be ready to clarify the values of different groups and offer values adequate to the specific situational demands (Sánchez Vidal, 1999). I have proposed a framework to analyse ethical or value questions in complex (conflicting or uncertain) social situations (Sánchez Vidal, 2002). It consists of four steps:

(a) identify relevant social *actors* (persons, groups, institutions and so on)
(b) ascertain the main *values* (declared or implicit) of each actor
(c) detect available *options* of action
(d) anticipate *consequences* of each choice for the different actors.

An examination of the first two steps enables the identification of conflicts and convergences; while scrutiny of the last two helps to predict social actors' reactions to proposed actions.

CLASS EXERCISE

1. Individually or in a small group, choose a social issue that requires the attention of a community psychologist. Examples of such issues are drug addiction, community violence, discrimination against people with disabilities, or the promotion of healthy relationships. Try to choose an issue that is relevant to your community.

2. Using the template provided in Table 3.5, devise value-based actions that address the issue of your choice. For example, you may wish to promote self-determination by making sure that community members are consulted about appropriate interventions.

CONT'D

3. Once you have completed the table, discuss and compare your suggestions with actions generated by other students and groups.

Table 3.5 Template for holistic value-based actions to address social issues

Values	Actions
Personal Self-determination	
Health	
Caring and compassion	
Relational Respect for diversity	
Collaboration and democratic	
Collective Social justice and accountability	
Support for community structures	

Chapter glossary

collectivism a belief in the importance of groups and communities that shapes attitudes and behaviours of citizens

communitarianism a school of thought that strives to restore citizens' responsibilities towards the collective as a means of advancing social well-being

context the social, cultural, natural or built environments that surround our lives and affect our cognitions, emotions and behaviours

holism a school of thought that emphasizes the importance of taking into account context and the various parts of social or natural phenomena in trying to explain them or change them

individualism a belief in the importance and supremacy of individuals over groups or collectives

kibbutz an Israeli collective society, ranging in number from a few dozen to several hundred people, where members share property and the means of production and engage in collective decision-making processes

liberalism a school of thought that upholds the rights of the individual in society and espouses individual solutions to problems in life

moral theory philosophical and ethical reasoning that helps individuals and groups to decide what is the right and just course of

action under a particular set of circumstances

psycho-centric a tendency to locate explanations for behaviour and problems in psychological dynamics such as cognitions and emotions, often at the expense of other contextual factors influencing human beings

synergy the positive effect of multiple forces coming together

values a set of principles, based on moral reasoning, that guide our behaviour

vision an image of a desired state of affairs worth striving for

■ **RESOURCES**

1. The World Bank conducted an extensive study of the experiences of poor people around the world. The various reports found in http://www.worldbank.org/poverty/voices/ describe what poor people value, what they need, and what actions they recommend. An excellent synthesis of the studies may be found in http://www.worldbank.org/poverty/voices/synthes.pdf.
2. The following website offers guidelines for ensuring participation and collaboration of community members in research projects. It offers suggestions for inviting community members to express their views on issues affecting their lives. Visit http://www.umich.edu/~irwg/research/collguid.html.
3. The Communitarian Network publishes materials and discussions related to values in contemporary society. They have an interesting website where you can view interviews with Amitai Etzioni and articles published in their newsletters and journals. Visit http://www.gwu.edu/~ccps/.

4

Ecology, Prevention and Promotion

Chapter Organization

The Ecological Metaphor	◆ What Is the Ecological Metaphor?: *Interdependence; Cycling of Resources; Adaptation; Succession* ◆ Why Is the Ecological Metaphor Important?: *Perceived Environments; Objective Characteristics of Environments; Transactional Approaches* ◆ What Is the Value-base of the Ecological Metaphor? ◆ How Can the Ecological Metaphor Be Implemented? ◆ What Are the Limitations of the Ecological Metaphor?
Prevention and Promotion	◆ What Are Prevention and Promotion?; *Prevention; Health Promotion* ◆ Why Are Prevention and Promotion Important? ◆ What Is the Value-base of Prevention and Promotion? ◆ How Can Prevention and Promotion Be Implemented?: *Risk Factors, Protective Factors and High-risk Approaches to Prevention; Universal Approaches to the Promotion of Health and Well-being; The Effectiveness of Prevention and Promotion* ◆ What Are the Limitations of Prevention and Promotion?

Chapter Summary	**COMMENTARY: Social Class, Power, Ecology and Prevention**

Class Exercise	**Glossary**	**Resources**

Warm-up Exercise

1. Reflecting on your childhood, think of some risk factors or stressful situations that threatened your sense of well-being.
2. What were some of the resources or protective factors (personal qualities, relationships, situations) that helped you deal with those stressful situations?

In this chapter, you will learn the definition, rationale, value-base, action implications and limitations of two of the key principles on which community psychology (CP) has been built:

- the ecological metaphor
- prevention and promotion.

We elaborate on each of these concepts that we briefly introduced in Chapter 2.

The Ecological Metaphor

What Is the Ecological Metaphor?

The ecological metaphor can be defined as the interaction between individuals and the multiple social systems in which they are embedded. Community psychologist Jim Kelly introduced four principles of the ecological perspective: interdependence, cycling of resources, adaptation and succession (Kelly, 1966; Trickett, Kelly & Todd, 1972). To illustrate the usefulness of these principles, we consider the example of the deinstitutionalization of people with serious mental health problems (a problem that Bret Kloos treats in more depth in Chapter 21). From the 1850s to the 1950s, people with serious mental health problems in western nations were institutionalized in large mental hospitals. Beginning in the 1950s, governments began a policy of deinstitutionalization. The inpatient populations of mental hospitals shrank dramatically, with hospitals in some locales being closed, and people with mental health problems were discharged into the community (Rochefort, 1993). How do the principles of the ecological metaphor help us to understand this change and its impacts on people and communities?

Interdependence

The principle of interdependence asserts that the different parts of an eco-system are interconnected and that changes in any one part of the system will have ripple effects that impact on other parts of the system. As we noted in Chapter 2, the ecological metaphor draws attention to three interdependent levels of analysis: personal (micro), relational (meso) and collective (macro). All of these levels are interconnected with each smaller level nested within the larger levels (see Figure 4.1). Deinstitutionalization provides a clear example of this interdependence. The closing or downsizing of mental hospitals led to former patients being discharged to poor living conditions in the community, including substandard housing (and, increasingly, homelessness for many) and inadequate support services. The ripple effects of deinstitutionalization also included uninformed and unprepared communities, with community members often displaying prejudice and rejection rather than welcoming acceptance of people with mental health problems. Families were also stressed and burdened by their having to assume the role of primary care providers, with little or no support. Attending to the unintentional side effects of a systems change is an important implication of the principle of interdependence.

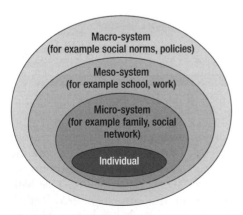

Figure 4.1 Nested ecological levels of analysis

Source: Prilleltensky, Nelson & Peirson (2001a)

Cycling of Resources

This principle focuses on the identification, development and allocation of resources within systems. One clear finding from the experience of deinstitutionalization is that, with a few notable exceptions, resources were not reallocated from mental hospitals into community support and housing programs, as was needed (Kiesler, 1992). Psychiatric wards in general hospitals were created, but these are short-stay facilities. Without adequate support following discharge, people with mental health problems experience a 'revolving door' of readmission to, and discharge from, these programs. The cycling of resources principle also draws attention to potential untapped resources in a system. Traditionally, society has regarded the formal mental health service system as *the* resource. However, with deinstitutionalization, non-traditional sources of support have been identified, organized and used to address the problems faced by people with serious mental illness. These include a person's social network, non-professional community helpers or volunteers and self-help organizations (both for mental health consumers and family members). The cycling of resources principle suggests that the community can be a valuable resource to people with serious mental illness and their families.

Adaptation

The principle of adaptation suggests that individuals and systems must cope with and adapt to changing conditions in an eco-system. In the wake of deinstitutional-ization, communities have had to adapt to the integration into their ranks of people with ongoing mental health problems; community support workers and programs have had to cope with inadequate funding and waiting lists for limited community services; families have often had to become primary care providers; and people with mental health problems have had to contend with stigma, poor housing, poverty and inadequate support services (Capponi, 2003). When housing, community support and self-help are available to help support individuals, the potential for recovery, community integration and quality of life is enhanced (Aubry & Myner, 1996; Nelson, Lord & Ochocka, 2001a).

Succession

Succession involves a long-term perspective and draws attention to the historical context of a problem and the need for planning for a preferred future. There are many explanations for why deinstitutionalization occurred. It is often argued that the advent of psychotropic medications helped to reduce psychiatric symptoms in this population and hastened their release from hospital. But this is only a partial explanation. Scull (1977) found that hospital downsizing began before these drugs were developed. Scull argued that the rising costs of the institutional care and the development of public welfare systems were the major reasons for deinstitutional-ization. It was becoming less expensive for governments to maintain people with mental health problems in the community than in institutions. However, deinstitu-tionalization created a whole new set of problems, but in a different context. In looking at deinstitutionalization in hindsight, most observers and critics agree that there was very little planning or anticipation of problems. As a result, some 50 years later, communities continue to struggle with the question of how they can adequately house and support people with serious mental health problems so that they can enjoy a desirable quality of life.

Why Is the Ecological Metaphor Important?

Community psychologists use an ecological metaphor in their emphasis on people in the context of social systems, because they believe that mainstream psychology has focused too much on individual psychological processes and neglected the important role that social systems play in human development. Community psychologists need to understand the pathogenic or oppressive qualities of human environments – those that block personal growth and create problems in living – and the positive qualities of environments that promote health, well-being and competence (Cowen, 1994). We need to know the characteristics of competent communities, communities that promote liberation and well-being (Iscoe, 1974).

It is also important to recognize that environments sometimes affect different individuals in distinct ways. This has been called a person–environment interaction. One case of a person–environment interaction of particular interest to community psychologists is that of 'person–environment fit'. In this case, a certain quality of the environment provides a good fit (or has a positive impact) for only some individuals. An example of this is provided by Canadian community psychologist Pat O'Neill (1976) in a study of fourth grade girls in conventional and open-space classrooms. Open-space classrooms are organized into large open areas with few partitions and teachers are flexible in their teaching approach. He found that students who were high in divergent thinking (creativity) had higher self-esteem in open classrooms than in conventional classrooms. Thus, open space classrooms had a positive impact on self-esteem, but only for those children high in divergent thinking. O'Neill (2000) introduced the idea of cognitive CP as a way of highlighting the importance of both individual and environmental qualities and the interrelationship between the person and the environment. Think of what type of environment is a good fit for you. If you are a private person, a noisy university residence with several roommates is not likely to be a setting in which you would be comfortable.

Since mainstream applied psychology has focused on individuals, there are many ways of thinking about individuals (psychoanalysis, behaviourism, humanism) and assessing their characteristics (for example personality, IQ and other tests of individual differences). In contrast, the study of social environments is in its infant stages of development. Community and environmental psychologists have been instrumental in developing ways of conceptualizing and assessing human environments (Linney, 2000; Moos, 2003; Shinn & Toohey, 2003). The study of cross-level relationships is a complex undertaking (Shinn & Rapkin, 2000; Shinn & Toohey, 2003). Community psychologist Jean Ann Linney (2000) has recently reviewed three ways of thinking about and assessing environments: (a) participants' perceptions of the environment, (b) setting characteristics that are independent of the behaviour of participants, and (c) transactional analyses of the dynamic relationship between behaviour and context. We briefly consider each of these three approaches, which can be applied to both neighbourhoods/communities and settings (for example schools, community organizations, workplaces).

Perceived Environments

Rudolf Moos (1994) and colleagues have emphasized the importance of the social climate or atmosphere of a setting. The key notion with this conceptualization of environments is the emphasis on people's *perceptions* of the environment. Most people can think of settings that they have experienced as oppressive and settings that were experienced as empowering. Moos has argued that there are three broad dimensions of different social environments: relationships, personal development, and systems maintenance and change. We can apply each dimension to a familiar setting – a school. The relationship dimension is concerned with how supportive or cohesive the setting appears to be. Are the teachers caring and compassionate? The personal development dimension addresses the individual's need for self-determination. Does the school provide opportunities for autonomy, independence and personal growth? The systems maintenance and change dimension is concerned with the balance between predictability and flexibility. Does the school provide clear expectations, yet at the same time demonstrate an openness to change and innovation? Too much predictability in a school can produce boredom and resentment, because it may reflect rigid authoritarianism and resistance to change. Too much flexibility, on the other hand, can produce confusion due to continuous uncertainty and flux. Moos and colleagues have developed self-report questionnaires tapping these three broad dimensions and specific sub-dimensions to assess classrooms, families, community programs, groups and work settings (Moos, 1994).

Objective Characteristics of Environments

A second approach to the assessment of environments is to examine characteristics of settings that are more objective and independent of the behaviour of individuals who participate in those settings. Different types of measures (for example observational methods, demographic and social indicator data) are used to assess qualities of environments, such as the physical and architectural dimensions, policies and procedures, and environmental resources. One example of an observational method cited by Linney (2000) is the PASSING approach designed by Wolfensberger (1972) to assess the extent to which facilities for people with disabilities reflect the construct of normalization. Wolfensberger (1972) defined normalization as the 'utilization of means which are as culturally normative as possible in order to establish and/or maintain behaviours and characteristics which are as culturally normative as possible' (p. 28). External observers spend several days observing these settings to come up with ratings on a number of different dimensions, including physical integration of the setting with the community, the promotion of resident autonomy, social integration within the neighbourhood, and many more (Flynn & Lemay, 1999).

Another way of assessing environments is to examine demographic and social indicator information about the community or setting. Such information provides an aggregate description of the characteristics of the individuals residing in the community (age, socioeconomic status, ethnic background) and characteristics of the community (types of housing, crime rates, rates of people under treatment for different psychosocial problems). An example of how one can use an objective approach to the assessment of environments is provided in Box 4.1.

Box 4.1   **Objective Assessment of School Atmosphere**

Rutter et al. (1979) used both observational and social indicator/demographic information in a study of 12 inner-city secondary schools in London, England. The major goal of the research was to identify characteristics of school atmosphere and to see if those characteristics related to students' rates of delinquency, behavioural problems, academic achievement and attendance over the three years they were enrolled in these schools. Some of the measures of school atmosphere were gathered through observational methods. Students had better outcomes in schools that showed a strong academic emphasis, as indicated by the total amount of teaching time, starting the class on time, assigning homework, planning departmental curriculum, displaying students' work and frequently using teacher praise for students. Other qualities of the school that were related to positive outcomes were good care and condition of the school, encouragement of student responsibility and participation, low teacher turnover rates and the number of experienced teachers in the school. While the researchers demonstrated an association between school atmosphere and student outcomes, these relationships could be due to other factors, such as the characteristics of the students. To control for this selection factor, the researchers used the method of social indicator and demographic assessment to describe the qualities of the students at the time they entered the school. Students with higher verbal aptitude and who came from higher socioeconomic status backgrounds had better outcomes three years later than those who were lower on these dimensions. *But the important finding of the study was that the school atmosphere measures predicted outcomes over and above the characteristics of the students at the time they entered these schools. School atmosphere does make a difference for students.*

Transactional Approaches

Linney (2000) describes transactional approaches as those that include both the behaviour of individuals and characteristics of the environment. One transactional approach is the concept of 'behaviour settings' developed by Barker (1968). The two main components of a behaviour setting are a standing or routine pattern of behaviour and the physical and temporal aspects of the environment. There are implicit guidelines on how to behave in behaviour settings. For example, a classroom science lesson and gym period are different behaviour settings, and the behaviour of people in these settings can be better predicted on the basis of the setting than on the characteristics of the people in the setting.

One interesting extension of the behaviour settings concept is Barker and Gump's (1964) theory of understaffing. They asserted that as the size of an organization increases, the number of people available to staff the different behaviour settings also increases. Furthermore, they hypothesized that, in small organizations, individuals would experience more invitations and pressure to take responsibility for staffing the different settings than they would in large organizations. In a study of high schools, they found support for this theory of understaffing. Students in smaller schools, including students with academic and social difficulties, were involved in a wider range of activities than students in larger schools. This approach to the understanding of environments has important implications for the CP value of participation and collaboration. Small, more intimate environments are apt to pull for more participation than larger, more impersonal environments. One downside to small settings, such as high schools, is that the number of activities in which students can participate is often restricted.

What Is the Value-base of the Ecological Metaphor?

The ecological perspective addresses the value of holism. Western science and ways of thinking about the world have emphasized linear, reductionistic and fragmented ways of understanding. In psychology, people are broken down into component parts (learning, perception, cognition) and are examined as isolated entities. Moreover, the researcher is a detached, objective scientist who is viewed as independent of the people he or she is studying, and the professional is an 'expert' helper. The ecological perspective revives the emphasis on holistic thinking, feeling and acting, that was evident in Gestalt psychology.

The holistic emphasis of the ecological perspective is also quite similar to the world view of aboriginal people. Connors and Maidman (2001) assert that the roots of tribal culture lie in holistic thought, which involves 'interdependence between the environment, people and the spirit' (p. 350). In the traditional world view of aboriginal people, there is a strong emphasis on the interconnection of people with their spiritual roots and the natural environments and on balance and harmony. Aboriginal holistic thinking also incorporates values (for example bravery, respect, cooperation) in the form of teachings which guide community members, unlike western science which claims to be value-neutral. The medicine wheel is a symbol of holism:

> This form of thought is often symbolized by the sacred circle or medicine wheel, which contains the teaching about the interconnection among all of Creation. The circle is a symbol that represents the knowledge offered by holistic world-views shared by aboriginal people. From this perspective, elements that affect change in a person are simultaneously seen as impacting on the person's family, community, nation and surrounding environment. (Connors & Maidman, 2001, p. 350)

How Can the Ecological Metaphor Be Implemented?

Jim Kelly and Ed Trickett have expanded on the four principles of the ecological perspective and have outlined their implications for preventive intervention (Kelly, 1986) and the conduct of research (Trickett, Kelly & Vincent, 1985). The major implication of the ecological metaphor for research is that research needs to be conducted in a much more collaborative, participatory manner than mainstream psychological research (Trickett, 1984; Trickett et al., 1985). Since CP research is carried out in the community with community partners, it stands in contrast to the mechanistic approach of experimental psychology and other basic sciences that are conducted in laboratories in which the variables under study are tightly controlled. Community members and settings are stakeholders in the research, who want to ensure that their needs are met. In community research, people are active participants in the research process, not passive subjects.

Moreover, community researchers are not exclusively detached, objective scientists. They are human beings with interests, agendas, values and feelings. Community psychologists are passionately concerned about disadvantaged people and social issues; they want to change the world, to make communities more caring and just. We believe that it is important for community psychologists to write more about their experiences and describe their standpoints in their research reports and writings. In Part IV, we elaborate more on the implications of the ecological perspective for community research.

Trickett (1986) has identified several implications of the ecological metaphor for intervention. First and foremost, the spirit of the ecological approach to intervention is distinctive. Not only are problems framed in terms of a systemic analysis, but the process of the intervention is one that is participatory and collaborative. Trickett (1986) captures this spirit in the following passage:

> The spirit of ecologically-based consultation is to contribute to the resourcefulness of the host environment by building on locally identified concerns to create processes which aid in empowering the environment to solve its own problems and plan its own development. This spirit is concretized in the kinds of activities engaged in by the consultants, which further highlight the distinctiveness of the ecological metaphor. (p. 190)

The spirit of ecological intervention is one of working *with* rather than *on* people.

A second implication for community intervention is that attempts to change one part of the system will have side effects on other systems, and that these side effects will often not be anticipated. The ecological metaphor suggests that social change is not linear. Attempts to solve a problem may lead to new problems in another context (Sarason, 1978). The case of deinstitutionalization of people with serious mental health problems cited earlier is an example of this. A third implication of the ecological perspective is that the intervention should not focus exclusively on the attainment of outcome goals for participants in a specific program. While it is important to see how individuals benefit from programs, the ecological perspective draws attention to goals at multiple levels of analysis. A successful ecological intervention builds the capacity of the setting to mobilize for future action and create other programs. The extent to which setting members participate in and take ownership for the intervention are also important.

Fourth, there are implications of the ecological metaphor for the role and qualities of the interventionist. Since ecological intervention is flexible and improvisational in nature, consultants must be able to form constructive working relationships with different partners from the host setting. They must problem-solve, think on their feet, be patient and take time to get to know the setting and the people within it. They must not jump into offering solutions, but must tolerate the ambiguities and frustrations that inevitably occur in any intervention, and help the setting to mobilize resources from within or to identify external resources. They must also be creative and attend to issues of entry and exit from the setting (Kelly, 1971).

A fifth implication of the ecological metaphor for community intervention is that the dimension of time is highlighted. The changing nature of eco-systems and human adaptation requires a long-term time perspective. Contemporary social problems have both historical roots and future consequences. When community psychologists examine social issues and problems from an ecological perspective, they consider these issues and problems at multiple levels of analysis and over a long-term time perspective.

Finally, it is important to consider both individual and setting characteristics in community intervention. For example, research by O'Neill (2000) and colleagues has shown that social change tends to occur when there are recent improvements in social conditions (an environmental characteristic) and when people have a sense of injustice and a belief in their personal power to effect change (individual characteristics).

What Are the Limitations of the Ecological Metaphor?

The ecological metaphor has value in providing a systemic and holistic perspective for the understanding of human experience and behaviour and it has led to the development of different ways of understanding and assessing human environments. To date, however, CP has tended to focus on micro and meso levels, to the neglect of macro-level structures and interventions. In the 1980s, Janet Cahill (1983) pointed out how different dimensions of the macroeconomy have an impact on mental health. Moreover, the macroeconomic trends that Cahill described have worsened since the publication of her article (for example larger gaps in income between the rich and poor, greater capital mobility). Inattention to the macro level of analysis is not a limitation of the ecological perspective, but rather a gap in the extent to which community psychologists have focused on larger social structures.

One limitation of ecological and systems perspectives is that in their emphasis on circular causality (the idea that everything is causally related to everything else), they do not take into account or highlight power differences within eco-systems. For example, the phenomena of child maltreatment and violence against women can be understood in terms of an ecological perspective, with multiple layers of influence. But it is also important to recognize that some players have more power than others in any eco-system and that those individuals who abuse power must be accountable for their actions. Abused women and children are not architects of their abuse. This is why the ecological metaphor needs to complemented with the concept of power (Trickett, 1994), which we consider in the next chapter.

Prevention and Promotion

What Are Prevention and Promotion?

Prevention

Prevention is a concept that has been around for some time. In the 18th century people believed that disease resulted from noxious odours, 'miasmas', that emanated from swamps or polluted soil. Improving sanitation resulted in a decline in the rates of many diseases (for example typhoid fever, yellow fever). George Albee (1991) has recounted one of the important stories in the history of prevention, that of John Snow and the Broad Street pump. In the year 1854 in London, John Snow determined that an outbreak of illness was traceable to one source of drinking water. People who drank from the well at Broad Street, but not other wells, were the ones who became sick. Removing the handle on the Broad Street pump and providing an alternative water source prevented the disease of cholera. An important lesson from this story is that prevention is possible even without knowledge of the causes of a problem. No one knew exactly what caused cholera, but this did not stop Snow and others from engaging in community action that led to successful prevention outcomes.

Prevention has its roots in the field of public health. The thrust of the public health approach to prevention is to reduce environmental stressors and to enhance host resistances to those stressors. In the case of smoking, public policy could attempt to restrict advertising and sales to young people (an environmental change) and programs could teach ways of resisting peer pressure and commercial exploitation (enhancing host resistances). The public health approach to prevention has been very successful in reducing the incidence (the number of new cases in a time period) of many diseases, yet this approach is effective only with diseases that have a single identified cause, be it a vitamin deficiency or a germ. The problem with this approach when applied to mental health and psychosocial problems in living is that very few of these problems have a single cause (Albee, 1982). This is how the ecological perspective is related to prevention. Most psychosocial problems are multiply determined, with micro, meso and macro factors all playing a role in causation.

Community psychologists have taken the lead in translating the idea of prevention into concepts, research and programs that are applicable to psychosocial and mental health problems. For example, George Albee (1986, 1996a) has drawn attention to the issue of politics and power in prevention, arguing that prevention should be a basic feature of a just society. Another community psychologist, the late Emory Cowen, played a pioneering role in prevention theory, research, practice and training.

As we noted in Chapter 2, primary prevention strives to reduce the incidence or onset of a disorder in a population, whereas secondary prevention is not really prevention, but rather early detection and intervention. There are three defining features of prevention (Nelson, Prilleltensky & Peters, 2003). First, with successful prevention, new cases of a problem do not occur. Second, prevention is not aimed at individuals but at populations; the goal is a decline in incidence (the rates of disorder). Third, preventive interventions intentionally focus on preventing mental health problems (Cowen, 1980).

A typology of prevention has been promoted by the Institute of Medicine (IOM, 1994). *Universal* preventive interventions are targeted to the general public or a whole population group that has not been identified on the basis of individual risk. An example of a universal preventive intervention for physical health is childhood immunization. Selective preventive interventions are targeted to individuals or subgroups of the population whose risk of developing problems is significantly higher than average. A Head Start or other early childhood programs for all children living in a socioeconomically depressed neighbourhood is an example of a selective prevention intervention. *Indicated* preventive interventions are targeted to high-risk individuals who are identified as already having minimal, but detectable signs or symptoms or biological markers, indicating predisposition for the mental disorder, but who do not meet diagnostic criteria. An intervention to prevent depression in children with one or both clinically depressed parents is an example of an indicated preventive intervention. (NIMH Committee on Prevention Research, 1995, pp. 6–7) (original emphasis)

Prilleltensky, Peirson and Nelson (2001) have noted that universal, selective and indicated approaches to prevention differ in two ways (see Figure 4.2). First, they differ with respect to the timing of an intervention. Universal and selective approaches take place before a problem has occurred, but indicated approaches are used during the early stages of the problem. Second, they differ with respect to the

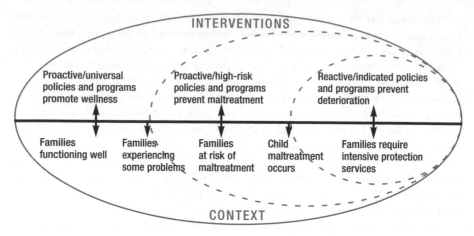

Figure 4.2 The promotion–prevention–early intervention continuum
Source: Prilleltensky, Nelson and Peirson (2001a)

population served. Everyone is served in a universal intervention; only those who are 'at risk' are served in a selective intervention; and only those who are already showing signs of a problem are served in an indicated intervention. In this book, we use the term prevention to mean primary prevention, which includes both universal and selective (or high-risk) approaches.

Figure 4.2 illustrates how these different types of prevention can be applied to the prevention of child maltreatment. The line that bisects the oval represents the timing of the intervention. The right-hand side of the line is the reactive end of the continuum (working with families in which a child has already been abused), while the left-hand side of the line represents the proactive end of the continuum (working with families in which child abuse has not occurred). The ovals represent the populations served by the prevention approach. The large oval indicates that the universal approach serves everyone; the next largest oval (with broken lines) represents a sub-set of the population (families that are at risk of abuse); while the smallest oval (again with broken lines) represents an even smaller sub-set of the population (families in which a child has already been abused). Whereas clinical intervention focuses on a small sub-set of the population after problems have developed (reactive approach), prevention works with larger segments of the population before problems have developed (proactive approach).

Health Promotion

Complementary to prevention is the concept of health promotion. Where prevention, by definition, focuses on reducing problems, promotion can be defined as the enhancement of health and well-being in populations. In practice, health promotion and prevention are closely related. For example, universal interventions that promote healthy eating, physical activity and fitness, and abstinence from smoking have also been shown to prevent cardiovascular disease (Pancer & Nelson, 1990). Cowen (1996) identified four key characteristics of mental health promotion or well-being: (a) it is proactive, seeking to promote mental health; (b) it focuses on populations, not individuals; (c) it is multidimensional, focusing on 'integrated sets of operations involving individuals, families, settings, community contexts and macro level societal structures and policies' (p. 246); and (d) it is ongoing, not a one-shot, time-limited intervention. See Box 4.2 for some of the ways that wellness can be promoted.

Box 4.2   Routes to Psychological Health and Well-Being

Cowen (1994) argues that there are several key pathways towards mental health promotion.

1. *Attachment.* Infants and preschool children who form secure attachments to their parents and caregivers early in life fare well in later life. Home visitation programs that work with parents and their infants are one example of a strategy to promote attachments.
2. *Competencies.* The development of age-appropriate and culturally relevant competencies is another health promotion strategy. School-based social competence (for example social problem-solving skills, assertiveness, interpersonal skills) enhancement programs are one promising approach.
3. *Social environments.* Another pathway to the enhancement of health and well-being is to identify the characteristics of environments that are associ-

ated with health and then direct social environments towards those characteristics that have been shown to be important for well-being. Changing family, school, community and larger social environments can be used to promote health.
4. *Empowerment.* Empowerment refers to perceived and actual control over one's life and empowering interventions are those that enhance participants' control over their lives. An empowerment approach stresses the importance of providing opportunities for people to exercise their self-determination and strengths, so that they are in control of the intervention.
5. *Resilience and resources to cope with stress.* The ability to cope effectively with stressful life events and conditions is another key pathway to health and well-being. Life stressors are often seen as presenting an opportunity for growth, if the person has the resources to manage the stressors.

Why Are Prevention and Promotion Important?

'An ounce of prevention is worth a pound of cure.' 'A stitch in time saves nine.' These proverbs get to the heart of why prevention is important. Once problems occur, they are very difficult to treat. Often one problem cascades into another. Treatment methods can be helpful, but many people experience relapse or reoccurrence of problems. Moreover, even if treatments were 100% effective, there are not nearly enough trained mental-health professionals to treat all those afflicted with mental health and psychosocial problems in living. As we noted in Chapter 1, the prevalence rates of psychosocial and mental health problems far outstrip available human resources. Albee (1990) has stated that 'the history of public methods (that emphasize social change) has clearly established, no mass disease or disorder afflicting humankind has ever been eliminated by attempts at treating affected individuals' (p. 370).

Another argument for primary prevention and health promotion is that they can save money in the long run. Both institutional and community treatment services provided by professionals for health, mental health and social problems are very costly. The costs of hospitalizing a person for one day is several hundred US dollars in most western countries and it is not uncommon for therapists to charge $100 US for an hour of therapy. Some research has documented the cost-effectiveness of prevention programs. For example, a longitudinal evaluation of the High/Scope

Perry Preschool, a preschool educational program for economically disadvantaged children living in a community in Michigan in the US, found the following:

> Compared to the no-preschool group, the preschool group had higher rates of employment and self-support, a lower welfare rate, fewer acts of serious misconduct and a lower arrest rate. For every dollar invested, the 30-week program returned six dollars to taxpayers and the 60-week program returned three dollars. (Schweinhart & Weikart, 1989, p. 109)

What Is the Value-base of Prevention and Promotion?

Prevention and health promotion focus on the values of health and well-being. Many people think of health or mental health in negative terms, as the absence of disorder. But a broader view of health can be framed in positive terms, as the presence of optimal social, emotional and cognitive functioning within a health promoting and sustaining context. According to the Epp (1988) report *Mental Health for Canadians: Striking a Balance*:

> Mental health is the capacity of the individual, the group and the environment to interact with one another in ways that promote subjective well-being, the optimal development and use of mental abilities (cognitive, affective and relational), the achievement of individual and collective goals consistent with justice and the attainment and preservation of conditions of fundamental equality. (p. 7)

According to this definition, mental health is defined ecologically in terms of transactions between the individual and his or her environment, not just in terms of qualities of the individual. The value of health, which underlies the concepts of prevention and promotion, holds that health is a basic human right. Article 24 of the United Nations Convention on the Rights of the Child (United Nations, 1991), for instance, asserts 'the right of the child to the enjoyment of highest attainable standard of health', while Article 19 asserts that children should be protected from harmful influences on their health: 'State parties shall take appropriate legislative, administrative, social and educational measures to protect the child from all forms of physical or mental violence, injury or abuse, neglect or negligent treatment, maltreatment or exploitation, including sexual abuse.'

How Can Prevention and Promotion Be Implemented?

As we noted earlier, there are two interrelated approaches to prevention and promotion: one focuses on risk reduction for mental health problems and the other on community-wide approaches to health promotion (Cowen, 1996, 2000).

Risk Factors, Protective Factors and High-Risk Approaches to Prevention

Since the early 1970s, a substantial amount of research has confirmed that most psychosocial problems are associated with many different risk factors. A risk factor is any factor that is related to the occurrence of a problem (Rae-Grant, 1994). Moreover, the effects of risk factors may be exponential. That is, most people can withstand one risk factor without being adversely affected, but when there is a 'pile-up' of risk factors, the impacts may be particularly devastating. For example, Rutter (1979) found a fourfold increase in subsequent rates of psychiatric problems when two risk factors were present in childhood and a 24-fold increase when four risk factors were present in childhood.

Some individuals, however, demonstrate resilience in that they are able to withstand exposure to many risk factors (Cowen, 2000). These individuals have protective factors, which are resources (for example coping skills, self-esteem, support systems) that help to offset or buffer risk factors. Albee (1982) views the incidence of mental health problems as an equation:

$$\text{Incidence} = \frac{\text{Risk factors}}{\text{Protective factors}} = \frac{\text{Organic causes} + \text{Stress} + \text{Exploitation}}{\text{Coping skills} + \text{Self-esteem} + \text{Support systems}}$$

This formulation is ecological and transactional in nature (Felner, Felner & Silverman, 2000). As Rae-Grant (1994) has shown, risk and protective factors can occur at multiple levels of analysis. For example, risk factors can occur at the individual (low self-esteem), family (marital discord or separation) and community (living in a violent community) levels of analysis. Similarly, protective factors can be individual (good coping skills), family (a warm and loving relationship with one parent) or community (opportunities for socialization, recreation or skill development) in nature. An example of a selective intervention program is the Prenatal/Early Infancy Project described in Box 4.3.

Box 4.3   The Prenatal/Early Infancy Project

This project was developed by David Olds and colleagues in 1977 in Elmira, a semi-rural community in upstate New York. This community was extremely economically depressed and had the highest rates of child maltreatment in the state. Nurse home visitors worked with first-time mothers during the prenatal period, continuing until the children reached two years of age. This was a selective or 'high-risk' approach to prevention of child maltreatment, because the women who were selected were low-income, unmarried or teenaged. The mothers were randomly assigned to the home visit program or to a control group that received transportation for health care and screening for health problems but no visits. The home visits focused on promoting parent education, enhancing informal support and linkage with formal services. The nurses completed an average of 32 visits from the prenatal period through to the second year of the child's life. The results of the evaluation showed that during the first two years after delivery, 14 per cent of the poor, unmarried teenage mothers in the control group abused or neglected their children, as compared with 4 per cent of the poor, unmarried teens visited by a nurse (Olds et al., 1986). Many other positive outcomes were found for the mothers and their children in the short term, including the fact that the program resulted in a cost saving. However, it is the long-term findings that are the most striking. In their analysis of the poor, unmarried women, Olds et al. (1997) found that nurse-visited women had higher rates of employment than the women in the control group, as well as lower rates of impairments due to alcohol or substance abuse (41% vs 73%), verified child abuse or neglect (29% vs 54%), arrests (16% vs 90% according to state records), convictions, days in jail, use of welfare and subsequent pregnancies by the time the children were 15 years of age. Also, compared with those whose mothers were in the control group, the children whose mothers participated in the home visitation program had significantly fewer incidents of running away (24% vs 60%), arrests (20% vs 45%) and convictions and violations of probation (9% vs 47%) at age 15 (Olds et al., 1998).

The risk and protective factor formulation is based on the broader approach of social stress theory. As we noted in Chapter 1, community psychologist Barbara Dohrenwend (1978) introduced social stress theory to CP as a framework for understanding both how social environments can have negative impacts on individuals and how social interventions can be designed to prevent social stressors or reduce the negative consequences of social stressors. A central thesis of social stress theory is that stressful life events and changes, particularly negative life events, create stress reactions in individuals and that the long-term consequences of these stress reactions can be negative, neutral or positive. That is, stress presents an opportunity for growth, as well as the potential for negative outcomes. Moreover, Dohrenwend (1978) asserted that there are a variety of psychological and situational factors that can moderate the impacts of stressful life events. For example, a person with a good social support network or good coping skills may adjust well to a stressful life event such as marital separation, whereas a person without such resources may fare worse. Such moderating factors are also referred to as 'protective factors' or 'stress-meeting resources'.

Since Dohrenwend's (1978) initial formulation, there has been a great deal of research and further theorizing about social stress in CP (Sandler, 2001). One of the advances of this research is that there is now a greater understanding of the role of particular life events, such as job loss (Dooley & Catalano, 1980, 2003) and divorce (Sandler, 2001), in contributing to psychosocial problems. In particular, research has helped to clarify the mechanisms by which stressful life events can have negative impacts on individuals. Sometimes stressful life events set in motion a variety of additional problems or ongoing life strains to which people must adapt. For example, unemployment leads to ongoing financial strains that impact on one's marital, family and social network relations. Thus, it is not just the stressful life event that is the problem, but all that ensues in the aftermath of that event. Irwin Sandler (2001) has found that the adversity of divorce can negatively impact on children's academic competence, self-worth and coping skills, which, in turn, can have a negative impact on children's behaviour. Thus, research has clarified the role of mediating factors (for example academic competence, self-worth, coping skills) that link stressful life events with negative outcomes for individuals. Community psychologists have used knowledge gained about mediating and moderating factors to design preventive interventions to reduce the negative impacts of stressful life events such as job loss (Price, Van Kyn & Vinokur, 1992) and parental divorce (Sandler, 2001). For example, mentoring programs have been successfully used to enhance the support and offset stressors faced by children or young people who are lacking social support (DuBois et al., 2002; Rhodes & Bogat, 2002).

Universal Approaches to the Promotion of Health and Well-being

Over the past few years, there has been an increasing focus on health and the promotion of well-being (Cicchetti et al., 2000; Cowen, 1994, 2000; Prilleltensky & Nelson, 2000; Prilleltensky et al., 2001a). Health promotion approaches are often provided on a universal basis to all individuals in a particular geographical area (for example neighbourhood, city, province) or particular setting (for example school, workplace, public housing complex). Moreover, health promotion is more likely to focus on multiple ecological levels than on risk reduction, which is more often aimed at individuals.

While many of the original prevention programs in mental health used the risk reduction or selective approach, focusing on at-risk individuals, more recently there has been a greater emphasis on setting-wide and community-wide approaches to prevention. These more environmental approaches to prevention focus not only on specific prevention programs, but more broadly on building the capacities of organizations and communities. A major focus of these interventions is developing partnerships or coalitions of various community stakeholders to plan, implement and evaluate the intervention (Foster-Fishman, Berkowitz et al., 2001; Wolff, 2001). Community-wide approaches have been used to address a variety of issues, including substance abuse, HIV/AIDS, heart disease, immunization, teenage pregnancy and child development (Roussos & Fawcett, 2000).

The Effectiveness of Prevention and Promotion

While the rationale for prevention is compelling, prevention and promotion need solid research evidence on which to base practice. One of the frequent criticisms of prevention is that practitioners implement programs that have not been proved to be effective and that are uninformed by research. Fortunately, the research base supporting the effectiveness of prevention and promotion programs has grown substantially since the early 1970s. In 1977 Cowen characterized prevention as progressing by 'baby steps,' but by 1996 he spoke of 'lengthy strides' in prevention. In a 1988 publication, a task force of the American Psychological Association (APA) on prevention identified only 14 prevention programs with a research base (Price et al., 1988), whereas the publication of a more recent APA task force on *Prevention: Promoting Strength, Resilience and Health in Young People* is filled with information on a variety of effective prevention programs for children and young people (Weissberg & Kumpfer, 2003). By the early 1990s, Durlak and Wells (1997) had located 177 controlled studies of prevention programs for children and young people and found that overall these programs were quite successful in preventing problems and promoting well-being.

In addition to the growth in the amount of research on prevention, there has also been growth in the application of prevention to a variety of different populations and issues. For preschool children, preschool education programs (for example Head Start in the US, Zigler & Valentine, 1997), family support programs (for example home visitation for parents, Olds et al., 1986), multi-component programs (for example the Perry Preschool, Schweinhart & Weikart, 1989) and programs with a skill-building emphasis (for example the interpersonal cognitive problem-solving program [ICPSP], Shure, 1997) have been found to improve cognitive and/or social–emotional outcomes in children and to prevent child maltreatment and other negative outcomes for children, both in the short term and through adolescence and early adulthood (MacLeod & Nelson, 2000; Nelson, Laurendeau et al., 2001; Nelson, Westhues & MacLeod, 2003; Weissberg & Greenberg, 1998). School-based prevention programs have been found to be successful in promoting school-aged children's social–emotional learning and preventing both externalizing (that is, conduct) and internalizing (that is, shyness, anxiety) problems (Durlak, 1995; Lorion, 1989; Greenberg et al., 2001; Weissberg & Greenberg, 1998). School-based and family support programs have also been successful in preventing a variety of negative outcomes for adolescents, including smoking, substance abuse, risky sexual behaviour, school failure/dropout, delinquency/violence and violence against women in dating relationships (Lavoie et al., 1995; Nation, Crusto et al., 2003). While much of the research in prevention focuses on children and young people, there have been successful applications with adults, including serious and widespread problems, such as depression (Price et al., 1992) and HIV/AIDS (Peterson, 1998). See Box 4.4 for a list of principles of effective prevention programs.

Box 4.4 **What Are the Principles of Effective Prevention Programs?**

What are the ingredients of effective prevention programs? Based on a review-of-reviews of prevention research, community psychologist Maury Nation and colleagues (Nation ct al., 2003) uncovered nine key principles.

1. *Comprehensiveness:* Multi-component programs that strive to address several different ecological levels and contexts are more important than single-focus programs.
2. *Varied teaching methods:* Programs need to teach skills through interaction, 'hands on' methods, as well as increasing knowledge and awareness.
3. *Sufficient 'dosage':* Programs need to be sufficiently long and intensive to have positive preventive impacts (Nelson, Westhues, & MacLeod, 2003).
4. *Theory driven:* Programs need to be based on a sound theoretical framework that is supported by research, such as the risk and protective factors formulation.
5. *Positive relationships:* Programs for children need to promote positive relationships with parents, teachers, peers, mentors and others.
6. *Appropriately timed:* Programs need to be well-timed to address specific developmental issues for children, young people and adults.
7. *Sociocultural relevance:* Programs must be tailored to the norms of the population served and include them in planning and implementation.
8. *Outcome evaluation:* Programs should have clearly specified outcome goals that make them amenable to research on the effectiveness of the program.
9. *Well-trained staff:* Programs must provide training for staff to properly implement the program.

What Are the Limitations of Prevention and Promotion?

While in the past prevention in mental health has been ignored or dismissed by psychiatry and the medical profession (for example Lamb & Zusman, 1979), more recently the medical profession has become more enamoured of prevention. Recently, psychiatry has broadened the definition of prevention to include 'comorbidity prevention' (preventing the development of a second disorder when a person already has one disorder) and 'relapse prevention' (preventing a person who has been successfully treated from having a relapse) (NIMH Committee on Prevention Research, 1995). Stretching the definition of prevention in this way takes the field back towards 'tertiary prevention' and away from true prevention and promotion, as we have defined them. Moreover, the Institute of Medicine's (1994) emphasis on 'prevention science', focuses rather narrowly on the prevention of psychiatric disorders, as defined in the latest version of the *Diagnostic and Statistical Manual*, through risk reduction approaches. As Albee (1996a, 1998) and Cowen (2000) have noted, this focus diverts attention from non-medical model approaches, such as health promotion, competence enhancement, empowerment and social change approaches to prevention and promotion.

The 'prevention science' approach tends to 'medicalize' and 'depoliticize' prevention. We are critical of this approach, not because we are against science, but because the particular form of science being promoted by the medical profession is very narrow in emphasis. Selective approaches to prevention, which predominate, are often carried out with low-income people because poverty, low social class and unemployment are one set of major risk factors for many different mental health problems (Perry, 1996). Moreover, selective approaches typically address the bottom half of Albee's (1982) equation (that is, promoting protective factors), rather than the top half of the equation (that is, reducing stress or exploitation). Also, programs which promote protective factors tend to be person-centred or family-centred, ignoring the larger social environment (Febbraro, 1994). One final criticism of prevention as it is currently practised, is that prevention is something that is done *by* professional 'experts' *to* 'at risk' people. Professionally driven approaches may not address what these so-called 'at risk' people need or want, they may be disempowering and create dependencies on service systems, and they tend to focus on deficits rather than the strengths of community members.

More recently, some prevention programs have become more community-driven, with residents in low-income communities actively participating in the planning and implementation of prevention programs in their communities. These programs are not only driven by community members, but they are designed to change or create meso-level settings in the community to foster the well-being of families and children. Moreover, Nelson, Amio et al. (2000) have proposed concrete steps for value-based partnerships in prevention programs, that include processes for inclusion, participation and control by disadvantaged people in the design of prevention programs.

There are some promising examples of partnerships for prevention between schools, parents and communities. One is the Yale–New Haven School Development Program (Comer, 1985), which began in two schools in a low-income African-American community in Connecticut and has now been implemented in more than 550 schools in the US (Weissberg & Greenberg, 1998). This program is based on: '(a) a representative governance and management group, (b) a parent participation program and group, (c) a mental health program and team, and (d) an academic (curriculum and staff development) program' (Comer, 1985, p. 155). There is a strong emphasis on parent participation in school programs and school governance in this program. A three-year longitudinal evaluation of this project found significant improvement on measures of school achievement and social competence for children participating in the intervention compared with children in similar schools (Cauce et al., 1987). A more radical approach to school-based prevention has been implemented in another Connecticut community, using emancipatory and African-centred education as the core philosophy (Potts, 2003). At the Benjamin E. Mays Institute, which serves 100 African-American male students in middle school, the focus is on the development of African identity and students as agents of social change. According to community psychologist Randolph Potts (2003):

> African history and wisdom teachings provide more than just additional content for primary prevention programs. The Akan symbol *sankofa* represents the African teaching that reclaiming and understanding history are essential for understanding present circumstances and moving forward into the future. For children of African descent, understanding both the African cultural legacy of intellectual achievement and the contemporary structures of domination are essential in preparing them to confront conditions that are destroying their communities. (p. 178)

An evaluation of this program has shown that students in the Benjamin E. Mays Institute score significantly higher on grade point average in tests of maths and writing skills and on a measure of African identity, than children from other middle schools in the same community.

While the direction towards more community-driven approaches is a positive one, prevention needs to move even further towards macro-level analyses and interventions. Albee (1986, 1996a, 1998) has argued that prevention should be linked to social justice rather than the medical model. A social justice approach to prevention strives to address the causes of the causes through social change efforts. Thus, prevention should not just be focused on changing individuals, families or communities, but on larger social structures in which people and settings are embedded. To translate this rhetoric into action, we believe that prevention should encompass not just programs, but also social policies. Since economic inequality is a major structural cause of psychosocial problems (Cahill, 1983; Hertzman, 1999; Wilkinson, 1996), policies that strive to reduce this, such as those practised in western and northern European countries, show the forms prevention can take at the macro-level (Peters et al., 2001). Not only have countries like Sweden been successful in reducing the level of economic inequality in their society, but as a result the literacy and numeracy skills of children in the bottom economic quintile in Sweden are vastly better than those of children in the bottom economic quintiles in the US and Canada (Hertzman, 1999). These findings suggest that there needs to be more emphasis on advocating change in social and economic policies to promote social justice and well-being.

Chapter Summary

We conclude this chapter by noting that the principles of ecology and prevention tend to focus on personal and relational values, to the neglect of collective values, on ameliorative rather than transformative change, to surface manifestations of larger social problems rather than unequal power relations and to a focus on well-being rather than liberation. Ecology and prevention help to define and differentiate CP from clinical psychology, but they can inadvertently lend support to the existing societal status quo. Nevertheless, ecology and prevention are useful and important principles for CP, and community psychologists can push the boundaries of these concepts more towards the macro level of analysis. Examination of structural causes of human suffering and macro-level policy change to reduce economic inequality are ways that these principles can move towards a more transformative agenda.

COMMENTARY: Social Class, Power, Ecology and Prevention   *George W. Albee*

The ecological metaphor clearly has much to offer in our efforts to understand that an action has effects in many areas, some unforeseen. As is pointed out in this chapter, CP has tended to focus on micro and meso levels, to the neglect of macro-level structures and interventions. The example chosen – deinstitutionalization of mental cases in the US – also needs to be considered at macro levels. I would include social class and political power among important macro forces.

From 1850 to 1925 there were a vast number of immigrants from Europe who landed in America. The Irish, Scandinavians, Eastern European Slavs and Jews, Southern Italians – mostly peasant and impoverished people – arrived in the hope of a better life for themselves and their families. Living in overcrowded cities they worked hard, were exploited and their children were educated. But because of the excessive stresses, their rate of mental disorders quickly overwhelmed the small retreats and mental wards. Mental disorders were declared to be brain diseases common to people who were seen by the ruling class as biologically inferior. Huge mental hospitals (asylums) were built and (inadequately) funded by the state governments to house the insane. Theses places quickly became the overcrowded hell-holes described as *The Shame of the States* (Deutsch, 1948). The chronic mental cases were/are mostly from the lowest social classes where few family resources were/are available for their care. Chronic mental cases require long-term care and there is no alternative to tax-supported programs.

In the 1950s a Joint Commission on Mental Illness and Health was appointed by Eisenhower and the US Congress to find an alternative to the huge state hospitals. The Commission's final Report, *Action for Mental Health* (1961), recommended establishing 4000 Comprehensive Community Mental Health Centers where, through a single door, all persons with mental disorders could find help. Day care, in-patient beds, community support programs, individual treatment, consultation education and research would be available in these centres. This promising program was brought to a halt by the powerful opposition of US medicine. It was socialized health care! Psychiatrists and other staff were to be paid federal salaries and this violated the conservative political opposition to using federal tax dollars to solve social problems and to provide health care.

But the states, delighted at the prospect of saving the enormous costs of running the state hospitals, went on closing them down as planned. The hapless inmates were mostly dumped into the streets. (They could apply for welfare only if they had a permanent address – but without welfare they could not pay for a permanent address.) So hundreds of thousands were doomed to live under bridges and in bus stations and packing crates.

What is the macro message?

1. One's social class determines the availability of medical care and social support. Today, the group with the highest rate of mental disorders, drug use, mental retardation, alcoholism, sickness and early death is the migrant farm workers.
2. The ruling ideas of a society are those that support the ruling class. Serious poverty affects

millions. It is hardest on children and women, on the elderly, on the physically and mentally handicapped. Proposals to raise the minimum wage, to provide health care for the uninsured, to build low-cost housing, all contradict the view of the ruling class that we must rely on hard work, prayer, individual initiative and volunteers to correct social injustice. Spending federal tax money to support the poor and passing federal regulations to protect the handicapped is socialism and must be opposed.

An understanding of the importance of primary prevention is essential for CP. There is a mistaken focus on one-to-one treatment in present-day clinical psychology. Few realize (or will admit) the truth of the public health dictum: *No disease or disorder has ever been treated out of existence*. No matter how successful our individual treatments, curing one person at a time does not reduce the incidence (new cases) of a disease or disorder. Only successful primary prevention reduces incidence. Some examples:

1. Reducing lead in the environment reduces the number of cases of brain damage. (Strategy: eliminate lead paint, lead toys, lead in gasoline.)
2. Reducing the stresses of poverty (low wages, overcrowded and unsanitary housing) reduces the rate of child abuse and neglect associated with childhood emotional and learning problems. (Strategy: raise the minimum wage.)
3. Provide support groups. Isolated persons are at high risk. A wide range of support groups – Scouts, clubs, home visitors and so on, has been shown to reduce psychopathology.

Primary prevention and promotion are aimed at developing interventions that affect groups. The members of these groups may be at risk, but they are not yet affected. For example, there are many effective programs for ensuring that infants are born full-term and of normal birth weight. Such infants are at lower risk later for many negative conditions. Low-birth-weight infants are at high risk. The goal of primary prevention is to increase the number at low risk and decrease the number at high risk. Working with premature infants is admirable, but it is not primary prevention.

In recent years the National Institute of Mental Health has stretched the concept of prevention to include interventions at early stages of the development of a mental condition in individuals. While this may be good medicine, it is not primary prevention. It is a strategy to allow allocation of tax dollars to treatment that can count as efforts at prevention. Treatment is profitable. Primary prevention is often costly (of tax dollars) and is opposed by political conservatives.

One of the ruling ideas of the conservative society argues that each mental disorder is a separate disease with a separate cause and therefore requires a separate strategy for prevention. This so-called 'scientific prevention' opposes the position that many different mental disorders may have the same cause – the stresses of poverty, for example. The 'scientific prevention' model argues that there is a specific biochemical cause for most mental disorders and that research funds must go into the search for each specific biological cause of each specific disorder listed in the American Psychiatric Association's (1988) *Diagnostic and Statistical Manual IV*. This Manual is unreliable and invalid (Kutchins & Kirk, 1997) but this is not a concern as 'scientific prevention' is far less costly (of tax dollars) than alternative models that require efforts at social changes to achieve social justice.

Social class is a major variable for CP (Perry, 1996). It is a macro variable to which more attention should be paid. Poverty causes pathology (Mirowsky & Ross, 1989). If mental disorders are learned in a pathological social environment, like poverty, (with homelessness, exploitation, family disruption, child neglect and so on), then there is hope for primary prevention. Truly meaningful prevention means building a just society. It means reducing poverty, the stresses of injustice, the loneliness in a society based on consumerism. Of dozens of examples, space will permit only one.

Recent research has come to the clear conclusion that the wider the income differences between rich and poor in a country, the worse the health, the lower the life expectancy, the higher the rate of violent crime, the more people in prisons and the worse the mental health of the population. In those societies where the income gap between rich and poor is small there is more social cohesiveness – people are more sensitive to the needs of others, violent crime is far less common, there is less emotional distress and fewer people die young as a result of stresses and selfish preoccupations. This set of observations has been confirmed repeatedly and is generally accepted in social medicine and public health.

The US is far down the ranking on all these pathologies – not because of the structure of our health care, the number and training of our physicians, the quality of our hospitals, the brilliance of research by our pharmaceutical firms – but because of the wide (and growing) gap between rich and poor. Dozens of studies demonstrating the crucial importance of social cohesion for mental health and its relation to the income gap, are summarized in Wilkinson (1996) *Unhealthy Societies: The Afflictions of Inequality.* He cites a wide range of research studies showing that when the income gap widens in a community, a region (state) or a country there is an increase in crime, child abuse, depression and death rates.

The variables are clear and measurable: data on income by social class are gathered routinely for other purposes, rates of death are objectively countable, as are rates of objective diseases and crime rates. The relations are clear. Inevitably the question arises: If the research evidence contradicts the ruling ideas of a society what should be the position of the community psychologist? It is an important question for each of us.

Domestic Violence: An All Too Familiar Story

A young couple emigrated from Portugal to Canada. In Portugal the man was an auto mechanic and the woman worked at home doing sewing and embroidery. They came to Canada seeking a better life. The man found it difficult to find a job equal to his training and eventually accepted a job cleaning offices. He initially forbade his wife to work, but as their family grew (3 children), she eventually took a job in a garment factory. A retired Portuguese woman helped by providing child care. In spite of both partners working, the two combined were able to bring in only a very low income. The man started to blame the woman for encouraging him to move to Canada, for having three children and for the problems that they were experiencing. Communication between the two became quite strained and the man began to withdraw from his family and spend more time with male friends. The woman assumed responsibility for running the household and for all child care and child rearing. The man became physically abusive to the woman when she started to work outside the home. The woman did not know there was a shelter for abused women in the community. The man left for a week and when he returned he was unapologetic and remained verbally abusive.

CONT'D

The couple began to sleep in separate beds and communicated very little. The woman was too ashamed to tell any family members about the violence.

1. Use the principles of ecology to help you understand what is happening with this

couple and their family in the context of the larger community and society.

2. How could the principles of prevention and promotion be applied to prevent domestic violence and promote family well-being?

Chapter glossary

adaptation how people adapt to the demands of different environments

behaviour setting a way of thinking about settings that is characterized by a standing pattern of behaviour and time and space dimensions

circular causality the notion that people influence environments, as well as environments influencing people

cycling of resources a focus on the resources within an eco-system, how they are distributed and how they can be used

holism a value that emphasizes interrelationships and interconnections

ecological metaphor a way of thinking about people and their environments that is borrowed from biology and stands in contrast to the mechanistic metaphor that is dominant in psychology

incidence the number of new cases of disease in a population or

community within a specified time period

interdependence the notion that different elements and levels of an eco-system are interconnected

mediating factors the mechanisms that link stressful life events with psychosocial problems

miasmas noxious odours emanating from swamps that were believed to cause disease

normalization a philosophy in the field of disabilities that emphasizes approaches that promote community integration, rather than segregation or exclusion

person–environment fit the idea that the adaptation of the individual is a function of the interaction between the individual and the environment, with some environments providing a more favourable setting for some, but not all, individuals

primary prevention reduction of incidence

protective factors resources that moderate, buffer or protect individuals from the adverse consequences of risk factors

risk factors stressful life events, life strains or other conditions that increase the likelihood that an individual will develop a problem in living

secondary prevention early detection and treatment

selective (high-risk) prevention prevention that is aimed at individuals considered to be at risk of developing problems

social climate the perceived or felt environment, consisting of three broad dimensions: relationships, personal development and systems maintenance and change

succession a long-term time perspective on people and systems

universal prevention prevention that is aimed at everyone in a population

Prevention Journals and Websites

Applied and Preventive Psychology, http://www.nd.edu/~japp/.
Journal of Prevention and Intervention in the Community,
    http://www.haworthpressinc.com/store/product.asp?sku=J005.
Journal of Primary Prevention, http://www.kluweronline.com/issn/0278-095X/contents.
Ontario Prevention Clearinghouse, http://www.opc.on.ca.
Prevention Science, http://www.kluweronline.com/issn/1389-4986/contents.
Prevention and Treatment, http://journals.apa.org/prevention/.
Prevention Connection: Promoting Strength, Resilience and Health in Children, Adults and Families,
    http://www.oslc.org/spr/home.html.
Prevention Yellow Pages, http://www.tyc.state.tx.us/prevention/.

RESOURCES ■

5
Community and Power

Warm-up Exercise: Community, Power and You

We would like you to think about the four following situations:

1. A situation in which you experienced a sense of community through bonding, close relationships and attachment.
2. A time when you felt excluded and isolated.
3. A situation in which you felt empowered to do something or achieve something.
4. An occasion in which you felt powerless and without a sense of control.

Write down how you felt in each one of these situations.

In this chapter you will learn about community and power. The specific aims of the chapter are to:

- define and critique the concepts
- study their value-base
- identify their implications for the promotion of well-being and liberation and for the perpetuation of oppression.

Have you done the warm up exercise? How did you feel when you experienced a sense of community? Did you feel supported, appreciated? Did you feel constrained? What about power? Did you feel good when you were in control of a situation? Did power ever get to your head? Most people experience both sides of community and power: positive aspects and negative aspects.

Positive aspects of community include social support, cohesion and working together to achieve common aims. Negative aspects of community include rigid norms, conformity, exclusion, segregation and disrespect for diversity. Positive aspects of power include the ability to achieve goals in life, a sense of mastery and a feeling of control. Negative aspects of power include the capacity to inflict damage or to perpetuate inequality. Our challenge as community psychologists is to promote the growth-enhancing aspects of community and power and to diminish their negative potential. We want to use community and power to promote social justice and not to stifle creativity or perpetuate the status quo.

Our work is difficult because it is highly contextual. It's hard to make rules that apply to all contexts. On one hand, we know intuitively that sharing happy and sad moments with friends and others is beneficial for personal well-being. On the other hand, groups can exert powerful norms of conformity that suppress the creativity and individuality of their members. Similarly, we know that disempowered people could use more political power to advance their legitimate aims, but that doesn't mean that more power is always a good thing, neither for disempowered nor for over-empowered people. Being disempowered does not make a person into a righteous individual. These potential scenarios teach us that the outcomes of community and power are highly contextual. We need to know the specific circumstances and dynamics of community and power before we endorse either of them. Who will benefit from a set of community norms? Who will gain and who will lose from giving a certain group of people more power? What is the impact of community and power for well-being and liberation? These are the key questions that we want to address in this chapter.

Community and Power

Community psychology (CP) has traditionally emphasized the role of community over power in promoting well-being. The sense of community metaphor discussed in Chapter 2 dominated the field's narrative for its first decade or so. In a corrective move, Rappaport (1981, 1987) introduced the concept of empowerment to indicate that power and control over community resources would be just as important as a feeling of communion. As we will see in this chapter, the concept of empowerment has limitations of its own, but at the time it was introduced it served an important function: it drew attention to power dynamics affecting well-being. Feminist critics of empowerment like Stephanie Riger (1993) pointed out some risks inherent in the concept. First, she reminded us of the danger of swinging the pendulum too much towards individual power and forgetting the need for sense of community. Second, she recognized that empowerment may become another psychological variable that would lead to individual changes instead of social changes. Riger's critique is reminiscent of Bakan's (1966) distinction between agency and communion. Agency is the power to assert ourselves, whereas communion is the need to belong to something larger than ourselves. The conflict between these two complementary tendencies is played out in the field of CP through the tension between empowerment and community.

In this book, we wish to avoid dichotomies such as community or power. We wish to push the CP agenda further and claim that psychological empowerment and empowering processes are not enough without social justice and a redistribution of resources (Speer, 2002). At the same time, achieving power without a sense of community, within and across groups, may lead to untoward effects (Nisbet, 1953). Without empowerment we risk maintaining the status quo and without community we risk treating people as objects. Let's explore this thesis and the ways in which these two concepts complement each other.

What Are Community and Power?

Community

At its most basic level, the word community implies a group or groups of citizens who have something in common. We can think of a geographical community such as your neighbourhood or country or we can think of a relational community such as a group of friends or your religious congregation (Bess, Fisher, Sonn & Bishop, 2002). Members of a relational group may share a culture or a common interest. There are countless forces and dynamics that bring people together. Some of us feel quite close to the community of community psychologists, while others feel close to the fans of a sports team or to members of a religious group. Some of us can feel close to these three groups at the same time. We can belong to multiple communities concurrently. Of the multiple meanings of the word 'community' we have chosen to concentrate on two that are important to the work of community psychologists: sense of community and social capital.

Sense of community. Seymour Sarason (1974), one of the founders of the field of CP, identified sense of community as central to the endeavour of the field. In his view, sense of community captured something very basic about being human: our need for affiliation in times of sorrow, our need for sharing in times of joy; and our need to be with people at all other times. He defined sense of community as:

> the sense that one belongs in and is meaningfully a part of a larger collectivity; the sense that although there may be conflict between the needs of the individual and the collectivity, or among different groups in the collectivity, these conflicts must be resolved in a way that does not destroy the psychological sense of community; the sense that there is a network of and structure of relationships that strengthens rather than dilutes feelings of loneliness. (Sarason, 1988, p. 41)

Since Sarason's (1974) coinage of the term, others have tried to operationalize and distil the meaning of sense of community, all in an effort to understand the positive or negative effects of this phenomenon. McMillan and Chavis (1986) are credited with formulating an enduring conceptualization of sense of community. According to them, the concept consists of four domains: (a) membership, (b) influence, (c) integration and fulfilment of needs, and (d) shared emotional connection. These four domains of sense of community sparked a great deal of interest and research in the field of CP. A special issue of the *Journal of Community Psychology* in 1996 (volume 4) and a recent book on the subject summarize very well progress in the area (Fisher, Sonn & Bishop, 2002).

The interest in communities is justified in a world where groups intersect and experience conflict over resources. We live in a world where communities of various identities share space, time, work, past, present and future. Each community has to value its own diversity as well as the diversity present in other groups.

What, on the surface, may look similar may hide vast differences. Not all aboriginal people share the same culture (Dudgeon, Mallard, Oxenham & Fielder, 2002), nor do all immigrants experience the same challenges (see Chapter 17). We can talk about a community of women, within which there are obviously multiple communities of chicanas, aboriginal, African-American, privileged, poor, disabled and able-bodied women. Every time we invoke a group of people, there are going to be multiple identities within it (Arellano & Ayala-Alcantar, 2002; Serrano-García & Bond, 1994). Communities may define themselves in exclusive terms reminiscent of apartheid or in inclusive terms reminiscent of solidarity.

Social Capital. While sense of community attracted a lot of attention within CP, allied terms such as 'community cohesion' and 'social capital' gained currency in other disciplines such as sociology, community development and political science. We find much in common between these two concepts and CP (Perkins, Hughey & Speer, 2002). In essence, they speak about the potential of communities to improve the well-being of their members through the synergy of associations, mutual trust, sense of community and collective action (Kawachi, Kennedy & Wilkinson, 1999; Veenstra, 2001). In short, they deal with the intersection of people, well-being and community. The main difference between sense of community and social capital lies in the level of analysis. Whereas sense of community is typically measured and discussed at the group or neighbourhood level, social capital research has looked at the results of cohesion at state and national levels. Community psychologists Douglas Perkins and Adam Long (2002) maintain that sense of community is only a part of social capital. They suggest that social capital consists of four dimensions: (a) sense of community, (b) neighbouring, (c) collective efficacy and (d) citizen participation.

In his widely popular book *Bowling Alone: The Collapse and Revival of American Community*, Robert Putnam (2000) distinguished between physical, human and social capital:

> Whereas physical capital refers to physical objects and human capital refers to properties of individuals, social capital refers to connections among individuals – social networks and the norms of reciprocity and trustworthiness that arise from them. (p. 19)

In our view, social capital refers to collective resources consisting of civic participation, networks, norms of reciprocity and organizations that foster (a) trust among citizens and (b) actions to improve the common good. Figure 5.1 shows the various dimensions of social capital identified by Stone and Hughes (2002) in their study of social capital in Australian families. As may be seen, social capital entails networks of trust and reciprocity that lead to positive outcomes at multiple levels of analysis, including individual, family, community, civic, political and economic well-being. Figure 5.1 summarizes the types and characteristics of networks. Density, size and diversity are key factors in the quality of community connections. Another important feature of this figure is that the hypothesized outcomes influence the very determinants of social capital. Some of the outcomes, such as civic participation, may generate more social capital. Accordingly, we should see determinants and outcomes of social capital as exerting reciprocal and not unidirectional influence on each other.

Social capital, in the form of connections of trust and participation in public affairs, enhances community capacity to create structures of cohesion and support that benefit the population and produce positive health, welfare, educational and social outcomes. Vast research indicates that cohesive communities and civic partic-

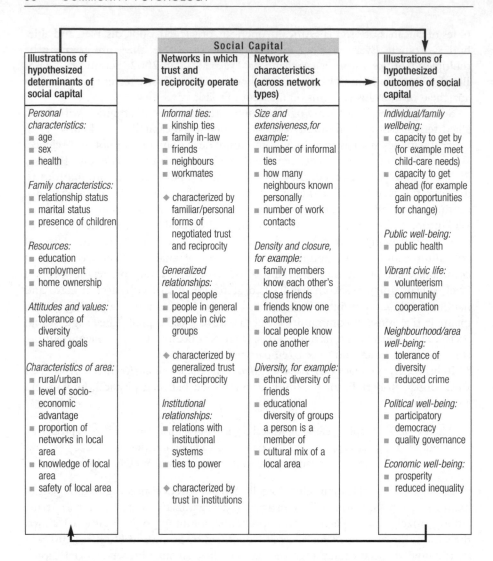

Social Capital			
Illustrations of hypothesized determinants of social capital	Networks in which trust and reciprocity operate	Network characteristics (across network types)	Illustrations of hypothesized outcomes of social capital
Personal characteristics: ■ age ■ sex ■ health *Family characteristics:* ■ relationship status ■ marital status ■ presence of children *Resources:* ■ education ■ employment ■ home ownership *Attitudes and values:* ■ tolerance of diversity ■ shared goals *Characteristics of area:* ■ rural/urban ■ level of socio-economic advantage ■ proportion of networks in local area ■ knowledge of local area ■ safety of local area	*Informal ties:* ■ kinship ties ■ family in-law ■ friends ■ neighbours ■ workmates ◆ characterized by familiar/personal forms of negotiated trust and reciprocity *Generalized relationships:* ■ local people ■ people in general ■ people in civic groups ◆ characterized by generalized trust and reciprocity *Institutional relationships:* ■ relations with institutional systems ■ ties to power ◆ characterized by trust in institutions	*Size and extensiveness, for example:* ■ number of informal ties ■ how many neighbours known personally ■ number of work contacts *Density and closure, for example:* ■ family members know each other's close friends ■ friends know one another ■ local people know one another *Diversity, for example:* ■ ethnic diversity of friends ■ educational diversity of groups a person is a member of ■ cultural mix of a local area	*Individual/family wellbeing:* ■ capacity to get by (for example meet child-care needs) ■ capacity to get ahead (for example gain opportunities for change) *Public well-being:* ■ public health *Vibrant civic life:* ■ volunteerism ■ community cooperation *Neighbourhood/area well-being:* ■ tolerance of diversity ■ reduced crime *Political well-being:* ■ participatory democracy ■ quality governance *Economic well-being:* ■ prosperity ■ reduced inequality

Figure 5.1 Summary of core measures of social capital and illustrative examples of its determinants and outcomes

From: Stone & Hughes (2002). Reproduced with permission from the Australian Institute of Family Studies

ipation in public affairs enhance the well-being of the population. Communities with higher participation in volunteer organizations, political parties, local and professional associations fare much better in terms of health, education, crime and well-being than communities with low rates of participation. This finding has been replicated at different times across various states, provinces and countries (Putnam, 2000; Schuller, 2001; Stone & Hughes, 2002; Wilkinson, 1996).

Box 5.1   Measuring Social Capital

The following are partial sample items taken from the *Social Capital Community Benchmark Study* sponsored by the Saguaro Seminar at Harvard University. The complete tool is available at http://www.cfsv.org/communitysurvey/docs/survey_instrument.pdf.

5. This study is about community, so we'd like to start by asking what gives you a sense of community or a sense of belonging. I'm going to read a list. For each one say 'yes' if it gives you a sense of community or a sense of belonging and 'no' if it does not.

   Your old or new friends
   The people in your neighbourhood
   Your place of worship
   The people you work with or go to school with

6. Generally speaking, would you say that most people can be trusted or that you can't be too careful in dealing with people?

16. Overall, how much impact do you think people like you can have in making your community a better place to live?

20. Which of the following things have you done in the past twelve months:

Signed a petition?
Attended a political meeting or rally?
Worked on a community project?
Participated in any demonstrations, protests, boycotts or marches?
Donated blood?

33. I'm going to read a list. Just answer 'yes' if you have been involved in the past 12 months with this kind of group:

   An adult sports club or league, or an outdoor activity club?
   A youth organization like a youth sports league, the scouts, 4-H clubs, and boys and girls clubs?
   A parents' association, like the PTA or PTO, or other school support or service clubs?
   A neighborhood association, like a block association?
   A labor union?
   A support group or self-help program?

34. Did any of the groups that you are involved with take any local action for social or political reform in the past 12 months?

Power

Since the 1980s, community psychologists have discussed empowerment more often than power per se (Speer, 2002; Zimmerman, 2000). For that reason, we begin with a brief review of the former.

Empowerment. Empowerment refers to both processes and outcomes occurring at various levels of analyses (Prilleltensky, 1994a; Zimmerman, 2000). Empowerment is about obtaining, producing or enabling power. This can happen at the individual, group or community and social levels. Rappaport claimed that empowerment is 'a process: the mechanism by which people, organizations, and communities gain mastery over their lives' (1981, p. 3); whereas the Cornell Empowerment Group defined it as 'an intentional ongoing process centered in the local community, involving mutual respect, critical reflection, caring, and group participation, through which people lacking an equal share of valued resources gain greater access to and control over those resources' (1989, p. 2). The latter definition starts talking about the process but ends with an emphasis on outcomes: control over resources. We agree with Speer (2002) that a balance must be reached between research and action on empowering processes and empowered outcomes. Otherwise, we risk sacrificing one for the other. Not only are the two components equally important, but they are mutually reinforcing as well. Based on the work of Zimmerman (2000) and Speer and colleagues (Speer & Hughey, 1995; Speer, Hughey, Gensheimer & Adams-Leavitt, 1995), we represent in Table 5.1 the various domains

Table 5.1 Empowerment processes and outcomes at multiple levels of analysis

Levels of Analysis	Processes	Outcomes
Individual	training in critical thinking participation in action groups mentoring experiences connecting with people in similar situations training in value-based practice	consciousness raising participation in social action assertiveness expanded options in life sense of control mentoring others
Organizational	shared leadership training in group facilitation participation in decision making sense of common purpose participation in social action	increased resources enhanced connections solidarity with other groups influences public opinion
Community	access to government participation in civic organizations political education target local issues	improved quality of life enhanced health and well-being democratic institutions improved access to services coalitions for well-being tolerance of diversity
Societal	struggles for democracy struggles for liberation solidarity across social groups resisting globalization political and economic literacy	redistributive policies support for disadvantaged people governmental accountability control of resources by poor progressive social policies resists economic neo-liberalism

Expanded from Lord and Hutchison (1993), Speer and Hughey (1995) and Zimmerman (2000)

and dynamics of empowerment at four levels of analysis. Similar to Figure 5.1 on social capital, some of the outcomes are reinforcing of the processes. Better empowerment outcomes should generate more empowerment processes and vice versa.

The concept of empowerment stimulated much discussion in CP, with two special issues of the *American Journal of Community Psychology* dedicated to it in 1994 (Serrano-García & Bond, 1994) and 1995 (Perkins & Zimmerman, 1995). Yet, despite much progress in the field, some key issues remain underexplored. In our view, these issues pertain to the multifaceted and dynamic nature of power. Empowerment is not a stable or global state of affairs. Some people feel empowered in some settings but not in others, whereas some people work to empower one group while oppressing others along the way. A more refined concept of power is needed to understand better the concept of empowerment and its nuances.

From Empowerment to Power. Power is everywhere; it's in interpersonal relationships, families, organizations, corporations, neighbourhoods, sports and countries. Power can be used for ethical or unethical purposes. It can promote well-being but it can also perpetuate suffering.

A more dynamic conceptualization of power is needed, one that takes into account the multifaceted nature of identities and the changing nature of social settings. Moreover, we need a definition of power that takes into account subjective and objective forces influencing our actions as community psychologists.

In the light of the need for a comprehensive conceptualization of power, we offer a few parameters for clarification of the concept. Based on previous work, we present them as a series of ten complementary postulates (Prilleltensky, in press).

1. Power refers to the capacity and opportunity to fulfil or obstruct personal, relational or collective needs.
2. Power has psychological and political sources, manifestations and consequences.
3. We can distinguish between power to strive for well-being, power to oppress and power to resist oppression and strive for liberation.
4. Power can be overt or covert, subtle or blatant, hidden or exposed.
5. The exercise of power can apply to self, others and collectives.
6. Power affords people multiple identities as individuals seeking well-being, engaging in oppression or resisting domination.
7. Whereas people may be oppressed in one context, at a particular time and place, they may act as oppressors at another time and place.
8. Because of structural factors such as social class, gender, ability and race, people may enjoy differential levels of power.
9. Degrees of power are also affected by personal and social constructs such as beauty, intelligence and assertiveness; constructs that enjoy variable status within different cultures.
10. The exercise of power can reflect varying degrees of awareness with respect to the impact of one's actions.

We expand here on the first and main postulate of our conceptualization of power. We claim that power is a combination of ability and opportunity to influence a course of events. This definition merges elements of agency or self-determination on the one hand, with structure or external determinants on the other. Agency refers to ability whereas structure refers to opportunity. The exercise of power is based on the juxtaposition of wishing to change something and having the opportunity, afforded by social and historical circumstances, to do so. Ultimately, the outcome of power is based on the constant interaction and reciprocal determinism of agency and contextual dynamics (Bourdieu, 1990; Martin & Sugarman, 1999, 2000).

People who are born into privilege may be afforded educational and employment opportunities that people on the other side of town could never dream of. Privilege can lead to a good education, to better job prospects and to life satisfaction. These, in turn, can increase self-confidence and personal empowerment. Lack of structural opportunities, such as the absence of good schools or economic resources, undermines children's capacities for the development of talents, control and personal empowerment (Bourdieu & Passeron, 1977; Prilleltensky, Laurendeau, et al., 2001).

Another defining feature of power is its evasive nature. You can't always tell it's there. Nor can you tell how it's operating. Power is not tantamount to coercion, for it can operate in very subtle and concealed ways (Bourdieu, 1986, 1990; Foucault, 1979a). According to social critics such as Bourdieu, Foucault and Rose, people come to regulate themselves through the internalization of cultural prescriptions. Hence, what may seem on the surface to be freedom may be questioned as a form of acquiescence whereby citizens restrict their life choices to coincide with a narrow range of socially sanctioned options. In his book *Powers of Freedom*, Rose (1999) claimed that:

Disciplinary techniques and moralizing injunctions as to health, hygiene and civility are no longer required; the project of responsible citizenship has been fused with individuals' projects for themselves. What began as a social norm here ends as a personal desire. Individuals act upon themselves and their families in terms of the languages, values and techniques made available to them by professions, disseminated through the apparatuses of the mass media or sought out by the troubled through the market. Thus, in a very significant sense, it has become possible to govern without governing *society* – to govern through the 'responsibilized' and 'educated' anxieties and aspirations of individuals and their families. (p. 88) (original emphasis)

The point is that if governments or rulers want to exert power over their dominion, they don't have to police people because people police themselves through the internalization of norms and regulations (Chomsky, 2002). The problem with this is that many groups absorb rules and regulations that are not necessarily in their best interests, as can be seen in Box 5.2.

Box 5.2   The Power to Delude Ourselves?

In April 2002, I, Isaac, travelled to California to teach a course at Pacifica Graduate Institute in Carpinteria. I took a shuttle from the LA Airport to Carpinteria. The driver, a congenial young man, started talking with passengers about the economy, the cost of living in California, housing and traffic. He shared with us that he had a BA in chemistry and that he worked full time in a laboratory. In order to afford the cost of living in California, he also drove a shuttle bus from the Los Angeles Airport several times a week, on weekends and after work. He had two demanding jobs. While talking about the economy he said that he is in favour of a flat tax, because 'the rich should not be punished for being rich'. I thought to myself, here is this guy who is working probably 80 or more hours a week and cannot afford the cost of living in California, and he is favouring a most regressive tax system that benefits the rich and disadvantages people like him because there are fewer public resources, little public housing, and poor social services. I then arrived at the hotel and went to the gym. As I was cycling on the exercise bike I turned on the TV which was tuned in to the Suzie Orman show. Suzie gives financial advice over the phone. One of her stock phrases was that your net worth was a reflection of your self-worth. She told people that if they did not achieve financial wealth it was because they did not think they deserved it! Here I was, a community psychologist trained in thinking that people's problems have to do with contexts and circumstances and opportunities in life, and in less than 30 minutes I encountered two cultural discourses completely undermining my message. Is culture so powerful that it can delude people into thinking that if they have problems it's their own fault? Was the driver deluding himself? What type of social power was at play in the case of the driver and in the case of Suzie Orman?

Power, then, emanates from the confluence of personal motives and cultural injunctions. But, as we have seen, personal motives are embedded in the very cultural injunctions with which they interact. Hence, it is not just a matter of people acting on the environment, but of individuals coming into contact with external forces that, to some extent, they have already internalized. The implication is that we cannot just take at face value that individual actions evolve from innate desires. Desires are embedded in norms and regulations (Bourdieu, 1990; Bourdieu & Passeron, 1977). This is not to adopt a socially deterministic position however; for even though a person's experience is greatly shaped by the prescriptions of the day, agency and personal power are not completely erased (Bourdieu, 1998; Martin & Sugarman, 2000).

Think, for example, about eating disorders. It is pretty clear that this psychological problem cannot be dissociated from a culture that exalts thinness. Whereas many women may wish to lose weight for health reasons, many others pursue thinness because it is culturally and socially prescribed. We cannot simply say that women have the power to lose weight or be healthy if they want to. We cannot claim that they have the power to decide what is good for them, for that would be a simplification. When many of us internalize norms that may be counterproductive to our own well-being, this process restricts our choices. Seemingly, we can do whatever we want. We can exercise or we can binge and vomit, but our choices are highly circumscribed by norms of conformity we have made our own, not necessarily because they are good for us, but because we are subjected to social influences all the time. Instead of rebelling against societal practices that feed us junk food and junk images, we censor ourselves. No need for physical chains, many of us wear psychological chains.

Why Are Community and Power So Important?

Community

Sense of community, social support and social capital can produce beneficial results at the individual, communal and societal levels. Different kinds of social support may be given and received. Instrumental support refers to the provision of resources, such as lending money, helping a neighbour with babysitting or sharing notes with a student who couldn't make a class. These are concrete actions that people take to help each other. Emotional support, in turn, refers to the act of listening and showing empathy towards others. When a friend shares a problem with you, you show emotional support by being there, listening non-judgementally and making yourself available. Bonding, sharing and building relationships through common experiences can activate either type of support.

Social support can increase or restore health and well-being in two ways (Cohen & Wills, 1985). First, social support can enhance well-being through bonding, affirming experiences, sharing of special moments, attachment and contributions to one's self-esteem. The more support I have the better I feel and the more likely I am to develop well-being and resilience in the face of adversity (Prilleltensky, Laurendeau, et al., 2001). There is an accumulated positive effect of having had good interpersonal experiences. According to our model of well-being, relational well-being leads to personal well-being. The second mechanism through which social support enhances well-being is by providing emotional and instrumental support in times of crises. As we noted in the previous chapter, the stressful reactions associated with divorce, moves, transitions or death may be buffered by the protective influences of helpful, supportive relatives and friends.

Cohen and Wills (1985) posited the buffering hypothesis to indicate that social support may serve to enhance coping and to mitigate the negative effects of stress. In their view, social support may prevent the perception of events as stressful because people have sufficient instrumental and/or emotional resources to cope with untoward situations. A person with sufficient supports may not experience a situation as stressful, whereas others, without supports, may perceive the situation as very threatening. A father who suddenly becomes unemployed but who has a partner with a stable job and parents with economic resources may not experience the loss of a job as does a father with no parents, no back-ups and several kids to feed. The very phenomenon of unemployment is experienced differently by the two men.

But social support can buffer the effects of stress even when situations are perceived as stressful. In the case of the man with supports, he will not worry as much about his children because others will come through. In the second case, the father has good grounds to worry about feeding his family. In effect, Cohen and Wills (1985) postulate that supports can help in reducing the very perception of a threat and in increasing the act of coping with the threat.

Various channels lead to the positive effects of social support (Barrera, 2000). We can think of agents and recipients of support, where the former is the one providing the help and the latter is the one benefiting from it. Relational well-being is characterized by relationships in which people assume the dual roles of agents and recipients. Support may be given and received from a single agent to a single recipient (friends talking to each other), from a single agent to multiple recipients (grandmother helping her daughter and grandchildren with shopping and cooking), from multiple agents to a single recipient (a self-help group where various participants encourage and support a person going through a hard time) and from multiple agents to multiple recipients (a group of women raising funds and lobbying the government to help refugee women). In some cases, the recipients are single individuals, whereas in others they are small or large groups. Let's explore the significance of social support for the various recipients.

At the individual level, compared with people with lower supports, those who enjoy more support from relatives or friends live longer, recover faster from illnesses, report better health and well-being and cope better with adversities (Cohen et al., 2000; Ornish, 1997). At the group level, studies have shown that women with metastatic breast cancer have better chances of survival if they participate in support groups. After a follow up of 48 months, Spiegel and colleagues (1989) found that all the women in the control group had died, whereas a third of those who received group support were still alive. The average survival for the women in the support group was 36 months, compared to 19 months in the control group. Richardson and colleagues made similar claims of a sample of patients with hematologic malignancies. They claimed that 'the use of special educational and supportive programs designed to improve patient compliance are associated with significant prolongation of patient survival' (Richardson, Sheldon, Krailo & Levine, 1990, p. 356). Finally, Fawzy and colleagues (Fawzy et al., 1993) found that patients with malignant melanoma were more likely to die or experience recurrence of the disease if they did not receive the group intervention that the experimental group received. Out of 34 patients in each group, of those who received group support, only 7 had experienced recurrence and 3 had died at the five-year follow-up, compared with 13 and 10, respectively, in the control group. Altogether, these three teams of researchers found that social support can enhance health and longevity in the face of deadly diseases.

In the psychological realm, self-help groups provide support for people experiencing addictions, psychiatric conditions, weight problems and bereavement. In addition, support groups are also available for relatives and friends caring for others with physical or emotional problems. Estimates of participation in self-help groups in the United States range from 7.5 million in 1992 to 10 million in 1999 (Levy,

2000). Moreover, self-help/mutual aid groups can be found in many countries throughout the world (Lavoie, Borkman & Gidron, 1994a, 1994b).

Keith Humphreys is one of the leading researchers in the field of self-help groups. In a study of people with substance abuse problems, Humphreys and colleagues found positive results for African-American participants attending Narcotics Anonymous and Alcoholics Anonymous. The sample of 253 participants showed significant improvements in employment, alcohol and drug use, legal complications and psychological and family well-being (Humphreys, Mavis & Stoffelmayr, 1994). In another study Humphreys and Moos (1996) compared the outcomes of self-help groups versus professional help on people who abused alcohol. The outcomes were positive for both groups, but the cost of the self-help option was considerably lower. As in these two examples, there is a vast amount of research documenting the positive effects of self-help groups. The research provides evidence that lay people can be very helpful to each other, even in the absence of professionals leading the groups.

The helper–therapy principle, according to which the provider of help benefits from assisting others, has been documented in a variety of groups and settings Roberts, Salem et al., (1999) showed that providing help to others predicted improvements in psychosocial adjustment of people with serious mental illness. Kingree and Thompson (2000), in turn, demonstrated that mutual help groups helped adult children of alcoholics to reduce depression and substance abuse. Kingree (2000) also found a positive correlation between levels of participation in the group and increases in self-esteem. Borkman (1999) theorizes that members of mutual help groups nurture each other through circles of sharing. Members normalize each other's experiences and provide non-stigmatizing meaning to their struggles in life. These hypotheses have been confirmed by, among others, the case of GROW, a self-help group for people with psychiatric disabilities that originated in Australia (Yip, 2002).

But the benefits of participating in mutual help groups extend beyond the participants themselves. Caregivers who attend these groups are better able to assist family members and others in need of help. Positive effects were reflected on children and elderly family members who require the attention of the middle generation (Gottlieb, 2000; O'Connor, 2002; Tebes & Irish, 2000). Children whose parents participated in mutual help groups, for example, exhibited fewer depressive symptoms and better social functioning than children whose parents did not attend such groups. The results were sustained at the six-month follow up (Tebes & Irish, 2000).

At the community level, the research demonstrates that communities with high levels of social cohesion experience better health, safety, well-being, education and welfare than societies with low levels of cohesion. Based on US research, Figure 5.2 shows the positive effects of social capital on a number of well-being indicators. Putnam created a measure of social capital based on 'the degree to which a given state is either high or low in the number of meetings citizens go to, the level of social trust its citizens have, the degree to which they spend time visiting one another at home, the frequency with which they vote, the frequency with which they do volunteering and so on' (Putnam, 2001, p. 48). He then compared how states with different levels of social capital fare on a number of indicators. Putnam compared states on measures of educational performance, child welfare, TV watching, violent crime,

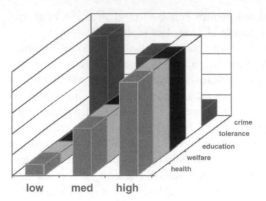

Low social capital states: Alabama, Mississippi, Georgia, Louisiana
Medium social capital states: Illinois, Kansas, California, Ohio
High social capital states: Vermont, North Dakota, South Dakota, Minnesota

* The trends reflected in the graph are based on research summarized by Putnam (2000) in *Bowling Alone: The Collapse and Revival of American Community.* New York, NY: Simon & Schuster.

Figure 5.2 The effects of social capital in different states of the USA

health, tax evasion, tolerance for equality, civic equality and economic equality. The trends in Figure 5.2 are representative of the results overall. States with high levels of social capital and social cohesion enjoy better rates of health, safety, welfare, education and tolerance. As can be seen in the graph, there is a clear gradient: the higher the level of social capital, the better the outcomes.

Of particular interest to us is whether social capital and social cohesion can increase health and well-being. There is evidence to support this claim. In a survey of 167,259 people in 39 US states, Kawachi and Kennedy (1999) lent strong support to Putnam's claim that social capital reinforces the health of the population. Convincing evidence making the link between social cohesion and health is also presented by Berkman (1995), Kawachi et al. (1999), Veenstra (2001) and Wilkinson (1996). Whereas the previous sets of studies investigated the effects of social support on individuals, researchers like Putnam, Berkman, Kawachi and Wilkinson assessed the aggregated effect of social cohesion on entire populations, demonstrating that a sense of community and cohesion can lead to population health.

Recent research in economics demonstrates that fluctuations in gross domestic product (GDP), inflation, unemployment and unemployment benefit levels influence the overall well-being of entire countries. Using data from hundreds of thousands of Europeans from twelve different countries, researchers found that when unemployment and inflation go up, well-being goes down, and when unemployment benefits and GDP go up, so does well-being (DiTella, MacCulloch & Oswald, 2001). In Switzerland, Frey and Stutzer (2002) found that levels of well-being are not affected only by economic measures, but also by democratic participation in referenda. Cantons with higher degrees of referenda and citizen participation report higher degrees of happiness than those with lesser citizen involvement. Taken together, the European research shows that circumstances do matter. Indeed, the average level of subjective well-being is affected by economic and political conditions and not only for those in extreme conditions, for the studies showed effects for the population as a whole.

In a recent and comprehensive review of the literature, Shinn and Toohey (2003) catalogued the effects of community characteristics on their members. Neighbourhoods with high socioeconomic status (SES) are predictive of academic achievement, whereas communities low in SES and high in residential instability are predictive of negative behavioural and emotional outcomes such as conduct disorders and substance abuse. In these poor neighbourhoods, residents also tend to have poor health outcomes, as measured by cardiovascular disease, poor birth weight and premature births. Not surprisingly, exposure to violence tends to be associated with poorer mental-health outcomes, depression, stress and externalizing disorders.

In addition to these correlational studies, Shinn and Toohey report the outcomes of a longitudinal experimental study called 'Moving to Opportunity'. In this study, families living in poor communities in Chicago were given the opportunity to move to other parts of the city or to more affluent suburbs. Children who moved to the suburbs did much better than those who moved within the city, on a number of outcomes. Compared with children who moved within the city, children who moved to the suburbs were much more likely to graduate from high school (86% vs 33%), attend college (54% vs 21%), attend 4-year university/college (27% vs 4%), be employed if not in school (75% vs 41%) and receive higher salaries and benefits. In a similar project in Boston, children who moved to more affluent parts of the city experienced dramatic decreases in the prevalence of injury and asthma (74% and 65%, respectively) compared with controls. In New York, behaviour problems for boys who moved to low-poverty areas were reduced by 30–43% relative to controls.

It is interesting to note that people adapt to contextual conditions in order to enhance the resiliency of their children. In low-risk neighbourhoods, low level of parental restrictive control was associated with high academic achievements, whereas in high-risk conditions, high level of parental control predicted academic success. High-risk situations require high levels of parental intervention for optimal outcomes (Shinn & Toohey, 2003). This finding shows that individuals are not mere victims of adverse conditions, but many of them adjust and adapt their behaviour to the context of their lives.

Power

People can use power to promote social cohesion or social fragmentation. But power does not inhabit humans alone. Power is vested in institutions such as the church, business corporations, schools and governments (Bourdieu & Passeron, 1977). Power is important because it is central to the promotion or prevention of the goals of CP: well-being and liberation. Without it, the disempowered cannot demand their human rights. With too much of it, the over-empowered are not going to relinquish privilege. With just about enough of it, it is possible that people may satisfy their own needs and share power with others in a synergic form (Craig & Craig, 1979).

Power to Promote Well-being. Well-being is achieved by the simultaneous, balanced and contextually sensitive satisfaction of personal, relational and collective needs. In the absence of capacity and opportunity – central features of power – individuals cannot strive to meet their own needs and the needs of others.

Personal and collective needs represent two faces of well-being (Keating & Hertzman, 1999a; Marmot & Wilkinson, 1999). The third side of well-being concerns relational needs. Individual and group agendas are often in conflict. Power and conflict are intrinsic parts of relationships. To achieve well-being, then, we have to attend to relationality. Two sets of needs are primordial in pursuing healthy relationships between individuals and groups: respect for diversity and collaboration and democratic participation. Respect for diversity ensures that people's unique identities are affirmed by others, while democratic participation enables community members to have a say in decisions affecting their lives (Prilleltensky & Nelson, 1997). Without power to exercise democratic rights, the chances of promoting the three dimensions of well-being are diminished.

Power to Oppress. Power can be used for ethical or unethical purposes. This is not just a risk of power, but part of its very essence. For French social scientist Pierre Bourdieu, social capital is power. It is power because it encompasses networks and resources available to serve personal and class interests (Bourdieu, 1986, 1990; Bourdieu & Passeron, 1977). Unlike authors such as Putnam who tend to emphasize the positive in social capital, Bourdieu is concerned with some of its negative effects. Like Bourdieu, we are concerned with the possibility of social capital and power being used to oppress others.

Oppression can be regarded as a *state* or *process* (Prilleltensky & Gonick, 1996). With respect to the former, oppression is described as a state of domination where the oppressed suffer the consequences of deprivation, exclusion, discrimination, exploitation, control of culture and sometimes even violence (for example, Bartky, 1990; Moane, 1999; Mullaly, 2002; Sidanius, 1993). A useful definition of oppression as process is given by Mar'i (1988): 'Oppression involves institutionalized, collective and individual modes of behavior through which one group attempts to dominate and control another in order to secure political, economic and/or social-psychological advantage' (p. 6).

Another important distinction in the definition of oppression concerns its *political* and *psychological* dimensions. We cannot speak of one without the other (Bulhan, 1985; Moane, 1999; Walkerdine, 1996, 1997). Psychological and political oppressions co-exist and are mutually determined. Following Prilleltensky and Gonick (1996), we integrate here the elements of state *and* process, with the psychological and political dimensions of oppression. *Oppression entails a state of asymmetric power relations characterized by domination, subordination and resistance, where the dominating persons or groups exercise their power by the process of restricting access to material resources and imparting in the subordinated persons or groups self-deprecating views about themselves. It is only when the latter can attain a certain degree of conscientization that resistance can begin* (Bartky, 1990; Fanon, 1963; Freire, 1972; Memmi, 1968).

The dynamics of oppression are internal as well as external. External or political forces deprive individuals or groups of the benefit of personal (for example, self-determination), collective (for example, distributive justice) and relational (for example, democratic participation) well-being. Often, these restrictions are internalized and operate at a psychological level as well, where the person acts as his or her personal censor (Moane, 1999; Mullaly, 2002; Prilleltensky & Gonick, 1996). Some political mechanisms of oppression and repression include actual or potential use of force, restricted life opportunities, degradation of indigenous culture, economic sanctions and inability to challenge authority. Psychological dynamics of oppression entail surplus powerlessness, belief in a just world, learned helplessness, conformity, obedience to authority, fear, verbal and emotional abuse (for reviews see Moane, 1999; Mullaly, 2002; Prilleltensky, 2003b; Prilleltensky & Gonick, 1996).

What Is the Value-base of Community and Power?

We have already established the complementarity of values for personal, relational and collective well-being in Chapter 3. In a similar vein, Newbrough (1992a, 1995) has argued that CP should try to reach an equilibrium among the principal values of the French Revolution: liberty, equality and fraternity. In our view, however, the desired equilibrium has not been reached because the field has paid more attention to fraternity than to the other two values. Unlike the value of solidarity, which has been enacted through the concept of community, the values of liberty and equality have not found similar expression in concepts such as power and justice (Prillel-tensky & Nelson, 1997). To achieve personal liberty and collective equality, which are closely intertwined, we sometimes need to resort to conflict. If collaborative means failure to produce a more equal distribution of resources, then conflict may be necessary. The absence of conflict rewards those who benefit from the current state of affairs, for the status quo is to their advantage. Hence, for as long as they produce the desired results, we would prefer conflict-free and fraternal means of promoting well-being. But if they don't, we have to consider more assertive means (Hughey & Speer, 2002). We could try to persuade companies to provide better conditions for their workers or we could create support groups for workers experiencing stress. Furthermore, we could negotiate with factory owners to put in place better working conditions such as ventilation, proper lighting and more breaks. But if the owners deny all requests, workers may consider a strike or more confrontational means of action.

The erosion of social cohesion since the 1960s, at least in the US, has been amply documented by Putnam (2000). This is a reminder that it is not enough to reflect on the virtues of community structures; somebody has to support them! In the age of economic neoliberalism and globalization, governments are under great pressure to reduce community and social services either to cope with lower taxes or to reduce them. This has been the trend since the 1980s. As a result, we see less investment in communities and more tax cuts that benefit the rich (Gershman & Irwin, 2000; Sen, 1999b). In the light of these developments, now more than ever we need social movements to fight for the restoration of community services and for social investments (Bourdieu, 1998; Kim et al., 2000).

How Can Community and Power Be Promoted Simultaneously?

The literature is quite abundant in examples that promote either a sense of community (for example, Fisher, Sonn, & Bishop, 2002) or empowerment (for example Perkins & Zimmerman, 1995; Serrano-García & Bond, 1994), but not so vast in cases that promote both simultaneously. Based on their research with community mental health groups, Nelson, Lord and Ochocka (2001b) proposed the empowerment-community integration paradigm. With input from various stakeholder groups they identified values, elements and ideal indicators for the promotion of the new paradigm. The key values for this paradigm are psychiatric consumer/survivor empowerment, community integration and holistic health care and access to resources. The principles, which correspond respectively to liberty, fraternity and equality, seek an integration of empowerment and community interventions. (See website.)

As found by Nelson and colleagues, the three values are needed for the well-being of psychiatric consumer/survivors. In our view, this integration is really imperative for the promotion of individual, group, community and societal well-being (see also Table 5.1). Social support by itself promotes a sense of community but it does not rectify power imbalances, whereas combative social action addresses power inequalities but doesn't necessarily promote cohesion.

Power and community may be invoked to promote well-being, engage in oppression or, finally, strive for liberation. *Liberation refers to the process of resisting oppressive forces. As a state, liberation is a condition in which oppressive forces no longer exert their dominion over a person or a group.* Liberation may be from psychological and/or political influences. Building on Fromm's dual conception of 'freedom from' and 'freedom to' (1965), liberation is the process of overcoming internal and external sources of oppression (freedom from) and pursuing well-being (freedom to). Liberation from social oppression entails, for example, emancipation from class exploitation, gender domination and ethnic discrimination. Freedom from internal and psychological sources includes overcoming fears, obsessions or other psychological phenomena that interfere with a person's subjective experience of well-being. Liberation to pursue well-being, in turn, refers to the process of meeting personal, relational and collective needs.

The process of liberation is analogous to Freire's concept of conscientization, according to which marginalized populations begin to gain awareness of oppressive forces in their lives and of their own ability to overcome domination (Freire, 1972). This awareness is likely to develop in stages (Watts, Griffith & Abdul-Adil, 1999). Through various processes, people begin to realize that they are the subject of oppressive regulations. The first realization may happen as a result of therapy, participation in a social movement or readings. Next, people may connect with others experiencing similar circumstances and gain an appreciation for the external forces pressing down on them. Some individuals will go on to liberate themselves from oppressive relationships or psychological dynamics such as fears and phobias, whereas others will join social movements to fight for political justice (Bourdieu, 1998). While a fuller exploration of interventions will be given in Chapters 8, 9 and 10, we offer below some parameters for intervention at different levels of analysis.

Individual and Group Interventions

Research on the process of empowerment shows that individuals rarely engage in emancipatory actions until they have gained considerable awareness of their own oppression and have enjoyed support from other community members (Kieffer, 1984; Lord & Hutchinson, 1993). Consequently, the task of overcoming oppression should start with a process of interpersonal support, mentoring and psychopolitical education. It is through this kind of support and education that people experience consciousness-raising (Hollander, 1997; Watts et al., 1999).

The preferred way to contribute to the liberation of oppressed people is through partnerships and solidarity. This means that we approach others in an attempt to work with them and learn from them at the same time as we contribute to their cause (Nelson, Ochocka, Griffin & Lord, 1998; Nelson, Prilleltensky & MacGilli-vary, 2001). The three community mental health organizations studied by Nelson et al. (2001b) dedicated themselves to empowering people with psychiatric problems. At their best, these organizations provided support and empowerment to their members, affording them voice and choice in the selection of treatment, caring and compassion, and access to valued services and resources. Similarly, action groups studied by Speer and colleagues offered citizens better resources such as services and housing, but connectedness at the same time (Speer & Hughey, 1995; Speer et al., 1995). In both sets of studies, the groups acted as communities of support and communities of power.

Community and Societal Interventions

Joining strategic social movements is perhaps the most powerful step that citizens can take to transform unacceptable social conditions. In some cases these will be global movements, in others they may be regional or community-based coalitions. In North America community-building efforts have proved useful in bringing people together to fight poverty. Snow (1995) claims that 'community-building can enable the underprivileged to create power through collective action' (p. 185), while McNeely (1999) reports that 'community building strategies can make a significant difference. There is now evidence of many cases where the residents of poor communities have dramatically changed their circumstances by organizing to assume responsibility for their own destiny' (p. 742). McNeely lists community participation, strategic planning, and focused and local interventions as being central to success. Similar initiatives have taken place in Europe to address the multifaceted problems faced by residents in large public housing estates. Community organizing helped many poor neighbourhoods throughout the UK to demand and receive improved social services such as health, policing and welfare (Power, 1996).

In their research of block booster projects in New York, Perkins and Long (2002) found that sense of community and communitarianism predicted collective efficacy, which is encouraging because collective efficacy may be a precursor of social action. A similar and encouraging result was reported by Saegert and Winkel (1996) who found that social capital increased empowerment and voting behaviour at the group level.

These interventions work at the personal, relational and collective levels at the same time. By participating in social-action groups, citizens feel empowered while they develop bonds of solidarity, a phenomenon that is particularly prominent in women-led organizations (Gittell, Ortega-Bustamante & Steffy, 2000; hooks, 2002). The feelings of empowerment and connection contribute to personal and relational well-being; whereas the tangible outcomes in the form of enhanced services and quality of life contribute to collective well-being. In comparing two social action groups, Speer and colleagues found that members of the organization that invested more in interpersonal connections reported their group to be 'more intimate and less controlling. They also reported more frequent overall interpersonal contact and more frequent interaction outside organizing events. Members of the community based organization also reported greater levels of psychological empowerment' (Speer et al., 1995, p. 70). Their research illustrates how an organization can promote empowerment and community at the same time.

What Are Some of the Risks and Limitations of Community and Power?

Community

Social capital may be used to increase *bonding* or *bridging*. Whereas the former refers to exclusive ties within a group, the latter refers to connections across groups. Country clubs, ethnic associations, farmers' associations and men's groups increase bonding. Coalitions, interfaith organizations and service groups enhance bridging (Agnitsch, Flora & Ryan, 2001). There is a risk of bonding overshadowing the need for bridging. If every group in society was interested only in what is good for its own members, there would be little or no cooperation across groups. Bridging is a necessity of every society. It is a basic requirement of a respectful and inclusive society. However, there are examples of groups investing in bonding to prevent bridging. Classic examples include the Ku Klux Klan and movements that support ethnic cleansing.

If bonding leads to preoccupation with one's own well-being and the neglect of others', we see a problem. The problem is even greater if social capital is used to promote unjust policies or discrimination. 'Networks and the associated norms of reciprocity are generally good for those inside the network, but the external effects of social capital are by no means always positive' (Putnam, 2000, p. 21). Proponents of mindsets such as NIMBY (not in my backyard) and coalitions of elite businesses exploit their power and connections to achieve goals that are in direct opposition to the values of CP. 'Social capital, in short, can be directed toward malevolent, antisocial purposes, just like any other form of social capital .... Therefore it is important to ask how the positive consequences of social capital – mutual support, cooperation, trust, institutional effectiveness – can be maximized and the negative manifestations – sectarianism, ethnocentrism, corruption – minimized' (Putnam, 2000, p. 22).

Another serious risk of the current discourse on social capital is its potential deflection of systemic sources of oppression, inequality and domination. There is a distinct possibility that social capital may become the preferred tool of governments to work on social problems because it puts the burden of responsibility back onto the community (Blakeley, 2002; Perkins, Hughey & Speer, 2002). We believe that communities should become involved in solving their own problems. But that is *part* of the solution, not the *whole* solution. No amount of talk about social support can negate the fact that inequality exists and that it is a major source of suffering for vulnerable populations. Social support can buffer some of the effects of inequality, but it would be ironic if it was used to support the same system that creates so much social fragmentation and isolation. Hence, we caution against social capital becoming the new slogan of governments. Furthermore, we call on people to create bonds of solidarity to enhance, not diminish, political action against injustice. We concur with Perkins et al. who claim that 'excessive concern for social cohesion undermines the ability to confront or engage in necessary conflict and thus disempowers.' (2002, p. 33).

Power

Too much power in the wrong hands and too little power in the right hands are two problems associated with power. Of course, we don't always know which are the 'wrong hands' and which are the 'right hands.' But, in principle, we know that certain groups are clearly over-empowered. In 2002, newspapers and magazines worldwide were decrying the unrestrained power of corporate executives. The collapse of corporations such as Enron and Worldcom, due in part to the unrestrained power of chief executive officers and their ability to doctor the books, left thousands of people with no pension plans and thousands of others with no life savings (for example, Gibbs, 2002). We don't want to give more power to corrupted corporate leaders, nor, for that matter, to racist demagogues or unreformed sexists.

Far too often, not enough power gets into the hands of the marginalized. A number of barriers stand in the way of the disempowered (Gaventa & Cornwall, 2001; Serrano-García & López Sánchez, 1994; Speer & Hughey, 1995; Speer et al., 1995). Superior bargaining resources are the first instrument of power in the hands of the powerful. Those with resources to pay lawyers and send their children to elite schools have more access to power than those with fewer resources. In the case of a dispute, those with the lawyers, the money and the connections can outweigh the position of the disadvantaged.

By setting agendas and defining issues in a particular way, power is also exercised by excluding issues such as inequality, privilege, oppression, corruption and power differentials from discussions and public debate. The third barrier to power and participation is defining issues in such a way that people do not realize that power is being taken away from them. Callers to the Suzie Orman show (see Box 5.2) are being robbed of power when they believe that their 'net-worth is a reflection of their self-worth'. They are buying into myths and cultural messages that prevent them from fighting injustice. Instead, they are told to go to therapy to improve their self-esteem. This is a forceful way to deny people the power of political and economic literacy (Bourdieu, 1990, 1998; Bourdieu & Passeron, 1977).

Finally, we caution against covering the whole human experience with a blanket of power. Power is vitally important in fostering well-being and liberation. Moreover, it is ever present in relationships, organizations and communities. But we want to think that there are spaces in human relations where power differentials are minimized, where people feel solidarity with others, where empathy outweighs personal interests and where love and communion are more important than narcissism (Craig & Craig, 1979; Dokecki, Newbrough, & O'Gorman, 2001; hooks, 2000, 2002). The complementary risk is that we fail to see power where power is present, for masking power is perhaps one of the gravest risks in the pursuit of well-being and liberation.

Chapter Summary

In this chapter we explored the concepts of community and power. These two concepts are the root of sense of community and empowerment, both of which have been hailed as defining metaphors for CP. We considered geographical and relational communities and explored sense of community and social capital. The research demonstrates that cohesive communities achieve better rates of health, education, tolerance and safety than fragmented ones.

The benefits of social support extend beyond the individual. Social networks improve outcomes for children, adults and for the community as a whole. While the positive outcomes of cohesion and social capital are many, it's important to remember that group unity can be used to exclude 'others'. It is equally important to keep in mind that social capital and the call for community may be used to excuse governments from investing in public resources (Blakeley, 2002). In other words, community and social capital may be used to deflect responsibility from governments.

Whereas bridging and bonding are desirable qualities of healthy communities, they can restrict opportunities for challenging power structures and for engaging in productive conflict. Although social capital can contribute to health and welfare, it can also depoliticize issues of well-being and oppression (Perkins et al., 2002).

The ability of communities to promote well-being and liberation is linked to the power of the group to demand rights, services and resources. We explored the concept of power and noted its multifaceted nature and applications. For us, power is a combination of ability and opportunity. In other words, power is not just a psychological state of mind, but a reflection of the opportunities presented to individuals by the psychosocial and material environment in which they live. Of particular interest to us is the potential of power to promote well-being, to cause or perpetuate oppression and to pursue liberation. Personal empowerment has to be complemented by collective actions (Cooke, 2002). We identified three main barriers to power, based on the ability of the powerful to (a) use resources to reward and punish behaviour in line with their interests, (b) set agendas, and (c) create cultural myths and ideologies that perpetuate the status quo. We noted that our work is challenged by the fact that it is not always clear who needs more power and who needs to be disempowered. Knowledge of the values, the context and the various interests at play is the best antidote to dogmatism. We can see too much power in certain places and not enough of it in others. Both are serious risks, for we don't want to be oblivious to power, nor do we want to project it where it doesn't belong.

COMMENTARY: Parents Involved in Schools: A Story of Community and Power

Paul Speer

Several years ago my wife Bettie became an active participant in the Parent Teacher Organization (PTO) of our children's school. One of the tasks she undertook was to develop a school handbook that provided important information for school families: school rules and procedures, parking at the school, procedures for snow days, where to go with questions and so on. In preparing the handbook, Bettie drafted a mission or role statement of the PTO vis-à-vis the school. The statement asserted that the role of the PTO was to support and enhance the educational opportunities in the school, to facilitate exchange of information between parents and teachers and to serve as a parents' liaison with the school administration when parents raised concerns. At a meeting of PTO officers and the school principal, the group balked at the point in the mission statement asserting that

the organization could serve as a mechanism for addressing parental concerns about the school. The principal felt this was not the role of the PTO, some officers voiced the view that the PTO's role was exclusively as a 'support' organization and other officers complained that a statement regarding 'parental concerns' was 'too controversial'. Bettie urged that the PTO served as a mechanism by which parents could raise concerns, particularly to the administration, as no such mechanism existed for the school. She was corrected by other parents who, with the nodding approval of the principal, revealed that if a parent had a concern about school policies or procedures, he or she should bring it up with the principal.

Power is Pervasive

Bettie's experience reveals many of the power

dynamics discussed in this chapter. For me, some of the most important are how unconscious forces and ideologies operate to reinforce the status quo – to the detriment of our values for justice and equality. When the idea that there should be a mechanism for addressing concerns gets defined by parents – not the principal – as controversial, it not only contradicts the very nature of a democratic process but reveals a form of self-imposed regulation that represents the hallmark of power (Haugaard, 1997). A common myth is that individuals susceptible to power, persuasion and manipulation are generally not well educated. Interestingly, the parents involved in the PTO were mostly very well educated – I believe all had college degrees and several had post-graduate degrees. But, as this chapter points out, one of the most important aspects of power is the ability to distort knowledge – to shape what people know or how they view the world. This mechanism is not bound by education, race, class or gender. How do we come to 'know' that PTOs are for fundraising and not for participating in school governance? How did this understanding come about for the well-educated group of parents in this organization? An important contribution of this chapter is the explicit attention it provides to the unconscious mechanisms through which power is exercised. These mechanisms are under-appreciated and largely ignored by psychologists, but nevertheless pervasive in community contexts.

Blending Power and Community

Perhaps the greatest insight of this chapter is the blending of the concepts of power and community. In my experience with community organizing, the development of social power comes only through gathering the strength of many individuals into a unified collective. To build a unified collective requires tremendous effort and time, but more fundamentally, it requires (in a non-economic context) building a sense of community that can operate within and across groups, in what the field of social capital calls both 'bridging' and 'bonding' forms of social capital. The conscious development of a collective with a strong sense of community will not always be successful – it depends on the context of that community and the experiences, interests and values of the individuals within that community. Organizing is about learning and understanding the experiences and interests of a group of individuals. To develop such knowledge and understanding requires building relationships with numerous individuals. In community organizing, one of the key organizing principles is: power flows through relationships (Speer & Hughey, 1995).

This process does not seem too difficult, but putting this principle into practice requires skill, commitment, time and a passion for justice. I've witnessed many failed attempts to organize communities and the reasons for these failures are many. Often, organizing efforts identify the issue to be organized a priori – organizers attempt to form groups working on substance abuse or housing or education. Organizing in such a way undermines the process of listening, thus limiting an understanding of the interests and values of individuals in a community. When outsiders, be they organizers, experts or funders, define in advance the issues for a community, the result is a weakened organization and an organizing process that resembles an exercise in manipulation. Most importantly, the activity produced in 'issue-defined' organizing efforts generally has little sustainability – and thus little power.

Another common shortcoming to community work when issues of community and power are not viewed together is that participation is encouraged as an end in itself. In many contexts, we view citizen participation as essential for democracy and a key method of building community and developing empowerment. But what of Bettie's experience in the PTO? Did participation there build power or cultivate community? These questions are not easily answered – they are very complex. A particular strength of this chapter is that it communicates some of the complexity and nuances involved in community work and issues of power. Too often community psychologists oversimplify these issues. Citizen participation, for example, is generally held to be a 'good thing'. I am not disputing this, but I would suggest that powerful interests have shaped many of the settings and niches in which we can participate and, as a result, our participation has been defined in very narrow, limited ways. At the PTO, Bettie participated in fundraising to bring educational opportunities to the school (dancers, rappers, puppeteers and so on) but the educated, involved and resourced parents kept participation focused on fundraising and away from deeper issues of equity and justice in that school (tensions in our school existed around 'well-connected' parents selecting their children's teacher thus producing 'designer classrooms' and segregated seating in the school lunch room due to seating assignments based on whether kids were part of the free or reduced lunch program). In that school setting, parent participation served to keep the 'system' intact, not to address issues of fairness.

Power and Conflict

The irony is that community and power, which are so often considered as separate or even dichotomous constructs, are so intimately linked. I've witnessed many efforts to develop one without the other, but successful organizing efforts usually attend to both relationship and cohesion within the organization as well as a strategic use of power beyond the group. However, there is one final observation to make about a noteworthy contribution in this chapter. The issue of conflict is presented as important to consider in the development of power. This perspective is not often shared, but it is critical to the development of power. While conflict is never desirable, efforts to change the status quo will eventually confront those with interests served by the status quo. In my children's school, PTO officers had the ability to influence what they wanted in the school so they felt no need to provide a mechanism for others. Those benefiting from existing relationships will not acquiesce based on reason, morality or justice. If these conditions are to change, conflict is inevitable. How that conflict is played out, however,

has numerous options. Unfortunately, many believe that conflict is to be avoided – suppressed even – regardless of the conditions around which it arises. Such a perspective serves to maintain the status quo. There are many types of conflict; for example, conflict between fathers over a call in little league sports is all too common and a form of conflict that I would argue should be avoided. In contrast, there is rarely conflict about capital outlays within city budgets, but for neighbourhoods with no public investment (which exacerbates private disinvestment) strategies to pressure for change are needed.

In my experience, and in the presentation of this chapter, conflict is a fact of life in community work. When working to make change, conflict is inevitable. Attention to the role of conflict, knowledge of the unconscious mechanisms of power and development of the relationships between power and community are critically important for community psychologists.

Chapter glossary

community a group of people affiliated on the basis of common bonds, such as geographical location, religion, profession, nationality or other

power the capacity and opportunity to influence the course of events in one's personal life or in the life of others in the community

self-help/mutual aid groups of

people who congregate in order to help each other with a particular challenge in life

sense of community the feeling derived from belonging to a particular group where the individual experiences bonds of affection, influence, companionship and support

social capital collective resources

consisting of civic participation, networks, norms of reciprocity and organizations that foster trust among citizens and actions to enhance the common good

stress-buffering hypothesis theory describing how social support may enhance coping and mitigate the negative effects of stress

RESOURCES

Websites in Community Psychology

1. For an interesting project on community capacity (headed at the time of writing by community psychologist David Chavis), visit the Association for the Study and Development of Community on www.capablecommunity.com.

2. For information on the role of social capital in international community development, you can visit a site operated by the University of Sussex in collaboration with the UK government department of International Development. Go to www.id21.org/insights/insights34/insights-iss34-art02.html.

3. *ISUMA – The Canadian Journal of Policy Research* has devoted its second volume to social capital. You may read online state-of-the-art articles by leading authors in this field. Visit http://isuma.net/v02n01/index_e.shtml.

4. The Saguaro Seminar at Harvard University is interested in promoting social capital. Visit at www.bettertogether.org.

5. Robert Putnam has an interesting website on his book *Bowling Alone*. You can read an overview of the book on www.bowlingalone.com.

6. The Poverty and Race Research Action Council offers resources on how to promote community development and community organizing. The Council aims to use social research to reduce poverty and racism. You can visit them at www.prrac.org.

6
Commitment, Accountability and Inclusion

Chapter Organization

Commitment and Accountability	◆ Commitment to What? Accountability to Whom? *To Values; To Self; To Others; To Community; To Profession* ◆ Why are Commitment and Accountability so Important? ◆ What is the Value-base of Commitment and Accountability? ◆ How can Commitment and Accountability be Promoted? ◆ What are the Limitations of Commitment and Accountability?
Inclusion	◆ What is Inclusion? ◆ Why is Inclusion Important? ◆ What is the Value-base of Inclusion? ◆ How can Inclusion be Implemented? ◆ What are the Limitations of Inclusion?
Chapter Summary	**COMMENTARY: Living Up to Community Psychology Goals and Values**
Glossary	**Resources**

Warm-up Exercise

1. There must have been occasions in your life when you recognized injustice and suffering. It is quite likely that at the time you thought to yourself: 'Something must be done about this; this is not right.' Now for the hard part.
2. How often have you pursued your conscience and what have you done about it?
3. If you have followed your conscience with actions, what factors helped you to follow your conscience? Please include in the list psychological, sociological, cultural, and political reasons for acting on your moral impulse. You can think of different levels of analysis (micro, meso and macro) and how they influence your decisions.
4. If you have not followed your conscience, what factors inhibited you from doing so?
5. Compare your actions and reasons with other students and friends.
6. What were the predominant reasons for acting or not acting on your moral impulses?
7. How satisfied are you with the way you responded to the injustice you observed?

Following and questioning your conscience are difficult tasks. In this chapter you will learn to:

■ reflect on your commitment and accountability to issues of injustice and suffering
■ recognize sources of action and inaction on moral issues
■ overcome forces of inaction through the concept of psychopolitical validity, and
■ enact commitment and accountability through the value of inclusion.

> Easier said than done.
> Walk the talk.
> The road to hell is paved with good intentions.
> Fight the good fight.
> Walk a mile in my shoes.

What do these proverbs have in common? They talk about commitment and accountability and human imperfections. Moreover, they talk about the risk of hypocrisy and the certainty of contradictions. In Spanish, the word *consecuente* is more common than the English 'consequent', which refers to being consistent with one's ideals. In liberation psychology, which has its origins in South American liberation theology, people talk about being consequent with one's ideals (Fals Borda, 2001; Martín-Baró, 1994; Montero, 2000a). In community psychology, as in liberation and feminist psychology, we aspire to be consequent with our values. This can make for an interesting but complicated life. Interesting because community psychologists are explicit about living their values and melding their professional and personal lives (O'Neill, 1989; Prilleltensky, 2001). Complicated because there is no rest from scrutiny. Once we declare our values we are exposed to criticism for not living up to them. It is far easier to hide our values than to commit to them in public. As human beings, we embody personal contradictions (Jaggar, 1994).

In this chapter we discuss ways of being consistent with our values. We do so by addressing commitment, accountability and inclusion. We will analyse these concepts and examine ways of being in harmony with our belief system. This is not to imply that all community psychologists believe in exactly the same credo, for differences abound, but there is enough in common to unite them through the values presented in earlier chapters. In essence, this chapter is about ensuring that all the previous principles outlined in the book are put into effect. Because of their function in upholding all the other values, we call commitment, accountability and inclusion, meta-values. That is, superordinate values that make sure the rest of the values are in place (see Chapter 3). We can pronounce all kinds of ideal values, but if we lack commitment and accountability, they remain in a theoretical sphere without application at community level. Complacency lurks everywhere. How can we fight it?

Commitment and Accountability

Commitment to What? Accountability to Whom?

Commitment to a cause such as social justice requires emotional and material investments (hooks, 2002). It requires time, dedication, thought, and perhaps even sacrifice. What do we commit to? In our view, we commit and are accountable to five principal entities: values, self, others, community and profession.

To Values

As noted in Chapters 2 and 3, values are guiding principles that help us behave in ethical and defensible ways. They are a set of action-oriented beliefs. In their absence, we wouldn't know what to propose to improve society, nor would we know how to assess the current state of affairs or progress in our communities.

But values are only as good as the people who practise them. Values don't have an independent existence other than as ideas. While it is imperative to refine our values and get the 'right ideas', values, as cognitive entities, don't expect accountability of us. It is people, ourselves included of course, who expect accountability. We should be careful to avoid the philosophical fallacy, according to which good ideas should necessarily lead to good outcomes. We need vehicles for action, and, more importantly, we need to internalize and embody our values and be accountable to ourselves and others. We are the first to admit that this is a high calling, and we, the authors, often fall short. It is a struggle. We don't want a life of guilt, but we don't want an unexamined life either. How do you resolve this conflict between aspirations for high moral standards and human failings?

To Self

This book pursues the dual and complementary goals of liberation and well-being. In line with personal interests, most people aspire to achieve these goals for themselves (Swartz, 1997), and while attention to self, as opposed to others, varies across cultures, a commitment to one's personal development and well-being is ubiquitous.

We earlier identified values for personal, relational and collective well-being. As you will remember, for reasons reviewed in Chapter 3, committing to any particular set of values in isolation creates a dangerous imbalance. Making a commitment to advance my personal well-being, through values such as self-determination and personal control, can undermine relational well-being. For looking after only my own well-being diminishes the chance that I'll care equally for others. Too much power in my hands translates into too little power in others' hands. The same logic applies to collective values. Total commitment to collectivist values leads to conformity and squashes personal freedoms. Our call is to improve personal well-being through relational and collective well-being, and to enhance collective well-being through relational and personal well-being. There is a tripartite relationship between the values.

But being committed to one's well-being is quite different from being accountable to oneself. How do I monitor whether I'm being true to my values? How do I account to myself that my actions are congruent with my beliefs? This is no simple process. We explore below enabling factors as well as traps. We are forever at risk of manipulating our thoughts and actions in order to bring them in line with our declared values. Human beings want to avoid cognitive dissonance at all cost. Our position, as noted later in this chapter, is that without help and monitoring from others, it's very difficult to maintain a close alliance between our deeds and our values. Subjective forces and psychological dynamics imperil the commitment to ethical principles (Flyvbjerg, 2001). Not because we are necessarily immoral beings, but because we are not moral machines operating on ethics software.

Countless intrusions interfere with the smooth operation of our values: a culture of self-indulgence, vested interests, economic considerations, ignorance, vanity, need for control, and others (Bourdieu, 1998; Damon, 1995). In short – our humanity. How to reconcile the part of our humanity that wants to be value-driven and the part that wants to be interest-driven is an open question. This process is further complicated by restraining environments. As a young professional wishing to promote alternative values, you may not have a smooth ride. In response to a call by postgraduate students from the UK, Dennis Fox wrote the piece reproduced in Box 6.1. Have a look and see how you feel about it. You can discuss it with friends and your instructor.

Box 6.1

In response to a request by *PsyPAGS Quarterly*, a UK postgraduate student journal (www.psypag.co.uk), Dennis Fox wrote this piece about commitment and politics in psychology. Reprinted with permission of the author and the journal.

THE SUITABILITY OF POLITICAL DEBATE IN PSYCHOLOGY August 17, 2002

Dennis Fox

My dictionary defines 'suitable' thus: 'of the right type or quality for a particular purpose or occasion.' The question posed – 'Is the discipline of Psychology a suitable site for Political debate?' – requires considering that debate's 'purpose or occasion.'

If your goal is to build a traditional career, the answer is usually 'No.' Students will discover an unpleasant truth: most future bosses and colleagues won't consider your insistence on psychology's relevance to oppression or capitalism appropriate for a new hire who might corrupt impressionable undergraduates. They'll dismiss you as either immature or dangerous.

If you do find a job, the gatekeepers who define 'suitability' won't disappear. To them, a science committed to objective inquiry might address the psychology of politics, if your research generates impressive statistics. But making psychology itself an arena of political debate violates the myth that science is objective rather than passionate. As for the politics of the discipline of psychology – well, that's best left to sociologists.

On the other hand, raising political issues is essential if your 'purpose or occasion' is to examine how psychology's assumptions and practices affect, and are affected by, societal forces. To investigate how an unjust status quo is maintained – and how to change it – you cannot help but notice human psychology's relevance. Pointing that out, and proposing values you think psychologists should embrace, may piss off the wrong people, but it's the honest thing to do.

There are ways to straddle a middle ground, at least until tenure provides somewhat more protection:

1. Address political issues as a small part of your work, spending the bulk of your time doing empirical research on traditional topics. Once you succeed on the mainstream's own terms, you have some leeway to raise political questions on the side – you've demonstrated that your political critique isn't based simply on an inability to follow the rules. Of course, it's pretty time-consuming to produce impressive empirical research and also do serious critical work. You may give up, especially if you find the traditional work boring or useless. But who said being critical was going to be easy?

2. Do conventional empirical research on politically tinged topics. The acceptability of qualitative research has increased, but a nice, neat experimental manipulation demonstrating some dynamic of oppression impresses mainstreamers, especially if published in a prestigious journal. The same is sometimes true for review articles or essays. In both cases, you have to tone down the language to get past reviewers, but if you write a book, you're allowed to admit in the preface that your research was motivated by deep political concerns rather than simple scientific curiosity.

3. Find a niche that tolerates political motives and alternative methods. This is more easily done in specializations like community or feminist psychology, which began as attacks on societal institutions. Although both fields have gone more mainstream, psychologists who see themselves as advocates may still find a home there. Outside North America, critical psychology itself is growing, with journals, degree programs, and conferences. You might make a career publishing in non-mainstream journals. That's a good option for some, though marginal to psychology's core.

4. Find a niche outside psychology, perhaps an inter-disciplinary department less concerned about psychology's status mania. This option, however, marginalizes the political debate even further.

Psychology plays a key role in the mechanisms of power. Psychologists who object to how societal institutions use their power will find a way to ask uncomfortable questions. Proceed carefully. Find others to work with – in collaboration there is strength.

But in any case, proceed.

Dennis Fox, associate professor of legal studies and psychology at the University of Illinois at Springfield, is co-editor of *Critical Psychology: An Introduction* and co-founder of RadPsyNet: The Radical Psychology Network (http://www.radpsynet.org). He's never had a job in a mainstream psychology department. His work is available at http://www.dennisfox.net; email: df@dennisfox.net

To Others

By 'others' we mean people who are close to us in our work and in our personal lives. Caring is not an abstract ideal performed only in heroic acts of self-sacrifice; it is also very much an act of mundane relevance. Caring and compassion for our children, partners, co-workers and friends are all expressions of love and commitment (hooks, 2002; Mustakova-Possardt, 2003). This notion is intuitively and easily understood. What is not so easy to apprehend and operationalize is how to be accountable to all those people. Where do we learn how to give and receive feedback? Who taught us to put in place structures of mutual accountability? How does a patriarchal society convince its male members that dialogue is more virtuous than psychological and physical dominance?

Ingrid Huygens has been developing, practising and studying structures of accountability in a bicultural environment for many years (see Chapter 16; Huygens, 1997, 2001a, 2001b; Mulvey et al., 2000). Her approach is based on two principal tenets. First, on the recognition of injustice and suffering inflicted by one party on another, in this case by pakeha, or white-European New Zealanders, to the Maori people of Aoteroa/New Zealand. And second, on the establishment of processes and structures to make sure that relationships between pakeha and Maori people are based on fairness, mutual respect, and responsibility for past and present injustices. Huygens puts this into practice by subjecting the nature of collaborations among pakeha and Maori people to the scrutiny of the latter. This is to ensure that past injustices are addressed and not perpetuated. Confronting previous and current wrongdoings is the trademark of this approach. Though labour intensive, Huygens (2001a) reports that the rewards of this work are uniquely satisfying.

To Community

Caring is proximal and distal at the same time. Whereas proximal caring refers to the compassion and support we display towards those close to us, distal caring reflects our concern for those who are not physically or emotionally close to us, yet worthy of our respect and obligations. We may not come into contact with poor or hungry children on a daily basis, but they are deserving of our concern nonetheless. Likewise, we may not witness first hand the plight of textile workers in Southeast Asia or the discrimination sustained by women in totalitarian and patriarchal regimes. Yet, if we are persuaded by the notion of proximal and distal caring, we will concern ourselves with justice and fairness, not only in our immediate environment, but wherever injustice and unfairness occur. Thus, we worry about immediate as well as distal geographical and relational communities.

Whereas convenience, logistics and opportunities can make it easier to do our community work close to home, that should not stop us from contributing to other communities. There are many ways to show caring for those who are physically removed. How much effort to expend on local versus global issues is an open question, one that requires personal deliberation and considered attention.

It is hard enough to commit people to transparency and accountability in close relationships, let alone in communities that can be amorphous entities. Who exactly am I accountable to in my community? What structures exist to monitor the accountability of citizens towards their community? And who is going to sit in judgement on me to tell me whether I behaved or misbehaved towards my neighbours? A Pandora's box of rights and responsibilities is opened by our suggestion that we should be accountable to somebody or something in our community (Etzioni, 1998). Compared to the reigning silence, we wouldn't mind some lively debate on these issues.

Emergent and imperfect as they might be, there are some exemplars of accountability to communities. Huygens (2001a) is documenting the work of treaty educators in Aoteroa/New Zealand. Treaty educators collaborate with organizations to facilitate accountability to the Maori people and to the Treaty of Waitangi, which outlines the rights and obligations of pakeha and Maori cultures towards each other. The treaty had been dormant for decades, and it is only in the last 15 years that intensive work to revive it has taken place. Treaty educators strive to raise awareness of white domination, privilege and oppression of Maori people. Partnering organizations create committees and structures to advance the process of reconciliation.

Counter examples of despotic accountability also exist. We have all seen in the media the burnt or mutilated bodies of men and women who 'disobey' community norms, only to end up as paraded corpses for 'all to see'. In August 2002, news broadcasts announced a death sentence by stoning of a Nigerian woman who had a child out of wedlock. These are gruesome reminders that accountability should not come at the expense of the liberty of the individual. This is not the accountability we're talking about. Fanatic regimes use accountability to terrorize the population and bring them into line with official rule.

The accountability we propose is to people who suffer from exploitation and marginality, not to those who use and abuse their power for personal, governmental or corporate interests. Furthermore, our accountability extends to those who are committed to bringing about a more just society.

To Profession

We choose to devote part of our energies to the development of community psychology (CP). This profession has much to offer for the promotion of liberation and well-being. There are many ways for psychologists to make a difference in the world (Prilleltensky & Nelson, 2002). Strengthening CP research and action is an important one for us and, we hope, for you too.

Multiple approaches, methodologies and interventions co-exist in CP. Although we welcome its pluralism, we sometimes wonder about priorities in CP. In this book, we make a case for prioritizing well-being and liberation, which are our two main priorities at this time. To guide our commitment to these two priorities we propose the concept of *psychopolitical validity* (Prilleltensky, 2003b, in press).

This type of validity is built on two complementary sets of factors: psychological and political. Hence, the term 'psychopolitical'. This combination refers to the psychological and political influences that interact to promote well-being, perpetuate oppression, or generate resistance and liberation. Psychopolitical factors help explain suffering and well-being. At the same time, this combination of terms denotes the need to attend to both sets of factors in our efforts to change individuals, groups and societies. As a result, we propose two types of psychopolitical validity: (a) epistemic and (b) transformational. Whereas the former refers to using psychology and politics in understanding social phenomena, the latter calls on both sets of factors to make lasting social changes.

Table 6.1 Guidelines for epistemic psychopolitical validity in community psychology research

Concerns	DOMAINS		
	Collective	Relational	Personal
Well-being	Accounts for role of political and economic power in economic prosperity and in creation of social just ce institutions	Studies the role of power in creating and sustaining egalitarian relationships, social cohesion, social support, respect for diversity and democratic participation in communities, groups and families	Studies role of psychological and political power in achieving self-determination, empowerment, health, personal growth, meaning and spirituality
Oppression	Explores role of globalization, colonization and exploitation in suffering of nations and communities	Examines the role of political and psychological power in exclusion and discrimination based on class, gender, age, race, education and ability. Studies conditions leading to lack of support, horizontal violence and fragmentation within oppressed groups	Studies role of powerlessness in learned helplessness, hopelessness, self-depreciation, internalized oppression, shame, mental health problems and addictions
Liberation	Deconstructs ideological norms that lead to acquiescence and studies effective psychopolitical factors in resistance	Studies acts of solidarity and compassion with others who suffer from oppression	Examines sources of strength, resilience, solidarity and development of activism and leadership

Adapted from Prilleltensky (in press)

Table 6.2 Guidelines for transformational psychopolitical validity in community psychology action

Concerns	DOMAINS		
	Collective	Relational	Personal
Well-being	Contributes to institutions that support emancipation, human development, peace, protection of environment and social justice	Contributes to power equalization in relationships and communities. Enriches awareness of subjective and psychological forces preventing solidarity. Builds trust, connection and participation in groups that support social cohesion and social justice	Supports personal empowerment, sociopolitical development, leadership training and solidarity. Contributes to personal and social responsibility and awareness of subjective forces preventing commitment to justice and personal depowerment when in position of privilege
Oppression	Opposes economic colonialism and denial of cultural rights. Decries and resists role of own reference group or nation in oppression of others	Contributes to struggle against in-group and out-group domination and discrimination, sexism and norms of violence. Builds awareness of own prejudice and participation in horizontal violence	Helps to prevent acting out of own oppression on others. Builds awareness of internalized oppression and role of dominant ideology in victim-blaming. Contributes to personal depowerment of people in position of privilege
Liberation	Supports networks of resistance and social change movements. Contributes to structural depowerment of privileged people	Supports resistance against objectification of others. Develops processes of mutual accountability	Helps to resist complacency and collusion with exploitative system. Contributes to struggle to recover personal and political identity

Adapted from Prilleltensky (in press)

We pay equal attention to psychological and political factors. Psychological factors refer to the subjective life of the person, informed by *power dynamics* operating at the personal, interpersonal, family, group and cultural levels. Political factors, in turn, refer to the collective experience of individuals and groups, informed by *power dynamics and conflicts of interest* at the interpersonal, family, group, community and societal levels. In both sets of factors we emphasize the role of power in the subjective or collective experience of people and groups.

Psychopolitical validity, then, derives from the concurrent consideration and interaction of power dynamics in psychological and political domains at various levels of analyses. Hence, we can talk about psychopolitical validity when these conditions are met. When this type of analysis is applied to research, we talk about *epistemic psychopolitical validity*. When it is applied to social interventions, we talk about *transformational psychopolitical validity*. To illustrate these concepts, we refer you to Tables 6.1 and 6.2, respectively.

To understand issues of well-being, oppression and liberation at the personal, relational and collective domains, we turn our attention to Table 6.1. Each cell in the table refers to issues of power and their manifestation in political and psychological spheres. Needless to say, this table is not exhaustive or inclusive of all the fields of CP. Rather, it concentrates on the priorities of well-being and liberation, two issues we regard as crucial.

Table 6.1 may be used to guide our commitment to CP research. Furthermore, it may be used as an accountability device. We can monitor the extent to which we study the priority areas described in the table. In a sense, these guidelines serve the function of a vision; a vision of what type of research we need to pursue in CP.

The same can be said about the guidelines for transformational validity. Table 6.2 integrates levels of intervention with key concerns for CP: well-being, oppression and liberation. This is a vision of preferred interventions. We would show high degrees of commitment and accountability if we pursued all these interventions. As a monitoring system, Table 6.2 helps to keep track of our interventions. Are we intervening primarily at the personal level? Do we focus too much on oppression to the neglect of liberation and well-being? Have we neglected the collective domain? The templates presented in Tables 6.1 and 6.2 can be used by research and action teams and by investigators wishing to assess progress in the field as a whole.

Why Are Commitment and Accountability so Important?

You are probably the best person to answer this question. We can only talk about why commitment and accountability are important to us. For us, commitment and accountability provide meaning to our actions. In their absence, the entire building of values collapses. What good is it to have values if there is no commitment to them? We value commitment for the same reason we value other principles; they provide a compass in our pursuit of meaning. Some people call it spirituality, others call it purpose in life. This is the part of our humanity that is driven by values and transcendence (Dalai Lama, 1999; Mustakova-Possardt, 2003).

What is your passion? Do you want to make a difference in the world? Is there a topic that excites you or upsets you? Do we want to go through life without reflecting on our actions? We think it's better to pause and reflect and commit ourselves to a set of values. Accountability makes life hard because it means producing some sort of a report card on our behaviour. This is, we think, a reasonable expectation in our pursuit of spirituality and a value-driven life.

In psychology and other disciplines there has been an emerging trend towards the pursuit of meaning in our work. Today, various strands within psychology converge in their desire for meaningful engagement with subjective forces, with community members and with social struggles. Critical, feminist, liberation and community psychologists have invested in creating meaning in their various roles. There is a need among many psychologists across the world to engage in meaning-seeking activities. We believe that many psychologists strive to integrate their professional lives with their civic lives through meaningful engagement. By meaningful engagement we mean involvement in activities that integrate the epistemological, moral, political and social commitments of psychologists with their professional endeavours.

A psychology for meaningful engagement examines the silent issues, those issues that are either too controversial or complicated for positivist psychology. Critical psychology and CP delve into the complicated relations between values, interests and power (Dokecki, 1996; Dokecki et al., 2001; Prilleltensky & Nelson, 2002). In each and every one of our interactions with students, clients, research participants or community members our values intersect with our own interests and the interests of others. To complicate matters, our behaviour is determined largely by our own power and the power of our partners. In the end, the way we behave towards others is the result of a struggle between our own values, interest and power, and those of others (Dokecki, 1996; Flyvbjerg, 2001). These are difficult connections to disentangle, but worth exploring nevertheless. If we neglect them, we can only achieve superficial commitments and limited accountability.

What Is the Value-base of Commitment and Accountability?

We make a distinction between common and meta-values. Social justice, caring and compassion and respect for diversity are examples of the former, whereas commitment and accountability are examples of the latter. In simple terms, meta-values refer to the values that look after all other values. In order to promote any of the values presented in Chapters 2 and 3 we need to commit ourselves to the basic principle of action. Commitment and accountability are superordinate principles that we invoke in order to pursue all other principles. Before we take steps to address injustice or discrimination, we commit ourselves to do something about important things in life.

But after we commit ourselves to doing something, how do we know what we're doing is the right thing? For this, we need accountability, to ourselves and others. We need to spell out how to achieve accountability, otherwise it can remain an enticing but unfulfilled promise.

How Can Commitment and Accountability Be Promoted?

As with many other phenomena in psychology, patterns of moral behaviour begin in childhood, through educational and socialization processes (Damon, 1995). Community psychologists bring to the profession a reservoir of experiences dealing with values, ethics, morality, commitment and accountability (Dokecki et al., 2001; O'Neill, 1989). In this regard they are no different from other people.

Unlike the sixties, which saw an effervescence of political consciousness, the eighties, the nineties and the first few years of the new millennium seem to promote political apathy (Ralston Saul, 2001). Stating and standing up for one's values is like swimming against the tide. With the exception of some new social movements (for example, Freeman & Johnson, 1999), everything else about western culture goes in the opposite direction: self-indulgence, consumerism and political cynicism (Ralston Saul, 1995).

Some community psychologists (Pancer & Pratt, 1999) and social scientists (Damon, 1995; Mustakova-Possardt, 2003) are investigating the sources of activism and volunteerism. Role models, opportunities to contribute in society through school and religious congregations, social consciousness and family influences all shape the future of a prospective activist and volunteer. Furthermore, some community psychologists are trying to intervene to increase social and political awareness. Some strategies include educational activities in schools, social action with special interest groups, and others (Watts et al., 1999).

To translate the vague idea of accountability into action, we recommend a series of steps. Table 6.3 describes roles, tasks, facilitating factors, potential subversions and mechanisms of accountability for community psychologists. We are not content to point out jobs without thinking about potential distortions of good intentions. The first two columns of the table may be seen as cognitive and behavioural tasks: imagining vision and values, talking to people, cooperating with stakeholders. This is very prescriptive. In other words, this is what we suggest people do to increase their commitment and accountability. But, as community psychologists, we know that this is not good enough. We also need to think about the context in which such actions take place. This is why we pay attention to facilitating factors and structures that may encourage, support and enable the person to engage in commitment and accountability.

What Are the Limitations of Commitment and Accountability?

Even after all the prescriptions and precautions put forth in Table 6.3, there is a chance that individuals will miss the mark. Good processes may be subverted and altered to suit personal interests. Let's have a look at the first row of Table 6.3. Under potential subversions we see that people may confuse personal preferences with well-justified values. This is very common in the organizational development literature (see for example Kanungo & Mendonca, 1996; Senge, 1990) where employers and employees put forth visions that satisfy their personal and corporate interests, but not necessarily those of the community they serve. When dealing with vision and values there is always the danger of engaging in platitudes that sound nice but lack substance or justification.

Substituting the need for personal change with personal forgiveness is a potential subversion we have witnessed. Instead of owning up to personal wrongdoings men and women choose to 'forgive themselves'. Forgiveness is good if it comes with a commitment to change, not if it serves to exculpate abusive husbands or exploitive bosses.

Tokenism is another distortion of commitment and accountability. Popular participation in decision-making processes is not an easy outcome to achieve. Easier and more expedient is choosing a few selected members of a community to repre-

Table 6.3 Seeking commitment and accountability in community psychology

Role of Community Psychologist	Tasks	Facilitating Factors	Potential Subversions	Measures of Accountability
1. Clarify personal and organizational position with respect to values for personal, relational and collective well-being	Engage stakeholders in dialogue about ways to balance personal, relational and collective well-being	Knowledge with respect to balance between values and processes of consultation and collaboration	Confuse personal preferences with values and remain at level of abstraction without translating values into action	Consult with others about limitations and contradictions in values selected
2. Promote state of affairs in which personal power and self-interests do not undermine well-being or interests of others	Develop critical self-awareness of how personal interests and social power suffuse professional role and may undermine collective well-being	Creation of safe space for dialogue about value and ethical dilemmas	Replace need for personal change with self-acceptance and/or distort values to coincide with narrow personal interests	Subject personal and organizational process of consciousness-raising to scrutiny by stakeholders affected by the work
3. Enhance solidarity and common interests among citizens, volunteers, service providers and psychologists	Create partnerships among public, volunteers, workers, and community psychologists	Prolonged engagement in the organization and community and establishment of mutual trust	Engage in token consultative processes that do not afford public meaningful input	Create leaderships structures with meaningful input and representation from various stakeholder groups
4. Confront people and groups subverting values, abusing power, or allowing self-interests to undermine the well-being of others in the organization or in the community	Engage in constructive conflict resolution with individuals or groups undermining vision and values	Clear procedures for conflict resolution, and a culture of openness and critique	Use power and legitimacy to confront people in order to suppress opposing views, or use conflict resolution to avoid excluding people from organization	Subject to scrutiny of partners psychologists' efforts to confront people and groups subverting vision and values

Adapted from Prilleltensky (2001)

sent others' interests. While convenient, this can easily turn into tokenism, claiming to have had a collaborative process, when in fact only a fraction of the population was represented.

The last two potential subversions presented in Table 6.3 deal with power. Commitment and accountability cannot take place without using one's power. Too much power leads to its abuse, whereas too little power may lead to its abuse by others (Dokecki, 1996). It is possible to use one's power to silence other people. But it is also possible for others to take advantage of our lack of assertion to advance agendas that are damaging to the community. With power, and we all have a measure of it, comes responsibility; the responsibility to confront those who exploit privilege and the duty to include others who have a stake in our work and values. One of the main commitments and the best measure of accountability we may have is inclusion.

Inclusion

What is Inclusion?

The term 'inclusion' has its roots in the field of disabilities (Oliver & Barnes, 1998). In particular, parents and advocates of individuals with developmental disabilities have promoted the idea and practice of inclusion and community because of widespread practices of segregation and exclusion of adults and children with developmental disabilities (O'Brien & O'Brien, 1996; Schwartz, 1997). Historically people with developmental disabilities have been labelled by professionals (with psychologists playing a lead role in this) with such pejorative terms as 'mental defectives', 'feeble-minded', 'idiots', and 'morons'. The eugenics movement, which we noted in Chapter 1, advocated that this 'tainted' group should be segregated and sterilized so that they would not mix with mainstream society. The stigma and shame that families with a child with a developmental disability experience, and that such children experience themselves, have persisted. Today, many people with developmental disabilities are surrounded by a 'sea of services', in institutions, special schools, special classes within schools and special living facilities (McKnight, 1995). Parents and advocates have contested this approach and reclaimed language with terms like 'inclusion', 'mainstreaming', and 'community integration'. The language of inclusion suggests that the community, not people with disabilities, needs to change; communities and community members need to become more welcoming and hospitable to people with disabilities (O'Brien & O'Brien, 1996; Schwartz, 1997).

The principle of inclusion goes beyond people with disabilities; it applies to a variety of groups that have been subjected to social exclusion. Inclusion is becoming an organizing principle that applies more broadly to people who have been discriminated against and oppressed by virtue of their gender, sexual orientation, ethnoracial background, abilities, age or some other characteristic. Sexism, heterosexism, racism, ableism and ageism are all forms of social exclusion. Inclusion is an antidote to exclusion and can be conceptualized at different ecological levels of analysis. At the individual level, inclusion entails the recovery of a positive personal and political identity – the development of a personal story of empowerment. At the relational level, inclusion means welcoming communities and supportive relationships. At the societal level, inclusion is concerned with the promotion of equity and access to valued social resources that have historically been denied to oppressed people.

Community psychologist Meg Bond (1999) has argued that inclusion entails both a culture of connection and the legitimization of varied perspectives. The notion of connection, which has been emphasized by feminist writers as important for women's growth and empowerment (Jordan et al., 1991), focuses on interdependence, team work, relationships, and sense of community. Connection stands as an alternative to the emphasis on individualism that is widespread in the western world. The idea of varied perspectives suggests that, in any setting, there are multiple perspectives that reflect people's unique circumstances and experiences. It has been observed that disadvantaged people understand the idea of multiple perspectives very well because they learn the norms and perspectives of their own group and they also have to learn the norms and perspectives of the dominant group in order to cope with and survive that reality (Bond, 1999). In other words, disadvantaged people live in two different worlds and have to bridge those two worlds every day of their lives.

On the other hand, advantaged people have more trouble understanding multiple perspectives. Advantaged people are often oblivious to the life experiences and circumstances of disadvantaged groups, because they do not have to cope with those realities or be accountable to disadvantaged people. Moreover, legitimization of these varied perspectives counters the belief that there is one true, external reality and one single standard against which everyone should be judged.

Bond and Mulvey (2000) have made a distinction between representation and perspective that is important for the principle of inclusion. Representation refers to the participation and inclusion of disadvantaged groups (for example, the representation of women in CP), while perspective refers to the unique and varied perspectives of disadvantaged groups (for example, the inclusion of feminist perspectives that challenge male domination). Representation is a necessary but insufficient condition for inclusion; the incorporation of perspectives that are critical of the status quo is needed as well. Together, representation and perspective enhance the voices of disadvantaged people, providing them with opportunities to name their experiences rather than being silenced and suffering in that silence (Reinharz, 1994).

The principle of inclusion is closely tied to that of accountability and commitment. Bond (1999) has argued that forces supporting exclusion are lack of accountability and differential privilege. When dominant groups are not accountable for their impact on subordinate groups, exclusion and oppression of the subordinate group occur. In contrast, inclusion is promoted when dominant groups become aware of their relative power and privilege and are accountable for their impact on the subordinate group. But inclusion has been difficult to promote because dominant groups have historically held on to their power and privilege, as US black activists Stokely Carmichael and Charles Hamilton wrote during the 1960s:

> Whenever a number of persons within a society have enjoyed for a considerable period of time certain opportunities for getting wealth, for exercising power and authority, and for successfully claiming prestige and social deference, there is a strong tendency for these people to feel that these benefits are theirs 'by right.' The advantages come to be thought of as normal, proper, customary, as sanctioned by time, precedent and social consensus. Proposals to change the existing situation arouse reactions of 'moral indig-

nation.' Elaborate doctrines are developed to show the inevitability and rightness of the existing scheme of things. (Carmichael & Hamilton, 1967, p. 8).

Often, disadvantaged people do things for advantaged people so that they do not have to do such work themselves. For example, feminist sociologist Dorothy Smith (1990) has observed that: 'Women do the clerical work, the word processing, the interviewing for the survey; they take messages, handle the mail, make appointments, care for patients' (pp. 18–19). Smith observed that when women do this, men don't have to take responsibility for any of this work and are therefore unlikely to be conscious of what this work involves. Advantaged groups can rationalize power differences by constructing and adopting dominant social narratives about disadvantaged people that are of the victim-blaming variety. Moreover, these dominant social narratives, while highly irrational, are clung to tenaciously by privileged groups. Consider, for example, bigoted white people who assert that black people are lazy, when at the same time, black people perform a myriad of services for these same white people, such as cleaning their homes, cooking and serving them food, and so on. When challenges to their assumptions about disadvantaged people break through these defences, advantaged people often find these experiences to be eye openers.

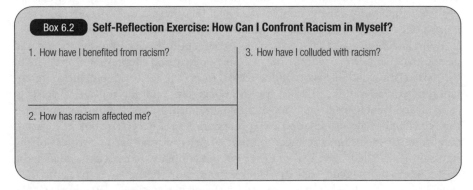

Box 6.2   **Self-Reflection Exercise: How Can I Confront Racism in Myself?**

1. How have I benefited from racism?

2. How has racism affected me?

3. How have I colluded with racism?

Why is Inclusion Important?

Failure to promote inclusion leaves the door open for oppression to occur. Sexism, heterosexism, racism and ableism are all forms of exclusion that have psychological and political dimensions (Moane, 1999; Prilleltensky & Gonick, 1996; Watts & Serrano-García, 2003). Moreover, these different forms of exclusion sometimes intersect, such that some disadvantaged people experience double or triple jeopardy. For example, black feminists have written about how black women have to overcome both white and male supremacy, and heterosexual supremacy in some cases (Hill Collins, 1991; hooks, 2002). While invited contributors go into much more depth and specificity about the problems facing women, minorities, people who have experienced unemployment, poor people, gay, lesbian, bisexual and transgendered people, and people with physical and mental health disabilities in Part V of this book, here we provide a broad overview of the problems that are created for these populations when the principle of inclusion is ignored.

Psychological oppression is the internalized view of self as negative, as unworthy of social and community resources (Bartky, 1990; Prilleltensky, 2003). African-American psychologist Kenneth Clark described the depth of psychological oppression in African-Americans in his book *Dark Ghetto*.

> Human beings who are forced to live under ghetto conditions and whose daily experience tells them that almost nowhere in society are they respected and granted the ordinary dignity and courtesy according to others will, as a matter of course, begin to doubt their own worth. Since every human being depends upon his [sic] cumulative experiences with others for clues as to how he should view and value himself, children who are consistently rejected understandably begin to question and doubt whether they, their family, and their group really deserve no more respect from the larger society than they receive. These doubts become the seeds of a pernicious self- and group-hatred, the Negro's complex and debilitating prejudice against himself. The preoccupation of many Negroes with hair straightening, skin bleachers, and the like illustrates this tragic aspect of American racial prejudice – Negroes have come to believe in their own inferiority. (Clark, 1965, pp. 63–4)

Psychological dynamics of oppression entail surplus powerlessness, low self-esteem, belief in a just world, learned helplessness, conformity/compliance and obedience to authority (Prilleltensky & Gonick, 1996). It is little wonder that people who are subject to exclusion and discrimination come to devalue themselves when one considers the countless ways in which other people and society as a whole send messages of devaluation. Often dominant narratives about disadvantaged people take the form of self-fulfilling prophecies, in which individuals conform to the low expectations that others hold of them. As Clark (1965) stated: 'A key component of the deprivation which afflicts ghetto children is that generally their teachers do not expect them to learn' (p. 132).

This psychological oppression arises out of a political context that can be conceptualized at different levels of analysis. Oppression is experienced both in the context of interpersonal relationships in the community and in the broader social context. A distinction has often been made between overt acts of discrimination at the relational level and more covert acts that are indicative of systemic or institutional discrimination. For example, Carmichael and Hamilton make this distinction in their discussion of racism and white power.

> Racism is both overt and covert. It takes two, closely related forms: individual whites acting against individual blacks, and acts by the total white community against the black community. We call these individual racism and institutional racism. The first consists of overt acts by individuals, which cause death, injury, or the violent destruction of property. This type can be recorded by television cameras; it can frequently be observed in the process of commission. The second type is less overt, far more subtle, less identifiable in terms of specific individuals committing the acts. But it is no less destructive of human life. The second type originates in the operation of established and respected forces in the society, and thus receives far less public condemnation. (Carmichael & Hamilton, 1967, p. 4)

For example, consider how women are excluded and oppressed. At the interpersonal level, there is abundant research demonstrating that violence, sexual harassment, and sexual abuse and assault of girls and women are widespread (Bond, 1995).

Furthermore, violence and assault are nearly always accompanied by verbal and emotional abuse, with women being subjected to degrading and damaging language that assaults their character and integrity. Violence is but one mechanism that is used by men to silence women (Reinharz, 1994); it is part of a larger pattern of systemic oppression of women that is rooted in social, economic, political, religious and ideological systems (Albee, 1996b; Albee & Perry, 1998). El-Mouelhy (1992) has described the practices of son preference, malnutrition, economic blackmail, bride burning, female circumcision and sexual enslavement that are used to contain women in many countries in the world. Moreover, sexism, like other forms of exclusion, is experienced by women on an everyday basis (Bond, 1999; Smith, 1990). The dynamics of sexism and patriarchal structures are elaborated on in Chapter 18.

What is the Value-base of Inclusion?

The principle of inclusion is based on the values of relativity and respect for diversity. Vive la difference! These values challenge the traditional paradigms in psychology that 'adopt an implicit faith that the single standard of white, middle-class society is, on an absolute basis, superior to all others' (Rappaport, 1977, p. 22). Dominant groups have constructed differences among people along some dimension, such as skin colour, equated those differences as deficits of the supposedly inferior group, explained those deficits in terms of biological or cultural factors, and used this narrative to legitimize mechanisms of exclusion of the subordinate group (Teo, 1999). The values of relativity and respect for diversity, espoused by CP, challenge this view.

> Community psychology … is an attempt to support every person's right to be different without risk of suffering material and psychological sanctions … Rather than trying to fit everyone into a single way of life, the community psychologist must become an agent of the local community. This will often require the community psychologist to work toward providing socially marginal people with the resources, the power, and the control over their own lives, which is necessary for a society of diversity rather than of conformity.' (Rappaport, 1977, pp. 1 and 23)

The recognition that there is diversity within diversity is another important insight of this perspective.

How can Inclusion be Implemented?

There are two broad viewpoints regarding the best way to promote inclusion. These two viewpoints differ with respect to the construction of similarity/difference. One approach minimizes the differences between groups, the beta bias approach, while the other maximizes the differences between groups, the alpha bias approach (Hare-Mustin & Maracek, 1988). Hare-Mustin and Maracek (1988) suggest that research on gender that is driven by the beta bias approach emphasizes the similarities of women and men. Another example of beta bias is the construct of androgyny, which integrates supposedly typical female and male qualities. According to this viewpoint, individuals, regardless of differences, are seen as people first; the focus is on the person, while characteristics such as gender, race or ability are relegated to the background. This 'gender-blind' or 'colour-blind' approach is guided by humanistic valuing of the person. Programs for children from different ethnoracial groups that emphasize similarities are an example of how this viewpoint can be put into action. Such programs have been shown to reduce prejudicial attitudes and ignorance of groups that are typically the target of prejudice (Williams & Berry, 1991). Emphasizing similarity rather than difference is one way of building community and inclusion.

In contrast, the alpha approach focuses on differences. There are at least two different ways in which differences can be constructed. Mukherjee (1992) and Watts (1992) have made a distinction between multicultural (cultural pluralistic) and anti-racist approaches to diversity. These two broad approaches can be applied to many facets of diversity, not just race and culture. The former approach is one that is culture-specific or population-specific and promotes an affirmative diversity (Trickett, Watts & Birman, 1993). Affirmative diversity means that the uniqueness, special qualities, strengths and positive characteristics of the group are emphasized. For example, feminist psychologists have argued that women place special emphasis on relationships, caring and connection (Jordan et al., 1991). The psychology of women, gay and lesbian psychology, the psychology of disability, and ethnoracial psychologies were all developed by psychologists from these backgrounds as an alternative to mainstream approaches which constructed the differences of these groups from dominant social groups as defects (Trickett et al., 1993). Moreover, these population-specific psychologies are a reflection of the larger pride movements (for example black pride, gay pride) within society, which strive to broaden social standards about what is not just acceptable, but desirable.

This approach has been implemented particularly in the context of multiculturalism. Overall this approach focuses primarily on culture and towards the goal of educating people about minority groups, celebrating cultural differences and strengths, and developing multicultural organizations and policies that reflect and support diversity. Heritage language programs and culturally sensitive interventions are examples of this approach at the individual and small group levels of analysis (James & Prilleltensky, 2002; Mukherjee, 1992). The development and control of alternative systems and services by a particular ethnoracial group, such as aboriginal people (Connors & Maidman, 2001), reflects how this approach can be implemented at organizational and community levels. At a broader societal level, Canada's policy of multiculturalism stands as policy initiative that strives to promote cultural pride and ethnoracial identity in contrast to 'melting pot' policies and ideologies (Naidoo & Edwards, 1991). In this regard, it has been found that the well-being of immigrants and refugees is related to their mode of acculturation. The pattern of acculturation that results in the least stress is that in which individuals retain a strong identity with their indigenous culture and strive to integrate into the host culture (maintaining a balance between the old and the new) (Williams & Berry, 1991). Thus, policies of multiculturalism are important for inclusion (see Chapter 17 for an elaboration of these issues).

The second beta bias approach to promoting inclusion, anti-racism (anti-sexism, and so on), focuses more on differences in power (Mukherjee, 1992; Watts, 1992). The goals of the anti-racist approach are the empowerment of disenfranchised groups and overcoming systemic barriers to participation and access to valued resources. This approach strives to broaden the opportunities for excluded groups. Whereas the multicultural approach is more liberal-reformist, the anti-racist approach with its emphasis on power is more transformative. As Mukherjee (1992) stated:

> Quite simply, the purpose of anti-racist change is to move our educational institutions from 'exclusive clubs' to 'inclusive organizations' in which: (a) there will be equity of results in academic achievement, curriculum, assessment and placement, staffing and community/school relations for all races and cultures; (b) there will be shifts in individual behaviours and attitudes; and (c) there will be willingness and ability on the part of everyone to recognize and challenge racism wherever it arises. In short, anti-racist education is not about equality of opportunity, sensitivity and dealing with individual acts of racism alone. More fundamentally, it is about voice, representation and participation in all aspects of the educational system for people who have been traditionally excluded from the curriculum and the institution; it is about challenging those dominant ideas, beliefs and assumptions that support such exclusion; and it's about actively confronting those individual behaviours and attitudes which perpetuate those dominant ideas, beliefs and assumptions. (p. 145)

Like the multicultural approach, the anti-racist approach can be implemented at different levels. At the individual and small group levels, consciousness-raising groups and programs for disadvantaged people can be implemented to develop critical thinking, a positive identity and social action. An example of this is a program for young African-American men, which links consciousness-raising and sociopolitical development with African-American spirituality (Watts et al., 1999). Consciousness-raising groups for women are another example.

At the community and societal levels, inclusion can be promoted through participation in social movement organizations (Morris & Mueller, 1992). The guiding vision of social movement organizations is a society free of racism, sexism, heterosexism, poverty, violence and environmental degradation, a society that celebrates diversity, shares the wealth, and practises equality, peace, sustainability and preservation of the natural environment. Often the goal of social movement organizations is to change social policies. To promote inclusion at the societal level, policies that strive to create equity (for example pay equity for women, affirmative action) are the end results towards which the activities of social movement organizations are directed.

Community psychologists can work in solidarity with social movement organizations through value-based partnerships to promote inclusion (Nelson, Prilleltensky & MacGillivary, 2001). Such partnerships are challenging for professionals and relatively privileged groups. In genuine or authentic partnerships, those who are disadvantaged have voice and can name their experiences, while those who are advantaged listen, learn, and validate the stories and experiences of those who are disadvantaged. People who are privileged take responsibility for the negative impacts of their actions on disadvantaged people, whether they are intentional or not (Bond, 1999). There is also a reduction of the power imbalance in the relationship between advantaged and disadvantaged groups with disadvantaged groups exerting more power, and advantaged groups having reduced power.

Value-based partnerships between advantaged and disadvantaged people are not linear or rational; rather they are often emotion-laden, touch people's blind spots, and can be conflictual and messy (Bond, 1999; Nelson, Prilleltensky & MacGillivary, 2001). Church (1995) speaks of 'working together across differences'; Lord and Church (1998) talk about 'partnership shock'; and Bond (1999) uses the term 'connected disruption' to describe these partnership processes. As we noted earlier, it is difficult for advantaged people to understand that they are privileged and to become accountable for that privilege. However, feminist community psychologists have taken the lead in showing how reflexive and participatory approaches can be undertaken in partnership with disadvantaged groups to promote inclusion (Mulvey et al., 2000). For example, as noted above, New Zealand community psychologist Ingrid Huygens has provided examples of partnerships between dominant groups and disenfranchised groups to eliminate racism (Huygens, 1996a) and violence against women (Huygens, 1996b).

What are the Limitations of Inclusion?

The central issue with which the principle of inclusion is concerned is that of diversity. As we have seen, one can approach the issue of diversity in one of two ways, maximizing differences among people (alpha bias) or minimizing differences among people (beta bias). Each approach has its limitations.

As we noted in the previous section, there are two approaches that reflect an alpha bias approach. One emphasizes the unique strengths and special qualities of diverse groups, while the other emphasizes differences in power among groups. There are limitations to both of these approaches. While the former approach is valuable in its emphasis on pride and the recovery of positive identities, a limitation of this approach is that it tends to ignore differences in power. On the other hand, the latter approach is valuable in highlighting inequities in power, but limited in its dismissal of the importance of the special qualities of diverse groups. In many ways, the tension of these two approaches mirrors the tension between the principles of power and community, which we discussed in the previous chapter.

There is also a danger in minimizing differences (the beta bias approach). As Hare-Mustin and Maracek (1988) point out, the beta bias approach overlooks social context and obscures existing power differences. Treating everyone as if they are the same, when they are not, can lead to approaches that strive to adjust the subordinate group to that of the dominant group ('she's as good as any man') and/or fail to address the lack of power and resources of the subordinate group. If we are all the same, then no one needs any special supports or consideration.

> Women and men typically have different access to economic and social resources, and their actions have different social meanings and consequences. Beta bias can be seen in recent social policies and legislation that try to provide equal benefits for men and women, such as comparable parental leave and no-fault divorce. Beta bias can also be seen in educational and therapeutic programs that ignore aspects of the context. They groom women for personal or professional success by providing training in what are deemed 'male' behaviours or skills, such as assertiveness, authoritative speech patterns, or 'male' managerial styles. Such programs make the presumption that a certain manner of speaking or acting will elicit the same reaction regardless of the sex of the actor. (Hare-Mustin & Maracek, 1988, p. 458)

In their discussion of alpha bias and beta bias, Hare-Mustin and Maracek (1988) argued that the 'true' nature of different constructions of gender (whether men and women are similar or different) cannot be known. Rather, they argue that what is important are the meaning and consequences of those different constructions. Similarly, Rappaport (1981) has asserted that most social problems are paradoxical in nature, meaning that there are often two equally compelling perspectives that can be used to understand the problem. Moreover, Rappaport suggested that community psychologists should be wary of pursuing one-sided solutions to social problems, because one approach, by itself, is incomplete. Alternatively, he recommended dialectical thinking, considering multiple solutions to complex social problems. Consistent with Rappaport's argument, we have noted that both alpha bias and beta bias approaches to inclusion have strengths and limitations. The challenge for community psychologists working in partnership with diverse and disadvantaged groups is to find some balance between the different approaches towards the goal of inclusion.

Chapter Summary

In this chapter, we introduced the concepts of commitment, accountability and inclusion. We argued that commitment and accountability are meta-values necessary for the promotion of the values that underlie CP. Inclusion is a closely related concept which suggests that the many forms of diversity existing in communities around the world should be embraced, rather than labelled as defective. Commitment, accountability and inclusion are tools for bringing people together to develop relationships and ways of living that are more respectful, just and compassionate.

COMMENTARY: Living up to Community Psychology Goals and Values *B. Ortiz-Torres*

Many times in my career teaching community psychology I have heard this question from my students: 'And how do you do that?' They refer to my constant reminder of the need to live up to our discipline's values and goals. Many times they have told me that my answer sounds like a declaration of faith but that they need more specifics. This chapter constitutes a concrete demonstration of what it means to be guided by the values of the discipline. But, be careful – this is not a cook book; this is a sophisticated analysis, well grounded in theory, as well as in a profound reflection of our goals and values.

Nelson and Prilleltensky take an in-depth look into the art of being a community psychologist rather than at the 'science' of CP. Ingrained in this art is the imperative to assume the political responsibility of our profession.

The authors make us face what seems to be logical but is only implicit in our professional culture: if we, as community psychologists, are not accountable, then there is no need to stress

the role of values in the discipline. Although it has always seemed apparent, the relationship between commitment and accountability has not been discussed enough within our discipline. Nelson and Prilleltensky have done a great job specifying and showing how accountability is a necessary consequence of professing a specific set of values, since these do not have the inherent quality of 'accountability'. Not only is this relationship made explicit, but concrete answers are provided to the question: 'to whom are we accountable?' In this work there is no room for confusion about who our 'clients' are, or for whom we work – it is clearly spelt out to whom we should be committed.

Accountability is a crucial issue when we are faced with the forces of isolation and individualism so dominant in our contexts. I feel that, fortunately, in academic settings we are continuously under the scrutiny of our students who constantly check whether we are living up to our discourse and rhetoric.

The present analysis of values, accountability and inclusion has an underlying appreciation for divergence and balance that should help in understanding complex issues. This is particularly true in the discussion of power and collective values. In adopting this approach, the authors are just doing what they preach: promoting divergent and complex analyses (Rappaport, 1981).

We are faced here with exercises and questions that are not typically presented in text books. The authors invite students to engage in some soul-searching, and what I find most interesting is that this is not proposed as an isolated process, but there is a call to make it relational (see Warmup Exercise: 'Compare your actions and reasons with other students and friends'). The subjective language used by the authors should facilitate the reflection with which students may want to engage. There is a constant questioning, an appeal to the student to confront typical dilemmas faced by community psychologists. The authors have been able to put themselves in the readers' shoes and walk them through this process of analysis, reflection and introspection. Nothing is left loose in this discussion, we find very specific ways to implement inclusion; we always see a practical component.

There is one potential risk in engaging in this reflection: students may end up thinking that only extraordinary or exceptional individuals can become community psychologists. The challenge is not to get discouraged but to be clear about the need for students to explore their values and aspirations and make sure they are compatible with those of the discipline.

This chapter covers research and action with a great variety of exemplars of both. However, the emphasis is on action and the authors are constantly alluding to tools and vehicles that facilitate an action orientation. The templates included in the tables are excellent; they have the potential for structuring and organizing material not only for students but for professionals as well. A valuable quality of these templates is the integration of diverse levels of analysis.

According to my reading of this chapter, the link between commitment and accountability on the one hand and inclusion on the other is not readily apparent. From my perspective, inclusion is the main vehicle for action. Inclusion is the vehicle that helps us translate values into action and good intentions into accountability. Therefore, I disagree with Nelson and Prilleltensky when they claim that values and accountability are the main vehicles for action. Values and accountability are guiding principles that may or may not be enacted in specific professional practices and behaviours. They do not, however, have an inherent action component. Inclusion, in my mind, does have this quality.

I did not find the term 'validity' particularly appealing in the context of this chapter, probably because it reminds me of measurement and psychometrics – two domains from which I have distanced myself in my practice as a community psychologist. 'Validity' suggests recognition by those who prefer social systems to stay unaltered or unchanged, and I am sure this is not what the authors value and strive for. I do not believe CP should prove to be valid, but to be purposeful, useful and necessary in the psychopolitical domain.

I am concerned that the reader might be left with the impression that subjectivity is only possible at the individual level – a likely interpretation of the distinction Nelson and Prilleltensky make between psychological and political factors. The collective can also be subjective. In fact, this is the realm in which the relational nature of subjectivity is more evident. Furthermore, CP has been developing methods and strategies to be able to capture subjective expressions of extra-individual interactions (van Uchelen, 2000).

While painful, the process of reflection and insight found in this chapter is crucial for our discipline. The more we do this kind of work, the closer we get to a shared vision of what CP should be.

---

cont'd

inclusion policies and practices that support diversity and give voice and choice to individuals, groups and communities which have been traditionally marginalized

individual racism discriminatory acts or gestures by individuals

institutionalized racism policies, practices and norms embedded in cultural patterns and social structures that perpetuate racial discrimination

meta-values a special category of values that makes sure other values are enacted and respected

multiculturalism an approach to dealing with diversity that affirms the unique value of different groups

psychopolitical validity the degree to which research and action take into account power dynamics operating in psychological and political domains and in the interaction between them

representation inclusion and participation of groups with varying degrees of power in decision-making processes affecting their personal and collective lives

social exclusion experience of living at the margins of society, often due to discriminatory policies and practices of groups or governments against people who are different from the mainstream

transformational related to structural and social change

■ **RESOURCES** ■

1. Free the Children is an organization started by Craig Keilburger when he was a young teenager. This Canadian boy travelled the world to learn about child labour and children's rights. His organization is an example of commitment to a cause and accountability to his stakeholders, the children who need help. Visit their website at http://www.freethechildren.org/.

2. Students like you can make a difference. In the US, students have made a partnership with the labour movement to improve wages of workers and to stop exploitation in sweatshops. Students show commitment to this cause and get support from established organizations. Check this out at http://www.aflcio.org/articles/studentactivism/.

3. Wyatt Resources helps workers in the public sector with information on various aspects of their work. They have an excellent website on applied ethics that can complement many of the arguments raised in this chapter. Visit them at http://www.wyattresources.net/ethics.html.

4. Watch the video *Hollow Water*, produced by the National Film Board of Canada (48 minutes), http://www.nfb.ca/. This a powerful video about diversity, power, oppression and liberation experienced by one First Nation community in Manitoba, Canada. Torn apart by years of abuse and struggling to confront their past, this documentary charts a moving journey of healing and change and through an alternative approach to justice grounded in spirituality, community and traditional native teachings and practices.

5. A group of community and critical psychologists created a coalition to be more accountable to the values of justice and equality: PysACT (Psychologists Acting with Conscience Together) organizes collective actions that psychologists can take to promote values for personal, relational and collective well-being. Visit www.psyact.org.

Part III

Tools for Action

What can community psychologists do to promote liberation and well-being through social, community, organizational, small group and individual interventions? This is the main question concerning Part III of the book. To suggest useful and meaningful action, we have to know the level of analysis and target of intervention. We begin with the big picture and work our way down to the smallest unit of analysis – the individual. The four chapters will make it clear, hopefully, that we have to target multiple levels of intervention in our efforts to promote liberation and well-being. Even if we are limited in our ability to act on multiple domains, we have to insure that our actions promote synergy across domains.

Chapter 7 provides an overview of the philosophy, roles and skills of community psychologists as change agents. Unlike professional schools that propose rigid distinctions among the personal, the professional and the political, we argue that such distinction is untenable and even incongruent with the values of CP. As we note in the chapter, CP begins at home. To exert a positive influence, community psychologists can act as insiders or outsiders. Insiders work in organizations and push for beneficial changes there. Outsiders put pressure on organizations from the periphery. There is plenty to change in society and its institutions to justify effective roles as either insiders or outsiders; but whatever role you choose, it's important to distinguish between ameliorative and transformative work. Amelioration refers to changes that do not challenge fundamental structures of injustice and inequality, whereas transformation refers to structural changes that go to the root of the problem. Not all of us may be able to engage in transformative work. That's understandable, but it's important not to deceive ourselves thinking we are making fundamental changes when we are not.

To promote liberation and well-being, either as an insider or an outsider, a community psychologist requires a set of skills. Chapter 7 introduces individual skills (effective communication, consultation, leadership), group skills (facilitation, conflict resolution, organizational development) and community skills (community development, advocacy, mobilization, partnership building). These skills, further elaborated in the remainder of the section, can be applied in a variety of human, health, social, alternative and social change settings. To put the skills into context, we introduce a cycle of praxis consisting of vision, needs, cultural context and action.

Chapter 8 is about social interventions. We don't take anything for granted. We question the values and assumptions of social interventions, and we critique their limitations. But, shortcomings notwithstanding, there is little doubt that social interventions have the power to influence millions of people through the actions of governments and social movements. The chapter is divided into two main sections: What community psychologists can do in government and what they can do in social movements (SMOs) and non-government organizations (NGOs). Within government, community psychologists can promote legislation, policies and programs that invest in human development, promote equality, and protect natural resources and public institutions.

In the second part of Chapter 8 we identify roles for community psychologists within SMOs and NGOs: coalition builders, networkers, organizational leaders, researchers and writers, program evaluators, speakers, activists and others. These various roles help in recruitment, public education campaigns, protests, strategic planning and political efficacy overall. The chapter offers a wide-ranging menu of options for community psychologists to act as agents of change in society at large.

Chapter 9 deals with interventions at the community and organizational levels. We connect the two because most community work happens in, and through, organizational settings. We apply the lenses of amelioration and transformation to examine the effects of community and organizational interventions. At the organizational level we ask what community psychologists can do to promote both amelioration and transformation within the organization and within the community served by the institution. Our assumption is that stagnant organizations cannot promote change in the community. Furthermore, organizations that do not promote the well-being of workers cannot be effective in promoting the well-being of citizens. We review the characteristics of empowered and empowering organizations and identify roles for community psychologists that will enable them to bring about the desired qualities. It is in this context that we introduce emotional intelligence competencies and draw their implications for transformational work.

At the community level, we concentrate on the role of community psychologists as partnership makers, change makers and knowledge makers. These three roles capture, we believe, the main tasks and interests of our profession. A partnership maker embodies seven qualities: inclusive host, visionary, asset seeker, listener conceptualizer, pragmatic partner, research partner, and trend setter.

The final chapter of this section, Chapter 10, addresses the dynamics involved in small group and individual interventions. In keeping with the theme of accountability introduced in earlier chapters, we ask how we can change ourselves, others and society when we are very much part of the system that resists change. We also struggle with the tension between ameliorative and transformative work. Is it fair to expect people who suffer exploitation and oppression to become activists when they are hurting? Is it fair not to expect them to do this and treat them only as victims? We offer some paths towards resolution of these dilemmas. In doing so, we articulate the skills that a community psychologist would want to rely on in individual and small group work. Our framework for this chapter combines the seven qualities introduced in Chapter 9 with stages of change. We believe that people don't jump towards personal or social change. People require a warm-up period prior to committing to any kind of lasting change. Therefore, we strongly suggest being in tune with people's readiness for change. Once a change has been accomplished, we must endeavour to make it sustainable and to disseminate it to other communities of interest.

7

An Overview of Community Psychology Interventions

Warm-up Exercise

In the field of education, much has been written about school improvement, school change, and educational reform. Based on your extensive experience in schools, make a short list of a few ways that schools and education could be improved.

After you have made this list, try to cast aside all your assumptions about schools and education and think again, a little harder this time, about how schools and education could be radically restructured. Make a short list of some more fundamental changes in education.

Compare the two lists. How do they differ? How hard was it to make the second list? Why?

The goals of this chapter are for you to learn about:

- the community psychologist as an agent of social change
- the differences between ameliorative and transformative interventions
- different settings for community psychology (CP) interventions.

The core concepts and framework that we introduce in this chapter serve as a foundation for the remaining chapters in this section, in which we go into more depth about interventions at the social (Chapter 8), organizational, community (Chapter 9), small group and individual (Chapter 10) levels of analysis.

The Community Psychologist as an Agent of Social Change: Connecting the Personal, Political and Professional

In this section, we discuss the role of the community psychologist as an agent of social change. However clear we are as community psychologists about our values, the world of action is one that is complicated and rife with conflicts, contradictions and ethical dilemmas. When we try to change the status quo, we inevitably run up against many obstacles and much resistance, including our own blind spots and weaknesses. Creating social change is a struggle. Our values are constantly challenged in the intervention work that we do. Sometimes we experience value conflicts and have to decide which values are most important in a particular context. At other times, we have to choose between many different ways of implementing our values.

The Making of a Community Psychologist

We believe that being a community psychologist is a question of identity, a definition of who we are and who we want to be. Each community psychologist is a whole person. As whole people, our personal, political and professional selves are intertwined. Through consciousness-raising about social issues and analysis of power dynamics, community psychologists come to connect the personal and the political parts of their identity, as feminists have asserted for some time. One cannot be a community psychologist in one's public life at work and then go home to one's private life and 'turn off' the values that inform one's work as a community psychologist. Rather the personal and political, the private and public, and the professional and citizen parts of the community psychologist come together through a journey of personal growth, empowerment and political awareness.

Moreover, each community psychologist has a unique personal journey that brought her or him to the field. As Ira Goldenberg (1978) observed some time ago:

> Social interventionists are not born, they are made ... The making of a social interventionist can best be understood in terms of a process through which certain classes of events become the experiential ground for subsequent social actions which, if not defined as 'deviant,' are acknowledged to fall outside the mainstream of expected or anticipated behavior. The process itself, which is rarely smooth or predictable, is punctuated by specific circumstances which are no less socially salient than they are personally significant. (pp. 29 and 34)

Goldenberg (1978) goes on to note that while there are seldom dramatic, life changing events in the biographies of social interventionists, each person experiences some critical event or events that push her or him along the road to CP and social intervention. He then relates several critical events in his life that shaped him into a social interventionist. Training in CP is a process of socialization into the identity of a community psychologist. Students in training are provided with the analytical tools to make sense of critical incidents in their lives and current field placements in community settings. Personal reflection in the context of group support facilitates the making of a community psychologist.

Like Goldenberg (1978) and others (for example, Sloan, 2000a), we believe that community psychologists need to be reflexively aware of their values, experiences and power, and to relate their personal biographies. Our values and social analysis are not fixed entities, but rather constantly emerging perspectives on both where we are currently and where we want to be. Reflexivity is an important antidote to arrogance, dogma and believing that we have the right answer. The point is that personal, political and professional growth are ongoing processes, not end states.

Reflexivity is necessary to unpack personal privilege (see Chapter 22, Box 22.1). Striving to understand personal privilege and developing accountability mechanisms to oppressed groups are ways to reveal blind spots and promote further growth. An example that illustrates this point is male privilege. The two of us, Geoff and Isaac, grew up in sexist, patriarchal societies, in which many privileges were and are bestowed upon us, simply by virtue of our gender. While we believe that we have come a long way, 25 years ago the two of us were undoubtedly blind to many of the issues faced by women in society and in our own field of CP (Bond & Mulvey, 2000). It is painful to realize that you have been guilty of sexist thoughts and acts and of colluding with social systems that were and are oppressive to women. This is why consciousness-raising and reflexivity need to be ongoing processes for community psychologists.

Finally, we want to make clear that connecting the personal and political comes through our relationships with others. It is important to build a support network and sense of community and to have places where we can be nurtured, sustained and challenged in our growth as community psychologists. Community psychologists need a peer group of like-minded people from psychology, other academic disciplines and the community, committed to social justice and social change. As feminist writers have pointed out, the growth and empowerment process is relational in nature. Moreover, we need to be genuinely supportive of one another and appreciative of our strengths. There is a danger that personal growth can be stifled if the group climate is one of competition and evaluation, focusing on who is the most 'pure' or righteous in the enactment of their values.

Can I Make a Living Disrupting the Status Quo?: Community Psychologists as Insiders and Outsiders

If CP is more of a social movement than a profession (Rappaport, 1981), we must ask how community psychologists are going to make a living. Who is going to hire and pay them to disrupt the status quo? Not surprisingly, community psychologists find employment based on their professional credentials rather than their values or political beliefs. Most often doctoral-level community psychologists are hired to work in university, research, or government policy settings, and masters-level and doctoral-level community psychologists work in a variety of human service settings, including health, education, mental health, child welfare and children's mental health, counselling, and so on. While these settings may hire community psychologists, they will nevertheless resist efforts by community psychologists and others to change the status quo. In a previous publication, we identified some ways in which community psychologists working as insiders in a variety of these settings can challenge the status quo and strive to shift the paradigm of practice (Prilleltensky & Nelson, 2002). Program managers, teachers/professors, and researchers can work within their organizations to promote social change. There are always dangers and concerns about 'rocking the boat', but many settings provide at least some latitude for change.

We also believe that there are other settings that might be more congruent with the community psychologist as a social change agent. Seldom do we see or hear about community psychologists working in labour unions, international non-government organizations (NGOs) that focus on social justice issues, or social movement organizations, but we believe that these social change organizations are ripe for partnerships with CP trainees and graduates (Prilleltensky & Nelson, 1997). CP training programs could pursue partnerships with these more non-traditional settings to promote more of a social change orientation.

Community psychologists can also work outside the system for social change. Those who work independently, or for one setting, can be hired to work as external evaluators, consultants, or researchers for another setting. They can often have considerable influence in working for social change in these outsider roles. There are also situations in which community psychologists are not invited by a setting but work as unsolicited interventionists. In other words, the community psychologist approaches a setting or community to partner on some project or intervention. Finally, community psychologists can work in their private lives as outside change agents. As citizens, they can join and participate in a variety of social change organizations and activities.

The Community Psychologist as a Professional

While community psychologists work collaboratively with community groups and de-emphasize the 'expert' role, they are trained professionals who have a set of core competencies. These competencies include: values, social ethics, and the ability to think critically; knowledge of CP theory, research and action; and a variety of community practice skills (Murray et al., 2001).

The knowledge and skill base of CP is rooted in values, social ethics and critical thinking. The values frame community interventions. Critical thinking encompasses the ability to: identify the often hidden assumptions that underlie community intervention; examine how arguments are constructed and based on different paradigmatic assumptions; analyse the role of power in community interventions; and reflect on how one's social position, including race, gender and social class, affects the construction of different intervention approaches (Murray et al., 2001).

Community psychologists must also have a broad base of knowledge related to community intervention. An understanding of CP intervention theory and intervention theories from other disciplines is essential. This includes knowledge about critical, ecological analyses of social problems and theory related to prevention, social change, alternative settings, citizen participation, community and organization development and social policy. As Glidewell (1977) pointed out many years ago, community psychologists must also have an understanding of different intervention approaches and their assumptions, knowledge about different intervention strategies, from macro social to small group, and research regarding their effectiveness.

Finally, it is not enough to be knowledgeable about community intervention. Community psychologists must also have applied intervention skills. Julnes, Pang, Takemoto-Chock, Speidel and Tharp (1987) argued that skills in conceptualization, intervention, evaluation and description are important for community psychologists. Similarly, Lykes and Hellstedt (1987) stated that community psychologists need to develop skills as participant–observers, evaluators, intervenors–change agents and planners–designers. More recently, Thomas et al. (1997) proposed that there are three broad sets of skills that cut across the different roles noted by Lykes and Hellstedt (1987) and Julnes et al. (1987). These include: (a) technical skills (for example skills in grant writing, research, evaluation), (b) collaboration skills (for example consultation, networking, partnering) and (c) personal-effectiveness skills (for example communication and interpersonal skills).

Elsewhere, we have suggested that the skill set for critical community psychologists can be conceptualized ecologically at multiple levels of analysis (Prilleltensky & Nelson, 2002). At the individual level, community psychologists need skills in communication, assertiveness, consultation with individuals, leadership and the ability to be open to personal growth and consciousness-raising. At the level of the group and organization, skills in group process facilitation, group intervention and organization development (including visioning, team-building, program and intervention planning) are important for CP. At the community and societal levels, key CP skills include working in solidarity with disadvantaged people, community development, community organizing, networking, coalition-building, advocacy and influencing social policy. All of these important skills require professional training in applied settings. The need for supervised, process-oriented and competency-based training in diverse field placements, and practical workplace experiences in applied settings has been underscored by many different community psychologists (Bennett & Hallman, 1987; Julnes et al., 1987; Lykes & Hellstedt, 1987; Thomas et al., 1997).

Summary

In this section, we have discussed a number of issues relating to the community psychologist as an agent of social change. Becoming a community psychologist involves more than acquiring professional credentials. It is a process of identity development in which the community psychologist develops a self-critical awareness in the context of his or her life experiences in the larger social and political milieu. This identity development involves connecting the personal, political and professional parts of oneself. We noted different ways in which community psychologists can function as insiders and outsiders, disrupting the status quo and creating social change. While few settings will employ people as social change agents, we discussed some possibilities that permit community psychologists to make a living and bring about change. Finally, we provided an overview of some of the core competencies and skills that characterize community psychologists as professionals.

The Focus of Community Psychology Interventions: Amelioration vs Transformation

In this section we examine the focus of CP interventions, making a distinction between ameliorative and transformative interventions (Prilleltensky & Nelson, 1997). Ameliorative interventions are those that aim to promote well-being. Transformative interventions, while also concerned with the promotion of well-being, focus on changing power relationships and striving to eliminate oppression. Community psychologists have also used the systems theory concepts of first-order and second-order change to capture this distinction (Bennett, 1987; Rappaport, 1977; Seidman & Rappaport, 1986). First-order change, amelioration, creates change within a system, while second-order change, transformation, strives to change the system and its assumptions. Ameliorative and transformative interventions can be contrasted along several dimensions, as is shown in Table 7.1.

Framing the Issues

How social issues are framed often dictates what interventions will be used to address those issues (Seidman & Rappaport, 1986). Ameliorative interventions tend to frame issues as problems and as technical matters that can be resolved through rational–empirical problem-solving (Sarason, 1978). Power dynamics are ignored or minimized in this formulation. For example, one might examine the issue of teenage pregnancy by studying its prevalence and the negative life outcomes that follow (for example failure to complete education or gain employment, mental health, drug and alcohol problems, and so on), and the risk and protective factors that help to explain the prevalence of this problem. Poverty may be constructed as a risk factor, but there is no class analysis or analysis of power dynamics that challenges existing social structures. Programs to help prevent teenage pregnancy through increased knowledge of birth control, or support groups or educational programs are developed to address this problem and promote the well-being of the mothers and their babies.

Transformative interventions, on the other hand, frame issues in terms of oppression and inequities in power and emphasize the strengths of people rather than their deficiencies. While research and problem-solving are used to address the issue, the overall focus is on liberation from oppression and changing the social systems that give rise to teenage pregnancy. Gender, race and class are examined as intersections of oppression, and vulnerable young women are engaged in a process of consciousness-raising about themselves and their political reality. The larger macro context of global capitalism is seen as overarching specific risk and protective factors at the micro and meso levels of analysis. The increasing numbers of women living in poverty with few real opportunities for economic advancement and the correspondingly increased wealth of a small segment of the population (both corporations and individuals) are examined in relation to the problem of teenage pregnancy to understand the 'causes of the causes'.

Table 7.1 Distinguishing characteristics of ameliorative vs transformative interventions

Characteristics	Ameliorative	Transformative
Framing of issues and problems	Issues and problems are framed as technical matters that can be resolved through rational–empirical problem-solving; power dynamics are ignored. Scientific problem-solving is in the foreground; power is in the background.	Issues and problems are framed in terms of oppression and inequities in power that require liberalizing solutions, as well as research and problem-solving. Power, oppression and liberation share the foreground with scientific problem-solving.
Values	Since issues and problems are framed in technical terms, the value emphasis of the intervention is often ignored. However, the values of holism, health, and caring and compassion are implicitly given the most emphasis. Values are in the background.	Values play a central role in the conceptualization of the intervention. While the values of holism, health, and caring and compassion may be present, greater emphasis is placed on the values of self-determination, participation, social justice, respect for diversity and accountability to oppressed groups. Values are in the foreground.
Levels of analysis	Issues and problems are examined in terms of an ecological perspective that is attuned to multiple levels of analysis. However, interventions are often targeted at improving personal and relational well-being. Intervention at the personal and relational levels is in the foreground.	Issues and problems are examined in terms of power dynamics that are conceptualized as occurring at multiple levels of analysis. Intervention occurs at all levels of analysis, but there is concerted effort to improve collective well-being. The collective level of analysis is in the foreground, even for interventions at the personal and relational levels.
Prevention focus	Prevention is aimed primarily at the enhancement of protective factors, including skills, self-esteem and support systems.	Prevention is aimed primarily at the reduction of systemic risk factors, including, racism, sexism and poverty.
Desired outcomes	The primary desired outcome is enhanced well-being, which is conceptualized apolitically and narrowly at the individual level of analysis. Specific outcomes include: the promotion of individual well-being, which includes self-esteem, independence and competence; the prevention of psychosocial problems in living; and the enhancement of social support. Outcomes at the individual level of analysis are in the foreground.	The primary desired outcome is enhanced well-being, which is conceptualized in terms of power at multiple levels of analysis. Specific outcomes include: increased control, choice, self-esteem, competence, independence, political awareness, political rights and a positive identity; enhanced socially supportive relationships and participation in social, community, and political life; the acquisition of valued resources, such as employment, income, education and housing; and freedom from abuse, violence and exploitation. Outcomes at multiple levels of analysis that emphasize power-sharing and equity are in the foreground.
Intervention process	The intervention process may be 'expert-driven', but usually involves collaboration with multiple stakeholders from the community.	The intervention process involves a partnership in which community psychologists work in solidarity with oppressed groups and possibly other stakeholders from the community. Conscientization, power-sharing, mutual learning, resistance, participation, supportive and egalitarian relationships, and resource mobilization are in the foreground of the intervention process.
Roles for community psychologists	Since issues and problems are framed as technical matters that can be resolved through rational–empirical problem-solving, the role of community psychologists is to lend their professional expertise to the community to solve problems. Program development and evaluation are emphasized. The professional expertise of the community psychologist is in the foreground, while the political role of the community psychologist is in the background.	Since issues and problems are framed in terms of oppression and inequities in power that require resistance and liberalizing solutions, the role of community psychologists is to work in solidarity with oppressed groups to challenge the status quo and create social change. Social and political action is emphasized, along with program development and evaluation. The political role of the community psychologist shares the foreground with the professional role.

Values

Since issues and problems are framed in technical terms in ameliorative interventions, the value emphasis of the intervention is often ignored or in the background of the conceptual framework. However, the values of holism, health, and caring and compassion are implicitly given the most emphasis in ameliorative interventions. Programs to promote health and prevent problems in living most often focus on skill-building and the development of social support networks, as mentioned in the previous section.

In contrast, values are in the foreground and play a central role in the conceptualization of transformative interventions. While the values of holism, health, and caring and compassion are present, greater emphasis is placed on the values of self-determination, participation, social justice, respect for diversity and accountability to oppressed groups. These latter values are consistent with the thrust of transformative interventions that strive to reduce power inequities (Prilleltensky & Nelson, 1997).

Levels of Analysis

Ameliorative interventions examine issues and problems in terms of an ecological perspective that is attuned to multiple levels of analysis. However, interventions are often targeted at the personal and relational levels. Prevention programs that strive to enhance competence and build social support are examples. When the macro level is addressed, power dynamics are ignored. For example, macro level health promotion interventions may aim to change social norms and practices regarding eating, drinking, smoking and exercise to prevent heart disease or other health problems. Issues of power and exploitation, such as the role of tobacco companies in promoting nicotine addiction, or the fast food industry (McDonald's, Coca Cola) in promoting poor diet and obesity, are seldom addressed.

In transformative interventions, issues and problems are examined in terms of power dynamics that are conceptualized as occurring at multiple levels of analysis. Intervention occurs at all levels of analysis, but there is concerted effort to change power relationships. The collective level of analysis is in the foreground, even for interventions at the personal and relational levels. An example of this is a smoking prevention program that Isaac developed with the Latin American community in Kitchener-Waterloo, Canada, in which children and parents engaged in social action against cigarette companies (Prilleltensky, Nelson & Sanchez Valdes, 2000).

Prevention Focus

Albee's (1982) equation, presented in Chapter 4, asserts that prevalence is equal to risk factors divided by protective factors. Prevention programs then should strive to reduce risk factors and enhance protective factors. Ameliorative prevention programs primarily address the bottom half of the equation, the protective factors, including coping skills, self-esteem and support systems. The risk factors include both biological (organic) factors and environmental systemic (stress and exploitation) factors. Transformative preventive interventions strive to address systemic factors, including racism, sexism and poverty (Albee, 1982). Most CP prevention programs are ameliorative in nature and do not address these macro systemic risk factors. One exception, briefly noted in Chapter 4, is the program of African-centred, critical pedagogy used in the Benjamin E. Mays Institute (Potts, 2003).

Desired Outcomes

The primary desired outcome of ameliorative interventions is enhanced well-being, which is conceptualized apolitically and narrowly at the individual level of analysis. Specific outcomes include: the promotion of individual well-being, which includes self-esteem, independence and competence; the prevention of psychosocial problems in living; and the enhancement of social support. Outcomes at the individual level of analysis are in the foreground.

The primary desired outcome of transformative interventions is enhanced well-being, which is conceptualized in terms of power at multiple levels of analysis. Specific outcomes include: personal changes (for example increased control, choice, self-esteem, competence, independence, political awareness, political rights and a positive identity); relational changes (for example enhanced socially supportive relationships, freedom from abuse and violence, and participation in social, community, and political life); and the acquisition of valued resources (for example employment, income, education, housing, freedom from exploitation) (Nelson, Lord & Ochocka, 2001a, 2001b; Prilleltensky, Nelson & Peirson, 2001b). Outcomes at multiple levels of analysis that emphasize power-sharing and equity are in the foreground.

Intervention Process

Ameliorative interventions are often 'expert-driven' (Nelson, Amio et al., 2000). The community psychologist uses her or his knowledge of risk and protective factors and program models to design the intervention. While the community psychologist may play the lead role in designing ameliorative interventions, there is also collaboration with multiple stakeholders from the community.

In contrast, the intervention process in transformative interventions involves a partnership in which community psychologists work in solidarity with oppressed groups and possibly other stakeholders from the community (Nelson, Prilleltensky & MacGillivary, 2001). Conscientization, power-sharing, mutual learning, resistance, participation, supportive and egalitarian relationships, and resource mobilization are key aspects of the intervention process.

Roles for Community Psychologists

Since ameliorative interventions frame issues and problems as technical matters that can be resolved through rational–empirical problem-solving, the role of the community psychologist is to lend her or his professional expertise to the community to solve problems. The roles of program developer and program evaluator are emphasized. The professional expertise of the community psychologist is in the foreground, while the political role of the community psychologist is in the background. Goldenberg (1978) argues that the roles of social technician and social reformer characterize the ameliorative approach. Social technicians and reformers work with those who hold power; they identify with and accept the goals of existing settings; they emphasize adaptation to social conditions; and they do not believe that basic change is needed.

Since transformative interventions frame issues and problems in terms of oppression and inequities in power that require resistance and liberalizing solutions, the role of community psychologists is to work in solidarity with oppressed groups to challenge the status quo and create social change. Social and political action is emphasized, along with program development and evaluation. The political role of the community psychologist shares the foreground with the professional role. In contrast to the previously mentioned roles of social technician and social reformer, Goldenberg (1978) argues that social interventionists work with oppressed groups; they do not identify with or accept the goals of existing settings; they emphasize consciousness-raising; and they believe that fundamental social change is needed. This is the role community psychologist Ed Bennett has taken in his work with Old Order Amish people (Bennett, 2003; see also Chapter 23). Bennett worked with this group to assist them in preserving their traditional lifestyles and community by challenging bureaucratic and legal obstacles to their way of life.

Summary

As we have shown, ameliorative and transformative interventions differ in many ways. Currently, most CP interventions are ameliorative in nature. Prevention programs, support programs and community development initiatives are typically designed to promote well-being at the individual and relational levels. Transformative interventions that strive to change the status quo through an alteration of structural conditions and power relations are less well-developed than ameliorative interventions. Our point here is not to suggest that ameliorative interventions are not worthwhile; they are useful and important. Rather what we are suggesting is that greater emphasis needs to be placed on transformative interventions. Unless we challenge unjust social conditions and power inequities, we will forever be engaged in ameliorative interventions.

The need for a shift in emphasis from amelioration to transformation is much like CP's initial shift in emphasis from treatment to prevention and from individual to community interventions. Treatment and individual interventions are needed, but they can never prevent or eliminate problems in living. We believe that it is time for a new shift in emphasis in CP interventions that promote social justice.

Settings for Interventions

Community psychologists work in a variety of settings. In the UK, for instance, many community psychologists work in community mental health settings delivering social support services. Others work for early intervention programs such as Sure Start (see Chapter 22, Box 22.2, and web resources at the end of this chapter). In

South Africa, community psychologists also work in a variety of programs and projects, within government and non-government organizations (NGOs), dealing with violence reduction and prevention, child health, injury prevention, reconciliation, and mental health (Seedat et al., 2001). In Canada and the US, many community psychologists work in agencies delivering a variety of human, education and health related services, including health promotion, social skills in schools and home visiting programs. In Australia and New Zealand, some community psychologists work in government agencies dealing with aboriginal issues (see Chapter 16). In South America, our colleagues work also in grassroots organizations (see Chapter 24 and Montero, 1994a).

In our view, there are four main settings in which we can practise the trade of CP. Human services, alternative settings, and settings for social change provide an opportunity for us to use our training and skills in a professional capacity. But there is one more setting where our professional skills and our lives intertwine – home.

Community Psychology Begins at Home

By 'home' we mean the place where we live, study, train, work and play. In other words, it is not just what we do from 9 to 5, or what we do when we wear the official hat of community psychologist. It is what we do all the time. Since values and social ethics inform all aspects of our human experience, not just our professional work, community psychologists try to promote these values in all spheres of life. The values we presented in Chapters 2 and 3 apply to relationships with our family, peers, co-workers, fellow students and community members. It would be inconsistent with the value of accountability to witness injustice at home and remain silent, just as it would be absurd to behave compassionately towards community members but despotically towards family members.

This does not mean that we have to behave like formal professionals all the time and that we have to treat our friends and relatives as if they were in need of help. Not at all – it simply means that we try to incorporate our values at home as much as at work. We do this naturally, because it is part of who we want to become, not because we are supposed to wear a badge of community psychologist all the time.

This natural integration of values into our lives makes our profession exciting. It affords us an opportunity to become more integrated human beings, trying to do what is beneficial for us, our partners, relatives, friends, and our communities at the same time. Box 7.1 offers some examples of what community psychologists working in universities can do to integrate their values in their workplace.

Box 7.1   Sample of Activities on a University Campus

- Faculty members from CP and other disciplines organized an anti-racism teach-in in response to psychology research conducted at another university that suggested that black people are inferior to white people, who, in turn, are inferior to oriental people.
- Male faculty members from CP and other disciplines formed a group 'Men Opposed to Violence Against Women'. This group successfully advocated with faculty members from the Women's Studies program for the funding of a Women's Centre on campus. This group also shared teaching materials related to sexism and violence against women to incorporate into their courses. They also participate in an annual remembrance ceremony for women at another university who died at the hands of a male student who 'hated feminists'.

- Faculty and students from CP and other disciplines organized a teach-in, 'Dismantling the Welfare State', in response to the neo-liberal policies of the newly elected provincial government, focusing on funding cuts to social assistance, health, education, social services and programs for battered women.

- Through protest activities, financial and moral support, CP faculty and students joined with faculty and students across campus to support university staff members who went on strike over issues related to job security.

Human Services

'Human services' is a generic term for organizations providing health, mental health, disability, housing, community, and child and family services, among others. These organizations can be: part of government; funded by government; funded by charities; or private agencies. Some human-service agencies receive funding from a combination of sources – government, charities and foundations. In Table 7.2 we see some examples of the various settings, along with possible roles for community psychologists.

Examples of human services include community mental health centres, children's mental health services, counselling agencies, alcoholism and substance abuse treatment facilities, child welfare agencies, community-based correctional services, and services for people with disabilities. These services are typically staffed by psychologists, social workers and a variety of other health and social service professionals, and afford community psychologists an opportunity to redefine ways of helping.

Community psychologists can promote change as insiders or outsiders (see Chapter 9). In either case, chances are that some resistance will be encountered from management and workers alike. Sometimes the resistance derives from diverse strategies; sometimes it derives from divergent values. If the former is the case, a

Table 7.2 Settings, examples and roles for community interventions

Settings	Examples	Roles
Human services	Community mental health agencies Independent living centres Department of community services Department of public health School board Child and family services	Program developer Program manager Program evaluator Human resources manager Health promoter Unit manager
Alternative settings	Women's shelters Community economic development corporation Resource centre for people with HIV/AIDS Self-help group run by community members Immigrant and refugee advocacy centre	Social advocate Team leader Community developer Group facilitator Board member
Social change settings	Public interest research group Social policy institute Social change movements Trade and labour unions Political parties	Researcher Organizer Public speaker Policy developer Writer

partnership for change is possible. If the latter is the case, we may have to reconsider our ability to work with organizations that do not share our vision and values. To guard against unpleasant surprises, Cherniss (1993) pointed out that before considering an intervention in a human service organization, it is important to consider such questions as:

- Whose interests will be served?
- Is there value congruence between the change agent and those with whom she or he will be consulting?
- What form will the intervention take (for example, action research, consultation, skills training)?
- What previous interventions have been tried and with what success?

Along with our colleagues Leslea Peirson and Judy Gould, the two of us consulted with a children's mental health agency in a review of its mandate. A value-based approach was used as the foundation for organizational change (Peirson, Prilleltensky, Nelson & Gould, 1997; Prilleltensky, Peirson, Gould & Nelson, 1997). As consultants, we negotiated with the agency to have an advisory committee with representation from management, staff, board members, parent-consumers, service-providers from other agencies and members of the community at large. The primary guiding values of the mandate review were self-determination (what stakeholders want), collaboration (participation of stakeholders), and distributive justice (how stakeholders believe the agency should allocate scarce resources). Focus groups and survey questionnaires were used to gather data regarding the agency's values and vision, needs, resources and mission from a wide range of stakeholders, including young people involved with the agency, non-referred young people, parent–consumers, non-referred parents, agency workers and board members, school personnel and other service-providers. This approach was designed to be highly inclusive in gaining input on stakeholders' views about what the mandate of the agency should be.

When we were first interviewed for the job of the mandate review, we explicitly acknowledged our bias in favour of prevention, and staff were concerned that we would impose our agenda on them. We indicated that while we were biased towards prevention, decisions about prevention vs treatment would be made by them, not us. In the end, the staff also wanted more prevention! We had an initial disagreement on strategies for children's mental health, but not on values. We asked agency staff and other service-providers how they would allocate the budget of the agency to different service areas. Respondents indicated that 39% of the budget should be devoted to prevention and consultation programs. While the agency did provide some prevention programs at the time of the review, these findings suggested that it should increase its commitment to prevention. In our follow-up with the agency, we found that several of the final recommendations and directions were being implemented by the agency. Another interesting finding emerged from this change process. When young people were asked what mattered to them, they stressed the importance of employment opportunities, making sure parents, teachers and service-providers listen to and understand them, youth support groups for different problems, and prevention programs. In other words, the young people wanted community change and community-oriented intervention approaches, not traditional clinical services. For us, these findings underscored the value of involving the young people themselves in the process of change.

Geoff and his colleagues witnessed the transformational work of psychologists and other service providers in the field of community mental health. Mental health services began to shift from institutional settings to community programs beginning in the 1960s. It was assumed that this process of deinstitutionalization would lead to more humane and effective practices, but there has been increasing recognition that many community mental health programs have retained the values and character of the institutional settings that they were designed to replace. While there have been changes in language (for example, 'patients' are now 'clients') and emphasis (that is, more emphasis on rehabilitation and psychosocial deficits rather than medical treatment and psychiatric diagnoses), the underlying values of community treatment and rehabilitation are similar to those of institutional treatment (Nelson, Lord & Ochocka, 2001a, 2001b).

Along with his colleagues John Lord and Joanna Ochocka, Geoff documented the process and outcomes of the transformation of mainstream community mental health services in their community (Nelson et al., 2001b). They found that organizational renewal processes which were based on the emerging paradigm of empowerment and community participation led to changes in organizational practices and programs, which, in turn, led to positive impacts on the people served by the organizations. The organizations that were studied engaged in a conscious reversal of power in which mental health consumers were encouraged to come forward and play a major role in organizational decision-making and the provision of services and supports. They found that with the change occurring in mainstream organizations and the creation of a consumer-controlled, self-help organization, that change extended beyond the organizations to the community level.

Alternative Settings

Alternative settings are voluntary associations that are created and controlled by people who share a problem or an oppressive condition. Within alternative settings there is a strong emphasis on: creating a supportive community, non-hierarchical structures, holistic approaches to health, consensual decision making, horizontal organizational structures that promote participation and power-sharing, building on the strengths of diverse people who do not 'fit' into existing programs and advocacy for social change. Such settings are formed as an alternative to mainstream organizations that are not based on these same values and which often blame the victims for not adjusting to existing social conditions (Reinharz, 1984). Community psychologists can assist in the creation of such settings, as well as with ongoing consultation.

Self-help/mutual aid organizations, which we described in Chapter 5, are an example of an alternative setting (Humphreys & Rappaport, 1994). Self-help/mutual aid groups have several characteristics. They are small groups in which people who share a common problem, experience, or concern come together to both provide and receive support. Members are equals, and the groups are voluntary and not for profit. There is a wide variety of such groups and organizations including the following: loss-transition groups (for example bereavement groups, separation/divorce support groups), groups for people who do not have a problem themselves but who have a family member with a problem (for example parent support groups, Al Anon and Alateen), stress, coping, and support groups (for example AA, psychiatric survivor groups), and consciousness-raising and advocacy groups (for example Mothers Against Drunk Driving, women's groups). There is a large range of different types of self-help groups available to people, and it has been estimated that in the US, more than 10 million people participate in a self-help group every year (Kessler et al., 1997).

How should professionals relate to self-help groups? When self-help group members are asked this question, they basically state that they want professionals to be 'on tap but not on top' (Constantino & Nelson, 1995). In other words, self-helpers want professionals to practise good partnership, emphasizing respect, collaboration, equality and appreciation for the knowledge and experience of self-helpers. One vehicle through which professional and self-help collaboration has occurred is through self-help clearing houses and resource centres (Madara, 1990). Self-help clearing houses are organizations which promote the self-help concept through information and referral, education, networking, consultation and research. Community psychologists can assist self-helpers through research and evaluation, consultation, and advocacy. However, it is crucial that community psychologists act in an enabling manner rather than in a way that promotes professional dominance and consumer dependency.

Box 7.2   Community Psychologists Help in Alternative Setting

Our colleagues Mary Sehl (1987) and Ed Bennett used a community development approach to create an 80-unit housing cooperative with affordable rents for new Canadians. Sand Hills Cooperative Homes became a springboard for a variety of other community-based initiatives. For example, Isaac became involved with Latin American families in the Sand Hills project, and together they formed the Latin American Educational Group. Using a participatory action research approach, the group identified the need to promote the Spanish language skills of children and prevent smoking (Prilleltensky, 1993). Heritage language classes were created, as well as a smoking prevention program with a community action component which addressed the role of cigarette companies in promoting youth addiction to tobacco (Prilleltensky, Nelson & Sanchez Valdez, 2000; Prilleltensky, Martell, Valenzuela & Hernandez, 2001).

Settings for Social Change

Of all the settings where community psychologists can practise their trade, this is perhaps the most neglected and, at the same time, the most important area. On the continuum of transformation, this is the end where most profound change may be accomplished.

Community psychologists have an opportunity to participate in social movements as organizers, consultants, researchers, and as citizens exercising their democratic rights to have a voice (Maton, 2000). There are social change and social movement organizations, described in Chapter 8, that have great potential to go beyond amelioration and towards transformation.

As we have argued elsewhere (Prilleltensky & Nelson, 1997), there are a number of social movement organizations (SMOs) with which community psychologists could ally themselves. These include anti-poverty movements (see Chapter 15);

feminist movement organizations (see Chapter 18), peace organizations and environmental organizations (see Chapter 23), among many others. These organizations are often coalitions of groups and individuals who view themselves as a part of broader movements for social change. The guiding vision is one of a society free of racism, sexism, heterosexism, poverty, violence and environmental degradation, a society which celebrates diversity, shares the wealth, and practises equality, peace, sustainability and preservation of the natural environment.

Some social movements begin with efforts by alternative settings. Some of the social issues identified in Chapter 2, such as discrimination, racism, powerlessness, stigma and others, have been picked up by groups that have grown into social movements. Some psychiatric survivor self-help organizations have been vocal in protesting against psychiatry and for the civil and social rights of people who have experienced mental health problems (see Chapter 21). Rape crisis centres have been a focal point for feminists organizing for social change (Campbell, Baker & Mazurek, 1998). Examples of feminist social action include organizing public demonstrations to raise awareness about violence against women (for example, Take Back the Night marches in the US), lobbying different levels of government to influence legislation regarding violence against women, and the development of programs to prevent violence against women (Campbell et al., 1998). Similarly, self-help organizations for people with disabilities have actively lobbied for resources and for the rights of citizens with disabilities (see Chapter 20). The Independent Living Centres (ILCs) movement in the US and Canada is a good example of advocacy by people with disabilities. ILCs are cross-disability, consumer-driven, and community-based self-help organizations that have a sociopolitical analysis of disability (Hutchison & Pedlar, 1999). ILC advocates have pushed for a new paradigm approach to disability policy and practice, emphasizing consumer control, housing, employment, mutual support, and civil rights.

In order to guide the process of change in social justice organizations, we have to be clear about values, social and cultural context, people's needs and strategic action. Table 7.3 describes a cycle of praxis whereby we address these four different points.

Table 7.3 Cycle of praxis

Dimensions	State of Affairs	Subject of Study	Outcome
Vision and values	What should be the ideal vision? What values should guide our vision?	Social organizations that promote a balance among values for personal, relational and collective well-being	Vision of justice, well-being and empowerment for oppressed communities
Cultural and social context	What is the actual state of affairs?	Psychology of individual and collective as well as economy, history, society and culture	Identification of prevailing norms and social conditions oppressing minorities
Needs	How is the state of affairs perceived and experienced?	Grounded theory and lived experience	Identification of needs of oppressed groups
Action	What can be done to change undesirable state of affairs?	Theories of personal and social change	Personal and social change strategies

From Prilleltensky and Nelson (2002)

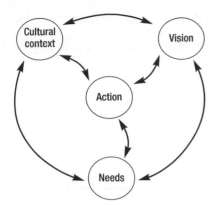

Figure 7.1 The cycle of praxis
From Prilleltensky and Nelson (2002)

As noted in Figure 7.1, this is a constant cycle of reflection and action. Each one of the four elements of praxis addresses a specific set of questions and has a concrete outcome. When the outcomes of the four components come together, they create a powerful synergy. This is what we are after when we participate in settings for social change. The cycle of praxis can be applied not only to social change, but to processes of organizational and community renewal as well.

While social change organizations can be effective in seeking transformation, sometimes they can perpetuate injustice within them, as we will see in Chapter 8. Group members can have different views, styles and backgrounds. This can create strain, tension and sometimes internecine conflict. In our experience, it is not important that coalition members agree on everything. What is important is that members strive to find common ground to advocate on those issues on which there is agreement. To guard against our personal tendencies to monopolize agendas or neglect others' contributions, we recommend looking at the tools for social change in Box 7.3.

Box 7.3   Tools for Working for Social Change
Courtesy of Professor Douglass St. Christian, Department of Anthropology, University of Western Ontario, Canada

1. Practise noticing who's in the room at meetings – how many men, how many women, how many white people, how many people of colour. Is the majority heterosexual, what are people's class backgrounds? Don't assume you know people. Work at being more aware.
2. Count how many times you speak and keep track of how long you speak. Count how many times other people speak and keep track of how long they speak.
3. Be conscious of how often you are actively listening to what other people are saying as opposed to just waiting your turn and/or thinking about what you'll say next.
4. Practise supporting people by asking them to expand on ideas and get more in-depth information before you decide to support the idea or not.

5. Think about whose work and contribution to the group gets recognized. Practise recognizing people for the work they do and try to do it more often.
6. Work against creating an internal organizing culture that is alienating for some people. Developing respect and solidarity across race, class, gender and sexuality is complex and difficult, but absolutely critical.
7. Be aware of how often you ask people to do something as opposed to asking other people what needs to be done.
8. Remember that social change is a process, and that our individual transformation and liberation is intimately connected with social transformation and liberation. Life is profoundly complex and there are many contradictions.

Summary

In this section we reviewed settings for interventions. Unlike other professions that advocate a separation between personal and professional life, in CP we are pleased to combine our professional values with our personal lives. Hence, the practise of CP begins at home. Home means the places where we live, work, study, socialize and play. We can wear the official hat of community psychologists in diverse settings, including human services, alternative settings and social change organizations. Our roles in social change organizations may be guided by the cycle of praxis, which includes four interacting components: vision and values, cultural and social context, needs, and action.

Chapter Summary

The aim of this chapter was to provide an overview of CP interventions. The next three chapters expand on social, community, organizational, small group and individual interventions. As community psychologists we blend the personal, the political, and the professional. This amalgam of roles enables us to be as influential as we can in our personal, civic and occupational lives. To be as useful as we can, we need to develop technical skills, aptitudes for collaboration, and personal effectiveness skills. These skills may be used for amelioration or transformation. Whereas amelioration refers to interventions designed to promote well-being, transformation refers to interventions aimed at changing power relations in society that underpin many of the barriers to well-being in the first place. We drew a clear distinction between these two types of interventions based on values, problem definition, levels of analysis, prevention focus, desired outcomes and intervention processes. The last section of the chapter dealt with four settings for interventions: home, human services, alternative settings and social change.

COMMENTARY: Virtues and Vocation: Community Psychology and Social Change

M. Brinton Lykes

As a community psychologist I have chosen (or been chosen) to combine university teaching and collaborative work in communities with ongoing conflict or those surviving and/or recovering from war and state-sponsored violence (Guatemala, the north of Ireland, and South Africa). Geoff and Isaac's invitation to comment on their excellent overview of CP interventions was an opportunity to reflect upon those experiences within the framework of a lucid and challenging characterization of the community psychologist as social change agent. Below I offer several experiences and my reflections in the hope of concretizing and complementing the challenges they have extended to community psychology/ists.

Virtues and Vocation: Reflexivity in the Borderlands
As a young, white, woman from the Southern United States I made a 'preferential option for the poor' in response to the Latin American bishops in Medellin, Colombia, who urged the first world (sic) to engage in the struggle for economic and political justice in the majority world. Years of anti-racism activism and solidarity work on behalf of

the majority were later tempered by a growing awareness of gender oppression and my own marginalization within church-based and left-wing social movements. Increasingly I realized that fundamental social change was not, at least in most contexts, an end-state achieved through short-term armed struggles but rather a lifelong process of internal and external transformation. About this same time my urgency to quiet the uncertainty of 'who' and 'whose I am' abated and I began to 'live the questions', embracing CP as a vocation, that is, my call to be human.

As Geoff and Isaac argue, there are many sites in which community psychologists can engage in social change work – and we have only begun to creatively explore our options. Yet these sites are not neutral but deeply influence how others view our work – and how we experience ourselves in it. For example, although an activist with years of volunteer social justice and social change work, I earn my living as a US professor with tenure. As such, my private university salary is greater than that earned by 90% of the world's population and this privileges me in multiple ways in a world characterized by increasing inequality. My decision to engage my activism and my intellectual/academic skills and interests through activist or passionate scholarship (DuBois, 1983) and to work among rural peasants in zones of armed conflict situates me in communities where a yearly wage is less than my daily pay. As significantly, in order to maintain that salary I conform to certain workplace expectations (for example, 'publish or perish') that are sometimes at odds with the immediate needs and desires of my community collaborators. To resolve those conflicts, I selected participatory action research (PAR) as a tool for engaging in social change work while documenting our grassroots work. I proposed a joint publication to reflect my commitment to both participation and collaboration.

Although I had been invited by them to come to Chajul, the rural Mayan women with whom I worked there sometimes viewed me with suspicion. On more than one occasion during our 10 years together I have found myself with 'mud on my face'. For example, for the sake of transparency in our *photovoice* project (see below) I explained to the local project coordinators why 30% of the grant was paid to my university. I was embarrassed – even ashamed – that in order to secure release time and sabbatical leave so I could collaborate full time in community-based activism we had to 'buy my time' at a rate that made no sense in this local context.

Previously I had sought to bypass university policy by working in Guatemala during my university vacations or without pay, seeking funds only for my travel, and contributing any funds above that to the local project. Increased pressure from the university to secure 'funded research' as well as the real costs of the PAR project required additional funds and all were delighted when we secured them. The grant ensured that I was meeting the university's demands and that we could do our joint work. But it also repositioned me vis-à-vis my Mayan partners. I had been living a gap between my values and commitments and my everyday practice, the 'working the hyphen' (Fine, 1992) between a US university economy and the poverty of war and rural life. The grant exposed me as a concrete beneficiary of privilege in the midst of their poverty, raising questions about commitments to equality and change. My solidarity and our collaboration were called into question. I was ashamed, embarrassed, humiliated – but also felt misunderstood and angry as I absorbed the complexity of re-presenting power and privilege.

Once back on 'my own turf' I have re-examined these moments of humiliation and contradiction and come to see them as opportunities to cultivate humility, a virtue not frequently associated with either US citizens or professionals. 'Humility', 'human', 'humiliate', and, some have argued, 'humour' (Gilbert, 1996) all share a common Indo-European root, *dhghem*, a word most frequently translated by the English word 'humus' (*American Heritage® Dictionary of the English Language*, 2000). The decayed vegetable matter (or mud) that nurtures plants is highly valued in traditional, agrarian societies. I have had multiple opportunities to cultivate humility in Chajul and have found that the virtue has nurtured my relations – and my work – in these borderlands.

Amelioration or Transformation in the War Zones

My work in Chajul, accompanying local communities in the development of psychosocial community-based programs to respond to the social suffering consequent to war and state violence (see, for example, Lykes, 1994, 1997), sits at the intersection of western psychological theory and practice and Mayan traditional beliefs and traditions. It seeks to foster psychological well-being, social consciousness and active resistance in culturally specific ways. The scars of war are deeply seated in the individual, the society, the culture and across generations. Thus, I have sought to work with ADMI (Asociación de la Mujer Maya Ixil – Nueva Amanacer/Association of Maya Ixil Women – New Dawn) to strengthen the community's capacity to collectively heal these wounds and to move forward through the development of innovative grassroots community projects that promote progressive social change and community mental health (see also Lykes & Liem, 1990 and www.martinbarofund.org for other examples of similar work).

In one of these actions I collaborated with 20 Mayan women from diverse religions, political commitments, ages and educational backgrounds in a PAR project using *photovoice* (Wang, 1999; Wang & Burris, 1994) as a resource (Women of PhotoVoice/ADMI & Lykes, 2000; Lykes, 2001b). The work occurred in the transitional spaces created in a post-war context as internationally brokered (CEH, 1999) and Catholic church sponsored (ODHAG, 1998) truth commissions were releasing their reports of the government's responsibility for the majority of the atrocities committed during Guatemala's nearly 36 year civil war. In contrast to official commissions that by definition focused on documenting the past, the women of ADMI sought a process whereby their stories of past atrocities could serve to reconstruct the present and contribute to a better life in the future.

Prior to our PAR project I had facilitated workshops wherein they had developed skills and organized several economic development projects, a bilingual after-school program for children, and ongoing reflection/action groups for women. The *photovoice* experience created spaces for restorying their lives in the wake of war's terror; further developing their capacities as women; 'negotiating' conflicting community stories about key events in Chajul during the war; extending their work with women to neighbouring villages (many of which were rebuilding after massacres and/or being burned to the ground during the early 1980s); and strengthening their organization as a site for the defence of Mayan women's rights.

Although time does not permit a full discussion of this ongoing collaboration (see Lykes, 1999) the framework provided by Geoff and Isaac enables me to situate this work within a wider discourse of CP. ADMI is an alternative setting, an NGO, but also a protagonist in several social movements seeking Mayan rights and gender equality. As an NGO it renders important economic and psychosocial services to women and their families both within Chajul and in neighbouring villages. It has created multiple culturally embedded yet transformatory spaces wherein women can 'heal themselves' and rethread local community. As significantly, through critically reflecting on their experiences – through storytelling, dramatizations, photography, and interviews – women have come to tolerate difference and conflict and to more fully understand and critique the powerful ties between poverty and war, racism and gender oppression.

I have served as consultant, workshop designer and facilitator, co-investigator, editor, grant-writer, liaison to funders, babysitter, and member of the family over 10 years of accompanying ADMI in a range of activities. I have drawn on my understanding of our relationships and our work to interrogate dominant metaphors that shape psychological knowledge about the individual (Lykes & Qin, 2001) and about war and its effects (Lykes, 1996, 2001c). As significantly, our collaboration at the intersection of amelioration and transformation promotes individual and community well-being and collective action towards creating a more just and equal world.

In working this hyphen I am challenged to rethink not only western psychological theory and practice and my privileges as a university professor but also the practices of participation and empowerment that characterize PAR and CP. Triantafillou and Nielsen (2001) argue that the 'capable and empowered subject' who emerges through participatory practices such as those described here is not someone to whom power has been transferred but a 'modern citizen in the western liberal sense' (p. 63). As an autonomous subject she is committed to the realm of the social through concrete norms, 'games of truth', and power relations where she must engage herself as subject and object. Those of us working as social change agents, particularly those who situate ourselves at the interstices of western and traditional cultures and societies, need to be reflexively self-critical, not only of ourselves and of psychological theory and practice, but of the ideology and praxis of participation and empowerment. The borders that I have crossed to collaborate with the women of ADMI pale in comparison to the selves and the worlds they now straddle in some small part as a result of our collaborative and my social change praxis.

Chapter glossary

alternative setting settings that are designed to be alternative to, and are often in opposition to, mainstream or traditional settings (for example an alternative school)

ameliorative an approach to intervention that focuses on improvement rather than fundamental change of underlying assumptions, values and power structures, also known as *first-order change*

framing, reframing how social issues are conceptualized or understood; transformative interventions involve reframing the way issues are typically understood

praxis the integration of theory and practice in social intervention, it includes attention to cultural context, vision, action and needs

reflexivity the subjectivity and social location of community psychologists in their roles as social interventionists, including the privileges that they enjoy

social interventionist one who engages in transformative social change, as contrasted with social technician and social reformer roles

social movement organization an organization that is specifically dedicated to transformative social change

transformative an approach to intervention that focuses on fundamental change of underlying assumptions, values and power structures; also known as second-order change

■ RESOURCES ■

1. Mark Burton and Carolyn Kagan maintain the website for community psychology in the UK. The website contains very useful information. Visit www.compsy.org.uk and click on the general leaflet about community psychology at Manchester Metropolitan University. The leaflet provides an excellent overview of roles and skills for community psychology interventions.

2. The Radical Psychology Network maintains an active list of resources. There are many links for practising psychology critically and applying critical psychology concepts in field work. Visit www.radpsynet.org/applied/index.html for materials related to this chapter. For general information go to www.radpsynet.org.

3. The Radical Social Work Resource List contains useful materials on working for transformation in human services: www.geocities.com/rswsg/resource.html.

4. The Consortium for the Advancement of Social and Emotional Learning is supported by the work of many community psychologists working in schools. Roles and skills for work in this field are covered in www.casel.org.

5. Many of the skills covered in this chapter relate to working with others in groups and communities. An excellent overview of community collaboration may found at www.communitycollaboration.net.

8
Social Interventions

Chapter Organization

Introduction

What are Social Interventions?	◆ In the Belly of the Beast ◆ Challenging the Status Quo

What is the Value-base of Social Interventions?

Why are Social Interventions so Important?	◆ What is the Role of Community Psychologists Working in Government? *Investing in Human Development; Promoting Equality; Protecting National Resources and the Public Sector* ◆ What are the Strengths and Limitations of Government Social Interventions? ◆ What are some of the Dilemmas Faced by Community Psychologists Working in Government? ◆ What is the Role of Community Psychologists in Social Movements and Non-Government Organizations? *Roots of Social Movements; Preparing for Action; Collective Action Srategies* ◆ What are the Strengths and Limitations of SMOs and NGOs? ◆ What are the Dilemmas Faced by Community Psychologists Working in SMOs and NGOs?

Chapter Summary	**COMMENTARY: Towards Transformative Social Interventions**
Glossary	**Resources**

Warm-up Exercise

Psychologist Martin Seligman published a book in 2002 called *Authentic Happiness*. In reviewing factors that lead to happiness, he makes the claim that 'objective good health is barely related to happiness' (p. 58). With respect to education, climate, race and gender, he also makes the claim that, 'surprisingly, none of them much matters for happiness' (p. 58). In discussing social conditions, Seligman laments that, 'changing these circumstances is usually impractical and expensive' (p. 50). Finally, he noted that, 'most Americans [he means citizens of the US], regardless of objective circumstances, say they are happy' (p. 51).

In a small group, discuss the following questions:

1. Do you agree that health, education, climate, race and gender do not matter much for happiness?
2. What are the implications of his statement that changing social conditions is impractical?
3. Why is it that most citizens of the United States, regardless of objective circumstances, say they are happy?

After reading this chapter you will be able to answer the following questions:

- What are social interventions?
- Why are they important?
- What is the value-base of social interventions?
- How do social interventions promote well-being and liberation?
- What are the strengths and limitations of social interventions?

Introduction

Meet Richard Wilkinson, world-renowned health scientist based in the UK. Through the publication of *Unhealthy Societies: The Afflictions of Inequality* (1996), Wilkinson changed the way many people think about health and well-being. He reported in the book the results of comparative studies on health, inequality and longevity. Main conclusion: Unless we change the social environment in which people live, our chances of improving health and well-being are minimal (see also Gray, 2001). Based on his studies, Wilkinson (1996) regrets the current state of affairs in the helping professions.

> Sometimes it is a matter of providing screening and early treatment, other times of trying to change some aspect of lifestyle, but always it is a matter of providing some service or intervention. This applies not just to health, but also to studies of a wide range of social, psychological, developmental and educational problems. What happens is that the original source of the problem in society is left unchanged (and probably unknown) while expensive new services are proposed to cater for the individuals most affected. Each new problem leads to a demand for additional resources for services to try to put right the damage which continues to be done. Because the underlying flaw in the system is not put right, it gives rise to a continuous flow, both of people who have suffered as a result, and of demands for special services to meet their needs. (p. 21)

The US Institute of Medicine concurs. In a recent study by the Institute, the research committee recommends the endorsement of a 'social environmental approach to health and health intervention' (Smedley & Syme, 2000, p. 3). The co-chairs of the committee reported that 'societal-level phenomena are critical determinants of health ... Stress, insufficient financial and social supports, poor diet, environmental exposures, community factors and characteristics, and many other health risks may be addressed by one-to-one intervention efforts, but such efforts do little to address the broader social and economic forces that influence these risks' (Smedley & Syme, 2000, p. 3). Their point is that 'fixing individuals' without 'fixing societies' is obviously not enough. Make no mistake; this situation applies not only to health but also to psychosocial problems, discrimination, exclusion and marginality. We cannot eliminate racism one-racist-at-a-time when the cultural norms uphold discrimination.

It is not enough to change 'downstream' individual-level factors such as lifestyle factors and biochemical pathways to disease. We also have to change 'upstream' societal-level factors such as public policies.

While we applaud the change in focus from the personal to the collective, we question whether the new focus will lead to transformational or merely ameliorative changes in society. Are more social services the answer to oppression and discrimination? Will more bandaid solutions reduce the effects of economic insecurity? We think not. Though necessary, it is insufficient to shift focus from the personal to the social level. Once we work at the social level, we have to make sure that we will try to transform systems of oppression and inequality. We do not want to perfect systems that ultimately contribute to oppression and ill-health.

Meet Linda Stout, Founder of the Piedmont Peace Project in North Carolina, seasoned activist and author of *Bridging the Class Divide and Other Lessons for*

Grassroots Organizing (1996). Stout shares our concern for making social change, not just social aid.

> Many people and organizations *confuse social service with social change*. Too often, people try to deal with whatever problem is at hand with 'bandaids,' by treating the symptoms of social problems rather than the causes. It's very tempting for activists to do this ... to respond to whatever emergency is happening at the moment – to fix it quickly with whatever is within reach – rather than stop and look at the bigger picture. As Kip Tiernan of Rosie's Place, a women's shelter in Boston, tells it, women are so busy trying to pull the babies that are drowning out of the river that they never stop to go to the head of the river to see who's throwing them in. (Stout, 1996, pp. 105–6) (original emphasis)

Linda Stout knows. She has been involved for many years in social action and social change. She knows the difference between bandaids and structural change. Stout worked with poor people in the Carolinas and beyond on literacy, voter registration, disarmament, gays and lesbians rights and other causes that made her a true believer in systemic change. She is not content with cosmetic changes or more services.

> People often think social service – giving poor people things to help them out – is all that is needed to fix things. This kind of service is important, but it falls short of changing the systemic oppression that is the root of the problem. Social service is not the same as organizing people for social change. Providing services does not result in social change. (Stout, 1996, p. 106)

A recent review of social, community and preventive interventions in the *Annual Review of Psychology* discusses violence as a public health problem and health promotion across the lifespan (Reppucci et al., 1999). The authors call on community psychologists to become more involved in policy making. But we have to be cautious that the type of policy making we do is not going to perpetuate the status quo, as it often does. Edelman (2001) noted that what is sold to the public as a major rewrite of policies is really no more than a minor edit on old scripts. Power structures remain unchanged, while the appearance of change is confused with the real thing.

Our challenge is to move from social services to social change and from amelioration to transformation. Whereas amelioration is about treating the victims of the system, transformation is about changing the system itself. Systemic change is called second-order change, whereas minor reform within existing structures is called first-order change (Watzlawick, Weakland & Fisch, 1974).

In this chapter we explore social interventions (SIs) and discuss their implications for second order change and for transformation. In the next chapter we discuss community and organizational interventions. Here we concentrate on large-scale interventions driven by either governments or social movement organizations (SMOs) and non-governmental organizations (NGOs).

What Are Social Interventions?

Social interventions are intentional processes designed to affect the well-being of the population through changes in values, policies, programs, distribution of resources, power differentials and cultural norms (Bennett, 1987; Maton, 2000). By intentional processes we mean interventions that are methodically planned and carefully executed. To achieve well-being at the personal, relational and collective domains, we have to attend to the various components provided in the definition above. To alter values without altering policies and programs is ineffectual. Re-writing policies without allocating more resources to the poor is merely window-dressing.

Our definition, we agree, sets a very high standard for what constitutes a valid SI. We expect this to change values, programs, policies and power relations. This is, indeed, a tall order. But, we argue, if we want to achieve transformation, as expressed in Chapter 7, then we must make an effort to go beyond the current state of affairs. We approach this task with conviction but also with great humility. We acknowledge that others before us have tried and understood the enormity of the task. This is not a deterrent, but rather a call to humility.

In general terms, SIs can be driven by government or by NGOs. Within government, community psychologists can work as 'insiders', trying to implement policies and programs that liberate people from oppressive forces (including government itself). Outside government, community psychologists can act as 'outsiders' in SMOs (for example the women's movement; the disability rights movement) and NGOs (for example block associations in the US, community safety groups; Greenpeace, Amnesty International, The Children's Defence Fund) (Hall, 1995).

In the Belly of the Beast

To the average citizen, governments look like huge and amorphous structures that have a life of their own. Yet, they consist of real people, sitting in offices, making decisions that affect the lives of thousands and sometimes millions of people. Change in government policies is never quick, but community psychologists have an opportunity to influence policy directions by being inside the 'belly of the beast' (Phillips, 2000; Shonkhoff & Phillips, 2000). Through the collection of taxes, governments have enormous resources at their disposal. How to use the money is a question of intense debate within government and across the political divide (Lavalette & Pratt, 1997).

From the outside, government may seem ugly, 'political' and contentious. In fact, it often is. But if we don't become involved, who will? If we resign ourselves to the exclusive role of outsiders, we will never have direct access to decision-making power or influence. This is a definite risk. Many people are put off by the idea of politics. The media have managed to equate politics with corruption and waste. But the fact is that politics is the vehicle for the transformation or preservation of just or unjust policies. It is possible that well-intentioned people may wish to pursue other avenues for social change, but it is essential to realize the strengths and limitations of each approach.

Governments are not monolithic entities. That is, not all parts of governments follow the same policy, and not all members of a particular ministry agree on policies and priorities. The challenge for community psychologists is to insert themselves in places where change can be promoted and to find sufficient supports within and outside government for their work. True, the work is hard, but the rewards can be enormous. Changing policies that will improve the well-being of millions of people can be very satisfying. Imagine if you were instrumental in implementing a more progressive taxation system, redistributing wealth from the top 10% of the population to the bottom 30% (George, 2002). Or if you were able to secure unemployment insurance for people made redundant due to plant transfers to developing countries. Or what if you participated in legislation to extend medical insurance to the entire population? (In 2003, in the US, there were 43.6 million people without any kind of health insurance). Those would be pretty major achievements.

Challenging the Status Quo

Often, governments are at fault for failing to provide adequate resources for disadvantaged communities. When policies and practices discriminate, or fail to protect those with less power, it is time to challenge the status quo. In this chapter we will review SIs that vary in the degree to which they challenge the structures of power. Some social movements, such as the Civil Rights movement in the US and the Anti-Apartheid movement in South Africa challenged power structures and sought to change the distribution of rights among black and white people (Freeman & Johnson, 1999; Seedat et al., 2001). Other SIs target local government and are satisfied with less ambitious aims, such as better services or public transport (Speer & Hughey, 1995). Yet other organizations, such as health coalitions, seek to prevent HIV/AIDS or to improve services for people with substance abuse (Foster-Fishman, Berkowitz, et al., 2001; Foster-Fishman, Salem, Allen & Fahrbach, 2001).

Either from the inside, from the belly of the beast, or from the outside, challenging the status quo, the principle to remember is that we are there to link the immediate concerns of citizens with larger structures of inequality. We should not deny the immediate needs of abused children or rape victims. They must be carefully looked after. But if we want to prevent future instances of rape and child abuse, we have to look upstream. We should keep one eye on the river and one eye on the bridge.

What is the Value-base of Social Interventions?

We have to distinguish between the overall values we wish to promote and the particular values we need to advance in a concrete situation. The values expressed in Chapters 2 and 3 call for the promotion of personal, relational and collective well-being. Our aim is to balance values of self-determination, caring and compassion, and respect for diversity with principles of social justice and sense of community. As John Ralston Saul (2001) observed, the merit of values is judged by their relative contribution to an overall state of well-being, achieved through tension and balance among complementary principles.

For a first step, this seems enough. We keep in mind the complementary set of values – not a single value, but a set of values – discussed in Chapter 3. But this is only the first step. Next, we have to ascertain what values are neglected in a particular social context and devise strategies to bring them from the background to the foreground. We agree that sense of community is a desirable aim for human societies, but if it turns into pressure to conform, the overall well-being of the individual is bound to suffer. We also agree that social justice must be fought for when it is absent; its pursuit, however, should not detract from caring about the partners with whom we collaborate.

Box 8.1   **Fighting for Justice, Oppressing your Partners**

Linda Stout, whom we met earlier in the chapter, is a community organizer and social activist. She founded the Piedmont Peace Project in North Carolina and worked on many political campaigns, including voter registration, literacy projects, nuclear disarmament, worker's rights, welfare issues and others. Linda grew up poor and could not get the education she always wanted. Among activists, she was different. She didn't speak like them, she didn't have the middle-class manners other activists had. She was a lesbian in a mostly straight culture. Linda did excellent organizing work and always believed in fighting for the poor and the oppressed. She knew that fighting oppression would not be easy. She encountered opposition from local government, police and angry citizens who didn't agree with her views. What she didn't know, or was prepared for, was the discrimination that she would face within progressive social movements. This is what Linda had to say about her plight:

'Because we are all products of the world we live in, it is understandable that oppression is also a problem within progressive movements. Most people involved in progressive organizations see themselves as fighting oppression that is 'outside,' in the larger society. We all agree that our goal is to end oppression in the world. However, what we have found is that very often it is oppression on the inside that keeps us from achieving our goals. Progressive people from the oppressor group carry into their organizations all the things they've been taught about the group they serve and oppressive ways of behaving toward the 'other.' Usually without intending it or seeing it, middle-class progressive people behave in ways that disempower low-income and working-class folks; whites do the same to people of color, men to women and heterosexuals to gay, lesbian and bisexual folks.' (Stout, 1996, p. 89)

In Box 8.1 we are reminded of our proclivity to privilege some values at the expense of others. When that happens, there are dire consequences for the cause of social justice and for its promoters. Linda's story reminds us that we all face contradictions in our values. While seemingly everyone was working for poor people's rights, some activists were discriminating against their own colleagues. Lesson? Values should not drive only the outcomes of SIs but also their very processes. Value-driven processes are goals in themselves. Because of that, we have to concern ourselves with the value of accountability. How can we make changes in societies and how can we be held accountable for our actions? As noted in Chapter 3, without accountability, all the other values remain theoretical. Goethe put it well, 'knowing is not enough; we must apply. Willing is not enough; we must do.'

Why are Social Interventions so Important?

There are several answers to this question. The first and obvious one is that without SIs we can forget about the promotion of well-being and liberation. If we were living in an ideal society, devoid of conflict and blessed with plenty, we may not need to worry about liberation and struggles. But that is not the case.

The second answer is that we need SIs because individual and organizational approaches are not adequate to address the range of problems that we collectively face (Maton, 2000; Mullaly, 2002). As noted elsewhere in the book, individual interventions are prone to blame victims, to be ineffectual, to stigmatize and to deflect attention from structural predicaments (see in particular Chapters 2 and 13). Social

Table 8.1 Ameliorative vs transformative social interventions

Setting/Role	Ameliorative	Transformative
Government/Insider	Contribute to population health Prevent epidemics Social supports Public education Provide basic necessities	Support full employment Equity legislation Progressive taxation system Eliminate poverty Universal health insurance Universal family support
SMOs and NGOs/Outsider	Demand more services Pressure to improve community Increased participation in local politics Funds for charity, research and demonstration projects	Oppose economic colonialism Resist globalization Fight exploitation Support networks of resistance Depowerment of powerful Create links of solidarity Sustainable communities Promote culture of equality Teach psychopolitical awareness

interventions are also important because they address power differences and their impact on health and well-being (Prilleltensky, in press). Finally, SIs are our main vehicle for the promotion of transformational or second order change. We present in Table 8.1 a summary of SIs that work on either amelioration or transformation.

In this review we mention briefly ameliorative interventions but concentrate primarily on SIs that are, or have the potential to become, transformative. We review the actions of governments, NGOs and SMOs and the roles of community psychologists within these settings. In the next chapter we consider the case of citizen participation in community development, organizations, partnerships and coalitions.

What is the Role of Community Psychologists Working in Government?

For radicals and activists, this title doesn't make sense. After all, isn't government the main culprit of many of our social ills? This is only partly true. Although it is fashionable to blame governments for most of our problems, we have to remember that they are the custodians of public resources. Of course, some do a better job than others at safeguarding our natural resources and protecting public institutions, but that doesn't make government antithetical to the idea of well-being; it only makes some of its policies antithetical to it (Chomsky, 2002).

Let's consider first some of the ameliorative actions of governments (see Table 8.1). In some countries, Departments of Health make sure the water is potable and that every child is vaccinated. They also promote healthy eating and exercise (Marmot & Wilkinson, 1999; Smedley & Syme, 2000). Departments of Education provide free education and literacy training. Ministries of Transport make sure that cars do not emit illegal levels of pollutants and that most regions have access to adequate public transport. These are some of the bread-and-butter activities of governments and they rarely challenge the societal status quo; they don't question the power structures. Although in wealthy countries we take these activities for granted, poor governments struggle to provide any kinds of water and transportation at all (Kim et al., 2000).

Some governments, however, engage in more than amelioration. Rich and poor countries alike can create profound changes in the well-being of the population. Some can even contribute to the liberation of oppressed groups within them. But national governments, especially in the southern hemisphere, are subject to regulations imposed by the International Monetary Fund (IMF) and by the World Bank that interfere with their ability to improve quality of life. In countries of the northern hemisphere, corporations put pressure on governments to cut taxes and reduce public spending. The common name for the influence of corporations and the IMF on governments is *globalization* (Gamble, 2001; Pilger, 2002; see also Chapter 15). Fighting globalization has become an important role for governments bent on protecting the sovereignty of their countries. We explore several roles for government at the national and international levels (Chomsky, 2002; Kim et al., 2000; Korten, 1995; Sen, 1999a).

Investing in Human Development

Sen (1999a, 1999b; 2001) challenges the dominant doctrine that economic growth inflicts short-term pain for long-term gain. Sen claims that investments in education, health and social services in fact contribute to economic strength. He challenges the received wisdom that 'human development is a kind of luxury that a country can afford only when it grows rich' (Sen, 1999a, p. 10). Based on evidence from East Asia, including Japan, Sen demonstrates that policies in favour of comprehensive human development do not retard, but rather enhance economic prosperity. 'These economies went comparatively early for massive expansion of education and other ways of broadening the entitlements that allow the bulk of the people to participate in economic transactions and social change. This happened well before breaking the restraints of general poverty; indeed, that broad approach greatly contributed to breaking the restraints of poverty' (Sen, 1999a, pp. 10–11).

Investments in education, health and social facilities enabled East Asian economies to work on economic deprivation quite successfully. Their major shortcoming, however, was not to plan for the possibility of sudden destitution that comes with economic cycles and recessions. As a result, during the 1997 economic crisis millions of working people suddenly became poor or even destitute in countries such as Indonesia, Thailand and South Korea. 'Even though a fall of 5 to 10 percent of total national income (or of GNP) is comparatively moderate, it can decimate lives and create misery for millions' (Sen, 1999a, p. 40).

According to Sen, protective security is as important as economic progress. Many of the tiger economies of Asia neglected to install safety nets to catch the victims of economic downturns. This is when the lack of democracy can be most severely felt. For recessions hit most harshly the poor, who, without unions or protective institutions, fall rapidly into destitution. 'The victims in Indonesia may not have taken very great interest in democracy when things went up and up. But when things came tumbling down for some parts of the populations, the lack of democratic institutions kept their voices muffled and ineffective' (Sen, 1999a, p. 40).

In Latin America, economic crises have had the similar effect of increasing poverty and exacerbating inequality. Based on data from 48 growth and recession periods for 12 Latin American countries, Janvry and Sadoulet (2001) argue that recessions are systematically devastating for the poor. They also note that the gains lost during recessions are not recovered in future spells of growth.

> A 1 percent decline in GDPpc in a recession episode eliminates the gains in urban poverty reduction achieved by 3.7 percent growth in GDPpc under early growth, the gains in rural poverty reduction achieved by 2 percent growth under early growth and the gains in inequality reduction achieved by 9 percent growth under late growth. Recession has a particularly strong ratchet effect on inequality since subsequent growth is unable to compensate for the higher level of inequality achieved. (Janvry & Sadoulet, 2001, p. 37)

At the national level, economists and community developers debate the merit of rapid economic growth as a means of overcoming poverty. Sen (1999b) makes the point that 'the impact of economic growth depends much on how the *fruits* of economic growth are used' (p. 44, italics in original). He further observes that the positive connection between life expectancy and Gross National Product (GNP) per head works primarily through investments in health care and poverty removal. In other words, growth per se does not necessarily translate into human development, unless it is properly invested in health, education, social security, social services and employment programs.

Indeed, during the 1997 crisis, the failure of some Asian countries to invest the gains of economic growth in human development resulted in devastation for millions of people (Sen, 1999a). But there is another route to human development and poverty alleviation that is not linked to rapid or elevated economic growth. 'In contrast with the growth-mediated mechanism, the support-led process does not operate through fast economic growth, but works through a program of skillful social support of health care, education and other relevant social arrangements' (Sen, 1999b, p. 46). This is exactly where community psychologists can make a difference.

The success of this approach is seen in countries such as Costa Rica, Sri Lanka and the State of Kerala in India (see Box 8.2). These places achieved rapid reductions in mortality rates and marked improvement in living conditions without much economic growth.

Box 8.2   Well-being and Liberation in Kerala

With a GNP per capita of less than $700 per year in 1994, Kerala and Sri Lanka had life expectancy at birth of 73 years. In contrast, with a GNP per capita of $4000, Gabon had a life expectancy of only 54 years. Brazil, with a GNP of nearly $3000, had a life expectancy of 63 years in 1994. Sen (1999a, 1999b; 2001) concludes from these figures that it is not only growth that will bring prosperity but rather a wise distribution of available resources across the entire population.

The celebrated case of Kerala deserves attention because it reflects vastly different trends to the rest of India and because it demonstrates the power of social policies in poverty alleviation. Parayil (2000), Franke and Chasin (2000) and Kannan (2000) document the success of Kerala in achieving human development rates that are comparable to developed nations.

The question is how Kerala managed to achieve these positive indices of human development. Through a series of government land reforms and redistribution of resources, as well as highly participatory social programs, Kerala managed to invest in social programs dedicated to economic equality and to the improvement of health and education. For more details on Kerala's case, see also Box 22.3.

In poor or rich countries, community psychologists can play several roles in the promotion of human development. They can work in any one of the following state, provincial or federal ministries: human services, community services, child and family services, health, urban planning, multiculturalism, care of the elderly, disabilities and others.

A key role for community psychologists working in any of these government departments is *program developer*. Governments develop multiple projects in the fields of health, education, community development, mental health, recreation, multiculturalism, urban planning and others. Program developers work with various levels of government to implement new initiatives. In Ontario, Canada, for instance, a government officer worked with several communities to implement the Better Beginnings Better Futures program, an early intervention and prevention project. She collaborated with various communities and teams of researchers in implementing the initiative. Started in the early 1990s, the government officer wanted community members to be well represented in the planning and execution of the program. In order to insure resident participation in the various stages of the program, she instituted a procedure whereby all committees should consist of at least 51% of local residents. This enabled a great deal of resident participation throughout the many sites of the project in Ontario. Although seemingly a simple intervention, the psychologist opened the door for community members to gain meaningful participation (Pancer & Cameron, 1994). Consistent with the values of community psychology expressed in Chapter 3, this government psychologist made a difference from within government.

As community psychologists, our skills in collaboration and partnership creation can make a positive contribution to programs, as would our knowledge on what works, what doesn't and how to evaluate programs (Nelson, Amio et al., 2000; Nelson, Prilleltensky & MacGillivary, 2001). Government interventions such as the Better Beginnings Better Futures and the many programs in Kerala require resident participation, collaboration across sectors, value-based partnerships and a social change agenda that goes beyond amelioration. By engaging community members in the process of human development, community psychologists can play a role in the empowerment of disadvantaged groups.

Another important role for community psychologists within government is that of *health promoter*. Community psychologists can assist in disseminating health messages and using the media to draw attention to the risks of excessive drinking, sedentary lifestyles, smoking, and fatty foods. The media have been used successfully in various countries to improve health and prevent the risks of cardiovascular disease and lung cancer (McAlister, 2000). In addition, community psychologists in government can work with various human service organizations to increase the support they give to people with severe mental health problems (see Chapter 21). In the region of Waterloo, Ontario, the department of health and community services has employed several graduates of Wilfrid Laurier University's community psychology program. Graduates of the program work for local government in health promotion campaigns, program evaluation, human resource management and other health related posts. In all these jobs, community psychologists can nibble at the conventions of ameliorative interventions and push the envelope towards more transformative ways of health (Murray & Campbell, 2003; Prilleltensky & Prilleltensky,

2003a & 2003b). We discuss below some of the dilemmas faced by community psychologists pushing for change within the fortress of the status quo: government itself (Bolam & Chamberlain, 2003).

Program evaluator is another important role that community psychologists can assume in local, regional and national governments. In the City of Port Phillip in Melbourne, Australia, two community psychologists, Peter Streker and Michelle Keenan, head an Alliance for Community Health and Safety. Working for the municipal government, they brought together many partners to implement a health and community safety plan. Rooted in CP values, the alliance tries to move beyond ameliorative interventions (see website).

Peter and Michelle, the two community psychologists, work as coalition builders, meeting facilitators, planners, evaluators, community consultants and policy developers. They gradually try to institute a value-based approach that is congruent with transformational ideals. Their commitment to this type of approach is demonstrated by their willingness to evaluate their own work in light of transformational standards.

Promoting Equality

Based on international comparisons Wilkinson (1996) arrived at the conclusion that countries with a smaller gap between rich and poor produce healthier outcomes for their citizens than do countries with a large gap. Because of more egalitarian income distribution, the life expectancy of Japanese people dramatically increased by 7.5 years for men and 8 years for women in the 21 years from 1965 to 1986. This dramatic increase took place between the years 1965 and 1986. Japanese people experience the highest life expectancy in the world, almost 80 years, in large part because in that period of time they became the advanced society with the narrowest gap in income differences. Communities with higher levels of social cohesion and narrow gaps between rich and poor produce better health outcomes than wealthier societies with higher levels of social disintegration. We have known for a long time that poverty is a powerful predictor of poor health (Marmot & Wilkinson, 1999), but now there is strong evidence that equality and social cohesion are also powerful determinants of well-being.

As Wilkinson observed, social cohesion is mediated by commitment to positive social structures, which, in turn, is related to social justice. Individuals contribute to collective well-being when they feel that the collective works for them as well. Social cohesion and coherence are 'closely related to social justice' (Wilkinson, 1996, p. 221).

The job of promoting equality is particularly challenging for community psychologists. It is challenging because most societal structures reflect and reproduce inequality (Korten, 1995; Ryan, 1994). As *policy developers*, community psychologists have a chance to influence, to some extent, policies, programs and practices that affect inequality. Based on research, information provided by social planners, government priorities and values, policy developers create new laws and programs that can affect the lives of millions of people. This type of work is very well suited for community psychologists, as it integrates knowledge of research, community needs and interventions (Phillips, 2000). The work of Shonkoff and Phillips (2000) on early childhood development is an example of policy development that can influence inequality in education. Working for the National Research Council and the Institute of Medicine in the US, they formed a committee of experts that formulated recommendations for early interventions. Many of their policy recommendations deal with closing the gap between rich and poor children.

Overcoming inequality in schooling is a major arena of intervention for community psychologists. Rhona Weinstein (2002), recipient of the 2001 award for contributions to theory and research in CP, outlined possibilities for action for community psychologists at research and policy levels. Education, for Weinstein, is a basic human right of which many minority children are deprived due to discriminating policies and practices in schools and communities. In a famous 1954 case in the US, Brown vs Board of Education, Kenneth Clark, a former president of the American Psychological Association, submitted evidence regarding the deleterious effects of segregation on the mental health of black children (Clark, 1974). That evidence was highly influential in promoting racial integration in schools. If full equality in education were achieved in most countries, a truly transformational leap could take place in the world.

Another potentially transformative intervention is the development of policies that redistribute wealth and income. Community psychologists can develop policies for demonstrating the positive effects of equality on well-being, as shown by Wilkinson (1996) and try to develop policies to implement progressive tax laws that redistribute wealth from the richest echelons of society to those in need, such as single parents without supports (George, 2002). Alternatively, they can develop policies that challenge exclusion (see Chapter 14 for examples of social exclusion in the UK) and discrimination (see Chapters 16, 18, 19 and 20 in particular).

As *action researchers*, community psychologists can influence policy processes through the dissemination of relevant data. Wilkinson (1996) made a persuasive case for linking health and equality. He presented the data in such a way that governments started to pay attention. Community psychologists can refine the science of research dissemination in order to maximize the impact of studies linking inequality with oppression and ill-health (Mayer & Davidson, 2000). Some useful but hitherto unappreciated dissemination strategies include videos, summary bulletins, newsletters, workshops and consultation sessions. In our project on family wellness for the Canadian government we developed summary bulletins in English and French. We distributed thousands of them across the country and made presentations and audio conferences to spread the message. Some Canadian provinces are now using the materials to reconsider their child welfare policies (Prilleltensky, Nelson & Peirson, 2001a; see also Chapter 22).

Psychologists with a social, community and developmental orientation have secured influential positions as advisors to legislators and policy makers. In a few cases, psychologists have successfully run for public positions (see Lorion, Iscoe, DeLeon & VandenBos, 1996). To strengthen the connection between CP and public policy we recommend more training programs such as the one developed at the Florida Mental Health Institute (Weinberg, 2001) and more policy-oriented research (Solarz, 2001).

Protecting National Resources and the Public Sector

We move now from the national to the international scene. Whereas in the past powerful countries invaded territories and dispossessed people of their resources by brute force, in the present, international lending agencies pressure poor countries to open their markets to foreign competition (Gamble, 2001). Whereas in the past, raw materials and slave labour were extracted from colonies, nowadays economic empires expect the poor to buy their products (Korten, 1995; 2001). In many instances, as in the case of Haiti (Aristide, 2000), countries became poor precisely because of a history of colonization, oppression and dependency. Forceful contact with colonizers not only depleted environmental resources but also tarnished social traditions of native groups. In the case of indigenous Australians this resulted in economic deprivation, psychosocial problems and health outcomes comparable to so-called Third World countries (see Chapter 16).

As poor countries depend – often because of histories of colonization – on foreign loans, lending institutions like the International Monetary Fund (IMF) dictate terms and conditions that wipe out social services, health care and public education (Gamble, 2001). Economic growth and efficiency, touted as the only way to prosperity, require the privatization of public utilities and services, resulting in massive unemployment of public sector workers and in restricted access to health, education (Korten, 1995; Shaoul, 2001) and sometimes even water, as in the case of Ghana (see www.africapolicy.org and www.challengeglobalization.org for updates).

The case of rice producers in Haiti illustrates the dynamics of globalization quite well. Governments are forced to open markets and lift restrictions on imports; local producers have to compete with cheaper foreign products that are either subsidized or produced with more efficient equipment. Once the local competition is eliminated, prices go up and fewer people have access to them (Aristide, 2000; Korten, 1995; Weisbrot, 1999).

At the national level, poor countries indebted to the IMF and to the World Bank spend considerable amounts of money servicing their debts. In the case of Mozambique, the country spends 25% of its income from exports on debt payments. This prevents the country from investing in its own population. If only half of the debt service payments were spent on health care, the lives of the 115,000 children and 6,000 mothers who die in childbirth would be saved (Weisbrot, 1999). These facts reinforce the need for poor governments to fight the debt and resist the interference of the IMF in their affairs (see also Chapter 15).

As if promoting equality at the national level was not difficult enough, imagine how hard it would be to challenge global policies. Psychologists working in government have limited opportunities to resist globalization. If they live in rich countries, most of their governments espouse globalization because they want access to new markets. If they live in poor countries, their governments have limited options for resisting globalization. Opposing globalization is something that may be easier to do from outside government. In the next section of this chapter we explore some opportunities to use psychological research and action in solidarity work at the national and international levels (see, for example, the work of Psychologists for Social Responsibility at www.psysr.org and PsyACT – Psychologists Acting with Conscience Together www.psyact.org).

It would seem that community psychologists are better positioned to defend public services than to fight global economic trends. One way they can do this is by linking with external groups to put pressure on government to be accountable to the people. Community psychologists can open doors to citizens to enter the halls of power and learn the rules of the game. In one telling case, residents of Better Beginnings Better Futures communities organized themselves, with the help of government psychologists, to fight budget cuts in their funding. The programs withstood various changes in governments and several ministers with shifting political agendas.

Protecting and enhancing services for people with serious mental health problems is a policy arena worth exploring. Nelson, Lord and Orchocka (2001b) documented changes in mental health policy at the provincial and regional levels in Ontario. Their study shows how government professionals partnered with NGOs, such as the Canadian Mental Health Association, to enhance services for people with serious mental health problems. The historical analyses demonstrate that government gate-keepers can be very powerful in either locking or opening the gate to winds of reform. In the case of Ontario in the 1980s and 1990s, the Ministry of Health and the District Health Council of Waterloo Region collaborated with consumer/survivor groups in shifting the paradigm in the way government responded to the needs of people with serious mental health problems. While the story is still unfolding, valuable gains were made with the help of government insiders and activist outsiders. Holding keys to the halls of power is a stratagem that community psychologists should not take lightly.

What are the Strengths and Limitations of Government Social Interventions?

The resources held by governments enable them to create profound change: sometimes positive sometimes negative. The benefits can be classified into four categories:

- *Breadth*. Government action on health, education, transportation, housing and human rights can reach far and wide and touch almost every citizen of the country. New laws banning smoking or discrimination against same-sex couples affect everybody in urban and rural regions. This benefit may be regarded as wide horizontal impact.
- *Depth*. Changes promoted by governments affect not only vast geographical regions, but within each location they affect human beings deeply. Each individual is deeply affected by human rights legislation or a progressive taxation system. Government interventions have the potential to lift children and families out of poverty and to prevent epidemics by massive immunization campaigns.
- *Duration*. Once a change is written into the law, interventions can last a long time. New educational policies can last decades, as can mental health initiatives such as deinstitutionalization. The longevity of the changes can have profound impacts on people's lives.
- *Sustainability*. Once a commitment is made, resources are likely to be made available until a change in power takes place.

Some of the weaknesses of government action can be gleaned from preceding discussions. In brief, they are:

- *Ameliorative.* The first risk of government action pertains to its ameliorative nature. Almost by definition, governments do not want to alter power structures. This would constitute self-depowerment, a noble aim but not one characteristic of people in office. As a result, we face interventions that engage in bandaid approaches (Taylor, 1996).

- *Conservative.* In a similar vein, many policies concentrate on changing individuals and not the social environment. Even with the best of intentions, governments often end up blaming the victim (Ryan, 1971).

- *Regressive.* In some instances, governments are not only conservative, they are outright regressive. Privatization in the UK is a case in point. Initiated in full force by Margaret Thatcher, the result of privatization has been a deterioration of public services and unemployment (Shaoul, 2001). Very similar was the fate of Canadian public policy under the governments of the 1980s and 1990s (Barlow & Campbell, 1995). The decimation of the public service and safety nets in developing countries has resulted in massive hunger and homelessness (Sen, 1999a, 1999b).

What are Some of the Dilemmas Faced by Community Psychologists Working in Government?

Governments change, and with them their philosophy and pilots. The crew does not get to choose the pilot. If the pilot's philosophy is congruent with the crew's, there will be a smooth ride, but if it differs, it is usually the crew who have to change their views. We know a few psychologists who started their jobs under one government and were compelled to resign when governments changed. They found it nearly impossible to work with people whose philosophies were antithetical to their views of health and well-being. From being supporters of consumers and enablers of community action one day they were expected to cut services and impose top-down managerial styles the next. To survive under adverse circumstances workers need the support of their peers and superiors. The dilemma of working for someone whose ideology you do not share is a difficult one. Not all psychologists can afford to resign and look for another job, especially when governments are cutting down funding for social services.

Another serious dilemma is what Prilleltensky, Walsh-Bowers and Rossiter (1999) called 'systemic entanglements'. This is a situation in which psychologists have to be accountable to several 'masters'. Psychologists working in schools present a case in point. They have to report to their professional supervisors, to school principals, to superintendents, to area managers and others. And, of course, they feel that their primary mandate is to help children. When various superiors have conflicting perspectives on what is good for the child and the family, the psychologist find herself in a dilemma. Being able to resolve this dilemma is not always easy. Clarity of roles and expectations, as well as a degree of autonomy, are vital. But this requires cooperative partners, which one cannot always take for granted.

A related dilemma derives from clashes of values. When the psychologist believes in resident participation in design and delivery of programs but his or her colleagues are less than enthusiastic, conflicts arise. Siding with the community members can stigmatize you and antagonize your peers – not a cheap price to pay for your values. We always recommend working with a group of supporters in peer supervision, either inside or outside the organization. Situations such as those just described require support and understanding by people who know your work (Rossiter, Prilleltensky & Walsh-Bowers, 2000; Rossiter, Walsh-Bowers & Prilleltensky, 2002).

What is the Role of Community Psychologists in Social Movements and Non-Government Organizations?

We move from the work of 'insiders' to the role of 'outsiders' (Hall, 1995). In general, social movements and social movement organizations (SMOs) tend to be more transformative than non-government organizations (NGOs). Yet, many social movements collaborate with NGOs and vice versa. Sometimes NGOs are part of networks that support social movements. Hall (1995) explains the relationship between the two. Social movements share the following three features:

1. *Social Change:* social movements promote or resist some kind of social change in order to uphold an explicit set of values
2. *People Power:* people come together to promote or resist the change, and
3. *Collective Action:* people undertake collective actions such as sit-ins, strikes, marches, media campaigns, protests and others.

Some, but not all, NGOs try to advance the three features of social movements. Others can be very conservative. Here we concern ourselves primarily with NGOs that support social movements in line with the goals and values of CP, as explained in Chapters 1, 2 and 3. Examples of social movements include the women's movement, the human rights movement and the environmental movement, which are supported, respectively, by NGOs such as the National Organization of Women in the US, Amnesty International and Greenpeace (Freeman & Johnson, 1999). In contrast to these movements, which are in line with the values of CP, some movements oppose the principles of liberation and well-being that we espouse and uphold instead patriarchal institutions (Green, 1999; Tarrow, 1998).

As 'outsiders' social movements have fewer resources than governments do. In fact, the very essence of social movements is often predicated on getting more resources. We explore below some of the processes leading to the emergence of social movements and some of the strategies used to obtain more material or symbolic resources (Bourdieu, 1998). Depending on context, strategy, traditions and leadership, movements may use more or less contentious strategies to get their points across (Della Porta & Diani, 1999; Katsiaficas, 1997; Tarrow, 1998).

Roots of Social Movements

Based on the work of social movement scholars and activists (Bourdieu, 1998; Della Porta & Diani, 1999; Freeman & Johnson, 1999; Gerlach, 1999; Hall, 1995; Kahn, 1982; Katsiaficas, 1997; Stout, 1996; Tarrow, 1998), we identify the following roots of social movements.

Suffering and Deprivation. People are driven to action when some of their basic human rights are denied (Hall, 1995; Tarrow, 1998). We can think of suffering and deprivation as the opposite of well-being and liberation. Manifestations of suffering are present at the collective, relational and personal domains. Concrete examples of suffering derive from the lives of poor people. At the collective level, poor people in the southern hemisphere suffer from two sets of devastating experiences: (a) *insecurity, chaos, violence* and (b) *economic exploitation*. Narayan and colleagues (Narayan, Chambers, Shah & Petesch, 1999; Narayan, Chambers et al., 2000; Narayan, Patel et al., 2000) interviewed thousands of people who commented on the fear of living with uncertainty, deprivation and lack of protection.

In the struggle for survival, the social relations of the poor also suffer. Suffering at the relational level is marked by: *heightened fragmentation* and *exclusion;* and by *fractious social relations*. The personal dimension of suffering in poverty is characterized by: *powerlessness; limitations and restricted opportunities in life; physical weakness; shame and feelings of inferiority;* and *gender and age discrimination*. Impotence in the light of ominous societal forces such as crime and economic displacement fuels the sense of powerlessness. This type of suffering engenders justified rage and indignation in many poor people. When the suffering is tied to an assessment of the power differentials leading to it, consciousness-raising takes place.

Consciousness-raising. Suffering in itself is not enough to generate action. People have to connect their plight to external factors. Otherwise, fatalism and internalised oppression ensue (Moane, 1999). Bombarded with messages of incompetence, many poor people believe they are to blame for their misfortune (Prilleltensky, in press; Stout, 1996). Connections between personal suffering and external roots of oppression and exploitation are the beginning of consciousness-raising (Cerullo & Wiesenfeld, 2001; McLaren & Lankshear, 1994). It is only when people begin to unveil the societal causes of oppression that a new awareness ensues. Although this is only the first step in bringing about change, it is highly liberating because people discover that they are not to blame for their suffering and that they have the capacity to challenge the status quo (Cerullo & Wiesenfeld, 2001; Freire, 1972; Hirsch, 1999).

Congealing Events. Although discrimination and exclusion may be the daily bread of many people, changes in consciousness often do not take place until there is a crisis or a catalytic event that puts suffering in sharp relief. Such was the case when Rosa Parks occupied a 'white' seat in a bus in Montgomery, Alabama on December 7, 1955, triggering the bus boycott and the formation of the Montgomery Improvement Association, which was very influential in the civil rights movement (Freeman, 1999).

Political Opportunities. Despite the presence of the three conditions above, efforts to create a movement may be thwarted by political repression. If the regime does not permit freedom of expression or association, organizers will encounter barriers (Hall, 1995; Tarrow, 1998). The regime has to be democratic enough to enable people to organize without fear of repression or violations of human rights. At the same time, the political climate has to be such that popular support will be gained for the emerging movement.

Preparing For Action

The next step in the formation of social movements is the progression from consciousness to action. Collective action requires coordination and sophisticated levels of organization, communication and strategies. In this section we review some of the necessary factors in the transition from awareness to preparation for action.

Multiple Sources of Support. Some scholars argue that the presence of diverse organizations within the movement is a vital condition for action. If some organizations face difficulties, others assume the leadership and continue the preparation. In fact, not all organizations need to have precisely the same ideology; it is enough to have an agreement on broad issues.

Gerlach (1999) studied the structure of social movements and concluded that there are two main characteristics that make them resilient. The first one is the fact that they consist of multiple groups that serve different and complementary functions. The second feature is that these diverse groups share symbolic and concrete resources. They have common reading materials, invite the same speakers to talk to their groups and often have overlapping memberships.

People with serious mental health problems have been subjected to oppressive treatments by 'well-meaning' helpers (Whitaker, 2002; see also Chapter 21). Their oppressive experiences congealed into a large social movement to reclaim their rights and ability to participate in their treatment (Chamberlin, 1990; Nelson, Lord & Ochocka, 2001b). Psychologists played a role in the anti-psychiatry movement and in the consumer/survivors movements. The history of these movements shows that they rely on various groups and that they share members and an ideology.

Congruence of Interests. While disagreements across organizations are common and expected, it is important to emphasize common interests and goals. For a social movement to engage in action, partners have to agree on certain actions that will advance the overall well-being of the affected population. 'Purists' remain isolated and fail to collaborate because they expect everyone else to think exactly like them. Diversity within movements has to be accepted and managed carefully (Della Porta & Diani, 1999). Organizations may not have shared values, but they may have shared opposition, which is often enough to engage in a common struggle.

Communications Network. One of the factors that ensure collective action is disseminating information to as many people as possible about a particular concern. Newsletters, websites, public rallies, media campaigns, are all important in letting people know that there is an injustice that must be addressed (Freeman, 1999). The role of *networker* is an important one for community psychologists (Foster-Fishman, Berkowitz et al., 2001).

Organizational Effectiveness. Organize, organize and organize! This is the lesson we derive from organizers such as Si Kahn (1982) and Saul Alinsky (1971). Each organization within the social movement has to perfect the art of internal and external effectiveness. This requires a delicate balance between attending to the needs of their members and completing tasks. Two threats assail organizational effectiveness. One is the lack of attention to members' needs for personal attention (Speer et al., 1995). The other is the lack of attention to task-orientation. We have to be good at both. Without attending to members' voices we neglect relational and personal wellness. Without attending to specific tasks we neglect the aims of the movement.

As *organizational leaders*, community psychologists can help in devising a strategic plan, establishing democratic decision-making processes, inspiring members, monitoring the implementation of actions and taking the pulse of the membership to know whether people are, overall, satisfied with the work, or feeling disaffected or burnt out. In essence, the leader has to keep an eye on the internal health of the organization and the external effectiveness of its actions (Maton & Salem, 1995).

Resource Mobilization. This refers to the infusion of human, intellectual, organizational and material resources into emerging movements. 'According to this model, strain leads to discontent, from which grievances result, yet the movement will remain dormant until resources are infused' (Hall, 1995, p. 6). Jenkins (1999) compared three movements launched by Californian farm workers since World War II and came to the conclusion that the one that succeeded, the United Farm Workers, did so because of the mobilization of essential resources. 'The crucial ingredients for the UFW's success were the mobilization strategy adopted by the union organizers and major changes in national politics that enabled the UFW to mobilize sufficient external resources to compensate for the powerlessness of farmworkers' (Jenkins, 1999, p. 278).

Psychologist David Hallman and the United Church of Canada mobilized their resources to stop Nestlé from distributing infant formula in developing countries. David Hallman (1987) described his role working for the United Church of Canada on the boycott of the Nestlé corporation. Nestlé was the major marketer of infant formula, developed in the 1800s by Henri Nestlé, to women in developing nations. Advertising in hospitals and free samples were provided to new mothers, with infant formula as a symbol of western affluence and progress. By the time the free samples were exhausted, mothers' breast milk had dried up and they were forced to use formula. This resulted in increased rates of infant malnutrition and mortality brought about by poor conditions for the use of formula in developing countries, including lack of clean water, lack of refrigeration, mothers' diluting formula because they found it expensive and difficulty sterilizing bottles and teats. All of these conditions can increase infants' exposure to sources of infection.

As these problems became evident to health care workers, a coalition of community groups across the world was formed in 1977 to oppose the promotion of formula. The Infant Formula Action Coalition (INFACT), which consisted of religious organizations, health care organizations, women's groups, nurses, the La Leche league and others, decided to conduct an international boycott of Nestlé products. The United Church of Canada donated David Hallman's time to work with INFACT and the boycott committee. In 1984, three years after the boycott started, Nestlé met with INFACT representatives and resolved all issues, thus ending the boycott. This social intervention illustrates the importance of coalitions and their mobilization for social change. What is remarkable about this intervention is that there was an organized worldwide outcry and opposition to a major international corporation which had a successful impact that has benefited babies throughout developing countries. And a community psychologist was behind it!

Collective Action Strategies

When discontent has matured into organization and when frustration has turned into motivation for change, it is time for action. A number of strategic actions have proven efficient in the past.

Recruitment. Numbers count. Every social change organizations needs volunteers and paid staff to spread the message of change, to talk to new recruits, mail information, talk to the media, go to protests, learn about issues and write briefs. Strategic recruiters go to places where discontent is latent or manifest and where large numbers of sympathisers may be found. Faith and religious organizations often offer support for social justice causes (Hall, 1995; Speer & Hughey, 1995)

Media Campaigns. The role of the media cannot be underestimated. As French sociologist Pierre Bourdieu noted, 'the media are, overall, a factor of depoliticization, which naturally acts more strongly on the most depoliticized section of the public .... Television (much more than the newspapers) offers an increasingly depoliticized, aseptic, bland view of the world and it is increasingly dragging down the newspapers in its slide into demagogy and subordination to commercial values' (1998, pp. 73–4). The challenge to counteract this trend has to be taken seriously by psychologists interested in social change. Effective social movements nurture writers who can express the movement's views in mainstream and alternative media.

The skills of community psychologists as *researchers and writers* cannot be underestimated in media campaigns. In Chapter 20 you will see how community psychologists helped to mobilize people with disabilities in letter-writing campaigns. Social movements require up-to-date information to educate their own members and the public about issues of concern. Information on the source, scope and effects of pollution or discriminatory policies and practices can be vital for strategic actions such as recruitment or media campaigns.

Increasingly grassroots organizations wish to evaluate the effectiveness of their actions (Dimock, 1992). Programs and actions may be measured against values and/or outcomes (see website). Community psychologists can help organizations to find out whether their efforts are congruent with their own values and with predicted or desirable effects. As *program evaluators*, community psychologists can contribute to the improvement of campaigns and collective action.

Writers can express information and the values of the movement in impassioned ways. Dennis Fox, a psychologist and co-founder of the Radical Psychology Network (www.radpsynet.org), often writes for the popular media to raise awareness about social issues and social injustice. His articles and commentaries may be read on www.dennisfox.net.

In addition to writers and researchers, social movements need eloquent *speakers*. Movements need articulate representatives who can speak with confidence in front of a TV camera or a city council. While in graduate school, CP students often make presentations to colleagues in class and at conferences. These experiences strengthen their public speaking skills and their ability to debate issues. These competencies cannot be underestimated, particularly when working with marginalized people who often feel intimidated by audiences (Stout, 1996).

Coalitions. As indicated by Gerlach (1999) (Multiple Sources of Support, above), effective social movements are most resilient when they share the load. In the case of the Pro-Choice movement in the United States, for instance, Staggenborg (1999) found that more progress was achieved by the work of coalitions than by the work of individual organizations. Furthermore, she found that established organizations with paid staff were more efficient in their coalition work than informal groups staffed mainly by volunteers. Similar findings were reported in a special section of the *American Journal of Community Psychology* dealing with community coalition building (Wolff, 2001). In fighting poverty, Narayan, Chambers and colleagues (2000) report that 'coalitions representing poor people's organizations are needed to ensure that the voices of the poor are heard and reflected in decision making at the local, national and global levels' (p. 265).

As *coalition builders* community psychologists can help in the identification of shared goals and missions (Nelson, 1994). Applying principles of collaboration, community psychologists can bridge differences and create bonds of commonality where shared values exist. Building value-based partnerships for solidarity is a task that calls for many community psychological skills. To promote the values of caring and compassion, health, self-determination, power sharing, human diversity and social justice, we need to engage with partners in four skilful tasks: building relationships and trust among partners; establishing clear agreements and norms of reciprocity; sharing power and resources; and challenging ourselves to make sure that we do not perpetuate, consciously or unconsciously, oppressive practices (Nelson, Prilleltensky & MacGillivary, 2001).

Lobbying and Political Influence. Franke and Chasin (2000) concluded that 'Kerala's quality-of-life achievements result from redistribution. But why has redistribution occurred in Kerala?' (p. 24). According to the authors, the answer lies in the century-long history of popular movements in the State. 'These movements have gone through many stages, from caste improvement associations to trade unions and peasant associations to Communist parties to the Kerala People's Science Movement' (Franke & Chasin, 2000, p. 24). These social movements have forced the government to listen to the concerns of the poor and have lobbied successfully for the introduction of poverty alleviation measures. The importance of social movements in reducing poverty cannot be underestimated. The case of Kerala demonstrates that governments can respond to social movements and coalitions. Through participatory democracy and civic associations, citizens created enough pressure on government to institute land reform and other distributive policies that enhanced the well-being of the poor.

Protest. Sometimes the only way to get attention is to engage in contentious actions such as disruption of meetings, occupation of premises, road blockades, petitions or civil disobedience. In Edwardian Britain, women campaigning for the vote chained themselves in public spaces to make their point. In 1930, Gandhi marched 380 kilometres to the sea to protest about the salt monopoly of colonial interests in India (Brazier, 1999). In Copenhagen, young people called attention to homelessness and abuse in the 1970s through a number of occupations of vacant buildings. A well-known occupation took place in 1971 in Christiania, an abandoned military base, where the Children's Liberation Front was established and provided housing and employment opportunities for hundreds of young people for several years (Katsiaficas, 1997). When I (IP) visited Christiania in 1978 it was still going strong.

Community psychologists Speer and Hughey (1995) studied the strategies of the Pacific Institute of Community Organizing (PICO). While not exactly a social movement in scope, PICO can mobilize large numbers of people for protest and local action. The organization usually goes through a cycle of assessment, research, action and reflection. Social movements engage in similar, if more prolonged, phases. Community psychologists can contribute to each one of these phases as *community researchers, planners of action* and *organizational leaders*.

The application of psychological knowledge to social action is a mission currently undertaken by Psychologists for Social Responsibility (www.psysr.org). Protest is a tool that has been used efficiently by people with serious mental health problems to combat their oppressive treatment by the medical system (Nelson, Lord & Ochocka, 2001b). As may be seen in Chapter 20, people with disabilities have also used protest to draw attention to their discrimination.

What are the Strengths and Limitations of SMOs and NGOs?

Social movements may not have the resources governments do, but they have the potential to create consciousness to change government itself. Anti-colonial movements, labour movements, human rights movements, the women's movement – all have had an enduring impact in the past century (Brazier, 1999). Some of the clear strengths of movements are:

Transformative. Movements seek radically to alter oppressive power structures. Anti-apartheid movements in South Africa and civil rights movements in the US managed to transform the way millions of people are treated in law and in front of each other (Freeman, 1999; Seedat et al., 2001).

Participatory. Unlike government interventions, which can be top-down, social movements recruit, rely on and reach out to people who are disenfranchised and oppressed. Poor and disadvantaged people have an opportunity to participate in creating their own destiny. In Latin America, community psychologists collaborate with social change movements in enhancing community participation (Cerullo & Wiesenfeld, 2001; de Souza, 2001; Montero, 1993, 2000a; Rosa, 1997).

Integrative. Social movements, at their best, promote not only social change but also meaning in life (Matustik, 1998). The women's movement promoted not only changes in policies, which are crucial on their own right, but also changes in personal philosophy (hooks, 2000, 2002). Such collective action fostered a new way of life, a new way of relating and a new way of being in the world. Women in the movement were concerned not only with changing governments and corporations, but also with transforming sexual and family relationships. It was about a philosophy of life as much as anything else. The same can be said of the work of activists in El Salvador, who fought not only the government but also forms of oppression at every level in the community. The outcome of this was devotion to a cause and a passion for meaning in life (Rosa, 1997).

But with strengths come weaknesses. These are some that concern us:

Unaccountable. Due to the informal structure of some social movements, some people allow themselves liberties that would not be tolerated in more formal structures. Katsiaficas (1997), for instance, noted the aggression displayed by some youngsters in the youth movement in Europe in the 1970s and 1980s.

Contradictory. As noted in Box 8.1, Stout (1996) reported the inconsistent behaviour of some of her peers. While highly concerned about social justice on the outside, some neglected basic values on the inside. Contradictions are pervasive and must be carefully monitored. Means of accountability articulated in Chapter 6 may be brought to bear on these two points.

Transitory. Some movements, such as the student movement in France in 1968, do not manage to survive the initial stages of formation. Following the student uprising, some gains were achieved and some changes were made to educational policy. However, as Tarrow (1998) pointed out, the movement did not last long. Associated with this risk is the threat of cooptation (Salem, Foster-Fishman & Goodkind, 2002).

Insular and Internecine. Some movements become so focused on the rights of their own members that they fail to establish bonds of solidarity with others who are also oppressed (Benhabib, 1996). Worse still, some engage in internal fights that detract from the cause of solidarity (Della Porta & Diani, 1999; Tarrow, 1998).

Indifferent to Diversity. While solidarity with other oppressed groups is healthy, indifference to their unique circumstances is not. Assuming that one type of oppression is similar to the next violates the principle of diversity and diminishes self-determination (Prilleltensky, in press).

What are the Dilemmas Faced by Community Psychologists Working in SMOs and NGOs?

First and foremost, income is an issue. It is hard to get well-paid jobs in SMOs and NGOs. Jobs are scarce and they are often only temporary. Without a guaranteed source of income, it is hard to make a living from activism. Many community psychologists volunteer their time to work for a variety of causes.

A second dilemma pertains to expectations and task orientation. Social movements consist of people from diverse backgrounds, some of whom may not be used to efficient ways of working. Adjusting to the norms of the organization is a challenge for people who are used to being very efficient with the use of their time.

Similar to dilemmas presented in government positions, value clashes can also occur in SMOs and NGOs. We have to make choices whether to confront peers or let go of minor misdemeanours. But what to do when basic norms and values are violated? What if we risk internal solidarity by pointing out the unethical behaviour of a well-respected leader? These are not easy situations. Nourishing open communication processes and measures of accountability similar to those developed in Chapter 6 can help. Linda Stout (1996) faced many risks when she confronted her board members in the Piedmont Peace Project. She challenged them to renounce their homophobic tendencies. It was not easy for her, but she decided that certain values cannot be compromised. She took a risk and stood by her convictions.

As a young person, I (IP) took some risks by the mere act of reading progressive literature. Once I had to go to the youth movement to burn some books because we heard that the police might raid the centre. I did not endure any pain or suffering, but many of my friends and relatives did (see website). Proceed with caution was a must then and it is a must today. In some parts of the world, transformative activity can cost you your life.

There are no set answers for these dilemmas. What we can recommend, as we have in the past, is to unite with like-minded people in sharing ethical dilemmas and searching for solutions (Prilleltensky, Walsh-Bowers & Rossiter, 1999; Prilleltensky, Sanchez, Walsh-Bowers & Rossiter, 2002; Rossiter et al., 2000, 2002).

Chapter Summary

Community psychologists have opportunities to promote social change as insiders working within government and as outsiders working in SMOs and NGOs. In both settings there are ample opportunities to promote well-being and liberation. While governments tend to concentrate on ameliorative functions such as risk reduction and social aid, social movements seek to change structures of inequality. The former engage in policy development, legislation and funding of new programs, the latter in collective action such as protests and civil disobedience. In both instances it is possible to pursue well-being and liberation. Government work is not antithetical to emancipation. Under pressure from women's movements, a sea change in levels of human development took place in Kerala.

While some social movements proliferate, others dwindle. On the one hand we witness youthful and courageous opposition to globalization, on the other we face massive apathy to poverty and victimization. Some governments dismantle the public sector at the same time as they tout prevention and promotion. Contradictions abound within governments, social movements and within our own lives. Our challenge is to keep our values front and centre and to create opportunities for transformation where amelioration reigns. But over and above these challenges, the biggest challenge for community psychologists is simply to get there, to be part of social movements, to document their work, to assist them and to reach a new level of congruence between our philosophy and our actions (Prilleltensky, 2001; Prilleltensky & Nelson, 1997, 2002).

COMMENTARY: Towards Transformative Social Interventions   *Dennis Fox*

The most useful contribution of this useful chapter on Social Interventions is its discussion of dilemmas facing community psychologists who work within governmental agencies, non-governmental organizations and social movement organizations. Too often, recruiters of all stripes make one-sided appeals urging students to use their skills to further one project or another, without emphasizing the difficulties inherent in any such effort. As Geoffrey Nelson and Isaac Prilleltensky point out, every choice forces one to navigate through difficult circumstances, leading to both hope and despair.

Citizens who remain hopeful, but sceptical of entreaties to enlist, can better contemplate the pros and cons of different forms of action. Those determined to spend a lifetime fostering social change and advancing social justice must determine for themselves how to retain their motivation beyond the exciting cause of the moment. Burnout

is a serious problem for movement activists and even for many in more traditional government and NGO settings.

My own biases from within the US make me especially sceptical of efforts to work as an insider within government. Nelson and Prilleltensky share this bias; even as they point to important examples of using one's position within government to advance socially useful work, they remind us that bandaid solutions don't go nearly far enough and that government is by nature conservative. Yet, perhaps reflecting their own dilemma posed by seeking to guide students in useful yet practical directions, they find more enthusiasm than I could summon about the prospects for justice-focused government work. As someone critical of government's role in maintaining rather than opposing injustice, I urge students to contemplate this route with careful deliberation.

Although it is sometimes possible to do useful work inside the belly of the beast and although government involvement may seem necessary to sustain comprehensive social interventions aimed at changing 'values, policies, programs, distribution of resources, power differentials and cultural norms,' pressure to avoid challenging the underlying system – as Nelson and Prilleltensky point out – is often overwhelming. Too often, rather than opposing globalization and other elitist corporate programs designed to reshape the world to meet corporate needs, governments serve those same corporate interests. Too often, government efforts aim to dampen popular support for change by supplying the appearance of justice rather than the reality (Fox, 1999). Even the tools we think will help us transform society often turn out to be less adequate than we had hoped. A bulwark of state control, law more often inhibits social change than advances it (Fox, 1993b, 1999; see dennisfox.net/links.html#law for law schools explicitly focused on justice.)

Thus, although Nelson and Prilleltensky note the risk of cooptation for those who work in social movement organizations, the risk is even greater for those in government, where lifetime careers can be destroyed if one pushes the boundaries too far, and where the attractions of climbing a career ladder 'inside the loop' frequently dampen reformist zeal. Change advocates inside government too often find themselves settling for policies that, while tolerable or even humane, have little transformative potential. So although I appreciate the chapter's optimism about using government against itself and although I'd rather have government agencies filled with reformers than automatons, more attention should be paid to bureaucratic imperatives that make transformative efforts unlikely to succeed. In my view, not every project that's socially useful leads to useful social change.

There are three additional problems with government efforts to ameliorate social problems – the first, somewhat ironically, with efforts that actually provide needed services. Community psychologist Seymour Sarason (1976) warned almost three decades ago that programs advanced by modern centralized states often damage two important values congruent with those advanced by Nelson and Prilleltensky: personal autonomy and psychological sense of community. Because the impetus for change comes from outside, community members direct their attention and expectations to external authorities rather than to themselves and their peers; this fosters dependency and apathy rather than liberation and participation. Thus, in this sense, there's another dilemma

for those who work inside government: how to provide services and meet important needs while also enhancing, rather than inhibiting, people's ability to work with others. Sarason urged community psychologists to pay more attention to this 'anarchist insight', and indeed community psychologists should find much of interest in anarchist suspicion of centralized authority (Fox, 1985, 1993a).

Second, emphasizing the kinds of social change possible within traditional governments and advanced by traditionally pragmatic policy-oriented NGOs, can lead to an unnecessarily restricted vision of what transformative change might mean. For example, in the top half of Table 8.1, the 'insider' goals identified as transformative (progressive taxation, universal health insurance and the like) are designed to make our current system more bearable (more fair and less destructive), not to replace the system with a fundamentally different one. If accomplished, this would ease injustice and make life measurably better. But it would also leave intact the underlying system of corporate and state power.

The third problem with government work is that emphasizing program evaluation and similar roles identified by Nelson and Prilleltensky as key to instigating change leads to an exaggerated belief that injustice exists because of bad data rather than elite power. Demonstrating to authorities, for example, that inequality leads to ill health is unlikely to persuade them to create an egalitarian society. Although more data always seems useful, the lack of data is rarely the most crucial barrier to resolving our most serious societal problems (Fox, 1991). Data gathering and dissemination is necessary for effective amelioration, but we shouldn't expect it to lead to transformation unless government authorities have first been forced to embrace transformation for other, more political, reasons.

So what's a budding transformational community psychologist to do?

If CP is – or is trying to be – a psychology of liberation, then we have to confront government as well as other sources of injustice. Governments do react to pressure for change, but rarely generate their own. It's our job to help create that pressure. Thus, social movement organizations of the kind Nelson and Prilleltensky describe are crucial for building concerns to boiling point, at which time government is more likely to respond, regardless of whether its agencies are filled with reformers or automatons. One dilemma is how to do that effectively and honestly, without overwhelming our audience, burning ourselves out, or accepting invitations to become rock-no-boat insiders beholden to governments or large non-governmental funding sources.

Fortunately, social movement activists have generated a large literature on how to analyse the sources of oppression and injustice, mobilize resources, raise consciousness and, in many other ways, work more effectively. In addition to the sources cited in the chapter, especially useful is the pamphlet *Principles for Promoting Social Change* (undated) written by peace psychologist Neil Wollman and others (Wollman, Lobenstine, Foderaro & Stose, undated) and published by the Society for the Psychological Study of Social Issues, a long-established organization of liberal activist psychologists. Wollman and others also have useful material on the website of RadPsyNet: The Radical Psychology Network (radpsynet.org). Isaac Prilleltensky and I co-founded this international network in 1993 to foster beneficial interaction among psychologists and psychology students who want to make transformational change a reality.

Nelson and Prilleltensky remind us that successful social movements have altered the course of history. Indeed, government endorsement of social interventions most often comes in response to persistent popular pressure. Fortunately, working towards building that pressure often provides movement participants with the satisfaction of doing the right thing while also enabling them to meet others with similar values, share their useful skills and learn new ones, and build a values-based life. Although we should keep in mind the potential drawbacks of movement work – the authors note internal contradictions, insularity, narrowed focus and the like – modern movement organizations are increasingly open to acknowledging and dealing with such drawbacks. Helping overcome them may be the most significant role for community psychologists who want to bring about a more just world.

Chapter glossary

ameliorative interventions purposeful activities designed to alleviate the results of living in unjust and prejudicial societies

coalition a group of groups dedicated to achieving social, economic or health goals for a particular sector of the population

health promoter person assigned the role of improving an aspect of the population's health

human development refers to comprehensive improvement in the education, health, housing, social and economic conditions of a population

internecine struggles within social movements or political parties

NGOs non-governmental organizations dedicated to fostering a particular cause for the improvement of human and/or environmental well-being

program developer person collaborating with others in developing a governmental or non-governmental project

resource mobilization infusion of material, intellectual and human resources into social change efforts

social interventions are intentional processes designed to affect the

well-being of the population through changes in values, policies, programs, distribution of resources, power differentials and cultural norms

SMOs social movement organizations dedicated to challenge the status quo and to transform conditions that have an impact on human and/or environmental well-being

transformative interventions intentional processes designed to alter the conditions that lead to suffering

RESOURCES

1. The January–February 1999 issue of *The New Internationalist* (Issue No. 309), a progressive magazine, covers The Radical Twentieth Century with multiple references to social movements and human development. The magazine may be read online at www.newint.org.
2. Five classic resistance texts:
   a. *The Second Sex* by Simone de Beauvoir (1989). New York: Vintage Books.
   b. *Opens Veins of Latin America* by Eduardo Galeano (1973). New York: Monthly Review Press.
   c. *Pedagogy of the Oppressed* by Paulo Freire (1993). New York: Continuum.
   d. *The Wretched of the Earth* by Frantz Fanon (1991). New York: Grove Weidenfeld.
   e. *Monopoly Capital* by Paul Baran and Paul Sweezy (1996). New York: Monthly Review Press.
3. Watch the documentary *Rebel with a Cause* portraying the work of Saul Alinsky.
4. Extensive documentation on women and social movements in the US 1775–2000 may be found at http://womhist.binghamton.edu/.
5. *Mobilization* is a new academic journal devoted to theory and research on social action. http://www.infonex.com/mobilization.

9

Organizational and Community Interventions

Warm-up Exercise

When consulting with organizations, community psychologists are typically hired by managers and executive directors. Historically, unions and workers have been suspicious of psychologists because they side with the management and not with the workers. As a community psychologist,

1. What do you tell workers in organizations who may be afraid that you will serve the interests of management and not the interests of workers?
2. What do you do tell managers about the need to listen to workers' concerns?
3. How do you balance the interests of workers, managers and, last but not least, the interests of the community served by the organization?

After reading this chapter you will be able to answer the following questions:

- What are organizational and community interventions?
- Why are they important?
- What is the value-base of organizational and community interventions?
- What are the roles of community psychologists in organizational and community interventions?

- What are the strengths and limitations of social interventions?
- What are the dilemmas facing community psychologists in this type of work?

In this chapter we link organizational and community interventions because most efforts for liberation and well-being take place in, or through, organizations such as human services, voluntary agencies or alternative settings (see Chapter 7). To enable community change, first we have to persuade our own organizations to contribute to the process. Organizations possess human and material resources that are crucial for initiating and invigorating ameliorative and transformative interventions. But we should not take it for granted that organizations will rally behind social change; or that they will examine critically their own role in promoting suffering and oppression, either in their own workers or in the communities they serve. In a multi-site study exploring the ethical dilemmas of mental health workers in agencies and clinics, we found that most organizations: fall short of supporting their own workers in resolving daily dilemmas; and resist changes that may diminish management control or increase worker and stakeholder decision-making power (Prilleltensky, Sanchez et al., 2002; Prilleltensky, Walsh-Bowers & Rossiter, 1999; Rossiter et al., 2000; Rossiter et al., 2002). Box 9.1 is a reminder of how difficult it is for organizations to think outside the square.

Box 9.1   What To Do When You Find You Are Riding a Dead Horse

1. Change riders
2. Buy a stronger whip
3. Say 'This is the way we've always ridden'
4. Appoint a committee to study the horse
5. Arrange a visit to other sites to see how they ride a dead horse
6. Increase the standards for riding dead horses
7. Appoint a group to revive the dead horse
8. Create a training session to improve riding skills
9. Compare the state of dead horses in today's environment
10. Change the requirements so that the horse no longer meets the standard of death
11. Hire an external consultant to show how a dead horse can be ridden
12. Change performance requirements for the horse
13. Increase funding to improve the horse's performance
14. Declare that no horse is too dead to beat
15. Buy a computer program to enhance dead horse performance

Retrieved from http://www.lotsofjokes.com/cat_269.htm

These studies reinforced in us the belief that even well meaning institutions can be unresponsive to the needs of workers and clients alike. As we saw in Chapter 7, community psychology (CP) begins at home, where we live, where we work, where we volunteer. It would be unpsychological for us to expect to contribute to others' well-being and liberation when we suffer from oppression and indifference in our own backyard. It would be equally unpsychological for us to promote well-being in the community at large when we ignore the plight of those next to us at work. Therefore, we deal in this chapter with interventions that promote the well-being of workers in organizations and of citizens in communities. We look at organizational development as an end in itself, designed to improve the life of workers; and as a means to an end, the promotion of well-being and liberation in disadvantaged communities. These organizational aims are congruent with the principles and values of CP (Boyd & Angelique, 2002; Keys & Frank, 1987; Shinn & Perkins, 2000; Tseng et al., 2002).

What are Organizational and Community Interventions?

Inasmuch as community psychologists strive to promote liberation and well-being in marginalized groups, we are interested in organizational and community interventions that foster these two goals. Communities depend on organizations for their improvement, while organizations justify their existence by assisting communities. Community interventions always occur through the efforts of people organized in either formal institutions or loosely based grassroots agencies, NGOs or social and political movements.

Re-organizing Organizations

For us, organizational interventions are systematic methods of enhancing an institution's capacity to promote the personal, relational and collective well-being of their workers and community stakeholders. This definition is congruent with Maton and Salem's (1995) characterization of empowering organizations, according to which empowering settings enable workers, service recipients and community stakeholders to experience greater self-determination (personal well-being), social support (relational well-being), and awareness of political forces impinging on their lives (collective well-being). The interconnection between the three levels of well-being was illustrated in a church-based organization where social bonds and close relationships contributed to both psychological empowerment and effective collective action (Speer et al., 1995). While the organizations studied by Maton and Salem concentrated on consumer well-being, the groups studied by Speer and colleagues went beyond members' well-being and focused on political action for community change. The leap from well-being to liberation is not an easy one. Some organizations, such as the ones reported by Maton and Salem, do a good job at empowering their own members, but don't always engage in political action or coalition formation. Others, like the ones explored by Speer and colleagues, manage to focus more attention on issues of power, oppression and disadvantage. In this chapter we wish to explore organizations that re-organize to contribute to the internal well-being of their own workforce, and to the external struggles of oppressed groups.

Politicizing Communities

By community interventions we mean efforts by organized groups and agencies to enhance the well-being of community members marginalized by social practices of exclusion, cultural norms of discrimination, and economic policies of injustice and inequality (Ife, 2002; Mullaly, 2002; Rappaport, 1977). Community well-being, as noted in Chapter 2, is predicated on emancipation from oppressive forces. Therefore, we are not content to improve narrow aspects of health, such as better hygiene or diet awareness, when systemic conditions of inequality perpetuate hunger. Similarly, we are not satisfied to improve charity services when the conditions that lead to charity in the first place continue unabated. In the language of Chapter 7, we seek to develop community interventions that go beyond amelioration and move towards transformation. This is not an 'either/or'. We do not advocate the elimination of social supports because they do not eliminate economic exploitation. Services are very much needed. What we do advocate is the pairing of ameliorative and transformative thinking and action (Prilleltensky & Nelson, 1997, 2002). We recommend intervening in communities in such a way that they receive services and resources and increase their political awareness and capacity for mobilization at the same time. Hence, we put emphasis here on strategies that ameliorate and, concurrently, have the potential to transform. Although these strategies are not the norm but rather the exception, a recent issue of the *American Journal of Community Psychology* contains examples of interventions that combine skill enhancement with sociopolitical awareness (Watts & Serrano-García, 2003). In Chapter 23 Bennett describes how his community development work has a clear transformational focus.

What Values Justify Organizational and Community Interventions?

In principle, all the values presented in Chapters 2 and 3 justify the need for organizational and community interventions. We have noted before that well-being emanates from the confluence of balanced value systems. Thus, well-being takes place at the intersection of holism, health, caring and compassion, self-determination, participation, social justice, respect for diversity and accountability. When the salience of one or more of these values obscures the presence of others, the balance is shaken. Different organizations and communities emphasize some values more than others. Although our assessment is not definitive, it seems to us that most organizations and communities pay attention to health and caring and compassion, and, to some extent, to diversity and participation. Few, however, are the organizations and communities that place social justice, holism and accountability front and centre (Prilleltensky, 2001). Not by coincidence, the three neglected values have to do with power. Social justice has to do with the fair and equitable distribution of burdens and resources in society, something that cannot happen unless those with power relinquish some of it. Similarly, accountability cannot be fulfilled unless there is a transfer of power away from dominant sectors. Holism, which can be deceiving because it is often narrowly interpreted, is not only about the natural environment, but also about the social context. And power, as we know, is an immanent part of the social ecology. Unless we view power and its unequal distribution as a central determinant of health and well-being, we will continue to shift pieces within the present configuration of injustice, without challenging injustice itself (Ife, 2002).

The very neglect of power inequality warrants organizational and community interventions that do more than ameliorate. In his analysis of community coalitions, Himmelman (2001) arrives at a similar conclusion. Without power equalization coalitions cannot go further than community betterment. With it, they can approximate community empowerment. A similar conclusion was reached by John (2003) in her exploration of children's movements, participation in civic life and alternative schools. In studying children's parliaments in India, alternative schools in the US, and youth participation in local government in the UK, she realized that meaningful and lasting changes occurred only when children and young people were afforded, or simply took, power away from adults. The inspirational examples documented by John (2003) point to the need to redistribute power, not only across gender, race and social class, but also across ages. Her study reinforces the assumption that power and control over one's life is not only a health-giving experience, but a sine qua non for lasting and effective change.

Why are Organizational and Community Interventions so Important?

We spend most of our lives in organizations, either as workers or recipients of services, such as education. Think about your life. As a student, you probably spend about 14 years of your life in school. Once you leave university, you are very likely to join a workplace. If you do sports, you practice in an organizational setting. If you volunteer, you do so in an agency. People spend most of their lives in one kind of organization or another. The way organizations operate has an impact on you, your family and society at large.

Organizations can promote life satisfaction and creativity (Lubinski & Benbow, 2000; Marmot & Feeney, 1996) or can induce a great deal of stress, as in the case of workplace strain, bullying and harassment (Beehr & O'Driscoll, 2002; Bond, 1999; Svyantek & Brown, 2002; Thomas & Hite, 2002). In a compelling longitudinal study, Marmot (1999) showed that the level of control exercised by different people within an organization has powerful effects on health, well-being and even mortality. The less control people have, the higher the risk of dying (see Box 9.2).

Box 9.2   Occupational Status, Control, and Risk of Death

Michael Marmot, a former Australian, was knighted for his ground-breaking research in England. Marmot studied the lives of thousands of British civil servants for over 25 years. After he eliminated all other possible sources of health and illness, he realized that those workers who experienced little control over their jobs were two, three, and even four times more likely to die than those who experienced a lot of control over their jobs.

Marmot (1999) divided the civil servants into four groups: managers, professionals, clerical and office support. Managers had the most amount of control over their jobs whereas the group called 'office support' had the least. Professionals were second and clerical staff third. Compared to managers, professionals were twice as likely to die, clerical staff were three times as likely, and the last group, which included people with few skills, were four times more likely to die. This is a persuasive argument for augmenting the level of control people can have in organizations.

Intervening in communities is just as important. The gradient observed in mortality rates among British civil servants is replicated in social classes at large. Gradient means an increase in risk with an increase in disadvantage. In a recent longitudinal study of 18,751 people in Oslo, McCubbin and Dalgard (2002) found that powerlessness was a very strong predictor of distress and ill-health in the population. Just as the lowest paid and lowest skilled workers in the Marmot study had the highest risk of death, so people in the lowest occupational level in Oslo experience the greatest amount of powerlessness and distress (see Figure 9.1).

Within countries, the poor, the unemployed, refugees, single-parents, ethnic minorities and the homeless have poorer indices of health than more privileged groups (Blane, Bruner & Wilkinson, 1996; Marmot & Wilkinson, 1999). This applies not only to poor countries, but to rich countries as well. Homeless people in western countries, for example, are 34 times more likely to kill themselves than the

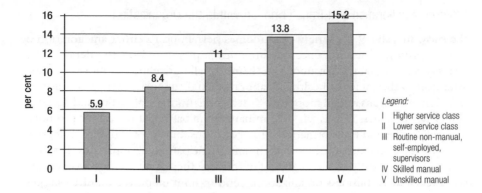

Figure 9.1 Percentage of people in distress by occupational status as measured by the Hopkins Symptom Checklist (HSCL-10)

Based on a longitudinal study of 18,751 people in Oslo. The HSCL-10 is a short version of the HSCL-25 measuring psychological distress. The pattern of the chart remains the same when controlling for age and sex. Used with permission from the authors (McCubbin & Dalgard, 2002).

general population, 150 times more likely to be fatally assaulted, and 25 times more likely to die in any period of time than the people who ignore them on the streets (Shaw, Dorling & Smith, 1999).

In addition to the pressing need to narrow the economic gap, there is some urgency to increase social cohesion, solidarity and a psychological sense of community (Fisher, Sonn & Bishop, 2002; Mustard, 1996). Inspiring community interventions, like the one carried out in Kerala (see Chapter 8) and others reported in North America by Repucci et al. (1999), show that mobilization can deliver positive effects in reducing hunger, malnutrition, violence and addictions, and in enhancing community health, social capital and quality of life.

What are the Roles of Community Psychologists Working in Organizations?

We identify two potential roles for community psychologists working in organizations. The first one is the promotion of amelioration and transformation within the organization. The second role is the pursuit of amelioration and transformation in the community served by the organization. These roles may be fulfilled either as internal or external agents of change. To be effective, community psychologists require certain skills. The skills we present extend the emotional competencies of effective leaders documented by Goleman (1995, 1998). Whereas Goleman's skills of emotional intelligence apply primarily to organizational efficacy, we discuss the implications of such skills for transformational work. Finally, based on the work of Prochaska and colleagues on processes of change, we describe the steps necessary to succeed in organizational development (Prochaska, Norcross & DiClemente, 1994; Weick & Quinn, 1999).

Promote Amelioration and Transformation within the Organization

We show in Table 9.1 a variety of outcomes pertaining to either amelioration or transformation. The difference in outcomes is predicated on the depth of the changes and the values that underpin them. Ameliorative interventions pay more attention to the values of health, collaboration and support, whereas transformational interventions attend more to self-determination, social justice and accountability. Some values, such as self-determination and participation, can be promoted in ameliorative and transformational interventions, but in very different degrees. The literature on employee involvement and participation demonstrates that organizations vary greatly in the degree of autonomy they grant to their workers and volunteers. Most business organizations tend to limit employee input to suggestions for problem-solving activities (Klein, Ralls, Smith Major & Douglas, 2000; Wadell, Cummings & Worley, 2000; Weick & Quinn, 1999), whereas human services and alternative settings usually afford workers and volunteers more voice and choice (Cherniss, 2002; Cherniss & Deegan, 2000; Maton & Salem, 1995; Nelson, Lord & Ochocka, 2001b; Sarason, 1972). This may reflect the fact that the latter 'focuses on empowerment and well-being' and the former on 'productivity and profitability' (Shinn & Perkins, 2000, p. 635). It should be noted, however, that within each type of organization, business, public sector or human services, there is also great variability in the amount of control and participation given to workers.

Interventions to enhance worker participation take place in small groups where colleagues discuss ways to improve productivity or service delivery. Some of these

Table 9.1   Ameliorative and transformative interventions in organizations

Population Served by Interventions	Ameliorative	Transformative
Workers within the organization	Collaboration across units Moderate participation Autonomy Caring and compassion for colleagues Conflict resolution plans Policies against harassment and bullying Family friendly policies Peer support Personal development Stress reduction Prevent burnout Improve communication	Accountability across and within levels of organization Attention to issues of social injustice Full participation in decision-making processes Meaning-seeking activities Attention to power differences Oppose discrimination Equalize power
Community, citizens, clients and consumers	Caring and compassion toward clients and citizens Workers contribute to civic associations through charity Partnerships for health and well-being Reinforce community structures Advocacy on behalf of clients Provision of new or better services	Mission of social change Allow community stakeholders full access to decision making Respect the environment Make community politically aware Accountability to disadvantaged members of community Support clients in resisting oppression and injustice

initiatives have been called Total Quality Management (TQM) or Quality of Working Life (QWL). In essence, groups are formed to analyse processes and outcomes of work and ways to enhance effectiveness and satisfaction. The nature of the groups varies greatly, with some being initiated by management, some by external consultants, and some by union–management committees (Johnson & Johnson, 2000; Klein et al., 2000). Depending on their origins and intent, groups can exercise more or less influence, can be permanent or sporadic, tokenistic or serious. The impact of such groups may very well depend on the depth of the changes generated by them, and on the actual control afforded by management.

Although it is hard to generalize because of the variability in teams and forms of worker participation, several reviews documented positive effects for both productivity and worker satisfaction (Johnson & Johnson, 2000; Klein et al., 2000; Shinn & Perkins, 2000; Weick & Quinn, 1999). Reviewers seem to agree that the overall impact on productivity and worker satisfaction depends on the duration, intensity, and actual – as opposed to perceived – control over jobs. When these conditions are present and long lasting, organizations improve their services and workers feel better about their jobs. When interventions are short-lived and half-hearted, positive results fade quickly. If means of increasing worker participation and control were profound, institutionalized and endorsed by management, we could say that an ameliorative change has turned into a transformative one. Thus, it is not only the type of values endorsed that make a difference between amelioration and transformation, but also the degree to which the values are fostered.

Reducing stress in the workplace is an aim of many managers, consultants, and worker themselves. Strategies to alleviate stress include participation in decision-making, structural innovations, ergonomic approaches, role-based interventions, social support, and provision of information. In a comprehensive review of the literature, Beehr and O'Driscoll (2002) found that most interventions had only modest effects on stress reduction. Some of the most promising strategies included worker participation in decision-making and role clarification. Role ambiguity, role conflict and role overload are three serious causes of strain. Making sure that workers know what is expected of them, that they do not have unrealistic caseloads, and that they have management support for their duties are useful ways of decreasing strain (Beehr & O'Driscoll, 2002).

Role ambiguity is very common in human service organizations. In several of our studies, workers in clinics and family agencies reported dilemmas related to caseloads, territoriality, diffused responsibility, and lack of support by supervisors and management (Prilleltensky, Sanchez et al., 2002; Prilleltensky, Walsh-Bowers & Rossiter, 1999; Rossiter et al., 2000, 2002). Participants reported that peer support, management backing, and the creation of a safe space for sharing dilemmas were essential components of effectiveness, satisfaction, and sometimes even 'emotional survival'. Social support in the workplace has long been recognized as an important correlate of worker well-being (Kyrouz & Humphreys, 1997; Milne, 1999; Quick, Quick, Nelson & Hurrell, 1997; Shinn & Perkins, 2000; Stansfeld, 1999).

Transformational interventions that enhance the well-being of workers can be found in both the human and business sectors. In the human services sector, including health, mental health, disabilities, education and employment organizations, transformational workplaces tend to have horizontal structures with minimal hierarchies. In addition, they tend to make decisions by consensus and to flatten power differentials within the organization (Reinharz, 1984; Riger, 2000). Many feminist organizations were created with visions of equality and mutual accountability (hooks, 2002). Self-help organizations often espouse egalitarian structures as well, as do alternative settings that are value-based, mission oriented and human-focused (Cherniss & Deegan, 2000). In reviewing the creation of alternative settings in human services, Cherniss and Deegan noted that 'the self-development of the staff and the health of the organization were considered to be two of the most important priorities' (2000, p. 374).

In business organizations we are also witnessing an increase in the number of co-operatives and worker-owned enterprises (Quarter, 1992; Quarter & Melnyk, 1989). Many of these organizations emphasize human, social and environmental aims and not just the economic bottom line. Korten (1999) documents the spread of such initiatives around the world. These co-operative forms of ownership increase worker well-being, economic security, collective responsibility and environmental awareness. According to Korten (1999), 'we are only beginning to tap the possibilities for organizing economic activity with a minimum of hierarchy and central control' (p. 178).

The creation of transformative workplaces is challenging (Cherniss & Deegan, 2000; Goldenberg, 1971; Korten, 1999; Sarason, 1972). Most pioneers point to serious, but not insurmountable barriers. Key obstacles include balancing effectiveness with decentralization of control, economic viability in a world of competition, and meeting the needs of the individual and the collective at the same time. These are exciting places for community psychologists to practise their trade.

Promote Amelioration and Transformation in the Community Served by the Organization

Improving quality of life for workers is only part of a community psychologist's job. The other part is to enhance the well-being of consumers, citizens and communities at large. Caring and compassion and client participation in decision-making processes go a long way in humanizing social services and empowering people who experience disadvantage. Re-designing organizations with consumer well-being in mind is an appropriate task for community psychologists.

In a longitudinal study of three empowering organizations, including a program for African-American university students, a religious group and a self-help group for people with psychiatric disabilities, Maton and Salem (1995) recognized some distinct features that contributed to the well-being of participants. These organizations had:

- Inspiring leaders
- Growth-oriented belief systems
- Strength-based philosophies
- Structures that enabled learning and role rotation
- Focus on self and community
- Comprehensive systems of social support
- High sense of community.

As in the case of organizational change, transitioning from amelioration to transformation in communities is hard. In fact, such a move is a test of our resolve to push CP to new horizons. Paul Speer and his colleagues have been studying an organization that is trying to make change rather than simply cure (Speer, 2002; Speer & Hughey, 1995; Speer et al., 1995). Pacific Institute of Community Organizations (PICO) is a community-organizing network with affiliates in 25 cities across the US. PICO helps to organize communities to demand more resources for children, families, crime prevention, poor neighbourhoods, and people with addictions and other social problems. This organization is very clear on the need to transcend therapeutic models and to use community power to access more resources. Three principles support PICO's organizing efforts:

- Empowerment can only be realized through organizing
- Social power is built on the strength of interpersonal relationships
- Individual empowerment must be grounded in a dialectic of action and reflection

PICO is successful in empowering its members and in getting results. Like other empowering organizations, this one allows members to rotate in their roles and to engage in a variety of tasks. Some of the jobs done by members and volunteers include getting information from public officials, asking politicians difficult questions, mobilizing communities for rallies, arranging transportation, arranging media coverage, facilitating meetings and so on. Some of the results include better resources for communities and increased awareness of the political dynamics oppressing the poor and the disenfranchised. In one campaign PICO obtained from city council and private corporations $9 million for substance abuse treatment and prevention.

Community psychologists can learn from and assist organizations and communities to change. This can be done from within the organization, as internal agents of change, or from the outside, as consultants or volunteers. We explore these different roles in the next sections.

Internal and External Agents of Change

Community psychologists can help organizations and communities from the inside or the outside (see Table 9.2). Graduating community psychologists often get jobs as program planners, managers in human services, program evaluators, or directors of community services or government departments. Other community psychologists open their own consulting firms and work for other organizations on

Table 9.2 Internal and external agents of change in organizations

Internal Agents of Change	External Agents of Change
Managers	Organizational consultant
Executive director	Member of the community
Administrator	Conflict resolution mediator
Staff member	Trainer
Member of the board	Program evaluator

contract. Alternatively, consultants get government grants to help community organizations deliver a service or evaluate their programs. Both of us, Geoff and Isaac, have worked as internal and external agents of change. We worked in community mental health settings as clinical, school and community psychologists, and both of us provide consultation to a wide range of agencies and groups, including psychiatric consumer/survivor initiatives, community-based prevention programs, self-help groups for immigrants and refugees, community mental health organizations, health promotion foundations, child and family services, local government, youth organizations, advocacy and social action groups. Some of the work we do as consultants is on contract but we also do a lot of external consulting for free. We feel privileged to have good paying jobs in universities that afford us the opportunity to spend time volunteering in the community; it is a privilege we do not take for granted.

As either internal or external agents of change, community psychologists can exert more or less control over the process of change. Depending on the level of control exercised, Dimock (1992) identified six possible roles for agents of change. In decreasing order of control, they are:

- *Director:* manager or administrator who makes decisions and gives instructions in order to control the intervention
- *Expert:* System analyst or organizational consultant who diagnoses problems and uses knowledge to tell others what to do
- *Consultant:* Community developer and consultant who makes suggestions and whose influence derives from respect and trust
- *Resource:* Group trainer or resource provider who helps group to collect data and provides training in planning skills
- *Facilitator:* Process consultant, helper or group observer who assists with group processes
- *Collaborator:* Staff, board or community member who is interested in change and joins groups or teams planning and carrying out interventions.

As internal or external agents of change, community psychologists can fulfil any one of these roles. We caution, however, against the adoption of director or expert roles, as they tend to alienate partners. However, it is possible to be a manager or executive director, but still work in a very collaborative manner; the position does not have to dictate the intervention style. We favour intervention styles that are collaborative and that share control across levels of the organization and the community, not only because they are in line with our values, but also because they are more effective (Bond, 1999; Dimock, 1992; Ife, 2002; Johnson & Johnson, 2000; Klein et al., 2000; Prilleltensky & Nelson, 2002; Shinn & Perkins, 2000).

Emotional Competencies and their Transformational Potential

To be effective as internal or external agents of change community psychologists require a set of skills. In previous chapters we reviewed the conceptual foundations of CP theory, research and action. In this section we want to emphasize some of the interpersonal and emotional competencies required to interact with people in organizations and communities. Goleman (1995, 1998) integrated a great deal of research concerning the personal and interpersonal skills that predict satisfaction in families, work, school and communities. He called this set of skills 'emotional intelligence'.

Table 9.3 Emotional competencies and their transformational potential

Emotional Competencies	Transformational Potential
Personal competence	

Self-awareness
  Emotional awareness
  Accurate self-assessment
  Self-confidence
	Self-awareness
	  Recognizing personal experiences of oppression
	  Understanding impact of oppression on self
	  Sense of agency

Self-regulation
  Self-control
  Trustworthiness
  Conscientiousness
  Adaptability
  Innovation
	Self-regulation
	  Monitoring effects of oppression on behaviour
	  Ethical behaviour in all domains of life
	  Accountability for actions
	  Appreciation of impact of change on self
	  Willingness to be challenged

Motivation
  Achievement drive
  Commitment
  Initiative
  Optimism
	Motivation
	  Pursuit of liberation and well-being
	  Commitment to change, liberation and well-being
	  Ability to mobilize self and others
	  Work with others to maintain hope

Social competence	

Empathy
  Understanding others
  Developing others
  Service orientation
  Leveraging diversity
  Political awareness
	Empathy
	  Appreciating others' experiences of oppression
	  Promoting others' sense of agency
	  Transformational orientation
	  Respecting and valuing minorities' experiences
	  Perceiving effects of power dynamics in groups

Social skills
  Influence
  Communication
  Conflict management
  Leadership
  Change catalyst
  Building bonds
  Collaboration and cooperation
  Team capabilities
	Social skills
	  Persuasive in promoting need for justice
	  Active listening and use of plain messages
	  Fair resolution of differences
	  Inspiring self and others to do their best
	  Promotion of change for liberation and well-being
	  Solidarity with people who are marginalized
	  Value-based partnerships
	  Fostering synergy, fun and satisfaction in group

Goleman's work provides a valuable foundation for understanding what is required to become an effective change maker. However, his contributions do not emphasize the same value-base or transformational goals that we deem important for CP. Goleman does not necessarily critique the exploitive nature of the corporations he studied, nor does he emphasize the need to use emotional intelligence to overcome oppression and injustice. Hence, we present in Table 9.3 the main emotional competencies identified by Goleman (1998) and their transformational potential. We agree with Goleman that these skills are vital for communicating effectively with others and exerting influence in respectful ways. He is very clear that change needs to take into account how other people feel about it. In our view, Goleman's main contribution is to personal and relational well-being. We are interested in distilling the implications of his theory for collective well-being as well.

The left-hand side of Table 9.3 lists the emotional competencies required to get along with others, to get along with oneself, and to get self and others to work for change. The right hand side of the table shows the implications of such skills for transformational change in organizations and communities. Whereas the top half of the table deals with personal competencies such as self awareness, self regulation and motivation, the lower half lists social competencies such as empathy, communication skills, conflict resolution and leadership. In a review of studies of work organizations, Cherniss and Adler (2000) found that individuals who excel at their jobs also have many of the skills that characterize emotional intelligence.

Goleman's emotional competencies concentrate on the values of caring, compassion, and collaboration at the interpersonal level. We see in them potential to contribute to social justice and accountability at the collective level. If Goleman highlighted personal and interpersonal intelligence, we want to develop the concept of collective intelligence, or the ability of the individual to think about the well-being of the collective, and the capacity of the collective to act on behalf of the individual. As community psychologists, it is our job to find ways to promote collective intelligence, not just interpersonal skills.

Steps for Organizational Change

Now that we know what emotional competencies are needed to foster and sustain change in organizations, we can use them to make progress through the different stages of change. All phases of organizational development require a combination of self-awareness, self-regulation, empathy and social skills. Self-awareness is required to assess: how organizational dynamics affect your own well-being; and your confidence to challenge the system. Self-regulation is required to make positive use of self-awareness in instigating change, while motivation is needed to get the process of transformation under way. Empathy, in turn, is needed to understand how the status quo and alternative modes of operation affect co-workers and partners. Social skills are essential in negotiating with multiple stakeholders the various tasks, aims, and processes of innovation, being always mindful of how power differences affect the different players in the organization. Each phase of change calls for the synergy of the various emotional, interpersonal and transformational competencies described in Table 9.3.

Prochaska and colleagues postulated a theory of change that has been successfully used and applied to individual and organizational change (Prochaska et al., 1994; Weick & Quinn, 1999). The theory describes predictable and necessary stages of change. Table 9.4 applies concepts of the theory to organizational work. For each one of the steps we describe key questions for planning and implementation. These questions should help you and other community psychologists trying to produce change and recruit support for it.

The first two stages of change relate to pre-contemplation and contemplation. In pre-contemplation it is possible that nobody, except perhaps you, or a few silent

Table 9.4 Steps for organizational change

Steps	Aim: What do we want to achieve?	People: Who should be involved?	Tasks: What needs to be done?	Accountability: Who will do it?	Timetable: When will it be done?
Pre-contemplation	Create awareness	Allies in change	Inform others	Choose effective people	Decide on period of time to raise awareness
Contemplation	Create need for change	Allies and potential allies	Identify specific problems and spread information	People with credibility in organization	Enough time to build momentum for change
Preparation	Choose specific goals and areas of change	People with influence and credibility	Gather data about problem and devise plan	Internal and/or external consultants with representative group	Have clear timelines for preparation phase
Action	Carry out most effective interventions	Everyone affected by the proposed change	Multiple tasks associated with changes	Involve multiple agents of change	Decide ahead of time on schedule as too much time diminishes credibility
Maintenance	Put in place systems for sustainability	Everyone affected by change	Key activities to sustain and institutionalize change	As many people as possible	Offer maintenance activities at regular intervals
Evaluation	Evaluate process and outcomes of change	Consult with as many people affected as possible	Quantitative and qualitative techniques of evaluation	Internal and/or external evaluators	Ideally conduct pre-, during and post-evaluations
Follow-up	Become a learning and empowering organization	As many people affected by intervention as possible	Institutionalize learning circles and cycles	Decentralize responsibility for learning cycles and circles	Continuous cycle of learning

others, are aware that something needs to be done about an unsatisfactory situation. In which case, somebody needs to raise consciousness about the problem. In contemplation you are already planting the seed to move the process forward. Discontent may turn into positive action. But for others to listen to you, you need to stay connected while creating a minor (or major) disturbance to the status quo. Bond (1999) coined the concept *connected-disruption* to describe the job of community psychologists within organizations. According to her we have to be able to point to unjust practices and still remain engaged with most people in order for them to listen to us.

> I characterize this prescription for change as connected disruption. Confronting our collective complacency with organizational arrangements that preclude meaningful involvement across gender, race, ethnicity, sexual orientation, and disability involves a process of developing a disruptive edge yet doing so while staying in relationships with others. It involves connecting to individuals while disrupting organizational culture. (Bond, 1999, p. 351)

The third step, preparation, involves the planning and design of innovations or alterations to the current system of work, service delivery, or communication patterns, whatever the case might be. During the action phase, it is very important to make sure that all stakeholders affected by the new system of work are involved. Once again, not only is it in line with our values, but it is also the most efficacious way of going about change because it creates ownership, commitment and account-ability (Dimock, 1992; Goleman, 1998; Johnson & Johnson, 2000).

Once the action has been initiated, it is crucial to put in place systems for moni-toring accurate implementation of the intended changes. The sustainability and dissemination of innovations depend on a careful plan for making the innovation or new program an integral part of the institution (Dalton et al., 2001). In the absence of maintenance and monitoring systems, change is likely to be weak and short lived. Although parts of the next step, evaluation, cannot be undertaken until changes have been introduced into the system, some aspects of the evaluation can be under-taken during the implementation itself. This will enable a formative assessment of how things are going. By observing the change process itself, we are able to feed back useful information that can improve and refine the innovation while it is being introduced. We call this process *action research* (Reason & Bradbury, 2001), and you will learn more about it in Chapters 11 and 12.

An ideal follow up to any process of organizational development is for the setting to become a learning organization itself, one that constantly evaluates and adjusts its operations in line with its values, goals and changing contexts. The learning organi-zation involves everyone in the process of improving the personal and interpersonal well-being of workers and the collective well-being of the community (Senge, 1990; Senge & Scharmer, 2001). This model has also been called the *continuous change process* (Weick & Quinn, 1999).

What are the Strengths and Weaknesses of Organizational Interventions?

The strengths of organizational interventions derive primarily from their *potential to affect the lives of thousands or millions of people*. Organizations affect our lives in multiple ways. The sooner we make workplaces, schools, civic institutions and government departments more participatory, value-based and transformational, the sooner we will be able to improve the lives of workers and communities alike. As social change happens in, through, and because of organizations, the potential to use organizations to produce larger changes is significant. Given that community psychologists work or volunteer in organizations, they have many opportunities to make a change. This potential notwithstanding, we realize that change is a hard and humbling enterprise.

We have to be conscious of traps and threats. *Complacency and resistance* are major barriers to change. Swimming against the tide can be emotionally draining and potentially risky. Challengers of the status quo risk exclusion, marginalisation, labelling and potential unemployment. The forces of resistance are almost always stronger than the forces of change (Beehr & O'Driscoll, 2002; Dimock, 1992; Hahn, 1994; Klein et al, 2000; Waddell et al., 2000; Weick & Quinn, 1999).

The ubiquitous risk of cosmetic changes is called *tokenism*. It is a technique used to introduce small changes that create the appearance of change but in fact help to prevent transformations. Sullivan (1984) calls this phenomenon *dislocation*, by which he means 'a process whereby something new is brought into a cultural system and has the ability to mute the partial critical insight of that cultural system' (p. 165). Changes of a minor nature are introduced into organizations with the purpose of creating an aura of innovation, changes that invariably delay attention to more structural issues.

An exclusive *inward focus* is another potential deviation that needs to be monitored. Some organizations invest in development only to advance the *interests of upper management or privileged stakeholders* (Alvesson & Willmott, 1992; Baritz, 1974; Hollway, 1991; Lawthom, 1999). Business and human service organizations alike have also been criticized for starting *half-hearted initiatives* that create expectations of improvement but amount only to passing fads that strengthen the status quo (Prilleltensky, 1994b; Prilleltensky & Nelson, 2002).

What is the Role of Community Psychologists Working in Communities?

The skills and processes required for organizational change apply to community change as well. In many cases, community psychologists represent one organization in working with another. Neighbourhood centres, schools, community mental health clinics and universities all interact with each other and with government in starting new programs or policies. But if the skills are similar, the contexts are different. We are moving from one level of analysis to another, a larger one. Inter-organizational work is becoming prevalent in CP, and for good reasons. No one organization has the power to enhance community well-being on its own. Inter-agency collaborations can mobilize multiple partners for interventions with synergistic outcomes (Foster-Fishman, Salem, et al. 2001; Wolff, 2001). Given the promise of partnerships for community change, we chose to concentrate a part of this chapter on the role of *partnership maker*. The creation of coalitions is really a prelude to community change. Hence, we also discuss the role of *change maker*. Finally, we discuss the role of *knowledge maker*, which should always accompany intervention efforts.

Partnership Maker

To make a change in an organization you need to find allies. Similarly, to make a change in a community you need partners. Table 9.5 describes seven steps in the creation and actualization of partnerships for change. In each step the community psychologist assumes a particular role. She wears different hats depending on the phase, but she always keeps all the hats in her bag, just in case, for partnerships are very dynamic and boundaries across phases often blur. Still, it is useful to identify the primary role in each step. Based on our previous work and reports of other community psychologists we identify seven main roles for the seven main tasks of partnerships (Elias, 1994; Foster-Fishman, Berkowitz et al., 2001; Nelson, Amio et al., 2000; Nelson, Prilleltensky & MacGillivary, 2001; Prilleltensky, 2001; Prilleltensky, Martell et al., 2001; Prilleltensky, Peirson et al. 1997; Wolff, 2001).

- *Inclusive host:* Whether you are initiating the partnership yourself, or you have been invited to one, you need to behave like an inclusive host. Power differentials are always at play in partnerships, primarily when community members with little or no formal education join the group. We think it is very important to contribute to a climate of respect and mutual support.
- *Visionary:* Once we are comfortable with each other, the business of change begins. We caution against skipping this stage. As a collective, partners need to establish a common vision for the project. Our role is to help in visioning outcomes and processes for the collaborative work.
- *Asset seeker:* This is an important role for two reasons. First, in line with the values of self-determination, collaboration and respect for diversity, we want to afford everyone an opportunity to express her or his views about what needs to be done. Each person has the right to express an opinion, regardless of expert status. Second, and just as importantly, valuable knowledge emerges from everyone in the partnership: citizens, professionals, and volunteers alike. We will never know what material or conceptual assets people bring unless we look for them.
- *Listener conceptualizer:* To define the problem cooperatively we need to listen carefully to what all the partners are saying. Next, we need to formulate the problem in light of previous research and local knowledge.
- *Pragmatic partner:* At this stage we wear the doer hat. The time has come to take action, and to do it with others. However, we should not forget the previous roles. We still need to be inclusive hosts, asset seekers, and good listeners. We have to be able to read the context and assess the group's readiness for action. To do so, we invoke the set of emotional and transformational skills presented in Table 9.4.
- *Research partner:* Throughout the planning and implementation, we study the work of the partnership. We engage partners in evaluating the process and the outcomes of the work.
- *Trend setter:* It is not enough to have an excellent pilot project that gets forgotten soon after it was born. We have to ensure that partners adopt the innovation and disseminate it widely. We have to create enduring trends, not just passing fads.

Table 9.5 Roles, steps, tasks and challenges for the development of community partnerships

Roles and Steps	Tasks	Challenges for Community Psychologists
Inclusive host Create partnerships	■ Include members of the organizations and communities where the intervention is to take place ■ Create a welcoming and friendly climate for partners	■ Abandon the role of the expert and share power with partners ■ Reduce barriers to participation for partners
Visionary Clarify values and vision and derive working principles	■ Collaboratively clarify values and vision to guide the project ■ Derive working principles and ground rules for how the group and programme should work	■ Engage in self-reflexive analysis of personal values ■ Be open to being challenged by partners ■ Be aware of value incongruence and strive to reduce it
Asset seeker Identify and amalgamate the strengths of different partners and approaches	■ Identify and build on strengths of different partners ■ Integrate deductive and inductive approaches to planning and implementation	■ Work to overcome self-doubts and mistrust of community members ■ Value the experiential knowledge of community partners ■ Find common ground and respect differences to bridge the worlds of community members and professionals
Listener conceptualizer Define the problem collaboratively	■ Collaboratively define and analyse the problem in terms of power differentials, oppression and injustice ■ Focus on the strengths of the community	■ Reconcile differing views and build consensus regarding a plan of action ■ Build ownership and support for actions
Pragmatic partner Develop and implement the intervention collaboratively	■ Collaboratively decide on what type of intervention to implement ■ Ensure that necessary human and material resources are available for intervention	■ Share with partners knowledge from literature about successful interventions ■ Ensure that CP values are respected throughout the entire process
Research partner Research and evaluate collaboratively	■ Use both deductive (quantitative) and inductive (qualitative) approaches in program evaluation ■ Research and evaluate each of the steps	■ Institute continuous cycle of learning in the partnership ■ Clarify roles of partners
Trend setter Disseminate and institutionalize	■ Share knowledge and lessons learnt with others ■ Build mechanisms for making partnership and interventions integral part of agencies	■ Move beyond pilot stage and consider sustainability a priority ■ Think long term even while confronting the challenges of the short term

Adapted from Nelson, Amio, Prilleltensky and Nickels (2000)

In March 2003, Isaac and Scot Evans from the Community Research and Action Program at Vanderbilt University began a consultation process with Oasis Youth Center in Nashville (www.oasiscenter.org). The process illustrates many of the seven roles of partnership makers. What is wonderful about the consultation process, which is still going on, is that people in the organization are magnificent partnership makers themselves. The aim of the consultation was to work with the organization to move it from ameliorative to transformative mode. Following a presentation by Isaac on the topic, a group of workers, including the executive director, decided to form a T-Team, short for transformative team.

During our first meeting, which followed shortly after Isaac's presentation, everyone behaved like an inclusive host. Aware of some tensions among various branches of the organization (youth shelter, counselling, youth leadership), Scot and Isaac wanted to make this process as inclusive as possible. This was not hard. Everyone who attended the meeting emphasized the need to have all voices heard in this renewal process. Representatives from all the branches were invited to subsequent meetings.

As soon as we started the process we realized that if we wanted to move the organization from merely reacting to problems to transforming the conditions that lead to problems, we needed a new mission statement. We all engaged in a visioning exercise that started within the committee but spread throughout the organization. Through a participatory action research process, members of the T-Team interviewed co-workers, parents and youngsters about their visions of personal, relational and collective well-being.

Soon after the new mission statement was adopted, the T-Team began identifying areas of strength within the organization, areas where the mission statement is already being enacted, and enacted well. This was an exercise in asset seeking. Oasis wanted to recognize and celebrate what it was doing well. But not all aspects of the organization aligned well with the new mission statement. The T-Team started doing some focused listening. We all tried to identify what issues prevented the organization from becoming more transformative. From this listening phase we moved to problem solving. We are all trying to be pragmatic and research partners, seeking solutions and researching alternatives to the current ways of serving young people in the community. We are not at the stage yet of being trendsetters, either within the organization, or within the community, but we are systematically reviewing all aspects of the organization, trying to find ways to match words to actions. One of the first places where changes took place was in the youth shelter. Following the adoption of the mission statement, staff started to involve young people much more in the operation of the shelter, giving them more choices and opportunities to participate in decision-making processes. Counsellors in Oasis are re-developing their intake forms to reflect a strengths-based approach and the youth leadership team received a grant to engage in youth activism. Our work continues to evaluate all branches of the organization, in the hope of moving from partnership makers to change makers.

Change Maker

How do we make sure that partnerships do not end up reproducing the status quo? After all, collaboration is a powerful tool used by protectors of the status quo. Business elites and conservative groups strike alliances to repel threats to the dominant social order (Barlow & Campbell, 1995; McQuaig, 1998). The risk of dislocation, reviewed in the context of organizations, applies equally to partnerships and coalitions. It is entirely possible that coalitions for health, safety and prevention divert attention from political reform. Hence, we make a distinction between partnership maker and change maker. For us, change makers have to elicit in themselves and others the transformational potential of emotional competencies. This involves asking hard questions such as *whose interests the coalition represents, whose power will be enhanced, whose values will be upheld, and whose lives will be improved by the intervention* (Lord & Church, 1998).

The emotional competencies for transformation reviewed earlier are a resource for community change. They just need to be focused on how the interventions will improve the lives of those with less power, less access to services and less influence. Organizations such as PICO strive to keep a focus on social change, as do consumer/survivor organizations struggling to change not only psychiatry, but also society's perceptions of people with mental health problems (see Chapter 21). Going back to Table 9.1, we want to make sure that our interventions transcend amelioration and move towards transformation.

Some radical transformations occur when people renounce the dominant system of consumerism and form communes and co-operatives such as Mondragon in Spain and the Israeli kibbutzim (Ife, 2002). In co-operatives of that kind people make major changes by adopting a simpler and more environmentally friendly lifestyle. These are examples of self-contained communities where co-operation is the primary value. Transformational changes in communities that are contiguous with the dominant capitalist system are harder to sustain.

Nation, Wandersman and Perkins (2002) review the work of several North American community development corporations (CDCs) and comprehensive community initiatives (CCIs). These partnerships address health, psychological, social, economic and urban issues. The Bedford-Stuyvesant Restoration Corporation, for instance, implemented political and economic action that culminated in better social services, improved housing and new retail stores. Other efforts improved health habits and rates of child immunization. These and other achievements, obtained through community development, group mobilization, advocacy and political lobbying, tended to fade away due to lack of sustainability. For interventions to be effective, and to last, the authors recommend four strategies:

1. *Comprehensiveness:* In line with the value of holism expressed in Chapter 2, the authors recommend intervening at multiple levels and targeting multiple issues at the same time. According to them 'a piecemeal approach rarely produces the critical mass needed to turn around distressed communities' (Nation, Wandersman & Perkins, 2002, p. 15).
2. *Empowerment:* Citizen participation and capacity building are emphasized to embed the intervention in the life of the community.
3. *Identification and utilization of assets:* Similar to the role of asset seeker in creating partnerships, the authors recommend 'identifying, mapping, developing, and using indigenous social, physical, and economic assets' (Nation, Wandersman & Perkins, 2002, p. 16).

4. *Sustainability:* Community psychologists need to procure the continuation of material, human, environmental, social and political resources to maintain the momentum for change.

The Massachusetts Area Health Education Centre supports health and human service coalitions (Wolff, 2000). This coalition seems to enact most of the prescriptions suggested by Nation, Wandersman and Perkins. In addition, and crucially, the coalition seems to inch towards transformation.

Knowledge Maker

Community psychologists have much to learn from successful and failed interventions. Each intervention consists of mini-cycles of interventions. By studying the enabling and inhibiting factors each step of the way, they can improve the next cycle, and the one after that. We call this a *formative evaluation*. At the end of a project or a major initiative, it is time to take stock of what has been accomplished, what has been learnt, and what could be done differently in the future. We call this *summative* or *outcome evaluations*. An action research approach that promotes learning by all stakeholders, throughout the whole process, ensures that important lessons are not lost along the way (Elias, 1994; Flyvbjerg, 2001; Reason & Bradbury, 2001). Part of the community psychologist's job is to nurture a culture of knowledge.

What are the Strengths and Limitations of Community Interventions?

The strengths and limitations of community interventions can be gleaned from a review on citizen participation and community organizations. Wandersman and Florin (2000) report that the main effects of citizen participation are related to physical and environmental conditions of the community, levels of crime, provision of social services, interpersonal relationships, sense of community, satisfaction with place of residence, personal efficacy and psychological empowerment. Although these are positive and encouraging findings, their review does not reveal outcomes associated with increased political activity or direct social action. *Most effects appear to be associated with ameliorative – as opposed to transformative – actions.* Herein lie the main benefits and shortcomings of community interventions.

There is little doubt that community interventions can improve quality of life. Tangible outcomes in the form of reduced crime, abuse, violence, and improved health, cohesion and urban civility make a difference in the daily lives of community members (McNeely, 1999; Power, 1996). Our challenge, however, is to blend the pursuit of short-term care and compassion with the long-term struggle for justice. For it is only when justice prevails that political, economic and social resources can be distributed fairly and equitably.

What are some of the Dilemmas Faced by Community Psychologists Working in Organizations and Communities?

Once you are trained to identify injustice at the interpersonal, organizational, community and societal levels, it is hard to keep it a secret. Once you associate with people who share your passion for making a difference, it is hard to ignore norms of oppression. What's the problem, you may ask. The problem is that many others may not share your passion or convictions. When opposition mounts, you face a tough choice: struggle and resist, or acquiesce. As Bond (1999) claimed, it is hard to remain connected with the people who perpetuate injustice. The dilemma is how far you can challenge the system before you begin paying a price in the form of exclusion, labelling and disconnection. The opposite dilemma is no less pressing: How to live in harmony with your values if you do not enact resistance?

The foregoing dilemmas refer to taking action. A further quandary is what type of action to take. What to do when we are aware that, despite much rhetoric, we are stuck in ameliorative mode? David Chavis (2000) has been involved in community development for 25 years. He has worked for many citizen committees and organizations. His capacity-building efforts have made a major contribution to many block associations in the US. To what extent that type of work leads to transformation and not just amelioration is not very clear. Chavis (2001) himself criticizes community coalitions for not pushing the social justice agenda far enough.

Chapter Summary

In this chapter we considered how community psychologists could make a difference in organizations and communities alike. We drew a distinction between interventions that ameliorate conditions of suffering and disadvantage and those that seek to make more profound transformations. This challenge pervades CP work. Typically ameliorative changes attend to values such as caring, compassion, health and a measure of participation. Transformative interventions, in turn, promote social justice, accountability, and meaningful participation and empowerment. To promote either type of change, we require skills that can be strategically applied at different stages of the intervention. Emotional competencies are important for working effectively with people in groups, organizations and partnerships. To ensure that emotional competencies are used for social change, we pointed to their transformational potential.

Discrete steps can be followed to increase the likelihood of success in organizational and community interventions. Following the theory of change proposed by Prochaska and colleagues we outlined a sequence of steps for raising awareness of problems, planning, implementing and evaluating new initiatives.

At the community level, we identified three primary roles for community psychologists: partnership maker, change maker and knowledge maker. Most of the skills and steps discussed in the organizational context may be applied in the community context and vice versa. The functions performed by the partnership maker (inclusive host, visionary, asset seeker, listener conceptualizer, pragmatic partner, research partner and trend setter) can be assimilated into the job of the organizational developer. The emotional competencies identified for organizational work are equally valid in coalition formation (Cherniss, 2002). Likewise, the dilemmas experienced in organizations make life harder in community settings as well.

COMMENTARY: Power and Participation in Context   *Meg A. Bond*

In this chapter, the authors emphasize several innovative ideas as they cover the wide-ranging topic of systems change. The chapter helps to demonstrate how integrally linked organizational and community interventions truly are by pointing out the importance of addressing issues of power in *both* types of interventions. In this commentary, I would like to expand on the particular themes of power and privilege by reflecting on some of the dilemmas and tensions that can emerge as well as on some implications for the change agent role of community psychologists. The conceptual backdrop here is the ecological imperative for understanding the individual in the context of relevant system dynamics.

Power and Participation
The chapter authors emphasize the role of participation for addressing concerns about social justice and power inequalities. The chapter summarizes compelling research that documents the positive health effects of having more involvement and control over one's work and life. In addition, the authors acknowledge that participation can significantly alter the substance and form of interventions. Although participation is suggested as an intervention of choice, in order to promote increased participation, it is important to recognize the peculiar organizational, small group, and interpersonal dynamics involving issues of power and privilege that make this easier said than done and which, at times, can actually place participation and social justice at odds. A few cautionary words follow:

Remember That Representation Is Not Enough
Sometimes attempts to promote shifts in power arrangements involve increasing the representation of more varied groups in decision-making settings. Participation of previously marginalized groups (such as women and/or members of ethnic/racial minority groups) is fostered by inviting members of these groups to 'sit at the table' with others as decisions are made about issues ranging from task assignments and job design to community development and budget priorities. Increasing representation of 'minority' groups is indeed a useful step towards greater equity among workers or community members from varied roles and backgrounds, yet can be akin to ameliorative approaches. Fully raising issues of equity involves more than elevating voices of underrepresented groups. Social justice involves a process of confronting systems of privilege that lead to the differential distribution of resources. Just moving a few new representatives into powerful positions does not, in and of itself, change the orga-

nization's or the community's way of operating. The values or practices that guide the distribution of resources (such as the use of testing to determine resources distribution to schools or the simple use of seniority to determine promotions – both of which tend to disadvantage people of colour) are not necessarily altered just by changing who is making the decision.

Beware of Illusions
Truly transformative interventions must contend with issues of power and privilege not only as reflected in opportunities for participation or formal structures but also in terms of the informal interpersonal dynamics that shape the actual practice of participation. For example, the authors suggest that minimal hierarchies are a step toward transformative change. This can be helpful, but not in all cases. It depends largely upon the nature of the *informal* power structures within the organization. One important lesson from feminist movement organizations is that a structure that masks differences in power and influence by organizing itself as a collective can be more 'tyrannical' than a visible, explicit hierarchy that can be commented upon (Ferree & Martin, 1995; Freeman, 1972). Different verbal abilities, comfort with collective arrangements, and a history of experience in the movement can give some members more power than others, even when the philosophy is feminist and the official hierarchy is 'flat' or 'minimal' (Freeman, 1972). In some situations, the illusion of participation and power sharing can actually further silence those who feel they are not being heard. There can be a sort of mystification born of their sense that they do not see any clear structural barriers to their participation, and thus blame themselves for not having more influence. It is important to avoid idealizing an absence of differentiated roles.

Notice the Subtle Divides
The daily interpersonal and small group dynamics are powerful determinants of not just which individuals are invited to participate but what groups are heard. In many community and organizational settings, the potential for interpersonal differences in power and influence to parallel gender, racial and cultural divides is strong. For example, in one long-term consultation, I observed the ways in which organizationally choreographed 'worker empowerment' efforts can actually impede social justice goals when the perspectives and style preferences of the demographically dominant group (white male workers) determine the flow,

substance, and decision making approach adopted in team meetings. Most of the women were not taken seriously, particularly if they did not talk sports at the water cooler before the meeting; the men of colour were heard only until they voiced a dissenting perception (see Bond, 1999). When engaging workers as partners, there is a risk of reifying team and organizational norms that are built upon the preferences of the majority group, and, ironically, the dynamics can play out in such a way that only those workers who are members of the majority group become fully able and/or comfortable to participate. More transformative approaches need to recognize that the privilege to define dominant norms, values, and preferred interpersonal styles is differentially distributed among organization members.

Avoid Casting Blame

These cautionary notes are not meant to imply that the dynamics that have the *impact* of subverting equality involve any *intentional* effort to curtail the empowering potential of participation. Rather they are strange, common system dynamics that are typically quite invisible to participants – particularly to those participants who have some power to define dominant norms (in the same way that fish are unlikely to be aware of water until it is no longer there). If participation is sought without attention being paid to the great diversity and informal power differentials among participants in terms of how they would prefer to participate and whether the substance and style of their participation would be syntonic with the organizational culture, not all voices and perspectives will necessarily be represented – in spite of everyone's best intentions!

Effective Change Agents: Seeking Authentic Shifts in Power Relations

What skills, perspectives, and sensibilities can help us be effective change agents as we tamper with these complex dynamics and idealistic goals? A stance of 'connected disruption' can be helpful as it emphasizes both the importance of participation and involvement while also acknowledging the importance of disrupting organizational and cultural arrangements that are blind to privilege (Bond, 1999). I believe you need to work in partnerships that embrace differences but that also actively recognize system dynamics where supposedly 'equally valuing' the voice of dominant groups can actually silence nondominant group members. Revealing and elevating minority perspectives is disruptive and signals a loss of power for the

majority to define the prevailing version of 'reality'. As change agents, we may well need to support participation in a more differentiated manner, where not all who 'come to the table' are treated the same way. One of my students captured this spirit in the following vision for her work: 'May the troubled be comforted, and may the comfortable be troubled' (Sanborne, 2001).

In this chapter, the authors provide some important guidance about change-agent roles as they extend the notion of emotional intelligence to 'collective intelligence', defined as 'the ability of the individual to think about the well-being of the collective and the capacity of the collective to act on behalf of the individual'. The authors call upon community psychologists to 'find ways to promote collective intelligence, not just interpersonal skills'. To extend this discussion, I suggest that attention to 'the well-being of the collective' requires empathy and members' ability to reach out and understand that others may see and experience the world differently. The 'capacity of the collective to act on behalf of the individual' can build upon reconsideration of who is accountable to whom and a willingness to be disruptive when the collective becomes complacent about any arrangements that only support the genuine participation of a privileged few.

Power and Privilege as the Common Thread

As glue for the chapter, the authors articulate a critical link between organizational and community interventions. Other texts often treat organizational interventions as if they were only another 'type' of community intervention. Organizations are where most people spend most of their time and thus a central context for our lives. So in one sense, the workplace *is* a 'community' and deserves attention as such. However, as the authors point out, it is also the case that organizations are the primary vehicle through which we direct our work with communities. We need to express – and experience – justice, respect and involvement in this context in order to develop the foundation for such work with others. If we feel inconsequential, disrespected and diminished in our workplaces, it certainly makes it difficult to support the empowerment of others. Finding authentic ways for all voices to matter is the uniting challenge.

Attending to the nuances of power and privilege that accompany participation as well as bringing the values and operations of our workplaces into line with the values that guide our work with communities are both common sense and profoundly radical.

community interventions efforts by organized groups and agencies to enhance the well-being of community members marginalized by social practices of exclusion, discrimination and injustice

consultant a person who works with an organization or community and assists them in achieving their goals

contemplation phase in which people realize that something needs to change

emotional competencies set of skills required to handle self and others in a respectful and efficient manner consistent with a set of cogent values

external agent of change the role assumed by community psychologists or others who wish to push for changes from outside an organization or community

internal agent of change the role assumed by community psychologists or others who wish to change a practice from within an organization

organizational interventions systematic methods of enhancing an institution's capacity to promote the personal, relational and collective well-being of their workers and community stakeholders

pre-contemplation state of affairs in which people do not realize the need to change a practice or a situation

1. Volume 34, number 1 of *The Community Psychologist* (Winter 2001) contains a special section on liberation psychology edited by Rod Watts. You will find there some examples of interventions that move from amelioration towards transformation.

2. A special issue of the *American Journal of Community Psychology* (2003, volume 31, Issue 1–2, pages 73–201), edited by Rod Watts and Irma Serrano-García, is entirely devoted to liberation and responses to oppression. That special issue also contains examples of transformative interventions.

3. A special section of the *American Journal of Community Psychology* (2001, volume 29, number 2), edited by Thomas Wolff, deals extensively with the issue of community coalition building.

4. You studied in this chapter some of PICO's interventions and strategies. You can visit their website on www.piconetwork.org.

5. A group of community psychologists has developed a web-based community toolbox that contains user-friendly guidelines for community development. Visit http://ctb.ukans.edu.

6. Another valuable website, http://www.capablecommunity.com/, is that for the Association for the Study of Community Development. David Chavis, a community psychologist, is the president of this organization.

10
Small Group and Individual Interventions

Warm-up Exercise

For us to change and to help others to change, we need to understand how social influences prevent us from transforming our attitudes and behaviour. In particular, we need to understand our relationship to our own power and privilege. Many theories claim that society influences us. We claim that society does not just influence us; society is in us. It is not just a matter of society shaping our ways; we embody society within ourselves. Therefore, it is very hard to be critical of society when we are it, and it is very hard to be critical of ourselves when society doesn't want us to be critical of the status quo. We are part of the status quo; we are the very society we wish to criticize.

To explore our blind spots then, consider the following group exercise:

1. Form in class a group of four or five students.
2. Make a list of privileges you enjoy in life.
3. Share your list with the group.
4. Discuss with the group how your privileges may come at the expense of others.
5. Contemplate what privileges you may be willing to give up.
6. Discuss what group norms may help you to give up some of your own power and privileges.

After reading this chapter you will be able to answer the following questions about small group and individual interventions:

■ What are they and why are they important?

- What is their value-base?
- How do they promote well-being and liberation?
- What is the role of community psychologists in promoting them?
- What are some of the limitations and dilemmas they pose for community psychologists?

Is it fair to expect community members wounded by interpersonal and social oppression to change society while they are hurting? At what point do we expect people who have been damaged emotionally and socially to turn their attention to the plight of others? If we expect them to do so too soon they may not be ready or it may not even be fair. After all, they may need some time and space to nurse their wounds and recover, spiritually and psychologically, from experiences of subjugation and minimization. On the other hand, if we don't connect their plight to the plight of others, in some form of solidarity, we may end up isolating them and their source of discomfort even further. There seems to be a unique paradox at play here. Without some kind of individual attention and space, individuals may not process their own sources of suffering and alienation; but with too much space and individual attention they may not connect their own suffering to the suffering of others, or join hands with others to overcome the forces pressing them down. The paradox may be resolvable if we time individual and small group interventions right and if we connect them to larger efforts at social transformation.

It is entirely possible that citizens experiencing psychosocial emergencies (for example abuse, depression, homelessness, crime) may be depleted and unable to turn their attention to the psychopolitical sources of personal, relational and collective suffering. Some of them may justifiably want to focus on the pain of abuse, depression or eviction. Some of them want food and school supplies for their children now. They cannot wait until a radical social transformation takes place. And they are right. So we, community psychologists and community workers of all stripes, rally behind their cause to demand psychosocial emergency help now. But our political awareness tells us that something must be done to stop these tragedies from happening in the first place. Something tells us that it's not fair that some live in opulence and others in destitution. But the unceasing demand for services and emergency supplies barely leaves time for transformative work. So we, community psychologists and community workers of all stripes, face a serious dilemma: When do we stop looking at the individual emergencies in order to put out the fire that is causing so many burns in the first place? It may seem out of place to worry about politics when children cannot eat now. It may seem utopian to think of a better society when homeless families are on the streets now. But if we fail to dream and we fail to put out the fire, more and more casualties will continue to require our immediate attention and nobody will have the foresight to think about the future, or the other children who will become homeless and hungry if we don't act now.

In the context of this dilemma we explore the role of individual and small group interventions. Our premise is that individual and small group interventions must be connected to the large socioeconomic spheres that dictate so much of what transpires at the local and micro levels of experience and analysis. Hence, we are in favour of providing psychosocial emergency services, provided they are accompanied and paralleled by efforts at social transformation. Otherwise, however well intentioned they might be, individual and small group interventions strengthen the status quo by giving the message that what ought to change is primarily psychological and not sociological. By the same token, we oppose societal interventions that neglect the psychological needs of individual members and force social changes without community consultation (Community Mental Health Project, 1998; Lewis, Lewis, Daniels & D'Andrea, 2003).

Think of yourself as a practising community psychologist. You are under pressure to look after psychosocial emergencies such as abuse, neglect and teenage pregnancy, but you know that you cannot expend all your energies treating the casualties of social decay. If you do, you'll have no time or stamina to prevent them in the first place. Well, most of us community psychologists feel that way. In this chapter we review the benefits of individual and small group interventions but we caution against glorification of their virtues, lest we forget that psychosocial emergency treatments have their limitations. Not surprisingly, their usefulness is a question of timing, balance and context.

Community psychology (CP) is closely connected to clinical psychology. In fact, many pioneers in CP were trained as clinical psychologists and many community psychologists still practise today in clinical settings. One could argue that it would be hard to be an empathic community psychologist without some kind of clinical training. Others could equally argue that treating individuals out of context is poor practice. Best practice lies, once again, in timing, balance and context. If all we do is therapy while neglecting people's circumstances, our practice is out of balance. If all we do is try to restructure communities without attending to people's inner struggles and feelings, we are equally off balance.

If citizens are hurting so much that they cannot attend to others, the timing is not right for them to engage in solidarity work. If the focus remains on the individual for too long, balance is offset. If the context violates individual rights and forces conformity, we turn our attention to personal needs. In the case of services for children, Levine and Levine (1992) documented how dominant ideologies created imbalances in attention to either personal or social issues. The lesson for us is to be alert to historical trends so that we may restore balance when necessary.

Hitherto we have turned our attention to interventions with people who require some form of help. But this is only one way of using individual and small group interventions. These strategies may also be used with people who do not necessarily hurt but can, and want to, fight injustice. The foci may change, but some of the tools are the same. In both instances we need to be good listeners, good communicators and good challengers of the status quo. Hence, in this chapter we present individual and small group interventions as means of coping with adversity and promoting social transformation (Vera & Speight, 2003). In many cases, our work with one group or one person may encompass both aims: coping and transformation. Sometimes it will be a matter of what comes first. In other cases we may be able to work on both simultaneously. We have to remember that people are neither victims nor selfless activists all the time. Many of us fluctuate between feeling hurt and gathering our strengths in support of social change. People who require help in coping with adversity can also support others. They are not permanently in 'client' mode. They also have a sense of agency that needs to be nurtured and validated, for their own sake and for the sake of others (Freedman & Combs, 1996; Morgan, 2000; White, M., 1988/9; 2000). This applies to adults as much as to children (John, 2003).

This preamble alerts us to the many uses of individual and group interventions. They can be used in supporting the unwell, but also in channelling the transformational energies of the well-enough. Let's see how we can do this in our work and personal lives.

What are Small Group and Individual Interventions?

Situations requiring small group and individual interventions are as diverse as the sources of oppression and suffering. Our holistic notions of health and well-being require that we intervene at the personal, relational and collective levels. Problems of abuse, homelessness and discrimination have multiple sources and multiple manifestations. While the problems go beyond any one individual's scope of action, the repercussions are often felt deeply at the personal level (McWhirter, 1994). To help individuals cope with problems in living and to strengthen their personal resources we devise individual and small group interventions. These interventions identify people's assets and build on their resilience. However, these strategies are not meant exclusively for people experiencing psychosocial challenges, for they can also be used to generate social change with people who are fortunate not to experience severe challenges.

For us, then, individual and small group interventions are paths and strategies towards coping and social transformation at the same time. Interventions of this kind may occur in mental health centres, community centres, adult education programs, schools, as part of a prevention program or as a component of mutual help projects. Furthermore, they may be directed by community, clinical, school or organizational psychologists, natural helpers, mentors, lay people or community workers. The crucial component for us is that people working with individuals and small groups follow the values and principles of CP articulated in earlier chapters. This means constant attention to the balance among values for personal, relational and collective well-being. This type of work requires the skilful combination of compassion and empathy with the ability to challenge preconceived notions of community members. All of it in such a way that trust may be built between the helper and the community member (Corey & Corey, 2003).

We want to be clear though that some mental health problems require the specialized treatment of clinical psychologists or counsellors. However, there are many issues in life that may be addressed with the help of natural helpers in the community such as youth leaders, pastors, mentors, friends, teachers and relatives. Hence, personal and small group work happens in parenting groups, counselling sessions, mutual help associations and so on (Levy, 2000).

Chapter 2 outlined the two main goals of CP: well-being and liberation. Driven by these goals and by the values expressed in Chapter 3, the task is to develop skills that can put these visions into action. The remainder of the chapter deals with that challenge.

What are the Values Supporting the Work with Small Groups and Individuals?

While all the values articulated in Chapters 2 and 3 play a role in well-being and liberation, the need for some values may be more pressing for some people than for others. People's needs, in turn, are greatly determined by the context of their lives. Hence, we cannot predetermine what combination of values will be most helpful to a woman before we know her situation. Victims of abuse, during a certain phase of their recovery, may need more compassion than assertiveness and self-determination. They may not have the emotional wherewithal to deal with the abuser or with the system that often re-victimizes them. But after a certain period of mourning or reflection or participation in self-help groups, victims may be ready to fight the system and help others who have been equally victimized. As discussed in Chapter 5, empowerment is closely linked to mentoring relationships and participation in action groups. Connecting with others in similar situations is a source of support and growth; it's comforting and energizing at the same time (Kieffer, 1984; Lord & Hutchinson, 1993; Nelson, Lord & Ochocka, 2001b).

The question we have to ask ourselves is what does this person need right now? As we progress in our work, we have to ask ourselves how her needs have changed over the course of our relationship. These are questions we cannot answer for ourselves. Our partners in the helping relationship have a big say in what they need. We accompany them on their journey, but we don't necessarily tell them where to travel, even if at times we may suggest a different course of action (Ivey & Ivey, 2003; Morgan, 2000; White & Epston, 1990).

It is possible that in our work with privileged people we may foreground the value of accountability (Goodman, 2001). There is much wisdom in the saying 'may the troubled be comforted and may the comfortable be troubled'. A call to accountability may trouble the privileged, for it requires self-examination and personal scrutiny. Most of all, it requires change and perhaps even a degree of depowerment. But however uncomfortable this may make us and them, it's one of the only ways we have to restore justice and equality: demanding accountability and a measure of self-depowerment (see Chapter 16 for an elaboration of this concept).

Why are Small Group and Individual Interventions Important?

This question has a three-part answer. They are important because they enhance personal, relational, and collective well-being. As may be seen in Table 10.1, the effects of individual and small group interventions may be felt at all these levels. Whereas some individual interventions may concentrate on the emotional well-being of the person in front of us, others can target relational or societal domains such as norms of aggression or social capital (Lewis et al., 2003).

At the personal level, research has documented some of the beneficial effects of counselling and therapy. Positive outcomes include better coping, higher sense of control, improved life satisfaction, renewed appreciation for one's voice, enhanced self-concept as well as other positive effects (Perez, DeBord & Bieschke, 2000; Seligman, 1995). These positive outcomes concern primarily a person's well-being.

Table 10.1 Potential contributions of small group and individual interventions

Concerns	Domains		
	Personal	Relational	Collective
Well-being	Effective coping Resilience Better quality of life Voice and choice Dignity and self-respect Respect Sense of control	Supportive relationships Caring and compassion Participation in decisions affecting one's life Respect for diversity in relationships Better parenting	Enhanced social capital Higher educational outcomes Reduced prevalence of mental health problems Economic productivity Sense of community Improved safety
Liberation from oppressive forces	Overcome internalized oppression Personal de-blaming Personal empowerment Expression of anger Protest against personal and social injustice Clear connections between personal and social injustice	Support people to leave abusive relationships Prevent emotional abuse in family, school and work Join with others in struggle for liberation Accountability in relationships Relationships based on 'power with' instead of 'power over'	Group action against patriarchy and other forms of domination Links with other solidarity groups More leaders in social movements Citizens with political consciousness Education about sources of injustice

Equally beneficial outcomes include liberation from oppressive psychological, social or political forces (Prochaska et al., 1994). Emancipatory outcomes at the personal level include overcoming internalized oppression, personal de-blaming, empowerment and making the connection between personal suffering and political circumstances. Personal well-being is closely tied to political well-being (McWhirter, 1994; Moane, 1999; Prilleltensky & Nelson, 2002).

Working with individuals or small groups can also have positive effects in the relational domain. They can improve relationships, balance power dynamics and increase participation in decisions affecting one's life and others. The benefits of individual and small group work can radiate outwards and create positive ripple effects. If I learn in a group how to identify my own biases and how to communicate with others better, those who surround me at work and at home will benefit from my participation in such group (Barrera, 2000; Borkman, 1999; Cohen et al., 2000; Ornish, 1997).

At the collective level, this kind of work can strengthen social capital, reduce the prevalence of mental health problems, improve community safety, and even generate social action to challenge oppressive norms (Putnam, 2000). We are reminded of Margaret Mead's 'never doubt that a small group of people can change the world. Indeed, it is the only thing that ever has.' Research demonstrates that empowerment is a very relational construct. Few are the people who empower themselves without joining groups or getting support from others (Kieffer, 1984; Lord & Hutchinson, 1993).

In addition to these beneficial outcomes, let's not forget that all our work in organizations, communities and social movements reviewed in earlier chapters relies heavily on our ability to work with people – another useful legacy of clinical and counselling psychology. There is, in fact, a great deal of correlation between our ability to listen empathically and to be a small group facilitator and our ability to be effective in any kind of organization. As Goleman (1995, 1998) noted, there is a core set of emotional intelligence skills that are transferable from setting to setting.

How do Small Group and Individual Interventions Promote Well-being and Liberation?

Individual and small group interventions can, and often do, go together. A common intervention in community psychological work is home visiting. In many early intervention programs, parents work with a nurse, a psychologist, a community worker or a volunteer. Mothers are often given advice on how to stimulate their infants and what to expect from them at different developmental phases. Often these mothers also attend parenting groups where they share experiences and learn from each other.

People who are effective changers go through identifiable stages. We introduced in Chapter 9 stages of change. Prochaska and colleagues observed that people move through different phases when they get ready to make changes in their lives (Prochaska et al., 1994). In this chapter we apply these phases to individual and small group work. Our dual emphasis is on how people work to alter circumstances oppressing them; and create changes to give up some of their power and privilege. Whereas the former concentrates on forms of empowerment, the latter deals with forms of depowerment (see Chapter 16). In this section we deal with both kinds of change.

Table 10.2 Steps for interventions with individuals and small groups

Steps	Work with Individuals	Work with Small Groups
Pre-contemplation	■ Explore sources of oppression and suffering ■ Explore need for accountability	■ Review reasons for coming together ■ Legitimize group's existence
Contemplation	■ Refine and define areas of work ■ Think about personal, relational and collective changes	■ Refine and define areas of work ■ Establish principles for working together ■ Validate misgivings and hesitations
Preparation	■ Choose specific goals and areas of change ■ Warm up to idea of doing things differently	■ Devise plan for achieving personal and group goals ■ Have timelines for preparation phase
Action	■ Experiment with actions to overcome oppression ■ In cases of over-empowerment, explore ways of sharing power and increasing accountability	■ Balance attention to participatory processes with concrete actions ■ Decide ahead of time on schedule but remain open to changes as group evolves
Maintenance	■ Put in place systems of sustainability that will reinforce personal empowerment or depowerment, as the case might be	■ Develop norms and procedures to sustain and institutionalize change either in people's behaviours or in social changes pursued
Evaluation	■ Evaluate process and outcomes of change, not only at the end of a trial period but throughout work phase as well	■ Group conducts formative and summative evaluations of the work
Follow-up	■ Procedures are in place for individual to check with self and others to see if changes are maintained	■ Institutionalize procedures to help group members to remain accountable to each other

During the various phases of change there are certain jobs that need to be done. In this section we describe the tasks community members embark on. In the next section we focus on what we, as community psychologists, need to do to enable community members to be effective change agents.

Helping encounters come in many forms. In some instances service providers and service recipients are paired because of a third party order. Such is the case when a court mandates a young person to see a probation officer or when a school principal sends a child to a counsellor. In other cases help is voluntarily sought from a social worker or a psychologist. In yet others, it happens because the community psychologist is part of a project and people trust her and come to her with their personal issues.

Pre-contemplation

During *pre-contemplation* people are usually exploring what is bothering them. Some may feel uneasy or unhappy but may be unable to articulate the source of oppression or concern. A milestone is achieved when they can verbalize what is bothering them and what may be the source of the problem. Whereas some people may be the subject of oppressive relationships or discriminatory practices, others may be exerting too much power over others, causing themselves and others pain and suffering. But being the complex beings that we are, most of us are somewhere in between these two poles of oppressed or oppressors. In fact, most of us experience some of both (Goodman, 2001). In some realms of our lives we suffer some form of minimization and exclusion; in others we do the same to other people. This requires that we, as helpers, view our clients and ourselves as potentially inflicting pain on others, directly or indirectly, wittingly or unwittingly, consciously or unconsciously. This interpretation rejects simple categorizations of people as either oppressors or oppressed. In pursuing well-being and liberation, we think that lasting changes come about when individuals reflect on their dual roles in life as contributors to well-being and possible oppression at the same time.

It is easier to recognize the victim rather than the aggressor within ourselves. We surely don't want to impugn our clients with crimes they have not committed, but nor do we want to create false dichotomies such as victim or oppressor. With this realization, it is possible that some of our clients, community partners or peers may wish to work on giving up some of their power. This process can take place in individual or small group work. In either case, the intervention can assist those of us who need to change something about ourselves in order to make more space for others.

In group work, the beginning stages also require that the group review its origins and aims (Dimock, 1987; Johnson & Johnson, 2000). In cases where the group is mandated, as in patients in psychiatric hospitals or young people in court-ordered treatment, there may be animosity towards the leader or other members of the group. Hence, we think it's important to spend some time clarifying feelings and legitimizing the group's existence, if such can be accomplished.

Contemplation

Whether it is in individual or small group work, we recommend that people spend some time during the *contemplation* phase defining the problem. It is all too possible and common to jump into action before knowing what the problem is. Ideo-logical influences are such in our society that people can seriously misjudge the source of their suffering. A common misattribution is to impute to oneself blame for things beyond one's control. Unemployed people blame themselves for losing their jobs and victims of spouse abuse blame themselves for not doing the right things. Advice programs, widely prevalent in North America, oversimplify problems and hosts are quick to diagnose a mental disorder. Judging by their popularity, their followers must be substantial. Contemplation requires that we explore carefully what we need to change and where we should channel our energies. Beware of actions that precede contemplation.

Group work also requires some contemplation with respect to values and work-ing principles. Do we have a leader? Do we make decisions by consensus? Do we rotate in our roles? Nothing is worse than starting a process with only an implicit understanding of how it 'should' work. People come to the table with varied expe-riences and expectations. The sooner we clarify them openly the better off we are. It is at this stage that misgivings and hesitations need to be aired. Otherwise they can fester like wounds, create resistance and undermine ownership (Nelson, Prilleltensky & MacGillivary, 2001).

Preparation

The *preparation* phase is very important. Eager clinicians send their clients to do something different, only to find out later that they were not ready for it. After all, change is hard and there is no reason why people should welcome it. Habitual modes of relating to others and thinking about ourselves are profoundly engrained in our individual and collective psyche. Imagery, visualization, concrete plans and achievable goals can all help in moving forward.

Action

Action, then, is only one more element in the equation, albeit an important one. People need a great deal of support to experiment with new ways of being and relating to the world. Some mechanisms for the promotion of resilience include person-centred changes such as enhanced self-esteem, while others entail envi-ronmental modifications. Action must take into account research on resilience, for it elucidates naturally occurring mechanisms that can be incorporated into help-ing processes.

Groups can act as powerful resources in introducing new behaviours in their members or getting rid of undesirable ones (Johnson & Johnson, 2000). The liter-ature on mutual help and organizing confirms that empowerment often grows out of social support and solidarity (Borkman, 1999; Levy, 2000; Speer & Hughey, 1995; Speer et al., 1995). But groups can be powerful in multiple ways, not all of them positive. Norms of conformity can suppress creativity, and power dynamics can further oppress vulnerable members. Hence, attention to process is crucial through-out the life of the group (Johnson & Johnson, 2000).

Maintenance

If you have ever tried to change something, you know how difficult it can be to sustain the new behaviour. If you tried to stop smoking or to lose weight, you probably know that starting is not as hard as keeping it up. This is why the stage of *maintenance* is so crucial (Prochaska et al., 1994). Planning for change without planning for maintenance is a recipe for failure. Imagine you decided to start exercising every other day for 30 minutes. You made a plan that read like 'exercise for 30 minutes Monday, Wednesday and Friday' but you did not plan exactly what time. What if somebody invites you to go out for a drink instead or if you just have too much to study? You may have had a good beginning, but you did not have a contingency plan or a maintenance plan. Groups can be powerful in creating norms of accountability. Alcoholics Anonymous creates pacts among its members that serve to maintain the gains newly acquired. Attending the meetings and sharing the personal odyssey towards sobriety helps people with addictions to keep the risk at bay.

Evaluation

Evaluation should not be relegated to the end of the change process. Nothing is more disappointing for group members or facilitators than to realize at the end that you had missed the ball from the beginning, that you didn't notice some people were disengaged, that therapy wasn't working, that there wasn't ownership of the process. To prevent this, it's important to build in reflective practice: structured moments where people can express their feelings about how things are going, either in group or individual quests for change (Patterson & Welfel, 2000). This requires the creation of a truly safe space where discontent may be expressed and achievements may be celebrated. Role modelling is crucial for formative evaluations to work. The message from the facilitator of change ought to be that mistakes happen, that things can go wrong, and that it is better to express discomfort as is felt. A skilled facilitator balances opportunities for process reflections with concrete actions and achievements.

Follow-up

Part of maintenance and evaluation is *follow-up*. Setting dates for reviewing new practices, assigning roles for championing new procedures, animating processes that keep an innovation alive are all parts of follow-up. Institutionalizing innovations is the culmination of change.

What is the Role of Community Psychologists Working in Small Groups and Individual Interventions?

In a nutshell, the role is to enable the progression from pre-contemplation to maintenance and follow up. But for this to occur, certain skills have to be developed. Table 10.3 describes seven roles that must be present every step of the way. While the discrete learning of these roles is vital, it is their integration that is crucial for

Table 10.3 Roles for community psychologists working with individuals and small groups

Roles	Work with Individuals	Work with Small Groups
Inclusive host	■ Make person feel welcome ■ Create a safe, friendly and non-judgemental climate for self-exploration	■ Abandon the role of the expert and share power with group members ■ Create a safe and friendly climate ■ Reduce barriers to participation ■ Develop working principles and ground rules for group work
Visionary	■ Collaboratively clarify values and vision to guide work ■ Expand realm of possibilities for alternative ways of being	■ Collaboratively clarify values and vision to guide work ■ Expand realm of possibilities for alternative ways of being
Asset seeker	■ Identify and build on strengths of individual	■ Work to overcome self-doubts and mistrust of group members ■ Value the experiential knowledge of group members ■ Find common ground and respect differences to bridge the worlds of different group members ■ Identify and build on strengths of the group
Listener conceptualizer	■ Collaboratively define and analyse the problem in terms of power differentials, oppression and injustice ■ If needed, confront people with contradictions and incongruence in their behaviour	■ Collaboratively define and analyse the problem in terms of power differentials, oppression and injustice ■ Reconcile differing views and build consensus regarding a plan of action ■ Build ownership and support for actions
Pragmatic partner	■ Collaboratively decide on what type of personal changes to implement ■ Ensure necessary preparation for plan of action ■ Support individual in attempts to change and experiment with new behaviours	■ Share with partners knowledge from literature about successful interventions ■ Ensure that community psychology values are respected throughout the entire process ■ Enable the group to problem-solve as it moves through stages of change ■ Balance attention to process with attention to outcomes
Research partner	■ Evaluate collaboratively how the process is going ■ Explore what can be done differently ■ Reaffirm commitment to change and process ■ Engage in self-reflexive analysis of personal values ■ Be open to being challenged ■ Be aware of value incongruence and strive to reduce it	■ Institute continuous cycle of reflection in the group process ■ Explore what can be done differently ■ Reaffirm commitment to change and process ■ Engage in self-reflexive analysis of personal values ■ Be open to being challenged ■ Be aware of value incongruence and strive to reduce it
Trend setter	■ Share knowledge and lessons learnt with others ■ Build mechanisms for consolidating changes and setting new trends	■ Move beyond pilot stage and consider sustainability a priority ■ Think long term even while confronting the challenges of the short term

success in facilitating change in individuals and small groups (Ivey & Ivey, 2003). What is expected of a skilled facilitator is to invoke the most appropriate role at the most opportune time.

Inclusive Host

The role of *inclusive host* calls for the creation of a welcoming atmosphere. In such a climate people feel safe to explore sources of oppression, avenues for empowerment, vulnerabilities, as well as personal and social privilege. An inclusive host makes space for all guests to feel at home. In a non-judgemental atmosphere people begin to consider aspects of their lives they didn't feel comfortable to explore before. This is the case in individual and small group interventions alike, although it is somewhat harder to achieve in the latter because of the gaze of multiple spectators.

An inclusive host strives to make all members of the group as accepting as possible. This requires a 'reading' of where people are at during the conversation. Skilful facilitators have a finger on the pulse of the group at all times. This is quite a sophisticated ability, as it requires identification of people's moods as individuals and as a group. Some of the questions inclusive hosts ask themselves are:

1. Is everyone feeling comfortable?
2. Is someone dominating the discussion in the group?
3. Are there some people who feel afraid to speak?
4. Have I made an effort to hear from all the people in the group?
5. Are people leaving the meeting enthusiastic or disappointed?

Once people feel comfortable and ready to do some individual or group work, it is important to help them envision a better, yet realistic, state of affairs. When people grow up in violent homes sometimes they come to believe that this is the way things are supposed to be. Their world of possibilities may be constrained by multiple factors including socialization, family experiences, community narratives and deprecating messages about one's group or personal abilities.

Visionary

It is the role of the *visionary* to expand the realm of possibilities, and establish values and principles to guide the work. Hence, in our role as visionaries we fulfil the dual task of aspiring to a better state of affairs and creating norms that will help us work together at the same time. In short, we envision the end and the means to achieve it. But we don't envision it by ourselves. We most definitely include the group and our associates in making the decision.

In individual work there are only two people making decisions about personal growth, coping strategies or social activism. In group situations, the process of crafting a vision and choosing values that guide the collaboration can be fairly involved. Some questions a visionary can ask him or herself at this stage include:

1. Have all people expressed their aspirations?
2. Are we able to think of alternative ways of being?
3. Have we established a process that is democratic and inclusive?

4. Have we had time to think about the norms that we all want to follow?
5. Is there collective ownership for the values and vision we have created?

Asset Seeker

As *asset seekers* it is our job to identify sources of resilience, strength and ingenuity in the people we work with (Ivey & Ivey, 2003). In individual encounters it is important to validate what the person in front of us is already doing well to cope with a problem or to fight injustice. Disenfranchised community members are used to hearing about their deficits, when in fact many of them have remarkable talent in coping with adverse circumstances. Within group settings it is vital not to leave anyone behind in our search for assets and strengths. People have experiential or academic knowledge they wish to have validated. To make sure we are effective in our search for assets we can ask the following questions:

1. Have I asked people how they cope with this difficult situation?
2. Have we discussed what each of us can contribute to the process?
3. Are we able to combine our strengths in a synergistic way?
4. Have I offered my input as an equal member of the group?
5. Have we explored different types of knowledge and wisdom that can help us in our collaborative work?

Listener Conceptualizer

A *listener conceptualizer's* main job is to attend carefully to what people are saying about their lives, challenges, struggles and aspirations. We cannot emphasize enough the importance of letting people speak and explain on their own terms what they are experiencing and hoping and feeling. It is not uncommon for eager helpers to rush to give advice before they have listened carefully. Each of us brings to the table multiple assumptions that can lead to unwarranted conclusions about other people's lives. It is best not to presume anything about people's lives or views before we check it out with them (James & Prilleltensky, 2002).

Once we have a good grasp of the issues and challenges ahead, we begin to conceptualize the problem and isolate the main factors causing and perpetuating suffering, injustice and oppression in personal, communal and social lives. As community psychologists we always have our antenna up for signals of oppression and exclusion. Power differentials and inequality figure prominently in the lives of people we work with (Community Mental Health Project, 1998; John, 2003; Lewis et al., 2003; Vera & Speight, 2003). Unlike other professionals in the helping fields, we do not necessarily concentrate on intrapsychic dynamics, although they may be an important part of the puzzle. For us, internal psychological processes are just one more element to consider. Ecologically speaking, we conceptualize problems in terms of micro, meso and macro spheres. As noted in Chapter 2, holism is the perfect antidote against reductionism in the formulation of problems.

As we come to our own conclusions about a problem in living or a challenge to work on, we have to recognize that our views may differ from the group or the individual we are working with (James & Prilleltensky, 2002). We have to consider the possibility that our conceptualization may be wrong or that it may take more dialogue for people to reach consensus on causes and possible solutions. Conflict is expected and unavoidable. The very way we deal with that may be therapeutic and growth enhancing.

To remind ourselves of the various tasks involved in being a good listener conceptualizer, we can use the following prompts:

1. Have I listened without interruptions to what people have to say about their issues?
2. Have I thought about it in ecological terms?
3. Have I expressed disagreement or alternative conceptualizations in a respectful way?
4. Have I thought about the influence of power inequality in this person's life?
5. Has the group agreed on the definition of the problem and possible solutions?

Pragmatic Partner

As we work our way through the steps, we approach the role of *pragmatic partner*. Problem definition is crucial, but action is what gets changes under way. When the group or the individual is ready to take action, we have to contribute our academic, professional and personal knowledge to the process of change. If a group wishes to use a confrontational technique with a school board, and you know that this strategy will alienate potential allies, as a pragmatic partner you want to discuss the merits of other options. If a victim of spousal abuse wishes to return to the marriage, and you know from her past experience and other research that this will probably not work out, as a pragmatic partner you want to raise the possibility that this may not be the best way to proceed. In either case, our alternatives have to be accepted by the people we work with. There is no point in forcing our views upon others who are not ready to listen.

As a pragmatic partner, your job is to listen, conceptualize, formulate actions and collaborate with your partners in carrying them out. This is an essential part of our job in working with individuals, small groups, organizations and communities: Our ability to identify transformational actions while keeping everyone effectively engaged at the same time. We discussed in the previous chapter the set of emotional intelligence skills that can help us not only in ameliorative, but in transformational work as well (see Table 9.3). These competencies come in handy when working with individuals and small groups. Questions that sharpen our skills as pragmatic partners include:

1. Have I considered with the group the risks and benefits of every course of action?
2. Have I consulted colleagues and the literature on the merits of various alternatives?
3. Is our work balancing attention to process with attention to outcomes?
4. Is the preferred action in accord with our values?
5. Do we have a contingency plan in case this strategy doesn't work?

Research Partner

Learning is truly a lifelong journey, and this is not just a cliché. Although we are able to extrapolate from one situation to another, more often than not new situations require a new lesson in how to solve problems. We have to be open to challenges and unexpected turns in our work. Therefore, we want to promote the role of *research partner*. This is not research in the narrow sense of experimental designs, but rather in the broad sense of exploring and evaluating how we're doing, what's working well, how people are feeling, and what we are doing wrong.

Table 10.3 identifies the various domains that need to be evaluated during our work with individuals and groups. Many of us are used to 'getting the job done'. While this quality may be a great asset, we have to be careful that in our rush to accomplish things we don't forget how we're accomplishing them. Evaluation is not a solitary activity but rather a collaborative one. Our partners in change have to be able to express their views on the process of our work together. Some questions we find useful at this stage are:

1. Have we created a space to reflect on how we're feeling about our work together?
2. What have we done to evaluate our intervention?
3. Are people feeling safe enough to express disapproval?
4. Am I open to challenges and criticism?
5. Have we practiced how to give feedback in respectful and useful ways?

Trend Setter

Perhaps the toughest part of the job is to make changes last, both in our personal and institutional lives. This is why we have to pay particular attention to our role as *trend setters*. To achieve a change is admirable, but to make it into a new trend is even more remarkable (Mayer & Davidson, 2000; Prochaska et al., 1994). This role supports maintenance and follow-up as described in Table 10.2. When starting new programs in the community so much effort goes into project development, recruitment and evaluation that sustainability is often not a priority. By the time funding runs out in a few years, there are rarely plans for the continuation of the initiative.

Long-term planning applies to individual, group or community change alike. The first priority is to institutionalize the innovation at the personal and local levels. Once that has been accomplished, it's important to take the message to other communities and groups (Mayer & Davidson, 2000). In Chapter 16 we can see how indigenous groups in New Zealand, in collaboration with treaty workers, strive to educate the entire population about Maori rights. Treaty workers have a systematic way of working with organizations so that education and affirmative actions may be institutionalized in government and private settings alike. It is not enough to raise the consciousness of a few people about the rights of aboriginal people – their plan of action includes a strategy for disseminating knowledge about past wrongs and possible ways of addressing them. This is an example of trend setting. The essence of trend setting is going beyond the initial goal. Remember: one swallow does not a summer make.

What can be done to make trend setting a priority? Some questions community psychologists can ask include:

1. What have we done to make sure that the changes we plan for are maintained?
2. How do we change the system, not just perceptions, in order to institutionalize innovations?
3. What group norms can we establish to help members sustain new behaviours?
4. How can we disseminate knowledge gained in one setting to others?
5. What do we know from the literature about institutionalizing innovations?

Trend setting is not only very challenging, it is also very exciting. Community members like being part of something new and transformative. Motivation increases when people realize that their contributions may transcend the local level. Think of environmental trends such as recycling and composting and you can appreciate how much rarer they were twenty or thirty years ago than they are today. At first environmentalists encountered much more opposition than they face today when trying to institute earth-friendly policies and practices. The same may be said of civil rights activists who fought an uphill battle to obtain basic human rights. While their struggle is far from over, new trends, such as affirmative action and disability rights legislation, make it easier for people of colour and people with disabilities to participate in society.

What are the Strengths and Limitations of Small Group and Individual Interventions?

We started this chapter with the concept of psychosocial emergencies. These are wounds that require urgent treatment. Abuse, neglect, violence, addictions, depression, homelessness; they all require immediate attention. And when properly given and carefully applied, sensitive one-on-one and small group interventions can help. People recover hope, feel empowered, join others in fighting inequality and enjoy the benefits of mutual support.

Research demonstrates that individual and small group interventions can help at the universal, selective and indicated levels (if you need a refresher on these concepts see Chapter 4). At the universal level, schools that smooth the transition from elementary to high school by grouping children in small clusters and restructuring the school environment deliver positive outcomes. In the School Transition Environment Project (STEP) in the US, the school was reorganized so that grade 9 students remained with the same group of students in the same part of the building for most of the day; they had a small group of teachers; and the class teachers handled many of the guidance-related issues for these students. Effectively this intervention created a smaller, more supportive environment within the context of a larger, more impersonal school. Compared with students in a control group, the students who participated in this new arrangement reported more positive attitudes towards school, had fewer absences and had better marks (Felner & Adan, 1988). This is a universal intervention in that all school children in the US participate in the program. They all receive individual guidance and they all work in small groups. Such a program has proved to be effective in enhancing academic performance and satisfaction with school overall.

At the selective level, families at risk for abuse or neglect, or children at risk for educational underachievement benefit from individual and small group interventions with parents and children alike. Geoff Nelson and colleagues conducted two meta analyses to find out whether programs such as home visitation and family preservation achieve reductions in abuse, and whether early intervention programs have lasting effects on children's educational well-being (MacLeod & Nelson, 2000; Nelson, Westhues & MacLeod, 2003). In both instances Nelson and colleagues found that individual and small group interventions work. Some work better than others and some achieve longer lasting results than others, but in general these analyses support the implementation of individual interventions with parents to prevent abuse and with children to enhance educational outcomes. Parents feel better about their children, obtain better employment and improve rearing knowledge and techniques. Children, in turn, become better learners and experience higher family and social well-being.

Sensitive home visitors help parents to remove blame and feelings of inadequacy. Trained group facilitators also help children of divorced parents to remove blame and feelings of inadequacy. Social support groups help people with addictions, mental health problems, physical disabilities and other afflictions to overcome exclusion, marginality and depression (Levy, 2000).

At the indicated level, individual and small group interventions are also effective in coping with adversities such as ill-health and serious mental health problems. In Chapter 21 we can see how people with psychiatric conditions benefit from mutual help and empowering approaches.

At all levels, through a process of personal affirmation and safe exploration, individuals and groups achieve higher levels of well-being. In the best possible world, the newly gained confidence and psychological health would be invested in helping others achieve higher levels of well-being and collective liberation. But often this is not the case. Self-actualization can easily turn into selfish actualization, a trend that has been inadvertently supported by traditional therapeutic approaches that reinforce individualism (Prilleltensky, 1994b).

At present, most preventive interventions are person-centred or small-group centred. This flies in the face of ecological formulations of problems. If problems reside in systems as much as in individuals, how come most of our psychological interventions put the onus of change on the victim and not on the system? Furthermore, most interventions wish to fix the person damaged and not the powerful ones inflicting the damage. These are inherent risks of individual and small group interventions. On one hand they are helpful, but on the other hand they divert attention from meso and macro sources of conflict.

A final caveat to keep in mind: the vast majority of individual and small group interventions are ameliorative in nature. They soothe wounds and react to pain, but do not confront their origins. In a sense, they follow the medical model of 'wait and they shall show up in your clinic' (Albee, 1990; Vera & Speight, 2003).

What are Some of the Dilemmas Faced by Community Psychologists Working with Small Groups and Individuals?

What right do we have to convince people to work for social change, to oppose convention, to rebel? If we are clear about our values, we are bound to share them with the people we work with. If we have an agenda for change, we will want to propagate it. Who is to say that our values will not seep into the work we do with individuals and small groups. That would not be a dilemma if people invited and allowed us to work for social change, but what about groups who think we can help them with addictions and we end up talking about how corporations exploit children and poor people and entice them to smoke? Aren't we politicizing the helping process? The answer is we most definitely are. The dilemma lies not in pretending we are apolitical when in fact we are not, but in introducing agendas community partners may not be ready for, or interested in. After all, community psychologists are well known for working on health and welfare related issues but not on radical transformation.

In our view, the ethical way to proceed is to share our convictions, our analyses and our strategies with people we work with. It is up to the partners to decide whether health can be isolated from corporate greed or not, and whether they see any connection between eating disorders and the fashion industry. If our partners refuse to make the connections or if they oppose our agenda, which is entirely possible, the collaboration may not work, in which case we gracefully exit the scene. We cannot be all things to all people.

We should not psychologize everything and think that people who exploit others are simply misguided or psychologically unhealthy. That may very well be true. But we must keep in mind that certain groups may expressly reject our values and wish us away. How wonderful it would be if we could easily tell who is misguided and who is a genuine despot. Until there is a quick procedure for such diagnosis, we are stuck with disclosing our values and seeing how far we can go with them.

Chapter Summary

This chapter merely touched upon ways of working with individuals and groups. Due to space considerations we could not expand on specific interviewing skills or group facilitation. Fortunately, there are excellent resources for learning the craft of interview and group processes (see Resources section below). In this chapter we chose to discuss the more likely roles of community psychologists and the likely stages people go through in their efforts to make personal or social change.

Prochaska's stages of change remind us that effective self-changers go through discernable steps, from pre-contemplation to maintenance and follow-up (Prochaska et al., 1994). There is merit in following their wisdom. Each phase builds on previous ones and skipping may cause unnecessary regressions. Action without contemplation may be misguided and contemplation without action may be frustrating. These phases are enabled by a set of skills and roles.

We recommended the use of seven roles, introduced in earlier chapters and applicable to work with both individuals and small groups: inclusive host, visionary, asset seeker, listener conceptualizer, pragmatic partner, research partner and trend setter. Mastery of individual skills is important, but their integration and activation at appropriate times is vital.

The dilemmas we posed at the beginning and the end of the chapter are not easily resolvable. How do we allocate our time between psychosocial emergencies and preventive measures? How can we tell if people who reject our values are simply misguided or genuinely disinterested in the well-being and liberation of others? For how long do we try to persuade others before we decide they need to be disempowered instead of empowered? When do we tell ourselves we have too much power and we need to find ways of giving it up? Answers will perpetually vary across contexts. But until all contexts look the same and before we can safely tell friend from foe, there is one simple answer: we struggle with each and every one of these dilemmas. At best, we will find colleagues to help us resolve them. At worst, we will pretend they don't exist.

COMMENTARY: Restorative Practices in Small Group and Individual Work

Mary Watkins

In Judaism humans are imaged as God's partners in creating, repairing and restoring the world (*tikkun olam*) so that justice, peace and love may come to flourish amongst us. Acts of restoration are not thought of as returning the present to some previous paradisiacal state, but restoring relations to what is most deeply desired though not yet incarnated. The kind of individual and small group work Nelson and Prilleltensky describe in this chapter can be read in the tradition of such restorative work. They are careful to differentiate therapeutic work that is ameliorative of individual suffering without being transformative of the underlying sociopolitical structures that give rise to such suffering. I would like to suggest, however, that the kind of work they describe creates a process and practices a way of being that embodies the changes they seek in the larger world, allowing amelioration and transformation to happen side by side.

bell hooks (1990) and Mary Belenky (1997; Belenky, Clinchy, Goldberger & Tarule, 1986) have called the spaces created through such work 'public homeplaces,' where the virtues of the home – care for others with particular attention to the vulnerable and the excluded – are extended to larger communities. Participation in the co-creation of such public homeplaces empowers participants to name their experience and then to deconstruct their understanding of it, taking care to contextualize it (historically, sociopolitically and economically). As Paulo Freire (1970) taught, such efforts for the development of critical consciousness open a group into shared dreams of a deeply desired future, from which acts of resistance to oppression and acts of creation towards a desired world can flow.

Nelson and Prilleltensky boldly and systematically articulate the scaffolding for such restorative work by exploring the steps for intervention with individuals and small groups: pre-contemplation, contemplation, preparation, action, maintenance, evaluation and follow-up. Such participatory groups begin with participants – including the leader – attempting to bracket their presuppositions about 'the problem'. A more open, problemposing inquiry is hosted that invites reflection on underlying assumptions and values. For instance, in an addiction recovery program, people might begin by wondering if 'recovery' is what they are aiming at (Stanley, 2003)? If so, what is each person feeling in need of 'recovery' from? What have they found helpful in previous efforts at 'recovery'? What needs to be recovered? What, in the wider community and culture, thwarts 'recovery' and what does, or could, support it? How have other efforts at 'recovery' they have been involved in understood 'recovery', and how did this affect how they were seen and came to experience themselves? Seeing-through the problem, deconstructing it, allows it gradually to be placed within a larger frame of understanding to which all the members can make contributions, freeing it from definitions that are overly professionalized, reductive or collusive with the status quo.

In such group work listening carefully to one's own experience is placed alongside careful listening to the multiplicity of perspectives available in the group. By virtue of this, the group can begin to think more complexly about the issue at hand, as well as begin to discern the threads of common experience from which possible joint action can emerge. Empowerment unfolds through articulation of experience and its deconstruction, through the practice of shared leadership and through the back and forth movement between reflection and action. Ongoing opportunities for the evaluation of goals, process and action provide a dynamic participatory experience that can become a model for other collaborative relationships that aim at transformative change.

Belenky, Bond and Weinstock (1997) present a moving example of the kind of ripple effect Nelson and Prilleltensky refer to. In their Listening Partners Project, groups of twelve mothers of young children from rural areas of Vermont met once a week for a year. These women were what Belenky et al. (1986) describe as 'silenced knows'. Often themselves victims of child abuse and neglect, they were largely brought up in authoritarian households where there was a marked absence of dialogue and opportunities for pretend play. Once mothers, they found themselves unable to resolve childcare dilemmas through verbal negotiation, often resorting to physical force. Through the kind of problem-posing small group work described by Nelson and Prilleltensky these women became able to listen not only to the thoughts of others but to their own thoughts, to express them and to risk entering into the give-and-take of dialogue. They became able to extend to their children the listening and opportunities for expression they had come to enjoy amongst themselves, mitigating against the use of force to negotiate issues of difference and questions of authority.

Nelson and Prilleltensky ask those of us involved in hosting individual and small group interventions to struggle with the possibility that work that focuses on individual healing and self-actualization may become a dead-end in terms of community or cultural transformation. They caution that while it may serve to address some of the wounds of its members, it often fails to either sufficiently insight the connections between personal suffering and taken-for-granted cultural arrangements or to weave the necessary threads of solidarity that enable members of a group to effect cultural change on a systemic level. The authors acknowledge that therapists and group leaders must be careful to discern whether an individual may be so depleted from psychosocial emergencies that he or she is unable to turn attention to psychopolitical sources of suffering, let alone commit time to changing them.

As we struggle to move more fully from an individualistic paradigm of the person to an interdep-endent one, these dilemmas begin to yield. An individual's liberation cannot be complete when the systems she is part of are oppressive. We know that the structure of relations in the world we inhabit become the scaffolding for our internal conversations as well as our roles in relation to others. When working therapeutically from standpoints within liberation psychologies, we see it as critically important for a person to be able to see the resonance between societal arrangements of power and both internal dynamics and one's relations to others. Such insighting allows one to understand that his/her suffering is shared by others and is not a sign of some wholly personal inadequacy. It also clarifies the cultural pressures and their dynamics that make it difficult for us to resist patterns that are disempowering and unhealthy. Without such clarification, we are at their mercy. Instead of putting off the understanding of the cultural level of our suffering until some of it is alleviated, we begin to see that such alleviation depends in part on this insight.

For instance, a young woman may come to individual or small group therapy complaining of depression, feelings of worthlessness and inferiority, unable to see a possible role for herself in the future. She is quiet in school, anxious when called on to voice her opinion. Individual therapy or a small group intervention might focus on her childhood, her relation to her mother, her father's view of her. As Nelson and Prilleltensky stress, however, holism is needed as 'the perfect antidote against reductionism in the formulation of problems'. How was she treated in school as a learner and a thinker? How are girls and women seen in her extended family? What is the message she receives about being a young woman from the media she is exposed to? While she may not become an activist for how media represent girls, she will begin to resist its messages and seek to extend herself into areas of challenge that she had previously avoided. It is also likely that her growing capacity to support her own strengths will extend to helping others resist cultural messages that encourage silence and conformity.

Some would argue that while it may be necessary to develop such insight, a person should be more focused on their own healing before he/she embarks on efforts at community or cultural change. The argument espouses that people who come to us to get 'their own house in order' should not be burdened with 'correcting the ills of the world'. Sometimes such a narrowing of focus is clearly a necessity. We need to leave room, however, for healing for the individual to come about through systemic change efforts in solidarity with others. Here the false divide between the internal and external, the private and the public is challenged.

To prepare others and ourselves to host and midwife such work we must learn to move fluidly between individual and small group work and cultural work on a broader, more systemic scale. While attention has been given to the extent that the small group participant can engage in cultural work while suffering under present burdens, even greater attention needs to be paid to the ethical demands placed on the practitioner of such work. For instance, in Taylor, Gilligan and Sullivan's research (1995) with Boston inner-city adolescent girls at risk for high school drop out and teenage pregnancy, they slowly faced the ethical demands their research resulted in. These girls felt failed by their teachers and their large urban public high schools, where they often felt completely on their own. They reported little continuity of relationship with teachers and counsellors. Their youthful aspirations for their futures were not met by adults who could help them avail themselves of opportunities and gather information needed to turn their dreams into reality. They experienced their teachers as unwilling to engage with them in the controversial issues they wondered and thought about the most. Without such supportive engagement many withdrew into a brittle independence; their adolescent dreams of who they could be met with bitter disillusionment.

Listening to these girls, the researchers say:

is to invite disruption, disturbance or dissolution of the status quo. To support the strengths, intelligence, resilience and knowledge of girls whose culture or class is marginalized by society is to support political, educational and economic change. It may be easier to sacrifice girls than to support their development and when girls sense this, it may be hard for them, with the best of intentions, not to give up on themselves and sacrifice their hopes. (Taylor, Gilligan & Sullivan, 1995, pp. 202–3)

For instance, over the years of their research they witnessed girls becoming pregnant who had previously clearly stated their intentions not to become teenage mothers. As they listened to the girls' experiences they became deeply disturbed by the fact that many of these pregnancies were the result of statutory rape and sexual abuse by adult men. This faced them with the ethical imperative of honouring what they heard by advocating for changes in public policy and providing services that would directly help the girls themselves.

Nelson and Prilleltensky use the term 'natural helper' to distinguish those who are gifted at assisting with the kind of work they describe without benefit of professional training. Such helpers, however, do not acquire their gifts 'naturally', but have had the benefit of experience of situations in which there is a give and take between listening and expression, where silenced knowings have been coaxed into more public dialogue and where the risk of seeing through arrangements of power that have been made to seem 'natural' are questioned and rethought. Such helpers – whether 'professionally' trained or not – encourage acts of resistance intrapsychically, interpersonally and culturally, seeing clearly the interdependence of these levels in our lives. By enlisting others to be what Nelson and Prilleltensky call 'research partners' with them, joint resistance begins to hold open a space where visions of what could be possible can arise along with actions on their behalf.

Glossary

depowerment the process whereby powerful people and groups relinquish some of their power in order to bring about a more equitable state of affairs among people and groups

emotional intelligence a set of personal and interpersonal skills that enable individuals to prosper and operate efficiently in social and organizational settings

psychosocial emergency situations that require immediate attention such as child abuse, neglect or domestic violence

status quo the current state of affairs

RESOURCES

1. For skills in working with individuals consult in particular the following authors listed in the reference section: Ivey and Ivey (2003), Corey and Corey (2003), McWhirter (1994) and Morgan (2000).
2. For skills in working with groups, please consult the following authors listed in the reference section: Dimock (1987) and Johnson and Johnson (2000).

Part IV

Tools for Research

The goal of this part of the book is to answer the question: how do we understand the nature of oppression and efforts to transform settings so as to promote liberation and well-being? To advance community psychology's understanding of its phenomena of interest and to promote social change, a variety of research approaches and strategies are required. In this part of the book, we consider the nature of CP research and the different methods that are used in that research.

In Chapter 11, we consider the goals, assumptions, values and processes of CP research. Mainstream psychological research has been dominated by the so-called 'scientific method' (positivism and post-positivism) that emphasizes the separation of the researcher and subject, detached objectivity, reduction of psychological phenomena to measurable and quantifiable bits of data, an analysis of cause and effect and hypothesis testing derived from theoretical propositions. The 'scientific method' has traditionally been viewed as *the* approach to research, rather than as one approach that is based on a certain set of assumptions. More recently, a set of alternative approaches to research has emerged in the social sciences. In contrast to the positivist approach, phenomenological, contextualist and constructivist approaches focus on human experience, language, subjectivity, textual or qualitative data and inductive, discovery-oriented research. We examine the assumptions, values, strengths and limitations of the positivist and constructivist paradigms.

Due to the value-laden, social-change focus of CP, a critical perspective on the subject matter under scrutiny is required. A third research paradigm, the critical paradigm, is evident in the work of feminist-standpoint, anti-racist, participatory and action-oriented approaches to research. We argue that the critical paradigm, which is congruent with the values of CP, provides an important foundation or meta-framework for research conducted from either positivist or constructivist approaches. The critical paradigm suggests that community research must be highly attentive to issues of power both in the goals and the process of the research and that research should be guided by the values and social ethics that we have put forward in this book.

In Chapters 12 and 13, we review some of the most frequently used methods in community research. We organize this presentation around the three principal research paradigms that we outline in Chapter 11: post-positivism; social constructivism; and critical approaches. In Chapter 12, we cover the methods associated with the post-positivist and social constructivist paradigms, while in Chapter 13, we focus on methods used in the critical paradigm. Rather than have a separate commentary and list of resources for each of these chapters (12 and 13), note that we have one integrated commentary and list of resources at the end of Chapter 13 that pertains to both of these chapters.

In Chapter 12, we review methods that are associated with post-positivism and social constructivism. While both quantitative and qualitative research can be used in both post-positivist and constructivist research, post-positivism emphasizes quantitative research and constructivism emphasizes qualitative research. For ease of presentation, we describe quantitative methods in the context of post-positivism and qualitative methods within the context of constructivism.

Various quantitative methods that are useful in community research are reviewed in Chapter 12, including survey and epidemiological approaches to community needs assessment and quantitative approaches to program evaluation that utilize experimental and quasi-experimental design. The use of structured questionnaires and interviews (measurement scales) is considered within this discussion, along with issues of reliability and validity. In contrast to the post-positivist paradigm, the constructivist paradigm tends to use qualitative methods, which have been ignored or denigrated in psychological research. Qualitative methods are also reviewed in this chapter, including case studies, life histories and narratives, ethnography, in-depth interviews, participant observation, discourse analysis and qualitative approaches to community needs assessment and program evaluation. Issues of how to analyse and establish the trustworthiness of qualitative data are considered.

In Chapter 13, we review research methods associated with the critical paradigm, focusing specifically on participatory action research. We suggest that the critical paradigm can be used to inform both critical realist and critical constructivist research towards the goals of liberation and well-being. Examples of research that is used to promote social change for disadvantaged people are presented in this chapter. Also in Chapter 13, we discuss the steps that community researchers follow when they enter a community to study a problem of interest. Establishing equal relationships with the individuals, groups and organizations hosting the research and developing an action agenda as well as a research agenda are emphasized. Practical examples are used to illustrate these points, as well as to emphasize the importance of the process and action orientation of critical community research.

The Foundations of Community Research

Warm-up Exercise

Since elementary (or primary) school, we have all learned about the 'scientific method'. Answer the following questions:

1. What are the key elements of the scientific method?
2. How can the scientific method be applied to the issues and problems that are of concern to community psychologists?
3. Do you see any limitations or problems in applying the scientific method to community psychology (CP)?

In this chapter, we lay the foundations of community research. We begin by clarifying the goals of community research. Next, we examine the assumptions and values of competing paradigms of community research. We end this chapter with a discussion regarding the processes of community research.

The Goals of Community Research: Towards Liberation and Well-being

In contrast to the traditional view of science as 'objective' and 'value free', we believe that community research, like any research, is value-driven. That is why it is very important for community researchers to be self-reflexively aware of their values, social position and relationship with those disadvantaged citizens with whom they are collaborating. Reflexivity also means being attuned to the ethical and power issues that inevitably arise in community research and the assumptions that underlie the research (Alvesson & Sköldberg, 2000; Willig, 2001). For us, the goal of community research is to construct knowledge that challenges the societal status quo and is useful for the liberation of oppressed groups and the promotion of well-being for all (see Box 11.1 for some principles of research aimed at promoting liberation and well-being). Our aim is to collaborate with oppressed people to facilitate the achievement of their goals. Unlike mainstream psychological research, CP research is action-oriented and strives to create social change. As Price and Cherniss (1977) pointed out some time ago, knowledge development and action are inseparable.

Box 11.1 **Principles and Agenda for a Critical, Humanist Social Science**

1. Choose and re-examine the political and value positions consciously and specify positions in terms of desired human conditions and outcomes.
2. Integrate these positions into every aspect and stage of the research.
3. Facilitate changes in the social orders which are conducive to the value position chosen.
4. Key components of a social science agenda include: the context of patterns of social life; actual patterns of social life; forces and processes that inhibit consciousness and understanding; how to overcome those forces and processes; both theoretical and active involvement in transforming social life.
5. Study free of all forms of domination, manipulation and exploitation.
6. Methods and designs follow from nature of the study and questions asked.

7. Integrity of research design is key requirement.
8. Integrity is intimately related to values and politics.
9. Avoid use of professional jargon.
10. Teach in a way that allows students a 'liberated space' (a counter-reality to institutional domination and control) to develop critical thought and consciousness, insights into the human condition and a personal commitment to human liberation and social justice.
11. Become involved in social–political liberation movements for mutual support and personal confirmation.

From: Gil, D. G. (1987). Social sciences, human survival, development and liberation. In K. Westhues (ed.), *Basic Principles for Social Sciences in Our Time* (pp. 118–29). Waterloo, ON: University of St. Jerome's College Press.

In our journey of mutual learning, we are guided by the values for personal, relational and collective well-being and liberation that we outlined in Chapter 3. Objectivity and subjectivity are both present and important in community research. In our experiences, we have found community research to be passionate, creative and personally, intellectually and emotionally challenging. We strive to integrate our moral values into the collaborative research that we undertake with oppressed groups. The ecological principle of interdependence (Chapter 4) suggests that community psychologists can pursue these goals through value-based research at multiple levels of analysis.

Personal Well-being and Liberation

Beginning with the individual level of analysis, community research with oppressed groups can help to chart the movement from oppression through resistance and empowerment to well-being of disadvantaged people (see Table 2.1 in Chapter 2). Studies of the process of personal empowerment, the development of positive identities, alternative personal stories and consciousness-raising that connects the personal and the political are important concerns for CP (Lord & Hutchison, 1993; Nelson, Lord & Ochocka, 2001a; Watts et al., 1999; Watts et al., 2003). Even if the focus of the research is on the individual, community research examines individual phenomena in their group, organizational and macro-social contexts (Nelson et al., 2001a).

Relational Well-being and Liberation

CP research that focuses on the relational level of analysis can examine the liberating and/or oppressive qualities of relationships, groups and organizations and outcomes that result from relationships and settings. For example, Maton and Salem (1995) have identified some of the following characteristics of empowering settings: a belief system that inspires growth and focuses on strengths, opportunities for member participation and contribution, social support, shared leadership and organizational power to effect community change. Research on the relationships, informal support and power-sharing that disadvantaged people experience in the context of self-help/mutual aid organizations is another important area of CP research at the relational level of analysis (Isenberg, Loomis, Humphreys & Maton, 2004; Nelson, Ochocka et al., 1998).

Collective Well-being and Liberation

The goals for social or collective change include greater social and economic equity, the development of group structures for further social change and increased control of social institutions by oppressed groups. We believe that CP research at the collective level should focus on social structures and policies that promote liberation and well-being of disadvantaged groups. Moreover, such research should challenge the societal status quo by exposing the damaging impacts of oppressive structures and policies. More CP research is needed on critical social policy analysis and mediating settings, such as NGOs, SMOs and alternative settings, whose mission involves social change. These meso-level settings mediate between oppressed groups and larger social structures and policies and have considerable potential for creating social change (see Chapters 8 and 9).

Assumptions and Values Underlying Paradigms for Community Research

Paradigms: Key Questions

Research methods in any field are guided by certain paradigms and related philosophical assumptions. In psychology, research methods are often presented to students as 'givens' and the paradigms from which the methods are derived and the philosophical assumptions that underlie those paradigms are typically unexamined and unchallenged. Remember from your introductory psychology course that psychology has its roots in philosophy. In this section, we examine the major paradigms of CP research and their assumptions. We have to warn you that the language and terminology in this section is based on the writings of philosophers of science and it is language that tends to be rather dense and difficult to understand. However, we will do our best to introduce complicated concepts in user-friendly ways. We want to make sure that the political, cultural, existential and social meanings of philosophical concepts are explicit and clear. Hence, we draw their implications for practical applications in community research.

Let's begin with the idea of a 'paradigm', a term that has become so popular and commonplace that one now hears about paradigms in TV commercials! A paradigm is a set of beliefs, a world view, a set of assumptions about the world and one's place in it. Paradigms are human constructions that represent the most informed and sophisticated view that its proponents have been able to devise to understand different phenomena (Lincoln & Guba, 2000). A dominant paradigm is one whose basic assumptions are so taken for granted by most people that to challenge them may be considered heresy. People believe that 'this is the way the world is!' Once upon a time, it was widely believed that the sun and stars revolved around the earth and that the earth was flat. It took some time for people to accept a change in paradigms.

In his 1962 book, *The Structure of Scientific Revolutions*, philosopher Thomas Kuhn challenged the prevailing belief that science progresses through the slow and steady accumulation of 'facts'. Rather he asserted that science progresses through the development of new paradigms. When the inconsistencies or problems of the dominant paradigm become evident, challenges are mounted and alternative paradigms begin to emerge. Such paradigm shifts are often met with scepticism and resistance, because they challenge people's basic assumptions about the world. In many respects the values and assumptions of CP, which we outlined in Chapter 1, represent an alternative paradigm to more traditional applied psychology. The power of paradigms lies in their ability to persuade audiences of the value of their arguments and principles.

With respect to science and research, paradigms represent a philosophy of science that addresses several questions (Guba & Lincoln, 1994; Lincoln & Guba, 1985).

1. *The question of ontology* – What is the form and nature of reality and what can be known about reality? Is reality something tangible that exists 'out there' and is it independent of the researcher? Or are there multiple realities that are constructed and interpreted in the minds of the researcher and the other stakeholders in the research?

2. *The question of epistemology* – What is the relationship between the researcher and what can be known? This question is closely tied with those related to ontology. If there is a single reality, then how can the researcher objectively capture that reality? But if one assumes that there are multiple constructed realities, then how can those multiple perspectives, including that of the researcher, be understood and interpreted? What constitutes valid knowledge? The issue of the objectivity and subjectivity of the researcher is important with respect to the question of epistemology.

3. *The question of ideology* – What are the underlying values, either implicit or explicit, that shape the research and the phenomena under study? Again, this depends on one's view of reality. If there is a single reality, then the values of the researcher, the participants and community members are not relevant to the research. But if one assumes that there are multiple constructed realities, then the values of all the stakeholders in the research matter a great deal. In this regard, it is important to pose and answer questions about power and the values that underlie the research, such as: whose research and whose knowledge? In other

words, whose voices are being amplified and who has control over the research agenda? Who will benefit from the research? How will the partners work together and how will conflict be addressed? (Harding, 1991; Lord & Church, 1998; Nelson, Lord & Ochocka, 2001b; Rappaport, 1990).

4. *The question of methodology* – How can the researcher go about finding out whatever she or he believes can be known? What tools can and should be used in the research to advance knowledge and promote change? Again, the research methods that one chooses depend upon one's assumptions about ontology and epistemology and one's ideology or values. In the next two chapters, we provide an overview of the different research methods that are available to community psychologists.

Three Paradigms for Community Psychology Research

In this section, we review three paradigms of community research: the *post-positivist paradigm*; the *constructivist paradigm*; and the *critical paradigm*. The distinction between the post-positivist paradigm (that emphasizes empirical-analytical knowledge) and the constructivist paradigm (that emphasizes meaning and experiential knowledge) has been made by several writers (for example Lincoln & Guba, 1985). The German critical theorist Jürgen Habermas (1971) took this debate one step further by introducing the critical paradigm (that emphasizes critical, emancipatory knowledge).

Over the past decade, several researchers, philosophers and psychologists have elaborated on the distinctions between these three research paradigms (Bhasker, 1975; Brydon-Miller, 2001; Lincoln & Guba, 2000). Feminist scholars have suggested that the three broad paradigms noted above capture the different approaches to feminist research: (a) feminist empiricism, (b) feminist postmodernism and (c) feminist standpoint theory (Campbell & Wasco, 2000; Harding, 1987b; Riger, 1992). Just as there is no one, single philosophy of feminism, there is no one, single philosophy of feminist research. In Table 11.1, we contrast these three research paradigms in terms of the questions of ontology, epistemology, ideology and methodology. This table is based upon similar, but much more detailed tables that were constructed by Lincoln and Guba (2000) and Blake Poland of the University of Toronto (in Murray et al., 2001).

The Post-positivist Paradigm

While you may be unfamiliar with the terms 'logical positivism' or 'rational-empiricism', you will be familiar with many of the defining qualities of this paradigm because it has been and continues to be the dominant paradigm of inquiry in the social sciences and psychology (remember the warm-up exercise about the scientific method?). Psychology has borrowed this paradigm from the natural sciences and adopted it as the scientific approach to guide all psychological inquiry. In their review of this paradigm, Lincoln and Guba (2000) note that there has been a shift from positivism to what they call post-positivism. While these two share much in common, post-positivism is a more modest version of positivism and most community psychologists who work from this paradigm are more closely

Table 11.1 Contrasting paradigms of community research

Assumptions	Paradigm		
	Post-positivist	**Constructivist**	**Critical**
Ontology (the nature of reality)	There is a single, external reality that can be imperfectly or probabilistically understood (that is, described, explained, predicted and controlled).	There are multiple realities that are constructed by the research stakeholders. There are no universal laws; reality is relative to the constructions of stakeholders.	There is an external reality that has evolved through history and is constituted of social and institutional structures.
Epistemology (the nature of knowing reality)	While external reality and the researcher are interactive, they are viewed as partially independent. Controls should be put in place to reduce researcher biases. Reality can be broken down (reduced) into component parts and causal mechanisms can be probabilistically understood.	The researcher, the research participants and community members are interdependent. The goal of the research is to understand and interpret the multiple realities of these stakeholders.	The researcher works in solidarity with oppressed groups and strives to amplify their voices through a process of dialogue and consciousness-raising. The function of deconstruction, reconstruction and construction is to challenge and transform knowledge and society.
Ideology (the role of values and politics in knowledge)	Since there is an external reality that is independent of the researcher, research which strives to explain that reality must be value-free. However, the researcher can play the roles of advocate and activist, using the research to promote social change.	Since reality is relative and multiply constructed, the values of the researcher, the research participants and community members are part and parcel of their constructions. Research is value-bound.	Since there is an external reality that is shaped by competing values, the critical researcher is morally obligated to use the transformative values that she or he shares with oppressed groups to guide the research towards the goal of social change. Researchers must be self-reflexively aware of their social position and values.
Methodology (the tools that are used to obtain knowledge)	Community research is primarily quantitative and uses reliable and valid measurement scales, both correlational (epidemiology, surveys) and causal methods (experiments, quasi-experiments). Qualitative methods are used to a lesser extent, particularly in the context of discovery (generation of hypotheses to be tested) or as a complement to quantitative methods.	Community research is primarily qualitative and uses a variety of different methods, including qualitative interviews and observations, ethnographies, discourse analysis, narratives and case studies. Quantitative methods are used to a lesser extent.	Community research is primarily participatory and action-oriented in nature. Both quantitative and qualitative methods can be used in the service of value-driven research for social change.

Based upon Lincoln and Guba (2000) and Blake Poland in Murray et al. (2001)

aligned with post-positivism (Cook, 1985). The movement from positivism to post-positivism is indicative of how paradigms are fluid and constantly emerging. However, it is important to understand that post-positivism has its roots in positivism. Thus, in this section, we note both the positivistic roots of post-positivism and how post-positivism differs from positivism.

Ontology. The positivist paradigm has its roots in the modernist thinking of rationalist philosophers (for example Descartes), the British empiricist philosophers (for example Locke) and more recently positivist philosophers of science (for example Popper). The modernist worldview, espoused by these Enlightenment thinkers (Gergen, 2001), asserts that there is an external reality that is driven by universal laws and that can be known (described, explained, predicted and controlled). The goal of science then is to discover these universal laws that correspond to the true nature of reality. An example of a positivistic law is B. F. Skinner's law of positive reinforcement, that any consequence that follows a behaviour that leads to a subsequent increase in the frequency of that behaviour is a positive reinforcer. In contrast to positivism, post-positivism holds that reality can never be fully apprehended, only partially and imperfectly understood. Post-positivism is much more tentative than positivism about the possibility of uncovering laws that apply universally. They would argue that Skinner's definition of reinforcement is circular and that what is reinforcing varies considerably from person to person.

Epistemology. Positivism subscribes to the dualistic position that the researcher and the research object (the participants and topic of study) are independent. The mind of the knower (the researcher) and what can be known (external reality) are separate from one another. To understand reality then, research must be objective and value-free, so that the biases of the researcher do not interfere with understanding the phenomenon of interest. Various methodological safeguards need to be put in place to control extraneous variables and reduce biases. Positivism further assumes that reality can be broken down (reduced) into component parts and causal mechanisms can be determined. Researchers develop a language of terms, concepts and theories that are believed to correspond to external reality. Theoretical constructs are operationalized or grounded in observable events and behaviours.

Post-positivism shifts this paradigm away from the position of dualism. The mutual influence of the researcher and the researched is acknowledged and taken for granted. However, it is still assumed that various methodological safeguards need to be in place to insure objectivity and the probable truth of findings about the nature of reality.

Ideology. 'Facts' and 'values' are viewed as distinctly different and separate in positivism. Research should be 'value-neutral' in pursuit of the truth about the nature of reality. Post-positivism, on the other hand, acknowledges that the values of the researcher do enter the research process. As was noted in the previous paragraph, the goal is to reduce the impact of value biases by introducing a number of methodological safeguards. However, post-positivist researchers believe that they can use research findings to advocate for social change.

From our perspective, values have been relegated to the background in the positivist and post-positivist paradigm. While seldom mentioned or acknowledged, the implicit value underlying positivism and post-positivism is that society will improve with the gradual accumulation of knowledge. In essence, this means that the societal status quo is upheld. As is shown in Chapter 15, this assumption of gradual social improvement through science is challenged by systems of exploitation and colonization that accompanied the scientific revolution. In the shift from feudal and agrarian societies to industrial and urban societies, capitalism became the dominant economic system. And with capitalism came the values of individualism, profit, competition and hierarchies of power. These values, which still compete for dominance today, are challenged by liberal-reformist values of holism, health promotion and caring and compassion – values which we believe focus on the amelioration of social problems, rather than social transformation and underlie post-positivism.

Methodology. Quantitative and laboratory methods, adopted from the natural sciences, are the primary tools used in post-positivist research. There is an emphasis on the development of reliable and valid scales to measure theoretical constructs (for example questionnaires that assess sense of community or empowerment). Moreover, hypotheses about the nature of reality are tested and verified (or falsified) through experimental and correlational research. While positivism has emphasized experimental laboratory methods, post-positivism utilizes more field research in naturalistic settings. Community surveys and program evaluation using experimental and quasi-experimental designs, which we describe in the next chapter, are typical of post-positivist community research. There is also an emphasis on using multiple research methods for the purposes of 'triangulating' research findings (determining the consistency of findings using multiple methods). Qualitative methods can be used by post-positivist researchers to triangulate quantitative findings. Qualitative methods are seen as particularly useful for the exploratory or discovery phases of research to generate hypotheses that can be tested.

Example of Post-positivist Research. Up until now, the discussion of the post-positivist research paradigm has been fairly abstract. What does this type of research look like on the ground? One social issue that has been of considerable concern to community psychologists is that of homelessness. An example of post-positivist research is an evaluation of a support intervention for homeless people conducted by community psychologist Paul Toro and colleagues (Toro et al., 1997). As an example of post-positivist research, this study assumed that there is an external reality, homelessness, and that interventions can be causally related to improvement in that reality. Quantitative, experimental methods were used in the study.

Toro and colleagues evaluated the effectiveness of an intensive case management program called DEPTH for homeless people in Buffalo, New York. 'DEPTH took an holistic approach that combined services with job training – placement and locating permanent housing and support services, all targeted to the individual's specific needs and oriented toward the long-term goal of helping the person escape homelessness' (Toro et al., 1997, p. 478). Over 200 participants were randomly assigned to the DEPTH program or to the typical services (usually emergency services, such as shelters) available to homeless people and followed up every 6 months over an 18-month period. Regardless of the program they were in, all participants improved over time in terms of fewer days spent homeless, better physical health and fewer self-reported stressful life events. However, those who participated in DEPTH reported a better quality of housing, fewer psychiatric symptoms and fewer stressful life events than those receiving the typical services.

Problems with the Post-positivist Paradigm. Psychology has been charged as guilty of 'scientism' and 'methodolatory', in its slavish adherence to positivism and quantitative methods (Murray & Chamberlin, 1999a). It is important to realize that positivism and its descendent, post-positivism, are not the only approaches to truth and knowledge.

Guba and Lincoln (1994; Lincoln & Guba, 1985, 2000) have identified specific problems of the positivist and post-positivist paradigms. While they argue that the two share many common problems, they also note how post-positivism has improved upon positivism. First, there is the problem of 'context-stripping' in positivist research. In reducing a phenomenon to the selection of certain pre-determined variables, important dimensions of the micro-, meso- and macro-contexts are often stripped away. To some extent, post-positivism strives to provide a more contextual analysis, but the larger macro-context is often ignored in post-positivism. Second, there is the disjunction of grand theories with local contexts and the inapplicability of group data to individual cases. This problem is acknowledged by post-positivists who believe that research findings in the social sciences are not universally true and generalizable to everyone. A third problem common to both positivism and post-positivism is the exclusion of meaning and purpose. Human beings are more than material objects; we are all involved in making meaning and purpose out of our life experiences.

Fourth, the discovery dimension of research is typically excluded with the emphasis on hypothesis-testing, verification or falsification. With the inclusion of qualitative methods, post-positivism begins to overcome these problems of exclusion of meaning and the discovery dimension. Fifth, there are the problems of the theory and value-ladenness of 'facts' and the interactive nature of the relationship between the researcher and the object of study. This problem is acknowledged somewhat by post-positivism. The researcher's choice of topics (what is worth studying), theoretical perspective (how the topic and research questions should be framed) and methods (what is the best way of learning about the phenomenon) all reflect the values and priorities of the researcher. There is no way the researcher can be separated from that which she or he is studying. Like any other activity, scientific activity takes place in a social, historical and political context, which shapes what is deemed to be worthy of study, worthy of funding and worthy of publication.

The Constructivist Paradigm

Social constructivism has recently emerged as an alternative human sciences paradigm of inquiry in the social sciences. This paradigm is in dialectical opposition to the dominant positivist and post-positivist paradigm. Many of the early explications of this paradigm contrasted constructivism with positivism (for example Lincoln & Guba, 1985). This alternative paradigm has tended to develop outside North America and outside psychology. However, a growing number of psychologists are importing the ideas of this paradigm into psychology (for example Gergen, 2001; Lincoln & Guba, 1985, 2000).

In comparison with post-positivism, constructivism is more phenomenological, interpretive, holistic and humanistic. The focus is more on language, communication, subjective human experience and the meaning that people make of their experiences in their historical, social, cultural and political contexts. It is an approach that has more kinship with the humanities than the hard sciences.

Constructivism also rejects the dominant discourses or grand narratives of psychology (for example psychoanalysis, cognitive social learning theory) and other disciplines (Leonard, 1994). For example, the French post-modernist Michel Foucault (1980) was critical of dominant, 'totalizing' discourses that reflect the power of one group to dominate another group. For Foucault, knowledge and power are inseparable and those in power use socially constructed knowledge for the purposes of exclusion and control. Foucault illustrated his argument with examples of how mainstream society constructs diversity as deviance. In *Madness and Civilization* (1965), he showed how society labels, confines and controls people with mental health problems in institutions. This is done through the legitimization provided by the so-called helping professions whose function is surveillance and control of 'deviants'. Psychiatry provides the grand narrative of the medical model about how people with mental health issues should be viewed and treated.

It is also important to note that social constructivism is more a family of approaches than a single entity. While there are many complexities, nuances and differences within this family of approaches, here we present a more simplified account that emphasizes the common themes of constructivism (for more of the distinctions, see Alvesson & Sköldberg, 2000; Schwandt, 2000).

Ontology. The constructivist paradigm has its roots in the idealist philosophy of Kant and more recently in what has been called post-modernism and post-structuralism (Gergen, 2001). A core assumption of this paradigm is that there is no single, external reality, but rather multiple, mental constructions of reality, that are based on people's experiences in context. In other words, in a social and community context, individuals make meaning of their experiences. Thus, reality is not some absolute, universal truth that can only be understood by scientists; rather, reality is dependent on the individuals and groups who hold such constructions, with no one construction being more or less 'real' or 'true' than another. Reality is relative to the people who participate in the study.

Epistemology. In contrast to the position of dualism in the positivist paradigm, constructivism espouses a position of monism or holism (Montero, 2002). That is, the researcher and the research object are assumed to be interrelated rather than separate. Moreover, research is subjective, value-laden and inductive. Since reality consists of multiple social constructions, the researcher and the participants co-construct or create the findings. Finally, language does not correspond to any external reality, but rather reflects the mental constructions of individuals.

Ideology. Values are an inextricable part of the research, as the researcher and the research participants bring their values into the research process. However, the assumption of relativism renders it impossible to prescribe one set of values over another (Gergen, 2001). Thus, the research is value-bound or influenced (Murray et al., 2001), rather than value-driven.

Methodology. Social constructions are generated through dialogue, reflection and a close working relationship between the researcher and the participants. Primarily qualitative methods are used to elicit and understand people's constructions and participatory processes are used to arrive at a consensus on the findings and their meaning. Qualitative methods are used to understand the values, interests and meanings that underlie language, discourses and texts. The primary data in qualitative analysis are people's words, not numbers or statistics. However, constructivists can also use quantitative methods in their research.

Example of Constructivist Research. Returning to the issue of homelessness, an example of the constructivist approach can be found in an article by Boydell, Goering and Morrell-Bellai (2000). These researchers conducted a qualitative study of 29 homeless individuals residing in Toronto, Canada. They were interested in understanding the participants' conceptions of self. Boydell et al. used the theoretical perspective of symbolic interactionism to understand the inter-relationships between sense of self and social context. A central premise of this theory is that it is through interactions with others that an individual creates personal identity. The authors conducted interviews with these individuals using an interview guide to inquire about their conceptions of self.

One of the main findings of the study was that the homeless individuals are motivated to have a positive sense of self. While they tended to construct their past selves in positive terms, they were more likely to report aspects of a devalued current self in terms of marginalization, stigma, isolation, feeling inferior to others and ashamed of their situation of homelessness. One participant made the following comment. 'I felt disgusted with myself, you know, that I messed up. I felt bad like, you know, like I was a nobody, you know? … There's times I just, you know, just feel what's the sense of my living now, you know' (Boydell et al., 2000, p. 31). This devaluation of self is experienced in the day-to-day contacts that these individuals have with other people. As one person said: 'Well, they all think I'm a lazy shiftless, no-good bum. Take your pick. I have no choice. It's like, believe me, if I could find work, I'd be very happy' (Boydell et al., 2000, p. 32).

How is this an example of constructivist research? The goal was not to test hypotheses or generalize the findings to all homeless people. The goal was to understand people's experiences and constructions of themselves. This was done by talking to homeless people and finding out from them about their experiences. In so doing, the research generated new insights into the lives of homeless people.

Problems with the Constructivist Paradigm. The primary critique of this paradigm lies in its basis in relativism. No one construction or moral position is deemed to provide a better understanding of reality than another. What is considered to be truth emerges from a consensual process of negotiation and the ability of a particular individual or group's construction to persuade members of a community of its value. A second challenge has been mounted by realists who argue that it is sheer folly to dismiss the material nature of reality. 'But there is a world out there. There is no denying the reality of the human body, of death or that the world is round' (Gergen, 2001, p. 806). Third, the constructivist paradigm has also been criticized as overly descriptive rather than explanatory. Finally, there is a danger in the researcher having too much control over the interpretation of findings in the constructivist paradigm.

The Critical Paradigm

The German critical theorist Habermas (1971) argued that the critical paradigm integrates the knowledge of the other two paradigms towards the goal of human liberation. For Habermas, both the empirical-analytic knowledge gained through positivism (and post-positivism) and the historical-hermeneutic knowledge (aimed at the understanding of meaning) gained through constructivism are both valid forms of knowledge. However, he argues that these two types of knowledge should be in the service of human liberation. Critical knowledge, which the other two paradigms cannot uncover, is necessary to reveal interests, power and ideology and to create social change (Carspecken, 1996; Flyvbjerg, 2001).

Ontology. The critical paradigm has its roots in Marxism, German critical theory and contemporary forces for social justice and social change, including feminism, anti-racism and queer theory (Leonard, 1994; Lincoln & Guba, 2000). This paradigm assumes that there is an external reality. However, unlike positivism, critical theory holds that reality is constituted of institutional and social structures that have been historically shaped by social, political, cultural, economic, ethnoracial and gender factors. Critical theory also assumes that there are social inequalities that are contested and that there are conflicts between dominant and subordinate groups.

Bhasker (1975) has advanced a position of critical realism as the ontology of the critical paradigm. He distinguishes between the unchanging 'structures and mechanisms that generate phenomena' and changing 'knowledge as produced in the social activity of science' (1975, p. 25). The former suggests an external reality, while the latter focuses on the social construction of knowledge; both of which exist, according to Bhasker. He argues further that values influence and are influenced by social reality and that values can be used to promote human emancipation and social transformation.

Teo (1999) distinguished three functions of critical knowledge. First, deconstruction can be used to critique mainstream psychological theories and research (see Fox & Prilleltensky, 1997, for critiques of various sub-fields of psychology). Critical analyses are particularly attuned to issues of values and power. Second, reconstruction can be used to reframe psychological issues through an analysis of power. Third, construction is the development of critical theories that take into account issues of oppression and power.

Epistemology. The researcher and the research object are assumed to be interrelated and research is value-laden. Research findings are mediated through the values of the researcher and the participants. The importance of the researcher working and being in solidarity with research participants who are oppressed and disadvantaged is emphasized. Reflexivity is another important concept for the critical paradigm (Alvesson & Sköldberg, 2000; Willig, 2001). Since the values of the researcher shape the research, it is important for researchers to be self-reflexively aware of their values and position in society.

Feminist standpoint theory is one example of the epistemological viewpoint of the critical paradigm (Collins, 1990; Smith, 1990). In contrast to the epistemological and moral relativism of constructivism, feminist standpoint theory 'claims that all knowledge attempts are socially situated and that some of these objective social locations are better than others for knowledge projects' (Harding, 1993, p. 56). Critical feminist research is done from the standpoint of oppressed women, including women of colour, poor women, aboriginal women, disabled women, and lesbian, bisexual and transgendered women. Through reflection and consciousness-raising, feminist standpoint research with women from oppressed groups has the potential to create critical knowledge that can transform society.

Ideology. Research conducted from the standpoint of the critical paradigm is value-driven (Prilleltensky & Nelson, 2002). Researchers and participants begin with a moral and political position that underlies the entire research enterprise. Moreover, the critical paradigm emphasizes the transformative values that we identified in Chapter 3, including self-determination, social justice, respect for diversity, inclusion and accountability to oppressed groups.

Methodology – There is an emphasis on dialogue and dialectical processes. Research is reflexive and transformative; findings are always a work in progress that are subject new insights and critiques as the research process unfolds. Highly participatory and social action-oriented approaches are used towards the goal of emancipation and change of oppressed groups (Flyvbjerg, 2001; Reason & Bradbury, 2001; Smith, 1999). Inclusion of the voices of disadvantaged people and democratization and demystification of the research process are emphasized in the critical paradigm (Brydon-Miller, 2001; Nelson, Ochocka et al., 1998; Stoecker, 1999). Both quantitative and qualitative methods are used, depending on the research question.

Example of Critical Research. Returning to the issue of homelessness, research from the critical paradigm begins with the assumption that homelessness is caused by social structural factors and that homeless people are an oppressed group that lacks power. Over the past few years, research by members of the Toronto Disaster Relief Committee has analyzed the problem of homelessness in Canada in terms of a social policy analysis. In a 1998 report to the United Nations, Hulchanski (1998) reported that between 1994 and 1998, the federal government of Canada spent nothing on social housing for low-income people; in spite of the development of national plans of action to end homelessness, the federal government of Canada has not created a program to address homelessness; recommendations stemming from an inquest into the freezing deaths of homeless men in Toronto have been ignored by the federal and Ontario governments; and all forms of assistance to homeless people are decreasing. More recent reports have linked the growth of homelessness in Canada with federal and provincial policies of free trade and tax cuts (Hulchanski, 2002; Shapscott, 2001). Homelessness has increased sharply, while government expenditures on housing, income support and social services has decreased. This critical research is driven by a value of social justice and focuses on a macro-level analysis of the problem.

Problems with the Critical Paradigm. There are two potential problems with this paradigm. First, there is the question of what values will be privileged over others. Values are ever changing and there is a danger that those who are oppressed may stifle the voices of others and become the new oppressors of those who dissent. A second, somewhat more difficult, problem to confront is when people's actions contradict their espoused values. We all slip from our ideals. Care must be taken to be reflexive, non-dogmatic and non-exploitative. Habermas (1975) developed the idea of an 'ideal speech situation' in which there can be an open dialogue regarding values, and participatory action researchers and feminists have likewise discussed the importance of highly participatory and interactive processes to promote reflexivity, share power and prevent exploitation (Brydon-Miller, 2001; Flyvbjerg, 2001; Isenberg et al., 2004; Olesen, 2000). We discuss these important processes later in the chapter.

Using the Paradigms

Having reviewed these three paradigms of community research, we are left with questions about their usefulness. It is not possible to determine what constitutes the 'the best' paradigm. We think it is more fruitful to think about the usefulness of these paradigms for the conduct of community research. We also want to emphasize that paradigms are constantly changing and that one can think of the three paradigms as 'transitional epistemologies', rather than as fixed entities (Harding, 1987a).

We believe that there are several different defensible positions that researchers can take vis-à-vis research paradigms. First, some researchers find it most useful to anchor all or most of their work in the assumptions of one particular paradigm. Second, some researchers do not dwell too heavily on underlying questions of ontology and epistemology, but adopt a pragmatic position of methodological pluralism, including a mix of quantitative and qualitative methods (Goering & Streiner, 1996). This pragmatic position often arises, as Murray and Chamberlin (1999a) noted, from the fact that some world-view clashes have been debated for centuries and remain unresolved (positivism vs constructivism) and that researchers do not want to be caught in the 'paralysis of analysis'. While the idea of pragmatically blending methods may sound useful, this approach side-steps important philosophical assumptions. We agree with Murray and Chamberlin (1999a) that whatever methods researchers use, they need to be clear on their assumptions.

A third approach that researchers can take is to match their research questions with the most appropriate paradigm. This assumes that different problems or questions need different approaches. If a researcher wants to know if a social intervention causally leads to improvements in indicators of well-being and liberation, then a post-positivist paradigm is called for. But if one wants to know about people's experiences of the intervention, then a constructivist approach should be used. This approach addresses both epistemological and methodological issues. And if we want to know how the intervention fits within the existing social order and whether it challenges or supports the status quo, a critical approach is needed.

CP, like most of the social sciences, is rooted in post-positivism. More recently, the field is beginning to open up to constructivist approaches. However, the critical paradigm has received the least attention in CP research. Our standpoint is that there needs to be greater use of the critical paradigm in community research. The critical paradigm puts values, power, reflexivity and attention to the macro-level of analysis more in the foreground (Flyvbjerg, 2001). We urge the field to use the critical paradigm to inform its research and we believe that there is potential for both critical realist and critical constructivist research in CP.

Processes of Community Research

Having outlined the goals and paradigms of community research, we now turn to a discussion of the processes of community research. In an article entitled 'Tain't what you do, it's the way you do it', community psychologist Jim Kelly (1979) argued that the process of community research and action is more important than the content of the research and action. Moreover, Ed Trickett, Jim Kelly and colleagues (Trickett & Birman, 1987; Trickett et al., 1985) advanced an ecological view of community research that emphasizes the dynamic relationship between the researcher and community members from the setting that hosts the research. The need for researchers to nurture this relationship through close collaboration, to attend to and strive to prevent unintended negative consequences of the research and to promote the development of community resources are underscored by their ecological conceptualization of the research process.

In line with the main theme of this book, we believe that an important question for CP research is: 'How do we put our values into action in the way we conduct community research?' The short answer to this question is that CP should adopt the approach of participatory action research, which Hall (1993) described 'as a way for researchers and oppressed people to join in solidarity to take collective action, both short and long term, for radical social change' (p. xiv). Participatory action research is particularly well-suited to CP, because it shares similar values, including self-determination, collaboration, democratic participation and social justice (Nelson, Ochocka et al., 1998; Ochocka et al., 2002).

While participatory action research is closely allied with the critical paradigm of research, it is not necessarily linked with any particular methodology. Thus, both quantitative and qualitative methods can be used in participatory action research (Reason & Bradbury, 2001). The key feature of participatory action research is that the researchers work in solidarity with disadvantaged people. Research is done *with* community members, not *on* them. Unfortunately, CP research has historically not emphasized participatory action research. In a review of research published in major CP journals and in interviews with senior community psychologists, Walsh (1987) found that CP research tended to emulate that of the natural sciences (the positivist and post-positivist paradigms). Few articles mentioned any aspect of the relationship between the researchers and research participants and community members. More recently, community psychologists have underscored the importance of collaborative research (Dalton et al., 2001; Jason et al., 2004; Tolan et al., 1990). But it is not just collaboration that is important, but rather a long-term commitment on the part of the researcher to work in solidarity with oppressed groups towards the goal of social change (Rappaport, 1990).

While values provide a foundation for the conduct of community research with disadvantaged people, translating lofty values into practice is often quite challenging. Through our experiences working on different projects with different groups of stakeholders, we have learned that it is useful to have practical guidelines to implement a value-based approach to community research. In this section, we touch on a few practical guidelines for community research, that we have elaborated on elsewhere (Prilleltensky & Nelson, 2002; Prilleltensky & Nelson, 2004).

Representation, Roles and Responsibilities

The first step in a collaborative research project is to decide who should be 'at the table' (Nelson, Amio et al., 2000). In line with the values of self-determination, democratic participation and inclusion, the disadvantaged group that is the focus of the research should be strongly represented in the research process. Disability groups have coined the phrase, 'nothing about me, without me' to capture the importance of this issue of representation (Nelson, Ochocka, et al., 1998). In addition to the issue of representation, the roles and responsibilities of those involved in the research need to be clarified. Elsewhere, we have suggested that it is useful to create different structures for different types of participation (Nelson, Ochocka, et al., 1998). A research steering committee can be formed to oversee the development and implementation of the project with representatives providing guidance and approving all steps in the research. One of the first tasks of the steering committee is to brainstorm the vision, values and working principles for the research project. This is important for ensuring that everyone is 'on the same page' and for establishing a foundation for working relationships for the duration of the project.

The steering committee is separate from the research team, which is responsible for implementing the research. Hiring and training disadvantaged people to work as researchers on the research team is one way of ensuing strong representation of disadvantaged people. We recommend that 51% of members of the steering committee and research team should come from the disadvantaged community as an accountability mechanism to ensure their strong representation in the research. Finally, the larger community of disadvantaged people needs to have input into the research process (Serrano-García, 1990). This can occur through community forums and other public meetings about the research. Also, steering committee members and researchers from the host community can play an important liaison role with their constituents, so that information can be widely shared.

Decision-making Power and Conflict Resolution

It is not just important to have the key parties 'at the table', but also to have all aspects of the research 'on the table' for discussion. Guidelines for decision-making need to be established that promote the value of power sharing (Nelson, Ochocka, et al., 1998). Also, conflict is an inevitable part of any relationship and should be expected in participatory action research. We all have 'blind spots' and we believe that conflict provides opportunities for learning about power inequalities. It is also important to address conflicts quickly and with clear and direct communication to minimize any potential damage. The role of the community researcher with respect to issues of decision making and conflict is to share power, to be open to learning from conflict and to help facilitate conflict resolution.

If oppressed groups do not have representation and decision-making power in the research, then the research can contribute to the further oppression of disadvantaged people (see Smith, 1999 for a discussion of how research has served to colonize people of aboriginal background). Like others (Perkins & Wandersman, 1990), we have found that due to past experiences, disadvantaged people often react to researchers and research with distrust and scepticism, or even cynicism as to whether they will gain any benefits from the research. The development of a written research partnership agreement, that outlines values, roles, responsibilities, conflict resolution procedures and so on, can be used to overcome these suspicions and promote power sharing. An example of an innovative code of participatory research ethics that was developed by researchers and representatives of the Kahnawake nation in Canada can be found in Box 11.2. Such protocols can serve as another accountability mechanism for researchers to the disadvantaged community.

> **Box 11.2** **Code of Ethics for Participatory Research with Aboriginal Communities**
>
> **Policy Statement**
> 'The sovereignty of the Kanienkehaka (the people) of Kahnawake to make decisions about research in Kahnawake is recognized and respected. The benefits to the community as a whole and to individual community volunteers should be maximized by the researchers. Research should empower the community goals of health and wellness, to promote healthy lifestyles, improve its self-esteem and to fulfil its traditional responsibility of caring for the Seventh Generation. (In Mohawk tradition, the Seventh Generation represents those as yet unborn.)'
>
> **The Principles of Participatory Research**
> 'The Kahnawake Schools Diabetes Prevention Project is a partnership of the Kanienkehaka (Mohawk) community of Kahnawake, community-based researchers and academic researchers. In this document these three groups are referred to as the three partners. The three partners will work cooperatively and collaboratively in the design, implementation, analysis, interpretation, conclusion, reporting and publication of the experiences of the project. Each partner provides ideas and resources that come from the experience, knowledge and capability of all its members. Together, through respect for each other, consultation and collaboration, they significantly strengthen the project and its outcomes. All three partners of the project share an understanding the community-based research is a powerful tool for learning about health and wellness, while contributing to the health of the community in which it is conducted.'
>
> **Dissemination of Results**
> 'No partner can veto a communication. In the case of a disagreement, the partner who disagrees must be invited to communicate their own interpretation of the same data as an addition to the main communication, be it oral or written. All partners agree to withhold any information if the alternative interpretation cannot be added and distributed at the same time, providing the disagreeing partner(s) do not unduly delay the distribution process.'
>
> Source: Macaulay, A. C., Delormier, T., McComber, A. M., Cross, E. J., Potvin, L. P., Paradis, G., Kirby, R. L., Saad-Haddad, C. & Desrosiers, S. (1998). Participatory research with native community of Kahnawake creates innovative code of ethics. *Canadian Journal of Public Health*, 89, 105–8.

Community and Support

Community research should also promote community and support. We see the role of the researcher as creating a welcoming atmosphere for participation and facilitating supportive relationships among the different stakeholders in the research (Nelson, Ochocka, et al., 1998; Ochocka et al., 2002). People need to be free to voice their concerns and issues and to have their knowledge and experiences validated and appreciated. To break down some of the built-in barriers to relationships that are normally constructed in a hierarchical fashion (researcher and participant), we have found it useful to set an informal tone to research meetings. Using 'check-ins' and attending to the personal and interpersonal aspects of the research is very important for building community and support. The research relationship should mirror the larger values guiding the research project.

Communication, Dissemination and Action

Clear communication is essential to community research. There is a need for regular and direct communication among all participants. We have found that the structures of a research steering committee and a research team, which meet regularly to share information, are important vehicles for communication. It is also important to have methods of communication that go beyond the core research committees so that information can be shared more widely. Summary bulletins, news reports and feedback sessions on the project are other valuable methods of communication.

Moreover, such written communication should be done on a periodic basis, not just at the end of the project, and should be written in accessible language that is free of research jargon. The use of videos and dramatic presentations are other more innovative ways of sharing the findings of research.

Project members also need to think strategically about how the research results can be disseminated to promote action and change (Price & Cherniss, 1977). To promote change, those involved in the research need to target their message at specific audiences with specific recommendations. Mobilizing support for the recommendations and creating pressure for change are important aspects of the dissemination process.

Chapter Summary

In this chapter, we laid the foundations of community research. We began by outlining some of the goals of community research that are congruent with the value-based approach to CP that we articulated earlier. Next, we outlined three broad paradigms that underlie community research. We compared, contrasted and critiqued each of these paradigms and discussed our standpoint regarding the value of each. Finally, we ended the chapter with a discussion of the processes of community research. We argued for the adoption of a participatory action research and provided some guidelines for the implementation of this approach to community research. In the next two chapters, we present and discuss specific community research methods that are associated with the three paradigms and provide examples of how these approaches can be used to promote social change.

COMMENTARY: Reconstructing Social Research   *Michael Murray*

Contemporary social research is a child of the Victorian era. This was the age of great scientific developments. The potential of explaining and controlling the power of nature seemed unlimited. Wondrous machines were developed. Psychology and social science arose in this era with similar ambitions to harness the power of humanity and to assist in the building of a new society (Rose, 1996). But whose interests were most served by these research pioneers?

The 19th century was an age of rapid social change. In Europe, millions of agricultural labourers were forced off the land with the collapse of the traditional forms of social organization and the introduction of machinery. They moved into the cities where they found work in the new factories. It was a period of great social unrest as these industrial workers began to assert their role in the growing capitalist society. Social scientists were keen to assist established governments maintain their rule of order. For example, LeBon conducted detailed examinations of the crowds participating in the

many popular uprisings that occurred in French society in the 19th century. His aim was to develop a scientific explanation of this threat to social order and to ensure the continuance of government by the ruling elite (see Moscovici, 1985).

This was also the great age of exploration and imperialist expansion. Social scientists often accompanied explorers and colonizers on their voyages of discovery and conquest and eagerly compiled reports of the new lands and new peoples. Museums were established that became hoarding houses to display the wonders of the new lands. Native people were captured and included in circus displays. In her critical review of the character of the social sciences Smith (1999) compares traditional social research with that of the colonizer. Both were concerned with imposing their view on that of the other, of shaping the world in their image. Like the colonizer, the traditional social researchers sought to grasp for their own purpose the knowledge and wisdom of the indigenous peoples.

Throughout the evolution of social science researchers paraded their value neutrality and their desire to follow closely the guidelines of natural science. They were keen to develop a social and human science that privileged measurement and control over understanding and emancipation. The science they sought to develop would contribute to the development of a better world organized on rational grounds and freed from the reign of ignorance and superstition. However, it was also a science in which the interests of the dominant class were served in preference to those of the disenfranchised and oppressed.

In the 21st century the challenge is to develop an alternative approach to social science that can contribute to broader human emancipation. As was emphasized in this chapter, the alternative requires adopting a clear ideological stance on the side of those who are oppressed rather than on the side of those who wish to exercise control. In this chapter particular reference was made to the work of Habermas. In this commentary I extend this critique to include the work of some Latin American scholars who have come to the fore in articulating an alternative agenda for social research. This is perhaps not surprising in view of their contemporary history of social and political oppression. However, although their critical social ideas may have evolved in that milieu they have wider currency in developing a critical social research agenda. It is important to refer to the heritage of two researchers in particular: Paulo Freire and Ignacio Martín-Baró.

Paulo Freire was a Brazilian, born in 1921. In his work with the poor and exploited Freire came to recognize the role of the traditional educational system as one of the instruments of social oppression. It contributed to maintaining a culture of silence among the disenfranchised rather than assisting them in identifying the social and political roots of their oppression and assisting them in developing a strategy of personal and social change. Freire criticized what he described as the traditional 'banking' model of education in which the student was conceived as a passive receptacle into which the teacher poured certain value-neutral knowledge. Such knowledge implied unquestioning acceptance of particular social arrangements within which poverty and inequality were endemic. The alternative was a 'pedagogy of the oppressed' (Freire, 1973) in which the teacher worked with the student to reveal the oppressive elements of social reality. Freire described this process as conscientization. Through this process the student and the teacher together began to challenge the established truths.

Applying such an approach to contemporary society helps to avoid the trap of accommodating social research to the needs of the powerful. As Ledwith (2001) has argued, community work often seems radical while adopting a very accommodative agenda to exploitative social arrangements. Similarly, community research can ignore the broader social and political context within which poverty and oppression exist. The challenge is to attempt to link the immediate concerns of the research project to the broader political concerns. Through participatory forms of research, both the researchers and the community begin to explore their social circumstances and to consider how to challenge the established social arrangements.

Ignacio Martín-Baró was a Jesuit priest and social psychologist who lived and worked in San Salvador during the recent period of military oppression until he was killed by the army there in 1989. Throughout his life he committed himself to developing a research practice that was linked to promoting the liberation of the poor and oppressed people in his country and throughout the world. Psychologists had to dispense with the false idea of value neutrality and instead place themselves clearly on the side of the oppressed. He termed this adopting the 'preferential option for the poor'.

For Martín-Baró (1994) the important issue was not the character of the research in terms of the particulars of its methodology but rather the purpose of the research. He saw the research process not as some sort of simple reflection of the world out there as traditional positivists might argue; it was 'not an account of what *has been done*, but of what *needs to be done*'.

His critique of Latin American psychology applies to much contemporary social research. He criticized it for its 'scientistic mimicry' by which he meant its uncritical acceptance of the models of natural science. He also criticized it for its lack of an adequate epistemology and referred explicitly to the positivism that he condemned as underlining 'the *how* of phenomena, but [which] tends to put aside the *what*, the *because* and the *why*' (p. 21). He criticized its individualism that ignored the social dimensions of humanity; its hedonism as an underlying motive for human arrangements that was equivalent to the assumed intrinsic nature of the profit motive; and its ahistoricism that ignored the changing nature of social reality. Instead, Martín-Baró argued for the building of a new liberation psychology from the bottom up. There is a need to redesign our psychological theories 'from the standpoint of the lives of our own people: from their sufferings, their aspirations and their struggles' (p. 25).

Today, as we attempt to build a new social science, these ideas provide not only an important starting point but also an inspiration. A community-based social science begins with an awareness of the grinding poverty and injustices facing so many of the world's population. It asks of privileged scholars how their work can contribute not only to a greater understanding of humanity but also to the alleviation of this suffering. The strategies that we can use are many and varied but the challenge is to place our small efforts within a broader movement for social justice. Research should indeed be part of the process of social emancipation, not just for the few but for the many.

In developing our research, the challenge is to work from the bottom up with particular communities. This does not mean accepting as sacrosanct their version of reality, but nor does it mean imposing an alternative viewpoint. The path is one of openness and humility to new forms of knowledge and social arrangements, while at the same time developing collaboratively an awareness of how the broader forms of social oppression impact on our everyday lives, and exploring new avenues of resistance and social change.

It means both an emotional as well as a rational commitment to change, and an awareness that personal change and emancipation are interwoven with social change and emancipation. On an emotional level it means experiencing the frustrations when things do not go as easily as you would like or when people do not agree with your perspective. On a rational level it means carefully assessing the weaknesses and strengths of particular engagements. A community researcher knows both when to encourage resistance and when to accept temporary retreats. She knows that comprehensive social change may be a long-term goal but even short-term victories can provide welcome breathing space and provide time to reassess where to go. It is through such experiences that the researcher and the community can grow in self-awareness and confidence.

Chapter glossary

constructivism a paradigm of inquiry that is based on idealism and which purports that reality is relative to the constructions of individuals, interdependent with the researcher, value-bound and which can be comprehended through an understanding of the meanings and experiences of individuals (for example feminist post-modernism)

critical paradigm a paradigm of inquiry that emerged from Marxism and critical theory, and which emphasizes an external reality that is historically determined, interdependent with the researcher, value-driven and which can be understood through critical analysis and inquiry using a variety of methods (for example feminist standpoint theory)

epistemology the nature of knowing or understanding reality

ideology a set of values or beliefs

methodology tools that researchers use to understand reality

ontology the nature of 'reality'

paradigm a set of beliefs, a world view, a set of assumptions about the world and one's place in it

post-positivism a paradigm of inquiry that emerged from positivism (or empiricism) and which emphasizes an external reality, that is somewhat independent of researchers and their values and which can be imperfectly understood through objective research (for example feminist empiricism)

RESOURCES

1. Centre for Research and Education in Human Services – a community research and education organization based in Kitchener, Ontario that has been a leader in participatory action research, www.crehs.on.ca.
2. Link to other participatory action research websites, http://www.goshen.edu/soan/soan96p.htm.
3. Institute of Development Studies – focuses on research related to social change, http://www.ids.ac.uk/ids/health/.

12

Community Research Methods:
Post-positivist and Social
Constructivist Paradigms

Warm-up Exercise

Read the Class Exercise at the end of the chapter.

1. What are some of the assets that are apparent from the description of this community?
2. What additional assets do you think may be present?
3. How would you go about finding more about the assets of this community?

Whereas the previous chapter examined the goals, paradigms and processes of community research, the focus of this chapter is on the methods of community research. Community research methods are the concrete tools that reflect more abstract philosophical assumptions that underlie different research paradigms. We use the research paradigms that we outlined in the previous chapter as the organizing framework for the methods presented in this and the next chapter. In this chapter, we consider methods that are used to understand oppression, liberation and

Table 12.1 Methods associated with the post-positivist and social constructivist research paradigms

Focus of Research	Paradigm	
	Post-positivist	Social Constructivist
Analytic	■ Primarily quantitative methods, including indicator approaches, epidemiology and survey research ■ Primary methodological concerns are reliability and validity of measurement and generalizability of findings to the population	■ Primarily qualitative methods, including grounded theory, case studies, narrative inquiry and discourse analysis ■ Primary methodological concern is trustworthiness of the data in capturing participants' different constructions of their lived experiences
Activist/Interventionist	■ Primarily quantitative evaluation methods, including program logic models, program monitoring and information systems, outcome evaluation and cost-effectiveness evaluation ■ Primary methodological concerns are internal and external validity	■ Primarily qualitative evaluation methods, using interviews, observation, program documents and other archival data ■ Primary methodological concern is trustworthiness of the data (as above)

well-being (analytical or basic research) and methods to overcome oppression and promote liberation and well-being (activist or interventionist research) for research operating from the post-positivist and social constructivist paradigms. See Table 12.1 for an overview of the different research methods.

While quantitative and qualitative research methods can be used by researchers operating from either the post-positivist or constructivist paradigms, post-positivist research has been primarily quantitative, and constructivist research has been primarily qualitative. Thus, in this chapter, we describe quantitative methods in the context of the post-positivist paradigm and qualitative methods within the context of the constructivist paradigm. However, we want the reader to know that there is overlap in the research methods used by the two paradigms (that is, post-positivist researchers sometimes use qualitative methods and constructivist researchers sometimes use quantitative methods).

Post-positivist Research Methods

Analytic Research: Indicators, Epidemiology and Survey Research

Indicator approaches, epidemiological research and survey research involve examining existing data or collecting new data on large samples of people in order to make generalizations about the population from which the samples are drawn. These approaches use quantitative methods to assess community needs and resources.

Putting Problems on the Map and Identifying Strengths: Needs and Resources Assessment

Needs and resources assessment is concerned with the following questions: What kinds of problems/needs are there in the community? What are the resources, capacities and strengths of the community that can be mobilized to address the problems/needs? What kinds of interventions are needed to address the problems and meet the needs in the community? The primary function of needs and resources assessment is to provide data for planning an intervention (McKillip, 1998; Posavac & Carey, 1997). Needs and resources assessment can show how widespread or prevalent a problem is and highlight some of the factors are that are related to the prevalence of the problem. The two primary quantitative methods used in needs and resources assessment are indicator approaches and surveys.

Indicator approaches include social indicators and indicators of service utilization that are likely to reflect the problems a community might be experiencing. Typically, indicator data have already been collected and the researcher's job is to access them and put them together in a meaningful and useful way. A variety of social indicators (for example age, income) are typically gathered by government bodies or planning agencies through a census (information on an entire population) or a survey (a sample of the population). Indicators of service utilization are those that show the number of people who use different health, social or community services. The utility of indicator approaches for needs assessment is that they can help pinpoint communities that might be selected for an intervention. Communities with a relatively high percentage of low-income families (a social indicator) and relatively high rates of police calls and families involved with mental health and child protection services (service utilization indicators) demonstrate a greater need for intervention than communities with lower rates on these indicators. However, in selecting a community for intervention, care must be taken not to further stigmatize these communities. That is why it is also important to examine the assets and strengths of communities (Kretzmann & McKnight, 1993).

An illustration of the usefulness of this approach to needs and resources assessment can be found in the Better Beginnings, Better Futures project in the province of Ontario described in Chapter 22. The provincial government developed a policy research demonstration project to promote the development of young children and prevent problems in living and invited communities across the province to become a Better Beginnings, Better Futures site. More than 50 communities applied, but only eight were selected. In their applications, communities provided indicator information on the needs of the community, along with information about community strengths and resources, both of which were considered in the process of site selection.

Epidemiological and survey methods involve collecting new information about a problem or need. In public health, epidemiology is used to document the *incidence* (the number of new cases) and *prevalence* (the number of existing cases) of a disease in a population, as well as factors that put people at risk of, or protect them from, developing the disease. Community psychology (CP) has been interested in the application of epidemiological approaches to the study of mental health and psychosocial problems (see Box 12.1 for an example). Moreover, Reinharz (1992) has argued that feminist survey research can be used to 'put a problem on the map by showing that it is more widespread than previously thought' (p. 79). For example date rape, child sexual abuse, sexual harassment and violence against women – problems that were previously unnamed – have, through feminist survey research, been shown to occur at alarmingly high rates (Reinharz, 1992).

Box 12.1   The Stirling County Study

One of the earliest epidemiological studies of mental health problems was carried out by Dorothea and Alexander Leighton and colleagues in a rural county in Nova Scotia, Canada. This study involved an in-person survey of about 1000 adults out of a population of about 20,000 people, half English-speaking and half French-speaking (Leighton, Harding, Macklin, MacMillan & Leighton, 1963). Most of the population lived in impoverished. small fishing villages of 200 to 500 people. The researchers tested the hypothesis that communities that were high in social distintegration would have the highest rates of mental health problems. They defined social distintegration much as current theorists define a lack of social capital (Chapter 5), as lack of membership in associations, absence of strong leaders, few sanctions against deviant behaviour, hostile interactions and poor communication. Not only did the researchers find high rates of mental health problems, but they also found support for their hypothesis that social disintegration is a major risk factor for mental health problems.

The researchers conducted a follow-up survey in 1962, 10 years after the original survey. Some interesting findings emerged (Leighton, 1979). One community, which was very high in social disintegration and rates of mental health problems in 1952, showed significant reductions in these two indicators over the 10-year period compared with other communities. Dorothea Leighton reported that major changes happened in the one community which showed improvement. First, the educational opportunities for children and adults expanded. A teacher was hired and worked with the adults, as well as the children, and helped them to reduce hostility, develop cooperation and social skills and engage in community problem-solving. The community mobilized to improve the school and they eventually made connections with a neighbouring community so the children could continue their education at higher grade levels in schools outside the immediate community. Second, economic opportunities in the community occurred, so that residents were able to increase their income. With higher income levels, the residents were able to improve their homes and to have running water and electricity. These longitudinal data show that improved social and economic conditions were associated with a decrease in social disintegration and mental health problems.

Sources: Leighton (1979) and Leighton et al. (1963).

Making Inferences about Populations

Epidemiology and survey research are closely tied with prevention and health promotion, which have a population-level analysis. Prevention and health promotion are the action steps that follow from epidemiological and survey research. The concepts of *population, sample, generalizability* and *sampling* are important in this type of research. Population refers to everyone in a defined geographic or social space; whereas a sample is a sub-set of people in the population. Samples are studied in epidemiological and survey research so that inferences can be made about the population from which they were drawn. Therefore, researchers strive to ensure that the samples that they study are representative of the larger population. Sample representativeness can be obtained if some method of random sampling is used to draw the sample from the population. In random sampling, every member of the population has an equal chance of being selected. Also, the larger the random sample, the more likely it is to reflect the population as a whole.

In the study of people from different cultures or ethnic backgrounds, post-positivist researchers take an 'etic' or outsider approach. The etic approach assumes that there is a single reality and that research can determine how participants from diverse backgrounds differ with respect to psychological constructs.

Measurement

Epidemiological and survey research utilize quantitative methods. Various measurement scales, administered as self-report questionnaires or through interview schedules, are used to evaluate theoretical constructs that are presumed to correspond to some external reality. Two key concepts related to psychological measurement are *reliability* and *validity*. First of all, a measurement tool must be reliable. That is, it must produce consistent or repeatable findings. Several different methods have been developed to test reliability (for example the test-retest method). Measurement scales must also be valid; that is, they must measure what they intend to measure. Typically, scales are validated through demonstrations that scores on the scale in question show significant correlations with other scales designed to measure the same or a similar construct. This is called *criterion validity*. The concept of *construct validity* includes both criterion validity (or what has been called convergent validity) and *divergent validity* (Cronbach & Meehl, 1955). Divergent validity is required to demonstrate that the scale is not significantly correlated with measures of presumably unrelated constructs.

An example of a measurement scale that is of interest to community psychologists is a questionnaire that assesses the empowerment of mental health consumer/survivors. This scale was developed by Judi Chamberlin, who is a mental health survivor, and colleagues in collaboration with consumer/survivors from several different self-help organizations in the US. They began by defining empowerment and its components, including learning about and expressing anger, having decision-making power and learning to think critically (Chamberlin, 1997). Next, they generated items that reflect these different components. After pilot testing and refinement, the authors created a 28-item scale (Rogers, Chamberlin, Ellison & Crean, 1997; see sample items of this scale in Box 12.2). Moreover, the reliability and construct validity of this scale have been established (Rogers et al., 1997).

Box 12.2 **A Scale to Measure Mental Health Consumer/Survivor Empowerment – Sample Items**

1. When I make plans, I am almost certain to make them work.
2. I feel I am a person of worth, at least on an equal basis with others.
3. Experts are in the best position to decide what people should do or learn. (Reverse scored)
4. People have a right to make their own decisions, even if they are bad ones.
5. People working together can have an effect on their community.

6. People have more power if they join together as a group.
7. Very often a problem can be solved by taking action.
8. Getting angry about something is often the first step toward changing it.

Source: Rogers et al. (1997).

Note: Items are rated on a 5-point scale from 'strongly disagree' to 'strongly agree'.

Testing Theory and Examining Relationships

Epidemiology and survey research go beyond determining how prevalent a problem is in a population to testing theoretically-derived hypotheses about factors that are related to the prevalence of the problem. In particular, this type of research can examine the role that risk and protective factors, that were defined and discussed in

Chapter 4, play in contributing to the problem. Low-income and unemployment, for example, are major risk factors for health and mental health problems (see Chapters 1 and 15), while social capital is an important protective factor for health and mental health (see Chapter 7). Moreover, longitudinal survey research can shed light on the causal role that risk and protective factors have in the development of psychosocial problems. Hypothesis-testing is a deductive approach in which one starts with a general principle (a hypothesis that derives from a theory) and tests that hypothesis in a specific situation.

Challenges and Limitations of Epidemiological and Survey Research

It is very challenging to mount these types of large-scale epidemiological and survey studies. Researchers need a great deal of technical expertise in surveys, sampling and statistical analyses, and ample budgets to conduct this type of research. Because of the level of expertise and funding required, it is difficult for community groups to use these methods for a needs and resources assessment.

One limitation of epidemiology and survey research is that the problems that are studied can become reified. That is, constructs such as 'mental illness' and IQ can be taken uncritically as some true reflection of external reality, when in fact those constructions are deeply embedded within the social context and may support the status quo. Critical analyses of 'mental illness' (Hare-Mustin & Maracek, 1997) and IQ (Cernovsky, 1997) have shown that these concepts need to be contested. Epidemiology and survey research can also individualize personal problems, even if at the population-level of analysis, which may lead to victim-blaming. Claims such as '30% of women in the population have experienced a depressive disorder' need to be subjected to critical scrutiny to uncover the role of power and social factors that contribute to women's experiences of depression and to avoid the problem of context-stripping that occurs in positivist research. For example, Poland, Coburn, Robertson and Eakin (1998) provide an excellent critique of population-health research on the socioeconomic determinants of health, arguing that this research is largely ahistorical and apolitical. Alternatively, they propose a critical, historical, political economy perspective on the socioeconomic determinants of health.

The etic approach to cross-cultural research is subject to the same problems. In comparing people from different cultures or ethnic backgrounds, researchers assume that the constructs are meaningful within the different cultures that are compared. However, often the psychological constructs that form the basis of the comparison are rooted in mainstream western research and are imposed on other cultures, for which they may not be meaningful and relevant.

Activist/Interventionist Research: Evaluation of Programs and Interventions

Post-positivist research is also used in the evaluation of social programs and interventions. Since the publication of Carol Weiss's *Evaluation Research: Methods of Assessing Program Effectiveness* in 1972, there has been considerable growth in the field of 'program evaluation' (see the Class Exercise at the end of this chapter), which has been defined as:

the systematic collection of information about the activities, characteristics and outcomes of programs to make judgments about the program, improve program effectiveness and/or inform decisions about future programming. Utilization-focused program evaluation (as opposed to program evaluation in general) is evaluation done for and with specific intended primary users for specific intended uses. (Patton, 1997, p. 23)

As Patton's definition suggests, program evaluation research is used to inform decision making on how a program can be improved or become more efficient (formative evaluation) or whether a program should be continued (summative evaluation). Since the inception of evaluation research, program evaluators quickly learned that empirical data are but one source of information that can have an impact on decision-making in what are often highly turbulent conditions within

Table 12.2 Matching evaluation purposes, approaches and questions in the post-positivist paradigm

Evaluation Purposes	Evaluation Approaches	Evaluation Questions
Planning – to develop a new program or intervention	Needs assessment – focus on needs/ problems and resources in a community	What kinds of problems/needs are there in the community? What are the resources in the community? What kinds of programs are needed to address the problems and meet the needs in the community?
Preparing for evaluation – to develop a working model of the program or intervention that is amenable to evaluation	Evaluability assessment – construction of a program logic model that includes three components: (i) clear and measurable outcome goals, (ii) an articulation of program activities and (iii) establishing a rationale that links program activities and outcome goals	Are the program outcome goals and objectives clear, specific, measurable and focused on change? What are the program components and activities? Is it reasonable to expect that the activities will achieve the goals?
Program improvement – improving the quality of program or intervention components (formative evaluation)	Process/implementation evaluation – focus on program implementation, intervention specification, input, effort, quality assurance, program monitoring, management information systems	Is the program offering the services it intends to offer? Are the program components being utilized? Are consumers satisfied with the quality of the program components that are offered? What information is being collected on program participants and activities?
Program effectiveness – to determine the effectiveness of the program or intervention in meeting its goals (summative evaluation)	Outcome evaluation – focus on effectiveness, goal attainment, change	How effective is the program in meeting its goals? Can the changes or attainment of goals be attributed to the program? Which program components contributed the most to goal attainment? Is the program ready to be disseminated on a more widespread basis?
Program efficiency – to determine if the program or intervention can be operated in a more efficient, less costly manner without loss of effectiveness	Cost-benefits/cost-effectiveness evaluation – focus on efficiency, comparison of costs and outcomes of different program alternatives	Does the program achieve its goals at a reasonable cost? Are there less costly ways of achieving the same or better outcomes? Is the program affordable?

and around social programs and interventions (Weiss, 1972). In other words, evaluation research is saturated with values and politics. Thus, program evaluators need to be clear about their values and skilled in working in with program constituents.

Many program evaluators utilize what they call a 'stakeholder' (Pancer, 1997) or 'empowerment' (Fetterman, Kaftarian & Wandersman, 1996) approach to evaluation. In this approach, evaluators begin by asking pre-entry questions (Cherniss, 1993), such as: Who wants the evaluation? Who are the stakeholders? Often, program evaluators work with program staff, managers and funders as the primary stakeholders. Using the concept of partnership that we have promoted throughout this book, the consumers of services, who are typically disadvantaged people, should also be major stakeholders involved in the evaluation.

Once the stakeholders have been identified, evaluators need to work collaboratively with them to answer other pre-entry questions, including: What do stakeholders want from the evaluation? What is the purpose of the evaluation? What are the evaluation questions? What type of evaluation is needed to answer the questions? Answering these questions is an important step in framing the evaluation. In Table 12.2, we provide an overview of the link between evaluation purposes, approaches and questions. In the previous section, we discussed needs and resources assessment, which is the first approach identified in the table. In the remainder of this section, we elaborate on the other evaluation approaches in Table 12.2.

Evaluability Assessment and Program Logic Models

Evaluability assessment and program logic models were introduced by Rutman (1980) to provide a framework for evaluation. Evaluability assessment seeks to determine whether a program or intervention is ready to be evaluated. A program must meet three criteria to be evaluated: (a) clear, specific and measurable outcome goals, (b) clearly articulated program components and (c) a rationale that links the goals and program components. It is common for program constituents to have difficulty articulating the outcome goals of the program in question, which leads to what Patton (1997) has referred to as the 'goals clarification shuffle'. Program staff become confused with evaluation jargon regarding goals, objectives and indicators. Also, the program components themselves are sometimes not clearly defined and their link to the outcome goals is tenuous. Program staff may expect changes in outcomes to occur when the intervention components are not powerful enough to effect a change.

The construction of a program logic model is a way of overcoming these problems (Pancer, 1997; Rush & Ogborne, 1991). First, outcome goals are identified in terms of the changes in individuals or systems that the program or intervention is striving to make. Sometimes when service-providers are asked about the goals of the program, they will respond in terms of services that they provide (for example 'The goal of this program is to provide home visitation'). Evaluators need to help program staff and consumers to differentiate between service goals and outcome goals. Service goals involve implementation of the program components, whereas outcome goals are the expected changes that occur as a result of the program components.

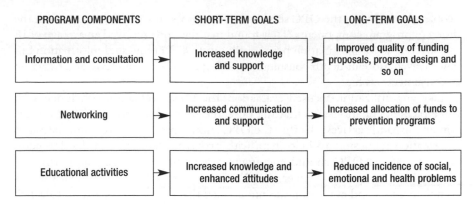

Figure 12.1 Program logic model for the Ontario Prevention Clearinghouse

In Figure 12.1, we present the program logic model that was developed for an evaluation of the Ontario Prevention Clearinghouse (OPC) conducted by Geoff and Mark Pancer. The OPC is an organization that was designed to support prevention and health promotion initiatives throughout Ontario (Pancer, Nelson & Hayday, 1990). The main program components include: (a) information and consultation (a toll-free telephone information and consultation service, with consultants and several computer data banks as resources), (b) networking referrals to other resource people pertinent to the caller's request and (c) educational activities regarding prevention, including a series of provincial Prevention Congresses (offered every other year) and workshops. In the short term, these program components should enhance the knowledge, support and attitudes towards prevention of those who use the OPC; and these short-term changes should lead to more proposals for prevention programs, more funding allocated to prevention and ultimately the reduction of health, education and social problems in the long term (see Figure 12.1). This logic model formed the foundation of a process and outcome evaluation of the OPC, which we describe next.

Process and Implementation Evaluation

Process evaluation involves an evaluation of the implementation of the program components rather than program outcome goals. As is indicated in Table 12.2, a quantitative approach to process evaluation focuses on collecting information about the people who use the service, indicators of the amount and types of utilization of the program components and consumer satisfaction with the program components (Pancer, 1997; Patton, 1997). Typically process evaluation is concerned with program improvement. Process evaluation is often used to assist a program in establishing a management information system, so that the program can routinely gather data relevant to the consumers who use the service and the utilization of program components (Posavac & Carey, 1997).

In the evaluation of the OPC, Nelson and Pancer (1990) assisted the OPC in the construction of a data base describing the characteristics of those people using the OPC and the nature of their requests. They also conducted a telephone survey of people who had used the OPC services to inquire about their satisfaction with the different program components. They found that the OPC received an average of 18 major requests for information per month; most (87%) requested information but few received more in-depth consultation (29%); and the overall level of satisfaction of consumers was high.

Like any utilization-focused evaluation, the OPC evaluation concluded with three recommendations: (a) that the OPC required additional funding to maintain and expand services; (b) that the OPC should provide more consultation to information requesters to help them with program planning and development; and (c) that the OPC should encourage more systems-centred approaches to prevention (Nelson & Pancer, 1990). Two years after this evaluation was completed, a second evaluation was undertaken that examined the extent to which these recommendations were implemented (Nelson & Hayday, 1995). First, the provincial Ministry of Health increased its portion of the OPC's operating budget from $50,000 a year to $384,000 a year. Second, the percentage of information requesters who received consultation increased from 29% to 65%. This was accompanied by increased satisfaction, more contact with other resource people, greater utilization of the information received, and increased knowledge and awareness of prevention and health promotion. Third, the OPC played a leadership role in advocating with anti-poverty groups for positive reforms to the province's social assistance system.

Outcome Evaluation and Research Design

Outcome evaluation is concerned with evaluating the extent to which the expected changes occurred as a result of the program or intervention (Posavac & Carey, 1997; Rossi, Freeman & Lipsey, 1998). Outcome evaluation is used to provide information about whether the program is valuable and should be continued and/or disseminated to other settings so that it can be implemented on a more widespread basis. In the OPC evaluation, participants were asked about changes relevant to the short-term outcome goals, such as whether or not their knowledge and awareness of prevention increased; whether or not they were able to contact more resource people with the aid of OPC than they would have been able to do on their own and so on. While the participants indicated that there had been changes as a result of their contact with OPC, it is difficult to conclude from this type of evaluation that there were changes and that they were due to the OPC. More convincing demonstrations of change require the use of some type of experimental (Fairweather & Davidson, 1986) or quasi-experimental design (Campbell & Stanley, 1966).

Consider an evaluation in which data relevant to the outcome goals are collected at two points in time: immediately prior to the intervention and immediately following the intervention. While this simple pre-test, post-test design can answer the question about whether or not change occurred in the outcomes, it cannot determine whether or not the change was due to the intervention. Campbell and Stanley (1966) refer to the confidence that one can have that the intervention was causally related to changes in outcome as *internal validity* and they described several threats to internal validity. History is one threat; the passage of time may account for any observed changes. Another threat is maturation. Imagine a program that is designed to improve children's academic or social competence. Perhaps the children would improve as a result of natural maturational processes. Or maybe the children's improvement was due to the experience of taking the pre-test. Testing improved their performance. There are many other threats to internal validity. Campbell and Stanley (1966) also noted the need for *external validity*, which refers to the confidence that one has that the findings are generalizable to other contexts.

Research designs are used to reduce these threats to internal validity and replications in different settings are used to demonstrate external validity. The most basic research design is the randomized controlled trial (RCT). In an RCT, participants are randomly assigned to intervention and control groups. That is, everyone has an equal chance of being assigned to either group. (Note that random assignment is not the same as random sampling, discussed earlier in the section Making Inferences about Populations). An RCT controls for history, maturation, testing and other threats to internal validity, because each group of participants should be equally affected by these factors. The only systematic way that they differ is in the terms of the intervention.

There are several examples of RCTs in CP, such as the evaluation of the intervention for homeless people described in Chapter 11 (Toro et al., 1997). It is also important to note that being assigned to the control group does not mean being denied services or supports. Rather, individuals in the control group tend to receive the services that are typically available to them, whereas those in the intervention receive supports that are more innovative or intensive than what is typically available. RCTs are typically used for what are called 'demonstration projects', in which the researchers examine the effectiveness of a new approach. When there are several RCTs demonstrating the effectiveness of the innovation, then the next step in the research and action process is dissemination of the project to other settings (Fairweather & Davidson, 1986). An example of this process of research and dissemination is the Lodge program developed by community psychologist George Fairweather (1972) for people with serious mental illness (see website).

In many situations, however, it is difficult to conduct an RCT. When such is the case, evaluation researchers often choose to use a quasi-experimental design which while not providing all the controls of an RCT, nevertheless approximates some of its controls. Quasi-experiments were introduced by Campbell and Stanley (1966) to provide some controls when random assignment is not possible. The most popular quasi-experimental design is called the *non-equivalent comparison group*, in which the evaluator seeks to find some group that is comparable to the intervention group, except for the intervention.

An example of the use of the non-equivalent comparison group design is provided in the evaluation of a multi-site, universal, primary prevention program for children and families called Better Beginnings, Better Futures, conducted by Ray Peters and colleagues, and described in Chapter 22 (Peters, 1994; Peters et al., 2000). First, all the communities in which the Better Beginnings projects were developed were compared with demographically similar communities. Samples of children and families were drawn from both Better Beginnings and comparison communities and these cohorts are being followed for 25 years to determine the long-term impacts of the project on participants. Another non-equivalent comparison group strategy that is being used is called the *leading cohort design*. Data were collected on a sample of grade 2 children and families before the projects started (these children constitute the comparison group) and they are being compared with the children who participate in Better Beginnings once they reach grade 2 (from junior kindergarten to grade 2, or four years of intervention).

One other useful quasi-experimental design is the *time-series design*. Like the simple pre-test, post-test design, the time-series design examines only one group over time. The difference is that data are collected at several different observation points, both prior to the intervention (baseline) and following the intervention. These multiple observations help to control for many threats to internal validity. This design can be used when the researcher has access to archival data that can be examined over time. For example, if a community development project wanted to examine the extent to which it reduced calls to police and other crime indicators in the neighbourhood in which the intervention was implemented, it would go backwards in time to generate a baseline of crime indicators and then forwards to see if crime started to drop with the introduction of the community development project.

Cost-effectiveness and Cost-benefits Evaluation

The focus of cost-effectiveness and cost-benefits evaluation is on efficiency (the relationship between effectiveness in achieving outcomes to effort expended to achieve outcomes). This type of evaluation seeks to answer the following questions: Does the program achieve its goals at a reasonable cost? Are there less costly ways of achieving the same or better outcomes? Cost-effectiveness and cost-benefits evaluation is done in the context of an outcome evaluation with some type of control or comparison group, or a time-series design. In addition to gathering data relevant to outcomes, the evaluator must determine the costs of the program (for example personnel, facilities, materials, equipment) and other services used by the consumer in order to have a fairly comprehensive comparison of costs across the different programs being compared (Yates, 1998). While cost-effectiveness compares the effectiveness to the costs of different program options, cost-benefits tries to quantify the benefits to participants in terms of monetary values (benefits could include employment income and savings in human service expenditures).

While difficult to conduct, cost-effectiveness and cost-benefits are important to CP. Government policy-makers are interested in these types of evaluations and the types of interventions that are developed by community psychologists and their partners have considerable potential to demonstrate cost-effectiveness or cost-benefits. Community psychologists have been instrumental in developing community-based alternatives to institutionalization for different populations. In a cost-benefit analysis of the Program for Assertive Community Treatment (PACT) for people with serious mental health problems, Weisbrod, Test and Stein (1980) found that the community-based program (PACT) had a better benefit–cost ratio (was less expensive and more effective) than the more traditional approach of hospitalizing people in a state psychiatric institution. Community psychologists have also argued that prevention and early intervention programs are more effective and less costly in the long term compared with traditional reactive approaches to intervention. In support of this, Schweinhardt and Weikart (1989) found that the Perry Preschool program in the US, a primary prevention program for disadvantaged preschool children, not only had significant impacts for participants when they reached their early 20s, but it also produced substantial cost savings. The 30-week program gave a return of $6 for every $1 invested, while the 60-week program gave a return of $3 for every $1 invested. The savings came from a reduction in costs for special education services in school, involvement in the justice system for criminal behaviour and welfare payments and from increased taxes paid due to higher earnings.

Challenges and Limitations of Post-positivist Approaches to Evaluation

In reducing programs to measurable processes, outcomes and costs, quantitative approaches to evaluation do not tell the whole story of interventions designed to assist disadvantaged people. In such evaluations, one seldom hears the voices of disadvantaged people and their experiences of such programs. Also, a major challenge in using this approach is that not all programs fit neatly into the straightjacket of different experimental and quasi-experimental designs. In contrast to the logical-empirical approach of program logic models and outcome evaluation, Etzioni (1960) conceived of programs in terms of a systems model with dynamic and interacting parts. One of the implications of this model, Etzioni argued, is that programs pursue other objectives besides the rational focus on goals. Programs strive to survive and cope with dynamic changes in the larger social–political environment, including funding cutbacks from government. Moreover, many of the programs that are amenable to post-positivist approaches to evaluation are those over which the researcher has some control. Such programs tend to be ameliorative in nature. More amorphous and dynamic social interventions that strive to be transformative are not as amenable to this type of evaluation.

Social Constructivist Research Methods

Analytic Research: Qualitative Approaches

Social constructivist research tends to rely much more on qualitative, naturalistic research. While qualitative research is used in education and many social science disciplines, it does not enjoy widespread use in psychology, which has by and large adopted a natural sciences model of research based on positivist assumptions (Kidder & Fine, 1997). While there has been more attention to qualitative research in some of the applied areas of psychology, including CP (see the list of special issues of psychology journals that focus on qualitative research in the Resources section at the end of the next chapter), qualitative research is still marginalized in psychology. We agree with Eric Stewart (2000) that qualitative research has much to offer CP, in that the two share an emphasis on diversity (including methodological diversity), understanding people in context and collaborative research relationships.

It is also important to realize that not all qualitative research is based on a constructivist paradigm. Kidder and Fine (1997) have made a distinction between what they call 'Big Q' and 'small q' qualitative research. The former is based on the constructivist paradigm, while the latter uses qualitative methods as a minor supplement to quantitative methods (for example adding some open-ended questions to a survey) and is rooted in the post-positivist paradigm. The focus of this section is on 'Big Q' qualitative research.

Characteristics of Qualitative Research

There are several characteristics of qualitative research (Kidder & Fine, 1997; Patton, 2002). First, qualitative researchers gather qualitative or textual data, including observations of behaviour, people's words and pictures. Big Q qualitative researchers rely on quotes or stories that are told by research participants and they do not attempt to quantify these data. Second, qualitative research is an immersion process for the researcher. The researcher enters the field and strives to get close to the phenomenon under study by immersing herself or himself in the context and lives of the participants for an extended period of time. There is a saying in qualitative research that the 'researcher is the instrument', which captures the shift of the researcher from being a detached outsider to an engaged insider. Third, qualitative research is naturalistic, with the researcher giving up control. The researcher does not attempt to manipulate any 'variables', and the research is situated in people's natural environments. Holism is a fourth characteristic of qualitative research. Rather than reduce the phenomenon under study to different components, the qualitative researcher strives for a holistic and contextual understanding of the phenomenon. Fifth, the subjectivity and emotions of the researcher and the participants are legitimate data in qualitative research. The research process is reflexive, with the researcher conveying experiential as well as intellectual understanding.

Sixth, qualitative research is inductive, moving from the specific to the general. While the researcher may have a hunch about the phenomenon under study, she or he does not begin with a hypothesis or theory to test. Rather, the research process is more open-ended, exploratory, adventurous and discovery-oriented. Often findings emerge that are surprising and the researcher constructs a grounded theory to understand these findings (Glaser & Strauss, 1967). Seventh, qualitative research is typically more concerned with depth than breadth. Whereas quantitative research emphasizes breadth and generalizability of findings by collecting data on large samples, qualitative research tries to provide a more in-depth understanding of the phenomenon of interest by gathering rich, qualitative data on a small number of participants or settings. Finally, despite being perceived by some as biased and lacking in rigour, qualitative research is in fact quite rigorous. The process of data analysis involves both creativity in developing the grounded theory and rigour in verifying the codes, themes and interrelationships that form the base of the theory.

Varieties of Qualitative Research

Qualitative research is quite diverse (Denzin & Lincoln, 2000; Patton, 2002; Willig, 2001) and there are several approaches that are useful for CP. First, *grounded theory* research is discovery-oriented and the role of the researcher is to construct a theory that emerges from the transaction between the data and the researcher (Glaser & Strauss, 1967). This is one of the most widely used approaches to qualitative research. *Case studies* are a second approach (Yin, 1994) and are characterized by their focus on the unit of analysis, one or several cases, as opposed to specific qualitative methods (Willig, 2001). Lincoln and Guba (1985) have suggested that the case study should be the unit of analysis in qualitative, naturalistic inquiry. The goal of case studies is to arrive at an in-depth understanding of a phenomenon in a particular context. An example of a qualitative research project that used grounded theory in the context of a single case study is Peirson and Prilleltensky's (1994) grounded theory of implementation of prevention programs and change in schools. These researchers identified factors that facilitated and inhibited the implementation of a prevention program in a high school and developed a grounded theory of the process of change.

A third method, *narrative inquiry*, focuses on how people make sense of their experiences through stories (Murray, 2000a). Julian Rappaport (1993, 2000) has argued for the utility of narrative methods for CP. Rappaport makes a distinction between personal stories, which are unique to the individual, and narratives, which have more common themes and are applicable across individuals. He further argues that there are dominant cultural narratives that provide the context in which individuals develop their personal stories, make meaning of their experiences and create their identities. For oppressed groups, the dominant cultural narratives are often terrorizing, stereotypical and stigmatizing (for example the dangerous mental patient). In contrast, alternative settings (for example self-help/mutual aid organizations) can provide an alternative, positive narrative from which individual members can fashion a more positive, joyful and hopeful personal story. Other narrative researchers have also pointed to the healing power of narratives in the context of health and illness (Murray, 2000a).

A fourth, and somewhat related method to narrative inquiry, is *discourse analysis* (Parker, 1997; Potter & Wetherell, 1987; Willig, 2001). While there are different approaches to discourse analysis, there is a common emphasis on the study of language. Moreover, what a person says, her or his talk, is constructed as an action with a purpose and meaning that must be understood in the context of the conversation. That is, the focus of discourse analysis is on what the talk is doing. This view stands in contrast to the mainstream positivist view that talk is a true reflection of the person's internal mental processes and structures (that is, cognitions, attitudes). Discourse analysis can be used to examine existing texts (for example newspaper or magazine articles) or data gathered through interviews or tape-recordings of conversation. Like narrative inquiry, discourse analysis can deconstruct the functions of dominant discourses (for example psychiatric professionals' medical discourse about 'mental illness') and alternative discourses (for example the stories of survivors of mental health problems and the mental health system). Fifth, *ethnographic research* strives to understand the culture of a setting and people. In contrast to the etic stance of post-positivist research, ethnography adopts an 'emic' or insider understanding of the culture and its assumptions.

While these different methods are typically associated with the constructivist paradigm, there are variations on the underlying assumptions of these methods. In some cases, grounded theory, case studies, narratives and discourse analysis may be more closely aligned with the critical realist assumptions of the critical paradigm (Alvesson & Sköldberg, 2000; Parker, 1997; Willig, 2001). Furthermore, the methods that we have briefly noted are by no means exhaustive of all the different methods of qualitative inquiry. For example, *hermeneutic/phenomenological* research (Alvesson & Sköldberg, 2000; Richardson & Fowers, 1997) is another major qualitative method.

Sampling in Qualitative Research

Since qualitative research is not concerned with generalizability to populations, it is not necessary to have the same large sample sizes that are found in survey and epidemiological research. Rather, the main issue in qualitative research is to purposefully select information-rich participants (that is, those people from whom the researcher can learn a great deal about the central issues which the research addresses) (Patton, 2002). Often, different stakeholders are sampled to obtain their constructions of the issues. Including multiple stakeholder groups permits an examination of issues across stakeholder groups so that one can discern both common and unique aspects of each stakeholder group's constructions of reality. A variety of different sampling techniques in qualitative research has been described by Patton (2002). Patton made the following statement about sample size in qualitative research.

> *There are no rules for sample size in qualitative inquiry.* Sample size depends on what you want to know, the purpose of the inquiry, what's at stake, what will be useful and what will have credibility and what can be done with available time and resources. (Patton, 2002, p. 244) (original emphasis)

One guideline for sample size is that one samples to the point of *saturation* or *redundancy*. That is, one continues to sample until little new information is gained from additional participants.

Data-gathering Methods in Qualitative Research

Qualitative Interviews. Interviews using open-ended questions (that is, questions that cannot be answered with a 'yes' or 'no') are widely used in qualitative research to understand people's lived experiences (Morgan & Krueger, 1997). Moreover, the qualitative researcher can use in-depth individual interviews or focus group interviews or some combination of the two, depending on the purpose of the research. Sometimes participants are interviewed only once, while in other research there may be multiple interviews with the same participants. Patton (2002) has also identified several different interview methods ranging from very unstructured to very structured: (a) the open-ended conversational interview, (b) the interview guide, in which there are a number of interview questions and probes, but which are not all necessarily asked and (c) standardized, open-ended questions, in which there are a number of interview questions, which are all asked in the same order and using the same wording. In line with the inductive and discovery-oriented nature of qualitative research, the skill of the interviewer in listening and in allowing the participant to determine the direction of the interview should not be underestimated in this type of research. Qualitative interviews are typically tape-recorded and later transcribed so that they can be coded.

Qualitative Observation. Qualitative researchers can also gather observational data, which provides information that participants may not talk about. Moreover, the researcher may observe something of which the participants are unaware. Qualitative observation is also important for understanding context, because the researcher can see people in their natural environments. As Patton (2002) noted, there are many variations in qualitative observation, including the level of engagement of the researcher (active participant vs more passive onlooker), the scope of the observation (very focused or narrow vs very broad and open-ended), and the duration of observation (single vs multiple observations). Most qualitative researchers attempt to become immersed in the setting, which means that they spend considerable time in observation and in relationships with the members of the setting. Generally, qualitative researchers take two different forms of field notes: (a) descriptive field notes about what they observe (including direct quotes) and (b) analytic or reflective field notes in which they record their impressions, insights, hunches and feelings.

Other Sources of Qualitative Data. Qualitative researchers can also use archival data, including program records and documents, newspapers, magazines and other sources from which they can extract textual data. In many qualitative research projects, the researcher uses more than one type of data-gathering.

Qualitative Data Analysis and Verification

Each approach to qualitative research has specific techniques for data analysis (for example grounded theory, discourse analysis, narrative analysis). However, these different approaches all tend to use some process of coding the data from transcripts, texts and field notes.

One often used method of data analysis in grounded theory is *constant comparison* (Glaser & Strauss, 1967). The first rule of the constant comparative method is that 'while coding an incident for a category, compare it with the previous incident in the same and different groups coded in the same category' (Glaser & Strauss, 1967, p. 106). The emerging coding system will be imperfect and will not always work, so 'the second rule of the constant comparative method is: stop coding and write a memo on your ideas' (Glaser & Strauss, 1967, p. 107). The aim of memo writing is to uncover the properties and dimensions of a code. Next, one begins to integrate the codes and their properties. At this stage in the analysis, the researcher makes a judgement as to whether a new incident exhibits the category properties that have been tentatively defined. The focus of this step in data analysis is on rule definition and making the properties of codes explicit. Initial coding generally stops when the codes are saturated (that is, no new codes emerge); all the data sources have been coded; and there is a sense of integration (Lincoln & Guba, 1985). An example of a code is that of 'Social Isolation', which emerged as a code in Lord and Hutchison's (1993) study of the process of personal empowerment. The key properties of social isolation they found were: neglect, lack of support and abandonment.

Once the initial set of codes has been developed, the next task in the analysis is

Table 12.3 Themes in the process of personal empowerment

Experiencing Powerlessness	Gaining Awareness	Learning New Roles	Initiating/ Participating	Contributing
Social isolation	Acting on anger	Connecting with other	Joining groups	Being a role model
Service dependency	Responding to new information	Linking with resources	Speaking out	Having influence
Limited choices	Responding to new contexts	Expanding choices/ opportunities	Expanding participatory competence	Increasing self-efficacy

Source: Lord and Hutchison (1993)

to develop more overarching theme codes or pattern codes, which subsume and link the more descriptive codes from the first level of analysis. Whereas initial coding breaks the data down into discrete codes, theme coding puts the data back together in a way that makes sense. In grounded theory, the theme codes are the conditions, context, actions and consequences of the phenomenon (Strauss & Corbin, 1998). In theme coding, the researcher uses questions (Who? What? When? Where? How? Why?) to create meaning out of the codes. Often researchers use charts, matrix displays or figures to clarify the theme codes and their inter-relationships. Table 12.3 is an example of a chart depicting theme coding in a qualitative study of the process of personal empowerment (Lord & Hutchison, 1993). Note that the themes are organized as the steps that are involved in the process of empowerment, with people moving from a state in which they experience powerlessness to a point in which they are contributing to community. The theme of powerlessness encompasses the codes of social isolation, service dependency and limited choices.

Lincoln and Guba (1985) argue that qualitative researchers must be able to establish the trustworthiness of their data. 'The basic issue in relation to trustworthiness is simple: How can an inquirer persuade his or her audiences (including self) that the findings of an inquiry are worth paying attention to, worth taking account of? What arguments can be mounted, what criteria invoked, what questions asked and what would be persuasive on this issue?' (Lincoln & Guba, 1985, p. 290). They propose four criteria for trustworthiness: (a) credibility, which means that one must adequately represent participants' multiple constructions of reality, (b) transferability, which refers to the extent to which the findings can be transferred to other contexts, (c) dependability, which is the extent to which findings are consistent or dependable and (d) confirmability of the data by others. Lincoln and Guba (1985) propose several techniques for establishing the trustworthiness of qualitative data, including: prolonged involvement in the setting and persistent observation, the use of multiple sources of information, multiple researchers and multiple methods to 'triangulate' or determine the consistency of the data, checking the interpretations of the data with participants, establishing an audit trail of the steps taken in the data analysis and providing a detailed description of the setting.

Qualitative Needs Assessment

Community researchers can use qualitative methods to assess the needs and resources of a community. Milord (1976) argued that key informant interviews, focus groups, nominal groups and community forums are non-epidemiological methods of needs assessment. Lord, Schnarr and Hutchison (1987) completed one of the first qualitative needs assessments of mental health consumer/survivors. They conducted in-depth interviews with 23 mental health consumer/survivors (16 people in four provinces and seven self-help group leaders) and one focus group interview (with five to nine participants) in each of the 10 Canadian provinces. The main needs that consumer/survivors talked about were housing, employment, friends and support, and the struggle for identity. The phrase 'a friend, a home, a job', have subsequently become a familiar refrain in the stories and discourse of mental health consumer/survivors (see Chapter 21).

Another technique that can be used in needs and resources assessment is *asset mapping* (Kretzman & McKnight, 1993). In asset mapping, participants are asked, through qualitative interviews, to map the strengths or assets of the community. For example, the Search Institute for developmental assets for children has identified many different assets, both internal and external, of children and young people that can protect them against stressful situations (see the website for the Search Institute, http://www.search-institute.org/).

Challenges and Limitations of Qualitative Constructivist Research

The major challenge that qualitative researchers face is the credibility of the methods. The academic community and granting agencies often do not understand or value qualitative research. Thus, gaining acceptance of these methods is a major challenge. With regard to limitations, qualitative research overcomes many of the problems inherent in quantitative research (for example context-stripping, narrowness, mechanistic simplicity). However, in the process, a new set of problems emerges (for example questionable generalizability of findings, an over-reliance on description). However, from our perspective, the main problems with qualitative research are not very different from those of quantitative research. Much of qualitative research lacks a critical perspective, fails to use participatory processes and has little focus on catalysing social change.

Activist/Interventionist Research: Evaluation of Programs and Interventions

Varieties of Qualitative Evaluation

Many of the methods and approaches to qualitative research that were described in the previous section are also applicable to the evaluation of programs and interventions. Qualitative interviews, observations and archival data can all be used in qualitative evaluation. Similarly, grounded theory, case studies, narratives, discourse and ethnographic methods can also be applied to evaluation.

There are two main approaches to qualitative program evaluation (Greene, 2000): the 'utilitarian pragmatism' of Patton (2002) and the social constructivism of Guba and Lincoln (1989). According to Greene, Patton's approach emphasizes the values of 'utility, practicality and managerial effectiveness' (Greene, 2000,

p. 984) and the primary evaluation audience is mid-level program managers and administrators. Patton (2002) borrows many of the concepts used in quantitative program evaluation, such as logic models, evaluability assessment and evaluation of process and outcomes, but he advocates gathering qualitative data for these types of evaluation. The evaluation purposes, approaches and questions used in Patton's (2002) approach to qualitative evaluation are similar to those that we described in Table 12.2. Patton's (2002) qualitative approach to evaluation could be considered to be more post-positivist than constructivist in orientation.

In contrast, the *fourth generation* approach to evaluation advanced by Guba and Lincoln (1989) rests explicitly on the assumptions of social constructivism and is concerned with how the program is experienced by different stakeholders (including managers, staff and consumers) and the meaning that the stakeholders attach to the program. This approach is guided by the principles of value pluralism, fairness in honouring stakeholder constructions and eliciting their claims, concerns and issues and a negotiated evaluation process. The primary method of fourth generation evaluation is the case study, which can include qualitative interviews, observations and an analysis of program documents. In addition to the criteria for technical adequacy of the evaluation findings (that is, the different criteria for trustworthiness mentioned earlier), Lincoln and Guba (1986) assert that the research process and findings must be fair (that is, a negotiated process in which all stakeholders have the opportunity to share their concerns, interpret the findings and influence the evaluation recommendations for change), authentic (that is, leading to increased understanding, appreciation and consciousness of the experiences of different stakeholders and their social contexts) and relevant to program stakeholders.

Challenges and Limitations of Qualitative Evaluation

While qualitative approaches to evaluation are not new (the first edition of Patton's *Qualitative Research and Evaluation Methods* was published in 1980), qualitative evaluation is still less accepted by government stakeholders than quantitative evaluation methods. In our experiences of evaluation, we continue to hear from government funders and managers that qualitative evaluation is 'soft' and 'subjective'. While qualitative methods cannot uncover causal mechanism or calculate cost-effectiveness, as can be attempted in quantitative evaluation, the more in-depth, stakeholder-based approach of qualitative evaluation is well suited to many different types of evaluation questions.

Chapter Summary

In this chapter, we reviewed a wide range of research methods that community psychologists can use in research with community groups. We examined methods associated with the post-positivist and social constructivist paradigms identified in the previous chapter as the organizing framework for this discussion. At this time, these two paradigms tend to capture some of the major emphases in different research methodologies. In the next chapter, we focus on methods that community psychologists use when working from the critical paradigm.

Needs and Resources Assessment Scenario

A group of concerned citizens and human service workers has approached you to help them conduct a needs and resources assessment of a neighbourhood. The neighbourhood consists of a mix of middle- to high-income families and low-income families. The group members perceive a lack of identity as a community (little sense of community), social isolation and lack of participation in community groups or events (in part, because there are few opportunities for participation), increasing vandalism (including constant harassment of convenience store workers by neighbourhood youngsters) and low levels of trust and safety.

There are two schools in the neighbourhood (one K-6 (primary) and one 7-8 (junior)); both have playgrounds and the 7-8 school has an athletic field. There is also a Mennonite church and a senior citizens' complex. Housing for low-income families is quite densely concentrated, with little green space and no common areas. The streets and yards are often littered and there are sometimes loud parties and fights. Police are called into the neighbourhood several times a week. Ontario Housing has 70 townhouse units in the area. There are also four apartment complexes, each with 20 units and 90 single-family residences, which house more middle- to high-income families. There is a bus route on one of the neighbourhood streets and residents can reach shopping facilities in 10 minutes.

The group which has approached you consists of two school principals (both of whom live in the area and attend the church), one school psychologist, the pastor and an outreach worker from the church, and a couple who live in the low-income housing. The senior citizens' home has been approached to become involved, but they are mistrustful and resent vandalism of their property by neighbourhood youngsters. The group wants you to help them check out their impressions of neighbourhood problems and concerns, identify neighbourhood strengths and find out what residents would like to see developed in their community. There is no money for the research, but the schools and church have indicated that they could provide some photocopying and other supplies.

Describe how you could use qualitative methods, including interviews, observation and a community forum to assess the needs and resources of this community.

Chapter glossary

asset mapping a technique used in needs and resources assessment to provide an inventory of the assets or strengths of individuals or a community

Big Q qualitative research research that does not reduce people's words or actions to numerical indices, but rather reports the textual data in the form of quotes or observations

case study the use of multiple methods to study one or more persons, programs or communities in depth

constant comparison a method of qualitative data analysis associated with grounded theory in which emerging codes or themes are constantly compared across cases in order to refine the codes and themes

cost-effectiveness/cost-benefits evaluation an approach to evaluation that examines both the costs and the effectiveness or benefits associated with a program or intervention

discourse analysis another approach to qualitative research that examines the functions of written and oral discourse

emic approach in contrast to the etic approach to cultural research, the emic approach involves the researcher immersing herself or himself in the setting to develop an in-depth understanding of the culture; the emic approach is used in ethnographic studies

epidemiology a public-health research approach that examines the incidence (number of new cases) and prevalence (number of existing cases) of a health problem in a community or population and the factors that are related to incidence and prevalence

etic approach an approach to research on people from different cultures in which the researcher is an 'outsider' who tries objectively to study the culture or compare it with other cultures

evaluability assessment an examination of the extent to which a program is amenable to evaluation as determined by the ability to construct a program logic model with clearly articulated program components, clearly specified outcome or change goals and a sound rationale that links the program components with the outcome goals

external validity the extent to which changes in outcomes can be generalized to other settings

Chapter glossary cont'd

generalizibility the extent to which the findings of a survey or epidemiological study can be generalized from the sample studied to the entire population; large, random samples are often used to enhance generalizability

grounded theory an approach to qualitative research and data analysis that involves inductively constructing a theory linking the main themes that emerge from qualitative data

indicator approaches social indicators (for example age, income, number of people living in poverty) and indicators of service utilization that are likely to reflect problems that a community might be experiencing; these data are typically archival (already collected)

internal validity the extent to which changes in outcomes can be attributed to the program or intervention

narrative inquiry an approach to qualitative research that involves examining the stories of individuals and communities

needs and resources assessment research that gathers information on the needs and resources of a community that are used for planning an intervention

outcome evaluation an evaluation that focuses on the extent to which the outcomes expected of the program were achieved

population all of the people in a community

process/implementation evaluation an evaluation that focuses on the adequacy of implementation of the components of a program

quasi-experiment a research design that strives to maximize internal validity by using comparison groups or control strategies that do not involve random assignment (for example non-equivalent comparison group design, time-series design)

reliability the consistency or repeatability of findings obtained from using a research instrument (for example test–retest reliability)

sample a sub-set of the population of a community

saturation a point at which no new codes or themes arise from the examination of additional cases (that is, participants) in qualitative data analysis

survey research research in which a sample of people are surveyed about some issue(s)

true experiment a research design that maximizes internal validity by randomly assigning participants to program and control conditions (that is, a randomized controlled trial)

trustworthiness the overarching criterion of data quality in qualitative data analysis, which encompasses the criteria of credibility (adequate representation of participants' multiple constructions of reality), transferability (the extent to which the findings can be transferred to other contexts), dependability (the extent to which findings are consistent or dependable) and confirmability of the data by others

validity the degree to which an instrument measures what it is intended to measure (for example if scores on an instrument are related to scores on a similar measure, then there is evidence of criterion or convergent validity)

13

Community Research Methods:
Critical Paradigm

Warm-up Exercise

In the previous chapter, you read about various approaches to evaluation. Imagine now that the university you are attending wants to conduct an evaluation of student services (library, bookstore, registration process, food services and so on). Think for a moment about how students could be involved in the development, implementation, analysis and interpretation of findings related to this evaluation. In other words, how could this evaluation be done with a high degree of student participation in all phases of the evaluation?

As was shown in the previous chapter, the post-positivist and social constructivist paradigms tend to be associated with specific research methods. What distinguishes critical research methods from post-positivist and constructivist research methods are less the specific methods used and more the processes and goals of the research. As indicated in Table 13.1, community psychology (CP) research operating from the

Table 13.1 Methods associated with the critical paradigm

Focus of Research	Critical Paradigm
Analytic	■ Quantitative and/or qualitative methods are used for problem analysis in a highly participatory research process involving a partnership between disadvantaged community members and researchers ■ Primary methodological concern is epistemic psychopolitical validity
Activist/Interventionist	■ Quantitative and/or qualitative methods are used for problem intervention and action in a highly participatory research process involving a partnership between disadvantaged community members and researchers ■ Primary methodological concern is transformative psychopolitical validity

Note that the dashed line separating the analytic and activist/interventionist research in the critical paradigm indicates that understanding and action are interlinked and typically inseparable assumptions of the critical paradigm includes both quantitative and qualitative methods. The key methodological element of the critical paradigm is that research is participatory and action-oriented.

Critical Research Methods

In the previous chapter, we made a distinction between analytic and activist/interventionist research methods. Note that in Table 13.1, there is a dotted line separating the analytic and activist/interventionist types of research. This is because these two types of research are more integrated in critical research and less separated than in the post-positivist and social constructivist paradigms. Consequently, in this section, we do not have separate sections on analytic and activist/interventionist research. Rather, they are treated together.

Analytic and Activist/Interventionist Research: Critical Participatory Action Approaches

The Foundations of Critical Research

Critical research has its roots in participatory research, action research, feminist research and anti-racist research. Brown and Tandon (1983) have pointed out that participatory research and action research stem from different traditions. Participatory research emerged from work with oppressed people in developing countries, particularly Latin America (see Montero, 2000a and Murray's commentary on Chapter 11). Moreover, participatory research is based on the assumption that oppressed people must be fully engaged in the process of research, education and change (Park, Brydon-Miller, Hall & Jackson, 1993; Tolman & Brydon-Miller, 2001). On the other hand, action research was introduced in North America over 50 years ago by Kurt Lewin (1946), who proposed cycles of problem definition, fact-finding, goal-setting, action and evaluation to simultaneously solve problems and generate new knowledge. Closely associated with organizational interventions, action research typically involves a partnership with organizational managers, not disadvantaged people. While having separate roots, many researchers today integrate participatory and action research into what is commonly referred to as *participatory action research* (Balcazar, Keys, Kaplan & Suarez-Balcazar, 1998; Nelson, Ochocka, et al., 1998; Reason & Bradbury, 2001).

Feminism is another foundation on which critical research is based. In contrast to liberal feminism which posits that women need to have equal opportunities to men, radical, socialist and anti-racist forms of feminism assert that more fundamental social change is required to address the structural problems of sexism, capitalism and racism (Campbell & Wasco, 2000). The mission of standpoint feminist research, as described in Chapter 11, is to expose and eradicate patriarchy and the oppression of women (Reinharz, 1992). While feminist research and participatory action research have different roots, they share much in common.

Campbell and Wasco (2000) have identified four themes that characterize feminist research methods. First, feminist research expands the range of methods. Feminists have pioneered the use of qualitative methods (Reinharz, 1992) and they have developed new methods, such as concept mapping. Campbell and Salem (1999) conducted focus groups with rape victim advocates to brainstorm how services could be more responsive to rape victims. The qualitative data were then quantified and statistical analyses were performed that yielded a map of key concepts. Second, feminist research connects women through 'openness, trust, caring, engagement, reciprocal relationships and solidarity among women' (Prilleltensky & Nelson, 2002). Third, feminist research strives to reduce power differences in the research relationship by engaging participants as co-researchers and co-analysts in the research process. Fourth, the emotionality of science is recognized in feminist research. Feminist standpoint researchers reject research dichotomies of the post-positivist paradigm, including reason/emotion, mind/body, objectivity/subjectivity. Emotion and subjectivity are treated as important sources of data in feminist research.

With respect to culture, ethnicity and race, critical psychology takes an altogether different stance from the etic approach of post-positivism and the emic approach of constructivism. The standpoint of critical research is explicitly anti-racist and focuses on oppression and power imbalances between people of different backgrounds. Smith's (1999) analysis of how research has historically served the function of colonizing people of colour by treating them as objects of curiosity, inferior to the standard of white Europeans, is an example of the critical perspective. Alternatively, Smith argues that research needs to be 'de-colonized' to promote liberation and well-being by working collaboratively with people of colour.

The Values and Principles of Critical Research

As we noted in Chapter 11, the critical research paradigm is value-based. Several authors have delineated some of the values and principles that underlie critical research (Balcazar et al., 1998; Nelson, Ochocka, et al., 1998). In Table 13.2, we

Table 13.2 Values and principles of critical research

Values	Principles
Self-determination and participation (empowerment)	■ Research should be attuned to issues of power and promote the power of disadvantaged people ■ Research begins with the experiences and concerns of disadvantaged people ■ Research process is democratized so as to maximize the participation of disadvantaged people in all aspects of the research ■ Research uses qualitative methods that give voice to disadvantaged people
Community and inclusion	■ Research strives to develop authentic and supportive relationships among researchers, disadvantaged people and other stakeholders ■ Research should be directed towards the goal of building solidarity for social change
Social justice and accountability to oppressed groups	■ Research money should be distributed in a way that provides job and training opportunities as co-researchers for members of disadvantaged groups ■ Research findings should be used for education and/or advocacy to create social change
Reflexivity	■ Research should use emergent (or flexible) research designs ■ Research should provide an educational component ■ Research should be demystified so that knowledge is accessible to all, not just researchers ■ Research should involve all stakeholders in the interpretation of findings and recommendations for change ■ Researchers and stakeholders should write about personal experiences and their perspectives in research reports

identify several values and related principles for critical research. Note that the values of critical research are congruent with the values of CP that we identified in Chapters 2 and 3.

First and foremost, critical research is guided by the values of self-determination and participation. That is, it is characterized by an agenda of empowerment (Rappaport, 1990; Ristock & Pennell, 1996). This means that critical research should: be attuned to issues of power and have as a goal the promotion of power of disadvantaged people; begin with the experiences and concerns of disadvantaged people; be democratized to maximize the participation of disadvantaged people; and use qualitative methods that give voice to disadvantaged people (Nelson, Ochocka et al., 1998; Ochocka et al., 2002). In this vein, Balcazar et al. (1998) assert that participatory action research has the potential to increase the 'awareness among people with disabilities about their own resources and strengths' (p. 107).

Second, critical research is characterized by its adherence to the values of community and inclusion. As corollaries of these values, research should: strive to develop authentic and supportive relationships among all those involved in the research enterprise; and be directed towards the goal of solidarity for social change. Stringer (1996) captures the essence of these values and principles in his characterization of action research as 'the search for understanding in the company of friends' (p. 160).

Third, social justice and accountability to oppressed groups are values that guide critical research. Social justice should be practised within the research project itself and also in relation to the broader social environment (Nelson, Ochocka, et al., 1998). Internally, funds from the research budget should be allocated in such a way as to provide opportunities for employment and training for the disadvantaged people who are stakeholders in the study. Externally, the research findings should be used for education and/or advocacy to create social change.

Fourth, critical research is based on the value of reflexivity (Alvesson & Sköldberg, 2000). Following from this value are the principles that critical research should: use emergent (flexible) research designs; provide an educational component for all stakeholders, including the wider community; be demystified so knowledge is accessible to everyone, not just research 'experts'; involve all stakeholders in the interpretation of findings and generation of recommendations for change; and provide opportunities for all stakeholders to co-present and co-author research reports, including personal experiences and perspectives (Nelson, Ochocka et al., 1998).

Roles for the Critical Researcher

Since critical research by definition involves active participation and control by disadvantaged groups, the traditional role of the researcher as the one who is in exclusive control of the research is clearly not applicable. What roles then can the CP researcher play in critical research? Stoecker (1999) has reflected on this issue and has suggested three possible roles. First, there is the role of initiator. While being an initiator appears to be at odds with the community-driven nature of critical research, Stoecker (1999) argues that researchers often invite community members to become involved in a research project (this is similar to the role of the unsolicited change agent described in Chapter 7). While the critical researcher may 'get the ball rolling', Stoecker cautions that for the research to be truly participatory, the researcher must be a skilled facilitator and organizer who is willing to give up power in working with community groups.

Second, there is the role of consultant. By consultant, Stoecker (1999) means that the professional is the person who does the research, which is a different definition of consultancy from that typically used in CP. Stoecker (1999) suggests that a community can commission a professional to do the research but needs to put in place accountability mechanisms and to ensure that the community remains the 'owner' of the research. Third, there is the role of collaborator, which is similar to what we mean by a partnership approach, in which the research is neither community-driven, nor researcher-driven, but rather some blend of the two.

Stoecker (1999) argues that each of these roles is inconsistent with a truly participatory action research approach when the research is viewed as a traditional research project. However, when one conceptualizes the research as one part of a larger and more long-term social intervention process, then the contradictions are less apparent. The choice of initiator, consultant and collaborator roles must be made in the context of the skills of the researcher and the degree to which other functional roles (facilitation, community organization, popular education, particpatory research) in the intervention are filled. Stoecker (1999) suggests that participatory action researchers should ask themselves the following questions to help them determine what role they should play in a particular intervention: What is the participatory research project trying to do (that is, what are its goals)? What are the skills of the researcher? How much participation in the research does the community need and want? What Stoecker is suggesting is that the role of the critical researcher is contextually dependent on the values, desires and needs of the community and that there are several different roles that the researcher can play.

The Process of Critical Research

As we explained in the previous chapter, the process of critical research involves a high degree of collaboration among researchers, disadvantaged groups and other stakeholders, with constant communication and feedback loops. Research is done with people, rather than on people. Several participatory action researchers have conceptualized the research process in terms of steps that one might follow in the research (Papineau & Kiely, 1996). For example, Taylor and Botschner (1998) have provided a very useful framework to guide program evaluation from a participatory action research approach (see Box 13.1).

Box 13.1   **Steps in Program Evaluation Using a Participatory Action Research Approach**

1. Organize a stakeholder group and clarify roles.
2. Identify your assumptions about people and research.
3. Highlight the context of the situation.
4. Identify the purpose of the evaluation.
5. Negotiate the evaluation questions.
6. Develop methods for gathering information.
7. Develop a data analysis plan.
8. Gather information.
9. Analyse the information.
10. Share the information.
11. Act on the results.

Source: Taylor, A. R. & Botschner, J. V. (1998). *The evaluation handbook.* Kitchener, ON: Center for Research and Education in Human Services

Critical research is typically not a single study or project in the traditional sense, as Stoecker (1999) pointed out in the previous section. Rather, critical research more typically involves a longer term commitment and immersion of the researcher in the issues, needs and context of disadvantaged people (Rappaport, 1990; Jason et al., 2004). This means that the researcher may play different roles and that there may be different research projects over time.

Quantitative and Qualitative Methods

As we noted in the previous chapter, critical research can use either quantitative or qualitative methods or both. Some community psychologists who work from a critical perspective have argued for this methodological pluralism (Campbell & Wasco, 2000; E. Stewart, 2000) and others who advocate the use of stakeholder and empowerment approaches to research tend rely on quantitative methods (Fetterman et al., 1996). On the whole, however, critical research tends to use qualitative methods, either on their own or in conjunction with quantitative methods. As we pointed out earlier in this chapter, qualitative methods are particularly valuable for giving voice to disadvantaged people and in providing a contextualized understanding of people's experiences.

There are also some researchers who espouse a research paradigm that is both critical and constructivist (Denzin, 2000; Guba & Lincoln, 1989). For example, Denzin (2000) argues for the importance of gender-specific and race-specific communities to provide critical, feminist, anti-racist interpretations of research findings towards the goals of human liberation. Similarly, Guba and Lincoln's (1989) fourth-generation evaluation is explicitly concerned with giving voice to disadvantaged people who are often the consumers of human services. Since science is politically and historically situated, and not purely value-neutral or objective as some would claim, we believe that issues of ontology, epistemology and methodology are secondary to the value base and social change goals of critical research. Therefore, there should be room for different methodological approaches to critical research, including both quantitative and qualitative methods and combinations of the two.

Applications of Critical Research

Critical research has been put into practice in the study of different social issues facing different disadvantaged groups. Feminist research has exposed and named different facets of the oppression of women (for example date rape, sexual harassment) and helped to create alternative settings, such as shelters for abused women (Reinharz, 1992; Ristock & Pennell, 1996; Chapter 18). Participatory action research has also been a good fit for research concerning the issues experienced by people with disabilities (Balcazar et al., 1998; Chapter 20), including people with mental health problems (Nelson, Ochocka, et al., 1998; Chapter 21), gay/lesbian/ bisexual/transgendered people (Chapter 19), immigrants, refugees, aboriginal people and people of colour (Macaulay et al., 1998; Papineau & Kiely, 1996; Smith, 1999; Chapters 16 & 17) and people suffering from various health problems and diseases (Gray, Fitch, Davis & Phillips, 2000; Murray, 2000b; Murray & Chamberlin, 1999b).

Participatory Evaluation

Since participatory action research is action-oriented, it is not surprising that this approach has been linked with program evaluation (Taylor & Botschner, 1998). For example, Whitmore (1991) conducted a participatory evaluation of a prenatal program serving low-income women in Halifax, Nova Scotia, Canada. The evaluator worked with a group of four of these women to conduct the evaluation. The women were paid for work as researchers on the project and they interviewed program participants. One of the co-researchers made the following comments about her relationship with the women who participated in the evaluation:

> You're dealing with a lot of people on social assistance and welfare. You're dealing with real hard-to-reach, low self-esteem people. And when they see anybody coming in that they think is high class or has anything to do with the welfare ..., they are scared to death that you're going to squeal on them, that people's going to coming around bothering and hassling them because ... It's so hard to get along with these [social workers], that ... you're high up there so that they can't trust you cuz you're right in with [the social workers]. But we're [single mothers, too;] we're not in with them [social workers] and we're not in there to tear [other single mothers] apart. And I think [the single mothers] really know that. (Whitmore, 1991, p. 1)

Whitmore (1991) pointed out that it is the process which is critical in this type of participatory evaluation. 'We spent considerable time building group trust, for the key to everyone's participation was motivation' (Whitmore, 1991, p. 5).

In another participatory evaluation, Papineau and Kiely (1996) worked with stakeholders (staff, volunteers, consumers) of a community economic development (CED) project for immigrant people in Montreal. This grassroots project provided training and technical assistance and a revolving loan fund to help immigrants start small businesses. The goals of the evaluation were to promote the empowerment of the stakeholders participating in the evaluation, plan and implement the evaluation and utilize the findings of the evaluation for program planning. Interviews with stakeholders indicated that all of these goals were met.

Although there is flexibility and the use of emergent research designs in participatory research and evaluation, it is important for the reader to understand that this type of research is not a completely open-ended, unstructured process. Rather, typically, there are concrete steps that evaluators follow to ensure a meaningful, participatory process (Papineau & Kiely, 1996; Taylor & Botschner, 1998; Whitmore, 1991). Whitmore (1991) noted that having a concrete and carefully structured sequence of tasks, a written contract with the co-researchers, attention to group process and publicity about the research findings were key factors in the success of the participatory evaluation briefly described above. Similarly, Papineau and Kiely (1996) provided stakeholders in the CED project with a blueprint for the evaluation process with concrete tasks for each phase of the evaluation.

Creating Change

How does a group use critical research to create change? We believe that there are at least five components for creating change in critical research: framing and interpretation; education; communication and dissemination; resource mobilization; and action. These components are part of a praxis cycle of values, theory, research and action that has as its objective the transformation of social structures towards the goal of social justice (Prilleltensky, 2001).

First, framing and interpretation provide the critical lens through which social issues are viewed, including both values and theories. We have argued throughout this book that problems need to be framed in terms of issues of power. This first step of framing sets the stage for critical research and action. As Rappaport and Stewart (1997) stated: 'In critical psychology, as in any academic/intellectual project, the power to frame the issues, define the terms of the debate and set the agenda for discourse is win the game before it happens' (p. 307). Participatory research that involves disadvantaged people in setting the research agenda can provide a framework that is critical of the status quo and is aimed at social change. Equally important though is the interpretation of data. Facts are not value-neutral and they do not speak for themselves. Rather research findings are given meaning and are interpreted through the lenses of the various stakeholders in the context of their historical, social, political and experiential realities (Denzin, 2000). As in any research, there is a danger of research findings being distorted. In its explicit political agenda of social transformation, the critical perspective is vulnerable to this problem. Criteria for the validation of data, be they post-positivist or constructivist, help to guard against this problem.

Second, critical research findings also have an educational function in raising the consciousness of different stakeholders about the issues under study. Moreover, the process of learning is mutual, involving an exchange among stakeholders, and ongoing learning as the research process and findings emerge (Nelson, Ochocka, et al., 1998). Third, in critical research, there is an emphasis on widespread communication and dissemination of research findings. It is not enough to publish the findings in a scholarly journal that will be read by only a select few. Rather, researchers and their partners need to consider all the different audiences for the research and devise multiple strategies for reaching those audiences. Single-page summaries, short summary bulletins and longer reports in accessible language are one method for communication and dissemination, as are oral presentations and workshops. But there is also room for more creative and potentially engaging forms of communication, including dramatic readings and scripts and video productions. Getting the message out through radio, television and newspapers can reach large numbers of people.

Fourth, communicating research findings to multiple audiences can lead to a process of resource mobilization for change. The question for the critical researcher and partners is which stakeholder groups and organizations can be organized to use the data for change. Once, these audiences have been organized, this leads to the fifth and final step of action or utilization of findings (Nelson & Hayday, 1995; Papineau & Kiely, 1996). One example of a project which utilized research findings for change is the development of a mental health housing coalition by Geoff and community partners. After conducting an assessment of the housing and support needs of mental health consumer/survivors (Nelson & Earls, 1986), Geoff and his colleagues organized a community forum on this issue. All the local candidates who were campaigning to be elected to the provincial government were invited to the forum. This forum attracted the attention of the press and led to the formation of the coalition to move from research to action. After several years of advocacy and education, the coalition, which ran on a minimal budget but with considerable representation from different stakeholder groups, was successful in increasing affordable housing and supports for people with serious mental health problems (Nelson, 1994).

Validation of Data

How does the researcher validate the data in critical research? This depends in part on the assumptions that underlie the research. The critical post-positivist researcher must be concerned with the traditional issues of reliability, construct validity and internal and external validity, whereas the critical constructivist researcher must be concerned with trustworthiness and authenticity. However, the critical paradigm invokes an additional concept for the validation of data, psychopolitical validity (Prilleltensky, in press). As we noted earlier in the book, psychopolitical validity has two components: epistemic and transformative validity. Epistemic validity is concerned with the degree to which community research and action is attuned to issues of power at multiple levels of analysis (personal, relational, collective). The more systematic the analysis of the phenomenon of interest in terms of psychological and political power, the more valid is the critical research and action. Transformational validity, on the other hand, is concerned with the degree to which community research and action strives to transform social structures. The more transformative and the less ameliorative the intervention (see Chapter 7), the greater the transformational validity of the critical research and action.

Just as Lincoln and Guba's (1985, 1986) criteria of trustworthiness, fairness and authenticity for constructivist research were in their early stages of development in the early 1980s, so too are these criteria of psychopolitical validity. We believe that these concepts will be of considerable heuristic value to critical researchers and that the criteria for these types of validity will be further clarified and enhanced over the next 20 years.

Challenges and Limitations of Critical Research

While critical research is appealing to some of us, a major challenge is that the standpoint of critical research is not well understood or respected by the academic research community. More traditional scientists bristle at the explicit political and value-based nature of this work. Relinquishing power and control over the research design and process can be viewed as compromising the integrity of the research. Thus, community psychologists who undertake critical research can anticipate resistance from their academic colleagues and granting agencies to their work (Balcazar et al., 1998; Gray et al., 2000; Isenberg et al., 2004). Balcazar et al. (1998) argue that traditional scientists view participatory action research and the use of experimental and quasi-experimental designs as incompatible and Isenberg et al. (2004) suggest that power-sharing in participatory action research may actually jeopardize the quality of the research. There are at least two responses to this challenge. First, experimental and quasi-experimental methods are not the only rigorous methods that researchers can use. As we have shown in the previous chapter, there is a rich tradition in qualitative research from which researchers can draw. Second, we believe that researchers can use a participatory and collaborative approach in the context of experiments or quasi-experiments. The Better Beginnings research, mentioned earlier and a study that Geoff and colleagues are currently conducting with self-help/mutual aid organizations for mental health consumer/survivors are examples that this integration is possible. While we agree with Isenberg et al. (2004) that power-sharing in participatory action research does not necessarily enhance the quality of the research, we argue that in many cases research with disadvantaged groups would not be possible if the researchers were not willing to share power. Researchers who were unwilling to share power are unlikely to get their foot in the door with disadvantaged groups.

Another challenge is that while the values and rhetoric of critical research may be appealing to some of us, critical research is very difficult to conduct. Reflexively, critical researchers need to ask themselves if they are really sharing power. Gray et al. (2000) observed in their participatory action research with breast cancer self-help groups that there is a tendency for researchers to develop a proposal for funding and then seek input from the stakeholders. Part of the tension in this situation is that the time available for proposal development is often short and there is a power imbalance between researchers and other stakeholders in terms of knowledge about research. As Papineau and Kiely (1996) observed, it takes time for stakeholders to get the 'big picture'. In spite of these constraints, we agree with Gray et al. (2000) that researchers can and should work more collaboratively with stakeholders in the proposal development stage, because it is at this stage that the research issues get framed.

Once the research is underway, another important issue is the length of the research process and the amount of stakeholder participation that is desired and required (Balcazar et al., 1998; Gray et al., 2000; Papineau & Kiely, 1996; Stoecker, 1999). We agree with Gray et al. (2000) and Stoecker (1999) that researchers and community stakeholders need to negotiate the purpose and time required for participation. In working with disadvantaged groups, Isenberg et al. (2004) suggest that in the name of power-sharing, researchers may side-step conflictual issues in their desire to be polite and respectful. Taking such a stance compromises the authenticity of the research relationships. Elsewhere (Nelson, Lord & Ochocka, 2001b), we have argued that conflict is part and parcel of partnerships between community psychologists and disadvantaged people and that community psychologists need to engage in, rather than withdraw from, such conflict. Balcazar et al. (1998) also noted that it is not uncommon for disadvantaged community members to challenge and criticize researchers. We believe that criticism and conflict present great opportunities for learning and questioning taken-for-granted assumptions, because conflict often arises from a collision of world views and experiences. Active listening and problem-solving are important skills for working through conflict. In conflict situations, there is a balancing act between standing firm for one's values and being open and flexible to new learning, and unfortunately there is no easy recipe for how to maintain that balance.

One other important challenge raised by Isenberg et al. (2004) that we want to comment on, is their observation that it is sometimes difficult to distinguish between who is oppressed and who is not oppressed. We believe that it is important to differentiate between where people are coming from (experiences of oppression) and their behaviour in research relationships. Understanding and acknowledging that some people have lived in oppressive conditions is crucial for critical researchers, but that does not mean that people who have lived such lives are not accountable for their current behaviour. Just as we have seen professionals act in an oppressive way, we have been in situations where one or more people from an oppressed background has behaved in a domineering and oppressive way in a community research or intervention project. Establishing a clear vision, values and ground rules for participatory research relationships can be used to address this difficult issue.

One last important challenge is the tension between research and advocacy. The culture of research is to be sceptical and cautious in one's interpretations of findings, whereas the culture of social movement organizations is to use whatever means are available to create social change. An example of this is provided in Gray et al.'s (2000) discussion of different approaches to advocacy that were taken by the researchers (more restrained) and the self-help group members (more exuberant). Balcazar et al. (1998) also note that there is the danger of reprisals from other segments of the community when a participatory action research group engages in advocacy. The distinction between what 'is' and what 'ought to be' could be helpful in working through this tension. Researchers and community members need to be clear on what the research findings mean, as well as how to use the findings to create social change.

We have spent some time on the challenges and limitations of critical research, because we want to convey the message that since this approach is explicitly participatory and action-oriented, the research process is complex and opens up a number of thorny issues. As community psychologists and community members gain more experience with critical research, we will be more informed and hopefully wiser about how to handle the many challenges that this approach poses and able to overcome the limitations of this approach.

Chapter Summary

In this chapter, we reviewed research methods that derive from the critical paradigm. Both quantitative and qualitative tools can be used in the critical paradigm, because critical researchers can be either critical realists or critical constructivists. Less important than one's epistemological assumptions about the nature of reality, critical CP research is primarily concerned with promoting liberation and social change. Consequently, the methodological tools that are central to the critical paradigm are creating value-based partnerships in solidarity with disadvantaged people. Such partnerships emphasize a high degree of participation of disadvantaged people in all phases of the research and using the research to create social change.

In closing, we wish to point out that the research methods and research paradigms that we described in these three research chapters are transitional in nature. In the future, new and different frameworks may prove more useful for understanding the different research tools that can be used in community research.

COMMENTARY: What's The 'Right' Method In Community Research?

Rebecca Campbell

Whew. I've just finished reading Chapters 12 and 13 and my head is spinning: with so many methods from which to choose, how do I know what's the 'right' method? How do I decide what's the 'right' approach: post-positivist, constructivist or critical? Analytic or activist/intervention? Nelson and Prilleltensky have written a wonderfully thorough summary of the numerous methodological choices facing community researchers. But precisely because this chapter so thoroughly covers multiple methodologies and methods, I am overwhelmed. So many choices, how do I navigate the field? I kept returning to Tables 12.1 and 13.1 (the methods associated with the different community research paradigms), hoping a big red 'You Are Here' sign would magically pop up and show me where I fit into the grander methodological scheme of things.

I suspect Nelson and Prilleltensky would say there is no 'right' answer, no 'right' method. Perhaps they would even say that this notion of what's 'right' is something we need to let go of anyway as it is a vestige of positivist ideologies. Perhaps, but the question 'What is right?' is one that I think many students, faculty and community practitioners ask themselves and are often asked by others. This question deserves further reflection because I believe the process of figuring out an answer is one of the most important developmental tasks for community researchers and practitioners. To me, the answer is: It depends. What's the 'right' method? It depends on …

… your research question. Some of the best methodological advice I ever got was from Julian Rappaport who told me that my method should fit my research question, not the other way around. I remember writing this down, thinking sure it was good advice, yet not really knowing what he meant, but hopeful that some day I'd figure it out. I can't speak for what he meant, but with time and practice, I came to understand this issue in my own way. I saw that my thinking and my students' thinking would sometimes became constrained and narrowed because we were working within the boundaries of a particular method. There were issues we didn't pursue, ideas we didn't follow up because the method didn't show us how to work with those alternative thoughts. When methods drive the research process, the questions must fit within the boundaries of the method. But when the questions drive the research process, methods will be selected, modified or combined based on their utility in answering the questions at hand. My

parents once told me, 'Never let anyone tell you what to think'. In this context, the corollary is: 'Never let a method tell you what you can study'. When we let our methods come first, they essentially do tell us what we can study. And consequently, we can only learn what that method is capable of revealing.

As Nelson and Prilleltensky noted in this chapter, positivist methodologies have traditionally excluded oppressed persons – their lived experiences being outside what most traditional methods could capture. Feminist scholars have noted that the methods of science reflect the social values and concerns of dominant societal groups (Campbell & Wasco, 2000; Harding, 1987b; Nielsen, 1990; Riger, 1992). As such, research projects in the social sciences have often ignored women and other oppressed groups. To the degree that the dominant group's view is imposed on the field as a whole, the potential for 'break-through conceptualizations' is decreased and the invigorating creative tension between scientific perspectives is hampered (McHugh, Koeske & Frieze, 1986, p. 879). As a result of this bias, the lives and experiences of oppressed persons have not been adequately captured through traditional scientific methods.

On the other hand, it's important not to romanticize post-positivist methodologies and assume that they will automatically capture the experiences of oppressed persons. Qualitative methods are not without their problems. For instance, Cannon, Higginbotham and Leung (1991) noted that because it is primarily white, middle-class individuals who volunteer for these in-depth, self-reflective studies, qualitative research is susceptible to racial and social class biases. In other words, the choices researchers make when implementing a method may have a profound effect on the degree to which the method is successful in capturing multiple perspectives. Method is only one part of the research process – how a researcher uses a particular method is just as important.

Selecting the 'right' method also depends on the researcher's identity. A researcher's values and beliefs are fundamental to the choice of methods and to how those methods will be implemented in the research process. In her book, *On Becoming a Social Scientist* (1979), Shulamit Reinharz advocated the 'integration of person, problem and method' (p. 369). She wrote, 'All projects should generate knowledge within the three components engaged in a research project: person, problem and method. In this scheme, self-knowledge (person) is a necessary and publicly relevant product of social research' (p. 370). Reinharz argues that the researcher's values are an integral part of the choice of method and the use of a method. To traditionalists, this is heresy as methods are supposed to be free of bias, but no part of science is value-free and objective. That we have believed for so long that methods are objective does not make them so.

As I mentioned previously, I wished my copy of Tables 12.1 and 13.1 came with a 'You Are Here' sign, but that's the key issue: Community researchers must find out where they are, what they believe and how they define their work. We have to create our own 'You are Here' sign because that sign helps you know what's 'right'. In the late 1990s I was working with a energetic group of feminist students to develop a community-based research project on sexual assault and this experience was instrumental in helping me discover what was 'right' for my program of research. In this study we wanted to hear the stories of rape survivors from different ages, races, ethnicities and social classes. We spent months trying to figure out how to recruit rape survivors to participate in our interview. The academic literature suggested that the 'right' method was random digit dialling or some other probability-based technique. One of the undergraduate team members asked me to explain random digit dialling (that is, households are called at random and asked if they would like to participate in a research survey). When I finished with my description, she said, 'You've got to be kidding. The 'best' thing to do is to call people at random and ask them if they've been raped? Who's going to answer that question? Is that any way to talk about something so painful and important in someone's life?' Although the technique is widely regarded as the gold-standard in sampling, our research team had many reservations about whether this method was right for the goals and values of our project.

We ultimately decided to design a sampling methodology that we thought made sense, and reflected our understanding of the needs and concerns of rape survivors, particularly those who had been particularly stigmatized by society. In my field notes for this project, I wrote, 'We'll just design something that makes sense and is respectful of the recovery needs of rape survivors. I'll figure out later on what the hell to call it.' And, with more digging in multidisciplinary literatures, I found that what we thought made sense did in fact have a name: adaptive sampling, a technique used primarily in the natural sciences (Thompson & Seber, 1996; see Campbell et al., (2004) for a discussion of how and why we selected and implemented this method). Our use of adaptive sampling in our project was unbelievably successful – we were able to hear from a diverse group of rape survivors, many of whom had never before talked about their assault (Campbell et al.,1999). The method was rigorous, yet respectful. Our decision to let our research questions, values and beliefs drive the method of the study ultimately improved the project. Once we let go of the notion of what was 'right' and tried to figure out what we needed, we found what was right for us.

Discovering where to place the 'You Are Here' sign is a fundamental task for community researchers and practitioners. If we let our questions drive our methods, then we need to be well-informed about various methodological options. We need to develop a scholarship of methods because not being aware of different choices is as limiting as letting the method drive the question. What is particularly useful about this chapter is that Nelson and Prilleltensky present a clear summary of the major methods of CP and discuss the problems and pitfalls of each method. What is 'right' is difficult to determine and may vary from project to project, researcher to researcher. By letting our research questions develop without the constraints of methods, and by allowing our values to have a voice in the research process, we can figure out what is right – at least for a while.

Glossary cont'd

initiator the researcher plays the role of organizer and facilitator in a participatory action research project

participatory action research a grassroots approach to research that emphasizes the participation of disadvantaged people in all phases of the research, which is aimed at the goal of social change

participatory evaluation an approach to the evaluation of programs or interventions that promotes the participation of the disadvantaged group in the evaluation

transformative validity a criterion of psychopolitical validity that emphasizes the extent to which the research can be used to create transformative social change

RESOURCES

Evaluation, Feminist and Qualitative Research Journals
Association for Qualitative Research
Canadian Journal of Program Evaluation/La Revue canadienne d'évaluation de programme
Discourse Processes
Discourse and Society
Discourse Studies
Evaluation and the Health Professions
Evaluation Practice
Evaluation and Program Planning
Evaluation Studies Review Annual
Evaluation Review
Feminist Research Center, links to feminist journals, http://www.feminist.org/research/pubjourn.html
Forum on Qualitative Research (on-line journal), http://www.qualitative-research.net/fqs/fqs-eng.htm
Grounded Theory Review
International Journal of Qualitative Methods
International Journal of Qualitative Studies in Education
Narrative Inquiry
New Directions in Program Evaluation
Qualitative Family Research
Qualitative Health Research
Qualitative Report

Part V

Putting It All Together: Addressing the Issues

The goal of this part of the book is to answer the question: How do community psychologists use the conceptual, action and research tools to create change regarding a number of different issues facing disadvantaged people? For this section, we invited authors to address specific issues and problems from the perspective of the framework of community psychology that we presented in Chapter 2.

In Chapter 14, UK community psychologists Carolyn Kagan and Mark Burton address the issue of marginalization, which is germane to all the chapters that follow in this section. The authors argue that marginalization entails both economic and social exclusion. Moreover, dominant groups in a society utilize an ideology of 'blaming the victim' to characterize the situation of marginalized groups. This leads to damaged identity, fatalism and internalized oppression. Kagan and Burton note, however, the resilience and resistance that often characterizes marginalized groups and individuals and they present tools, strategies and examples of how community psychology (CP) can strive to work with people to overcome marginalization. In Chapter 15, Tod Sloan from the US examines globalization, poverty and social justice, both historically and in the contemporary context. Many of the problems with which CP deals can be traced to socioeconomic inequality and poverty. Yet CP rarely addresses social class analysis. Sloan argues that global capitalism and corporate rule is leading to an increasing gap between the 'haves' and the 'have nots', as well as a variety of other social and environmental problems. In his analysis, Sloan points to the key role of ideology in perpetuating inequality, noting the particular importance of consumption in our current context. The need for CP to take these problems seriously is argued, and potential roles and strategies of resistance for CP are presented.

Chapters 16 to 21 address various facets of diversity. In Chapter 16, community psychologists, Marewa Glover, Pat Dudgeon and Ingrid Huygens from Australia and New Zealand examine issues of colonization and racism, focusing on indigenous people in Australia and New Zealand. The authors review the problems of colonization and racism from a historical and contextual perspective. Decolonization, depowerment and anti-racist interventions are considered as potential strategies that can be used to overcome the problems of colonization and racism. Australian community psychologists, Chris Sonn and Adrian Fisher, focus on issues related to immigration and culture in Chapter 17. The chapter focuses on trauma experienced by refugees and immigrants, settlement issues, racism, cultural diversity and the role that CP can play in promoting the well-being and liberation of this population. In Chapter 18, Heather Gridley and Colleen Turner of Australia analyse the issue of sexism, gender and power from a feminist CP perspective. The issue of diversity among women is considered, as well as the need for CP to embrace feminism.

In Chapter 19, Gary Harper of the US examines the problem of heterosexism and the oppression of gay, lesbian, bisexual and transgendered (GLBT) persons. Strategies for promoting well-being and liberation of the GLBT community are considered. Glen White of the US analyses ableism and the struggle for rights and resources for people with disabilities. In Chapter 20, he examines issues related to disability and the growth of the disability rights movement and user-controlled alternatives to traditional rehabilitation services. Bret Kloos of the US focuses on one group of people with disabilities in Chapter 21 – those with psychiatric disabilities or serious mental health problems. Since its inception, CP has been concerned with people with serious mental health problems, deinstitutionalization and community mental health. In this chapter, Kloos describes the paradigm shift that is occurring in some places that emphasizes empowerment, community integration, self-help and social justice.

In Chapter 22, Leslea Peirson of Canada examines the issues facing disadvantaged families. Community psychologists have focused on developing a number of interventions for preschool children and families. Such programmes have shifted from single-focus, preschool and home-based interventions to more multi-focused, community-driven approaches. These approaches are considered along with the important role that social policy plays in the empowerment of disadvantaged children and families. In Chapter 23, Canadian community psychologist Ed Bennett examines problems related to environmental degradation, which is another relatively neglected area of CP. Pollution, agri-business and global warming are some of the problems that are examined in this chapter, as well as the potential for sustainable alternatives.

Collectively these chapters cover a range of issues and problems that are of concern to CP. Moreover, all of the chapters utilize the main conceptual tools that we presented in the second part of the book. The concept of oppression is used to frame the problems experienced by different disadvantaged groups and social intervention strategies are proposed to move towards the goals of liberation and well-being.

Individually the chapters provide an in-depth examination of how CP can address each of the specific issues. The authors of these chapters bring their expertise, experience and passion to the issues. Each of them has been committed to addressing the injustices they describe and their work provides important exemplars and inspiration for students of CP. Let us now turn to the issues.

14

Marginalization

Carolyn Kagan and Mark Burton

Chapter Organization	
What is Social Marginalization?	**Poverty and Economic Marginality**
Impaired Social Support Networks and Social Marginalization	**Ideological Aspects of Marginalization**
Resistance and Resilience	**Why Does Marginalization Matter?**
The Relevance of Community Psychology to Marginalization	**Working Against Social Marginalization: Tools and Examples**

Chapter Summary	**COMMENTARY: Multiple Intersecting Oppressions**	**Glossary**	**Resources**

Warm-up Exercise – Marginality and the Economy

Once or twice a month a young man (we'll call him Tony) knocks on our door. He speaks with an impediment and begins his well-practised introduction about how he has been unemployed for more than a year so he thought he'd do something about it by selling some household items. The items are of poor quality and about 50% more expensive than in the shops, but some people buy them out of compassion, particularly if the weather is cold or wet. Tony of course knows that he is an object of pity and charity. Tony has to pay a fee to the company that runs the scheme. The company gave him a basic training and supplied the goods. He has to declare his earnings and after a few pounds his social security is reduced by what he earns. Some weeks he is no better off than if he were not working, but in a good week he has a little extra – the social security is not sufficient to live on for more than a short time and people build up debts.

In Britain, people who are disabled through significant levels of intellectual difficulty still receive reasonably high state benefits, but the state monitors their wealth very closely. If they manage to save more than a few hundred pounds, the state reduces their benefit level. Since the early 1990s social services departments have (because of central government policy) levied a charge for the assistance people receive. Few people have waged employment because this can lead to a change in benefit status, so they risk becoming worse off if they lose the job. They are therefore trapped in a position of economic dependency and subject to the official gaze.

Consider the following questions:

1. What might be the implications of government policy for a person's self-concept, self-esteem and confidence?
2. Is the state making reasonable provision that its money is well spent or is it proceeding from the belief that people are dishonest?
3. In what ways do the actions of the state combine to maintain the marginality of the people mentioned?

The goals of this chapter are for you to:

■ understand the nature of social marginalization
■ consider values that contribute to marginalization

- consider values that can counter marginalization
- establish the relevance of critical community psychology (CP) praxis for working against marginalization
- propose analytic and practical tools for working against marginalization
- reflect on some potential problems community psychologists face when trying to work against marginalization.

Marginality is an experience affecting millions of people throughout the world. Though various aspects of it will be considered in subsequent chapters, here we offer an introduction to the theme. Being poor, unemployed, discriminated against or disabled in an ableist society are serious risk factors. Being excluded from economic, social and political life can have adverse effects on individuals and communities alike. This chapter focuses on social marginalization to see how community psychologists can understand it and challenge it at the same time.

Marginalization is strangely ignored in the psychological literature. In preparation for writing this chapter we carried out a search of the PsycINFO database for the period from 1876 to the present day, using both 'marginalization' and 'marginalisation'. We found 52 items that included the term in the title – of these, only 17 actually dealt with the experience of social marginalization by people in positions of oppression, exclusion, vulnerability or discrimination: the others dealt with things as diverse as a statistical technique or the marginalization of certain professional groups or practices. Curiously, there was no entry at all from before 1982. Over 55,000 references are currently added to the database each year, so in the year 2000, for instance, there were two out of 55,000 or 0.0036 per cent of relevant references. Although there will be many more texts that deal with the question (but do not mention it in the title), this still looks like a remarkable neglect by the established field of psychology.

CP, in contrast, does have a history of dealing with marginalized people. People with mental health difficulties and the services developed to support them, have been at the heart of the discipline since its inception (Levine & Perkins, 1997; Orford, 1992). Over time, attention has widened to other marginalized groups (Speer, Dey, Griggs, Gibson, Lubin & Houghey, 1992). For example, there has been considerable and varied community psychological work on homeless people, a highly marginalized population (Shinn, 2000).

What is Social Marginalization?

Marginalization is a slippery and multi-layered concept. Whole societies can be marginalized at the global level while classes and communities can be marginalized from the dominant social order. Similarly, ethnic groups, families or individuals can be marginalized within localities. To a certain extent, marginalization is a shifting phenomenon, linked to social status. Individuals or groups might enjoy high social status at one point in time, but as social changes take place, they lose this status and become marginalized. Similarly, as people cycle through life stages they move in and out of marginal positions.

Let us consider the position of many civic organizations in South Africa under apartheid. Although excluded from the mainstream, these groups held important positions in the fight against apartheid. Post apartheid, their status changed. People prominent in resistance organizations, and indeed some of the organizations themselves, were incorporated into Government. In contrast, at the local level, those young men who had high status as 'freedom fighters' almost overnight became virtual outcasts as their reliance on violence had no place in the rhetoric of the new South Africa (see Noyoo, 2000). These are examples of shifts in marginalization that occur alongside social and political change. A different type of example would be found in communities or sectors of communities, in which social and economic changes propel people into marginality.

Charlesworth (2000) wrote a moving phenomenological account of working class life in a former steel-manufacturing town in England. In discussing the ways in which people's social position affects their identities and even their appearance, Charlesworth says that:

> It is the economic changes and the social conditions they ushered in that have consigned these people to a life of marginality which, naturally enough, manifests itself in their comportment, manner and style. (p. 160)

One of the local people in his book describes the hopelessness that such marginalization engenders:

> Ah get up some times an' it's just too much fo' mi, yer know, it creeps over yer, it just gets too much an' tha can't tek no mo'ore [...] It's heart breakin', it's just a strain all time an' tha just wants t' not live, tha just can't see n' point in thi' life (p. 160)

At certain stages of the life cycle the risk of marginalization increases or decreases. For example, the marginalized status of children and young people may decrease as they get older; the marginalized status of adults may increase as they become elders; the marginalized status of single mothers may change as their children grow up and so on. Even so, there are different risks within particular social groups at risk of marginalization. Eldering and Knorth (1998), for example, demonstrate that the risks of marginalization of immigrant youth in Europe vary with ethnicity, irrespective of the particular host countries or of degree of acculturation. Kagan and Scott-Roberts (2002), working with NGOs supporting families in the slums of Kolkata, India, illustrate how having a disabled child further marginalizes them. Similarly, Wenzel, Keogel and Gelberg (2000) draw our attention to the different risks faced by homeless women compared to homeless men. Taywaditep (2001), in turn, discusses forms of marginalization amongst gay men.

In his unjustly neglected book *Personality and Ideology* Peter Leonard (1984, p.180) defines social marginality as 'being outside the mainstream of productive activity and/or social reproductive activity'. This includes two groups, firstly a relatively small group of people who are voluntarily marginal to the social order – new age travellers, certain religious sects, commune members, some artists. Here, however, we are concerned with a second group: those who are involuntarily socially marginal. Leonard (1984) characterizes these people as remaining outside 'the major arena of capitalist productive and reproductive activity', and as such experiencing 'involuntary social marginality' (p. 181).

The experience of marginality can arise in a number of ways. For some people, those severely impaired from birth or those born into excluded groups (for example members of ethnic groups that suffer discrimination – the Romanies in Europe, indigenous people in Australasia and the American continent, African-Caribbean people in Britain), this marginality is typically life-long and profound.

For others, marginality is acquired by later disablement or by changes in the social and economic system. The collapse of the Soviet Union plunged millions into unemployment. In Manchester, our own city, neoliberal economic policies closed down the traditional industrial base and led to unemployment and various patterns of insecure and casual employment for many. As global capitalism extends its reach, bringing more and more people into its system, more communities are dispossessed of lands, livelihoods and systems of social support (Chomsky, 2000; Petras & Veltmeyer, 2001; Pilger, 2002; Potter, 2000). Indeed, we argue that capitalist development in its current globalizing phase inexorably creates increasing levels of marginalization throughout the world, particularly as collective safeguards – from indigenous cultures to trades unions and government welfare programs – are attacked.

Marginalization is at the core of exclusion from fulfilling and full social lives at individual, interpersonal and societal levels (see Chapter 2). People who are marginalized have relatively little control over their lives and have few resources available to them; they become stigmatized and are often at the receiving end of negative public attitudes. Their opportunities to make social contributions may be limited and they may develop low self-confidence and self-esteem. If they do not have work and live with support services, for example, they may have limited opportunities for meeting with others. A vicious circle is set up whereby their lack of positive and supportive relationships means they are prevented from participating in local life, which in turn leads to further isolation. Limiting social policies and practices restrict access to valued social resources such as education, health services, housing, income, leisure activities and work (see Chapter 8).

Although different people will react variably to marginalizing processes, some common social psychological pathways can be identified. We pay particular attention to processes that facilitate or prevent collective social action (see Burton & Kagan, 1996).

Poverty and Economic Marginality

People who are experiencing marginalization are likely to have tenuous involvement in the economy. Their sources of income vary. Some are waged, while others depend on state benefits or marginal economic activity such as casual work or charity (see, for example, Sixsmith, 1999). It is not unusual for people to combine or move between, these various ways of getting money in their struggle for survival. Poverty, dependency and feelings of shame are everyday aspects of economic dislocation and social marginalization.

Impaired Social Support Networks and Social Marginalization

A further problem is the relative or complete exclusion of marginalized people from social networks. Some people born into marginality will be able, at best, to access resources through strong social networks (for example, a person born with impairments into a rich family). Others will be able to access weaker networks, such as neighbourhood or church-based organizations. But often these sources of support will be weak or overburdened. In some poor communities, where unemployment is the norm and social problems are rife, tenants associations have reduced to a minimal role of working solely in the interests of those on the committee (see, for example, Kagan, Lawthom, Knowles & Burton, 2001). Strong associations such as trades unions are not available to economically marginalized people isolated from the world of work.

People who have become disabled, and those with a severely disabled child, often report rejection and isolation from their former friends and allies (see Box 14.1). Marginalization then means reduced opportunity to link with others in common action to solve problems. The result can be described as disempowerment.

Box 14.1   Listening to Parents of Children with Disabilities

The experiences of parents of severely disabled children in England can throw light on processes of marginalization and survival. One of us (CK) had been working with a group of parents of adult sons and daughters with severe and multiple impairments. The local authority where they lived had some money to support these parents and it had been agreed that the parents, not the professionals, should decide what it should be spent on. After a series of meetings, in which the parents had met each other, often for the first time, they agreed that what was needed was a 24-hour telephone line through which they could contact someone, 'just to listen', if needed.

On the whole they thought they managed pretty well, but every now and then things got too much for them. Senior managers from both the health and social services were invited to meet the parents and hear their suggestions. At this meeting they were concerned that a telephone line would not use up all the money available, and pressed the parents for more concrete (and expensive) ideas. After a while one of the mothers, who had become impatient with the professionals, stood up and said:

I have looked after my son for 35 years. For 35 years no one has come near me and asked what I wanted. For 35 years I have not dared to even think about how our lives could be different. Now you come along and ask me what I want? How can I tell you what I want? When I do, you don't want to hear. We have said we want someone to be available on the telephone. You say 'Don't you want a washing machine?' No, we want someone to listen to us.

The senior managers were humbled and the rest of the parents delighted. From then on, there were regular meetings between the parents and the services got a little better at listening to them.

Ideological Aspects of Marginalization

The above dimensions of marginalization, poverty/economic dislocation and disempowerment/social dislocation, can be regarded as primary material insults. But being a member of a marginalized group also brings the risk of psychosocial-ideological threats. The first of these is the definition of one's identity by others: the ideological definition of one's marginalized identity in the interest of dominant groups. What typically seems to happen is that the situation of marginalized persons is portrayed as a result of their own characteristics. What is essentially a social and historical phenomenon is presented as a biological or an intrapsychic event.

The problems that people face are then seen as of 'their own making', or at least as inseparable from their particular nature. The phenomenon is naturalized, seen not as a socially determined reality, but as something to be expected given the way the person is. This phenomenon has been called 'blaming the victim' (Ryan, 1971),

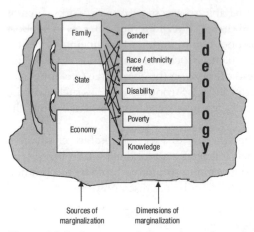

Figure 14.1   Sources and dimensions of marginalization and resistance

which is part of a more general 'culture of blame' (Farber & Azar, 1999). Examples of this will be encountered in the following chapters.

Psychology has often colluded with ideologies that blame the victim by offering endogenous causes of the situation in which oppressed people find themselves. These causes have reflected the scientific and psychological theory of the time, from MacDougall's use of instinct at the turn of the last century, through drives and personality traits, to the maladaptive cognitive structures that today's cognitive theorists claim to detect. The latter have some justification because oppressed people do internalize aspects of the existing social reality and its ideological 'story' (see Chapters 16, 17 and 19 for examples of this phenomenon).

Some psychological writers have offered analyses of what goes on in processes of internalization (for example Fanon, 1986; Martín-Baró, 1996a). Martín-Baró studied the phenomenon of fatalism in Latin American societies. Psychological explanations had hitherto considered this in terms of the character of the people concerned. It had been suggested that these personality characteristics develop in a specific cultural context, for example a 'culture of poverty' in which destitution leads to cultural patterns that are passed on from generation to generation.

Martín-Baró suggests other explanations. The first of these is fatalism's 'truth'. The impossibility of social change – poverty, debt, failed social movements – leads to an internalization of external reality. As a result, we see a correlation between the societal context and psychological structures. The oppressed classes assume that their destiny is out of their control. The structure condemns to failure whatever members of the poor classes do to 'get ahead'.

Secondly, Martín-Baró looks at fatalism as the internalization of social domination. He follows Fanon, who suggested that violence imposed by the colonizer is introjected, turned inward, by the colonized – it remains anchored in their bodies as repressed tension. Similarly for Freire (1970, 1994), the oppressed are immersed in a condition in which they are robbed and rendered helpless. Unable to get to the source of their condition, they take refuge in a fatalistic attitude, transforming history into nature. Impotence becomes proof of their worthlessness. The oppressor becomes an irresistible model for the oppressed, with whom they identify and whose orders they follow.

Finally, Martín-Baró identifies the ideological nature of fatalism. Fatalism saves the oppressor from having to exert coercive control; it induces a docile reaction to the demands of those who wield power. In keeping with fatalism, historical forces are rendered mythical, so they seem to resemble nature or God.

A further result of victim-blaming ideologies, imposed but assimilated, is the definition of one's reality by 'experts'. This is most obvious in the case of disabled people and those with mental health difficulties, where personal experiences become a set of pathologies with technical names and technological treatments.

Resistance and Resilience

Despite all the negative impositions of ideology, the situation of oppressed people is also characterized by resistance and resilience. In resilience there is the potential for an enhanced, reclaimed and reinvented identity. The very fact of being oppressed, of having fundamental rights denied or diminished, elicits attempts to rectify the situation. This can be negative and destructive, as in the vandalism and petty crime of disaffected youth in our cities or in the pathologies of self-destruction, addiction and depression. However, attempts at rectification can also be highly positive, as in collective action to improve social conditions. Potential or actual resilience and resistance can be key resources in CP praxis.

As people are affected by social forces and changing social relations and as they organize to resist oppression and reclaim what is truly theirs, they experience changes in identification and affiliation. A person who becomes unemployed is likely to lose both the social context and network of work and to begin seeing herself in other terms – not defined by her working life any more. This is likely to involve a struggle, often lost, to retain a positive self-concept and not be defeated by feelings of worthlessness and superfluity (Charlesworth, 2000; Leonard, 1984). Similarly, when people in the UK have to move house due to their age (Churchill, Everitt & Green, 1997) or due to housing policies, there are marked changes in how they feel about themselves and about the social contributions they can make.

People who engage in collective action describe how their sense of belonging and personal worth changes for the better (for example Kagan, Caton & Amin, 2001; McCulloch, 1997; Menchú, 1984; A. Stewart, 2000). It is important for community psychologists to understand these processes if they are to help in supporting community-based movements for change.

Why Does Marginalization Matter?

It is worth focusing briefly on why marginalization is actually a problem. There is something fundamental here to the very meaning of being human. It is common-place to find the assumption that the self precedes society and therefore that society is made up, in a cumulative way, from individuals (or in former UK Prime Minister Margaret Thatcher's words: 'There is no such thing as society, only individuals'). An alternative view can be found in the work of Karl Marx (see Sève, 1975) and G. H. Mead (1934). Both derived 'human essence' (Marx) or the 'self' (Mead) from the 'ensemble of social relations' (Marx) or the 'organized pattern of social relations and interactions' (Mead). In other words we become who we are through relationships. For people who are severely and involuntarily marginalized, their selfhood, their humanity, is threatened.

Reflecting what Thekaekara and Thekaekara (1995) found on peripheral estates of Britain, Charlesworth (2000, p. 60) puts it thus:

> No matter what one has done occupationally …[once marginalized] … there is no way one can escape the experience of a social context that is like a stagnant pond in which we are the suffocating organisms. There is an absence of the social conditions that make optimism and hope a realistic life strategy.

It is therefore unethical to do nothing about social marginalization: it is a major human problem, undermining the essence of humanity.

Based on multiple sources of evidence, Doyal and Gough (1984, 1991) argue that there are two fundamental human needs: *physical health* and *autonomy*. Autonomy is further divided into two levels, *autonomy of agency*, the ability to initiate actions; and *critical autonomy*, the opportunity for participation in political processes. People who are involuntarily marginalized, then, would have to be seen as having their fundamental needs compromised. Doyal and Gough go on to suggest that the human needs of health and autonomy can be achieved through a process of learning: learning as a social process, involving people interacting in social groups; learning from history, learning between groups within a society or across cultures, are all very important. In fact, they argue that the ability to translate lessons into practice is what they call 'human liberation' (Doyal & Gough, 1984 p. 22).

Box 14.2 **Doing Critical Community Psychology**

The process of learning and the ability to translate this into practice is a key area of possibility for critical community psychological praxis. The transfer of knowledge and skills and the strategic thinking often required to put them into practice, usually called 'capacity building', is one way in which community psychologists can shift resources to those who are marginalized. Two examples from our own work can illustrate this.

The first is a project that sought to enable community groups, interested in different ways in health and well-being (and which varied from oral history groups, to walking clubs for elderly people, to regeneration of housing projects), to understand and use meaningful methods of evaluation. The knowledge and skills of evaluation are usually retained by professional experts and rarely by marginalized people. Through a process of participatory and creative evaluation techniques, modelled directly in multi-project workshops, some of this understanding was transferred to approximately 150 projects (Boyd, Geerling, Gregory, Midgley, Murray, Walsh & Kagan, 2001).

The second project is one in which we are working with colleagues in Kolkata, India, to enable health workers in urban slums to understand, and be able to work with, families with disabled children in order to maximize the likelihood of their inclusion in local life. Not only are slum dwellers marginalized because of their place at the bottom of the caste hierarchy, families with disabled children are further marginalized. These families are often unable to maintain the levels of work necessary for basic survival. Furthermore, they lose social contacts by being confined to their homes. Some of the intermediary health workers, too, are marginalized by virtue of the fact that they work in the slums and receive little funding for their work. Many of those involved in the project work as volunteers and themselves live in the slum areas. Thus the work is about enabling intermediary health workers to develop the capacity to work with disabled children and their families and then to pass on this knowledge and skill to the families and those who live locally themselves. (See Kagan and Scott-Roberts (2002) for discussion of community psychological perspectives on the project.)

Dussel (1998; see also Alcoff & Mendieta, 2000), a Latin American philosopher of liberation, offers a critique of the conditions caused by the dominant geopolitical system from the perspective of the 'oppressed other', the victims of the system. He articulates a practical approach to ethics in a world where the majority are excluded from the possibility of producing, reproducing and developing their lives. He affirms the principle of liberation – the positive critical duty for us to work for liberation, whether that is through feasible reform of aspects of the system or feasible transformation of the system itself.

What Dussel and Doyal and Gough have in common is the view that human life is inseparable from the ability to enter into and critically negotiate, social relations. For marginalized persons, groups and communities, the inability to meet these expectations has negative repercussions for their biological and psychological well-being.

The Relevance of Community Psychology to Marginalization

Community psychology should be particularly well placed to help people respond to the challenge of their marginalization in constructive ways. Its refusal to restrict itself to the individual level and to attribute social problems to internal pathologies, as seen in Chapter 2, is a first step. By taking a transactional view that positions the personal, relational and societal planes as interrelated, interdependent and of similar importance, critical CP can attend to the various problems at the same time (see Chapter 3).

Let us take as an example some of the work we have undertaken, along with others, with people with learning difficulties, their families and services in the North West of England (Burton & Kagan, 1995; Kagan, 1997). As psychologists, we might have limited our activities to working with individuals, so as to enhance their skills and capacities. As social workers, we might have limited our activities to ensuring that disabled people and their families got full access to their welfare entitlements. As health workers, we might have limited ourselves to improving the health status of individual people.

As community psychologists, though, we extended our work to: regional and national policy development; facilitation of interagency work; training of professionals and education of disabled people and their families; facilitation of self-help groups; identification of service gaps and abuses; exposure of unequal access to social institutions; and facilitation of both organizational change and community development in order to be inclusive of disabled people and their families. This work led to increased capability and self-determination for disabled people and their families (personal well-being); less isolation and more community connection for disabled people and their families (relational well being); wider social changes stimulated by, and informed by, the experiences of disabled people and their families (collective well-being) (see also Chapter 20). As this is a process of countering marginalization, the work continues.

Working Against Social Marginalization: Tools and Examples

It is one thing to assert that a critical CP can help, but a more difficult matter to do so. There are constant dangers of reinforcing marginalization or unwittingly colluding with the forces that create it.

Box 14.3 **Example of Co-option through Participation**

An inner-city suburb had its slum housing replaced in the late 1960s. Ten years later the 'deck access' flats were acknowledged to be another housing disaster. The flats were damp and expensive to heat, children had nowhere to play safely and, because it was difficult to monitor who was coming into the vicinity of each flat, there were high levels of vandalism and violence. The city council stopped housing families there and the remaining families were found alternative accommodation. Nevertheless the flats suited some people, including students, single people and young childless couples, as well as craftspeople and small social firms. Because of poor construction the majority of the flats needed replacement, so in the early 1990s the council won funding from central government for a complete rebuild of the area. The agency set up to lead the redevelopment affirmed the importance of working closely with the local population (as well as the development companies), consulting and holding a number of participatory events, so the people concerned could take part in the redesign of their neighbourhood.

Community development activists were of course involved in this work and they were able to help local groups put forward proposals that were innovative on social, ecological sustainability and architectural grounds. Nevertheless, it soon became clear that the extent of this participation was to be limited. In terms of Arnstein's (1969) 'ladder of citizen participation', for example, only the first five rungs (which together only amount to 'non-participation' and 'tokenism') were reached, with none of the top three (citizen power)

rungs of partnership, delegated power and citizen control being attained.

Of the proposals made by local people, only two small schemes were approved, and the bulk of the redevelopment was almost indistinguishable from that in any other redeveloped inner-urban area, both in Britain and elsewhere. It was private capital that had the most influence on the design and operation of the new housing and structure of the neighbourhood. As Croft and Beresford (1992) for example suggest, the participation perhaps served some other purposes at a level of national (neoliberal) government policy: delay, incorporation/co-option and diversion of the energy of activists, legitimation of pre-determined decisions and plans and tokenistic involvement of minorities bypassing representative organizations.

The use of public participation and its limited success (from the perspective of those who participated), can be understood in terms of the broader policy context, whereby urban areas competed with one another for central government funds that supported redevelopment by large construction companies – to which the profits of course went. The participation by unrepresentative and ad hoc groups marginalized the already weakened structures of local democratic accountability, bypassing the local council. Nevertheless the whole enterprise could be cosmetically presented as an inclusive project where local voices were respected.

Based on local experience and knowledge and papers by Croft and Beresford, 1992; Mayo, 1997; Randall, 1995; and Thekaekara and Thekaekara, 1995. See also Cooke and Kothari, 2001, for a more sustained critique of the abuse of participatory methods.

But if there are dangers of co-option and tokenism, as seen in Box 14.3, there are also some powerful models for effective work. Although much of this comes from outside the field of psychology, psychological concepts and principles can be employed to strengthen and develop such approaches.

What could be called the Latin American model of liberatory praxis summarizes a vast body of work by educators, community workers, social movements and community psychologists. This is work done with, and in the service of, oppressed groups in that region (see, for example, Montero, 1994a, 1998b; Quintal de Freitas, 2000; Sánchez & Wiesenfeld, 1991). Particularly through the work of Freire (1970, 1994; Freire & Faundez, 1989) and Fals Borda (1988), this approach has been applied in countries of the southern hemisphere and in work with marginalized groups in core capitalist countries (for example Atweh, Kemmis & Weeks, 1998; Kane, 2001).

A key theme in liberation thought is that liberation is not a thing, nor can it be located in a moment in time. It is not something to be given, but rather it is a movement and a series of processes. It has origins in the interaction of two types of agents or activists: external catalytic agents (which may include community psychologists); and the oppressed groups themselves.

The Latin American notion of liberation proposes a strategic alliance between these two sectors. As seen in Chapter 8, a central idea is Freire's concept of *conscientization*. Martín-Baró (1996b) identifies three aspects of it:

1. The human being is transformed through changing his/her reality, through an active process of dialogue.
2. In this process there is a gradual decoding of the world, as people grasp the mechanisms of oppression and dehumanization. This opens up new possibilities for action.
3. The new knowledge of the surrounding reality leads to new self-understanding. Such learning is about the roots of what people are at present and what they can become in the future.

Freire is careful not to provide blueprints for this process, as every situation is different. However, two examples from British community psychologists working with people with mental health difficulties give some flavour of these ways of working.

Holland (1988, 1991, 1992) and Melluish and Bulmer (1999) worked with groups of women and men, respectively, in deprived urban communities. In both cases they started with people referred for psychological help and used group-work methods to build confidence and understanding. With the support of community psychologists, both groups were able to move beyond a focus on personal problems and individual explanations to a community action perspective.

The project by Melluish and Bulmer took account of working-class experience by emphasizing the role of the group rather than the individual, social instead of internal causes of distress and the role of action rather than introspection. The group focused on how to overcome feelings of resignation and passivity and how to start making changes at the community level. Personal commitment to the prevention of distress and suicide were also important. Their group became organizationally and economically self-sufficient without the input of the community psychologists.

It would be a mistake to see these interventions as relating only to people with mental-health difficulties. CP is concerned with well-being generally and with working with people who are marginalized in different ways.

The three aspects of liberation identified by Martín-Baró could be seen in some work that we did, by invitation, with some residents living on a run-down city housing estate, which was, somewhat unusually, placed in the prosperous countryside. Some women on the estate had begun to talk about how things could be made better for residents on the estate in the face of disinterested and negligent councils. They heard of the community psychologists through an unrelated article in the local paper and invited us to talk things through with them. Our initial brief had been no more than to show interest, discuss what was going on with the local women, give ideas and links to other projects and to use residents' experiences to spread understanding of what living in poverty was like in Britain. The very involvement of our university gave self-proclaimed strength to the women and helped them gain media interest in life and changes on the estate.

Through this dialogue, the women began to see how their lives were linked to political priorities within both the local councils and the government and to see that their scope for change was going to be limited. They also began to see how it would be necessary to broaden the base of interest and action on the estate. They chose two forms of action. The first was to clear rubbish from the centre of the estate. The second was to find out what residents thought about their housing. The rubbish clearing was met with suspicion at first, but as they persisted some others, including children, joined them. People would stop and talk and begin to open up:

> People have started to 'come out' (to members of our women's group) with regard to 'nuisance neighbours', domestic violence, homelessness and many other issues. But seem powerless to take the smallest action on their own behalf, but it's a start.

In relation to the housing, the women carried out a door-to-door survey, which meant they had to work together and to appreciate each other's strengths. More people joined in the activity and more people began to share information on the doorstep:

> I'm still delivering [information] and Heather now has two women who come round with her, surveying. Meg (age 78) is there for moral support and her daughter Kate … the survey is shocking and every day we hear more abuse stories. This week an elderly woman was *afraid* to ask for repairs … Families, such as one where the father had seriously abused his daughters then committed suicide, are 'coming out', no cure whatsoever for the girls (now women) and rage and anger acted out daily – their own children being first in line. So many broken people. The light on the situation yesterday was that people came out *asking* for information.

By this time there was a considerable group of residents becoming active and seeing possibilities for change in other directions. Over a period of about six months, they formed a residents' association that developed and steered a number of other community projects. They had a complex understanding of the constraints imposed upon their lives as well as of their own capabilities. Whilst the situation appeared optimistic, the residents were limited in what they could achieve and were thwarted at every turn by officialdom (see Kagan, Lawthorn et al., 2001, for a fuller account). Nevertheless, people on the estate have become more involved and active and have a stronger understanding of how they might improve things for themselves.

In the UK there is a major policy initiative that has the potential to reduce social marginalization. In 1997 the Government established the Social Exclusion Unit (SEU). Social exclusion is considered to be:

> A shorthand term for what can happen when people or areas suffer from a combination of linked problems such as unemployment, poor skills, low incomes, poor housing, high crime environments, bad health and family breakdown … It includes low income, but is broader and focuses on the link between problems such as, for example, unemployment, poor skills, high crime, poor housing and family breakdown. Only when these links are properly understood and addressed will policies really be effective. (SEU, 2001c, Chapter 1)

The SEU identified the costs associated with social exclusion. Human costs faced by individuals who experience social exclusion include underachievement in education and the labour market, low income, poor access to services, stress and ill-health. Social costs include reduced social cohesion, higher crime and higher levels of stress and reduced mobility. The social costs also include the financial burden of paying for crime, school exclusions, drug misuse, unemployment and lost tax revenue. Business, too, suffered from a less-skilled workforce, lost customers and markets and – like the rest of the population – higher taxes to pay the bills for social failure.

The SEU targeted a number of priority areas, including truancy and school exclusion, rough sleeping (homeless people sleeping on the streets), neighbourhood renewal, teenage pregnancy and young people leaving school. Each priority area has a platform of consultations (what is hailed as 'bottom-up' policy making) and action plans. The neighbourhood renewal program consists of nearly 600 recommendations for actions that are publicly audited (SEU, 2001b).

Paid work and access to the labour market dominates UK Government policy (Levitas, 1998; Williams, 2002). Even so, one of the current projects of the SEU is concerned with transport – thus broadening both the understanding of exclusion and its remedies (SEU, 2002).

Although these policies look promising, commentators have been concerned with the ways in which causes of exclusion are frequently seen to be located within individuals and their personal deficits (Colley & Hodkinson, 2001), thus rendering deep-seated structural inequalities invisible. It is a rights and responsibilities approach that focuses on individuals doing things differently, to fit with existing social structures, not necessarily an approach focusing on social change.

Much was made of the consultative, 'bottom up' approach of the SEU (Matthews, 2001; Morris, 2001). Similarly, much was made of the move to 'joined up Government' underpinned by the SEU. However, we can still see the ways in which different Government policies pull against each other in housing (Lemos, 2000; Shelter, 2002) and neighbourhood renewal (Home Office, 2002; LGA, 2002; SEU, 2001a). Problems have also been identified with the marginalization of groups from the process and with contradictory policies. Still, the identification of social exclusion as a Government priority opens possibilities for more community psychological work.

Chapter Summary

Community and government work should involve an alliance between the community psychologist and people at risk of marginalization. The professional contributes some general templates and understandings, some organizational know-how and some access to resources. Community members, in turn, bring their own commitment, their local knowledge and their lived experience. From the combination of these resources, action for social justice, supported by emancipatory research, can emerge. Ideas from psychology and related fields can create a synergy with local knowledge to bring about liberatory change (Burton & Kagan, 2000; Choudhury & Kagan, 2000; Kagan, 1995; Mollison, 1988).

One of the challenges to CP is, to use a well-known saying, to 'think global and act local'. Our analyses of marginalization must take account of the wider global picture and our actions must transcend national boundaries as well. Local compassion has to be accompanied by global solidarity.

As community psychologists we can work together to help evaluate what works best, what are the barriers to change and what action projects are all about (see Kagan & Burton, 2000). We would argue that to work at the margins of psychology, with one foot in and one foot out of the discipline, in partnership with those who are marginalized, demands particular ways of being. This work requires us to make personal commitments to social justice, not just in our work, but in our lives as well.

COMMENTARY: Multiple Intersecting Oppressions   *Lesley Hoatson*

I trained in Australia as a social worker and community developer and for many years have been an activist in low-income neighbourhoods. Nowadays I teach at a university in the poorest part of Melbourne. In all my work settings I struggle with how to be most effective when working alongside marginalized people. Early on I realized that to intervene and make a difference I needed an analysis of why the world was so unfair and how oppression was consciously and unconsciously used to keep people marginalized. Carolyn Kagan and Mark Burton's chapter begins to provide just such an analysis. Recognizing that marginalization is complex, they build a powerful understanding of how people become marginalized, its impact, how it is perpetuated and strategies that community practitioners might use to challenge it. I wish, though, that they had discussed in more detail why society tolerates and, some would argue, actively encourages the marginalization of classes and communities. I notice that the most powerful in society substantially benefit from keeping people marginalized. In my region, for example, large numbers of people are either employed on very low wages or they cannot find work. This environment profits employers because they have a ready pool of cheap labour, with workers competing to take whatever job is available. The fight for wage justice is sidelined in the knowledge that rocking the boat will only make you less attractive to employers, who, after all, have plenty of other people they can employ. It is in the interests of the powerful to impose on the less powerful so that they quietly accept their unfair place in society.

The authors identify that the experience of marginality can arise through being born into a marginalized group or acquiring marginality through some personal or structural mishap. Their diagram (Figure 14.1) introduces the idea of dimensions of marginality through gender, race, disability, poverty or knowledge, occurring from the individual

through to structural levels. Unfortunately they do not expand much on these concepts. Some writers, such as Mullaly (2002), identify marginalization as one form of a broader category of oppression. He argues that individuals have multiple identities associated with class, social roles, ethnicity, gender. The dominant group uses these socially constructed different identities as the bases for carrying out discrimination against less powerful members. Often psychologists and social workers treat these forms of oppression as a number of single sources when they should be seen as multiple, intersecting oppressions, which are both complex and potentially volatile. For example, Mullaly suggests that oppression based on patriarchy will not be experienced identically by all women, as it will be mediated in some way by a woman's class position, race, sexuality, level of disability and so on. Multiple oppressions are not just cumulative; the interactive effects of many forms of oppression increase exponentially as other forms of oppression are added.

He also points out that oppression not only occurs between the dominant and less powerful group, it also occurs within oppressed groups. Every so-called identity group (for example men, women, gay, lesbian, bisexual, heterosexual, disabled) contains a hierarchy of privilege and advantage that can lead people to hold on to relative advantages and support the status quo. This makes it much harder to build solidarity between and within marginalized groups.

Burton and Kagan comment on two other factors that prevent collective action. Marginalized people are likely to have tenuous involvement in the economy, with varying sources of income that make it a struggle to survive. They also see that marginality excludes people, either relatively or completely, from social networks. I would argue that while some marginalized individuals do have few networks, it is not necessarily exclusion from networks that occurs but as they later argue, exclusion from particular sorts of networks. I worked in a remote aboriginal community in central Australia in the early 1990s where local Pitjantjatjara people lived (and still live) marginalized lives in Third World conditions. Despite this level of marginality, most families had strong, dense networks of extended family support. Children, for example, were surrounded not only by parents but also aunts, uncles and grandparents who all took responsibility for child rearing. These families and communities did not have access, however, to what Granovetter (1973) called 'weak ties'. These refer to contacts (often occurring through 'acquaintances of acquaintances') that bridge into political and economic worlds, providing a more diversified set of exchanges. Marginal communities need ways of building these links and being empowered to lobby for better resources and employment.

It is pleasing to see Kagan and Burton explore the ethical question of why marginalization should be challenged. It leads me to think about what social justice is and what should we be fighting for when we are in partnership with marginalized communities. Most people answer this in terms of the redistribution of resources. Ife (2002) argues that while the former is important, unless changes are made to the basic structures and discourses of oppression, which create and perpetuate inequality, little change will occur. Just as Kagan and Burton note, having such a perspective challenges practitioners to work for a broad social change agenda at individual, collective and structural levels.

Kagan and Burton's case studies of people seeking help for personal troubles and eventually overcoming feelings of resignation and passivity to start making changes at the community level, are excellent examples of how psychologists can start working with marginalized people on this broader agenda. Recently I came across an article that gave wise advice about how to be effective at this level. A famous community development writer, Jack Rothman (2000) reviewed large numbers of community building projects and concluded that a number of characteristics were evident in those projects that successfully work alongside (rather than for) those marginalized. The best conditions can be found where:

- A baseline of capacity within the community either exists or can be built so that there is a sufficient degree of cohesion, internal organization and a level of leadership, knowledge and skills to carry out the necessary tasks.
- There is strong community commitment to working on the issues, with collaboration between groups with common interests and needs and collective decision-making processes.
- Projects are more likely to succeed if the projects are small scale, encourage participation in project design and are based around non-authoritarian approaches and participant ownership.
- The benefits are tangible (preferably quick, visible and local) and can be predicted by local people to outweigh the costs, that is the gains outweigh the effort.

While these principles provide direction for a local practice framework and complement Kagan and Burton's discussion of Freire's conscientization strategies, the authors rightly warn of the risk of local social action ending up as isolated community activism. Moving from local micro-practice to broader social change strategies that address marginalization and the processes that entrench it, is not easy. This is particularly the case when, as Mullaly argued earlier, marginalized people most often identify through a single source of oppression, such as being coloured or disabled. Investing in other groups is beyond their purview. Kagan and Burton's suggestion that we build alliances with those at risk of being marginalized is well placed. Such alliances need to assist community activists who stand up and speak for marginalized groups and need to create broad networks and coalitions for social change.

Chapter glossary

conscientization a term imported from the Portuguese *conscientizaçao* (from the Brazilian Paulo Freire), according to which a person or group achieve an illuminating awareness of social forces shaping their destiny and of their ability to transform that reality

fatalism the attitude or belief that one has little influence over what happens to one personally or to one's people

marginalization being involuntarily disconnected from the economic and social mainstream of the society in which one lives: generally involves being discriminated against, being poor, having limited personal and collective power and being excluded from social opportunities

naturalized used here to indicate the (implicit or explicit) suggestion that a phenomenon which has a social origin is regarded as either a natural or innate characteristic of a people

neoliberal/neoliberalism refers to the doctrine of the prime importance of the market in ordering society and defining value. Associated with policies that reduce state spending on health, education and welfare, constrain trade union and other collective rights and freedom. Linked with the monetarism of the Chicago school of economics practiced by the Pinochet (Chile), Thatcher (Britain) and Reagan/Bush (US) regimes and promoted by the International Monetary Fund and World Bank

phenomenological to do with personal, felt experience. Knowable through qualitative, participative and non-reductionist methods of enquiry

praxis the combination of theory and practice, each feeding the other. Usually implies a critical or radical orientation

■

RESOURCES

■

Websites

1. Our Community Psychology UK website: http://www.compsy.org.uk has links to a variety of resources relevant to marginalization, as well as to some of our other work in community psychology and related areas.

2. Information on the Latin American model of liberatory praxis can be found in several places: http://www.oneworld.org/cantera/education/index.html – an English language website based in Managua, explains the Freirian model of popular education, while for those who read Spanish, the following site is that of a Latin American-wide network of popular education centres: http://www.ceaal.org/.

3. The Instituto Paulo Freire in Brazil has some pages in English: http://www.paulofreire.org/

4. The Brazilian Landless Workers' Movement, the MST has a good site in English and Portuguese, covering the MST's history, its settlements and its educational program: http://www.mstbrazil.org/index.html.

5. The site for the World Social Forum, held annually in Porto Alegre, Brazil, contains links, articles and information on this innovative approach that advocates and works towards a different globalization that includes the marginalized: http://www.forumsocialmundial.org.br/home.asp.

6. More information on the British Government Social Exclusion Unit, including reports that can be freely downloaded, can be found at their site: http://www.cabinet-office.gov.uk/seu/.

7. *New Internationalist* magazine provides an international perspective on exploitation, diversity and discrimination, human rights, the abuse of power and alternatives: http://www.newint.org.

Films

1. The films of Ken Loach, for example, *Bread and Roses, Cathy Come Home, Kes, Raining Stones, Navigators, Sweet 16*, all deal with issues of marginalization and people's resilience and resistance to it.

2. Similarly the films, journalism and books of John Pilger have a great deal of material relevant to worldwide struggles of, and for, the marginalized. See http://www.johnpilger.com/.

15

Globalization, Poverty and Social Justice

Tod Sloan

Warm-up Exercise: The Student Anti-sweatshop Movement

Students on over 200 campuses in North America have organized to protest against conditions under which girls and young women in the Third World work as they produce university-licensed apparel such as T-shirts and gym clothes. The movement began in 1997 at the University of North Carolina in opposition to an exclusive $11 million contract with Nike. Students had become aware of horrendous fourteen-hour days worked in unhealthy conditions for highly exploitative wages in countries such as Indonesia and Honduras. Coalitions quickly formed with groups at other universities. Students and professors arranged teach-ins and seminars, met with administrators, and eventually held sit-ins to demand that universities fully disclose information on the factories that produce their licensed products, and require that these factories abide by codes of conduct and pay a living wage. Some campus groups have achieved their goals and others are still struggling to disentangle cash-strapped university administrations from their ties to lucrative contracts with corporations. The overall impact on global trade has been limited by the fact that university apparel sales constitute only 2% of the clothing sales in the US, but the debate has brought new energy to the global anti-sweatshop movement. Students are learning that solidarity with their local labour movement and with diverse coalitions is as important to success as international solidarity.

1.   What do you think of the Students Against Sweatshops campaign?
2.   If the university that you attend does not have a chapter of Students Against Sweatshops, do you think it should have one? How could one be started on your campus?
3.   What other sorts of actions could students organize to improve conditions for workers in developing countries?

For further information, see: Traub-Werner, Marion. (2002). Sustaining the student anti-sweatshop movement: Living workers' struggles. In M. Prokosch & L. Raymond (eds), *The global activist's manual* (pp. 191–8). New York: Thunder's Mouth Press

Figure 15.1 'Students Against Sweatshops' logos

In this chapter, I examine the relationship between corporate globalization and global poverty. After reviewing the rise of capitalist industrialization and its effects on what became the Third World, I discuss some of the general ways in which the globalization of capitalist consumerism is disrupting material and social well-being. My primary aim is to highlight the crucial roles that communities and citizens will play in determining the outcomes of the contemporary political struggles for global social and economic justice.

I often find myself wondering why, in a world where billions of dollars are spent on weapons, space exploration, cosmetics, spectator sports and popular music, can we not manage to shift resources to solve the problem of global poverty? It is hard to imagine a more urgent task. A third of humanity scrapes by on an income equivalent to $2 a day or less (United Nations Development Programme, 2000; World Bank, 2000). Such poverty is not just a lack of money as the World Bank's *Voices of the Poor* research project 'discovered' when 60,000 poor men and women were interviewed (see Box 15.1). Poverty is a lived experience associated with hunger, illness, inadequate housing, illiteracy, human rights abuses and social marginalization (Narayan, Chambers, et al., 2000). Technological and socioeconomic developments over the past 50 years have improved the situation of some social classes in particular parts of the world, but rapid population growth, continuing violent conflict and epidemic diseases in poorer countries have basically negated progress overall. Poverty is not due to there not being enough to go around – it stems from societal and institutional arrangements that do not give priority to meeting basic needs.

Box 15.1 **The Poor View Well-being Holistically**

Poverty is much more than income alone. For the poor, the good life or well-being is multidimensional with both material and psychological dimensions. Well-being is peace of mind; it is good health; it is belonging to a community; it is safety; it is freedom of choice and action; it is a dependable livelihood and a steady source of income; it is food.

The poor describe ill-being as lack of material things – food especially, but also lack of work, money, shelter and clothing – and living and working in often unhealthy, polluted and risky environments. They also defined ill-being as bad experiences and bad feelings about the self. Perceptions of powerlessness over one's life and of voicelessness were common; so was anxiety and fear for the future.

'Poverty is like living in jail, living under bondage, waiting to be free.' – *Jamaica*

'Poverty is lack of freedom, enslaved by crushing daily burden, by depression and fear of what the future will bring.' – *Georgia*

'If you want to do something and have no power to do it, it is *talauchi* (poverty).' – *Nigeria*

'Lack of work worries me. My children were hungry and I told them the rice is cooking, until they fell asleep from hunger.' – *an older man from Bedsa, Egypt*

'A better life for me is to be healthy, peaceful and live in love without hunger. Love is more than anything. Money has no value in the absence of love.' – *a poor older woman in Ethiopia*

'When one is poor, she has no say in public, she feels inferior. She has no food, so there is famine in her house; no clothing and no progress in her family.' – *a woman from Uganda*

'For a poor person everything is terrible – illness, humiliation, shame. We are cripples; we are afraid of everything; we depend on everyone. No one needs us. We are like garbage that everyone wants to get rid of.' – *a blind woman from Tiraspol, Moldova*

'I repeat that we need water as badly as we need air.' – *a woman from Tash-Bulak, The Kyrgyz Republic*

'The waste brings some bugs; here we have cockroaches, spiders and even snakes and scorpions.' – *Nova California, Brazil*

Conclusions from the World Bank's *Voices of the Poor* Project: (from the website at http://www.worldbank.org/poverty/voices/listen-findings.htm)

A Personal Journey

I was introduced to issues of global development early in my life as I travelled and lived abroad with my father, who worked for a small private foundation involved in Asian development. In the 1950s and 60s, US development projects were shaped by the larger context of the Cold War. The idea was to promote democratic institutions and market economies to squash the idea that state-controlled (socialist and communist) economies might meet people's needs more effectively. As I child I saw, but certainly did not understand, Japan recovering from World War II with US aid, Singapore beginning to boom and even Afghanistan beginning to open to western ways. As I rode in a bus to a little American school in Kabul in the mid 1960s, I saw young men and women in European dress going to Kabul University. Unfortunately, one of the last phases of the Cold War closed the doors on education in Afghanistan, as the US and the Soviet Union played out their differences in a manner that reduced that society to rubble and allowed the fundamentalist Taliban to take control.

What stood out most for me, however, was the sheer poverty of the urban poor wherever I went. I remember seeing boys standing barefoot in snow, children picking through garbage dumps for food, people with misshapen limbs dragging themselves along the street amidst cars and bicycles, and children no more than six or seven hawking nearly worthless items all day in hopes of a coin or two. These memories contrasted with my own middle-class lifestyle as a child, and later as an adult, and they tugged at me when I saw that people living in suburban middle-class neighbourhoods in the US lived as if they had no idea that a billion or more people on the planet suffer from extreme poverty.

Ten years of studies in psychology did absolutely nothing to remind me of global poverty, let alone poverty within the US. I think this is one of the major reasons to have serious concerns about the field of psychology as it is currently organized. How can a science of behaviour almost totally ignore the unequal economic conditions that affect psychological development so profoundly?

At any rate, my conscience was stirred by travels to Latin America during the 1980s and 90s, particularly to Nicaragua, where a brave revolutionary society was doing the best it could to meet people's basic needs first, and to develop an alternative to both communist and capitalist forms of development. Nicaragua unfortunately became one of the last victims of the Cold War and it remains one of the poorest countries in the hemisphere. I am haunted by a 1995 memory of three little children in Managua sitting in a small wagon, inactive and blank-eyed in the heat, while their mother sold towels at a busy intersection day after day. A few blocks away, a shiny new supermarket full of imported goods, guarded by security guards with submachine guns, serviced people pulling up in $50,000 sport-utility vehicles.

Back at home, these images and memories quickly fade and I have found it very difficult to figure out what we can do, especially as psychologists, to transform the realities of poverty. Nevertheless, I would argue that the very first value that should be listed in the psychologist's code of ethics is to devote one's expertise in the science of behaviour to address the most widespread sources of human suffering. High on the list along with war, violence and disease would be poverty.

Critical Community Psychology

My interest in critical approaches to community psychology (CP) (see Sloan, 2000a, 2000b) stems in part from my hopes that the major groups of psychologists will reorient themselves radically to address the needs of the poorest people and contribute to the sociopolitical changes that this will require. Community psychologists in the US have tended to do work that might modify and ameliorate families, schools, social services and neighbourhoods, but I fear that unless we significantly transform the underlying political and economic processes affecting all of these community-level institutions, we are simply part of the problem. We are improving systems that rely on the functioning of a larger system that is fundamentally flawed. When I look at the entire field of psychology through this lens, I begin to despair. But hope is occasionally rekindled as I see glimpses of broadening awareness and possibilities for change. For example, the American Psychological Association recently made an important statement on the need for psychologists to address the effects of poverty (American Psychological Association, 2000) and a few psychologists are involved in helping the United Nations meet its goals of reducing poverty by half by 2015. To attend more to the value of social justice and to engage in more transformative intervention, CP needs to understand the problem of poverty in the context of globalization. But the road will be long and hard.

If we, as community psychologists and citizens, are going to address larger political and economic structures, we need to know what those structures are and how they came to be that way. With this in mind, we turn now to some historical background on how globalization and poverty are intertwined.

Historical Context

What are the Origins of Contemporary Poverty Around the World?

World history is usually taught in a manner that fails to convey the grand sweep of events, inventions and movements that led to the current global situation. If one can manage to stand back a little from the biographies of kings and chronicles of war, what stands out is the enormity of the social and political changes associated with the rise of modern science and associated technologies. Just 500 years ago, the vast majority of the world's population lived in agrarian communities. Lives were simple, but most ways of life were self-sufficient and sustainable. When we look at surviving examples of self-sufficient life (indigenous peoples), we may think of them as poor, but that is a judgment imposed from an external point of view. Nowadays, roughly 75 per cent of humanity is urbanized, separated from agricultural processes, and embedded in highly interdependent systems of production, energy, transportation and commerce. Average urban lives are much longer and less physically challenging than pre-modern agrarian lives, but they are probably more complex at psychological and social levels. They are also not very sustainable in terms of their impact on natural environments.

Science and Modernity

Most historical accounts seem to concur with the idea that the magnitude of the changes that occurred over the past 500 years was indeed unprecedented. While explanations of the rise of modernity differ, certain factors are always acknowledged. The scientific method led to increased human control over natural and physical processes. All technologies, from weapons and transportation to medicine and farming equipment, benefited from scientific reasoning. As a consequence, the power of superstition, magic and religious authorities over human knowledge and action was reduced. The economies, armies and navies of countries with advanced science and technology became powerful. In particular, Europeans used this new power to colonize other regions of the world beginning in the 1600s. This was rationalized as a civilizing process, but massacres, slavery and exploitation were routine practices of the colonizing powers.

Industrialization and Imperialism

Philosophers of the Enlightenment period proposed rational ways of governing societies and, leaning on ideas such as democracy and equality, the rising commercial classes in Europe gradually displaced medieval nobilities to establish modern nation-states. The Industrial Revolution and the associated need for raw materials and new markets led to a second wave of colonization and conquest in the 1800s, known as the *era of imperialism*. During this period, the industrializing European powers consolidated at least a degree of control over most of the territory on earth. Wealth accumulated in European and US banks. This was reinvested in further industrial development, increasing the need for resources from the colonies. These resources (labour, minerals, food) were extracted on terms that were not favourable to progress in the colonies. In fact, centuries-old forms of agrarian subsistence were disrupted as colonial economies were organized for resource extraction rather than for local needs and the foundation for what was to become Third World poverty was laid. Previously autonomous communities became entangled in powerful webs of international commerce. Sustainable ways of life were replaced by labour-intensive systems of production serving the appetites and desires of distant populations: tea, coffee, cotton, silk, gold, silver, tobacco, hardwoods, fruit and so on.

Modernization

The world wars of the first half of the 20th century accelerated industrialization in Europe, Japan and the US and weakened European colonial powers in a manner that prepared the way for a wave of independence movements for colonies in the Third World. Real competition and the ideological divide between capitalist and socialist/communist economies led to further conflict in the second half of the 20th century – Korea, Vietnam, Central America and Afghanistan, for example. The Cold War diverted resources sorely needed for schools, housing, sanitation and other basic needs into weapons stockpiles. Decolonization was primarily accomplished by elites and the middle classes in the southern hemisphere, often on the basis of political rhetoric about meeting the needs of the poor. Indeed, poverty was a striking feature of the Third World as the colonizing powers withdrew. The solution proposed by the western economic powers and the western-trained elites of the Third World was known as *modernization*. Bundled in this concept were a number of processes experienced by Europe and the US over a span of two centuries: industrialization, urbanization, public education, literacy and democratization. None of these processes is inherently problematic (Sloan, 1997), but development was extremely uneven and often created new problems. Certain sectors, usually the middle classes of urban centres, saw improvement. Urban and rural poor, however, continued to suffer in most Third World countries as rural poverty fuelled migration to the cities, state bureaucracies bloated, foreign debts accumulated and local economies continued to be affected by local corruption and global economic conditions. Eventually, the framework of global geopolitics changed when the 1989 collapse of the Soviet Union left western elites thinking that countries that hold democratic elections and foster market economies and free trade had undoubtedly discovered the best form of government and economy.

Globalization

The term *globalization* achieved its current popularity in the 1990s as a new way of describing the process that is supposed to bring the benefits of science, democracy, free trade, communications systems and corporation-controlled capitalism to the entire world. (Some argue that globalization is merely a euphemism for capitalist modernization.) Quite a few individuals and groups are not convinced that this is the only possible path, as was shown in Chapter 2, and, ironically, one of their biggest concerns also happens to be democracy, or the lack of it, for example in international trade negotiations. The dramatic turn-of-the-century protests in Seattle, Washington, Prague and Québec against global financial and trade organizations such as the International Monetary Fund (IMF), the World Bank and the World Trade Organization (WTO) are only the tip of the iceberg of a broad social movement that aims to construct a different sort of global political and economic order (Korten, 2001).

The Political Economy of Development

At this point, I think it is important to lay out some very basic understandings about the economics of development. I fear that psychology has systematically made itself irrelevant to debates in economics and politics because it has failed to include broad socioeconomic concepts in the education of psychology professionals. Psychology's commitment to natural science models accounts for part of this narrowness, but actually the sheer success of the field has induced a certain over-confidence and blindness to its situation. Psychologists have a hard time recogniz-ing that the acceptance they find within the social system is partially due to their willingness to serve as conveyors of exactly the forms of individualism the system of exploitation requires (Fox & Prilleltensky, 1997).

A key sociological understanding, stated most radically by Karl Marx, is that human beings are the products of the social relations they experience. The term 'social relations' includes all dimensions of social life, from love and friendship to trading practices and legal systems. Human actors, in turn, can shape their social reality. This means it is impossible to determine whether there is an essence of humanity we could call 'human nature'. Are people naturally greedy or aggressive? According to Marx, this question cannot be answered. For example, the observed greediness or aggressiveness of individuals or social groups is the product of a complex interaction of historical, cultural, economic, technological and political relations that have shaped human action in a particular place and time. This key understanding led Marx and other social theorists, such as Max Weber and Emile Durkheim, to examine the roles of all these factors in the rise of modern society. Marx is, of course, best known for emphasizing the economic determinants of soci-etal development and since we are trying to understand the contemporary produc-tion of global poverty, we will review several concepts and perspectives that draw their inspiration from his work.

Capitalism

The term *capitalism* refers to a general economic system and associated way of producing goods. In capitalist economies, the means of production (factories, offices, tools, materials) are privately owned. Because of private ownership, profits from the sale of products are accumulated by individual owners or groups of owners and investors (corporations). Profits result when goods can be sold for more than the associated costs of materials, labour and equipment. In this process, capital accu-mulates and becomes the basis for other investment, either directly or through the banking system. In capitalist economies, workers are usually not in a position to earn enough to participate much in the accumulation of capital (except perhaps through pension plans over which they have little control). Instead, they compete with each other on the labour market, selling their time, energy and skills for the best wages they can get. The 'reserve army' of the unemployed serve to keep wages low, since 'there is always someone else who might want your job'. The result is a fairly impor-tant divide between those who own and direct the productive system and those who do the work, whether managers or workers. The persistence of this divide is noted in Marxist sociology by the term *class society*.

The raw effects of capitalist relations in modern class society have been softened to some extent by the effectiveness of labour unions and state welfare systems. Unions first formed to protect the interests of groups of workers in collective bargaining with the owners of the means of production. Government welfare systems emerged later as 'safety nets' to ensure the basic health and housing of the unemployed labour pool and the unemployable, particularly when the capitalist economic system is undergoing one of its occasional recessions or depressions. Both unions and welfare systems are under attack in the era of globalization for various reasons, in particular, because individualism and capitalism go hand in hand. Individuals are supposed to compete to survive in the free market. Collective bargaining by unions and taxes to support non-workers are perceived as brakes on businesses that might produce more jobs and better wages if left unhampered by constraints on individual competition. This debate will certainly continue for a few more generations!

The dynamic combination of modern science and technology with capital accumulation and investment led to the impressive achievements of the Industrial Revolution in Europe and the US. Production systems became more effective and efficient. Marx himself was impressed by this and assumed that agrarian societies would have to move through a capitalist phase of industrialization before moving on to socialist and communist economies. But, as seen above, the effects of capitalist industrialization were harsh. As feudal-era rural arrangements collapsed, poverty spread and urban centres expanded as workers flowed into cities. Meanwhile, the drive for access to raw materials and bigger markets for industrial products fuelled further European and American expansion and imperialism. When the former European colonies gained their independence in the post World War II era, most of them had not developed significant industry of their own. As mentioned above, they had been used, and continue to be used, by the colonizing powers as sources for raw materials and agricultural products. The newly independent countries of the Third World were encouraged and helped to 'modernize'. The effect of modernization in practice, however, was the reordering of society in ways that increased the efficiency of capitalist production and the accumulation of wealth by the powerful classes.

The thrill of independence was quickly displaced by new forms of exploitation, in a process that came to be known as *underdevelopment* (Clark, 1986). Goods and raw materials were bought cheaply in the peripheral societies and sold at high prices from the core, enriching middlemen and investors and leaving no local capital for development of the periphery. Elites in Third World countries had a share in profits but tended to keep their wealth in banks outside their own countries in order to avoid the wild economic swings of developing economies. Gradually, most Third World countries were encumbered with incredible debts incurred in the hope that development would follow. In many cases, interest payments alone have consumed up to a third or more of a country's gross domestic product.

To summarize, modernization conducted according to capitalist models left Third World countries only partly developed, with vast sectors of their populations stranded between previously self-sufficient agrarian lifestyles and unattainable middle-class urban lifestyles. Rampant unemployment, 40–70% of populations living below official poverty lines, high infant mortality – all these indicators of Third World suffering are fairly well known. Burdened by billions of dollars of debt, Third World governments had little room for action in response to poverty. They came increasingly under the control of the financial institutions of the world's economic powers. This was the general scenario that gave rise to the brouhaha about globalization and to the resistance against it.

Globalization and Its Effects

As a description of what has happened since the fall of the Berlin Wall in 1989, the buzzword *globalization* is useful only to a certain extent. At the most general level, globalization simply means the spread of a local practice or product to the entire world, for example, the use of e-mail or the availability of pizza or hamburgers. From this point of view, globalization actually started hundreds of years ago with the spice trade.

A second common use of the term globalization is slightly more specific, but still far too broad in its scope. It sees globalization both as a process and a result of that process. The primary drivers of the process of globalization are all events, forces and changes that are transnational, transcultural and transborder. These include: flows of capital, ownership and trade; telecommunications; transportation; political and military alliances; and international organizations. The results, according to Marsella (1998) are greater interdependence, shifting personal and collective identities and lifestyles, awareness of the global condition, increased linkages and chain reactions, and new levels and forms of control of processes such as trade, communications and finance. Marsella was one of the first psychologists to draw attention to the importance of these forms of globalization:

> Human survival and well-being [are] now embedded in an entangled web of global economic, political, social and environmental events and forces! ... The scale, complexity and impact of these events and forces constitute a formidable challenge for psychology as a science and profession. They demand a major disciplinary response, including a rethinking of psychology's assumptions, methods and interventions and a rethinking of psychology's roles in understanding and resolving the challenges now before us. (Marsella, 1998, p. 1282)

More recently, Arnett (2002) also examined the psychological impact of globalization, focusing on adolescent identity development. Unfortunately, he uses a watered-down definition of globalization that almost completely misses the economic tensions and contradictions that make globalization such a major political issue: 'Globalization has existed for many centuries as a process by which cultures influence one another and become more alike through trade, immigration and the exchange of information and ideas' (p. 774).

Friedman's (2000) popular account of globalization, *The Lexus and the Olive Tree*, captures these dynamic processes very well and helps reduce the vagueness of the concept of globalization by focusing on the globalization of electronic communications, democratic practices and financial systems. Even though Friedman supports globalization, he raises a few concerns about its consequences. In each case, however, he believes that the solution is simply more globalization (for example better communications systems, better representative democracies and better financial systems).

A fast-growing group of concerned citizens and non-governmental organizations (NGOs) around the world do not agree that the kinks in globalization will simply work themselves out eventually through more globalization. They begin by pointing out that the core economic practices driving globalization are inherently problematic. If these practices are continued, the global situation will only become worse. This core structure of globalization that has driven workers, students, human rights activists and environmentalists into the streets in protest is known as *corporate globalization* (Anderson & Cavanagh, 2000; Barlow & Clarke, 2001). It is essential to keep in mind that contemporary protests are not about the general versions of globalization discussed above. Very few people have problems with improved communications and cross-cultural exchange, for example. When western political leaders argue in favour of globalization, they are primarily referring to the expansion of capitalist market economies and 'free trade'. In order to avoid saying this, they often speak of spreading 'democracy', when they really mean pressuring governments to open their markets to foreign products.

Corporate globalization has been facilitated by financial policies of the IMF and the World Bank, known as 'structural adjustment'. These policies require debt-ridden countries seeking loans to slash government spending on education and health, privatize government-owned enterprises, shift economies towards production of exports and open themselves to flows of external capital. The extent to which the structural adjustment strategy is working is hotly debated. While conservatives argue that it is just a matter of allowing free markets enough time to stimulate economic growth, progressives claim that corporate-led globalization concentrates wealth and power in the hands of a few and leads to further impoverishment for the masses of humanity. They note, for example, that national markets have become increasingly volatile and national democratic processes are quashed by transnational corporate decisions. Government subsidies for basic needs, such as water and electricity, are removed as structural adjustment requires that these essential services be privatized. Jobs are lost as companies hop around the world to employ workers who will accept lower wages in countries that will not fuss about violations of labour rights. Families and communities are disrupted as workers migrate in hopes of finding employment. Environmental protections are weakened as countries compete for foreign investment by promising limited regulation.

Citing such major problems associated with 'globalization from above', Brecher, Costello and Smith (2000) propose a 'globalization from below' that would take into account the interests of the great majority of the world's people (see Box 15.2).

Box 15.2   **Draft of a Global Program**

1. Level labour, environmental, social and human rights conditions upward.
2. Democratize institutions at every level from local to global.
3. Make decisions as close as possible to those they affect.
4. Equalize global wealth and power.

5. Convert the global economy to environmental sustainability.
6. Create prosperity by meeting human and environmental needs.
7. Protect against global boom and bust.

Source: Brecher, Costello and Smith (2000) *Globalization from below: The power of solidarity*. Boston: South End Press. (pp. 68–9)

If it is not already obvious, I should make it clear that while I see some merit in the conservative position on globalization, my studies have convinced me that the basic operating principle of corporate capitalism (maximization of profits to enrich investors) runs counter to the interests of the vast majority of humanity and the earth's environment. A significantly different system for meeting human needs must be developed. This is a task that must be addressed by community psychologists and by all citizens in the 21st century. I look first at what we are up against and then discuss the tools we can develop to confront the challenge.

Ideology: A Key Concept

At the outset of this chapter, I asked how it is that the world has not yet solved the problem of global poverty. One can also ask, in light of what the world has experienced as a result of exploitation built into capitalist economics, why it is that so many people believe that it is a good system and blame themselves for their difficulties in making ends meet. My best answer to this question points to the power of the curious phenomena associated with ideology. *Ideology refers to a system of ideas and practices that sustain social relations of domination and oppression* (Thompson, 1984). It is essential to understand that we are not using this term in the more common, neutral sense used to denote any system of ideas, but rather in what is known as a 'critical' sense. The Marxist notion of 'false consciousness' (a tendency to see the unjust status quo as natural or given) is related to what I have in mind, but that implies a mostly cognitive process, as if changing ideology might simply involve improved education (Rosen, 1996). Ideological processes are always sustained not only by cognitive, but also by emotional, behavioural and institutional practices (Sloan, 1997, 2000a). A critical notion of ideology would always attend to the interaction of these different aspects of structures of social injustice.

In order to make headway in the eradication of global poverty, it is essential to analyse a central ideological structure involved in corporate globalization: consumerism. I define consumerism as the process that orients much of life around earning money in order to purchase unnecessary goods. Consumerism is a core ideological process sustaining globalization and it must be confronted if global poverty is to be eradicated.

At the behavioural level, consumerism simply requires that people purchase items that they do not really need in order to survive or enjoy life. Note that they do not actually need to use any of the products they buy – the system simply requires that purchases be made. At the emotional level, making purchases is made to feel good through an elaborate system of lifestyle advertising and status symbol construction (Korten, 2001). At the cognitive level, consumerism is justified as the driving force of economic growth, as evidenced by concerns about indicators of low 'consumer confidence'. Finally, at the institutional level, banks support consumerism through credit card offers and stores support consumerism by extending their hours of operation and redesigning malls as places to spend leisure time. In turn, politicians promise to work for policies that favour economic growth, reduce taxes, increase salaries and maximize disposable income for consumer purchases.

We must now add the fact that in order to engage in the direct behavioural component of consumerism, people must be willing to work longer hours than necessary to earn the extra money needed to buy products that are not essential to survival. The entire advertising industry serves to make people feel they must have products that they objectively do not need in order to live comfortably. Accordingly, advertisements increasingly focus on identity and status issues that will be resolved if one owns or uses a product. Consumerism does not feel like direct oppression or exploitation, but it is a form of domination nonetheless.

Along with many others, I have argued that consumerism has played a major role in destroying the fabric of community in western society (Sloan, 1997). It is clearly beginning to undermine community in the rest of the world. I saw this particularly in the contrasts between the isolated lifestyles of the new middle classes in Latin America and the more collective forms of life among the working classes there. People increasingly shift their free time and energy into either working for, or using, cars, consumer gadgets, entertainment products and toys. In general, these are used either privately or in small groups (watching TV, playing videogames, solitary hobbies). Dialogue, communication, social life, group life, creative action – all key components of a thriving community – tend to be displaced by shopping and isolated entertainment. (For example, I know a family of four that has six television sets to ensure maximum individual TV-watching pleasure.)

The news media, of course, do not do much to raise awareness of the global impact of consumerism or of the political and economic forces that want to protect the divide between the wealthy and rest of us. The news media pretend to offer a range of opinion, but actually actively exclude reasonable ideas and proposals that would disrupt current arrangements of wealth and privilege. The same media also tend to exclude third parties from political debates – so the public only gets to hear two candidates leaning toward the middle ground of public opinion. A complicated process, labelled 'manufacturing consent' by psychologist Noam Chomsky, seals off the ideological structure of corporate capitalist consumerism from effective criticism and we all pay the price (see the website for links to Chomsky's video on this topic). The process of manufacturing consent involves intense collaboration between the institutions, political parties, think-tanks and corporations that benefit from existing social arrangements and is designed to dull people's critical faculties and enhance their belief that things need to be the way they are.

Meanwhile, the resources that would be devoted in a rationally organized society towards the alleviation and eradication of poverty are squandered. Instead of meaningfully employing the world's labour energies in the production and equitable distribution of sufficient food, shelter, transportation, schools, health clinics, recreation centres and so forth, we have millions occupied in the production of unneeded products and other millions standing around as retail clerks waiting on consumers.

The various components of the ideological structure of consumerism are going to be very hard to unravel and replace with more consciously chosen and sustainable lifestyles. In the remainder of this chapter, I touch on a number of ideas, practices and strategies that may be relevant to this project. I do not claim to have worked all this out. In fact, as I write this, I am in the midst of a major life transition with hopes of making my work more effective in relation to this global problem.

Box 15.3 **Plump Eyelashes or Proper Education** *Elena Johnson*

While lipstick may enhance beauty, it cannot teach the ABCs. But if we were to take the eight billion dollars that Americans spend annually on cosmetics, we would have more than enough money to provide basic education for every human being on this planet. Such are the statistics in the 1998 United Nations' Human Development Report, which reveals how much we spend and how we could spend it better. It illustrates not only the disproportionate allocation of wealth in the world, but the frivolous use of this wealth by the richer populations of the planet. Some additional examples are as follows:

- Europeans spend $11 billion per year on ice cream, while nine billion dollars could provide clean water and safe sewers for the world's population.
- An estimated additional $13 billion could provide basic nutrition and health for everyone in the world. Meanwhile, Americans and Europeans spend $17 billion yearly on pet food.
- The poorest fifth of the world population consumes only 1.3 percent of all goods and services. The richest fifth, meanwhile, consumes 86 percent – that is, 45 percent of all fish and meat, 58 percent of energy, 84 percent of paper and 87 percent of vehicles.

The report credits the increase in consumption in this century with improving nutrition, housing, living standards and leisure time. However, researchers also found that rapid consumption growth is putting unprecedented strains on the environment. The two most urgent problems are deterioration of renewable resources such as water, soil, fish, forests and biodiversity; and pollution and waste, which exceed the earth's sink capacities of absorption and conversion.

The resulting environmental damage affects the poor most severely, locking people into a downward spiral of desperation and environmental degradation.

Poverty and underconsumption are not limited to developing countries. Over 100 million people in industrial countries suffer from these social maladies, according to the report.

The report outlines two basic choices for developing countries and for affluent societies. Developing countries could repeat the environmentally damaging

and socially inequitable industrialization and growth process of the past 50 years or they can progress to growth patterns that preserve natural resources, produce less waste and pollution, create employment for the poor and expand access to social services. Industrial countries, similarly, can continue the trends of the past half-century or adopt more eco-friendly and people-friendly consumption and production patterns.

The report's proposed agenda for action would:

- ensure that everyone has the minimum 'consumption requirements' such as sufficient food, clothing, housing, education, medical care and social services;
- create and use sustainable technologies and methods;
- shift incentives in tax and subsidy toward consumption that promotes human development;
- increase educated consumer choice by strengthening public action for information and environmental protection;
- lessen environmental damage and manage other impacts of consumption – poverty, inequality and shifting consumption patterns – through international action and co-operation;
- build better alliances among the environmental protection, consumer rights, poverty eradication, children's rights and gender equality movements; and
- act locally, by supporting sustainable local initiatives and synergy in the actions of the public, the government and the private sector.

A summary of the *United Nations Development Report* is available on the internet at <http://www.undp.org/hdro>.

Elena Johnson is in Environment and Resource Studies at the University of Waterloo.

Reprinted courtesy of *Alternatives Journal: Canadian Environmental Ideas and Action*, www.alternativesjournal.ca

The Promise of Global Community Psychology

Given that we are addressing the issue of global poverty from the perspective of CP, it is important to note that changes in the field itself will need to occur before it is up to the challenge. A leader in international psychology, Anthony Marsella (1998) boldly proposed an expanded vision and scope for CP that would take into account the effects of globalization on personal and community well-being. This would be a 'global community psychology'. As we reviewed the effects of globalization, the urgent need for such an approach became clear. Globalization may have some positive effects for some sectors, such as improved health and material standards of living, new meanings and purposes for life and freedom from oppressive traditions, but these changes, combined with negative effects, can be very disruptive if individuals are not supported by community structures that help them negotiate change. Changes associated with globalization can increase uncertainty, anxiety, depression and fear. Among groups with less support, these can lead to greater incidences of serious mental illness. Economic disruption and poverty can produce increased drug abuse, prostitution and crime. In short, rapid social change produces societal stress and confusion, which is linked directly to marginalization and alienation of certain groups and to identity confusion, emotional distress and behavioural problems. CP must address both the material and the psychocultural aspects of social change if it is to be effective.

Participatory Democracy

One of the more obvious solutions to the decline of community brought about by the western consumerist individualism is the construction or reconstruction of forms of community in direct response to the pressures that undermine community life. Among the promising possibilities are the following, each of which strengthens local ties: food co-operatives; community gardens; systems for sharing tools and bartering skills in neighbourhoods (see Box 15.4); agricultural, craft and manufacturing cooperatives; and co-housing projects that provide common spaces for intergenerational and mixed-income interaction. Each of these addresses one of the components of the problem – there will be no single solution, just a range of alternative ways of living that gradually emerge and become integrated with each other.

Box 15.4 **On Local Exchange Trading Systems**

In cities such as Ithaca, New York, communities have devised their own currencies, sometimes called 'time dollars' or 'green dollars', to reduce dependency on working for cash. These systems are set up in various ways, but usually involve a directory of members offering skills or products to other members. Time dollars are exchanged, or a tally is kept of each member's credits or debits, for helping to paint a house, baking a cake, fixing a bike, having a guitar lesson or a massage and so on. The benefits are numerous. People get to know each other and pick up skills. They don't have to spend time at their usual job just to earn money to pay for an expensive service.

See http://www.gmlets.u-net.com/ and http://ccdev.lets.net/ for more information

---

Underpinning these practical projects are the processes of citizen participation that can envision and organize them. Democracy must be deepened and practised across all spheres of life in which decisions are made that affect the quality of people's lives. In this case, democracy means much more than simply voting for or against a representative or a proposal. It means an open process in which all those who have a stake in the outcome have a chance to reflect carefully and develop an opinion, on the basis of adequate information, and move towards consensus on best outcomes with others who may be affected by the decision. The culture of deep democracy has not been well developed in advanced industrial society, so this is going to take a lot of practice.

A particular role for psychologists in this connection should be to insist that in order to realize the promise of deep democracy, the values that inform participatory decision-making must be implemented as fully as possible. Think of your own frustrations in meetings at work or school in which a group was trying to make a difficult decision. There is hope. Expert facilitators of group process point to the following values as central to effective decision making and offer methods for realizing them (Kaner, 1996):

- Full participation – participants feel free to express opinions that diverge from the trend of the discussion
- Mutual understanding – participants work to comprehend fully the positions and ideas of others
- Inclusive solutions – Decisions take into account and synthesize various proposals rather than excluding alternatives
- Shared responsibility – Participants who have worked on a solution feel they have a stake in making it work.

When these core values guide group process, not only do groups become more effective, their members learn more and develop leadership skills that transfer to other spheres of life. Community psychologists can be trained to serve as facilitators for all sorts of community dialogues and deliberative processes that are occurring in relation to visioning post-consumerist societies. Community psychologists can also play an important role in researching exemplary community projects in participatory democracy. The documentation of these exemplars can be widely shared and emulated in other settings to facilitate social change (for example Barker, 1999).

Linking the Global and the Local

The ideals of participatory democracy are difficult enough to achieve in local settings. They are even more complicated when national governments and international organizations interact with local communities affected by multinational trade. The challenge for the future is to preserve the advantages of a global economy and market without harming community, environmental and human resources. This can only be done by attending to issues of human rights and social justice at each of the interdependent levels that affect collective, relational and personal well-being (Edwards & Gaventa, 2001). International organizations, both governmental and non-governmental, national organizations, community-based organizations and citizens all need to be linked in new forms of networks and partnerships if the material and social needs of the world's poor are to be adequately addressed. Community psychologists occupy a crucial position at one of the main points of intersection of these various levels. The possibilities for action and related research are many, but all these possibilities require a fundamental shift in attitudes about citizenship and the professional roles of psychologists.

A first step in moving towards roles as citizen-professionals is to think through the issues involved in working in solidarity with oppressed groups (Nelson, Prilleltensky and MacGillivary, 2001). In particular, issues arising from the perceived power of the expert need to be addressed. A mode of practice that will need to be continuously reworked, both at the professional and the personal levels, is to achieve depowerment of the privileged participants in a project, program or campaign simultaneously with the empowerment of the members of the oppressed or disadvantaged group.

Important lessons can be learnt from the advocates of community participation in development planning. A mode of empowerment that has been practised extensively in Third World rural development projects is known as *participatory rural appraisal* (PRA) (Singh, 2001). This practice involves assembling knowledgeable members of a community to discuss needs and establish priorities for development. The practice developed partly in response to the failure of various projects that had not involved local communities in project planning. PRA certainly increased community input into planning, but recently serious questions have been raised. Cooke and Kothari (2001) are concerned that such practices may mask the fact that the important decisions about funding and projects are still made far from the communities that are affected by them. Participation may simply be a form of window-dressing to make projects appealing to donors and to get community buy-in to reduce obstacles to implementation. In some cases, participation has been advocated in order to disconnect development projects from radical political movements. If participants can feel a part of incremental change in concrete projects to improve housing, for example, they are less likely to push for changes in the political order. Cooke and Kothari (2001) advocate extensive participatory action research in order to determine the sorts of things that are happening under the rubric of participation. It is not a matter of avoiding participation in the future, but of ensuring that it is meaningful, effective and equitable.

Participatory solutions to poverty have been developed along other lines as well. Communities in India and Brazil have had considerable success with a process known as *participatory budgeting* (Fong & Wright, 2003). In Kerala, India and Curitiba, Brazil, for example, a major portion of the city budget is set aside for citizens themselves to allocate after reviewing the city's needs. Such forms of direct democratic planning are likely to spread, especially as cities attempt to tap citizen's visions for the future. More direct political action is possible as well and has often led to significant improvement in conditions. Barker (1999) documents how global political and economic realities can be addressed at the margins of power in remote local settings. These accounts also reveal the degree to which all situations are now penetrated by globalization and therefore need to be addressed globally as well as locally. The Students Against Sweatshops movement described at the beginning of the chapter is an impressive example of how local action can have a major impact on conditions far away.

Dozens of international NGOs and thousands of local non-profit organizations are working to transform the global economy in ways that would decrease exploitation and inequality. It is worth noting that the hopes resting with this 'third sector' (after government and the market), also called civil society, can only be realized if NGOs themselves operate in ways that prefigure the sort of deep democracy that will need to characterize social relations in a more equitable society. In many cases, NGOs duplicate the authoritarian bureaucracies of the corporate and government structures they are attempting to transform (Williams, 2001). They do this partly in the name of efficiency and to please donors, but in the long run, opportunities to practise full participation in decision-making are being bypassed.

With these principles and practices in mind, group after group can be mobilized into ever wider coalitions that will be able to organize strikes and boycotts, insist on major roles in the deliberations of world financial and trade organizations, shift government investments toward the needs of the poor, reduce the power of corporate decisions to affect communities in negative ways – the possibilities are endless.

Protecting Basic Human Rights

Finally, one of the most important things to keep in mind is the link between human rights work and poverty eradication (Van Genugten & Perez-Bustillo, 2001). Nobel prize laureate Amartya Sen (1999b) has argued that economic development cannot proceed fully unless it is accompanied by civil liberties, such as freedom of assembly and speech. Governments that protect human rights are ensuring that the fruits of economic development will be enjoyed more widely and reducing the possibility that corruption will interfere with the efforts of individuals and businesses that obey the law. The protection of human rights also means that community organizers and labour leaders can represent their constituencies without fear of reprisals from paramilitary groups or company thugs. Poor people's movements towards inclusion in civil society depend on protected spaces for meeting and protest. In recent surveys of the poorest (Narayan, Chambers, et al., 2000), it was discovered that abuses of basic human rights by police and bureaucrats ranked as high among their concerns as improved economic possibilities.

The United Nations has approved various human rights documents that have been ratified by most countries in the world, but these have been difficult to enforce. Nations tend to hide behind principles of sovereignty and are reluctant to allow international inspectors into prisons where political prisoners are being held. Progress in this area of global governance will be critical to the advancement of the world's poor. The recent establishment of the International Criminal Court is a good first step, since it will bring those responsible for genocide and state-sponsored violence to justice. Nevertheless, human rights violations are still daily occurrences for far too many of the world's citizens.

Chapter Summary

In summary, community psychologists confronting global poverty should expect to work as interdisciplinary participants in a broad social movement (Montero, 1998c). They will need to know as much about issues in global governance as about local practices. They need to be ready to catalyze change where it is ready to happen and to build the bases for change where it will be a long time coming. They will benefit from extended fieldwork in particular regions as well as from experience inside bureaucratic organizations such as the United Nations or development agencies and foundations. Students aiming for careers in global CP should therefore seriously consider starting with international service organizations such as the Peace Corps or its equivalents (mostly for language learning and cultural understanding) and then enrol in graduate programs that allow for practical, internships and participatory action research with international organizations working on poverty, community development and human rights.

I will conclude by saying that there is no right way to go about this work. Each person will have his or her own contribution to make. But this work is complicated and scenarios are complex. We can never know enough to be sure that what we are doing will work. The best corrective for this is to be deeply committed to working with others who share the goal of eradicating the misery of poverty. Only solutions that are imagined and realized collectively will endure. The fact that the beginning of the 21st century found the earth with one clear superpower, both militarily and economically, points to the possibility for a new global order (Hardt & Negri, 2000). Will it be characterized by neo-feudal relations, with special enclaves for the super-rich protected from the hungry masses by armed guards, or by a new level of civilization, where differences are resolved peacefully and the world's resources are shared equitably? My hope is that each of us will find ways to ensure that our work and our lives contribute to a global flourishing of social justice.

COMMENTARY: 'Be The Change You Want To See In The World'[1] *Suzanne Galloway*

I appreciate the thorough and refreshingly positive perspective Tod Sloan offers in his overview of global poverty and possible responses. My understanding of Sloan's presentation is that he identifies economic structures and institutions as creating and perpetuating global poverty. At the individual level, he recognizes that a complacent media and western ideology fuel the problem, especially our addiction to consumption. I respect and applaud the innovative and compelling long-term projects that Sloan advocates. However, with the exception of the Students Against Sweatshops example, I am concerned that these will do little to inspire hope or make change in the short term.

I agree that we need fundamentally to rethink the way we organize our change-making institutions so as not to unwittingly replicate the structures we seek to change. I also believe we need to take action on current concerns. Joanna Macy, a Buddhist writer and scholar, suggests that to make progressive change we need *both* 'holding actions' such as non-violent protest actions *and* also 'new social and economic structures, new ways of doing things' (Macy, 2000). In fact, failing to act will likely diminish both our sense of power and the actual possibilities of effecting change.

It is important to directly and immediately tackle the economic structures mentioned by Sloan, as they are increasingly reducing the power of citizens and governments. For example, the North American Free Trade Agreement (NAFTA) gave foreign corporations new power to sue governments whenever they think their 'rights' have been violated by a particular government measure (Dobbin, 2003). In 1997, the Canadian government banned the gasoline additive MMT because it is a suspected environmental and health hazard. Under threat of being sued by the manufacturer,

the Canadian government removed the ban on MMT and paid a US$ 13 million settlement. The MMT case illustrates how NAFTA limits governments' capacity to enhance or support environmental, health and other public values in the face of commercial interests.

International agreements have also undermined the choices made by democratic governments to support developing nations. In 1997, the World Trade Organization (WTO) ruled that the European Union's (EU) longstanding support of small banana farmers in the Caribbean must cease because it contravened provisions in the General Agreement on Tariffs and Trade (GATT). This case was brought before the WTO by the US government on behalf of Chiquita Brands, a US-based corporation which already controls 50 per cent of the EU banana market, while Caribbean island producers supply only eight per cent. The Prime Minister of Santa Lucia has pointed out that, without the preferential support of the EU, these countries 'would have little or no possibility of participating in the global trading system' (Barker & Mander, 1999, p. 26). These cases both illustrate how, as Sloan suggests, 'national democratic processes are quashed by transnational corporate decisions'.

Sloan mentions the connection between poverty and increased militarization. It is worth noting that the GATT encourages the war industry through a 'security exemption' that allows governments to subsidize corporations to build weapons (Public Education for Peace Society, 1999). Meanwhile, supporting farmers is considered unfair. Sloan also speaks of the need to protect human rights. Unfortunately, the economic options available to do so are restricted by the WTO. For example, the state of Massachusetts passed a law disallowing government contracts with companies doing business with Burma, a military state with an abhorrent human rights record. The legislation was very similar to the state's anti-apartheid legislation in the 1980s. Both the EU and Japan challenged Massachusetts' law as a violation of the WTO's Agreement on Government Procurement. Massachusetts' law was struck down by domestic courts before it went before the WTO tribunal, but it is chilling to realize how progressive economic measures that were once effective are now suspect under international laws.

It is becoming clear that free trade agreements such as the GATT or the proposed Free Trade Area of the Americas (FTAA) have as their primary agenda the unrivalled movement of money – not social equity, human rights or environmental health that are critical to reducing global poverty (Barlow & Clarke, 2001; Korten, 2001). As long as these free trade agreements are allowed to be signed, citizens and governments lose their power to make progressive change in the future. Currently, transnational corporations and government officials are negotiating to expand NAFTA to all of the Americas (excluding Cuba) and to expand the GATT to have explicit jurisdiction over services such as health care and education. Sloan identified powerlessness as a form of poverty. If we allow trade agreements to proceed unchallenged, we stand to be impoverished in terms of our societal resources and our ability to act.

In the face of issues of complex problems with global implications, many of us feel the 'uncertainty, anxiety, depression and fear' that Sloan identifies. I was disappointed to learn from Sloan's writing that there has been little examination of the psychological impact of globalization. I perceive that many are suffering from the thinly veiled despair that Sloan's tone frequently belies, despite his hopeful suggestions. While there is not the space to indulge in a discussion here, I believe that many refuse to allow themselves to explore fully their feelings about the state of the world, for fear of feeling overwhelmed by guilt or sadness (Macy, 1991). We are in a paralyzing dichotomy where many in the world are so impoverished they can do little, while others are so entrenched in affluence and complicity that they are immobilized.

A recent British study would suggest that taking action may in fact be the answer to this hopelessness and inertia. Psychologists at the University of Sussex found that people who get involved in campaigns, strikes and political demonstrations experience improvements in psychological well-being that can help them overcome stress, pain, anxiety and depression. The findings are consistent with other studies suggesting that positive experiences and feeling part of a group can have beneficial effects on health (Reuters, 2002).

Sloan suggests that 'hope is occasionally rekindled as I see glimpses of broadening awareness and possibilities for change'. I too have been inspired by seeing people working together for change, especially at the several anti-globalization protests I have attended. I resonate deeply with Naomi Klein's description of such events:

> These protests – which are usually week-long marathons of intense education on global politics … are like stepping into a parallel universe. Overnight, the site is transformed into some kind of alternative global city where urgency replaces resignation, corporate logos need armed guards, people usurp cars, art is everywhere, strangers talk to each other and the prospect of radical change in political course does not seem like an odd and anachronistic idea, but the most logical thought in the world. (Klein, 2002, p. F3)

I believe the sense of community and enchantment that is available at these events can help combat the malaise that encourages consumerism. As well as inspiring and informing masses of people, mass public protest does create change. For example, a proposed trade agreement with widespread implications, the Multilateral Agreement on Investment (MAI), was defeated through grassroots opposition.

There are many exciting avenues for change provided in Sloan's excellent analysis and suggested resources. I would like to add to his suggestions of international opportunities available to interested community psychologists. I would hope that those interested in participatory action and challenging professionalism would offer themselves to work on issues as identified by grassroots organizations in developing nations. Also, there are many opportunities to learn and contribute to global change in their home countries.

I agree with Sloan's assertion that 'there is no right way to go about this work'. And I also believe it is important that action accompany our theorizing, especially if we recognize that 'ideological processes are always sustained not only by cognitive, but also emotional, behavioural and institutional practices'. I conclude with the adage that we are more likely to act ourselves into new ways of thinking than to think ourselves into new ways of acting.

Note: [1] *Ghandi*

Chapter glossary

capitalism an economic system in which the means of production are privately owned and operated for profit

class society the basic social and economic structure of a capitalist economy in which wealth, capital and power are concentrated in the hands of a small elite class, leaving those at the bottom of the class society with minimal resources and power

consumerism the process that orients a large part of life activity around earning money in order to purchase unnecessary goods

corporate globalization the process by which transnational corporations are able to enhance profits and accumulate, facilitated by government policies and international trade agreements

globalization events, forces and changes that are transnational, transcultural and transborder in nature and which result in

enhanced global interdependence (for example telecommunications, trade)

ideology refers to a system of ideas and practices that sustain social relations of domination and oppression

imperialism the control of land and raw materials and the subjugation of people in the developing world by colonial powers

manufacturing consent a process of promoting acquiescence to, and compliance with, existing social and power arrangements that is promoted through the media and social institutions

modernization the processes of industrialization, urbanization, public education, literacy and democratization

participatory democracy an open process in which all those who have a stake in the outcome have a chance to reflect carefully and develop an opinion, on the basis of

adequate information, and move towards consensus on best outcomes with others who may be affected by the decision

participatory rural appraisal the practice of assembling knowledgeable members of a community to discuss needs and establish priorities for development

'safety net' systems that are set in place by governments to protect people from extreme poverty (that is, systems of the welfare state that provide employment, financial support, housing, health, social services and education)

structural adjustment policies of the World Bank and IMF that require debt-ridden countries seeking loans to slash government spending on education and health, privatize government-owned enterprises, shift economies towards production of exports and open themselves to flows of external capital

RESOURCES ■

Basic Facts and News

1. United Nations Development Program – for current data on world poverty – www.undp.org.
2. World Bank – data and information on development projects – www.worldbank.org.
3. Essential Action – fact sheets and reports on corporations – www.essential.org.
4. OneWorld – News on the general global situation – www.oneworld.net.
5. Canadian Social Research – dozens of helpful links on globalization – www.canadiansocialresearch.net/global.htm.
6. inequality.org – a website full of basic tables and articles on the unequal distribution of wealth, primarily in the United States.
7. Third World Network – news on international development (economics, environment, social) from the perspective of developing countries.
8. *Yes! Magazine* – a journal of positive futures – inspiring stories of progressive change and insightful essays – www.yesmagazine.org.

Policy Analysis

1. The Global Economy Project of the Institute for Policy Studies – excellent summaries of complex economic and political issues – www.ips-dc.org.
2. The Center for Economic and Policy Research – in-depth research papers – www.cepr.net.
3. International Forum on Globalization – an alliance of sixty activists, economists and researchers propose innovative solutions – www.ifg.org.
4. Alliance for Responsible Trade – alternatives to the Free Trade Area of the Americas – www.art-us.org.
5. Grassroots Economic Organizing Newsletter – info on networks of worker cooperatives – www.geonewsletter.org.
6. Program on Corporations, Law and Democracy – research on corporate responsibility – www.poclad.org.
7. CorpWatch – information on corporate power and resistance to corporate globalization – www.corpwatch.org.

8. The Co-Intelligence Institute – catalogues methods for practising deep democracy in various settings – www.co intelligence.org.

Organized Resistance

1. Mobilization for Global Justice – central organizers at Seattle, DC, Quebec protests – www.globalizethis.org.
2. Convergence des Luttes Anti-Capitalistes/Anti-Capitalist Convergence – decentralized 'affinity groups' working to challenge corporate globalization – various websites, start at http://www.abolishthebank.org/.
3. Global Exchange – creative projects confronting oppression and inequality – www.globalexchange.org.
4. Students against Sweatshops – over 200 campuses organizing to improve labour conditions – various websites.
5. Polaris Institute – a Canadian organization devoted to providing citizens with the tools and information to fight for democratic social change. Great accessible, educational materials here – www.polarisinstitute.org.
6. Voluntary Service Overseas – the Canadian version of the Peace Corps (see also Canada World Youth and Crossroad International, Frontier College) – www.vsocanada.org.
7. Bretton Woods Watch – watchdog over the World Bank and the International Monetary Fund.
8. The Catalyst Centre – a Canadian-based organization supporting grassroots action.

RESOURCES ■

16

Colonization and Racism

Marewa Glover, Pat Dudgeon and Ingrid Huygens

Warm-up Exercise

1. How does your cultural group affect your life?
2. What difference would it make if you had been born to indigenous parents? To European/Anglo parents? To parents who are colonial settlers in your country?
3. How would you notice if your cultural group was being treated unfairly?
4. If you woke up tomorrow to find that indigenous people freely determined their political authority and freely pursued their economic, social and cultural development, how would you notice?

The goals of this chapter are to:

- show how psychology has developed within a colonial, racist context
- introduce decolonization work in two societies shaped by colonization
- communicate the urgency of self-determination and social justice for indigenous peoples

■ suggest ways in which psychologists can support decolonization, including practical examples and student exercises.

Introduction

In this chapter an Australian Aboriginal woman, a Maori and a pakeha (white) New Zealander draw on their life experiences and work as psychologists to discuss colonization, racism and decolonization. Concepts essential to the pursuit of well-being and liberation for communities affected by colonization, such as self-determination and social justice, are explained and discussed. Case stories describe practical ways in which decolonization is being pursued in Australia and New Zealand. The authors discuss emerging issues and suggest ways in which psychologists can support decolonization and indigenous self-determination.

Colonization

The emergence of European capitalism, from the 1500s onwards, depended upon systematic exploitation of environmental and human resources in other lands, usually termed *colonization* or *colonialism*. Still continuing today, colonization follows standard processes whereby control over spirituality, land, law, language and education, health and family structures and finally culture itself pass from the indigenous people to the colonizers (Nairn, 1990). The outcome for indigenous populations has been poor health, social disruption, low educational achievement and suppression of culture, language and spirit.

Racism

When the inevitable end is the killing of the *wairua* (spirit)
We are dead living.
Racism means to kill us living. Racism is death.

> *(Tangata whenua workshop group, Auckland College of Education, 1983, in Nairn, 2002)*

Three forms of racism underpin colonization:

■ Personal racism, where an individual's negative stereotypes and attitudes towards other racial groups cause him or her to discriminate against those groups.
■ Institutionalized racism or structural racism, where the policies and practices of organizations deny members from an oppressed group access to resources and power.
■ Ethnocentrism or cultural racism, where the values, beliefs and ideas that are embedded in social representations endorse the superiority of one group over the other (Howitt & Owusu-Bempah, 1994; Jones, 1997).

Institutional and cultural racism 'privileges members of the dominant group in that the whole society is structured in ways that are familiar and natural to them' (Nairn & National Standing Committee on Bicultural Issues [NSCBI], 1997, p.133). As the Australian Psychological Society's position paper on *Racism and Prejudice: Psychological Perspectives* (1997) claims, 'It creates an atmosphere in which a group finds itself in a devalued position' and this in turn leads to personal racism so that 'those who are assumed to be inferior are treated differently and less favourably in multiple ways' (p. 10). Through a combination of these forms of racism, European colonists ensured that their own ethnic group was the primary beneficiary of colonial capitalism, leading to a dominant culture in Australia, New Zealand and elsewhere often called 'western'.

European Ethnocentrism and Assumed Universality

Because of its origins, colonization is deeply intertwined with European world-views. The institutions of the colonizing culture, which uphold and promote European worldviews, intentionally replace indigenous systems and come to dominate colonial society. Europeans have downplayed the role of disease, violence and treachery in this process and instead have attributed their cultural and economic dominance in other lands to their cultural 'superiority'. Western science has been used to construct the notion of race, which was used to construct the notion of the aboriginal (including Maori) as inferior. Thus, racism and colonization have been supported by western scientific theories of human evolution, eugenics, biological inferiority and cultural deficit models.

However, western science went one step further than cultural racism to assume universality for its worldviews. As a standard part of colonization, the European scientific paradigm was introduced as the only valid system of knowledge. Howitt and Owusu-Bempah (1994) describe the orientation of European social sciences as more than ethnocentric or culturally racist. They propose the term *Eurocentric* to capture the universality assumed by European worldviews.

Decolonization

Decolonization attempts to address the impacts of colonial capitalism, racism and Eurocentrism, in particular by making visible how colonization privileges the colonizers and exploits and disadvantages all others. It can refer to structural as well as psychological work and usually begins with making visible the processes and outcomes of colonization. Used in a psychological sense, it has links to processes such as 'conscientization' (Freire, 1972) and the 'liberation of consciousness' described by other practitioners such as Ivey, Ivey and Simek-Morgan (1993) or liberation psychology (Comas-Diaz, Lykes & Alarcon, 1998). Both indigenous and colonizer people have a part to play in effective decolonization work.

Decolonization is a process that assists indigenous people to identify as members of a racial group that has been systematically oppressed by a dominant culture; it enables them to take action towards social transformation. Facilitating an understanding of oppressive processes and affirming the legitimacy of a people's ancestral culture encourages cultural renewal (Dudgeon & Williams, 2000). Members of colonizer groups working on decolonization come to acknowledge their personal participation in the structural and cultural racism that maintains their group's economic and cultural dominance (Nairn, 2000) and to join others in collective work for change.

Decolonizing Australia and New Zealand

Colonization and Change in Australia

To understand the contemporary culture(s) of indigenous Australians and New Zealanders, both pre-contact and contact history needs to be considered. The indigenous people of Australia consist of two different cultural groups: mainland Aboriginal people and Torres Strait Islander people. Aboriginal people have been in Australia for 50,000 or even 150,000 years (Broome, 1994; Aboriginal and Torres Strait Islander Commission, 1998). For Aboriginal people land was not only a source of sustenance but also the materialization of the journeys of the ancestors from the time of creation. Land was not owned, but one belonged to certain areas. Groups and individuals had rights and obligations to their 'country'. These obligations included looking after the country, maintaining sacred sites and performing ceremonies to ensure the country's well-being. Attachment to land is very powerful for Aboriginal people today. Even for those not living in their country, there are still spiritual, psychological and familial bonds with places of origin (for a brief history of the impact of colonization in Australia, see Dudgeon et al., 2000).

Deeply entrenched cultural myths about Australia as *terra nullius* (empty land), about Aboriginal people bowing submissively to white settlers and about Aboriginal people inevitably dying off still inform many people's understanding of history in Australia. These myths, and this historical perspective, function to legitimize colonization and naturalize white interests. Over the past three decades or so, a history is emerging that challenges such Eurocentric myths and narratives and, from an indigenous Australian standpoint, identifies the genocide, denial of human rights, alienation from land and assimilation to European models of society.

Former Prime Minister Paul Keating was the first national leader to publicly acknowledge the devastation of Australia's colonial past that has been masked beneath triumphal nationalist accounts of 'discovery', pioneering spirit and Christian civility. In his launch of the International Year for the World's Indigenous People, Keating (1993) declared that European Australians had dispossessed indigenous people: murdered them, taken their land and smashed the culture, removed children from their parents in the assimilation process and practised discrimination and exclusion.

Amidst a fluctuating political climate in which more conservative forces describe such revisionist histories as 'black-armband' accounts, cultural renaissance has emerged as a key goal for indigenous people – celebrating survival, taking pride and joy in culture and identity and revitalizing language and cultural practices. Since citizenship was secured in the 1967 Referendum, there has been considerable social and political change, marked by such milestones as the goal of self-determination for indigenous Australians; Aboriginal land rights legislation; the formation of the Aboriginal and Torres Strait Islander Commission (ATSIC); the 1990 Royal

Commission into Aboriginal Deaths in Custody's focus on underlying social, cultural and legal issues; the establishment of the 1991 Council for Aboriginal Reconciliation; and the Mabo case and resultant Native Title Act of 1993.

In this wider context of change, constructions of mental health informed by indigenous people began to emerge. There was a move away from the disease model towards a focus on wellness, concepts of holistic health and culturally informed and appropriate approaches (Hunter, 1997). An increasing number of indigenous mental-health professionals began to contribute, participate and reclaim the authority to speak for, contextualize and determine indigenous mental health. As a result, a national consultation report, *Ways Forward: National Consultancy on Aboriginal and Torres Strait Islander Mental Health* (Swan & Raphael, 1995) emphasized a philosophical approach of empowerment and self-determination in the provision of mental health services for indigenous people (Swan & Raphael, 1995). Mental-health training courses for indigenous people were initiated and mental-health professionals were required to conceptualize mental health in different ways. Terms such as 'self-determination', 'quality of life' and 'well-being' have recently entered the vocabulary of mental-health professionals working in indigenous settings (Hunter, 1997).

Colonization and Change in New Zealand

The Maori migrated from Eastern Polynesia around AD 1000 or 1100 (Te Aweko-tuku, Neich, Pendergrast, Davidson, Hakiwai & Starzecka, 1996). Ancient Maori society was essentially tribal, with each iwi (tribe) being a nation unto itself (Te Awekotuku, 1991) and holding political authority as *tangata whenua* (people of the land) in their region. Colonization began in earnest in 1840, after The Treaty of Waitangi was signed by over five hundred tribal leaders. The Treaty allowed for the establishment of a settler government, guaranteed that iwi would maintain their *tino rangatiratanga* (sovereignty) and guaranteed protection over property rights and *taonga* (cultural and social properties) (Durie, 1996). The Treaty promised that Maori would have equal citizenship rights to other New Zealanders, implying equal opportunity and access as well as spiritual and cultural freedom.

An account of the impact of colonization from a Maori perspective can be found in Walker (1990) and from a pakeha (white settler) perspective in Nairn and McCreanor (1991). In contravention of the Treaty, white settlers established a national government excluding Maori and used the British army to force land sales and seize land. Overt legislation and policy destroyed the economic base and undermined the Maori spirit and culture. For example, the Tohunga Suppression Act of 1907 forbade the role of *tohunga* (people with superior knowledge in a particular area) and enabled Christianity to supplant the ancestral gods or spiritual guardians (Roberts, Norman et al., 1995). Following the Maori rural to urban shift in the 1950s and 1960s, tribal structures were discouraged on the grounds that they obstructed the assimilative process. As a result, third or fourth generation urban migrants were effectively cut off from any tribal links (Ratima, Durie, Potaka & Ratima, 1993). Today, Maori are over-represented among the unemployed, the poor, the ill and imprisoned.

Maori have been undergoing a process of decolonization. Past damage is being documented and acknowledged. Maori knowledge that has been submerged, hidden or driven underground is being revived (Smith, 1999). Different interpretations of the Treaty are still being debated, but the process of token reparation is underway. Principles (that is, of partnership, protection and equity) have been drawn from the Treaty and promoted as essential to the relationship between Crown agencies and Maori. Three developments have accelerated the move towards Maori sovereignty (Durie, 1996):

- The worldwide move by indigenous people towards self-determination and greater autonomy.
- New Zealand's reaffirmed commitment to the Treaty of Waitangi in the 1980s and the subsequent inclusion of the Treaty in the obligations (if not legislation) of Government.
- Recognition, by 1980, that Maori worldviews and Maori understandings of knowledge were themselves distinctive.

There is a higher level of awareness and debate of Maori rights in New Zealand now than in the 1970s. In this context, most professional associations (including the NZ Psychological Society) include in their ethical guidelines the rights of Maori people to culturally appropriate service; and many public services have attempted some form of organizational change to provide for Maori aspirations and needs.

Founding Concepts for Self-determination and Decolonization

The following concepts have their base in the activism of indigenous groups and their supporters, rather than in the western academy.

Indigenous Authority and Self-determination – *Tino Rangatiratanga*

A central concept around which change efforts have clustered in New Zealand has been *tino rangatiratanga* or the 'unqualified authority' of the indigenous people. Guaranteed in the Treaty of Waitangi, this means that Maori tribes have self-determined political power to define and resource their priorities. It means that the indigenous peoples are not just another minority group with special needs (Te Pumanawa Hauora ki Te Whanganui-A-Tara, 1993).

Australia, New Zealand and most western countries are signatories to the UN Charter that defines the collective rights of all peoples as the inherent 'right of self-determination' by which 'they freely determine their political status and freely pursue their economic, social and cultural development'. Thus, indigenous peoples have the full right to self-determination that all other peoples of the world have under international law, including all rights to decolonization and permanent sovereignty, as expressed in UN General Assembly Resolution 1514 (XV) of 1960.

Box 16.1 **Case Story: *Kaupapa* Maori Research**

In the New Zealand context, traditional and new Maori paradigms and theoretical frameworks compete for recognition in a research environment dominated by western knowledges. *Kaupapa Maori* research is an emerging methodology that seeks to facilitate and support decolonization and Maori development. The term *kaupapa* means to lay down the philosophy, thus *kaupapa* Maori establishes Maori epistemology and culture as that foundation. This case study outlines the key principles by which a growing number of Maori researchers are choosing to work.

Kaupapa Maori research is distinguished by Maori control and is frequently described as research by Maori, for Maori and with Maori. It takes for granted the validity and legitimacy of Maori, the importance of Maori language and culture (Smith, 1999, p.185). Emancipatory aims are a significant component: 'Intrinsic to kaupapa Maori theory is an analysis of existing power structures and societal inequalities. Kaupapa Maori theory therefore aligns with critical theory in the act of exposing underlying assumptions' (Pihama, 1996, p.16). However, there are differing views on the value of critical theory. Bishop (cited in Smith, 1999) disagrees, saying instead that critical approaches to research have 'failed' to address the issues of communities such as Maori and that the development of alternative approaches by Maori reflects a form of resistance to critical theory. Smith argues that *kaupapa* Maori is a 'local' theoretical positioning (p.186).

Maori control over the research extends to 'control over the agenda for research' (Smith, 1996, p.25). Priorities for research are most often defined by pakeha professionals rather than by the communities being studied. 'As a result, the key issues (as seen by the community) have often not been addressed and the research has often been primarily of academic value' (Pomare, 1992, p. 8). Further, most of this research on Maori has been 'obsessed with describing various modes of cultural decay' (Smith, 1999, p.87) and the common practice has been to measure Maori by comparing Maori with non-Maori (Kilgour & Keefe, 1992). There is an expectation 'that Maori outcomes will be the same as non-Maori outcomes and that non-Maori strategies can achieve the same level of effective outcomes for Maori as non-Maori' (Watene-Haydon et al., no date, p.492). This is an assumption that is rejected by some Maori. For example, Durie (1996) said this goal implies that '…the same measuring rod can be used for all people or that similar outcomes are desirable. That would be an assimilative device, totally

unacceptable to Maori and, more to the point, inconsistent with the finding that health and culture are inseparable' (p.7).

Research, instead, should focus on and celebrate progress (Glover, 1996). It should benefit Maori (Te Awekotuku, 1991). Research offers an opportunity to set right past impacts. Research can support social change, particularly *kaupapa* Maori research that, located within the wider struggle for *tino rangatiratanga*, openly 'addresses the prevailing ideologies of cultural superiority which pervade our social, economic and political institutions' (Smith, 1995).

Kaupapa Maori research is noted for its commitment to the involvement of Maori research participants and their communities throughout the various stages of the research (Ngawhika, 1996). Attending to ethics and accountability is a key requirement of researchers. Consultation with iwi authority structures may be conducted to determine research needs and priorities and to negotiate permission and access to communities.

Kaupapa Maori research is conducted in accordance with Maori *tikanga* (protocols) and upholds the *mana* (power and dignity) of all involved. Different relationships or interactions have specific cultural protocols that apply to them. For instance, 'there are cultural protocols that relate to the integrity of whakapapa (geneaology), which we see inextricably linked to the physical gene' (Mead, 1995, p.3). For Maori, knowledge itself is *tapu* (sacred). This *tapu* is put at risk when knowledge is shared, especially if the result is commercialization. If this happens the 'sacredness' and 'fertility' is lost and the knowledge becomes 'common' (Roberts, Norman, Minhinnick, Wihongi & Kirkwood, 1995).

For the reasons listed above, Maori regularly express concerns relating to the use of research data, security, control and ownership of data. The concept of *kaitiaki* (guardianship), rather than ownership, is important to Maori. As Jackson (1996) explains 'ownership which is a very Pakeha capitalist view' is designed to protect commercial interests (p.10).

How information is analysed is as important as the other issues already discussed. Analysis done in accordance with a Maori worldview uses a broad, holistic approach. The re-emergence of traditional Maori frameworks for assessing, monitoring and promoting evaluation has been paralleled by the development of new and appropriate models from which Maori may work.

'True' Histories for Colonized and Colonizer

Another founding concept of decolonization and anti-racism work in Australia and New Zealand has been the retelling of history. In the process of moving towards self-determination, indigenous people need to focus on an appreciation of themselves, prior to colonization, and an understanding of what happened during the time of colonization. Rethinking history is an important part of the process, as Smith states:

> Coming to know the past has been part of the critical pedagogy of decolonization. To hold alternative histories is to hold alternative knowledges. The pedagogical implication of this access to alternative knowledges is that they can form the basis of alternative ways of doing things. Transforming our colonial views of our own history (as written by the west), however, requires us to revisit site by site, our history under western eyes... Telling our stories from the past, reclaiming the past, giving testimony to the injustices of the past are all strategies which are commonly employed by indigenous peoples struggling for justice. (1999, pp. 34–5)

Box 16.2   Case Story: Decolonization in Australia by Pat Dudgeon

Indigenous people have been actively discouraged from education. The first official indigenous graduate from an Australian university was in 1968. Hence, participation in higher education is extremely challenging but empowering in a number of different aspects.

Curtin University has a twelve-month course that prepares Aboriginal students for tertiary studies. Called the Aboriginal Bridging Course, it has been operating for about 20 years. Hundreds of people have undertaken the course. Of those who complete, some have gone on to mainstream degrees, while others have gone into employment. For all, participation in the course has been a signpost in their lives. Like the birth of a child the experience is one that changes their lives.

Until recently, the true history of our people was not available to us. There were stories told by the elders of families and cultural ways that were practised and spoken about privately, but the dominant society did not acknowledge these. Many of us grew up being taught a history at school that ignored the presence in Australia, or worse painted a negative picture, of our culture and people. We were told we were savage, uncivilized and that we did not deserve the country as we did not put it to 'good use'. We were told that our people did not fight for the land, so even the pride of defiance was denied to us.

The Aboriginal Bridging Course teaches Aboriginal Studies from an indigenous perspective. For many students this is the first time they are offered a different view of their history and culture. The colonial past is close for Australians. Most families have living members that grew up on missions and reserves, were forcibly removed and lived under the various Aborigines Acts where standard human rights were denied and one had to seek permission from authorities to move location, work and marry. Many older people still have their

exemption papers that gave them conditional Australian citizenship. Until the 1960s, assimilationist policies towards Aboriginal people prevailed, hence many students grew up in hostile and racist environments, where cultural ways were hidden and not celebrated.

At the beginning of the course, students are sometimes hostile towards our approach and resist the process. They say that they do not want to be 'political' or become 'radical blacks'. However, in the process of learning about their history and identity, they often reframe life experiences they may not have previously defined as outcomes of racism or segregation. Some have an identity crisis causing them to rethink who they are, what happened in their families and how they have been 'lied to' by white society. The process of understanding their positioning in white society clarifies and explains why they have been feeling negative, angry, inadequate, disillusioned, marginalized and uncomfortable identifying as an Aboriginal.

After this introspective period, students go through a radical stage of anger and fierce pride in their cultural history and identity. During this period some students dislike white people as they are symbolic of the oppressive history and current inequity that our people have suffered. They often make negative comments about white society and white people, which can be difficult for non-Aboriginal lecturers. One of our indigenous lecturers decided not to come to the defence of white people and recommends that non-Aboriginal lecturers do not take these comments personally or become defensive. As she explains it, this is part of the decolonisation process for students. Becoming aware of their history and how they and their people have been oppressed assists in their healing and affirms the positives of their cultural identity.

Relearning history is a key process for the colonizing group also. Treaty education for pakeha in New Zealand re-tells the process of colonization from a less self-serving perspective than the standard story of a 'fair fight' 'won' by the colonizers and resulting in the 'best race relations in the world' (Nairn & McCreanor, 1991). As colonizer people learn, for example, of the relentless array of legislation passed by their settler governments to break down indigenous education, health and community support systems, they may experience critical shifts in their beliefs and feelings about local social justice.

Social Justice and the Role of Power in Colonization

Social justice is a core concept in any process to redress colonial injustice. There cannot be any reconciliation or decolonization to a position of injustice, that is, to accept and collaborate in an ongoing state of inequality, oppression, marginalization, poverty and powerlessness (Dudgeon & Pickett, 2000). Michael Dodson, former Aboriginal and Torres Strait Islander Social Justice Commissioner (Council for Reconciliation, 1995) says:

> Social justice must always be considered from a perspective which is grounded in the daily lives of indigenous Australians. Social justice is what faces you in the morning. It is awaking in a house with an adequate water supply, cooking facilities and sanitation. It is the ability to nourish your children and send them to a school where their education not only equips them for employment but reinforces their knowledge and appreciation of their cultural inheritance. It is the prospect of genuine employment and good health; a life of choices and opportunities, free from discrimination. (p. 22)

Social justice means that the history of our nations is recognized and, within this, the political and cultural oppression of indigenous people is acknowledged.

The Australian Council for Reconciliation endorses the following principles in the achievement of social justice for indigenous Australians:

- Equality not just before the law, but in the processes of living together at all levels.
- Respect for differences, without imposition and interference.
- The right to live as the cultural group chooses.
- Control of indigenous destinies and over social processes insofar as indigenous people wish to engage in them.
- Empowerment and self-determination and the resources to put this into effect (Council for Reconciliation, 1995).

In New Zealand, the Waitangi Tribunal hears any claim by a Maori group (including land claims) that some action of the Crown has been prejudicial to them and is in conflict with the principles of the Treaty (Temm, 1990), thus providing a process for redress for injustice.

Addressing Structural and Institutional Racism

In New Zealand, there has been a focus on structural and institutional racism rather than on personal racism or prejudice. Maori activism and the terms of the Treaty encouraged pakeha anti-racism groups to address structural racism in the 1970s. As pakeha Treaty worker Humphries puts it: 'overt personal racism is well understood. Despite its potential for hurt, this is not the form of racism that undermines the very essence of Maori existence. Rather, it is the denial of difference in ways of being human – imposed by pakeha, over and at the expense of those Maori...' (Kirton, 1997, p. 3). Making structural racism visible usually involves analysing the power structures in an institution and attending to which cultural group is making the decisions. Comparing the intentions of an institution (such as 'education for all') with its outcomes (Maori student achievement falling behind other groups and Maori students dropping out) reveals social injustice. Placing the responsibility for the disparity on the institution itself ('Education system fails Maori') helps to highlight how our institutions benefit the cultural group who designed them and imposed them on indigenous people.

Box 16.3   **Case Story: Pakeha Debate the Treaty by Ingrid Huygens**

In response to Maori calls for dialogue about colonization, pakeha anti-racism groups in New Zealand launched a national campaign in 1986 to educate our own cultural group. The aim of Project Waitangi was for pakeha 'to study and debate the Treaty of Waitangi in order to understand Pakeha commitments under the Treaty'. Targeting government, community and other public service organizations, pakeha educators used adult education methodology to present a more critical view of colonial history and to encourage participants to consider the complicity of their organizations in ongoing structural and cultural racism. Wherever possible, we would facilitate a sense of collective responsibility among staff for the racist outcomes of their institutions' services, and support actions for institutional change. Maori monitors observed and guided our workshops and led separate indigenous caucuses when they deemed necessary.

Evaluating the contribution of Treaty education to changes in institutional practices and outcomes is complex. Government services and charitable organizations, almost without exception, make reference to the guarantees of the Treaty in their charters, aims or constitutions. On the other hand, only a modest number of organizations, notably feminist and other values-based organizations (Huygens, 2001b) have attempted structural change to give expression to *tino rangatiratanga*, or unqualified indigenous authority.

We organized a national conference, drawing together representatives from tertiary educational institutions, local bodies, libraries, women's and church organizations to present their attempts to implement the guarantees of the Treaty in their organizations (Proceedings of Treaty Conference 2000). Their accounts covered time spans of three to 16 years, during which all the workplaces had been exposed to education about the Treaty and some had restructured

to give expression to indigenous authority. The following discursive themes arose from an analysis of the accounts:

1. All the pakeha organizational representatives involved in Treaty implementation accepted and affirmed indigenous political authority – they used language that implied a sense of accountability to this authority and a sense of commitment in relation to it.
2. Many described dissonance, tension and struggle in the process of organizational change.
3. Most had adopted a collective or team approach on the journey of attempting change.
4. In those few organizations where constitutional changes had given rise to Maori authority co-existing with pakeha structures, pakeha described a sense of 'right' relationship with Maori people (Huygens, 2001a).

Reflecting on these themes, it may be that affirming indigenous authority is a crucial shift in the thinking and practice of colonizer peoples who become active in decolonization work. As the constitution of the NZ Women's Refuge states, 'we consensually affirm the right of approval by Maori caucus... [in all organizational decisions]' (Campbell, 2000, p. 61). Experiencing the new relationship arising from dual and co-existing authority held by colonizer and indigenous groups may also be significant: '...a relationship between Pakeha/ *tauiwi* (non-indigenous) and Tangata Whenua... is based on the two groups maintaining their individual sovereignty' (McNamara & Moore, 2000, p.119). Finally, adopting a collective approach among the colonizer group may be critical, since the target of change is shared cultural institutions and practices in colonial settings.

Emerging Concepts and Issues

The concepts and themes in decolonization work by indigenous people have remained constant, since most features of colonization have continued. However, the exploitation of indigenous resources and denial of the legitimacy of indigenous worldviews have taken new forms, as follows.

Continuing Colonization

'We are still being colonised (and know it) and ... we are still searching for justice' (Smith, 1999, p. 34). One example of continued exploitation is 'genetic mapping projects' which attempt to map the genetic diversity of isolated and threatened indigenous communities. Research of this type has deep implications in terms of Maori beliefs about the sacredness and inherent power of *whakapapa* (genealogy). Indigenous beliefs continue to be overlooked as for example, when blood from the umbilical cord and the afterbirth is 'farmed' to be used in treatments for certain sorts of diseases. Blood and the placenta are regarded by Maori as highly sacred and subject to protocols to ensure the well-being of the concerned family is protected (Smith, 1999, p. 100). This ongoing exploitation of intellectual and genetic property, as well as the continued exploitation of land and peoples is sometimes termed 'recolonization' and, when applicable to vulnerable people in all countries of the world, 'globalization'.

The commercializing and commodification of culture is another ongoing colonizing practice, whereby the indigenous culture comes to exist as an exotic commodity to sell and indigenous activities are practised on terms controlled by the colonizing culture, such as for tourism (Nairn, 1990).

The New Assimilationists

When working in collaborative ways and working for indigenous people to establish indigenous paradigms, non-indigenous professionals need to be careful not to engage in disempowering practices. Their well-intended help and theories are sometimes elevated as 'the Indigenous Way'. Although it appears positive and supportive to the indigenous community, it may be a form of new assimilation whereby indigenous people serve as the vehicle for having the non-indigenous person's intellectual, emotional and political needs fulfilled. As Cram (1995) says 'many Pakeha researchers have built their careers on the back of Maori – their research satisfying the criteria set by Pakeha institutions but offering nothing back to the Maori community in return' (p.7).

Non-Maori control over and involvement in the conduct of Maori research remains a contentious issue (Smith, 1999). Some Maori are absolutely opposed to pakeha conducting research on Maori (Cram, 1995), believing non-Maori involvement is unnecessary and counter-productive. It is not only because of their poor record, or because their different historical, social and cultural view inhibits an accurate understanding of Maori, but also because their work can prevent Maori researchers from gaining access to the same funds and data (Glover, 2001).

Indigenous people themselves must remain vigilant as they are still co-opted to continue colonization. Maori have a word, *kupapa*, which means traitor, to refer to Maori people working for the Crown in a way that continues rather than deconstructs colonization.

Endorsing the Unique Status of Indigenous People

As a result of colonial capitalism's disruption to population groups over the past 500 years, including the creation of widespread economic refugeedom, colonial societies are composed of many cultural groups. However, the racism of Eurocentric societies creates a sense of competition for 'cultural space'. This situation is often used and manipulated by dominant as well as minority cultural groups to deny indigenous rights. Typical arguments are that 'multiculturalism leaves no room for biculturalism (or indigenous rights)' and that 'indigenous people are just another minority group'. In decolonization work, it is crucial to endorse the unique status of indigenous peoples while working with the complex histories and rightful claims of numerous cultural groups.

Individuality and Collectivity in Framing Human Rights and Responsibilities

In working towards social justice, a focus on both collective and individual rights is important because, although people are unique individuals, their humanity depends on their social and cultural context. Western democracy reinforces the notion that human rights are held by individuals and that one's political power is derived from individual citizenship granted by a nation state. Indigenous and tribal peoples are struggling to retain a basis for their rights as collectives, as well as to retain a non-derivative notion of political authority – the notion that their political authority is self-determined, collectively, by them. For example, the western process for obtaining informed consent to participate in research is highly individualized. Some information, such as genetic information is collective. Mead (1995) asserts that where the outcomes of research affect families and communities, they should have a role in determining consent.

Addressing Cultural and Constitutional Racism

Developments in European philosophy and science, such as feminism and post-modern social science have helped the western academy to embrace the notion that all human knowledge and social interaction relies on language and cultural understandings about the world and that all people have a 'culture' – the dominant group included. However, typical terms used for the culture of the dominant group are 'mainstream' and 'public'. Such usage renders invisible the Eurocentric basis of the dominant culture while pointing to everyone else as 'ethnic' or 'diverse'.

Dominant group members can contribute to reducing their cultural dominance by negotiating (rather than assuming) the legitimacy and authority of institutions and processes. In structural terms, this involves 'depowering' themselves (Huygens, 1997) and renegotiating with indigenous people the constitutions of societal structures, such as governments, organizations and services. New processes of accountability may be agreed upon whereby practitioners are monitored by indigenous supervisors and authorities (for example Huygens, 1999). The affirmation of indigenous authority has implications for all aspects of colonial life – for the status and methodologies of colonial law, philosophy and science as well as for constitutional, economic and social systems. In cultural terms, reducing Eurocentrism involves revealing and questioning the cultural values of the colonizers (for example Black, 1997; Kirton, 1997) so that the dominant group can learn to 'other' themselves and their culture (for example Huygens & Sonn, 2000).

The Role of Psychology/ists in Decolonization

The discipline and practice of psychology has emerged and grown within a colonial framework and has played a role in legitimizing European dominance and assumed universality in colonial settings worldwide. Many authors, such as Fox and Prilleltensky (1997) and Dudgeon and Pickett (2000), describe psychology as an example of a practice grounded in Eurocentric culture that purports to be objective and apolitical. Two fundamental assumptions underlying the discipline have particularly excluded indigenous people and indigenous realities. These are the assumption of universal applicability and a preoccupation with individualism.

Psychology has underlying assumptions of 'truth' based on collecting facts about human nature, without regard for cultural, historical and political contexts. This notion of universal truths supports the notion of 'progress' that, as time goes on, we will move closer to the 'truth'. Furthermore, the image of humankind is a homogenized one, with the differences between peoples as individuals and groups regarded as peripheral. Thus psychology proceeds to focus primarily upon the individual rather than the interactions between individuals and makes little reference to the cultural and historical context of individuals and groups. This decontextualized image of humanity has assimilationist implications as diversity, particularly cultural diversity, is ignored. As a result, there is inherent racism in all aspects of psychology: in its philosophical foundations, practices, training and in the mindsets of the professionals who collectively make up the profession. At times, psychology has directly collaborated with racist ideology and practice. As Howitt and Owusu-Bempah (1994) point out, academic discussions of race have frequently been incorporated into adverse and oppressive policies for those of other races.

Psychologists can progress the decolonization of psychology, or at least work to minimize the harmful impact of a colonizing psychology, at a number of levels. Below we suggest ways in which psychology can be decolonized at a fundamental theoretical level, at the levels of individual and community practice and within the broader political arena.

Deconstructing and Critiquing Dominance and Injustice

A range of psychological perspectives and approaches provide critiques and alternatives to the approaches used in dominant mainstream psychology. Some of these include critical psychology, CP, narrative and discursive psychology, feminist psychology and liberation psychology. Dudgeon and Pickett (2000) propose that these approaches can be inclusive of indigenous realities and endorse indigenous rights, because they challenge the dominant mainstream, they work towards social change and value the marginalized in their own cultural and political right.

Learning to Practise 'In the Presence of History'

Nairn and NSCBI (1997) propose that psychologists 'must be aware of the cultural preconceptions, both those of the discipline and their own, that shape their practice'. They must be able to practise 'in the presence of history' (Awatere-Huata, 1993; Tamasese, 1993) with a 'strong awareness of the social context' (Nairn & NSCBI, 1997, p.134). They should be aware of the sociopolitical systems in society and how these affect the client's cultural group (Sue & Sue, 1990). Psychologists need to be aware of their own assumptions, values and biases and have a critical awareness that acknowledges that they have grown up in a racist society.

Similarly, indigenous people need to be supported to identify positively with their own culture. For example, to support decolonization Maori researchers need to 'have some form of historical and critical analysis of the role of research in the indigenous world' (Smith, 1999, p. 5).

Affirming Indigenous Authority, Expertise and Self-determination

Dudgeon and Pickett (2000) urge that psychologists be prepared to engage with the indigenous client and community as novices on cultural matters, with a willingness to take and heed advice. Mechanisms need to be developed for collaboration and direction from the client groups, so that indigenous people themselves direct the engagement, whether in interaction between a psychologist and a client or in establishing services and developing policy. The aim is to enable 'culturally just encounters' within which there is 'an active balancing of the (cultural) needs and rights of those involved that appropriately includes their peoples' (Nairn & NSCBI, 1997, p. 134).

The Maori Nursing Council's work on cultural safety recognizes inequalities within professional interactions as representing in microcosm the inequalities that have prevailed through history (Ramsden, 1991). The cultural safety approach enables safe service to be defined by those who receive the service through accountability structures that put non-dominant groups in the position of monitoring the outcomes of cultural safety training and practice (Nursing Council of New Zealand, 1996).

Further along a perceived continuum of attendance to indigenous needs is the Bicultural Therapy Project. In this example, a Department of Justice Psychological Service developed a relationship with local tribes and enlisted their participation in extending the range of practitioners to include Maori experts in healing. Maori clients could work with a Department psychologist, a Maori expert or both. The psychologists did not become experts in Maori psychology, but rather learned to recognize the limits of their own expertise and to refer appropriately (Glover & Robertson, 1997; McFarlane-Nathan, 1996; Roger & White, 1997).

Nyoongar elder Wilkes (2000), patron of the Centre for Aboriginal Studies at Curtin University in Western Australia, recommends that mental-health professionals should never be afraid to approach Aboriginal clients to give them the option of seeing a cultural healer, thus demonstrating respect for the status of such people; and that Aboriginal healing experts need to be recognized with appropriate remuneration equivalent to that paid to white mental-health professionals. As he asserts, 'the well-being of Aboriginal clients depends upon the use of Aboriginal healers' (p. 522).

Listening, Protesting and Advocating

Indigenous people and their allies have used a variety of strategies and tools to facilitate change. Advocacy groups have formed and reformed to organize rallies, marches, petitions, sit-ins and land occupations. Arts, crafts, song, dance, storytelling and theatre have been utilized to educate and motivate change. Political lobbying, upskilling and infiltrating 'the system' to work from within are popular modern-day tactics. Whether tribal elders meet with Government officials to negotiate across the boardroom table, or Maori protestors cut down flagpoles or behead statues of colonizers, all of these actions are legitimate social change avenues. They have succeeded in gaining attention for desperate and urgent injustices, such as black deaths in custody. Psychologists can make an important contribution by aligning themselves with indigenous goals and becoming advocates for change.

Chapter Summary

In conclusion, although there are promising examples of psychology used in the service of indigenous rights, it remains to be seen whether the decolonizing approaches described in this chapter become part of a psychology agenda for well-being and liberation. We conclude with the words of Wilkes (2000) to psychologists in Australia:

> Reconciliation cannot take place until the mean spiritedness of the nation is itself healed .... All healers know that it is no good just treating the symptoms. Together we must deal with the cause .... As healers together, black and white, we are responsible for healing the mind, body and soul. (p. 522)

COMMENTARY: Decolonizing Community Psychology   *Randolph Potts*

An examination of the history of racism and colonization is essential in understanding and acting against social problems faced by oppressed peoples around the world. It is especially important for community psychologists and others seeking to impact systemic problems among 'racial minorities' (such as poor health, school failure, substance abuse and so on) to view these problems in their historical, political and cultural contexts. Furthermore, we need to be aware of how psychologists have participated in sustaining structural inequities that have engendered these very problems. This important and informative chapter originates very far from me geographically, but resonates intimately with major aspects of my own story as a person of African descent and a black psychologist in the United States of North America. I will comment briefly on three ideas presented in this chapter that I find particularly relevant for those engaged in intervention research and teaching: the importance of re-telling 'true histories' in working against processes and outcomes of oppression; resisting assimilationist pressures in research and pedagogy; and expanding the horizon of psychology to include anti-racism, social justice and liberation.

Pat Dudgeon shares a story of being taught in school a history that ignored or presented negative images of the Aboriginal people of Australia. Racist pedagogies have presented a variety of negative caricatures of indigenous peoples. These representations have ranged from demonized to docile and inept and in most cases present a people with no significant history or contribution to humankind prior to European contact. Martín-Baró (1994) identifies 'the recovery of historical memory' as one of the urgent tasks of a Latin American liberatory psychology. Recovery of historical memory means 'recovering not only the sense of one's own identity and the pride of belonging to a people but also a reliance on a tradition and a culture … rescuing those aspects of identity which served yesterday and will serve today, for liberation' (Martín-Baró, 1994, p.30). A similar message is presented in Hilliard's (1998) excavation of elements of African history and philosophy in service of black liberation. Hilliard provides examples of how the answers to major problems presently encountered by people of African descent may be found in the wisdom teachings of our ancestors. Retelling true histories helps in deconstructing the distorted images of indigenous peoples and distorted accounts of transactions between colonizer and colonized. Providing students with the tools for deconstructing misrepresentations of the African experience, reconstructing knowledge of African history and philosophies and constructing a better life for African people are what Akbar (1998) identifies as three critical methods for black psychology and education.

Another critical issue addressed in this chapter is one that is often raised in closed-door meetings of students of colour in CP, but scarcely, if at all in published literature in the field. The authors address a problem termed 'new assimilation', in which non-indigenous researchers use collaborative or 'mentoring' relationships with indigenous people for advancing the non-indigenous person's professional status and enabling the non-indigenous person to claim that their work represents 'the indigenous way'. Psychologists' appropriation of data from communities of people of colour, then 'processing' this information into manufactured commodities (books, articles and so on) from which political and economic benefits are reaped by the psychologists, has been called 'scientific colonialism' (Nobles, 1991). Another metaphor for new assimilation might therefore be 'scientific neo-colonialism', where colonizing methodologies continue but with indigenous people overseeing the mining of data. We see that struggles for self-determination also occur in institutions of higher education and in community research. Indigenous researchers are not always kaupapa but may often be confronted with pedagogy and mentoring that convey the idea that the more one masters the models and discourse of the dominant group, the more secure one's position as a researcher. The authors of this chapter point out that there are valid non-European methods of inquiry and conceptualizations of the human condition, as well as valid non-European critical voices against dominant paradigms in research. Marewa Glover's case story of kaupapa Maori research theory and methodology provides an example of research that is grounded in Maori epistemology and culture; requires Maori control over research involving Maori people; and includes a critical analysis of power inequities.

The discussion of new assimilation juxtaposed to kaupapa Maori theory and methodology touched upon some important questions that need to be further explored. First, what is (or should be) the relationship between kaupapa Maori theory, critical theory and CP values related to system-level change and empowerment? Second, given CP's expressed interest in 'incorporating diversity' and facilitating the entry of indigenous people and racial minorities into the field, is there a possibility of mentoring relationships that do not include pressures for assimilation? We see in this chapter that there are those who see kaupapa Maori theory as aligned with critical theory, given its critique of existing power asymmetries; those who see kaupapa Maori theory as resistance to critical theory, as critical theory has failed to adequately address cultural racism and the politics of culture; and those who see kaupapa Maori theory as possibly a 'local' critical theory. I believe that kaupapa Maori theory may be all of the above – a critical theory based in Maori culture that addresses the history of racism confronting Maori people and the history of Maori resistance. Similarly, critical theories grounded in and speaking to the African American experience have been termed 'critical race theory' (Ladson-Billings, 1997) and 'critical Africanist theory' (Murrell, 1997). Unlike other critical theories, kaupapa Maori and Africanist critical theories explicitly identify their cultural and historical origins and do not present themselves as 'universal'.

I have been very fortunate to have as mentors people with whom I share the same cultural space. Is there a possibility of mentoring relationships with members of hegemonic cultures that do not include pressures for assimilation? Freire (1997) puts the question more generally and bluntly, 'can one be a mentor/guide without being an oppressor?' (p. 324). Freire responds to this question by offering his definition of the role of a mentor. 'The fundamental task of the mentor is a liberatory task. It is not to encourage the mentor's goals and aspirations and dreams to be reproduced in the mentees, the students, but to give rise to the possibility that the students become the owners of their own history' (p. 324).

The authors of this chapter provide practical ideas on the political actions and self-critical work required for one to be able to take on the role of mentor or researcher as a liberatory task. A tremendous value of this chapter is that it very thoughtfully, clearly and with specific examples and suggestions, addresses the role of dominant group people in working against institutional and cultural racism, supporting decolonization, self-determination and social justice. The case story of Ingrid Huygens focuses on anti-racism work among the dominant group, working to dismantle structures of domination and supporting unqualified indigenous authority. In this story a fundamental problem is seen as racism. This is a radical departure from the typical story within US CP where the focus is mainly on prevention or skill/competency building. That story may acknowledge the presence of social injustice, but actions target skill/competency deficits and risk factors on the part of the person, family or community 'at risk'. Indigenous peoples and racial minorities have extensive histories of resistance and resilience, wisdom teachings and other cultural resources relevant to overcoming injustice and traditional systems of healing individuals and communities. I join with the authors of this chapter in calling upon CP to expand its horizons, confront racism within and around it and learn from indigenous expertise.

> And even as community psychologists we often come into the community mounted on the carriage of our plans and projects, bringing our own know-how and money. It is not easy to figure out how to place ourselves within the process alongside the dominated rather than alongside the dominator. It is not even easy to leave our role of technocratic or professional superiority and to work hand in hand with community groups. But if we do not embark upon this new type of praxis that transforms ourselves as well as transforming reality, it will be hard indeed to develop a Latin American psychology that will contribute to the liberation of our peoples. (Martín-Baró, 1994, p. 29)

CLASS EXERCISE

With all participatory work to raise awareness of racism and colonization, it is important to create contexts in which indigenous people are not exposed to further racism. You may want to consider the most appropriate groupings or caucuses in which to undertake these exercises so that participants can speak and share safely with others in their group.

- Using a self-reflective process, consider how you personally, professionally and politically, on a daily basis, contribute to, support or undermine: colonizing acts, redress of disparity and re-establishment of the centrality of indigenous life to indigenous peoples. Are you an ally? (See Dudgeon & Pickett, 2000; Dudgeon & Williams, 2000).

- Plan a program evaluation which attends to and critiques the disparity between universal intentions for all and differential outcomes for indigenous and colonizer service users. Show how your plan is an example of 'practising in the presence of history' and takes account of historical processes and social context.

- Create a research design that validates indigenous epistemologies and methodologies. Show how you have incorporated your own role in a way that is appropriate for your cultural background and how you would ensure your accountability and safety.

- Design a multi-level intervention to achieve constitutional and cultural changes in a service as well as improving service delivery to indigenous service users. Show how your intervention would support self-determination for indigenous people and contribute to 'right' relationships and 'culturally just' encounters.

Chapter glossary

assimilation attempts to remove cultural differences by having the indigenous or minority group discard their own culture in favour of the culture of a dominant group

colonization a process whereby a dominant group assumes control over the land and the economic, political, social and cultural institutions of an indigenous or pre-existing people

cultural racism the values, beliefs and practices of one culture are favoured by the dominant group while other values, beliefs and practices are ignored or suppressed

cultural renewal also **cultural renaissance** revival and revitalization of the suppressed cultural practices, language and knowledge

cultural safety mainstream delivery of services to a cultural group in a way which does not perpetuate colonization or cultural racism, that is, where the safe service is defined by those who receive the service

decolonization process of undoing or healing the ill effects and changes implemented with colonization

genocide policy and practice aimed at eliminating a race of people

indigenous the *tangata whenua* people of the land or original inhabitants of a country

pakeha white settler in New Zealand

reconciliation a movement to bring justice and equality to Aboriginal and Torres Strait Islander peoples in Australia

self-determination/*tino rangatiratanga* sovereignty, autonomy, the 'unqualified authority' or political power of the indigenous people to define and resource their priorities

social justice a situation in which all social and cultural groups have the power to define and resource their priorities

universal applicability notion of universal truths where differences between peoples as individuals and groups are regarded as peripheral

RESOURCES

1. The Canadian Labour Congress has an extensive website with resources on human rights, racism and aboriginal issues. Visit at http://www.clc-ctc.ca/human-rights.
2. The Australian Human Rights and Equal Opportunity Commission has extensive information on the plight of Aboriginal and Torres Strait Island people in Australia. Visit http://www.hreoc.gov.au/social_justice/.
3. Native Web Resources contains links to many useful sites dealing with colonization and aboriginal issues around the world. Their website is at http://www.nativeweb.org/resources/.
4. There is a very interesting world wide web for Maori organizations in Aoteroa New Zealand. http://www.maori.org.nz/.

17

Immigration and Adaptation: Confronting the Challenges of Cultural Diversity

Christopher C. Sonn and Adrian T. Fisher

Chapter Organization

Immigration and Refugees	Basic Definitions	Defining Culture
Cross-Cultural Transition: Challenges of Change	◆ Acculturation ◆ Oppression, Culture and Class ◆ Oppression, Race and Settlement	
Responses of the Receiving Community	Creating Settings and Support Systems	
Roles and Challenges for Community Psychologists	Chapter Summary	
COMMENTARY: Reflections on Immigration	Glossary	Resources

Warm-up Exercise – Exploring Social Identities

Before reading this chapter write your responses to the following questions on a separate sheet of paper. Once you have read the chapter respond to the questions again and then compare your responses.

1. What is your ethnic, 'racial' or cultural group membership?
2. What symbols or markers distinguish your group from other groups?
3. What does it mean for you to be a member of your group?

In this chapter you will learn about:

- individual and community responses to intergroup contact following immigration
- implications of within-group diversity and power for understanding adaptation
- experiences of oppression and their implications for community-building in a new context, and
- responses of the host community to immigrant and refugee groups.

Immigration and Refugees

Immigration and inter-cultural contact have been features of almost all societies throughout history. We can trace patterns of the movement of humans across continents and between islands through information held in archaeological artifacts, written histories and in the pictures and stories that peoples hand down from one generation to the next. Alexander the Great and Ghengis Khan give us images of the invaders killing or enslaving all before them. In much more recent times, we have seen, and still experience, the impact of colonization by British and European countries all around the world. The invasions of World War II saw the ultimate clash of cultures and the deep social and psychological scars that still remain for many people.

Today, immigration is a feature of most, if not all, societies. People choose to move to new countries for the sake of themselves and their families and the new countries welcome them by valuing the skills and knowledge that they bring. However, there are circumstances in which it is disruptive or worse, as immigration may not be by choice and the newcomers may be far from welcomed.

International immigration is now at its historical height. This trend is not likely to change (Martin, 2001) and many countries are struggling to come to terms with the massive numbers of people arriving at their borders. Most of the immigrants are people who are there by choice or because of the pushes of technological change and other impacts of globalization. However, there are also many people who have been displaced because of war and prolonged social unrest, political upheaval, drought and other natural disasters in their home countries. These broader level phenomena are all contributing in varying degrees to increasing immigration trends; the cultural diversification and transformation of host communities; and the displacement of many people (Fenton, 1999; Joppke, 1999).

As community psychologists, we are faced with the challenges of working with those who are newcomers to our lands, as well as with the existing population. Many of the newcomers have faced the traumas of war and torture. They have been uprooted, and their families, natural support systems, ways of life, food and religion have been thrown into chaos as well. We are often also faced by the existing residents of the host country who may perceive that their way of life and the things that they value are threatened by those who are coming in.

A second challenge for us is to understand the bases on which we work with these groups. That is, we must have a strong understanding of the culture into which we have been socialized in order to help our interpretations of the world and the ways things should work in it. We must also have a deep understanding of the assumptions of the psychology into which we have been socialized, its assumptions about people and how they operate. This is crucial to our ability to interact with people from cultures that are different from our own.

In this chapter, we explore some issues as they relate to our work with groups who immigrate, who are refugees or who suffer the impacts of colonization. We consider deeper issues and challenges that may develop following relocation and intercultural contact. We suggest that current conceptualizations of immigrant responses to intercultural contact are limited and that framing the issues in an ecological model will allow us to consider fully the issues of power and oppression in the settlement process. While most of this work focuses on the newcomers, we also examine the impacts on the residents themselves.

To help us in this endeavour, we draw upon Julian Rappaport's principles underpinning community psychology (Rappaport, 1977). He called upon us to consider three key elements when we work with and for groups in our communities. These principles are the *cultural relativism* needed to understand the bases of people's behaviours and belief systems; the *diversity* through which we understand and value differences between groups, as well as the inherent strengths and healing systems of those groups; and the *social ecology of person-environment fit* that guides us in developing and delivering services that aid in people's integration.

Basic Definitions

In the previous section we have used some concepts that require proper definition. These definitions will help us understand the different expectations that people hold and the ways in which the movement of people and contact between groups operate.

Those who move from one place to another have been distinguished into two broad categories, *voluntary* and *involuntary* (Martin, 2001; Ogbu,1994; Segall, Dasen, Berry & Poortinga, 1999). In addition to these two categories, groups can also be distinguished in terms of the *permanence* of the move.

Immigrants are people who have made a relatively free choice to relocate from one country, region or area, to another. This is seen as a permanent decision to make one's home in a new place. In most cases there is a combination of push and pull factors, in the home and receiving countries, that trigger relocation. For those who move voluntarily (for example skilled immigrants, sojourners) there is often an economic incentive.

For those who are forced to move, that is, *refugees*, survival is often the primary motivation. Recent waves of people who have fled, often under perilous conditions, from Afghanistan, Iraq, Sudan and China, fall under the broad category of refugees. They want to escape war, social disasters or persecution. They want to find new lives around the world. Some refugees have stated their intention to return to their homeland when circumstances improve. For others, there is the realization that they may never be able to go back.

A sub-set of immigrants are those who are referred to as *sojourners* – people such as international students, diplomats, military personnel and business people with international postings (and the families who travel with them). They move to another country to achieve certain objectives, within a specific time frame and intend to return home. Although they go for a limited period of time, sojourners still face many of the adjustment issues of immigrants in the host country, as well as re-adjustment issues when they return home.

Whatever the motivation for relocation, those who move are always faced with settlement challenges. *Intergroup contact* involves interactions between groups in specific sociocultural and political contexts and it has implications for group boundaries and identities. The relationships between groups are often characterized by unequal power relations – that is, groups have differential access to social, cultural and material resources. Immigrants and refugees are often in the less powerful positions. This power disparity can involve oppression.

The interactions and influence between groups is bidirectional, but because of the research focus on subordinate group responses, there is the impression that the process is unidirectional. However, there is sufficient evidence to suggest that greater attention is required to understand responses of the host (for example Esses, Dovidio, Jackson, Armstrong & Tamara, 2001), which is often the dominant community. For these groups, the responses are often influenced by perceived threats to ways of living, values and forms of expression (Fisher & Sonn, 2002).

For those who are coming to a new country the transition often entails the severing of community ties, the loss of social networks, resources and familiar bonds. And, of course, the loss of taken-for-granted systems of meaning. The experience is often traumatic. For some, the transition can be positive, as it entails hope for a better future for themselves and their children.

Some communities are able to integrate social and cultural systems from their home country into the new context (Sonn & Fisher, 1998). These systems provide members with social and psychological resources and opportunities for social participation that are central to successful adaptation.

Defining Culture

Broadly speaking, culture includes common values, beliefs and norms within groups who share an ethnic heritage, sexual orientation or socioeconomic class. Culture has been used to refer to those who share a corporate identity because of membership in an organization. Kagitcibasi (1996) views culture as a context for meaning. Essentially, people have argued that culture is knowable and can be described in objective terms and viewed as a creative and interactive process involving relationship between people and their social environment.

Culture, according to Lonner and Malpass (1994), is knowing the rules by which we live in a society. Culture is learnt and transmitted from one generation to another. Culturally based values, norms and behaviour are transmitted from one generation to the next through the processes of *socialization* and *enculturation* (Hughes, Seidman & Williams, 1993).

Socialization is the formal process of learning the rules and behaviours of our culture through education and child-rearing practices. *Enculturation*, in turn, is the informal learning that occurs in human life in our natural settings. The process is unintentional and often reflects the internalization of social regularities and norms required to be a member of a society.

There have been numerous efforts to describe and measure culture and cultural values. However, there is also debate about the all inclusive use of the concept of culture, the methodological problems associated with cross-cultural comparison and the epistemological assumptions underpinning conceptualizations of culture (Hermans & Kempen, 1998).

One approach that has been used is the idea of not simply monolithic cultures encompassing all members of a group, but cultural patterns or syndromes (Triandis, 1996a). According to Triandis:

> A cultural syndrome is a pattern of shared attitudes, beliefs, categorization, self-definitions, norms, role definitions and values that is organized around a theme that can be identified among those who speak a particular language, during a specific historic period and in a definable geographic period. (1996a, p. 408)

He acknowledges that it is extremely difficult to operationalize and measure culture, but argues that we can describe the various forms of cultural and social organization and gain insight into cultural differences.

Hofstede (1980) examined patterns of cultural differences among employees of organizations in more than 40 countries. He identified four dimensions along which these differences can be understood: power distance, individualism, masculinity and uncertainty avoidance. Following Hofstede, Triandis wrote extensively about individualism and collectivism (Triandis, 1995). According to Triandis (1996a, 1996b), cultures differ on their individualistic or collectivistic orientations, reflected in cultural patterns conceptualizing the self, interpersonal relations and social behaviour. For example, people in individualistic cultures view themselves as independent from others and give priority to personal needs, rights and goals. Those who are collectivistic are motivated, mostly, by group norms, duties and prioritize collective goals and needs over personal goals.

The central points are that cultures are diverse, complex and changing. Culture is central to human functioning, guides our behaviour and provides scripts for living. The important lesson for us, as community psychologists, can again be drawn from Julian Rappaport (1977). A key element of our work is to be explicit about our values and their impact on our interpretation of events and ways of working. As our values are typically based in our cultures, we must have a strong understanding of the spirit in which we have been raised. In addition, we must have a critical understanding of the professional culture into which we have been socialized.

Cross-cultural Transition: Challenges of Change

Acculturation

A strong research focus in cross-cultural and cultural psychology has been on understanding *acculturation*. Acculturation involves challenges and subsequent changes to one's culture. Acculturation reflects the adaptations that different cultural groups must make due to continuous, first-hand contact with others (Redfield, Linton & Herskovits, 1936). Often, acculturation is considered from the perspective of those with least power in the situation, for example, immigrants or refugees. While newcomers have to make the largest adaptations in order to live in a new community, the host group also has to make adaptations. However, most of the research has been concerned with the changes that those in less powerful positions have to make. For many indigenous groups, it is the power of the newcomers that transformed their lives – usually not for the best.

A number of different theoretical models have been developed to capture the experiences, processes and outcomes associated within acculturation and intercultural contact. These include mainly acculturation and social identity theory (Berry, 1997, 2001; Birman, 1994; Lafromboise, Coleman & Gerton, 1993; Tajfel, 1981). Some of these models are presented in Table 17.1. Berry's (1997) model of acculturation and immigrant adaptation contains four common responses to intercultural contact: assimilation, integration, separation and marginalization. These responses are characterized by shifts in attitudes and behaviour toward one's own and other communities. For example, group members may move away from their community of origin towards the host community (assimilation) or they may move towards their own community and away from the host group (separation).

These responses are characterized by different mental-health and social outcomes, with integration (or biculturalism) being the most favourable and marginalization the least. There is general agreement among these conceptual models that those who are better rooted in their home culture report better social and psychological well-being (Lafromboise et al., 1993; Phinney, Horenczyk, Liebkind & Vedder, 2001). One would need to ask under what circumstances individuals and groups respond by opting for assimilation or marginalization?

Although these models have been useful in clarifying the role of psychosocial factors in intercultural contact, there are issues that hinder a fuller understanding of the complex ways in which groups negotiate the challenges associated with intergroup contact. There is a tendency to oversimplify and present in a deterministic manner individual and community-responses. In addition, there is a failure to examine group-specific settings and social, cultural and material resources available in negotiating intergroup relations. Ethnic and racial groups have often been presented as passive victims of broader social forces, as lacking in competence (Sonn & Fisher, 1998; Watts, 1994a, 1994b) – a simple case of blaming the victims for their circumstances.

A more sophisticated, pseudo-acceptable, way of blaming the victims was identified by Rappaport, Davidson, Wilson and Mitchell (1975). In this, the environment or culture in which people live is blamed for their circumstances – it is not them, just their culture that makes them that way. Such a response denies the political and structural roots of these environments, roots that are usually outside the control of the people involved. While cultural relativity (Rappaport, 1977) is impor-

Table 17.1 Models of individual and group responses to intergroup contact

Author	Strategy	Characteristics
Bochner (1982)	Passing	Rejects culture of origin, accepts second culture
	Chauvinistic	Exaggerates first culture, rejects second culture
	Marginal	Moves between cultures
	Mediating	Integration of both cultures
Berry (1997)	Assimilation	Denounce culture of origin, moves into dominant culture
	Integration	Maintains culture of origin, participates in dominant culture
	Separation	Maintains culture of origin, minimal contact with dominant culture
	Marginalization	Little interest in culture of origin or dominant culture
Tajfel (1981)	Assimilation	Rejection of minority status
	Full assimilation	Denounce culture of origin and is accepted by dominant group
	Partial assimilation	Negative connotations maintained, not fully accepted
	Passing	Rejection of original culture acceptance of new one
	Accommodation	Retains identity and competes in terms of aspects dominant group values
	Internalization	Internalization of status of inferiority

tant in understanding why people behave the way they do, it is neither an excuse for behaviours that we cannot tolerate, nor should it be an excuse for denying services and help. Similarly, just blaming the newcomers does not pay adequate attention to the different sociopolitical forces that influence the acculturation and settlement experiences – it invokes an implicit assumption that the process is universal and the same for all groups and individuals.

Bhatia and Ram (2001) suggested that for some groups settling in the US, especially those who are 'visibly' different, experiences of *racism* have significant implications for the acculturation and settlement experience. In fact, Dion (2001) showed that visible minorities experienced rejection in housing and in other domains. Such experiences are likely to lead to responses that may not always be the most adaptive in adjusting to a new country.

Indeed, the responses presented in Table 17.1 are from members of the non-dominant group. These responses are focused on the behaviours and thoughts of individuals coming into with members of the dominant group. However, these responses also reflect the official policies imposed by governments in their efforts to re-settle immigrants. As highlighted in Box 17.1, the Australian government has had a series of policies and propaganda campaigns to manage and often discourage immigration and cultural pluralism. For many years, assimilation was the official policy. 'New Australians' were expected to fit in with the dominant British culture. This was assisted by the White Australia Policy which acted to exclude most potential immigrants who would be obviously different in race, religion and culture. The current model of multiculturalism has reflected a policy aimed at integration: the original culture is nurtured within the broader scope of the Australian community. In this way, the benefits of rootedness in home culture are maximized, while the dominant culture is enriched (Lafromboise et al., 1993; Phinney et al., 2001).

Box 17.1   **Words and Meanings in Immigrant Adjustment**

The ways in which immigrants and refugees are described carry powerful messages, often reflecting the government policies of the times. We will use some of these words, particularly from Australia, to illustrate a number of these issues.

Our favourite description of immigrants and others is *aliens*. This is the USA's use of the term 'aliens' for anyone who does not have citizenship – legal aliens, illegal aliens, permanent aliens, temporary alience. (From the Immigration and Naturalization Service website glossary: 'Alien – Any person not a citizen or national of the United States.')

New Australians. The wave of immigration to Australia after World War II saw a shift from British to southern Europeans accounting for the much bigger proportion of immigrants. The term 'New Australians' was used to indicate the *assimilationist* government policies in place.

The Ethnics. In the 1970s, the Australian government introduced a policy of integration rather than assimilation – the policy of *multiculturalism* (an integ-

ration strategy). In some ways, it was sold to the public as a celebration of the ethnic diversity of the population and the welcoming and sharing of various cultures. In this period the federal government had the Department of Immigration and Ethnic Affairs.

While many accepted the multicultural policy, the use of 'The Ethnics' became a mixed term, but often one of denigration, referring to immigrants from non-Anglo backgrounds as ethnics. For those who held assimilationist views, it was often used to target people who, supposedly, received special privileges.

Later, came a wave of refugees from Vietnam, usually from the south, after the fall. As they often came by sea, in leaky boats, they were referred to as '*boat people*'. Although not always positive in its use, it carried a note of respect for how they got here and from what they had escaped.

The last few years has seen a new wave of arrivals by sea, often from places such as Afghanistan and Iraq. Although most recognize them as refugees or asylum seekers, the Government has been strong in its use of other terms. 'Refugees' and 'asylum seekers' convey a special status – just like the earlier boat people. These new arrivals, however, were called *illegals* or *queue jumpers*, terms used to denigrate and demonize them. Of course, it denies these people their rights under international law – and denies the fact that there are no queues, indeed nowhere to queue, in the places from which they escaped.

It has been suggested that these terms reflect a change in government policy back to an assimilationist or even a new white Australia policy. Whatever the case may be, the terms reflect a hardening of official stance and policy regarding immigration and refugees.

Given these issues, we must consider immigrant and refugee responses in a holistic and reflexive manner. We must acknowledge the interrelatedness of people and systems and pay greater attention to the history of intergroup relations, to power issues and to diversity. These factors have direct implications for our community interventions. The notion of social ecology provides a conceptual tool for understanding the multiple ways in which groups adapt and interact. The ecological metaphor encourages us to recognize the embeddedness of people in contexts (Bronfenbrenner, 1977; Rappaport, 1977). This helps us to shift our focus from individualistic explanations that are prone to victim-blaming towards more holistic, system-oriented models of explanation.

Oppression, Culture and Class

Respect for diversity is a core principle of community psychology and is central to social ecology. Trickett (1996) strongly argued that we must consider diversity of contexts, as well as contexts of diversity, in community research and action. Ignoring within-group diversity will result in the homogenization of ethnic communities and will undermine within-group diversity.

In our research with Chilean immigrants in Australia it was evident that they shared a common history and cultural values (Sonn, Bustello & Fisher, 1998). Participants would often speak about their Catholic religion, *familismo,* and *respect* as cultural values central to their group. These values are important in affirming individual and group identities. However, within the community there were strong differences in terms of political allegiances, immigration history and socioeconomic background. These factors had a big impact on the nature of adaptation. For example, once a participant observed:

> If you think back to the 70s during the social depression [in Chile], people who were very much right wing left the country on their own. They were professional people and educated people ... they did what they had to do and so when other people came with government assistance they were very reluctant to mix with them.

Although people shared cultural symbols and practices that were important to community identity, social and political factors from the home country set them apart. In the new country, participation in immigrant organizations reflect social, educational and economic disparities that were evident in the home country.

It is clear that the community has, to some extent, reproduced an internal class structure and political allegiances based on the home culture. In the former country, economic opportunity, education and political allegiance afforded people differential levels of privilege and power. Power and privilege are evident in how group members speak about *educacion*. This notion means more than formal education; it reflects 'moral development and familial responsibility' (Goldenberg & Gallimore, 1995, p.187). Perceived lack of *educacion* was used to exclude and devalue others.

Oppression, Race and Settlement

According to Bhatia and Ram (2001), current theorizing about acculturation and settlement is based on the assumption that all groups experience acculturation in the same way. They argued that some groups, such as East Indians who settled in the US, have histories of colonization and continue to experience racial prejudice. History forms part of the collective memory of groups as they negotiate their individual and community identities, often in the context of ongoing institutionalized racism. Hence, they have strong implications for the settlement process. Not paying attention to these experiences would undermine our ability to work with groups for whom there are such salient factors.

Fenton (1999) drew on examples from Britain, Hawaii and Malaysia to show how the experiences of ethnic groups are constructed and negotiated in political and economic contexts. He argued that in many countries the division of labour is organized along 'ethnic' or 'racial' lines. In those contexts, ethnic groups come to occupy a particular niche within the division of labour. So much so that certain ethnic groups become synonymous with class position. Fenton cites a number of examples, including the Chinese merchant in Jamaica and the Indian cane grower in Fiji.

The creation of social settings is a central part of the adaptation process for immigrant communities. Yet, not all participate or desire to participate, in social settings within their ethnic and immigrant groups; often they seek opportunities for participation in the broader community. Participation in the broader community may well represent opportunities for social mobility – something they were denied in the home country because of their group membership. On the surface, the movement away from one's community may reflect assimilation or rejection of a minority status. The rejection of the minority status can be regarded as a positive achievement. However, it often comes at a cost, including the loss of contact with the home community, feelings of selling out and ambivalence about acceptance by the dominant group.

Close scrutiny of individual and group responses reveals a complex picture of how oppression is experienced and how it impacts adaptation. Birman (1994), for example, argued that Russian refugees to the US use different adaptation strategies in different social contexts. She suggested that in some circumstances individuals and groups may choose to assimilate to ensure group survival. Thus, assimilation may be the visible response in one setting, while integration is the response in another.

Lewis (2001) investigated the role of race, gender and ethnicity in the experiences of first generation 'coloured' South African women in Australia. Analyses of qualitative data show that many participants have a strong preference to identify themselves as Australian and intend to socialize their children as Australians. Many want little contact with their community of origin. The data show that participants often speak in negative ways about their community of origin, in particular about the experiences of oppression and exclusion in South Africa during the Apartheid period. The rejec-

Table 17.2 Watts' (1994a) model of sociopolitical development

Stage	Characteristics
Acritical	internalized feelings of inferiority and powerlessness
Adaptive	attempts to maintain positive sense of self through *accommodationist* strategies or *antisocial* means
Precritical	developing doubts about adaptation
Critical	develop understanding of forces maintaining oppression
Liberation	involvement in social action

From Watts, R. J. (1994a)

tion of the home community and imposed labels, as well as the decision to assimilate may be understood in terms of responses to oppression and colonization. In this case, people feel welcomed in the new community, but the motivation for assimilation and rejection of the home community is fuelled in part by the internalization of racialized myths about the home community (Sonn & Fisher, 2003).

Among these immigrants, there is a reliance on dominant narratives about identity and community that were internalized during the Apartheid period in South Africa (Sonn & Fisher, 2003). The negative stories, experiences and perceptions of life in the home country are often rooted in Apartheid ideologies and racist myths. In that country, ethnic groups were hierarchically arranged according to racial classification and received differential levels of access to material, social and educational resources. The desire to assimilate into the broader Australian community is not problematic, but reflects the internalization of oppression and the subsequent rejection of the home community. In this situation, there is more to the settlement process than the negotiation of the new culture; there are experiences of racialized oppression and experiences of rejection that complicate settlement and community-making.

For this group, community-building initiatives and social identity interventions have to include a focus on challenging negative stereotypes of race and class position. As a part of this process there can be an emphasis on developing an awareness of the social and political processes that impact community and individual development. In this respect, the work of Rod Watts and his colleagues (Watts1994a, 1994b; Watts et al., 1999) on sociopolitical development may be very helpful in informing interventions aimed at decolonization and consciousness-raising about internalized oppression (see Table 17.2). Watts' focus is on developing political understandings so that people can move from the uncritical acceptance of a status of inferiority to challenging the status quo.

The model has relevance for many different communities that are oppressed because it is concerned with deconstructing the social, cultural, political and historical factors that inform the structure of race relationships. It is about raising awareness regarding the sociopolitical basis of oppression and constructing alternatives that can form the basis for positive development and community participation.

Responses of the Receiving Community

So far, we have suggested that immigrant adaptation can be considered within an ecological model that recognizes the interrelatedness of people and systems. We have also suggested that we must pay specific attention to diversity that is reflected in the histories, stories and lived experiences of groups as well as the nature of power in communities. In addition to the experiences of immigrant groups, it is equally important to pay greater attention to the responses of the receiving community. Arguably, the receiving community also creates a set of discourses and understandings about those who come to settle. These discourses inform individual and community responses to immigrants.

Researchers have theorized about the responses of the receiving community (for example Hage, 1998). These responses often vary from acceptance through to outright rejection of newcomers. In Australia at the moment, there is considerable diversity in community responses to the arrival of refugees. Comments made in the media cover the whole range, from pleas for compassion to calls to turn the boats around. These views are expressed within a context in which politicians speak out against immigrants, as they 'take jobs from hardworking mainstream Australians'.

There is a growing body of work in Europe and North America exploring experiences of racism and discrimination among ethnic and religious minorities, including xenophobia and anti-semitism (for example Banton, 1999; Esses et al. 2001; Joppke, 1999; Ter Wal, Verdun & Westerbeek, 1995). According to this literature, there is a growing exclusionary response towards immigrants that is reflected in the rise of conservative political discourses. These political discourses advocate anti-immigration policies and exclusion. Banton (1999) cites literature that shows different forms of racial vilification against black people in Italy, attacks on Turkish and Yugoslav workers in Germany and attacks on immigrants and ethnic minorities in France, Sweden and Denmark.

It is easy to say that those in dominant positions are prejudiced or racist. However, this is too simplistic an explanation. There are deeper questions that must be asked, including what social, cultural, historical and political realities inform these social and psychological responses?

Realistic group conflict theory (Sherif, 1966) forms the basis of much of the research exploring this issue. Some have expanded this model in the instrumental model of group conflict, which posits that perceived competition over scarce resources impacts intergroup relations. That is, the perception that competitive outgroups threaten resources may result in hostility towards those groups. This hostility involves rejection and is reflected in ethnic prejudice and discrimination. Esses et al. (2001) argued that this perceived competition is a strong factor influencing attitudes toward multiculturalism. They also found a strong relationship between negative attitudes toward immigrants and people who believe in a hierarchical structuring of the world (Sidanius, 1993). This work suggests that social psychological phenomena play out in broader socio-cultural and political contexts.

More recently, there has also been considerable attention paid to examining the role of whiteness, as a form of privilege and dominance, in structuring responses to immigrants and refugees in North America (see Fine, Weis, Powell & Mun Wong, 1997; Frankenberg, 1993). Whiteness is seen as useful because it allows us to examine fairly deep and complex ways in which colonization and racism continue to impact immigrant and refugee groups. Whiteness shifts the focus from those in positions of relative powerlessness to an analysis of the social and cultural systems that maintain oppression in specific contexts. A focus of this work is on identifying forms of cultural racism (Jones, 1997).

Cultural racism is often very hidden and is reflected in collective schemas, stereotypes and ideologies; it is about examining the ways in which the images and impressions of non-dominant groups are portrayed in the mass media, as well as through scientific research and inquiry. In a sense, cultural racism is about examining and challenging dominant discourses about non-dominant groups. Mass media is an extremely powerful force through which public opinions and attitudes are conditioned and minority groups positioned and represented in stereotypical ways, if they are represented at all.

An examination of media coverage of government and public responses to the refugee influx allows us to explore the ways in which 'othering' works to distance, marginalize and dehumanize those who are different. These people are often referred to as asylum seekers, illegals and queue jumpers. They are given plenty of labels that 'other' them. Currently in Australia, many of the refugees are in detention centres, waiting for visa applications to be processed – some have been waiting for periods over two years.

Community responses to the issue raise a number of questions, including: How do people wittingly, and sometimes unwittingly, exclude others and deny them basic human rights? What are the social, cultural and political processes that characterize social exclusion and perpetuate oppression? What are the social and psychological benefits for those in dominant positions? These are questions that require urgent attention. They are not only about psychological issues and implications. There are broader concerns about the responsibility of nations such as Australia, the US, New Zealand and countries in Europe and Asia towards groups that have been oppressed.

Community psychologists have an opportunity to make a contribution to promote a better understanding of the refugee experience. One of the ways to achieve this is to engage in community-based education about the powerlessness of refugee groups and about the marginalizing impacts of labelling. The myths and misinformation must be challenged because they are embedded in social systems and everyday discourses that are often invisible to those in dominant positions. At the 8th TransTasman Community Psychology conference in Perth in 2002, all delegates at the conference endorsed and released a press statement condemning the involuntary detention of refugees. In this way groups can mobilize and raise community awareness and lobby politicians and policy makers about issues of oppression and the violation of human rights.

Creating Settings and Support Systems

Social support systems can play a significant role in facilitating individual and community responses to change (Heller & Swindle, 1983; Mitchell & Trickett, 1980). These systems operate in different ways to provide material, informational, instrumental and emotional support. Some researchers (for example Cox, 1989) have documented the individual and communal benefits of social settings within ethnic groups. These settings operate as *protective* mechanisms which *buffer* stressors associated with racism and other sources of adversity; they provide the contexts in which identities can be affirmed and skills can be developed.

Immigrant groups can transfer the positive experiences of community they had in their home countries to the new country through social networks and social support systems (Sonn & Fisher, 1996, 1998) . These systems are activity settings (O'Donnell, Tharp & Wilson, 1993) and can include social and sporting clubs, church groups and cultural associations. In the new country these social networks provide opportunities for participation and identity making, furnishing people with social and emotional support. Members have the opportunity to renegotiate cultural identities and find ways to support other community members in these settings. The sense of community nourished in these settings enhances personal, relational and collective well-being (Prilleltensky & Nelson, 2002; Sonn & Fisher, 1996; Sonn, 2002).

It is important to note that although there are many positives associated with internal support systems, there can also be a negative side to these because they can become very insular. A focus on maintaining community boundaries may inadvertently result in restricted opportunities for group members to participate in the broader community. However, the key concern is with providing structures and settings in communities that will provide members with opportunities for meaningful social roles, identities and networks. These systems link people to the broader society and are responsive to broader social pressures. In essence, they are core mediating structures that are central to the promotion of relational wellness and the enhancement of group and community capacity (Chapter 2 this volume; Sonn & Fisher, 1998).

Roles and Challenges for Community Psychologists

Robertson, Thomas, Dehar and Blaxall (1989) identified a number of possible roles for community psychologists: consultant, evaluator, researcher, planner, networker, trainer, negotiator and advocate. Although these roles seem relatively straightforward, they are actually complex and challenging because they involve the negotiation of values, roles and identities. These negotiations are an essential part of the process of working with different communities. If we fail to negotiate values, roles and identities in different contexts with different groups, we may run the risk of working in disempowering ways.

For example, based on my (Christopher) work with an Aboriginal group in Australia I have been able to identify some intense challenges associated with being an outsider to that community. I am an outsider because of my ethnicity and my position within the University as an educator. I am also an insider because of my own lived experiences of racism. In exploring issues with members of that community it became clear to me that I could unwittingly participate in oppressive practices because of a failure to critically examine my own privilege and power. For example, as part of a research project on Aboriginal students' experiences in mainstream education, I learned that for research processes and outcomes to be empowering we may need to examine deeper issues, including the assumptions we hold about knowledge and the processes that we use to legitimize some forms of knowledge over others. This was quite disconcerting because it challenged the foundations of my previous learning in psychology. It meant that I had to rethink the way in which we work with communities who are oppressed and critically reflect on my own role in oppression. This critical reflection is not easy because it involves consciousness raising about our own subjectivity and limits.

Some years ago I (Adrian) and my colleague Wally Karnilowicz (Fisher, Karnilowicz & Ngo, 1994), received funding to examine the delivery of disability services in the Vietnamese community. While we knew a lot about disabilities and service delivery, we knew little about Vietnamese culture and certainly did not speak the language. Drawing upon community psychology principles, we engaged with leaders of the Vietnamese community in an attempt to understand their perspectives of disabilities, the appropriate ways of delivering services and how to proceed with the research. We were welcomed by the community leaders because we were attempting to work with them and because we asked about their ideas rather than imposing our own. From this, they acted as sponsors for the research, assisting with many access issues.

What we learned from the initial contacts was that our understanding of the causes of disabilities and those of the Vietnamese people were poles apart – from our science-based knowledge to their belief in Karma. Services to be delivered were not to focus exclusively on the individual, but had to reflect the family-oriented nature of their culture, as well as the negative stigma that disabilities carried for the family.

A key part of undertaking the research was honouring the sponsorship of the community and the need to work within totally different cultural constraints. One important way in which this was played out was in the recruitment of a research assistant, with the selection panel including a senior member of the Vietnamese Community Association. He conducted about half of the interview in Vietnamese. One part of this was to assess the language competence of the applicants. However, a more important part was to test out their cultural knowledge and operation – to whom to give deference and when, how to approach families, understanding the generational order of extended families and others. These are cultural differences for which our training in western psychology had never really prepared us, but which are crucial for working with people from disparate cultural backgrounds.

Chapter Summary

In this chapter we discussed different concepts and models that have been used to understand the challenges of immigration and settlement. We suggested that much of the focus has been on the experiences of those in minority positions and that these communities have often been portrayed as passive victims of acculturative forces. Understanding the experiences within an ecological model means that we are able to look at multiple domains of adaptation. Such a model allows us to consider the different ways in which experiences of oppression and exclusion can impact settlement and adaptation. We showed that oppression related to class and race can impact community adaptation in the new country.

We also highlighted the importance of examining dominant and host community responses and policies because these have major implications for individual and community well-being. There are numerous challenges for community psychologists in working with both the new groups and the host community. The roles that community psychologists can take are diverse and will be challenging because intercultural work requires the negotiation of power, values and identities.

COMMENTARY: Reflections on Immigration   *Elba Martell and Eliseo A. Martell*

Reading this chapter brought to our consciousness perceptions, feelings and ideas associated with our own experiences as immigrants. Our reactions to the chapter are shaped, not only by our own experience of immigration, but also by the vicissitudes of other immigrants and refugees with whom we have worked since coming to Canada 12 years ago. Our interpretation of the chapter is further informed by writings describing the effects of the migration process on individuals and communities alike (Berry, 1992; Cole, 1998; Dunn & Dyck, 2000; Galuzzi, 2001; Hicks, Lalonde & Pepler, 1993; Porter, 1997). In writing this commentary we also draw from the work of Prilleltensky and Nelson (1997), Phinney, Ong and Madden (2000) and Rumbaut (1997).

We concur with the authors in that current conceptualizations of immigrant responses to interaction are limited. As we see it, political, social and economical power, ideology, dominant culture and oppression define migrants' and hosts' responses to each other. Furthermore, we agree that using the ecological framework of analysis to study the phenomenon of immigration provides an understanding of the structural forces that contribute to its dynamic nature.

War and other social traumatic events uproot and displace people. Power groups with the capacity to oppress, uproot and displace others make use of their resources to accrue more political influence and material resources. Refugees and immigrants move as a result of oppressive social, political and economic conditions in their own countries. The presence of war and other social traumatic events create situations of extreme vulnerability, uncertainty and powerlessness.

The vulnerability experienced by oppressed and persecuted people reminds me (Eliseo) of a traumatic event of my own. As I was working in the School of Medicine in El Salvador, an earthquake shook the building so powerfully that I was absolutely certain that I was going to die. Windows broke, shelves fell down and I felt that the building was going to collapse. I was sure that these were the last moments of my life and that there was nothing I could do about it. Social events that create this sense of vulnerability and powerlessness on a daily basis make many people leave their own country and seek refuge somewhere else.

For people who have been displaced, there is a deep sense of loss and suffering. In addition to being uprooted and losing their natural support systems, many immigrants and refugees lose the status and esteem associated with their professional standing in countries of origin. This leads to poor self-esteem and the urgent need to recover the lost occupational prestige in the host society. If they don't succeed in recovering their occupational standing, they will risk marginalization from the host society and from their own cultural group as well. We need to remember that, for many people, the status within their own cultural group can be as, or even more, important than their status within the host society.

In our work with immigrants and refugees we have observed many within-group responses to immigration. We have noticed that responses to the migration process are highly determined by structural conditions of the host society at a particular time. The dominant ideology of the host society creates the cultural framework for dealing with human diversity in general, and immigration in particular. This framework is reflected in laws, policies, social roles, hiring policies, access to resources, cultural stereotypes and even jokes. The political situation of the host society plays a role in the acceptance or rejection of immigrants and refugees.

Host societies usually assign a role to immigrants and refugees. We can see these roles through the media: a particular ethnic group always depicted as taxi drivers; others as housemaids. These stereotypes contribute to stigmatization and inferiorization of entire cultures.

Institutions, in turn, reflect the values of the dominant culture. When social or health services employ a foreign-trained professional as an interpreter, it is often difficult for the organization to see this person as other than a translator. This situation limits the possibility for more skilled employment within the agency.

In our experience, immigrant communities import their own customs to the new countries. Sometimes the re-enactment of old customs can lead to a healthy adaptation, but sometimes to the creation of ghettos that reinforce the sense of isolation from the host community.

We resonate with the authors' definition of culture as a dynamic set of norms, largely determined by temporal and geographical parameters affecting not only the immigrant community, but the host society as well. In our experience, the dominant culture tends to see itself as monocultural; but in fact most societies are multicultural and heterogenous. Despite attempts to homogenize the population, differences in ability, economic power, gender, race and sexual orientation disrupt attempts to paint the host society as harmonious and homogeneous.

The authors mention some of the possible roles that community psychologists may play in working with immigrant and refugee populations. They also describe what make these roles challenging. From our perspective, we think that an understanding of the interplay of structural issues, oppression and power imbalances might help to enhance the efficacy of those roles. Although the authors explain the role of culture and oppression, we feel that people working with immigrants and refugees need to learn more about the dominant culture and how many of the elements mentioned

in regard to the immigrant groups can be applied to the dominant culture as well.

The authors make reference to Watts' model of sociopolitical development (Table 17.2); they mention the need to deconstruct the social, cultural, political and historical factors that inform the structure of race relationship in different communities. We believe that people working with immigrants need to go through that process in regard to their own culture. As a worker, your economic position, societal status, race, ethnicity and value-orientation will very much influence the nature of the help extended to immigrants and refugees.

In conclusion, we believe that the interaction between immigrant and host communities must lead to mutual transformation. Both communities should arrive at a more progressive place where reciprocity prevails over stereotypes and where respect for diversity outweighs patterns of discrimination. This experience is not necessarily a pleasant one, as it challenges our own assumptions about others, about ourselves and about our culture.

Chapter glossary

acculturation the learning of a new culture and replacement of parts of one's old culture as a result of immigration or other forms of sustained intercultural contact

assimilation the loss of the features and practices of one's home culture and the adoption of the culture of the host (or dominant) culture. Often a feature of immigration policies which attempt to promote only the dominant culture

enculturation the learning of the rules and behaviours of one's culture through informal means, for example, observations

indigenous people the 'native' or traditional inhabitants of a land or area

intercultural contact the interaction across time of people from two or more different cultural groups. May be associated with differences in power and the subjugation of the less powerful group

integration the adaptation of newcomers and host culture so that there is a balance between features of the host culture and that of the newcomers – a process of accommodation in which both parties make changes

immigrants people who make a free choice to live in a new location or in a new culture, on a permanent basis

multiculturalism a policy of integration in which the less

dominant culture is nurtured within the broader dominant culture. A policy opposite to assimilation

refugees people who are forced to leave their home countries or locations for a new one because of factors such as war, natural disasters or political or religious oppression

socialization the formal ways in which people learn the rules and values of their culture – often in schooling

sojourners people who choose to live in a new country or culture for a defined period to achieve a specified outcome, for example overseas students or employees on international postings

RESOURCES

1. There are many resources available that can assist in working towards change. The United Nations High Commission for Refugees' website is one that has relevant information about the plight of refugees: http://www.unhcr.ch/cgi-bin/texis/vtx/home.

2. The European Research Centre on Migration and Ethnic Relations contains research reports and information about training in this area with a focus on issues in European countries. http://www.eumc.eu.int/.

3. There are other pragmatic strategies for working towards the emancipation of immigrants and refugees. These strategies can include writing to newspapers to present alternative views about issues; connecting with local community-based groups (for example the Refugee Rights Action Network in Perth, Australia) and others in your local community or area. Visit http://www.immi.gov.au/.

4. A number of journals have very good special issues related to this topic, bringing together research from a number of countries and perspectives. See, for example, *Journal of Social Issues* (2001) **57**(3); *Journal of Community and Applied Social Psychology* (2000) **10**(5).

18

Gender, Power and Community Psychology

Heather Gridley and Colleen Turner

Chapter Organization

Historical Context	◆ Why a Women's Movement?

Ecology, Prevention and Community in Gendered Contexts	◆ Ecology ◆ Prevention ◆ Community

Power, Subjectivity and Reflexivity, Diversity and Partnership in Gendered Contexts	◆ Power ◆ Subjectivity and Reflexivity ◆ Diversity ◆ Partnership

Vision and Values Guiding Feminist Community Work	Chapter Summary

COMMENTARY: Social Justice Includes Feminism	

Class Exercise	Glossary	Resources

Warm-up Exercise

1. Think of some ways that gender impacts on your life.
2. What would you be more (or less) able to do if you had been born a different sex? Would this be the case if you had been born somewhere else in the world?
3. If you awoke one day to discover that gender equality had miraculously been achieved worldwide, how would you notice?

The goals of this chapter are to:

- review the history of gender inequality in society and within psychology
- examine community psychology's (CP) potential contribution to gender equality
- identify and encourage feminist visions of wellness and liberation for women, and
- consider how we can participate in realizing such visions and values, as community psychologists and in our personal lives.

> Women
> constitute half the world's population,
> perform nearly two-thirds
> of its work hours,
> receive one-tenth of the world's income
> and own less than one-hundredth
> of the world's property.
>
> *(United Nations Report, 1996)*

A quarter of a century since feminism's 'second wave' was at its peak, the movement's basic aim of equality for women is far from being achieved on a global scale. A United Nations Population Fund report (2000) describes gender discrimination as a global health issue, directly associated with poverty, poor health and rapid population growth. In Beijing in 1995, the Fourth World Conference on Women adopted the slogan 'Women's rights are human rights', listing in its Platform for Action several key areas of concern to all humanity where women's rights still needed to be addressed. Under each of these headings were calls for global and local action. The areas most relevant and amenable to CP research and practice are related to health and well-being, participation in all levels of decision-making, power-sharing in a non-violent and just society, action on violence against women and equality of access to resources. Central to all of these is the operation of power.

In this chapter we examine CP's historical and potential contribution to gender equality. What would a vision of well-being and liberation for women around the world be and how can we know if we are part of the problem or part of the solution, as community psychologists and in our personal lives? If sexism is the problem, are feminisms the solution? Selected examples are used to anchor the chapter.

We write from within our 'natural communities' (Huygens, 1988) as white Anglo-Celtic Australian women, feminist community psychologists working for change within and beyond our profession.

Historical Context

Because We're Women

Because women's work is never done and is underpaid or boring or repetitious and we're the first to get the sack and what we look like is more important than what we do and if we get raped it's our fault and if we get bashed we must have provoked it and if we raise our voices we're nagging bitches and if we enjoy sex we're nymphos and if we don't we're frigid and if we love women it's because we can't get a 'real' man and if we ask our doctor too many questions we're neurotic and/or pushy and if we expect community care for children we're selfish and if we stand up for our rights we're aggressive and 'unfeminine' and if we don't we're typical weak females and if we want to get married we're out to trap a man and if we don't we're unnatural and because we still can't get an adequate safe contraceptive but men can walk on the moon and if we can't cope or don't want a pregnancy we're made to feel guilty about abortion and ... for lots and lots of other reasons we are part of the women's liberation movement.

Joyce Stevens (1975), Women's Electoral Lobby (Australia)

Why a Women's Movement?

Written for International Women's Day 1975, this declaration has a decidedly western flavour, reflecting the priorities that gained attention as women in relatively affluent countries began to raise their collective voices. Yet throughout history every society has practised some form of oppression of women. In response there have been ongoing waves of feminist consciousness and action.

Box 18.1 **Christianity's Fluctuating Track Record on Women** (drawn from Ellerbe, 1995)

■ Jesus Christ: included women among his friends and followers, affirming Mary's (non-traditional) *and* Martha's (traditional) roles.

■ Council of Macon (584AD) – 43 bishops and 20 other men voted, after lengthy debate, about whether women were human and had souls – 32 voted yes, 31 no!

■ Middle Ages – Hildegard of Bingen and other educated abbesses exercised much power within and beyond their convents, until reined in and restricted to contemplative, cloistered roles by papal decree.

■ The burning times – women were blamed for the Black Death pandemic, resulting in the 'holocaust' of up to a million women. Any woman who dared to cure without having studied (from which they were

banned) was to be declared a witch (*Malleus Malefi-carum – Hammer of the Witches*, manual of the Inquisition).

■ Early 21st century: Women priests ordained in (some) Anglican/episcopalian dioceses – but fewer permit bishops and Catholic and Orthodox churches have barred debate on the subject.

■ Churches are often in the forefront of conservative backlash on reproductive rights, blocking international aid funds for family planning programs, promoting homophobic discourses and retaining narrow definitions of women's roles.

■ Sexual abuse scandals challenge the patriarchal structures that have enabled and even sanctioned abuse on a previously unimagined scale.

In the 20th-century western world, the timing of so-called 'second wave feminism' paralleled the emergence of CP in the late 1960s. From the 1970s onwards, feminism drew on a range of perspectives, including liberal feminism (which emphasized equality), Marxist feminism (which made links with class and other forms of oppression), radical feminism (which argued that women should distance themselves from male norms), feminist psychology, postmodern feminism and feminisms within a range of cultural contexts (some African-American women preferred to describe themselves as 'womanist'). These various feminisms all work towards the common goal of improving women's lives. Each has its own views on how improvements may be achieved and indeed what constitutes improvement. The vigorous ongoing debates among feminisms can confuse outsiders and frustrate feminist theorists and activists themselves – yet why would it be assumed or even desirable, that all women, or all feminists, speak with a unified voice? (For a fuller introduction to feminist thought, see Tong, 1998).

Within psychology, both feminist psychologists and community psychologists developed critiques of mainstream psychology, while within the wider community, feminism and CP took their place alongside related human-rights movements, such as the gay liberation, civil rights, anti-apartheid and peace movements. In Australia and Aotearoa New Zealand in the same decade, Aboriginal and Maori activists were making their presence felt.

Feminist psychologists directed their critique towards psychology's 'mismeasure of women' (Tavris, 1992) and the individualization and pathologization of women's collective distress (Astbury, 1996; Caplan, 1995). Women had not participated equally in the establishment of psychology as a science and feminists mistrusted its application to women's lives. 'Psychology has nothing to say about what women are really like ... essentially because psychology does not know' (Weisstein, 1993, p. 197).

The 1970s feminist slogan 'the personal is political' meant that psychology was (and still is) fertile ground for feminist action and that political questions came to be seen as psychology's business. But some early attempts to paint women into the psychological picture were themselves subject to critique as perpetuating victim-blaming (for example by suggesting that women's 'fear of success' was the real reason for the glass ceiling) or reinforcing gendered stereotypes of masculinity and femininity – and leaving oppressive, inequitable social and organizational structures unchallenged (Mednick, 1989). Examining texts and courses on the psychology of women, Crowley-Long (1998, p. 128) concludes that 'feminist psychology has adopted a much too narrow political focus' in drawing almost exclusively from liberal feminist frameworks and positivist methods and not enough from radical and socialist alternatives. She argues that a broader frame of reference would be more inclusive of marginalized groups and more sensitive to 'social and economic forces that shape the lives of women from many diverse backgrounds'.

Community psychologists' critique of mainstream psychology emerged from its parent sub-disciplines of community mental health (clinical psychology) and applied social psychology. Their concerns focused less on measurement and therapy and more on the settings in which psychological research and practice took place – they set about broadening their applications (for example, prevention and macro-level intervention) and taking account of contexts (ecology and community). Thus they distanced themselves from 'the personal' as reflecting psychology's traditional victim-blaming stance and tended to take up 'public' ahead of 'private' causes as their intervention targets.

Anne Mulvey's (1988) landmark article noted commonalities between CP and feminism – they shared similar social critiques of victim-blaming ideologies, pushed beyond individual, adjustment–oriented solutions, called for new paradigms beyond the fragmentation and mystification of traditional disciplines and developed similar change models and strategies. Both focused on social policy, prevention ahead of 'cure,' advocacy, empowerment and the demystification of experts. Feminist consciousness-raising groups resonated with community psychologists' support for self-help groups and consumer-based movements.

But shared values and goals and the common experience of 'swimming against the tide' of mainstream psychology did not lead to much integration between the two emergent sub-disciplines. Even now, references to CP rarely appear in feminist psychology literature, while feminist community psychologists have struggled to have 'women's issues' acknowledged within CP's agenda. Replication of patriarchal patterns and power structures (Cohen & Gutek, 1991; Mulvey, 1988; Oliver & Hamerton, 1992) has seen a predominance of men in CP research, teaching, leadership and publications, while frontline practitioners and students are increasingly likely to be female, not to mention at least 50% of the populations we purport to serve. In organized CP (for example Society for Community Research & Action (SCRA), the Australian Psychological Society College of Community Psychologists), women are likely to be in maintenance or 'housekeeping' roles such as membership or professional development, while more prestigious and public roles (for example president, journal editor) have been predominantly (though not exclusively) 'men's business'.

Why does this matter? Salazar and Cook (2001) examined the nature and representation of research on violence against women in CP journals as compared with mainstream psychology literature. Useful research would be characterized by attention to diversity in participant selection, action-oriented methods and macro- rather than micro-level analyses. Although these characteristics were indeed more prevalent in CP research than elsewhere, there were so few articles on violence against women that the impact of the difference remains questionable.

How far have we come? The special double issue of the *American Journal of Community Psychology* (Bond et al., 2000a, 2000b) provides a rich menu of feminist research and action in CP. The special issue was organized around seven themes linking CP with feminist theory and research: contextualized understanding; attention to diversity; speaking from the standpoints of oppressed groups; collaboration; multi-level, multi-method approaches; reflexivity; and action orientation. In the same year, a special issue of the international journal *Feminism and Psychology* (Gavey, Lapsley & Cram, 2001) was dedicated to feminist psychology in Aotearoa, New Zealand, with significant CP content. Fox and Prilleltensky (1997) brought together a range of critical perspectives from the margins of psychology, enabling the possibility of dialogue between community and feminist psychologies as well as other non-mainstream approaches.

Ecology, Prevention and Community in Gendered Contexts

What do CP's founding fathers (and mothers) have to say about feminism/women's experiences? How far do their principles/approaches take us?

Ecology

CP's primary departure point from mainstream psychology was/is its emphasis on the central importance of context to any understanding of human behaviour. In practice, this might mean conducting research in naturalistic settings, working with family or community systems rather than individuals or seeking sociopolitical rather than intrapsychic explanations for presenting problems. Similarly, feminist theorists have argued for alternatives to reductionist approaches that narrow down and systematically decontextualize the phenomena to be studied.

Ecological models that promote holistic understandings of the interrelatedness of all human experiences can be helpful in addressing structural inequalities based on gender. For example, changes that occur in women's lives that are related to their reproductive systems (such as menopause as disease) are often represented as purely biomedical problems to be 'cured'. Psychological theories then add an 'emotional disorder' layer (for example PMS, 'empty nest syndrome') necessitating therapeutic 'treatment'. An ecological perspective would take account of society's expectations and valuing of women at different points in their lives – for example, the demands of parenting adolescents, caring for ageing parents, renegotiating work roles, having less access to retirement fund benefits and finding oneself devalued by the appearance of grey hair (which for men is sometimes considered an asset), all need to be factored into any understanding of women's lives at mid-life – not to mention the freedom and energy that might be available to post-menopausal women.

From a feminist perspective, the downside of ecological and systems models is that they usually lack any power analysis and can run the risk of promoting homeostatic 'status quo' solutions to problems that require fundamental change. Just as biological metaphors do not serve women well, with their implication that 'biology is destiny', ecological explanations can lead to victim-blaming or unwarranted implication of less powerful groups or individuals in causal explanations. Between the rhetoric of terms such as 'ecology' and 'prevention' and the reality that entrenched power is not easily given away, we need to keep asking what safeguards need to be in place to ensure that interventions don't work against the groups they were intended to assist. False Memory Associations and lobbying by men aggrieved by family law enforcement, are examples of backlash to apparent concessions to women's rights to safety and economic security.

Effective ecological conceptualizations must factor in a social justice component if they are to pave the way for ecological (systems-level) interventions that lead to social change. Theoretical models must involve naming of power differentials along with recognition of structural inequality as a primary cause of personal distress.

Prevention

CP students soon become familiar with the cliff rescue metaphor of prevention – the notion that it is better to repair the fence at the top of the cliff than to supply the ambulance and paramedics to rescue those who fall over the edge. But have we actually improved someone's quality of life if all we've done is remove a potential hazard? Suicide prevention programs that focus on taking sheets from prisoners' beds or raising the safety rails on a bridge do nothing to address the poverty and desperation behind disproportionate incarceration rates among indigenous communities or suicide rates among young men in rural communities.

It is also obvious that ambulances are still needed as well as fences. And prevention strategies can gain much from the experiences of those who have jumped or fallen over the metaphorical cliff. People living with HIV/AIDS continue to be heavily involved in designing and delivering prevention strategies, including 'safe sex' education campaigns.

A prevention approach to depression in women should address the oppression and abuse that underpin much of the everyday experience of women across a range of circumstances (Bostock, 1997). But many approaches that claim to be 'preventive' are narrowly focused on medical explanations and ameliorative solutions. This is all too evident in mental health initiatives that confine prevention to early identification of genetic predispositions to bipolar disorder, for example, or early detection of symptoms to encourage speedier referral for treatment, often with antidepressant medication only.

Community

There is increasing recognition in international development contexts that women's empowerment and education are the keys to real change in disadvantaged communities (Black, 1993; Van der Gaag, 1995). Grassroots community campaigns have often involved women fighting for the right to control their fertility, to limit the sale of war toys or to bear witness to the 'disappearance' of their children under repressive regimes.

The downside of community metaphors lies in the fact that a focus on public aspects of community can render women invisible by prioritizing 'public' over 'private' concerns. The minimization of domestic violence by police and other authorities as less serious than other forms of crime is a prime example. The uncritical acceptance of community as a 'spray-on solution' (Bryson & Mowbray, 1981) can be fundamentalist when it means the subordination of legitimate concerns for the greater good – women who were urged to leave the paid workforce to set up house in the post-World War II period were sacrificed to a narrow vision of community rebuilding. In such cases, a focus on community can have the effect of submerging women's voices to the louder notes (of usually male, often patriarchal leaders) within particular communities.

As early as 1981, when the concept of community had been in currency in public policy arenas for a decade, some analysts were questioning its claims to radicalism in the light of its 'systems-preserving effect' (Bryson & Mowbray, 1981, p. 255). They argued that the usage of the term 'community' often suited conservative interests in its emphasis on an essential unity or harmony of interests (rather than separation of interests from, say, a class or gender perspective); and 'in its use in characterizing a management model geared to minimizing government expenditure' (p. 265). The latter point has particular relevance for women, who are frequently expected to provide unpaid labour involved in what has come to be known as 'emotion work' (Winefield, 2001) – volunteering, telephone counselling, caregiving – when government responsibilities are devolved to communities as a cost-saving measure. Moreover, community consultation is a feel-good, widely supported notion, but can act to rubber stamp decisions imposed by power elites.

Power, Subjectivity and Reflexivity, Diversity and Partnership in Gendered Contexts

Power

> Psychology, with its individual focus, has particular difficulty understanding power relations as socially constructed frameworks that may be expressed by individuals, but are created in larger social contexts. (Burman, 1997, p. 146)

The operation of power is central to all feminist analyses. Why do so many men use violence against women? 'Because they can', was one police superintendent's pithy summing up. Whether measured in terms of information, institutionalized authority, resources, decision-making, coercion or privilege, power differentials can be seen to constrain or expand the choices available to women and men in a wide range of social contexts – not the pseudo-choice of coffee blends or mobile phone covers, but real choices about how life is to be lived, individually and collectively.

Feminist understandings of power have shifted from unitary notions of something bad when men have it and good when women have it towards recognition of its multiple levels of operation (Kitzinger, 1991). Recent theorizing and research on the operation of power between women provides examples of these complexities (Beckwith, 1999).

Box 18.2   Women's Work – Whose Labour?

The First World has become reliant on the skills of an elite of professional, educated women and expects them to continue in paid work, often for fifty or more hours per week. But neither the original 19th-century 'eight-hour day' nor current campaigns factored in the second (domestic) shift worked by many women or the 'emotion work' that is primarily women's work (Winefield, 2001).

Poor women have always acted as housemaids, wet nurses or nannies to wealthy families. Globalization of the control of resources now means that women from poor countries such as the Philippines, Mexico or Eastern Europe are forced by economic necessity to leave their own children behind (or sometimes, to prostitute them) to provide cheap immigrant labour, often illegal, in more affluent countries.

The exploitation of women in domestic work reproduces and widens the First/Third World divide and makes real and reciprocal feminist alliances between women structurally more difficult, both within the First World and between the First and Third Worlds (cf. Anderson, 2000). Privileged women with a conscience, like Naomi Wolf (2001), can see the inequities operating in their (our) lives:

> I learned that if I sat in a park with our baby and chatted with an immigrant nanny who was wiping the drool of a white baby ... within minutes she would show me a photo of her own children far away, whom she might not have seen for years. And her eyes would fill with tears ... These women must often cross oceans and leave their children, big kids and small, with relatives. They often live in rooms at the margins of other people's families ....so that they (the children) can have school uniforms and good food, education and a better chance at life. (p. 219).

Power is not something we have but something we swim in, a matter of discourse and practice rather than quantity. And like racism, its operation in sexist terms has become more subtle – it is rare, at least in western society, for women to be openly referred to as property, yet the notion is far from dead. A range of gendered power disparities can be seen to increase the risk of a woman experiencing violence within a relationship and to decrease her power to escape it.

The fact that gendered power differentials have narrowed dramatically over the past hundred years in societies where women can vote, be educated, earn an independent income, control their fertility and participate in sport and other hitherto 'unladylike' activities indicates that change, however slow, is possible. But the experience of women under regimes such as the Taliban in Afghanistan shows how fragile such gains can be.

Source: Horacek, 1994, *Unrequited Love*, Nos 1–100

Empowerment is a founding metaphor within both CP and feminism. But its critics have argued that it has been too easily reduced to simplistic New Age notions of individual power (Kitzinger, 1991). And conservative governments have co-opted the words 'self-empowerment' as a counter to the more radical demands of minority groups for self-determination. We think empowerment is more usefully understood as a process rather than an active verb (I cannot empower you, but our conversation or active engagement might be experienced as empowering to one or both of us). Ingrid Huygens (1995) asks 'What happens to rape when all women have learnt self-defence?' She argues that more attention needs to be directed towards 'depowering the powerful,' or at least towards creating space for power-sharing partnerships.

'Power does not have to be repressive – it can actually facilitate better, more satisfying lives for people' (Perkins, 1991, p. 136). The challenge for feminist community psychologists is to recognize both our relative privilege and relative powerlessness, as springboards to action. 'The personal is political' is an old feminist slogan, but in contemporary settings it means that community psychologists should always consider and acknowledge their relative power and privilege in any environment in which they work. Often that very power and privilege may be useful to the communities we are working with. At other times, our own powerlessness enables us to firmly align ourselves with other women's experiences of oppression.

Subjectivity and Reflexivity

Warning – you are about to enter big word territory!

Notions of subjectivity and reflexivity are drawn from postmodern, poststructuralist and social constructionist epistemologies that have challenged the heavy reliance of psychology (and most modern sciences) on a positivist paradigm of value-free, objective, measurement-focused research and a concomitant commitment to 'evidence-based' practice. As the name suggests, poststructuralist approaches question the existence of a single human consciousness or reality and hence emphasize plurality and tolerance of difference. While CP aspires to a more contextualized, ecologically valid and socially useful praxis, its entrenched North American hegemony has largely been impervious to the emergence in Europe and elsewhere of postmodern psychology. Critical psychology on the other hand has been influenced by the application of Marxist, feminist, Foucauldian (poststructuralist/postmodern) and psychoanalytic theories.

Where critical, community and feminist psychologies intersect is on the need to be context-specific in theory, research and practice. Each seeks to prioritize voices that need to be heard or that have been silenced on specific issues and this is where the notion of subjectivity comes into play – the recognition that truth claims based on objective, value-free science are unsustainable. Feminist psychologists were among the first to open up space for multiple subjectivities to be acknowledged within the discipline. By separating the universal 'he' into the gendered subject 'she/he', they exposed the supposedly impartial, depersonalized observer as just another form of the male gaze.

As Mulvey et al. (2000) observe in collating reflections by feminist community psychologists on issues of relative privilege, the 'relevance of concepts like voice [and subjectivity] to fostering progressive social change or to redistributing power depends on how they are understood and applied within particular, dynamic contexts' (p. 908). Such contexts are inseparable from issues discussed earlier of power, diversity and partnership – whose voices are privileged and whose muted? Who is constructed as 'other' vis-à-vis the subjectivities of authors, researchers, theory-builders and practitioners – 'the experts'?

Gavey (1989) presents compelling arguments for the incorporation of poststructuralist approaches within feminist psychology. Her work on the sexual coercion of women in heterosexual relationships was based on recognition that knowledge is 'socially produced and inherently unstable' (p. 459), along with language practices and the discourses in which they are constituted. Gavey gives an example of how a young woman might experience sexual coercion within a dominant 'permissive sexuality' discourse that makes sex very difficult for a 'liberated women' to refuse; alternative subject positions within different, non-dominant discourses (such as 'women's rights') lack an articulated and authorized language and are thus barely available to her:

> Discourses vary in their authority. The dominant discourses appear 'natural,' denying their own partiality and gaining their authority by appealing to common sense. These discourses, which support and perpetuate existing power relations, tend to constitute the subjectivity of most people most of the time (in a given place and time). So, for example, systems of meaning such as feminism are currently limited in their power because they are marginalized and as yet unavailable to many women. (Gavey, 1989, p. 464)

Gavey and other feminist scholars acknowledge that poststructuralist approaches have drawbacks of their own, partly because they demand a new jargon that seems highly academic and risks alienating the very women whose perspectives they claim to include, and partly because their strategies of discourse analysis and deconstruction do not necessarily lead to advocacy for non-dominant groups or action for social justice. But within psychology, poststructuralist (or social constructionist – see Gergen, 1985) approaches are a breath of fresh air in a discipline long dominated by adherence to a narrow and impoverished version of empirical science.

Diversity

Diversity often refers to cultural or ethnic diversity but can and should encompass class, age, religion, abilities and sexual orientation. Sampson (1993), John (1998) and many others have argued that mainstream psychology needs to diversify the 'voice' that authors (and authorizes) its claims to scientific status and its pronouncements on the nature of evidence and 'truth'. While cultural diversity is given lip-service and guidelines have been developed to guard against 'bias' in research and practice, institutionalized practices often work against equal power and participation by all the diverse groups, interests and individuals that make up the communities we claim to serve.

Promoting diversity is no simple matter of token representation or assimilationist melting pots. Dimensions of diversity are also commonly experienced as dimensions of inequality and discrimination, often with compounding effects. The

Australian Human Rights and Equal Opportunity Commission uses the notion of 'intersectionality' to conceptualize the consequences of the interaction between two or more forms of discrimination or systems of subordination. Racism is expressed differently towards women than men. Similarly homophobia is more likely to be expressed as violence towards gay men and experienced as invisibility by lesbian women. And indigenous women may be divided about whether to 'go public' on issues such as domestic violence.

During the 1990s there was a vigorous debate between established forms of feminism and the increasingly visible feminisms of the Third World and of indige-nous women and women of colour. The point is made that First World feminism has largely advantaged middle-class white women and has not had a flow-on effect to other women. Some reasons advanced include the fear that, in sharing new-found power, advantaged women (read we) risk losing favour, ground or personal power to men from whom the power was gained. Meara and Day (2000) point out that 'in the short term a more inclusive feminism is likely to have more integrity and less power' (p. 260).

Embracing diversity demands a commitment on the part of CP. First, to expand the range of voices represented in its publications, theory-building and applications from token inclusion to a critical, sustainable mass. Next, beyond the 'add voices' strategy, comes the challenge of complexity – of recognizing that we are all more than the sum of our demographic dimensions and that often as not, the dimensions are in conflict. And are we truly prepared for the field to be transformed by the inclusion as equal partners of multiple 'others' we had assumed to have fewer resources or had defined by perceived deficits – homeless substance users, young single mothers, women in veils, asylum seekers, indigenous elders, clothing outwork-ers …? Potts (1995) noted that minority students (add working-class communities and developing countries) are often drawn to CP ideals, only to find 'we colonize them out of their passions' by imposing an underdeveloped and narrow (read white, male, North American) vision of the field. Is that the best we can do?

Partnership

The notion of partnership implies equality, or at least an intention to work on an egal-itarian basis. A partnership may be forged for a particular, time-limited purpose, such as a grant application or on a long-term basis of shared interests. In CP contexts, the reference is often to partnership as a metaphor for the researcher–community rela-tionship (Dalton et al., 2001). However from a feminist perspective, the assumption that 'we' are the researchers and 'they' are the community is problematic – it may be more useful to think about partnerships as occurring at many levels and in a variety of combinations, rarely involving equal power.

At the interpersonal level, largely thanks to the women's movement, it has become increasingly common to refer to a spouse/lover/wife/husband as one's 'partner', to avoid the gendered and heterosexist assumptions in traditional couple/marital discourses and to promote the notion of equality in intimate rela-tionships. Partnership can also encompass initiatives that foster alliances, for exam-ple between women from different cultural backgrounds (Pheterson, 1990) or between women and men in the cause of everyday cultural reconciliation (McCart-

Source: Horacek, *Unrequited Love*, Nos 1–100

ney & Turner, 2000). Eisler (1988) documented archaeological evidence of partnership societies pre-dating the patriarchal dominance that has characterized sociopolitical governance across most known societies.

Like the term 'community', partnership rhetoric can be pressed into less than egalitarian service. An information pamphlet produced by a pharmaceutical company blithely declares: 'The relationship between you and your physician should be a *partnership*. Your physician's role is to diagnose, treat and prescribe, while the patient can contribute by complying with medication and treatment regimes and asking questions when necessary' – hardly a marriage to die for, nor the model of partnership we had in mind for feminist community psychologists!

At community and structural levels, there is increasing recognition of the value of partnership models. Such models respect the independence, agency and integrity of groups with less direct access to power and resources, such as consumer groups, children or local residents, while drawing on the leverage and skills offered by more enabled or privileged groups, such as a university-based research team, a peak advocacy body or a men's anti-violence network. Don Edgar (1995) makes a spirited argument for the importance of personal and structural partnerships between women and pro-feminist men in working to combat sexism: 'Women make gains partly through their own efforts, partly through the necessary protection of anti-sexist legislation, partly through the gradual re-education of men and partly through the support of men who have always been disgusted by the aggressive display of male power' (p. 13).

A cautionary note from the frontline is that what once operated as grassroots consultation may now be reframed as partnership, but often between top level representatives – hospital managers, chief executives of local councils, government bureaucrats, corporate developers – with some public meetings thrown in. Agencies may be keen to promote consumer representation, but real partnerships that offer an equal share in decision-making to those most affected and least empowered often founder at the point where radical change threatens vested interest. Beckwith and Shopland (2001) described a partnership project based on feminist critical theory that involved a collective of service providers and service users, as a philosophical and practical model for addressing collective power differences. The partnership process was embraced by clients and supported by workers, but resisted by management of the host organization, eventually leading to the disintegration of the process within its hierarchical context.

Vision and Values Guiding Feminist Community Work

We noted earlier that diverse feminisms all work towards the common goal of improving women's lives. We wonder what a world without sexism would look, feel, smell like? The Revolutionary Association of Women of Afghanistan (RAWA), who have been fighting for over twenty years for personal and political liberation in Afghanistan, provide a striking example of the determination of women in enormously difficult circumstances to fight for their vision of a just society.

Psychologists, or indeed any outsider working with communities, must recognize that in any community they are working with, for, or in, there *will be* women. This seems obvious, but women are often invisible under 'bigger issues' of poverty, crime, terrorism, war or more mainstream issues such as property development.

Beyond the acknowledgement that women are everywhere, the range of their voices should be sought out, considered and *included*. There is no one 'women's voice' in any debate, but usually a multitude of women's voices, sometimes in harmony with each other and in dissent with other voices and at other times in harmony with sections of their communities and not with each other.

Not only must women's voices be included, they must also be given *equality* with men's voices. After all, one of the most widely recognized goals of the women's movement is equality with men and also with each other.

The *process* of any activity is also historically important in feminist valuing. Consultation or action should therefore be planned and undertaken in accordance with clearly stated and transparent values. Equitable process is often bypassed in an era when the dominant market-derived rhetoric defines equality as a level playing field on which unregulated competition is free to produce winners and losers. 'Excessive commercialism of professional expertise is anathema to the feminist agenda and the values that support it' (Meara & Day, 2000, pp. 254–5). Relationships built in the course of community action should be positive and sustaining – in feminist and CP terms, the end never justifies the means.

For practitioners, CP and feminist work needs a balance between 'ambulance' work such as counselling, the provision of soup kitchens or home help, and proactive advocacy, structural reform and/or social action. One activity supports and enables the other, like an action research loop. Research, advocacy or social reform without connection to people living with 'the problem' risks being all head and no heart, while frontline work that is all heart risks futility and burnout. This balance has been operationalized in the policy of Victorian Sexual Assault Centres, where for each hour of working with survivors, workers spend another hour working in prevention and/or social action. Practice that encompasses such 'big picture' involvement as Reclaim the Night marches and rape law reform can be affirming for practitioners seeking channels for their accumulating rage – and more effective as action for social change.

Box 18.3   Putting Vision into Action: Stopping Violence Against Women

It was impossible to find any historical period in which there were no formulae ... specifying the conditions under which a wife was deserving of a good clout.

(Dobash & Dobash, 1979, p. 31)

This is my weapon, this is my gun; one is for fighting, the other for fun

(Traditional military drill chant, origin unknown)

Violence against women is as public as the tools of war, as global as gender inequality and as private as the family home. As such, it is one of the most pervasive yet least acknowledged human rights abuses throughout the world (Amnesty International, 2001; Heise, 1993). A feminist community psychology approach emphasizes the need for fundamental social change to remove the cultural supports of violence against women. How does each of the key principles outlined in this chapter apply to such a challenge?

Community: Tackling violence must be acknowledged as a community responsibility, not a private matter. Past approaches that see violence against women as an individual or a relationship problem will lead to practices that are victim-blaming and unsafe.

Ecology: Violence against women must be located in its full social and historical context of gender and power. At the relational level, violence must be viewed in terms of its controlling effects rather than stated intentions. However, ecologically derived explanations such as 'the cycle of violence' or 'the dance of anger' (Lerner, 1985) are challenged by feminists who argue that they assign women a role in precipitating or maintaining violent behaviour patterns by their intimate partners ('it takes two to tango!') (for example McGregor, 1990; Loughnan, 1999).

Prevention: Raising the status of women is essential. A systems-wide approach addressing the 'cultural facilitators' of violence against women is essential to ensure that legal, medical and social responses serve to expand the options available to women experiencing violence (Busch & Robertson, 1993).

Diversity: Respect for diversity is sometimes misinterpreted as cultural relativism, justifying a failure to intervene in the affairs of groups defined as 'other'. But violence is unacceptable in any form and attention to diversity means working from within the perspectives of minority-group women experiencing violence. Thus Aboriginal women in outback communities may prefer to tackle alcohol profiteers to reduce levels of violence associated with substance abuse; in Aotearoa, parallel development models of service delivery (Nikora & Robertson, 1995) aim to increase within-group accountability while promoting cultural as well as gender safety for Maori women; in Africa, peer educators dispel cultural myths surrounding the practice of female genital mutilation (FGM).

Partnership: At the relational level, equal partnership models need to replace the predominant patriarchal model based on power and control, now well past its use-by date. Community-level partnerships between women and men committed to ending violence against women need to be based on the 'depowerment' principle (Huygens, 1988) where the dominant group makes the changes and the less powerful group benefits. This requires firm accountability mechanisms and ongoing vigilance by all parties.

Subjectivity/reflexivity: Violence is both a social construct and a (painfully) lived experience – feminist theories define violence as a product of the social construction of masculinity and femininity, the sets of traditions, habits and beliefs which permit some men to assume dominance and control over women and thus, to assume the right to use violence as a means of exercising that control. At the personal level, a woman's subjective fear can be the best indicator of the dangerousness of her violent partner, regardless of any informal or professional risk assessment – yet her voice is often ignored, sometimes with fatal consequences.

Power: Questions that need to be asked of any theory of violence include:

- Does it deal with violence in terms of gender and power issues?
- Does it couch the problem in a gender-blind way (for example 'the violent couple')?
- Does it encourage the perpetrator to take responsibility for the violence?
- Does it blame the victim in any way?
- Does it directly confront the violence as a central issue *or* as a side issue to a 'larger' problem, a 'byproduct' of a bad relationship?
- Does it serve to limit perpetrators' power by enforcing legal sanctions?
- Does it work to expand victims' options in housing, income support, job opportunities, legal redress, crime compensation, parenting support?
- How does it serve to narrow the gender/power gaps at global, community and interpersonal levels that facilitate violence against women?

Chapter Summary

We have not offered in this chapter a definitive conceptualization of a world without sexism or misogyny or a vision of well-being and liberation for women throughout the world. We leave that task for you, the readers. In CP and feminist style, we have imagined roads leading to such a world and described useful tools for building, signposting and maintaining such roads. We have pointed to potholes, roadblocks and bad weather that make the journey mostly slow, often boring and sometimes dangerous.

Feminism's historical context reminds us that, in the words of a cigarette commercial, women 'have come a long way baby'. That history also demonstrates that most changes are incremental and many gains fragile – as feminist community psychologists, we need to be vigilant about co-option by commercial interests (such as tobacco companies), erosion of hard-won rights and the need to stay honest with ourselves – it is the ultimate privilege to be able to choose one's level of commitment to social justice.

COMMENTARY: Social Justice Includes Feminism *Colleen Loomis*

After reading the thought-provoking chapter by Heather Gridley and Colleen Turner, we can appreciate the rich histories and important applications of the interdependent fields of CP and feminism. The universal and complex nature of gender inequality exists in the context of communities, highlighting the need for CP to move towards meaningful integration with feminism. In the chapter, the authors take on the formidable task of presenting an overview of the study, research, practice and activism of CP and feminism, as well as offering a vision of an emerging field of feminist CP: a lot of information in a limited number of pages.

The model of feminist CP presented by Gridley and Turner is within the context of the English-speaking privileged countries. The chapter draws from publications predominantly from Australia, New Zealand, the UK and the US, although there is brief mention of women's movements in Afghanistan (see also Brodsky, 2003) and some African countries (see also Scott, 1995–96). Obviously, the theories and perspectives of many nations are missing. The absence of lesbian and bisexual perspectives in the chapter also is noticeable, as was the case in a special issue of the *American Journal of Community Psychology* on feminism and community (Bond et al., 2000a, 2000b). The present commentary is restricted even further to the context of the US.

The chapter provided a good stimulus for reflecting on my experiences in and visions for,

CP. In some ways the chapter's breadth of information and the mixture of technical terms from CP, feminism, epistemology, ontology and methodology overwhelmed me, even though I have studied these areas. I found it helpful to return to some of my earlier readings as well as to read (or re-read) some of the original sources and websites cited in the chapter. I encourage you to do the same. Essentially, the chapter inspired me to deconstruct and reconstruct my own interdisciplinary model of CP.

After presenting a history of the fields, the authors provided seven principles of feminist CP: ecology; prevention; community; power ;subjectivity/reflexivity ; diversity; and partnership. I make a brief comment on history and power analysis before suggesting a slightly varied and condensed model of CP in which feminism is an explicit value rather than a description of the type of community work.

Constraints notwithstanding, the authors attend to how history aids our understanding of similarities and differences between CP and feminism. Furthermore, it provides important criteria for our future work in solving the problem of gender inequality. In the US, for example, feminism was recognized as a movement in the 1800s and CP developed in the 1960s. In fact, feminism, along with other equality movements active at the time, provided the context in which the development of CP was possible (Bennett et al., 1966). Feminism's efforts to liberate women and girls provided valuable lessons that CP applies in its own efforts to liberate oppressed peoples (SCRA Mission Statement, 2002). Since its inception, CP has had a parallel and interdependent course with feminism (Kelly, 1990).

In the chapter, rationales are offered for incorporating feminist research traditions of power into CP. I agree with the authors that we need to investigate power analysis among the social contexts of oppressed groups. I know that this kind of information increases our understanding of dominant groups from a subordinate position (Riger, 1990, 1992). While reading the section on power and agreeing with the points made I noted four cautions that are not explicit in the chapter. In a separate publication, along with some colleagues I raise questions about the relationship between power sharing and social justice, posing alternative views to conventional research premises about power sharing (Isenberg et al., 2004).

My reading of the chapter on gender, power and CP raised different questions about the relationship between power analysis and feminist work. First, not all power is gendered. Non-gendered power differentials exist along other dimensions such as age, class, disability, seniority, race and so on. That is, simply saying we analyse and intervene in power dynamics does not make our work feminist.

Second, acknowledging a position of privilege in a power relationship does not change the power. While the authors' suggestion to make transparent our positions resonates with me, I know from experience (on both sides of a power dynamic) that acknowledging differences helps and is necessary but it is insufficient to achieve equality. We need to learn more about how to make real changes in power differentials, particularly in our research partnerships (cf. Nelson, Prilleltensky & MacGillivary, 2001).

Third, remembering that power is a relationship (Montero, 1998a), we must continue to attend to our professional relationships by training community psychologists how to develop, establish, negotiate and continuously renegotiate relationships. The two principles of power and relationship are inseparable; for me these principles become a single principle.

Finally, in order to have a more comprehensive understanding of power we must expand our research to powerful persons, groups and systems (that is, non-oppressed). 'Studying up' is not a novel concept but it is one rarely reflected in CP research. If we want to liberate the oppressed we need to examine the power of the powerful.

In my experience, feminism is a core value of CP. From this perspective the field's practice is premised on four principles: values; ecology; power; and action. This slightly revised and condensed model of CP shares characteristics with the one presented in the chapter, but explicitly focuses on CP's values and places feminism as a value of CP – subsumed under the value of social justice (cf. Maton, 2000; Serrano-García, 1994) or 'liberating oppressed peoples' (SCRA Mission Statement, 2002) – rather than suggesting a model of feminist CP.

Ecology subsumes diversity, while power relationships are negotiated through reflexive praxis. Action, in turn, includes prevention, promotion, teaching and research, as well as the methods to perform these activities. It seems to me that methods may be applied (constructively or destructively) to many substantive areas (cf. Isenberg et al., 2004), including but not limited to feminist issues. For this reason, I do not label the study of power and reflexivity (for example) as particularly feminist, although I credit feminism for some of the developments and advancements in these areas. As we conceive ways of integrating CP and feminism, let us be careful not to strip away the political impact of either field and end up with a diluted feminism or a diluted CP.

The chapter highlights that our implementation of a CP model that values feminism could be strengthened. We can raise awareness about our principles and reflect these principles (both in process and content) in our research, training and community service. Obviously, context shapes values. For example, it is clear that not all community psychologists (within or across local, national and international communities) value autonomy in the same way (Francescato & Tomai, 2001). I believe, however, that human rights is a universal value. And, gender equality is a human right. CP contributes to gender equality through research and practice. Additionally, because CP and feminism each have something unique to offer (in their respective various forms around the globe), in my opinion the best plan is to work collaboratively across paradigms. We should expect and demand collaboration between community psychologists and feminists in their common pursuit of social justice.

Exercise in Deconstruction: Questioning the Text

Find a newspaper or magazine article about women. It can be about women's health, women's work or any other topic involving the lives of women. The article can be from a printed or online magazine or paper. Read the text and try to answer the following questions.

1. What kinds of discourses surround, or are created within, a particular text? Is equality implicit in the text? Is patriarchy supported or subverted?

2. Where does the authority/authorship lie? Is the author imputing aspirations and attitudes to women or are women's voices given their legitimate place?

3. How are women's experiences made relevant?

4. Are gender relations visible in this text? What forms of masculinity and femininity are being made available here?

5. What are the political implications of the text? Is there a progressive message there?

6. Whose voices are represented mostly? Women (or men) in positions of privilege? Are the voices of the women most affected represented in the text? Minority women?

Chapter glossary

We have decided to group all the gender/sex words together so that readers can see how they relate to one another in the way we have used them.

equality in this chapter we have used equality, particularly between women and men, as the principle of 'being of equal value' rather than 'being the same as' or 'identical'

equal rights similarly this principle may require different actions or outcomes according to differing – but equally important – needs. For example women have a right to (and need access to) good quality appropriate medical care at the time they become mothers. Parents (and children) need, and therefore have equal rights to, a range of supports throughout childhood

feminism(s) various forms of feminism work towards a common goal of improving women's lives. A basic definition is 'advocacy of women's rights on the grounds of equality of the sexes'. According to Hughes (1994), feminism offers 'not only a set of strategies through which to improve women's material lives, but a critique and analysis of the very foundations of a society

which uses gender inequality to organize itself.' (p. 2)

gender is a much debated term. The classic way of differentiating sex from gender is to use 'sex' to distinguish two biological divisions of organisms – male and female – though this binary opposition is contested. Gender is defined along several dimensions, including how individuals are socialized. It is a variable set of practices. We all 'do' gender within the parameters of our age, culture, social class, sexual orientation, personality and circumstances

misogyny hatred and/or hostility towards all women

sexism the 1975 edition of the Shorter Oxford did not include 'sexism' but did provide a definition for 'sex kitten' as a 'young woman mischievously exploiting her sex appeal' – thereby demonstrating that even the Shorter Oxford is not immune to what it does not name! We define sexism as any beliefs, attitudes, practices and/or institutions in which distinctions between people's intrinsic worth are made on the basis of sex/gender. This discrimination can be systemic as well as individual

hegemony is the assumption of power or disproportionate control usually by a 'ruling class' or dominant group. Not only is political or economic control exercised by the dominant group, but it succeeds in projecting its own particular way of seeing the world, human and social relationships so that these are accepted as the natural order or 'common sense' by those who are subordinated to the ruling view

intersectionality is defined by Australia's Human Rights and Equal Opportunity Commission (HREOC) as the consequence of the interaction between two or more discriminations, for example sex and race or sex and sexual orientation

power central to feminist analysis of everything – traditionally measured in terms of individual or collective authority, information, resources, decision-making, coercion and privilege, power is increasingly described in terms of discourse, relationship and practice rather than quantity. In other words, power cannot be separated from how it is authorized and exercised

■ RESOURCES ■

1. For an overview of the situation of women in poor countries, visit
   http://womensissues.about.com/cs/thirdworld/.
2. For global and economic issues affecting women, visit http://www.twnside.org.sg/women.htm.
3. Interesting links to sites dealing with feminism, activism and politics may be found at
   http://www.euronet.nl/~fullmoon/w-active.html.
4. The Society for the Psychology of Women maintains an active website
   http://www.apa.org/divisions/div35/quarter.html.
5. The Center on Human Policy at Syracuse University published an interesting paper dealing with Women
   with disabilities: The double discrimination. The paper may be read at http://soeweb.syr.edu/thechp/
   womdis1.htm.
6. An excellent list of academic journals dealing with gender issues was published by the University of
   Trent, Nottingham and may be viewed at http://www.ntu.ac.uk/lis/library/gender.pdf i.

19

A Journey Towards Liberation:
Confronting Heterosexism and the Oppression of Lesbian, Gay, Bisexual and Transgendered People

Gary W. Harper

Chapter Organization

Defining Variations in Sexual Orientation and Gender Identity: The Power of Words	◆ Lesbian, Gay, Bisexual, Transgender: What's the Difference? ◆ Diversity and Culture
Heterosexism and Oppression	◆ Is It Homophobia or Heterosexism? ◆ Heterosexism as a Form of Oppression; *Cultural Heterosexism; Psychological Heterosexism* ◆ Multiple Membership and Layers of Oppression ◆ Consequences of Heterosexism and Oppression for LGBT People ◆ Reactions to Immediate and Chronic Oppressive Actions
Towards Liberation and Well-being	◆ LGBT Health Promotion and Prevention ◆ Building Community: LGBT People and Families Unite ◆ Collective Power: Gay Rights Liberation Movement and Community Partnerships ◆ LGBT Legal Issues and Public Policy: Towards Inclusion and Equity ◆ Commitment Through Research: Listening to the Changing Voices of LGBT People

Chapter Summary	**COMMENTARY: Thinking Outside the Box**	**Class Exercise**
Glossary	**Resources**	

Warm-up Exercise

After reading the material in Box 19.1 (see next page) respond to the following questions:

1. Have you ever heard any of the ideas, beliefs and/or myths that were presented in this section regarding gay, lesbian, bisexual or transgendered people? Where did you hear them?
2. Why do you think people hold these types of ideas/beliefs/myths?
3. Using the ecological metaphor presented in Chapter 2, how do you think these ideas/beliefs/myths get transmitted both within and across a community's various nested ecological levels? What role might power inequality play in the perpetuation and maintenance of these ideas/beliefs/myths?
4. How might these ideas/beliefs/myths act as barriers to liberation and well-being for lesbian, gay, bisexual and transgendered people?

Now read this passage again and instead of reading the words 'those people', insert a term that describes a group to which you belong (for example women, Christians, Asians and so on). What type of reaction would you have if your community held these beliefs about your group and about you?

Box 19.1 **'Those People'**

Imagine, if you will, growing up hearing about a group of people that exist in society who are 'defective' and who are all 'going to hell' because of who they are and who they love. You rarely see 'those people' on television, magazines or in movies and when you do they are usually the humorous characters that are viewed as unusual or silly. There may be a rumour that one actually lives in your neighbourhood or that someone has one in her/his family, but your parents forbid you to even talk about that possibility. Imagine the children at school telling jokes about the way 'those people' talk and act and you even hear jokes about a fatal disease that some of 'those people' acquire from engaging in 'inappropriate' or 'immoral' behaviours. You see news reports and 'made-for-TV movies' about some of 'those people' being beaten, tortured and killed for no other reason than being who they are. In school you learn about research that has attempted to uncover the biological defect that makes 'those people' the way they are and you hear about a type of therapy that can change 'those people' into 'normal' human beings. In another class you learn about laws that restrict 'those people' from having the same basic human and civil rights and legal protections as everyone else in society and that prohibit them from forming legal unions. You also hear rumours that 'those people' attempt to 'recruit' others, particularly the young, to be like them and that they should not be left alone with children because most of them are sexual predators who will sexually exploit the young. Now imagine thinking and feeling that you yourself might be one of 'those people' ... what would you do?

In this chapter I address the issue of heterosexism and the continued oppression of lesbian, gay, bisexual and transgendered (LGBT) people and communities. In addition, I present ways in which community members and community psychologists have promoted liberation and well-being through intervention and activism at multiple levels. In order to understand the issues that confront LGBT people, it is first important to understand the historical and current variations that exist in self-definition and in societal definition when it comes to different forms of sexual orientation and gender identification. It is difficult to find consensus on how to define the sexual lives and identities of people since sexuality is a very personal, and often private, aspect of our existence and is strongly influenced by societal and cultural factors (Diaz, 1998; Harper, 2001). I will use the acronym LGBT throughout this chapter to indicate the collective community of lesbian, gay, bisexual and transgendered people and LGB in instances where transgendered individuals have not been a part of the discourse.

Defining Variations in Sexual Orientation and Gender Identity: The Power of Words

As was presented in Chapter 2, Julian Rappaport (1998, 2000) has talked about dominant cultural narratives as being shared stories that are communicated through media and popular symbols, words and phrases to describe a particular group of people in a stereotyped fashion. These narratives are often used by members of dominant groups to continue the oppression of people who lack social power. It is important, then, to be aware of the meaning that society may attach to the words we use so that we are not participants in the continued oppression of disadvantaged people. Words can be powerful; they can both oppress and liberate. In this section of the chapter I will review relevant terms that will help you to understand the complexity of individuals and groups that are often classified under the umbrella phrase 'LGBT' and describe the historical roots of terms such as 'homosexual' that have been used to pathologize and marginalize LGBT people. In addition, I will discuss the importance of attending to diversity considerations when addressing LGBT issues in community psychology (CP), with an emphasis on the role of culture in defining sexual orientation and gender identity.

Lesbian, Gay, Bisexual, Transgender: What's the Difference?

Individuals in western societies who experience varying degrees of same-gender desire and attraction and engage in same-gender sexual behaviour are typically referred to by the terms 'lesbians', 'gay men', and/or 'bisexual women or men'. The focus here is on the individual's sexual orientation, which is defined by the identity of the person to whom an individual is physically and emotionally attracted. The term 'transgender', on the other hand, is focused on issues of gender identity and represents a range of individuals who do not conform to traditional societal expectations and roles for each gender such as transvestites, transsexuals, transgenderists androgynists and intersex people (Gainor, 2000). A transgendered individual's sexual orientation is not defined by her/his gender nonconformity, thus transgendered people may experience sexual attraction to females, males or both.

Therefore, group membership for lesbians, gay men and bisexual women and men is defined by their sexual orientation, whereas transgendered individuals' group membership is defined by their gender identity and gender nonconformity. Although the life experiences of these groups of people can vary tremendously, psychologists and other professionals from related disciplines often group them together under the acronym LGBT to represent a group of people who experience oppression and marginalization based on their sexual orientation or gender identity and who do not share the same basic civil rights as other citizens in many societies. In addition, members from these various groups may join together in their activism efforts in order to create social support, form a sense of community and increase solidarity.

The term 'homosexual' was first coined in the 1800s to categorize those who engaged in same-gender sexual behaviour as sick or deviant (Bullough, 1994; Donovan, 1992). Over the years the term 'homosexuality' has been associated with sin, criminal behaviour, uncleanliness and mental illness (Donovan, 1992; Hunter, Shannon, Knox & Martin, 1998; Pierce, 2001) – all of which serve to place LGBT people in the subordinate role of being categorized as 'deviant' individuals who are marginalized by mainstream society. One example of the relatively recent negative use of this term by larger societal institutions is the inclusion of 'homosexuality' in the Diagnostic and Statistical Manual (DSM) of Mental Disorders by the American Psychiatric Association. Although 'homosexuality' was removed from the DSM in 1973 as a specific mental illness, it was not until 1987 that all references to LGB sexual orientation were removed.

Dean Pierce (2001) has suggested that using the term 'homosexual' is one way that perpetuates the power of the majority group by creating what he calls 'the rule of symbolic opposites'. He suggests that the term 'heterosexual' is used to describe the more powerful majority group and that the term 'homosexual' is then the more negative hierarchical opposite and is even seen by some as the 'enemy' of heterosexuality. This type of hierarchical and opposing term serves to perpetuate a negative discourse about LGBT people. In 1991 the American Psychological Association's Committee on Lesbian and Gay Concerns published a set of guidelines for avoiding heterosexual bias in language and discouraged psychologists from using the term 'homosexual' because of its negative connotations with psychopathology and its primary focus on the sexual aspect of a person's identity.

Diversity and Culture

When we talk about LGBT communities, it is important to keep in mind that this category includes a range of different types of individuals who share some aspect of oppression related to their sexual orientation and/or gender nonconformity and that within each of these types there is also a diverse array of individuals who are members of other oppressed or marginalized groups with varying levels of social power (for example women, people of colour, people with disabilities). Although people may share membership in some of these identity groups, we must be careful not to make assumptions about each person's experiences and reactions as a member of these groups, since they can vary greatly (B. Greene, 2000). As community psychologists, we should be cognizant of the importance of recognizing this diversity within the larger LGBT community and strive to promote the inclusion of these various voices in our research and liberation efforts. Beverly Greene (2000) cautions against the silencing of LGBT people who are not members of the dominant group and suggests that 'the very act of defining the experiences of all lesbians and gay men by the characteristics of the most privileged and powerful members of that group is an oppressive act' (B. Greene, 2000, p. 39).

It is also important to keep in mind that the majority of the conceptualizations and definitions of LGBT people described in this chapter and other writings are those from modernized western civilizations and that some authors such as Mary Fukuyama and Angela Ferguson suggest that sexual orientation is a 'Western psychological construct not always found in or stigmatized across other cultures' (Fukuyama & Ferguson, 2000, p. 88). They point out that anthropologists such as Gilbert Herdt (1998) have demonstrated that same-gender sexual behaviour is quite common in other cultures and that those who participate in such activities are not stigmatized. American Indian culture offers another departure from traditional westernized conceptualizations of LGBT identification and allows for a range of sexual identity categories, as is characterized by the term 'two spirited' which serves to describe an individual whose identity is determined by social roles and spiritual powers rather than physical sex (Jacobs, Thomas & Lang, 1997). Contemporary use of the term 'two spirited' has been expanded to signify 'a fluidity of gender roles and sexuality beyond the dualistic Western notions of male/female and homosexual/heterosexual' (Walters, Simoni & Horwath, 2001, p. 135).

Box 19.2 illustrates the importance of considering the role of culture in defining sexual orientation and gender by discussing the cultural conceptualization of same-gender sexual behaviour in Mexico, Brazil and Peru. As was discussed in Chapter 2, this also emphasizes the need for community psychologists to listen to the stories and narratives of the people with whom we work as we strive to respect the unique social identities of people and communities. We must also engage in continual self-examination and reflexivity to assure that when working with LGBT people and communities we are not imposing our own cultural conceptualizations of sexuality, gender and sexual orientation onto another group, especially when we come from a position of relative power and privilege. In doing this we should examine our own biases to sex and gender related topics and acknowledge that discourse about sexual expression and desire may cause discomfort because of the often private and personal nature of sexuality, and that discussions of gender identity may challenge our very notions of what it means to be a 'man' or a 'woman' – issues that we often take for granted.

Box 19.2 **Latin American Conceptualizations of Sexual Orientation and Gender Roles**

Anthropological research on same-gender sexual behaviour in both Mexico (Carrier, 1989) and Brazil (Parker, 1989) has demonstrated the powerful position of gender roles in defining sexual behaviour and sexual orientation. In these cultures, participation in same-gender sexual behaviour is generally not stigmatized as long as the individual maintains her/his culturally appropriate gender role both in the sexual act and in social interactions, with the male role being that of the active partner (Mexico = *activo* or Brazil = *atividade*) and the female role being that of the passive partner (Mexico = *passivo* or Brazil = *passsividade*). Therefore, males who take on the active or penetrative role during anal intercourse with another man, or women who have sexual activity with other women and are passive sexually and socially, are not marginalized in some segments of Mexican and Brazilian culture. Men who do take on the active role in sexual activity with other men may further assert their masculinity by showing disdain for 'feminine' men and degrading them. Carlos Caceres and Ana Maria Rosasco (1999) have also found similar conceptualizations of gender and sexual orientation among men in Peru and stress the role that social class plays in how these cultural messages are internalized and activated. In their qualitative study of men who have sex with men in Lima, Peru, they found a diversity of sexual orientation subcultures organized around social class, sexual identity, gender self-presentation, degree of participation in the gay scene and participation in commercial sex. In these Latin American cultures, an important core belief underlying sexuality is that the gender of an individual's sexual partner is less important than their role during the sexual encounter.

Heterosexism and Oppression

In this next section of the chapter I review the meaning of the terms 'homophobia' and 'heterosexism' and discuss the implications of using these terms. I then discuss how multiple forms of heterosexism serve to oppress LGBT people and interfere with attempts at liberation and well-being, and differentiate between cultural heterosexism and psychological heterosexism. After discussing various forms of these types of heterosexism, I explore ways in which LGBT people who belong to other marginalized groups may experience multiple layers of oppression. In the last part of this section, I use the conceptual framework for CP presented in Chapter 2 as a basis for exploring the range of issues and problems that are experienced by some LGBT people as a result of heterosexism and oppression.

Is it Homophobia or Heterosexism?

The term 'homophobia' was first coined in the late 1960s by George Weinberg, a heterosexual psychoanalyst who used the term to describe heterosexual people's fear, contempt and hatred of LGBT people. 'Heterosexism' is a term that emerged after 'homophobia', and shares more in common with other terms such as 'racism' and 'sexism' that focus on multiple levels of prejudice and oppression experienced by a group of people. Gregory Herek, a psychologist who has conducted a great deal of research on negativity and stigma directed towards LGBT people, has defined heterosexism as 'the ideological system that denies, denigrates and stigmatizes any non-heterosexual form of behaviour, identity, relationships or community' (Herek, 1995, p. 321). Joseph Neisen (1990) stresses that heterosexism emphasizes the power that major social institutions possess and the way this power is used to subordinate any non-heterosexual lifestyle. The term 'heterosexism' also differs from homophobia in that it was created by activists within the Women's and Gay Liberation Movement to have political meaning and to offer a common language to discuss the systemic oppression of LGBT people (Kitzinger, 1996).

Some researchers and activists caution against the use of the term 'homophobia' since it focuses on individual-level thoughts, actions and behaviours of the homophobic person and does not recognize the societal level oppression that LGB people face (Blumenfeld, 1992; Hunter et al., 1998). This micro-level analysis makes it easier for people to isolate the negative experiences of LGBT people into discrete events and to lose sight of the macro-level changes that are needed to help liberate LGB people. This may be a more comfortable position for some people to accept, since they can then divorce themselves from the actions of an individual who engages in homophobic behaviour and do not have to take responsibility for being part of the larger social system that perpetuates the oppression of LGBT people.

Homophobia also suggests that the person who engages in homophobic thought or actions is experiencing some type of individual-level psychopathology and may even engender compassion for the homophobic person since she or he is 'suffering' from a 'fear' (Blumenfeld, 1992; Herek et al., 1991; Hunter et al., 1998). In addition, Celia Kitzinger (1996) cautions that the use of terms such as 'internalized homophobia' denote negative psychological states experienced by LGB people, since it describes a negative reaction to oppression. She points out that even though LGB people typically do not seek psychological services to change their homosexuality any more, they now seek the assistance of therapists in overcoming their internalized homophobia – shifting the focus from the powerful oppressor to the less powerful individual who experiences the impact of oppression (Kitzinger, 1996).

This discussion of the term 'homophobia' is an excellent example of how terminology that is used to describe the negative experiences of an oppressed group of people can be used (intentionally or unintentionally) to limit efforts at liberation and well-being by concentrating the focus on a micro-level analysis of a social issue as opposed to a macro-level analysis. In addition, it can work against the CP principle of ecology and promote the dominant culture's focus on individualism and promote victim-blaming, as in the use of the term 'internalized homophobia'. In community psychologists' efforts to be accountable to oppressed groups of people, we must be cognizant of the ways in which we conceptualize and discuss the actions of oppressive forces in society and the role that terminology plays in these efforts.

Heterosexism as a Form of Oppression

Given that heterosexism serves to subordinate and stigmatize LGBT people, it can be viewed as a major oppressive force in their lives. Celia Kitzinger (1997) suggests that because of the pervasiveness of heterosexism, 'Lesbians and gay men are oppressed in almost every aspect of our lives' (p. 204). This oppression is experienced at multiple levels of analysis (as described in Chapter 1), including the personal, interpersonal or relational and social or community. Although LGBT people may experience heterosexism and oppression in multiple forms within these various ecological systems, Gregory Herek (1992) and Ski Hunter and her colleagues (1998) assert that heterosexism is manifested in two primary ways: through societal customs and institutions (cultural heterosexism) and through individual attitudes and behaviours (psychological heterosexism).

Some forms of heterosexism within these categories are blatant and vengeful, whereas others may be more subtle (regardless of whether or not they are intentional) and may be perpetuated without the oppressor's conscious recognition that she or he is being heterosexist. Many non-LGBT people are not aware of the heterosexist nature of most societies, since heterosexist language, icons, images and messages are so pervasive within various realms of our existence. For example, LGBT people are traditionally non-existent in mainstream advertising. How many television commercials or magazine advertisements have you seen that include a same-gender couple purchasing a car, having a meal with their children or sharing a tender kiss?

Most heterosexual women and men have never been forced to question their sexual attraction to, or love for, members of the opposite gender, since they assume that their affectional feelings and emotions are just a natural or normal part of being a woman or man. For many LGBT people, on the other hand, these feelings of sexual desire and love for a person are often questioned on a daily basis, as they are constantly bombarded with messages regarding the deviance of the feelings and emotions that to them are natural and normal.

Cultural Heterosexism

Cultural heterosexism, which has also been referred to as institutionalized heterosexism (Blumenfeld & Raymond, 1993), is 'manifested in the belief in and promotion of the inherent superiority of the heterosexual sexual orientation, that it is the only acceptable form of affectional and sexual expression' (Hunter et al., 1998, p. 22). This level of heterosexism is promoted through various cultural rituals, customs and beliefs and is so pervasive in most modern westernized societies that it is taken for granted and rarely even noticed (Herek, 1995). Major macro-systemic and meso-systemic institutions such as government, the military, medical and psychiatric centres, schools, businesses, mass media, legal systems and religion create policies and codes of conduct that reinforce heterosexist attitudes, values and behaviours. These institutions have tremendous social power and control their constituents through systems of rewards and consequences that create incentives for conformity to heterosexist norms (Blumenfeld & Raymond, 1988). LGBT people experience cultural heterosexism in two primary ways – they are either hidden from the rest of society, and institutions and people of power do not acknowledge their accomplishments or even their mere existence, or they are stigmatized and discriminated against (Herek, 1992; Hunter et al., 1998).

Cruikshank (1992) has suggested that one method that heterosexuals have used to maintain power over LGBT people is to erase their lives and accomplishments from history. Ski Hunter and her colleagues (1998) point out that this has occurred in several instances such as the alteration of Greek poetry that described love between men and the alteration of Emily Dickinson's love letters to women. In addition, history books rarely reveal that several historical figures, such as Florence Nightingale, Billie Holliday, Virginia Woolf, Michelangelo, Alexander the Great and Oscar Wilde, were gay men or lesbians. In some instances the 'invisibility' of LGBT people is self-imposed, as individuals may chose to conceal their sexual orientation for fear that talking about their partner, love interests and general lifestyle will result in negative consequences such as harassment or victimization.

This protective desire to hide one's sexual orientation can lead to the living of a 'double life', whereby a person only talks about LGBT-related experiences with those friends, family and co-workers who are aware of the person's LGBT identity. LGBT people who are only 'out' to some individuals in their social and family networks may become quite facile at pronoun switching when talking about same-gender dating partners or love interests – using opposite gender pronouns around those who are not aware of their orientation and same-gender pronouns around those who are aware. Some individuals even adopt a different set of behaviours and language that is enacted around those to whom they are not 'out' in order to remain 'invisible'.

Discrimination is the other form of cultural heterosexism. In many instances LGBT individuals are not legally protected from abusive and discriminatory actions, as many oppressive legal ordinances and laws restrict LGBT-identified individuals from sharing the same basic human rights and privileges as those who do not identify as LGBT (Swan, 1997; Wetzel, 2001). For example, in the US this includes actions such as prohibiting same-sex marriages, restricting same-gender sexual activity, giving employers the right to terminate LGBT employees, allowing landlords the right to prohibit same-gender couples from cohabiting, prohibiting LGBT people from serving in the military, terminating parental rights of LGBT individuals and using sexual orientation as a factor in making restrictive custody decisions. Unfortunately many of these laws are not based on objective decisions regarding basic human rights for all people, but instead are strongly influenced by court justices' and lawmakers' views regarding the morality of same-gender sexual conduct (Feldblum, 2000, 2001).

Psychological Heterosexism

Psychological heterosexism represents individual-level heterosexism that may be manifested through both feelings/attitudes and behaviours and is usually discussed in terms of how it promotes and perpetuates violence against LGBT people (Herek, 1992, 1995). Ski Hunter and her colleagues (1998) outline three levels of psychological heterosexism: prejudice and stereotypes; harassment; and violence. The negative attitudes that some people have towards LGBT people result from prejudice and stereotypes, which often are created and promoted by people who have had either no contact, or limited interactions, with LGBT people. These negative attitudes can then lead individuals to engage in harassment or violence as they act out their perceived hatred of LGBT people. The perpetuation of negative stereotypes and myths represents one way in which people in the majority can use their position of power to influence others who have never come into contact with LGBT people, and also rationalizes their role in oppressing LGBT people (Rappaport, 2000).

Community psychologists have documented the shocking frequency of LGBT harassment and violence that occurs in North America and the negative impact it has on people who experience it (for example D'Augelli, 1989; D'Augelli & Hershberger, 1993; Garnets, Herek & Levy, 1990; Rosario, Rotheram-Borus & Reid, 1996; Schneider, 1991; Waldo, 1998). For many LGBT people, potential threats of violence are a daily concern. This is especially true for adolescents, who may experience bullying, harassment and physical abuse perpetrated by a range of individuals including peers, parents and teachers (Rivers & D'Augelli, 2001) in a range of settings including the young person's neighbourhood, home and school, thus adding to the traumatic nature of these events.

Box 19.3   Heterosexual Questionnaire

This questionnaire is for self-avowed heterosexuals only. If you are not openly heterosexual, pass it on to a friend who is. Please try to answer the questions as candidly as possible.

1. What do you think caused your heterosexuality?
2. When and how did you first decide you were a heterosexual?
3. Is it possible your heterosexuality is just a phase you may grow out of?
4. Could it be that your heterosexuality stems from a neurotic fear of others of the same sex?
5. If you've never slept with a person of the same sex, how can you be sure you wouldn't prefer that?
6. To whom have you disclosed your heterosexual tendencies? How did they react?
7. Why do heterosexuals feel compelled to seduce others into their lifestyle?
8. Why do you insist on flaunting your heterosexuality? Can't you just be what you are and keep it quiet?
9. Would you want your children to be heterosexual, knowing the problems they'd face?
10. A disproportionate majority of child molesters are heterosexual men. Do you consider it safe to expose children to heterosexual male teachers, paediatricians, priests or scoutmasters?
11. With all the societal support for marriage, the divorce rate is spiralling. Why are there so few stable relationships among heterosexuals?
12. Why do heterosexuals place so much emphasis on sex?
13. Considering the menace of overpopulation, how could the human race survive if everyone were heterosexual?

14. Could you trust a heterosexual therapist to be objective? Don't you fear s/he might be inclined to influence you in the direction of her/his own leanings?
15. Heterosexuals are notorious for assigning themselves and one another rigid, stereotyped sex roles. Why must you cling to such unhealthy role-playing?
16. With the sexually segregated living conditions of military life, isn't heterosexuality incompatible with military service?
17. How can you enjoy an emotionally fulfilling experience with a person of the other sex when there are such vast differences between you? How can a man know what pleases a woman sexually or vice-versa?
18. Shouldn't you ask your far-out straight cohorts, like skinheads and born-agains, to keep quiet? Wouldn't that improve your image?
19. Why are heterosexuals so promiscuous?
20. Why do you attribute heterosexuality to so many famous lesbian and gay people? Is it to justify your own heterosexuality?
21. How can you hope to actualize your God-given homosexual potential if you limit yourself to exclusive, compulsive heterosexuality?
22. There seem to be very few happy heterosexuals. Techniques have been developed that might enable you to change if you really want to. After all, you never deliberately chose to be a heterosexual, did you? Have you considered aversion therapy or Heterosexuals Anonymous?

(©1972, Martin Rochlin, Ph.D., available from http://monster-island.org/tinashumor/humor/quest.html)

Some acts of violence against LGBT young people are so severe that they result in death. Two relatively recent cases occurred in the US and were so shocking that they were heavily covered by the media. Both cases also resulted in the production of major movies that told the stories of these murders so that a wider audience could learn about these crimes. One incident involved a gay, 21-year-old University of Wyoming undergraduate student named Matthew Shepard. In 1998 Matthew was befriended by two young men in a bar, who lured him into their truck where they brutally beat and tortured him because he was gay. They then tied him to a fence in a remote area, continued to beat him with a gun and to burn him and then left him to die. After enduring 18 hours tied to the fence in freezing weather, Matthew was discovered but died shortly after due to his multiple injuries. A similarly shocking incident involved the rape and murder of a 20-year-old transgendered young man named Brandon Teena in Falls City, Nebraska. In 1993, after two of Brandon's male acquaintances learned that he was biologically a female but living as a man, they brutally raped and assaulted him. Brandon reported the rape to the local law enforcement agency and instead of offering him protection, the county sheriff told the two men that Brandon had reported the rape. One week later Brandon was murdered by the two men who had raped him.

Such acts of hatred and violence against LGBT people have been reported in several other countries as well. One highly publicized case in 1999 involved a 14-year-old male by the name of Jeff Whittington, who was viciously assaulted and murdered by two young men who assumed that he was gay, based on his effeminate behaviour. Jeff's attackers brutally beat his head, face and body and then proceeded to jump on his head. After the beating they left him in the middle of the street to die (Public Education Regarding Sexual Orientation Nationally, 1999). Activists in other countries have attempted to document the number of anti-LGBT murders in order to illustrate the need for social action efforts aimed at protecting LGBT people around the world. A report produced by LGBT activists in Brazil revealed that 130 gay men, lesbians and transgendered people were murdered in Brazil in 2000 (Mott & Cerqueira, 2001). An earlier report also indicated that in the previous decade there had been more than 1200 anti-gay murders in Brazil (Mott, 1997).

Multiple Membership and Layers of Oppression

LGBT people who are members of one or more other marginalized communities may experience multiple layers of oppression. Often LGBT people of colour, for example, must not only contend with the negative societal reactions to their sexual orientation and/or gender nonconformity, but also may experience racial prejudice, limited economic resources and limited acceptance within their own cultural community (Diaz, 1998; Martinez & Sullivan, 1998). Some LGBT people of colour even feel that because of negative attitudes and stereotypes that exist within their community, they must chose between identifying as LGBT or identifying as a member of their ethnic/racial group. This is perpetuated by a belief that the gay liberation movement and LGBT identification are white middle-class phenomena and that those people of colour who join this movement are rejecting their culture of origin and joining the white oppressor (D'Emilo, 1983; Fukuyama & Ferguson, 2000). Pat Washington (2001) has referred to the perpetuation of multiple layers of oppression against LGBT people of colour by non-LGBT people of colour as 'one subordinating group subordinating another' (p. 123). People of colour also may experience racial prejudice and marginalization within the predominately white, mainstream LGBT community. This may be manifested in an objectification and eroticization of LGBT people of colour by white LGBT men and women who are seeking to fulfil an exotic or passionate fantasy (Diaz, 1998; Han, 2001; Martinez & Sullivan, 1998).

This differential treatment in both the community of culture and mainstream white LGBT community, may lead some LGBT people of colour to experience varying degrees of visibility and invisibility within these communities and their identity as a LGBT person may change depending on the cultural context (Fukuyama & Ferguson, 2000; Morales, 1989). Maria Cecilia Zea, Carol Reisen and Raphael Diaz (2003) illustrated this phenomenon in an article where they reported that some Latino men that they interviewed said that they identify as 'gay' when they are in the context of a gay bar, but not when they are with their families. Other LGBT people may make themselves 'invisible' within their cultural group, as was demonstrated by Tremble, Schnedier and Appathurai's (1989) study of lesbian and gay young people of colour in Toronto, which revealed that they would often exclude themselves from cultural activities in order to avoid bringing shame to their families.

The interaction between race/ethnicity and sexual orientation may be further complicated when issues of power enter the equation, as switching or concealing an LGBT identity may result in varying levels of social power and opportunities for one's voice to be heard. Mariana Romo-Carmona (1995) suggests that for some LGBT people who experience multiple layers of marginalization, such as lesbians of colour, the act of being visible as a LGBT person can be empowering. She posits that '"Coming out" by the least powerful, most oppressed members of a society challenges the foundation of power, by individuals whom the power structure considers to be the least threatening' (Romo-Carmona, 1995, p. 90). She cautions that although this act can be empowering, it may also spark retaliation from those in positions of privilege who do not want to surrender power and social control.

Although the vast majority of research and writing about multiple identity concerns and layers of oppression for LGBT people has been related to people of colour, similar issues of invisibility, lack of acceptance and negativity have been reported by other groups of LGBT people as well. Tom Shakespeare (1999) conducted interviews with disabled LGBT people in Britain and found that one of their most distressing concerns was the hostility that they faced in either, or both, the LGBT and/or disability communities. This lack of acceptance and need for a cohesive community that unites multiple forms of identity has been echoed by those working with LGBT people with developmental disabilities as well (Thompson, Bryson & Castell, 2001). Within the deaf community, William Rudner and Rochelle Butowsky (1981) found that some LGBT individuals have maintained their invisibility by creating a set of signs in American Sign Language that are known only to lesbian women and gay men and serve to conceal certain aspects of their LGBT-related communication from straight deaf men and women.

Consequences of Heterosexism and Oppression for LGBT People

The multiple acts of oppression experienced by all LGBT people, regardless of their membership in other communities, can lead to a range of threats to their well-being and liberation. As discussed in Chapter 2, it is important to differentiate between the surface manifestations that may be experienced by marginalized people, such as mental health problems, and the root causes of these manifestations, which include a complex web of oppressive forces and power inequalities. The issues and problems experienced by LGBT people are multi-dimensional and are typically a result of society's negative reaction to them and the perpetuation of heterosexist actions and forces, not because of anything inherent in being LGBT. Gregory Herek's (1991) review of research on the mental health of lesbian women and gay men demonstrated that overall these individuals do not experience higher rates of negative mental health outcomes, with the exception of higher rates of suicide among LGBT youth and higher rates of substance use among lesbian women and gay men. Both of these psychosocial problems (that is, suicide and substance use) are strongly influenced by the root cause of oppression.

Reactions to Immediate and Chronic Oppressive Actions

Several of the 'Issues and Problems' discussed in Chapter 2 are experienced, to varying degrees, by some LGBT people as a result of society's reaction to them, including internalized oppression, fragmented identity and living a double life, poor mental health, psychosocial problems, social isolation and rejection, powerlessness and discrimination, harassment and violence. These issues are typically inter-related and not mutually exclusive, often impacting the individual in multiple interactive ways. The most frequently studied areas have been negative physical, psychological and psychosocial outcomes (for example depression, anxiety, suicide, substance use) experienced by some LGBT adolescents and adults due to their experiences of discrimination, harassment and violence (for example D'Augelli, 1993; D'Augelli & Hershberger, 1993; Garnets et al., 1990; Meyer, 1995; Rosario et al., 1996; Ryan & Futterman, 1998; Waldo, Hesson-McInnis & D'Augelli, 1998). These outcomes may be a response to immediate or direct acts of harassment and violence or to more chronic exposure to oppression.

One clear example of the direct impact of anti-LGBT violence can be found in a study conducted by Gregory Herek, Roy Gillis and Jeanine Cogan (1999). They examined lesbian women and gay men who were survivors of hate crimes over a five year period and found that they demonstrated more signs of psychological distress such as depression, anger, anxiety and post-traumatic stress, than lesbian women and gay men who had experienced non-prejudice-based crimes during the same time period. In addition, these negative health effects appeared to be maintained over a longer period of time than those resulting from random crimes.

Chronic and pervasive exposure to oppressive actions and systems may lead to internalized oppression, a broad term that has been used to describe the experience of an individual from an oppressed group accepting the negative societal views of the oppressor and experiencing self-blame and shame. For LGBT people, it has been suggested that internalized oppression may be expressed in both overt and covert ways (Gonsiorek, 1993). Overt expressions may take the form of self-deprecating comments and failure to access needed social supports due to internalization of messages that they are not deserving of such assistance; whereas covert expressions may be more difficult to detect since the individual may appear to exhibit a healthy self-acceptance, yet places herself/himself in situations that are destined to lead to distress.

Ilan Meyer (1995) has suggested that the chronic negative societal stressors and oppression experienced by LGBT people as members of a stigmatized numerical minority group leads to the experience of 'minority stress'. He has demonstrated, in a sample of gay men, that the minority stressors of 'internalized homophobia' (that is, directing negative societal attitudes towards the self), stigma (that is, expectations of rejection and discrimination) and actual experiences of antigay violence and discrimination are each independently related to psychological distress (for example demoralization, guilt, suicide, sexual problems). Rafael Diaz and his colleagues (2001) also demonstrated the impact of oppression on psychological distress with their sample of gay and bisexual Latino men living in the US. They asserted that the psychological symptoms exhibited by their participants (that is, social isolation/ loneliness and low self-esteem) could not be attributed to individual pathology and instead were 'deeply connected to a lifelong history and current experiences of social discrimination owing to sexual orientation and racial/ethnic diversity, as well as to high levels of financial hardship due to severe unemployment and poverty' (Diaz, Ayala, Bein, Henne & Marin, 2001, p. 93).

Although the most commonly studied psychosocial reactions to oppression for LGBT people have been suicide and substance use, the more recent and persistent threat of HIV and AIDS among gay and bisexual men in most industrialized countries has lead researchers to examine the potential role of oppression in increasing gay and bisexual men's risk for HIV infection. Caitlin Ryan and Donna Futterman (1998) have discussed the need to attend to the increased risk for HIV infection among LGBT young people, since the societal stigmatization and invisibility they face compound the existing high risk of infection with sexually transmitted diseases that all adolescents traditionally experience. Rafael Diaz and George Ayala (2001) have demonstrated a relationship between increased HIV sexual risk and experiences of homophobia, racism and financial hardship among Latino gay and bisexual men in the US. On a more individual level, Margaret Rosario and her colleagues (2001) have examined the impact of internalized homophobia/oppression within a sample of LGB youngsters in New York, where they found that more negative attitudes towards same-gender sexual expression (including attitudes related to their own sexual orientation) were related to increases in unprotected sexual activity.

Towards Liberation and Well-being

In this section I will discuss a range of social-change efforts focused on promoting liberation and well-being for LGBT people. I have organized my discussion of these initiatives in accordance with the conceptual framework for CP detailed in Chapter 2, with each section focused on a specific set of values and principles that have guided LGBT social-change efforts. It is important to keep in mind, though, that many of these initiatives have incorporated various combinations of the values and principles of CP. I have attempted to address the first principle of ecology throughout this section by illustrating that LGBT efforts at liberation and well-being have been enacted at many different levels within society, including person-centred health promotion approaches, family and peer-group level initiatives and interventions, community-level organizing efforts, institutionalized accountability and changes in legislation and public policy.

LGBT Health Promotion and Prevention

The concept of health promotion and prevention reflects the CP value of health and can be applied at multiple ecological levels through person-centred prevention, community-wide prevention and public health policy. Over the past few years, there has been an increasing recognition that LGBT people experience unique societal circumstances that may differentially impact their health and well-being. In the US, this shift has been partially due the collective efforts of LGBT activists, community members, researchers, clinicians and organizations such as the American Psychological Association (APA) and the Gay and Lesbian Medical Association (GLMA), who have been providing federal public health officials with documentation regarding the unique health needs of LGBT people and communities. Due to these united voices, the National Institutes of Health (NIH) released a program announcement calling for research on LGBT health on May 21, 2001 – the first of its kind to focus specifically on LGBT health issues. The announcement invites submissions of grant applications for behavioural, social, mental health and substance abuse research with LGBT populations. This action provides overt legitimization of LGBT research since the federal government has made a secure commitment to fund LGBT health research and represents a shift in LGBT public health policy.

The publication of the *Healthy People 2010 Companion Document for Lesbian, Gay, Bisexual and Transgender (LGBT) Health* (Gay and Lesbian Medical Association and LGBT Health Experts, 2001) was another major advance in the movement to increase people's awareness of the specific health and health-care needs of LGBT people and communities. This document contains 120 objectives and 12 focal areas from the *Healthy People 2010* document, a national prevention agenda produced by the US federal government in order to identify the most pressing preventable health threats and to establish goals to reduce them. The companion document is the first time that a separate publication focusing on the unique needs of LGBT people has ever been produced to accompany the US Healthy People public health agenda (which is published every 10 years).

Additional advances have been made in the form of other national publications and major health conferences focused specifically on lesbians and gay men. The Institute of Medicine released the first national report on lesbian health issues in 1999 entitled *Lesbian Health: Current Assessment and Directions for the Future*. This publication was the result of a NIH and Centers for Disease Control and Prevention-funded assessment of the available scientific data on the physical and mental health concerns of lesbian women, and included a review of the challenges faced by researchers who conduct research specifically focused on the unique health issues confronting lesbians (Institute of Medicine, 1999). National conferences designed to explore lesbian and gay health concerns have also helped to increase a focus on these populations. The first National Lesbian Health Conference was held in San Francisco in June 2001 and was co-sponsored by a number of groups and organizations, including two federal offices (Office on Women's Health within the US Department of Health and Human Services, and Office of Research on

Women's Health within the National Institutes of Health). Prior to this, the first Gay Men's Health Summit was held in Boulder, Colorado in 1999 and was followed by two other national summits in 2000 and 2003 and over twenty local US summits in 2001 and 2002. The latest summit in 2003 included participation from health advocates, community organizers, activists and researchers from Canada, Europe, New Zealand and the US. These summits are designed to support the health and well-being of men who identify as gay, bisexual and transgendered, through interactive workshops, seminars, community building and activism.

Building Community: LGBT People and Families Unite

Several specific groups of people within the larger LGBT community who share a common identity or membership in another group (for example ethnicity, age), as well as the families and friends of LGBT people, have engaged in community organizing and mobilizing efforts in order to increase their social support and improve collective well-being. Self-help groups and community-based organizations formed by individuals who share a common concern are examples of meso-level interventions that can combat the impact of social isolation experienced by oppressed people. The formation of community organizations and collective networks, and participation in community development initiatives can also create change for LGBT people and their allies at a macro-level by increasing community capacity and social capital.

Self-help groups have been helpful for parents who need assistance in understanding and coping with their child's sexual orientation (Savin-Williams, 1996). The most recognized and extensive of self-help groups is Parents, Families and Friends of Lesbians and Gays (P-FLAG), which is a non-profit organization that provides support group meetings, community education and advocacy for LGBT civil rights in more than 460 communities in the US through its local chapters and national office. P-FLAG began with a simple act of activism by a mother who witnessed her son being attacked at a gay rights demonstration in New York. In reaction to this event, Jeanne Manford marched with her son in the 1972 New York Pride Day parade and later, at the urging of many lesbian and gay people who asked her to talk with their parents, held a support group for parents in a local church (http://www.pflag.org).

Although Latina lesbians were involved in many of the social activist activities of the gay rights liberation movement in the 1960s, they began organizing in autonomous groups in the early 1980s in major cities in the US as a way to show solidarity and to provide support and assistance to each other (Romo-Carmona, 1995). Many of these women organized themselves as networks, as opposed to formal organizations that were often viewed as hierarchical, and groups such as Las Buenas Amigas were formed to create a safe space for Latina lesbians to build connections with other Latina lesbians in other parts of the world. In 1987 the first *Encuentro de Lesbianas de Latino America y El Caribe* was held in Mexico to create a space for Latina lesbians to unite and to show solidarity (Romo-Carmona, 1995). Groups such as Las Buenas Amigas were critical to the organization of this event and have also been involved in major lesbian and gay political movements and actions.

Nancy Nystrom and Teresa Jones (2003) describe the community organizing efforts of a small group of older lesbian women in the Pacific Northwest region of the US who met in 1996 to discuss the lack of support and resources for aging and older lesbian women in their community. These women formed the Elder Initiative (the name of the group was changed during the development process but was not revealed in the article to protect the confidentiality of the members), in an attempt to ensure the involvement of aging lesbians in planning efforts in their community and to increase social support through building connections among lesbian women over the age of 45. Within three years, membership in the group grew from 45 to 550 women and over time the women organized a range of efforts such as monthly workshops on health, grief and loss and social support; a newsletter and website to inform members about relevant community events and issues; and the Skills Bank which was a clearinghouse for home-repair projects, fundraising, networking and maintaining contact with the housebound (Nystrom & Jones, 2003).

Collective Power: Gay Rights Liberation Movement and Community Partnerships

Dalton et al. (2001) suggest that movements for social change and liberation that occurred among various oppressed groups in the US during the 1960s had a strong influence on the development of the field of CP and they cite the gay rights liberation movement as one of those motivating forces. The gay rights liberation movement is an example of a macro-level social change movement that occurred as a result of oppressed people joining together in an attempt to promote collective well-being.

Lesbian women and gay men actually began participating in a variety of community organizing and mobilizing efforts on social, organizational and political fronts many years before the New York Stonewall riot in 1969, which is often recognized as the event which marked the beginning of the modern gay rights liberation movement (Poindexter, 1997). In fact, the first organized gay civil rights group in the US was formed in Chicago in 1924 and was called the Society for Human Rights. Other formal gay and lesbian organizations also existed early in the 20th century, including the Mattachine Society, Daughters of Bilitis and ONE (Nardi, Sanders & Marmor, 1994; Poindexter, 1997). These early organizations served as venues for affiliation and community organizing around issues of harassment, politics and discrimination.

Community psychologists Linda Garnets and Anthony D'Augelli (1994) provide an excellent historical trajectory of empowerment efforts in lesbian and gay communities within the US, beginning in the 1950s. In tracing this history they demonstrate how lesbians and gay men have enacted Swift and Levin's (1987) four steps for translating empowerment into action. They demonstrate how lesbian and gay communities have identified *empowerment deficits* by documenting discrimination and prejudice based on sexual orientation; promoted *empowerment awareness* by analysing gay/lesbian history and providing public education regarding anti-lesbian/gay violence; *mobilized economic, social and political power* by forming social networks and political coalitions directed at confronting prejudice and discrimination; and attempted to *change levels of equity in society* by developing and implementing interventions that attempt to change social norms related to prejudice and violence, and to create formal legal and institutional protections against such harm (Garnets & D'Augelli, 1994).

An example of addressing collective power at the relational or meso-level of analysis is the formation of partnerships between community psychologists and LGBT people. For the past five years, some of my graduate students and I have been working collaboratively with a community-based organization that provides sexual health promotion services to gay and bisexual Latino and African-American male adolescents. We have worked together to reveal the various oppressive narratives that impact young gay and bisexual men of colour and have then used this information to help young people in the community modify existing narratives and create new narratives through the agency's health promotion program. In order to maintain a collaborative partnership and to work in solidarity with the agency and the young people, my graduate students and I actively participate in agency procedures and meetings, attend program activities (that is, street/community outreach and intervention sessions), participate in cultural and fund-raising events and generally 'hang out' at the agency and in the community (Harper, Bangi, Contreras, Pedraza, Tolliver & Vess, 2004).

LGBT Legal Issues and Public Policy: Towards Inclusion and Equity

Laws and public policies that restrict the human rights of LGBT people or fail to offer LGBT people the same legal protections as non-LGBT people serve as major oppressive forces. The CP value of respect for diversity and cultural relativity can be enacted at the macro-level through policies that are designed to provide a greater degree of equity for marginalized groups and to create a society that is more inclusive of all people. Within the past 20 years, several countries have made advances in laws and public policies that are beginning to provide LGBT people with the same basic human rights as non-LGBT people.

The US is one country that has evidenced recent victories in the fight for LGBT rights. The US Supreme Court has heard a growing number of cases related to LGBT legal rights over the past few years and the rulings of this High Court have had a tremendous impact on the way LGBT rights are viewed in the US (Feldblum, 2001). The court's most recent decision was a 6–3 ruling on June 26, 2003 that all sodomy laws that apply to consenting adults in private settings are unconstitutional and unenforceable in the US. This was a great victory for all LGBT people and is a step in the direction of securing equal human rights for LGBT people. The Supreme Court's 1996 ruling in *Romer* v *Evans*, which struck down Colorado's Amendment 2, was another notable action of this court. Amendment 2 would have removed the possibility that LGBT people could be legally protected against discrimination in Colorado. Although supporters of Amendment 2 claimed that LGBT individuals were being granted 'special rights' because of the discrimination protection they received under the law, in actuality the state's discrimination laws merely allowed for 'equal treatment', not 'special treatment' (Feldblum, 2001; Russell & Richards, 2003).

Rulings handed down by State Supreme Courts in the US also reflect a growing recognition of the ways in which LGBT people's civil and human rights have been violated and a movement towards offering protection and reconciliation to those who have been harmed. The example detailed earlier in this chapter where a county sheriff's failure to protect Brandon Teena lead to his tragic death, resulted in one such ruling. The Nebraska Supreme Court held the sheriff accountable for his failure to protect Brandon and this ruling is seen as strengthening law enforcement agencies' duty to protect LGBT crime victims (Lambda Legal Defense and Education Fund, 2001). Despite these advances, more changes still need to occur in order to offer LGBT people in the US the same legal rights and protections as non-LGBT people. The need for continued social change in this area is clearly illustrated by the fact that as of January 2003, only 13 of 50 states in the US have legislation that prohibits employment discrimination (Lambda Legal Defense and Education Fund, 2003). A growing number of individual cities and counties in the US have ordinances and laws that offer employment discrimination protection, but these do not hold the same weight as federal and state laws.

Other countries have also enacted a variety of legal and legislative mandates during the past five to ten years that demonstrate a positive change in the way that LGBT people's human rights are being viewed. For example, in 1996 the Republic of South Africa, which was quite oppressive toward LGBT people under apartheid, officially adopted a new constitution that guaranteed protection for lesbian, gay and bisexual people, making it the first country in the world to include such specific protections for LGB people. In 2000, the Netherlands became the first country in the world to legalize same-gender marriages. The Dutch law gives same-gender couples the right to legally marry and provides for all the same privileges and conditions as heterosexual marriages, including divorce and adoption rights. On July 12, 2002 the Ontario Superior Court became the first Canadian court to rule in favour of recognizing same-gender marriages when it ruled that prohibiting lesbian and gay couples from marrying violates the Charter of Rights and Freedoms and thus is unconstitutional. Despite attempts to appeal this ruling, on June 10, 2003 the Ontario Court of Appeal ruled that the common law definition of marriage should be changed to redefine marriage as the lawful union of two persons (regardless of gender), thus legalizing same-gender marriage.

National and international human rights groups have addressed other LGBT civil and human rights issues elsewhere in the world. In 1994 the United Nations Human Rights Committee determined that the sodomy laws of the Australian State of Tasmania violated the country's obligations under the International Covenant on Civil and Political Rights. The International Gay and Lesbian Human Rights Commission (1999) reported that this case was a landmark decision for international LGBT rights. Great Britain was recently charged by the European Court of Human Rights to lift its ban on LGB people in the military, since this exclusion violated the European Convention on Human Rights (Lyall, 1999). The United Nations became the first non-LGBT specific group with international presence and power to take a solid stand on the provision of equal rights to LGBT people when their High Commissioner for Human Rights recently moved to increase the United Nation's focus on human rights abuse and violations based on sexual orientation and gender identity (International Gay and Lesbian Human Rights Commission, 2001).

Commitment Through Research: Listening to the Changing Voices of LGBT People

An examination of the progression of LGBT-related research over the past few decades illustrates ways in which the CP value of accountability to oppressed groups has slowly been incorporated into scientific inquiry and how the voices of LGBT people are gradually being heard. Scientific research and literature on sexual orientation has progressed through several different stages since the 1950s. Early research focused on whether or not 'homosexuality' constituted a mental illness and included a progression of studies that eventually portrayed LGB people in a more positive light. Due to these early studies, which demonstrated that LGB people were not suffering from any type of psychological disturbance and the activism of several groups and individuals, the diagnosis of 'homosexuality' was removed from the DSM in 1973 (Bayer, 1981).

A second wave of research focused on the lesbian and gay experience, while an awareness of bisexuality emerged even later. This era of research revealed information about the coming-out process, about the effects of discrimination and violence on LGB people and about the lives of LGB people in their various roles as family members, partners, parents, members of the work force and citizens (Harper & Schneider, 2003). Although these studies gave voice to the life experiences of LGB people, they have been criticized for focusing more on the negative experiences, such as rates of victimization and suicide and less on the strengths and resiliencies of this population. In the 1980s the emergence of the HIV/AIDS epidemic fostered another new wave of research. Despite early popular press accounts of gay men as perpetuators of the epidemic, HIV-related research ultimately resulted in a greater focus on the strengths of LGB communities as it demonstrated how united grassroots efforts and activism resulted in major advances in the treatment, management and prevention of HIV/AIDS. These studies also focused more attention on LGB people and communities as underserved and understudied. This scientifically based awareness of the need for more research and services also assisted LGB activists in their social action efforts (Harper & Schneider, 2003).

Most recently, research related to transgendered individuals is beginning to emerge and the voice of this oppressed group is slowly being heard. Early research related to transgendered individuals was actually conducted in the early 1900s, but it was not scientifically based and consisted primarily of case studies conducted by psychiatrists with a Freudian orientation (Bullough, 2000; Pfaefflin, 1997). Recent research on transgender issues is being conducted using more scientific methods and closely echoes the early wave of gay and lesbian research that focused on the question of psychopathology. Some authors are challenging the inclusion of *transvestic fetishism* and *gender identity disorder* as psychiatric disorders in the current DSM-IV (for example Gainor, 2000), but more research that involves the voices and perspectives of transgendered individuals is needed to support the challenge.

Chapter Summary

As I have illustrated in this chapter, community psychologists are in a prime position to contribute to the social change efforts that are needed in order to liberate LGBT people. Unfortunately, several of the initiatives detailed in this last section have not been initiated by community psychologists, but by groups of LGBT people who joined together to fight an oppressive society. Tony D'Augelli was one of the first US community psychologists to write about the need for the field to actively address LGBT issues, and in 1989 noted that despite community psychologists' level of expertise in empirically describing social phenomena and community change and in implementing social action initiatives, they have not adequately addressed LGBT communities. An increasing number of community psychologists are working to increase the field's focus on LGBT issues, as illustrated by several recent issues of CP academic journals that are exclusively focused on efforts by community psychologists to promote liberation and well-being among LGBT people and communities. These issues are listed below in the 'Resources' section of the chapter and are unique in that they are the first special issues of these journals to be exclusively focused on LGBT issues.

The initiatives detailed in these special issues and throughout this chapter are a step in the right direction, but there is still much work to be done. Community psychologists need to join in solidarity with LGBT people and communities in a collaborative manner and work towards sharing their knowledge and talents to fight oppression and heterosexism. Social inequalities and oppression persist because those in power do not want to give up that power. With a united voice and strength in numbers we can challenge the negative societal forces that continue to oppress LGBT people and work towards increasing liberation and well-being for all LGBT people. Every action helps and you can help in this fight – something as simple as challenging heterosexist assumptions and statements in your day-to-day interactions, confronting a friend or family member who tells an anti-LGBT joke or educating a classmate about the forces that oppress LGBT people. This chapter and the readings and websites in the Resources section below will provide you with the necessary information in your efforts to combat heterosexism and oppression of LGBT people. Knowledge is power.

COMMENTARY: Thinking Outside the Box   *Janice Ristock*

When Geoff Nelson and Isaac Prilleltensky asked me to write a reflexive commentary on a chapter that focused on LGBT people for a CP text, I enthusiastically said 'yes' and read Gary Harper's chapter with much anticipation. I recalled how as a lesbian PhD student in a CP program I was told by my advisor not to write or do research on gay and lesbian issues if I hoped to get a tenure-track position in a university. She herself was an out lesbian who published on lesbian issues and offered this advice to me based on her own negative experiences as a tenured professor. While much has changed since then (the late 80s) and more people are doing research on LGBT issues (myself included), I still find that too much of the literature and research in our field excludes the experiences of LGBT people, so that I am usually in the position of reading against texts as a way of resisting

heterosexism and as a way of keeping my voice present and my identity visible. This chapter provided me with that still too rare opportunity to read with the text, in an act of solidarity, even though LGBT people are not a homogeneous group and our experiences are diverse. Most of all the chapter offered me hope that we are confronting and will continue to confront heterosexism in our field and work towards liberation. So it is in the spirit of solidarity and diversity that I also offer my critical reactions to some of the issues that Gary raises in the chapter.

The Power of Words and the Limitation of Categories

When reading the section on 'defining sexual orientation and gender identity' I immediately thought of a concrete example that illuminates the diversity of individuals who might be classified under the umbrella LGBT and that also exposes some of the assumptions we might hold about what these categories mean. When I was beginning a research project on the issue of violence in lesbian relationships I made a poster inviting lesbians to participate in the study. One of the first women who came forward explained to me that she was not sure if she qualified because she did not identify as a lesbian even though she was in a sexually intimate relationship with another woman who was physically abusive towards her. She told me that she was also in a heterosexual marriage (which was not abusive) and that she identified as 'gay'. This experience reminded me that LGBT people identify with a number of different labels – for example lesbians might prefer terms such as 'queer', 'dyke', 'butch', 'femme', 'gay', 'two-spirited' and so on. Although I was using the word 'lesbian' as a category that included any intimate relationships between women, no matter how they self-identified, I had to become aware of who would feel included and who would feel excluded by my exclusive use of the term 'lesbian' on the poster. This encounter reinforced the need to be reflexive when conducting research, and in this case caused me to change the wording of my posters and to challenge some of my own assumptions about how many women in same-sex relationships would identify with the term 'lesbian' (Ristock, 2002). It also reminded me of the limits of categories in capturing the complexity of people's lives.

The term 'queer', although not introduced by Gary, is one that some people, often younger people, are using to describe their non-conforming and unfixed gender and sexual identities. It is a term that is very challenging, firstly because it reclaims a pejorative label that was used by dominant culture to describe gays and lesbians and is now being used positively by some LGBT people to name themselves; and secondly because, for some people, the term is also a refusal to accept the available categories that we currently have to describe sexual and gender identities. The terms 'gay', 'straight' and 'bisexual', for example, often assume a fixed, stable, core identity, when for many people (and for those who take a postmodernist theoretical view of identity categories) that is not how they understand or experience their desires (Jagose, 1996). As the chapter points out, words are powerful and so it becomes very important for members of marginalized communities to be able to define, name and locate themselves more accurately.

Social Location and Knowledge from the Margins

Understanding the diversity of LGBT people is not only about seeing the way our experiences of heterosexism and oppression are different, as described in the important section on 'multiple membership and layers of oppression'. It is also about understanding and bringing forward the way our differing social locations (that is our personal histories, our class backgrounds, racial and cultural identities, our gender identities, our sexual orientations and so on) (Ristock & Pennell, 1996) provide us with diverse vantage points that affect what we see, the meanings we make and how our knowledge is heard or received. Because I think we should pay more attention to the way our social locations give us differing vantage points, I am wary of terms such as 'internalized oppression' and 'internalized homophobia' that were introduced in the chapter. In isolation they may make some sense. But step back to look at the individual in his or her community context and ask 'whose interests do these terms serve and whose vantage point do they reflect?' When using a term such as 'internalized oppression' the problem of oppression can too easily be placed back on the individual as his or her problem, taking the focus away from the source of that oppression in dominant culture. Why is it that we do not use corresponding terms for those who oppress or who inflict homophobic violence on others? Why use terms that mask the agency, resilience and strength of LGBT people who survive in spite of widespread oppression?

Gloria Anzuldua – a Chicana lesbian and feminist – writes about *mestiza* consciousness that she argues needs to be part of our research and theorizing:

> As a mestiza I have no country, my homeland cast me out; yet all countries are mine because I am every woman's sister or potential lover. (As a lesbian I have no race, my own people disclaim me; but I am all races because there is the queer of me in all races.) I am an act of kneading, of uniting and joining that not only has produced both a creature of darkness but a creature of light, but also a creature that questions the definitions of light and dark and gives them new meanings. (Anzuldua, 1990, p. 380)

I find her words powerful because they remind us that in addition to the negative experiences of being on the margins we also have a way of seeing the world that can offer new insights and new knowledge. In my view, it is precisely the role of community psychologists to bring forward these 'new meanings' so that our work will be less likely to serve the powerful and more likely to have us understand and confront the layered workings of oppressive power. For me, a feminist analysis that understands the interlocking nature of systems of oppression experienced by individuals in society is an important framework for helping us to challenge dominant discourses while validating the viewpoints that come from the margins.

Thinking Outside the Box: A Way to Well-being and Social Transformation

Bringing forward new meanings and perspectives from the experiences of LGBT people also requires us to think outside the box of established thinking. By that I mean we must continually engage in a reflexive practice where we ask ourselves: Who benefits and whose interests are being served by the way we currently understand an issue or develop prevention and intervention strategies? Whose voices are heard, whose voices are excluded? What difference does that make to our work?

Take the problem of homophobic bullying in schools. For many years this wasn't even recognized as a problem affecting young LGBT. Now that it has been acknowledged, our response has typically been to punish the perpetrator and offer the victim assertiveness training and supportive counselling as a way of re-building his or her self-esteem. Yet this individualistic intervention does nothing to disrupt the school culture of homophobia and violence that allowed and fostered the bullying in the first place. Some schools, however, are trying a different approach. They are opting for anti-homophobia education for all staff and students as a way of trying to build other structures of relationships in the school culture (Taylor, 2002). This is an example of community capacity-building that can both lead to the greater well-being of all staff and students (LGBT and heterosexual alike), and also transform an oppressive homophobic and heterosexist culture. It is an example of a new intervention that comes from thinking outside the box of established individualistic practices and one that addresses the larger goals of social empowerment and social transformation that I hope we never lose sight of.

CLASS EXERCISE

Over the period of one week, record the number of times you see LGBT identified people on television shows, commercials and in other forms of advertising (for example magazine ads, billboards and so on). When an LGBT-identified person is featured in one of these forms of media, record whether or not they are portrayed in the following ways: (a) caring/nurturing, (b) intelligent, (c) courageous/heroic, (d) serious/thoughtful, (e) monogamous, (f) spiritual, (g) overly sexual/promiscuous, (h) substance using, (i) masculine [for females]/ effeminate [for males], (j) self-indulgent/materialistic, (k) criminal/predatory. Compare the number of times the LGBT person is portrayed in a positive light (a–f) versus a negative light (g–k). Discuss your findings with other students in the class and explore the implications of these portrayals.

Chapter glossary

gay rights liberation movement the movement by the LGBT community and allies to end heterosexism and uphold the human rights of LGBT people

heterosexism like racism and sexism, this term focuses on multiple levels of prejudice and oppression experienced by LGBT people, including cultural heterosexism (institutional or systemic beliefs in the superiority of an exclusively heterosexual orientation) and psychological heterosexism (prejudice and stereotypes, harassment and violence towards LGBT individuals)

homophobia a term used to describe heterosexual people's fear, contempt and hatred of LGBT people

homosexuality because of its association with psychopathology and the DSM, and because it identifies people solely based on their sexual orientation, this is no longer the preferred term of the American Psychological Association or the LGB community to refer to people with a same-sex sexual orientation

internalized oppression the internalization of heterosexism by LGBT individuals, such that they experience negative self-esteem

LGBT lesbian, gay and bisexual refers to people who experience varying degrees of same-gender desire and attraction and who engage in same-gender sexual behaviour, while transgendered refers to a range of individuals who do not conform to traditional societal expectations and roles for each gender; LGB refers to sexual orientation, while transgendered refers to gender identity

two-spirited fluidity of gender roles and sexuality, rather than an 'either-or' position (man/woman, gay/straight)

■ RESOURCES ■

1. Adrian Coyle and Sue Wilkinson edited a special issue of the *Journal of Community and Applied Social Psychology* entitled 'Social Psychological Perspectives on Lesbian and Gay Issues in Europe: The State of the Art', 2002, **12**(3).

2. Janice Ristock and Danielle Julien edited a special issue of the *Canadian Journal of Community Mental Health* entitled 'Disrupting Normalcy: Gay/Lesbian/Queer Issues in Mental Health', which was published in Fall 2003.

3. Margaret Schneider and Gary Harper edited a special issue of the *American Journal of Community Psychology* entitled 'Lesbian, Gay, Bisexual and Transgendered Communities: Linking Theory, Research and Practice', 2003, **31**(3–4).

4. PFLAG – Parents, Families and Friends of Lesbians and Gays. 'PFLAG promotes the health and well-being of gay, lesbian, bisexual and transgendered persons, their families and friends through: support, to cope with an adverse society; education, to enlighten an ill-informed public; and advocacy, to end discrimination and to secure equal civil rights.' (http://www.pflag.org/).

5. GLSEN – Gay, Lesbian and Straight Education Network: Creating Safe Schools for Lesbian, Gay, Bisexual and Transgender People. 'GLSEN is the leading national organization fighting to end anti-gay bias in K-12 schools.' (http://www.glsen.org/).

6. Lambda Legal. 'Lambda Legal is a national organization committed to achieving full recognition of the civil rights of lesbians, gay men, bisexuals, the transgendered and people with HIV or AIDS through impact litigation, education and public policy work.' (http://www.lambdalegal.org/).

7. American Psychological Association Lesbian, Gay and Bisexual Concerns Office. 'The APA Lesbian, Gay and Bisexual Concerns Office has worked since 1975 to eliminate the stigma of mental illness long associated with same-sex sexual orientation and to reduce prejudice, discrimination and violence against lesbian, gay and bisexual people.' (http://www.apa.org/pi/lgbc/homepage.html).

20
Ableism

Glen W. White

Chapter Organization

Introduction	
Historical Context	◆ Developments in Early United States ◆ Developments in the Mid-Twentieth Century
The Struggle for Self-determination	**Media Portrayal Contributing to Ableism**
Challenges for Community Psychologists	◆ Power ◆ Diversity ◆ Partnership and Collaboration ◆ Subjectivity and Reflexivity ◆ Vision and Values Guiding Community Work
Examples of Research and Action	◆ Action Letter Portfolio ◆ Health Promotion Interventions for Women with Physical Disabilities ◆ Lessons Learned
Reflection and Application	**International Vistas**	**Chapter Summary**
COMMENTARY: Ableism: A Disability Rights Perspective	**Class Exercise**	**Glossary**	**Resources**

Warm-up Exercise

1. How does Hollywood usually portray people with disabilities? Does this portrayal affect the way you or others view people with various disabilities?
2. When you encounter a person with a severe disability, what is your first reaction? Why?
3. People with disabilities are often discriminated against in terms of jobs, education and housing. What can community psychologists do to help reduce these types of discrimination?

Introduction

Many people with disabilities report their community experience to be disconcerting. Experiences range from being invisible and unnoticed by others to being viewed as the objects of pity. People with disabilities are often thought to be incapable of contributing meaningfully to society. If they are invited to participate, they feel it is a great burden to continually prove themselves worthy of such involvement. It is abundantly clear that people with disabilities are marginalized by society in terms of attitudes (Enwemeka & Adeghe, 1982; Jackson & Mupedziswa, 1988; Okunda, 1981), employment (O'Day, 1999; Schriner, 2001), income levels (Kaye & Longmore, 1997), education (National Council on Disability, 1989), poor assistive technology (Werner, 1987) and access (Kaye, 1998). But perhaps one of the biggest challenges people with disabilities and chronic conditions face is the concept and barrier of ableism. Simply put, ableism is a non-factual negative judgment about the attributes and capabilities of an individual with a disabling condition. While other 'isms' such as sexism, heterosexism and racism have large existing literatures, there is a small but growing literature in the area of ableism (Burdekin, 1995; Charlton, 1998; Davis, 1995; Gokhale, 1985). These and many other issues prevent people with disabilities from fully participating in their communities and society in general. In order to understand the situation of people with disabilities we must explore the historical roots of ableism and the contextual issues which affect attitudes and actions toward this population.

Historical Context

Dating back to Greek and Roman societies the incidence and prevalence of disability was high, largely because of the strenuous and manual nature of most daily activities. In addition, disabilities due to injuries and diseases were common due to poor living conditions and the frequent occurrence of wars and pestilence (Garland, 1995). The practice of infanticide for infants born with obvious deformities was required by law in the city-state of Sparta and acceptable in other parts of Greece (Stiker, 1997). Interestingly, according to Stiker, those who had congenital abnormalities such as hearing, visual and or cognitive impairments that were not easily detected until later development were not as likely to be put to death.

Braddock and Parish (2001) provide an excellent overview of the institutional history of disability throughout the Middle Ages to modern society. During the Middle Ages the conventional wisdom concerning many disabilities and impairments (that is, psychiatric disability, deafness, epilepsy) suggested that the cause of such maladies were demonological or supernatural causes; the individual with the impairment was thought to be possessed. Treatment for these pour souls ranged from drinking unpleasant tasting concoctions to their execution as witches. As Braddock and Parish (2001) further note, starting in the mid 1200s members of religious orders and laypersons with an interest in mental illness established residential institutions to house and assist those with disabling conditions such as mental illness, cognitive impairments and, later, leprosy.

Developments in Early United States

The founding colonies in the US frequently adopted and adapted English law for their governance. Early laws in some communities included public welfare provisions for those who were poor or had infirmities that prevented them from working (Morton, 1897). In addition to these laws and policies, new treatments were developed to aid people with selected disabling conditions. Some of the earliest interventions targeted persons with mental illness. One signer of the Declaration of Independence in the US, psychiatrist Benjamin Rush, took an active interest in finding treatments to cure mental illness, including the development of mechanical devices to reduce sensory motor activity and heart rate pulse levels (Rush, 1812). Other treatment approaches common in the last quarter of the 1700s and early 1800s included prescribed dietary changes, enemas, bloodletting and cold showers.

The early 1800s brought new developments and leaders who worked to advance the education and welfare of persons who were deaf or blind. Thomas Gallaudet, an educator, founded the first deaf school in the US. After his education at Yale, Gallaudet became interested in deaf education and travelled to France where he studied sign language and other teaching methods at the Institut Royal des Sourds-Muets in Paris. In 1816 Gallaudet returned to the US with Frenchman Laurent Clerc, a teacher of the deaf, and founded the first free public school for the deaf in the US, the American Asylum for Deaf-Mutes (now the American School for the Deaf in Hartford, Connecticut). Later, Gallaudet's son, Edward, would direct the Columbia Institute for the Deaf and the Dumb and the Blind. (This institute is now known as Gallaudet University, the first US institution of higher education for the deaf, located in Washington, DC).

In the 1820s, Frenchman Louis Braille, an blind instructor at the National Institute for the Young Blind in Paris, modified the Barbier 'point writing' system, used to decode army messages, to assist blind students to read by using their fingers to lightly ride over a series of embossed dots and dashes on cardboard (Roberts, 1986). Following the trend in Europe around 1800, the first educational institutions for the blind began to be established in the United States. Originally founded as private philanthropic organizations, these included the Perkins School for the Blind, the New York Institution for the Blind and the Overbrook School for the Blind in Philadelphia.

As educational approaches to students who were deaf or blind became more widely disseminated, states started establishing and expanding the institutional model, where students who were blind or deaf were housed and educated away from their families and support systems. This institutional approach also became an emerging model for training individuals with intellectual disabilities, after a rapid building expansion in the mid 1800s (Braddock & Parish, 2001). Following the Civil War, the training approach towards helping people with mental retardation and mental illness was de-emphasized in favour of a more custodial approach, where institutions would house residents with intellectual disabilities throughout the course of their lifetime (Bicknell, 1895; Fish, 1892; Wilbur, 1888).

While these institutional approaches sought to deliver professional treatment to people with various disabling conditions, the person was objectified and the goal was to help 'fix' or restore the person to normalcy, a contrasting term to deviancy, which first appeared in the English language circa 1855 (Davis, 1995). This approach disempowered people with disabilities, as the problem was still ascribed to them, with little concern for environmental contributions to the disabling process.

Developments in the Mid-Twentieth Century

The practice of ableism continued unabated until the late 1960s. During the preceding decades, persons with physical disabilities, such as spinal injury, post-polio syndrome, cerebral palsy and those with head injuries were frequently restricted to their homes or other long-term care settings. There were few advocates for these individuals and they lacked leaders and models of empowerment that were emerging in other civil rights movements in the 1960s. In addition, there were no federal mandates or civil protections for citizens with disabilities.

They were denied equal access to the community including transportation, education, housing, medical care and employment.

During the latter 1960s the independent living movement was started through the personal experience and leadership of several persons with severe disabilities who were marginalized and discriminated against by those who were given the mandate to help people with disabilities. These early pioneers responded to this broad social injustice towards people with disabilities, experienced in virtually every sector (public, private, medical). Ed Roberts was one of the first leaders of this movement and his tactics and actions empowered him to increase his personal independence and challenge ableist attitudes and policies. Many others with severe disabilities would later follow his model for change (Levy, 1988).

Box 20.1   Ed Roberts – Pioneer in Independent Living

Roberts' earliest recollection of disability takes him to a day in 1946 when, like many six-year-olds, he heard his father say, 'Don't stare', when a woman with cerebral palsy came into view. At 13, his prejudices against people with disabilities were well entrenched. At 14, he contracted polio. Roberts reminisces, 'I was a very independent kid; suddenly I became a patient. My mother was told I'd become a vegetable because of my high fever. The doctors told her it would be better if I died.

Meanwhile, I was experiencing lots of self-hatred and powerlessness. I was a helpless cripple, dependent on an iron lung. I absorbed all the stereotypes: I would never marry, have a job or be a whole person. I tried to starve myself – the only way to commit suicide. In seven months my weight dropped from 120 to 50 pounds.' Fortunately, when the last home nurse quit, Roberts started eating again. Still, he stayed at home for five years, afraid to be seen by those who had no disability, ashamed to be seen by those who did.

The turning point came when, after years of high school by telephone, Roberts completed his senior year. There was nothing left to do but get out of the house. 'My worst fear came true', he recalls, 'Everyone stared. But that experience created a shift in my own perception: I could be a star, different in a positive way, not a helpless cripple. I decided if people wanted to stare, it was their problem, not mine.'

A mediocre student before the onset of polio, Roberts excelled over the telephone wires. 'I began to realize that the key to power was education.' Ironically, his high school principal thought ignition was the key that mattered. He maintained Roberts couldn't graduate because he had not taken driver education. 'You wouldn't want a cheap diploma', he intoned. Roberts and his mother threw the principal out of the house. With the help of a family friend on the community school board, Roberts got his diploma. 'It was a very important fight for me because I won. I learned that you must fight for your own rights, no matter what people say. And I learned it's important to win when you fight, to find a way to make it happen, to turn to the media if necessary.'

Turning to the media became necessary two years after the diploma victory. California's Department of Rehabilitation, rejecting Roberts as 'too disabled to work', refused to sponsor his university education. Roberts contacted the press. Within a week, the Department of Rehabilitation caved in. 'Public bureaucracies have a lot of trouble with negative PR', says Roberts. (Fifteen years later, he was appointed head of that very system. 'Better watch out when you reject people; it may come back to haunt you', he remarks in retrospect.)

Source: Used with permission from the Research and Training Center on Independent Living.

Now that we have set the contextual stage on the issue of ableism let's explore this topic from a community psychology (CP) perspective.

The Struggle for Self-determination

Persons with physical and/or sensory disabilities are often neglected when considering marginalized and disenfranchised groups. Yet, ironically, they offer significant opportunities for community psychologists to learn from, and to help develop tools, both to reduce the effects of ableism and to enhance personal empowerment and community change. Until recently, people with disabilities were spectators watching life pass them by – with little hope that they could have any meaningful role in society, whether it be developing a relationship with others, receiving the same educational opportunities as their non-disabled peers or obtaining employment without fear of discrimination. In the past decade awareness has increased regarding new and emerging disability populations such as persons who have chronic fatigue syndrome (Jason et al., 1999), multiple chemical sensitivity syndrome (Jason, Taylor & Kennedy, 2000) or neurological injuries due to violence (National Institute on Disability and Rehabilitation Research, 1999). Persons from these emerging groups face increased marginalization by society and a lack of responsiveness from social service providers who should be addressing their needs.

As noted, ableism has become increasingly amplified by the warehousing of individuals with disabilities in institutional settings; by the sensationalistic and inappropriate portrayal of people with disabilities in the arts and the media; by the tear-jerking and heart-wrenching national telethon appeals to give money to help the 'crippled children' live longer. As one example, the community of Arnhem, in the Netherlands held a major telethon appeal for people with disabilities and created hetDorp, a self-standing community where persons with mobility limitations could live. While such fund-raising was well-intentioned, hetDorp is a segregated community for people with disabilities and limits opportunities for its residents to become more integrated into the Arnhem and surrounding communities.

People with disabilities have had to contend with assigned identification resulting from medical models and categorical labels that are diagnosis and deficit driven. Some argue that ableists assign cultural prescriptions of disability based upon their own definition of normalcy.

Perhaps nowhere is ableism more frequently practised than in the medical and rehabilitation system that is supposedly designed to help people with disabilities to increase their participation in and quality of life. Ostensibly, such a system, designed

Table 20.1 Rehabilitation versus independent living paradigm

Issue	Rehabilitation Paradigm (Ableing Model)	Independent Living Paradigm (Enabling Model)
The problem defined	Disability or impairment Lack of vocational skills	Lack of autonomy Dependence on professionals
Problem focus	On the individual	In the environment In the rehabilitation process
Problem solution	Intervention by professionals	Peer counselling Advocacy Self-help Consumer control Barriers removal
Social role	Seen as patient or client	Seen as consumer
Who is in control?	Professionals	Consumer
Desired outcomes	Restore maximum function Obtain gainful employment	Living independently in the least restricted environment

Adapted from DeJong (1979)

to help prevent further deterioration and disablement, should emphasize and support the concepts of prevention, empowerment and choice. Gerben DeJong (1979), in his seminal article on 'Independent living: From social movement to analytic paradigm' provided a comparative analysis of the medical model and the more consumer-friendly independent living, or social model, used when working with people with disabilities. Table 20.1 summarizes DeJong's comparison of these two models.

DeJong points out that under the rehabilitation paradigm (ableing model), the problem resides in the person, who needs to be cured or rehabilitated to restore former levels of function and value. In contrast, under the independent living paradigm (enabling model) the need for cure or restoration is diminished when emphasis is placed on modifying the environment to better accommodate people with disabling or chronic conditions. Additionally, under the rehabilitation paradigm, professionals are considered the most qualified interveners to ameliorate professional-identified problems. In summary, the professional is in control and determines the outcomes to be achieved and whether or not they are successful. In contrast, the independent living model has strong resonance with the concepts of CP, especially with the emphasis on self-help, empowerment, consumer sovereignty and control. Lappé and DuBois (1994) describe a similar paradigmatic contrast with their 'New Model Emerging in Human Services' (p. 156), which shares many commonalities with the independent living model.

A poignant example of the non-empowering and ableistic approach that some health providers use with people with disabilities was captured in interviews with disabled women about their reproductive experiences. Many women said that the subject of sexuality was rarely discussed at home or in institutional settings (Nosek et al., 1995). In some cases medical staff treated the women as though they were ignorant (Walter, Nosek & Langdon, 2001). Nosek and colleagues captured the child birthing experience of a woman with bilateral amputations above the elbow. This woman reported that she was in labour for 30 hours and that she had both her artificial limbs removed during the delivery process. She was not allowed to see her baby and feed her after delivery.

Media Portrayal Contributing to Ableism

Another factor that contributes to ableism in the community and society in general is the issue of media portrayal of people with disabilities. The words society uses to identify and describe specific groups can affect how they are viewed and valued, whether the words are used to describe gender, race, religion, sexual orientation or in this case, actual or perceived level of ability. As Longmore (1985) discussed, ableist language and portrayal is ubiquitous, ranging from children's books and cartoons such as the evil Captain Hook and the stuttering Porky Pig to negative images in the film industry such as the crazed paraplegic Dr. Strangelove, who wanted to destroy the world, and the blind man with the extraordinary sense of smell in *The Scent of a Woman*.

While these misrepresentations may foster ableistic attitudes, perhaps more frequent and damaging are the numerous stories about people with disabilities in the print and broadcast news media. There is an irony in that people with disabilities are usually invisible to the media (Ruffner, 1984) and if they are reported at all, they are likely to be presented in one of two non-factual ways. First, as a human interest story about their unfortunate circumstances – in which case descriptors such as 'stroke victim', 'helpless cripple', 'wheelchair-bound', or 'confined to a wheelchair' are frequently used. The emphasis is not placed on the person but rather on the defects or specific disabling condition. Instead of the more appropriate 'person first' language such as 'person with a stroke', the word 'person' is often eliminated altogether and terms such as a 'polio victim' are used instead. The other approach used by print and broadcast reporters and writers is the overemphasis on the person with a disability being courageous or superhuman. Examples of this include stories of extraordinary achievements, such as the efforts of Mark Wellner, a paraplegic and US Park Service Ranger who scaled the steep cliffs of Yosemite, a large mountain cliff in western US, using only his hands. While this approach might seem more positive, it still draws attention to the disability first and to the person second. Unfortunately, this media portrayal is not limited to the popular literature, printed news and broadcasts.

The American Psychological Association's *Publication Manual* (2001), a respected guide for professional writing, recommends that 'The guiding principle for "nonhandicapping" language is the integrity of individuals as human beings.' (p. 69). However, ableist language continues to be sprinkled throughout many professional peer-reviewed research articles, often using archaic terms such as 'wheelchair-bound' and 'confined to a wheelchair' instead of one of the more acceptable terms such as 'person with a spinal injury' or simply, 'wheelchair user'. Box 20.2 contains one approach used to influence print and broadcast media to accurately portray people with disabilities in their reports.

Box 20.2   Influencing Media Portrayal of People with Disabilities

The Research and Training Center on Independent Living (RTC/IL) at the University of Kansas (2001) has just completed the 6th edition of *Media Guidelines for Writing and Reporting on People with Disabilities*. The 'media guidelines' were the end product of a media watch campaign conducted by RTC/IL researchers who read disability-related stories and video recorded local newscasts on disability issues and monitored them for person-first language and positive portrayals of people with disabilities. When the reporters used inappropriate language or portrayals, letters were written with specific suggestions for more appropriate language or portray- als. The recommended language was eventually incor- porated into the Associated Press Stylebook and was cited by the 4th and 5th editions of the American Psychology Association's *Publication Manual* as a resource for using person-first language when writing about persons with disabilities. Since 1985, our Center has distributed over one-million of these media guide- lines to consumer and professional organizations, reli- gious organizations, libraries, state and federal agencies and the countries of Australia, Wales, Peru, Ecuador, Spain and Mexico. For more information go to: www.rtcil.org

---

Challenges for Community Psychologists

As Nelson and Prilleltensky described earlier in the book, there are several emerging metaphors and concepts ripe for consideration and action by community psychologists. In the context of ableism we will discuss power, diversity, partnership/collaboration and subjectivity/reflexivity.

Power

People with disabilities have been and continue to be one of the most disenfranchised and unempowered groups in the community. For most, the issues raised are intensified because many people with disabilities have low incomes and cannot afford the assistive technology, therapy or medications required for even a moderate quality of life. Box 20.3 presents a true case of a 44-year-old woman with diabetes.

Box 20.3   Karen's Story

Karen had Type I diabetes most of her life. She regularly used insulin to keep her blood glucose levels regulated. However, the recommended levels were difficult to maintain. As the diabetes progressed, Karen became unemployed and moved into an apartment by herself, having the help of a personal care assistant for a couple of hours each day. As the diabetes progressed further Karen suffered impaired circulation in both legs, and eventually required above knee amputations. Following rehabilitation, Karen worked in a direct marketing business selling products from her home. This enterprise was mildly successful, however, since she relied on Medicare to help with her staggering medical expenses, she was allowed to make only a very minimal outside income due to federal eligibility regulations. Thus, while Karen wanted to work and increase her income, there was a disincentive to do so.

During the cold winters Karen started staying in bed with several blankets and quilts to keep warm. Karen explained that she kept her thermostat set between 50 and 55 degrees to save money on her heating bills so that she could pay for the expensive diabetes medications she needed each month. Karen died about a year later.

This case demonstrates a system-induced disempowerment. Early Medicare and Social Security regulations were made by policymakers who had little understanding of how these laws would eventually affect people with disabilities. The programs were focused on older, retired people who were no longer expected to work. Sadly, there was no voice for younger people with disabilities on these issues. If the voice was present, it was without power. For people with disabilities living in many developing countries, especially where local and national economies are severely depressed, this voice is further muted by the cacophony of needs and politics of daily survival from non-disabled citizens.

Since the 1980s community psychologists have been working with persons with disabilities to help increase their participation and empowerment in the community. Some achievements for persons with disabilities include setting agendas for community development (Whang, Fawcett, Suarez de Balcazar & Seekins, 1982), participating in self-help and social support groups (Suarez de Balcazar, Seekins, Paine, Fawcett & Mathews, 1989) and decreasing unauthorized parking in handicapped parking spaces (White, Jones, Ulicny, Powell & Mathews, 1988). In addition, Seekins and Fawcett wrote a series of straightforward guides to assist consumers with disabilities to give their personal testimony before policy makers (1982), write letters to public officials (1984a) and write letters to the editor (1984b) to raise community awareness of issues affecting people with disabilities. Fawcett, White, et al. (1994) further describe these efforts using a contextual-behavioural model of empowerment and illustrate this model with eight empowering case studies on people with disabilities. These case studies demonstrate 18 tactics for promoting empowerment within this population. Some of these tactics employ person/group approaches such as increasing knowledge about issues, the causes of problems and possibilities for change; other tactics use environmental approaches to promote empowerment such as removing or minimizing physical barriers and providing economic supports to reduce deprivation associated with poverty.

As people with disabilities have become more empowered they are starting to challenge ableistic practices, policies and attitudes. In the mid 1980s activist disability organizations, such as ADAPT (Americans with Disabilities for Accessible Public Transportation), started to address issues of social injustice for people with disabilities in the US, in a public and forceful manner. Before the Americans with Disabilities Act was passed (major civil rights legislation for people with disabilities), accessible public transportation was virtually non-existent. ADAPT identified when and where the American Public Transit Association (a national organization of public transportation operators) met for their national conventions and planned a series of 'ADAPT actions'. Wheelchair users and others with disabilities blocked the streets to keep traffic idle, while others chained their wheelchairs to public buses. They gained attention for the inequities in public-funded transportation, a system that was serving only non-disabled citizens. ADAPT leaders were eventually able to convince the Executive branch and Congress to include the right to accessible public transportation as part of Title III of the Americans With Disabilities Act, passed in 1990. Such tactics as non-violent demonstrations have been used in other countries, such as Peru, to gain attention from authorities concerning public disability concerns.

As community psychologists, working with people with disabilities, there is always a tension that has to be recognized and negotiated. Unfortunately, many individuals with disabilities have been ill treated or marginalized by the medical, rehabilitation and even research sectors.

Fawcett (1991) identified a comprehensive set of standards for community and behavioural psychologists conducting research with participants living in the community. The article identified several guidelines to help researchers avoid developing 'colonial' relationships with their research participants, among other caveats. As a community psychologist conducting research on disability issues, and a person with a severe disability for over 38 years, I am still viewed with a jaundiced eye by some in the disability community. Some disability advocates have accused social scientists of siphoning off money for 'disability research' that could be better used for advocacy or direct services. Parts of these allegations are true, in the sense that disability research may have rigour, but it is often without practical applications for key stakeholders. Actively involving the disability community to shape and have an active voice in the research process can help neutralize part of this distrust. As an example of this partnership, the Research and Training Centre on Independent Living convened a panel of 14 national leaders and experts in the field of independent living and specified chronic conditions to help create a national survey on full participation in independent living. This process was critical to obtaining ownership and buy-in from national disability organizations, as well as helping to create a survey that would be acceptable to responders with disabilities and chronic conditions. The survey has been disseminated through the Internet, email listservs and via surface mail. Once the survey is completed and the results tabulated, we will convene a town meeting with representative constituents to discuss identified disability concerns and strengths and discuss action plans to address such concerns and enhance the strengths. These collaborative partnerships provide constituents with knowledge and enable their assistance in the research and, later, dissemination process.

Diversity

When one thinks of diversity several categorical headings come immediately to mind; race/ethnicity, gender, age, religion, geographical representation, class bias and sexual orientation. I have observed that ability (inclusion of people with disabilities) rarely makes the list. This lack of inclusion of people with disabilities in the diverse fabric of community and society is emphasized when we examine the level of participation and quality of life. First, people with disabilities make up one of the largest minority groups. Kaye (1998) estimates that approximately 15% of US citizens have disabilities. According to Kaye (1998), people with disabilities, on average, are significantly poorer than their non-disabled counterparts. The poverty rate is three times higher for adults with working limitations than for those who are not limited in work activity. People with disabilities also experience much higher rates of unemployment compared to non-disabled workers. For example, Louis Harris and Associates (1998) found that two-thirds of working age people with disabilities in the United States are unemployed and only 20% are working full time. For those working-age individuals with visual impairments (cannot read print) this unemployment percentage increases to 74% (McNeil, 1993). It is likely that this figure is considerably higher for people with disabilities living in economically depressed countries.

Partnership and Collaboration

There has been a growing interest in involving people with disabilities as partners in community-based research with this population. This approach has been coined 'action research' (Karlsen, 1991), 'participatory action research' (Whyte, 1991) and more recently 'value-based partnerships' (Nelson, Prilleltensky & MacGillivary, 2001). As described in Part IV of this book, the hallmark of participatory action research (PAR) is that it empowers research participants to have an active role in shaping the research process. Some researchers suggest that this approach raises participants to a co-researcher role. Their insider status and local knowledge makes them equal co-researchers (Elden & Chisholm, 1993). The PAR philosophy values participants as experts based on their experiences and history with the particular research issue or problem that is being addressed. This relationship places the researcher in the role of learner to better understand participants' experiences with respect to their disabilities.

The PAR approach to value-constructed research has been used across various CP issues, including community health initiatives (Fawcett, Paine-Andrews, et al., 1994; Schwab, 1997), self-help groups (Chesler, 1991) and cooperative living (Whyte, Greenwood & Lazes, 1989). In addition, PAR has been used to better understand various disability populations, such as persons with psychiatric disabilities (Rogers & Palmer-Erbs, 1994), families with children with disabilities (Santelli, Singer, DiVenere, Ginsberg & Powers, 1998; Turnbull, Friesen & Ramirez, 1998), persons with developmental disabilities (Gilner & Sample, 1993) and adults with physical disabilities (White, Nary & Gutierrez, 1997). White, Nary and Froehlich (2001) describe how PAR can be integrated into the research process and provide examples of how it has been employed. Increasingly, the disability research literature describes the use of PAR philosophy. In fact, the *Canadian Journal of Rehabilitation* dedicated a special issue to PAR (Krogh, 1998).

Why is PAR so important in working with people with disabilities? As noted earlier, many people with disabilities have spent much of their lives dealing with the 'medical model' system in which professionals were trying to 'fix the problem', a problem that always resided within the person. Under this system, persons with disabilities have little or no say over treatment goals, procedures and outcomes of interest. The 'professionals' determined the priorities.

Of course, recruiting consumers and participants to come to the table is only the first step in creating stakeholdership on research and training projects. Finding enough room at the table for all the players is another challenge that community psychologists must address to ensure that there is actual power sharing in the process. However, our experience shows us that there are several personal barriers that can interfere with this process of power sharing. Personal interests and histories of involved constituents can frustrate the stakeholdership process. For example, we convened a meeting of key informants to help create a national survey on full participation in independent living. We invited national leaders from the disability rights movement, who are very open and upfront about their disability and use strong advocacy tactics to create social change. Other key informants at the table represented groups with chronic conditions such as chronic fatigue syndrome and multiple chemical sensitivity syndrome. The leaders associated with these groups stated that many with such chronic conditions might not even label themselves as disabled. The working process of creating the survey brought frustration to representatives from the chronic condition areas. The critical issue was how to frame the survey questions so that responders with chronic conditions would actually relate to the survey. Those from the disability rights movement talked about disability pride and being very direct about disability when creating survey questions. Those representing chronic conditions stated that if questions were only framed using the word 'disability' many people with chronic conditions would not identify with that label and view the questions as irrelevant. A dialogue on the philosophy of inclusion and independent living had to be convened so that key informants could better understand the importance of considering the optimal framing and taxonomy of survey questions to allow for a larger and more diverse response.

Another frustration we faced was the experience of dealing with the needs of a constituency that we knew little about. One of our stakeholders in the process was a person with multiple chemical sensitivity syndrome. This individual reported having very severe reactions to environmental contaminants, to which most individuals have a greater tolerance or immunity. One issue we thought hard about was weighing the factors of cost versus participation. In order to accommodate this individual (and a personal assistant), we had to pay for several days of driving and hotel rooms because this constituent could not fly due to environmental concerns such as jet fuel fumes and other passengers smoking in and around the airport. Additionally, the hotel room and meeting rooms had to be scrubbed with a special non-toxic substance to decontaminate common household cleaners that could be life-threatening for this individual. We also purchased three cases of water in special non-plastic bottles so that this participant could have adequate liquids for the duration of the trip. The expenses and time required to learn about and help coordinate accommodations for this constituent's needs were unexpected. However, our desire to have people with chronic conditions at the table made for a more inclusive and relevant survey instrument. This situation shows that community psychologists often have to work outside of what they know and push the limits of accommodations to ensure a more representative and inclusive process.

There has been a growing interest in and application of self-advocacy knowledge and skills and personal empowerment for people with disabilities. These skills are increasingly being used to address personal and community disability concerns (Balcazar, 1990; Bond & Keys, 1993; Nelson, Ochocka et al., 1998; White, Thomson & Nary, 1997). However, there is a growing number of disability advocates who strongly resist any involvement in a project or event in which they are not included as stakeholders. Some individuals and disability organizations have adopted the slogan 'Nothing about us without us,' which according to Charlton (1998) was first used by participants at an eastern European disability conference. As community psychologists and disability researchers extend their interests in working with people with disabilities, they will need to develop collaborative relationships with key informants from disability populations.

Subjectivity and Reflexivity

As community psychologists and behavioural disability researchers, we are committed to the use of rigorous methodology to produce evidence-based outcomes that contribute to the science and understanding of human behaviour. While we believe that this is a worthy goal, we also acknowledge that such outcomes are of little value unless we carefully consider their relevance to those to whom the research is directed (White, 2002).

We recently received a grant to establish the Rehabilitation Research and Training Center on Full Participation in Independent Living (see section on Resources at the end of the chapter), funded from the National Institute on Disability and Rehabilitation Research (NIDRR). This centre has a portfolio composed of 8 research and 14 training projects, each addressing ways to increase participation in independent living, with special emphasis on emerging disability populations such as those with chronic fatigue syndrome, multiple chemical syndrome, as well as people with disabilities from diverse cultures. Five community psychologists are working as part of the overall research team for this national centre.

To increase interaction and dialogue between consumers and researchers, our Research and Training Center has affirmatively recruited a national advisory board composed of disability researchers, consumers with diverse disabilities and consumers from underrepresented cultures. This board provides advice and feedback on the conduct of our research and training activities. In addition, each research project director consults with a consumer-empowered team which provides its viewpoint concerning research questions, goals, procedures, outcomes and dissemination of research and associated products. White et al. (2001) have described involvement of consumers as collaborators in community-based disability research and provided examples of how this partnership works in research and training activities.

To further increase the dialogue between researcher and consumer, staff from the Research and Training Center are committed to writing articles for consumer publications and speaking at consumer meetings and conferences (Research and Training Center on Independent Living, 2001). The centre is currently planning a consumer consensus conference, inviting consumers with disabilities to attend a national meeting where results from the formative research projects will be discussed with the audience. Feedback from this conference will help shape future research and training activities for the next three years of this five-year federal award.

Vision and Values Guiding Community Work

Our work is guided by values consistent with the aims of CP. In Chapter 3, several core values for CP were described. While we embrace all of these values, in particular, our work is guided by the values of health, self-determination, participation/collaboration, diversity and social justice. Living in an ableist society, people with disabilities encounter daily threats to the enjoyment of these values, which many non-disabled individuals take for granted. Potential barriers include very low income levels, physical and programatic barriers, discriminatory policies and the patronizing attitudes of employers, educators and even other family members.

To enact these values, we routinely use key informants – such as disability advocates, independent living experts and disability research scientists to help shape and guide our research goals, procedures and interpretation of outcomes. In addition, we are building capacity through affirmatively recruiting people with disabilities to pursue graduate training in the disciplines of behavioural and CP. Graduate students' expertise and personal experience is further articulated in weekly meetings or at our Research Group on Rehabilitation and Independent Living (see section on resources). The next section gives examples of our research and action activities for people with disabilities living in the community.

Examples of Research and Action

To illustrate the approaches our research has taken to prevent or reduce the effects of ableism, we cite two recent examples of our community-based work addressing the concerns of people with disabilities. First, we will discuss the Action Letter Portfolio and then conclude with a brief overview of a health promotion intervention for women with severe physical disabilities living in the community.

Action Letter Portfolio

People with disabilities frequently face problems of exclusion, discrimination and access. Yet many do not know how to take action to advocate for their concerns and the problems often go unresolved. The Action Letter Portfolio (ALP) is a social technology tool designed to help people with disabilities improve their advocacy letter writing skills (White, Thomson & Nary, 1999). The ALP package includes a manual that both outlines the components and methods of writing an action (or advocacy) letter and provides examples and practice lessons for manual users to learn and hone these skills. This self-administered guide helps users to write their own personal disability concern letters and allows them to compare their letters with standard letters included in the manual. Both letter content (that is, introduction to the problem, stating a rationale, providing evidence) and form (that is, inside address, salutation, closing) are taught as essential elements of an effective advocacy letter. The manual guides letter writers where to send their letter and how to follow up after sending it. The ALP also contains a section summarizing relevant disability laws (for example Americans With Disabilities Act, Fair Housing Amendments Act), which can be cited in the letters as supporting information and evidence.

This research project was developed using the PAR model. A researcher with a disability conceived the idea for the manual as a result of personal frustrations in trying to write a letter to an insurance company to advocate for a more durable and lightweight wheelchair than their guidelines allowed. The individual seeking the wheelchair wondered why no handbook or manual on writing effective advocacy letters existed. There were many reference books on how to write business letters; why weren't there guidebooks on how to write advocacy letters?

As part of the manual development, researchers sought exemplary advocacy letters from over 350 centres for independent living (CILs) across the US and then performed content and structural analyses to determine what made effective advocacy letters. In addition, researchers sought social validation from these CILs to see if such an action letter manual would be of value to their staff and consumers. Over 80% of the responders indicated it would be very valuable. As the manual was developed it was empirically tested with consumer-users to determine its effectiveness as a self-administered advocacy tool for addressing personal disability concerns in the community (White, Thomson & Nary, 1997). Since the manual was published, numerous state and national training sessions with consumers and workers have taken place.

Health Promotion Interventions for Women with Physical Disabilities

Physical activity guidelines issued by numerous organizations recommend accumulating 30 minutes of moderate intensity activity on most days of the week (National Institutes of Health, 1995; Pate et al., 1995; US Department of Health and Human Services, 1996). However, over 60% of US citizens are sedentary and do not achieve these recommended levels of activity. The sedentary level for people with disabilities is at a much higher 73% (Heath & Fentem, 1997). To find out more about the nature of this issue, investigators from our research centre surveyed women with disabilities across Kansas to identify barriers they faced in engaging in physical activities (Froehlich, Nary & White, 2002).

Following an assessment of barriers, we designed a pilot program to increase physical activity for women with disabilities. This pilot served to inform a large-scale, Center for Disease Control-funded study to increase activity levels of women with disabilities. This study used a randomized control trial to analyse the effectiveness of a community-based intervention to help women with severe physical disabilities to increase their weekly levels of physical activity (Final Report, 2001). The components of the intervention included an educational workshop on increasing physical activity, individual counselling to develop an activity plan, weekly activity logs for recording and reporting activities and peer support from another participant through weekly phone calls.

Participants reported that their overall physical activities increased by 54%. In addition, they more than doubled their amount of time doing cardiovascular activities. The study goal was remarkable because it encouraged women to self-direct their increases in physical activity in their homes or selected community sites. This approach was a more realistic alternative than regularly working-out at a fitness centre because of the barriers posed for the participants (cost, need for accessible transportation and lack of physical and programatic accessibility).

Lessons Learned

The Action Letter Portfolio project taught us that consumers with disabilities could learn how to write advocacy letters. They responded to our structured training scenarios by writing strong advocacy letters. However, when asked to create a letter based on their own personal disability concern, usually their written letters did not fully show the skills that participants demonstrated under training conditions. In future research in this area, participants should incorporate their personal disability concerns as part of the training process to increase the likelihood that skills will generalize from training conditions to real-life conditions.

The project on increasing physical activity for women with disabilities taught us that many participants want to exercise but barriers such as cost, transportation, attitudes and inaccessible facilities prevent them from doing so. We noted that if they are given appropriate information and provided with tools to self-monitor their progress, many women would increase their physical activity over baseline levels. Additionally, we discovered that social support that is arranged with a one-time workshop partner is not functional and that participants were more likely to recruit social support from a family member or friend with whom they have a deeper connection.

Reflection and Application

Our research has taken a very applied and pragmatic approach to evaluating personal and social problems and contexts. Most often the results have been ameliorative rather than transformative, with changes usually being made at the individual level. Part of this is due to our frequent use of applied behaviour analysis methodology, using single subject design methods to approach a particular research question. Such methodology is often directed at first-order change such as increasing a desirable behaviour (that is, physical exercise) or decreasing an undesirable behaviour (that is, powerlessness).

In our research over the past 20 years, I can think of two strong examples of transformation, where second order change has truly occurred. The first was the Media Watch Campaign, conducted by Elkins, Jones and Ulicny (1987). This project resulted from consumer complaints about inappropriate wording and portrayals of people with disabilities (see Box 20.2 for more information) and led to the development of a nationally recognized resource for the media on how to write about and report on people with disabilities. These guidelines have been incorporated into the Associated Press Stylebook and other nationally recognized organizations. Perhaps one of the clearest indicators that the guidelines are being used at the broader level is the frequency of requests we have from national associations for copying and quoting part of the guidelines – or outright plagiarizing them and putting their name on them!

The second example of transformation research was based on work done by Suarez de Balcazar, Fawcett and Balcazar (1988) and White et al. (1988). These research projects evaluated the effectiveness of upright signs to discriminate handicapped parking spaces from regular parking spaces. The latter study investigated the effectiveness of wording on handicapped parking signs to deter unauthorized parking in handicapped spaces. This study showed that handicapped parking signs clearly indicating the potential amount of fines that one could incur for parking illegally were more effective when compared to the standard handicapped parking signs. This information was presented to legislators from different states, who later passed laws requiring that fine amounts also had to be posted on the handicapped parking signs.

In this book, Nelson and Prilleltensky challenge us to think beyond ameliorative and towards transformative research and action. One should not be at the expense of the other, but we as community psychologists must think beyond the immediate outputs and outcomes of our research to broader changes and impacts. Part of this will come from careful planning and cultivation of contacts and collaborations, while other serendipitous opportunities will present themselves, for which we must be ready.

International Vistas

In this chapter we have examined the issue of ableism and its effects on people with disabilities. We discussed historical examples of how people with disabilities were treated and described how ableistic policies and practices today deter them from full participation in community life. Values and concepts that could reduce the effects of ableism were identified and two exemplary studies were presented on approaches that could be used to empower and enable people with disabilities to increase their participation and quality of life.

This chapter has discussed research activity and community applications with a focus on disability concerns in the US. It should be recognized that our approach is not to just 'throw money' at the problem until it is solved. We believe that employing PAR philosophy can help CP researchers and practitioners solve problems using local resources or tapping into natural contingencies. While much of our work is grant funded, we must ask the question, 'How can this community intervention be sustained once grant funding is depleted and researchers have left the setting?' Answers to this question do not come easily, but as we work closely with key informants and stakeholders, we will more likely increase the chances for functional, sustainable solutions to personal and community disability concerns that address ableism. Much of the social technology we use is transferable and adaptable. We have been privileged to work with disability leaders and constituents in Peru (White, Chapman, Jay, Branstetter, Mayo & Isola, 2000). Specifically, we have worked with Peruvian colleagues to conduct training on personal and systems advocacy. Training has been done with many different disability groups. Many challenges exist in order for *personas con discapacidad* to further their progress, however. The cultural tradition of Peruvians is to accept things as they are and not to make waves. Thus the concept of advocacy is unusual and needs to be discussed and adapted for their specific needs. Complicating the process of social change are the severe economic conditions affecting most Peruvians, with those with disabilities more proportionally so.

There are many needs for organizational and community development of Peruvian disability organizations. For example, the deaf club in Lima consists of approximately 150 individuals who have profound hearing loss or are deaf. However, many of these individuals cannot read and only have signing capabilities. Developmentally, the function of the deaf club is to provide a social atmosphere for its members. Elsewhere, disability groups tend to be fragmented and lack a critical mass for political and social change. For example, there are over 20 different national Peruvian organizations representing people who are blind. Unfortunately, many of these are focused on personal well-being versus relational and collective well-being. This self-determination approach is at the expense of building broader coalitions that can organize and create values of diversity, participation, social justice and accountability.

More recently, we have embarked on another project in Ho Chi Minh City, Vietnam with Ford Foundation International Fellow and colleague Hoang-Yen Thi Vo. Currently we are working on developing a disability concerns report survey to administer to people with disabilities in the Disabled Youth Association. There are many challenges in survey development and administration in a politically sensitive society that is very careful with information. In this regard, it was judged to keep a low profile regarding Ms. Vo's educational involvement and contacts with the United States when conducting this research. The participants in the process have nearly completed the survey construction phase. Next, the survey will be distributed to people with disabilities, within the parameters set by Vietnamese authorities. We anticipate one of the largest challenges will be how to interpret and report the survey findings. On the one hand we are establishing a baseline of needs and concerns of Vietnamese people with disabilities to provide clear information for future research and action. On the other hand we are cognizant that the results will have to be carefully framed to reduce severe political consequences preventing interventions to address problems.

Working with citizens with disabilities living in the community is challenging but rewarding. There are many personal, social and policy issues waiting to be tackled by aspiring community psychologists. The funding for research in this area is growing and many young scientists are giving serious attention towards careers in the field of disability research. As an example of the types of problems we encounter as community psychologists in the field of disability research, we have designed the Class Exercise, after the Commentary, for your thoughtful analysis and course of action.

Chapter Summary

The history of disabilities is marked by a slow but steady progression towards the recognition of the rights of people with disabilities. People with disabilities have long fought the subjects of seclusion and discrimination in order to receive better services and better recognition of their diverse needs. While benevolent attempts at helping people with disabilities can be seen over the last century, we know now that some of these efforts continued to disempower this population. Institutional approaches offered services that, however well-intentioned, continued to stigmatize people with disabilities by locating problems within people and neglecting the very environments that prevented full participation by people with disabilities in society.

The 1960s saw the emergence of the independent living movement, which contributed much to the dignity of people with disabilities. Pioneers of the movement fought social injustice towards people with disabilities in a variety of settings – medical, community, public and private. DeJong, a fervent promoter of the movement, observed that the rehabilitation paradigm (ableing model), continued to locate the problem within the person, whereas the independent living paradigm (enabling model) emphasized the need to alter the environment to better accommodate people with disabling or chronic conditions.

Our work illustrated how people with disabilities can work alongside community psychologists to overcome barriers through partnerships and social action. The more people with disabilities become involved in fighting discriminatory policies, the better the chances of eliminating environmental and attitudinal barriers that keep them from full participation in society. The Americans with Disabilities Act is a testament to the struggle of people with disabilities. Through policy and grassroots organizing, change is possible.

COMMENTARY: Ableism: A Disability Rights Perspective   *Ora Prilleltensky*

In his chapter, Glen W. White discusses the roots of ableism, provides a historical overview of the oppression experienced by people with disabilities and proposes ways in which community psychologists can join people with disabilities in their struggle for empowerment and self-determination. The examples of collaboration between stakeholders and researchers are particularly relevant.

This commentary aims to bring some of the issues raised in the chapter into sharper focus. Specifically, I address societal factors that continue to impinge negatively on the lives of people with disabilities and provide examples from my own research on women with disabilities and motherhood. This serves as a backdrop to the cautious attitude adopted by many people with disabilities towards professionals and researchers. Finally, I contend that disability researchers must ensure that the philosophy underlying their research projects, as well as its methodology and objectives, are consistent with a critical disability rights perspective.

Consider the following quote:

There would be no privacy screens or anything … they'd have us literally running around in our underwear … at ages 9, 10, 11, 12, you know, when you become painfully aware of your body

and you're becoming aware of the opposite sex as well … they weren't sensitive at all to how it would make you feel and how it would impact on you later on … I really see this as a sort of systemic abuse. (O. Prilleltensky, 2004a)

In this quote, one of my research participants was reflecting on her physiotherapy sessions at a school for children with disabilities in Canada in the late 1960s. I believe that it serves as a powerful reminder that damaging oppressive practices should not be regarded as belonging to some far, archaic past. In recent decades, personal narratives by women and men with disabilities have given voice to their lived experience. Often such narratives include testimonies of oppressive experiences and threats to self-determination. These are balanced with personal experiences of triumph, support and resistance. Far from wanting to sensationalize images of oppression, I believe that both ends of the spectrum can teach us a lot about factors enabling or hindering wellness. Personal accounts of living with a disability give voice to the pain associated with exclusion and marginalization. Women have been particularly vocal in this arena, arguing that their stories are another indication that the personal is indeed political. In other words, personal stories tell us much about the impact of oppressive practices and attitudes (Morris, 1992).

More often than not, experiences of prejudice, discrimination and powerlessness continue to be in the background and sometimes in the foreground of the lives of many people with disabilities. In addition to the economic, vocational and educational disadvantages noted in the chapter, people with disabilities continue to face formidable challenges in having their sexuality acknowledged (Milligan & Neufeldt, 2001), in forging and maintaining intimate relationships (Noseck, Young, Rintala, Young & Chanpong, 2001) and in securing services that would support them in their role as parents (O. Prilleltensky, 2003, 2004a, 2004b).

This phenomenon can be understood in light of the pessimistic, tragedy-oriented view of disability that was highly prevalent in the past in the medical and rehabilitation community and in society at large (Barnes, Mercer, Shakespeare & Taylor, 1999; Barton, 1998). If children with disabilities were regarded as tragic mistakes of nature, then little attention was given to the possibility that they would lead normal lives and engage in typical age-appropriate activities such as working and parenting.

Disability studies is a growing academic discipline that highlights the social, structural and economic barriers faced by many people with impairments. Disability activists argue that the very term 'disability' is not about physical or intellectual impairment. Rather, it is discriminatory and oppressive policies and practices that disable individuals who have impairments; thus disability is a socially created construct (Charlton, 1998).

Notwithstanding some variations between the British social model of disability (Oliver, 1990, 1996; Oliver & Barnes, 1998) and the US minority group model (Hahn, 1988; Olkin, 1999), both approaches highlight the deleterious impact of oppressive ideologies and discriminatory practices. These socially constructed factors are viewed as more problematic than the impairment itself in constricting the lives of people with disabilities. Rather than perceiving disability as a personal tragedy that clouds all other components of personal identity and inevitably leads to a reduced quality of life, both of these models highlight societal factors that prevent the full participation of disabled people in the larger community.

The political action and struggle of people with disabilities around the world has resulted in significant progress. No longer willing to put up with inadequate resources and professional control, people with disabilities have collectively fought for economic, legislative and social gains. In the US,

the formation of the Independent Living Movements in the 1960s and 1970s has been associated with greater individual autonomy as well as more political and economic freedom. The legislation of the Americans with Disabilities Act in 1990 has ensured that many of the aforementioned gains are not contingent upon people's goodwill, but are enforceable by law. In addition to these tangible gains, the paradigm shift from impaired bodies to societal barriers and systematic powerlessness has done much to improve the self-esteem and well-being of people with disabilities.

Regrettably, psychology, as a discipline, cannot be credited with being at the forefront of the struggle to empower people with disabilities. Psychologists and allied health-care professionals have been criticized by disability activists for espousing a personal tragedy orientation in their research and practice (Shakespeare & Watson, 1997). Rehabilitative efforts are typically designed to facilitate a speedy return to pre-injury or pre-illness levels of functioning (Barnes et al., 1999). The focus is on curing or at least minimizing the effects of the injury. If this is not possible, efforts are concentrated on the patient's adjustment to her plight. All too often, the physical impairment itself is perceived to be the cause of personal distress, with little consideration given to the role of such socially constructed factors as exclusion, discrimination and marginalization. Even when these factors are incorporated into the formulation of the problem, the target of change remains the individual with the disability.

The 'requirement of mourning' (Olkin, 1999, p. 79) is often taken as a given, along with the belief in stages of grief that one must go through if a positive adjustment is to be made. Those who are not distressed, despite their disability, may be perceived as being in a state of denial. Patients who question or oppose their professionally driven treatment regimens may be variously labelled as difficult, bitter or maladaptive.

Similar criticism has been levelled against psychological research that has traditionally focused on the effects of the impairment on mental health. The often unquestioned assumption is that the impairment itself presents the greatest obstacle or source of distress. However, people with disabilities typically identify social barriers and negative attitudes as the greatest impediment to well-being. Furthermore, psycho-social research on disability often focuses on its impact on non-disabled family members. Whilst the demands that disability may impose on families cannot be ignored, the perception that often remains with consumers of such research is that the person with a disability herself is the source of burden (Olkin, 1999).

Few people are familiar with the story of the Tavistock research on the practices of a residential care facility for individuals with severe physical impairments in the early 1960s. The residents themselves initiated the research in their hope to gain support for their demands for greater autonomy and control over their lives. One can only imagine the sense of betrayal they felt when the researchers, Eric Miller and Geraldine Gwynne (1972; in Finkelstein, 1998) concluded that such demands were unrealistic. Instead, they focused on the dual goal of ensuring humane care for the 'socially dead' (Finkelstein, 1998) and training staff to cope with job-related stress (Barnes, 1998; Finkelstin, 1998). This story provides a context for the following powerful quote from the Union of the Physically Impaired Against Segregation (UPIAS) in 1976:

> We reject the whole idea of 'experts' and professionals holding forth on how we should accept our disabilities or giving learned lectures about the psychology of impairment. We already know what it feels like to be poor, isolated, segregated, done good to, stared at and talked down to – far better than any able-bodied expert. We as a union are not interested in descriptions of how awful it is to be disabled. What we are interested in is the ways of changing the conditions of our life and thus overcoming the disabilities which are imposed on top of our physical impairments by the way this society is organized to exclude us …. We look forward to the day when the army of 'experts' on our social and psychological problems can find more productive work to do. (UPIAS, 1976, pp. 4–5)

From a critical disability studies perspective, progress has been made not due to the actions of professionals and social science researchers but often in spite of them (Barnes et al., 1999). It is activists and researchers with disabilities that deserve the credit for empowering people with disabilities and improving the quality of their lives, economically, socially and psychologically. Community psychologists who possess this knowledge will therefore understand the tension between researchers and participants noted in the chapter. They will further accept, and perhaps even encourage, the philosophy of 'nothing about us without us' adopted by a growing number of activists (Charlton, 1998).

The atmosphere of distrust is a healthy response to a disempowering history between researchers and consumers with disabilities. Increasingly, the latter demand more than token participation in research projects. They are interested in research projects that go beyond the personal experience of disability to explore the impact of ableist policies and practices. They want to see research projects that expose, examine and attempt to transform disempowering and ableist policies and practices in schools, hospitals and other meso-level organizations. Finally, critical disability theorists and activists are interested in exploring and challenging dysfunctional societal practices that perpetuate ableism, oppression and discrimination. Community psychologists who are interested in joining the struggle to end oppression are welcome.

CLASS EXERCISE

Community Research and Action: What Would You Do?

A group of concerned citizens with disabilities come to you about a problem they are frequently encountering in the community – unauthorized vehicles parking in spaces reserved for drivers or passengers with disabilities. This has been a growing problem and these individuals are turning to you for your thoughtful analysis to find a solution to this problem. After careful consideration you come up with a plan for intervention.

1. What is it? How do you approach these citizens with your idea? How do you use the PAR process as part of your plan for solving this problem?

2. How do you go about implementing the solution? Maintaining it? Who are the stakeholders that might help you with this?

3. What are the implications for policy change? At the local level? State/provincial level?

As Kelly (1987) describes, how will you determine if your intervention was effective at individual organizational and community levels? **

** To see how community psychologists addressed this actual problem see Reference section to find these articles: White, Jones, Ulicny, Powell & Mathews (1988) and Suarez de Balcazar, Fawcett and Balcazar (1988).

Chapter glossary

ableism a non-factual negative judgment about the attributes and capabilities of an individual with a disabling condition

congenital abnormalities disabling physical and cognitive conditions that are present at birth. Some refer to these as 'birth defects'

institutionalization popular in the 1800s and the first half of the 1900s, the practice of placing family members with cognitive, psychiatric or sensory (that is, blind or deaf) disabilities in state run institutions for long-term care

participatory action research (PAR) raises participants to co-

researcher roles that empower them to actively participate and shape the research process

self-determination the empowerment of people with disabilities by allowing them choice to live in least restricted settings and live their lives independently as possible

RESOURCES ■

General Information

1. Visit the Rehabilitation Research and Training Center on Full Participation in Independent Living at www.rtcfpil.org.
2. Visit also the Research Group on Rehabilitation and Independent Living at Kansas University: www.RGRIL.ku.edu.
3. In the United States, visit National Organization on Disability at www.nod.org.
4. See also American Association of People with Disabilities at www.aapd.com.
5. On March 21, 2002, Anna Diamantopoulou, Commissioner responsible for Employment and Social Affairs of the European Union delivered an important paper entitled 'Towards a Barrier Free Europe for People with Disabilities'. You can read the paper on line at http://europa.eu.int/comm/dgs/employment_social/speeches/200302ad.pdf.
6. A comprehensive directory on disabilities may be found at http://dir.yahoo.com/Society_and_Culture/Disabilities/Organizations/.

Journals

1. *Disability and Society*
2. *Disability Studies Quarterly*
3. *Sexuality and Disability*
4. *Rehabilitation Psychology*
5. *Journal of Disability Policy Studies*
6. *Journal of Applied Rehabilitation Counselling*
7. *International Journal of Disability, Development and Education*
8. *Canadian Journal of Rehabilitation*

Author's Note

This chapter was supported by the National Institute on Disability and Rehabilitation Research (Grant H133B000500). I wish to thank all of the consumers with disabilities who have helped to shape our Research and Training Center on Independent Living. In addition, I would like to acknowledge the help of Dr Katherine Froehlich-Grobe and Dorothy Nary for their thoughtful input on this chapter.

21

Creating New Possibilities for Promoting Liberation, Well-being and Recovery:
Learning from Experiences of Psychiatric Consumers/Survivors

Bret Kloos

Warm-up Exercise

Before beginning the chapter, take a moment to reflect upon what information and assumptions you have about serious mental health problems.

1. What is the story that comes to mind when you think about life events for a person diagnosed with schizophrenia?
2. What is the nature of her or his difficulties?
3. How can her or his problems be addressed?

Introduction

The overarching goal for this chapter is to examine how action and research can help people with serious mental health problems achieve their hopes for liberation, well-being and recovery. While much is written about the treatment of mental health problems, this chapter focuses on what CP perspectives can contribute. In terms of health promotion, I consider how community psychologists can assist efforts to obtain resources and promote practices that advance well-being (for example housing, work, meaningful social relationships). In terms of liberation, I describe what people with serious mental illnesses are doing to increase opportunities for their self-determination and to challenge definitions of mental health deviancy that oppress them. In terms of prevention, I appraise the strategies for prevention of serious mental health problems and argue that there must be more work devoted to primary prevention.

I have organized the chapter to provide readers with background information about serious mental health problems and needs for liberation before examining how CP principles and techniques can be useful. I begin by specifying what is meant by the terms *serious mental health problems* and *recovery*. Next, I review current and historical contexts of how communities have responded to the needs of people with serious mental health problems. Third, I discuss the emerging role that people with serious mental health problems have in changing societies' responses. Finally, I present examples of how liberation and well-being can be promoted in collaboration with people who have histories of serious mental health problems.

Definitions of Serious Mental Health Problems and Recovery

Serious Mental Health Problems

The term *serious mental health problems* refers to persistent psychiatric disabilities that can have a profound effect on a person's behaviour, thinking, emotions and relationships. These disorders include diagnoses such as schizophrenia, bipolar disorder and severe major depression. The designation of 'serious' or 'severe' is not meant to diminish the difficulties encountered by people with other psychiatric disabilities, but rather to refer to more extreme disturbances in living and everyday activities. The term also is associated with a high level of intervention that is typically prescribed to help people address the symptoms associated with these disorders. The terms *serious mental illness* or *severe mental illness* are used more often in mental health practice and research to refer to these diagnoses. However, I am using the term 'serious mental health problems' to underscore that the social experience of these disabilities is a major component of the problems encountered by people experiencing these disorders, not solely the 'illness' (Anthony, 1993).

Subjective Experiences of Serious Mental Health Problems

Serious mental health problems 'strike like a two edged sword' (Corrigan & Penn, 1999). They can profoundly disrupt personal functioning and have a simultaneously onerous set of social consequences as communities respond to a person's problems. In terms of personal functioning, people feel as if they have lost control of their lives. Thinking can be greatly distorted. For some people, beliefs of persecution or torment intrude, even when they doubt the authenticity of these feelings (for example being followed by government agents). In more extreme cases, people can feel as if their thoughts are being controlled or inserted into their heads. In some cases of schizophrenia, severe depression, bipolar disorder or with co-occurring substance abuse, people can experience auditory hallucinations. A person's emotions can change drastically, leading in some cases to their becoming depressed and lacking enjoyment of previously rewarding activities. In other cases emotions can fluctuate to alarming highs and lows. The ability to complete previously easy tasks can be greatly diminished. Unlike many media portrayals, the symptoms of people who have the same diagnoses can vary widely. What is common in people's experiences is that these symptoms are unwanted, often frightening and dramatically disruptive. These experiences shake one's confidence in oneself and lower self-esteem. They contribute to difficulty in social situations, isolation, lost opportunities and shattered personal dreams.

The social experiences of people with serious mental health problems often include encountering fear, discrimination and prejudice from fellow citizens who learn of their disabilities (Carling, 1995). Long-held expectations of participating in community life disintegrate. Aspirations for careers, university degrees, intimate relationships or making a commitment to a life partner are often lost or seem unattainable in the face of social responses to the personal difficulties associated with psychiatric disabilities. People with serious mental health problems have smaller networks of friends and support people (Segal, Silverman & Baumohl, 1989) and often report being lonely and feeling isolated (Davidson, Hoge, Godelski, Rakfeldt & Griffith, 1996). Perhaps it is not surprising that those with serious mental health problems have difficulty getting jobs, making friends or obtaining housing (Corrigan & Penn, 1999). Furthermore, the quality of their housing is much lower than the general population and, as a group, they must find new housing twice as often as people without serious mental health problems (Newman, 1994). This chapter examines community responses that can foster nurturing social experiences in response to these oppressive social consequences.

Recovery

The concept of *recovery* in mental health care has emerged with the acceptance of empirical findings that the course of serious mental health problems is not one of unavoidable decline and poor functioning (for example Harding, Zubin & Strauss, 1987; Strauss & Carpenter, 1974a, 1974b). First, articulated by mental health consumers and ex-patients (for example Chamberlin, 1978, Deegan, 1988), recovery emphasizes personal goals of experiencing hope, healing, empowerment and connection with others after life disruptions from serious mental health problems. Since the early 1990s, recovery has become increasingly accepted as an appropriate goal of mental health care in North America (Jacobson & Greenley, 2001; Nelson, Lord & Ochocka, 2001b). Recovery has been defined as:

A deeply personal, unique process of changing one's attitudes, values, feelings, goals, skills and/or roles. It is a way of living a satisfying, hopeful and contributing life even with limitations caused by an illness. Recovery involves the development of a new meaning and purpose in one's life as one grows beyond catastrophic effects of mental illness. (Anthony, 1993, p. 19)

It is important to note that proponents of recovery do not consider it to be synonymous with the notion of a cure. 'Recovery is distinguished both by its endpoint – which is not necessarily a return to "normal" health and functioning – and by its emphasis on the individual's active participation in self-help activities' (Jacobson & Greenley, 2001, p. 483). Recovery is about regaining a sense of purpose and self after a major life disruption. I will argue in this chapter that the concept of recovery is central to realizing liberation and well-being for those with serious mental health problems.

Examining Community Contexts for Responding to Serious Mental Health Problems

Balancing Competing Values and Resulting Consequences for People with Serious Mental Health Problems

There are competing tensions in how communities respond to people who experience disruptions in emotional, cognitive and interpersonal life. In western countries, we tend to emphasize the importance of people overcoming difficulties and value people's 'right' to live independently. We cherish the notion that individuals should decide for themselves where to live, work and with whom to have friendships. However, at the same time, we seek to maintain order and safety in our communities. When someone's behaviour is too bizarre or appears dangerous, we rely on professionals to take control of the situation, restore order and, when appropriate, offer the person assistance. With serious mental health problems, the values of self-determination and social order come into conflict when a situation, behaviour or person is considered deviant rather than simply different. Judgements concerning deviancy often lead to decisions about the need for *social control* that are at odds with the cultural value of promoting *self-determination*. Communities differ in which problems they want to assist, which they will not tolerate and which problems they will simply ignore. In their journeys to liberation and well-being, people with serious mental health problems inevitably have to respond to how their communities define and address deviance.

Designating a situation or person as deviant has far-reaching consequences for the person and for those making the judgement. The act of defining problems shapes how competing values are balanced. Identifying a situation as a problem can be a call to action that focuses resources to address the situation. However, the courses of action for addressing something as different or deviant are markedly different. The notion of a phenomenon deviating from a norm can be simply descriptive (for example the tallest student in a class) and would be labelled as a matter of diversity. However, categorizing someone as deviant because of some personal characteristic, such as mental or physical disabilities, injury, illness, race or ethnicity devalues that person (Wolfensberger & Tullman, 1982). Deviancy-based justifications are used to detain people with serious mental health problems (for example disturbing the peace, involuntary psychiatric hospitalization), take away individual rights (for example parental status, control of personal finances) and restrict resources (for example welfare supplements). Examples are also readily available from everyday life; when we see a person apparently talking to himself, many of us go out of our way to avoid interaction.

The prejudice and discrimination directed towards devalued people are often referred to as *stigma*. Erving Goffman (1963), who conducted seminal research on the stigma of mental health problems, described stigma as 'an attribute that is deeply discrediting' (p. 3). If a person had an attribute that discredited her in a particular community, it is easy to imagine community members would tolerate discriminating behaviour against that person (for example being banned from sitting on benches downtown). Stigma about mental health problems is widely held in western countries, although the 'negative stereotypes are not warranted and are overgeneralized' (Corrigan & Penn, 1999, p. 766). Research has documented how stigmatizing views about mental health problems are also held by well-trained mental health professionals (Keane, 1990; Mirabi, Weinman, Magnetti & Keppler, 1985). Corrigan and Penn (1999) have grouped research on media representations of serious mental health problems into three main thematic categories: people with serious mental health problems should be feared and thus excluded (for example the homicidal maniac); they are child-like, irresponsible and need care from others (for example the innocent, child-like man who can't make good decisions for himself); they are rebellious free spirits who do not accept the norms of community living. Stigma related to serious mental health problems can have a particularly pernicious moral tone, such as assuming that people with serious mental health problems have caused their illness or should be more in control of their disability than those with physical disabilities.

While stigma can translate into open discrimination, internalized negative images of oneself can destroy one's self-concept and radically limit personal goals, self-confidence and the opportunities that one is willing to undertake. Thus, the experience of being categorized as a deviant can bring unintended consequences for the person's hopes for the future and sense of self. Box 21.1 presents one view of the pain and cost associated with being labelled deviant because of mental health problems, as well as some ideas about alternative responses.

Box 21.1   **How Stereotypes About Deviance Can Oppress**

To me, mental illness meant Dr. Jekyll and Mr. Hyde, psychopathic serial killers, loony bins, morons, schizos, fruitcakes, nuts, straight jackets and raving lunatics. They were all I knew about mental illness and what terrified me was that professionals were saying I was one of them. It would have greatly helped to have had someone come and talk to me about surviving mental illness – as well as the possibility of recovering, of healing and of building a new life for myself. It would have been good to have role models – people I could look up to who had experienced what I was going through – people who had found a good job or who were in love or who had an apartment or a house on their own or who were making a valuable contribution to society (Deegan, 1993, p.8).

Competing Narratives about Serious Mental Health Problems

Understandings about the nature of serious mental health problems are often communicated as convincing stories. The ability to relate understandings of the world in the form of a narrative is a powerful, socially normative way to order experience and explain the meaning of phenomena (Rappaport, 1993; Schank, 1990). Narratives can be easily communicated, are more easily remembered than lists of facts or figures (Schank, 1990) and may be more persuasive (Pennington & Hastie, 1992). They can provide examples of particular reactions to life events or interpretations of them (Cain, 1991). Like fables or parables, they might also provide a guide for how to handle particular life experiences (Vitz, 1990). Although the viewpoints of narratives might also be expressed as propositions (for example 'schizophrenics' are dangerous), they are usually justified by relating a story, recounting a movie or making a literary reference to illustrate the veracity of the perspective.

Deviancy Narratives

Stories about deviance related to serious mental health problems are pervasive in our communities. A storyline common to most of these narratives runs something like this:

> Joe had not been getting adequate medical care for months. Those who knew him thought he had been acting very strangely, apparently hearing commanding voices instructing him to hurt himself or others. Unfortunately he acted upon the suggestions of those voices and was violent in a public place before he could be hospitalized (or locked up).

These 'dangerous deviant' stories are those most readily available about serious mental health problems to the general public (for example newspapers, movies) as their sensationalism captures our attention. Occasionally, the media communicate hopeful stories about people who had lost control of their lives and much of what they valued, but with the help of mental health professionals and medication, had regained control. These treatment and rehabilitation narratives tend to be emphasized in the experiences of mental health professionals. A narrative told by a mental health professional might look something like this:

> After struggling with disorganized thinking and paranoia, Maria was finally properly diagnosed as having schizophrenia with co-occurring substance abuse. Now she is taking appropriate medication regularly, attends substance abuse groups and participates in a social club rather than being isolated in her apartment for weeks at a time. Just like a person with diabetes or other chronic medical condition, she has learned to manage the symptoms of her illness with the help of competent medical care. Although she needs to be careful not to take on activities that are too stressful (for example having a job), if she follows professional advice, she will avoid many of the troubles she had struggled with or they will be greatly diminished.

Although this second type of narrative is more hopeful, both of these narratives emphasize the deviancy of the person or her functioning and the necessity of effective professional intervention. They perpetuate stigmatizing views of people with serious mental health problems to the extent that they restrict opportunities, assume lack of ability or perpetuate fear of a group of people based upon a diagnosis rather than basing such decisions on a person's abilities, interest or past experience.

In my experience, it is rare to hear other types of narratives about serious mental health problems in everyday conversation. These *deviancy focused narratives* prevail in western countries and shape public opinion and policy about serious mental health problems (Corrigan & Penn, 1999).

Empowerment Narratives

In the past 20 years, however, the predominance of the mental health deviancy narratives has been increasingly challenged by people with serious mental health problems, their family members and a small but growing number of mental health professionals (Carling, 1995; Nelson, Lord & Ochocka, 2001b). These emerging *empowerment narratives* emphasize the role that people with serious mental health problems can play in recovery and the contributions they can make to their communities. Their proponents observe that deviancy-focused narratives about serious mental health problems concentrate almost solely on people's problems to the exclusion of their current capabilities, potential capabilities and negative consequences of social control of serious mental health problems. Empowerment narratives document the contributions that people with serious mental health problems can make to their recovery and can offer hope to those struggling with serious mental health problems. Furthermore, they encourage all community members to broaden their perspectives on serious mental health problems. See Box 21.2 for an example of an empowerment narrative.

Box 21.2 **Example of An Empowerment Narrative**

I got married pretty young and had a lot of problems with my husband. I left him when he started abusing me, but I didn't know why I still felt so bad. My doctor put me on medications and I figured everything would get better, but I got worse. I went into the hospital again and again. I started really depending on medication itself to make things better. I wasn't putting all my effort into getting well, I don't think. But then I got involved with a self-help group where people cared about me, supported me and after awhile, challenged me to really start working on my mental health. I started bringing up problems and working on them. Eventually, I became a group leader. I felt pretty good about that because I had achieved something. People believed in me and that started helping me believe in me. In January, I started taking classes at the community college. I was pretty nervous about it, but I started thinking that I can do well in courses. My daughter moved back in with me and we found a church that works for both of us. I want to become an occupational therapist or something like that, helping other people out. I'd like to give back what I've been given.

In this emerging view, people helping an individual with serious mental health problems need to address concerns about diversity of ability and personal strengths, as well as their needs (cf. Carling, 1995; Nelson, Lord & Ochocka, 2001b). This requires deliberate efforts to recognize the individual's strengths, to persevere in creative efforts to promote and develop those strengths and a commitment to a view of recovery that supports the realization of individual and collective journeys to liberation and well-being. In all but the most exceptional cases, such a broadened scope of recovery can not be accomplished by only one approach to helping (for example clinical treatment, community development, self-help). This chapter is written from the standpoint that there is a limit to how much clinical practice can be revised to support well-being and liberation because of its problem orientation and focus on personal deficits. Similarly, case management approaches, such as Assertive Community Treatment (ACT) teams, are limited to the extent that they accept the charge of mental health systems to implement a higher level of supervision for people deemed to be having problems living in the community. However, as a growing number of mental health professionals have demonstrated, revised clinical and case management practices can be effective in addressing concerns of safety and deviant functioning, when viewed as being one resource that an individual can use to develop personal capacities and utilize opportunities that promote well-being, liberation and recovery.

Competing Tensions in Helping Professions

Before a brief discussion of historical context, I want to further ground our consideration of liberation and well-being for people with serious mental health problems in a dilemma frequently experienced by those in the helping professions. When social workers, nurses, mental health workers, psychiatrists and psychologists respond to help people experiencing serious mental health problems, they are conferred a social role of helping the person to fit into society. If one is evaluated as being too vulnerable to take care of oneself; at risk of harming oneself; or a danger to others, the role of these mental health professionals is to ensure the safety of the person and those who may encounter that person in crisis. Thus these helping professionals have the dual charge of being agents of compassionate care and agents of social control. Combining society's interest for compassionate care with interests in maintaining safety often puts these service providers in awkward situations where they have to choose one role over the other (for example when to involuntarily detain and hospitalize someone in the 'best interest' of the community).

Consider how you would respond to the needs of a person whose thinking, behaviour and life circumstances are routinely labelled as 'deviant' in society. Refer to Box 21.3 for a vignette and pragmatic questions about how you would balance competing tensions.

Box 21.3   How Would You Help Joseph Realize Well-being, Liberation and Recovery?

Joseph does not trust many people. Although he sometimes recognizes that it is hard for others to believe, he thinks that people put thoughts in his head or even broadcast what he is thinking on TV. Joseph often feels threatened by others and is quick to lash out if people 'invade his space'. In fact he has been arrested several times for assault and subsequently hospitalized against his will. Joseph wants to live in his own apartment and have a job, but he can't afford an apartment by himself and doesn't have any good references for employment. He has sold sex for money to sustain himself. Although he has had sexually transmitted diseases, he is not currently HIV positive. During warm months, Joseph sleeps on the street, but he tries to get a bed at a homeless shelter during the winter.

Now, imagine that you are a mental health professional assigned to work with Joseph. How would you answer the following questions:

1. *Social control:* What are your (and your agency's) obligations to protect Joseph from (a) getting into situations where he may be a victim of assault, (b) being exposed to harm from sleeping outside or (c) contracting HIV? Do you need to protect others from harm he may cause when he feels threatened?

2. *Deviancy:* How do you respond to business owners who don't want 'homeless, crazy people' scaring away customers? What can you do to address the discrimination that Joseph encounters when trying to buy a sandwich at a downtown store?

3. *Self-determination:* How can you help Joseph gain access to an affordable, decent apartment of his own? How can you help him to have more power over what happens in his life?

Which narratives about mental health problems did you draw upon to answer these questions? In my experience as a North American community psychologist working in clinical settings, the choices for responding to such a scenario revolve around maintaining safety and social control for all involved and maximizing the promotion of self-control and self-determination. This typically requires arranging for the best care and rehabilitation while challenging prevailing notions of mental health deviancy and systematically seeking alternative opportunities.

For the field of mental health, the central questions to consider are: what narratives about serious mental health problems are we promoting? and what are the consequences resulting from how we fulfil our social roles? I argue that these questions are best answered in any 'helping profession' when there is an open dialogue with people who we are trying to serve about what we can do to support them and what is helpful or harmful in our practice. The perspective and interventions promoted by community psychologists can make unique contributions to these efforts by helping to create community structures that are tolerant of diversity and do not primarily respond to deviance by isolating and pushing to the margins those who are deemed deviant.

A Brief History of Community Responses to Serious Mental Health Problems

Tension between these competing values and narratives has existed throughout history for people with serious mental health problems. For thousands of years, there has been a range of viewpoints in how to identify and how to respond to mental health deviancy/diversity. Accounts left by the ancients of western civilization record that societies often attributed very deviant and outlandish behaviour to be a sign of supernatural possession (Fabrega, 1990). During the European Middle Ages, severely aberrant behaviour was seen as a sign of demonic manipulation requiring exorcism or imprisonment. In some instances, bizarre behaviour was interpreted to be evidence of witchcraft and was 'treated' by public flogging or even capital punishment (Fabrega, 1990). However, in some spiritual traditions, experiences of visions and hearing voices have been (and are) celebrated rather than viewed as manifestations of mental health problems (Castillo, 1997). A few religious communities have provided sanctuary to those who have been cast out due to judgements of deviance (Kloos & Moore, 2000; Pargament, 1997): the town of Gheel, Belgium has been a place of sanctuary where people with serious mental health problems have participated as citizens for several hundred years (Morton, 2002). Native healers of many aboriginal peoples throughout the world have traditions of responding to emotional upset by restoring a balance of person, nature and spirit (Asuni, 1990; Hazel & Mohatt, 2001).

From the 4th century BCE, Greek and Roman forebears of modern western medicine viewed the disordered mind as an appropriate topic for scientific study. During medieval times, several physicians protested against demonizing practices such as those described above (Rappaport, 1977). Although the conceptualization of the phenomena associated with serious mental health problems was an advance, their methods of intervention were often crude by today's standards. 'Treatments' included submersion in vats of nearly freezing water, blood letting (that is, planned bleeding through laceration or parasite) and even using hot glass to burn the skin of patients (Fabrega, 1991). Although not recorded in graphic detail, it is likely that the most common practices of the 'average person' living in communities of the past are those that continue today: ignoring or not associating with people who are considered deviant; hiding them from view; or actively ostracizing them from their communities.

Communities' Settings for Addressing Serious Mental Health Problems

The history of modern mental health treatment can be traced to the actions of Phillipe Pinel in 18th-century France, where ostracizing and imprisoning people with serious mental health problems were the status quo. Pinel was interested in reforming these practices and instituting 'humane treatment'(Rappaport, 1977). He unshackled those who were chained and asserted that hospital care should be provided for those with serious mental health problems rather than prison. Similar convictions of compassion and justice led to the formation of hospitals and asylums for rehabilitation in the colonial US and England. While this shift in thinking has been called the 'moral treatment' movement, the emphasis on medical care and professionalization of that care eventually changed the dominant paradigm for understanding serious mental health problems from one of demonology or moral failing to one of illness (that is, the medical model).

The history of community responses to mental health care since the 18th century can be viewed as successive waves of periodic reform. By the middle of the 19th century, the local hospitals and asylums were viewed as inadequate; people whose behaviour was most aberrant were again detained in jails and prison. Reformers argued that specialized institutions needed to be created by regional governments that would be dedicated to the care (and segregation) of people with serious mental health problems. In the US, a new reformer emerged in the person of Dorothea Dix, whose advocacy led to the creation of state hospitals and sanatoriums (that is, the medical model). The mission of the 'mental hygiene' movement of the early 20th century was to reform psychiatric treatment and improve the regional mental hospitals which had become overcrowded and brutish, mirroring the prisons they were meant to replace (Rappaport, 1977). The movement took inspiration from Clifford Beers (1908), who spoke publically about his mental health problems in the service of making reforms and policy changes. Beers' book, *A Mind that Found Itself*, recounted his journey to well-being after developing mental health problems as a Yale University undergraduate. Beers influenced a Canadian physician, Clarence Hincks, who created the Canadian Mental Hygiene Association, the forerunner of the Canadian Mental Health Association. However, the opportunity for collaborative work to promote liberation of people with serious mental health problems was not realized as mental hygiene supporters emphasized training professionals as the primary means of reform (Rappaport, 1977). It would be another 60 to 70 years before people with serious mental health problems would re-emerge as powerful voices for the reform of societies' responses to serious mental health problems.

Over the past 50 years, the number of regional mental hospitals has been greatly reduced throughout most industrialized countries, as many have been closed and deemed not worth reforming (Fattore, Percudani, Pugnoli, Beecham & Contini, 2000; Manderscheid & Henderson, 1998; Newton, Rosen, Tennant, Hobbs, Lapsley & Tribe, 2000). Between 1972 and 1982, the number of hospitals with over 1000 psychiatric beds was reduced by 50–80% in Denmark, England, Ireland, Italy, Spain and Sweden (Freeman, Fryers & Henderson, 1985). Similar patterns occurred in North America and Australia (Carling, 1995; Newton et al., 2000). In many countries, community mental health centres were founded with the charge of developing care for serious mental health problems within the community contexts where people lived rather than at remote hospitals.

Unfortunately, the aspirations of these reforms were not realized as community support for people who were discharged from hospitals diminished in the face of seemingly endless demand for treatment and unmet need for services (Carling, 1995; Lamb, 1993). All too often, poverty, poor quality of housing, lack of employment opportunities, discrimination, social isolation and alienation have 'greeted' people in North America, Australia and Europe who have left large institutions to live in community settings (Carling, 1995; Chamberlin, 1978; Newton et. al., 2000). In the US, caseloads for mental health professionals have increased, while resources for mental health services have been cut (Torrey, Erdman, Wolfe & Flynn, 1990).

Italy provides a more successful example of a nation that radically changed its health policy to dismantle hospitals and provide care in community settings (Barbato, 1998; Fattore et al., 2000). In 1978, federal legislation outlawed building new psychiatric hospitals and closed many large institutions. *Community Psychiatric Services* were created for defined geographical areas that integrated acute psychiatric units of general hospitals with community-based psychiatric services, such as mental health centres, residential facilities, rehabilitative institutes and psychiatric outpatient centres. Typically, care is provided by multi-disciplinary teams. These policy changes have reduced the population of public psychiatric hospitals from 60,000 in 1978 to 15,000 in 1994. A similar reduction has occurred in private psychiatric hospitals (Barbato, 1998). This approach to mental health policy, and the approaches of other countries who have embarked on deinstitutionalization, emphasizes top-down planning by region that focuses on 'the overall management of disorder' (Fattore, et al., 2000). As with the reforms reviewed above, consumers were not involved in these reforms in a meaningful way.

Have you noticed in this brief historical overview that past reforms have a consistent ameliorative focus with very little consideration of transformative possibilities for how serious mental health problems can be addressed? Over the past 300 years, a focus on illness-related deviance has replaced demonology as the major explanation of serious mental health problems. However, by framing serious mental health problems as being primarily about illness, community responses are limited to treatment and rehabilitation and are necessarily ameliorative in focus. With one's attention focused on matters of illness, one cannot see problems arising from the social experience of serious mental health problems. Within a treatment and rehabilitation paradigm, it is highly improbable that intervention efforts will promote transformative change that liberates people with serious mental health problems from overzealous social control and stigma and fosters the development of recovery. A new paradigm is needed to help communities support recovery for people experiencing serious mental health problems.

Changing the Balance? The Emergence of Consumer/Survivors in Society's Efforts to Address Serious Mental Health Problems

Over the course of these 'modern' reforms in mental health practices, people with serious mental health problems were seldom included in formal deliberations and decisions about how communities can respond to the realities of mental health problems. By not including all stakeholders, these reforms often overlooked valuable resources for addressing mental health concerns, that is, the experience and input of people with serious mental health problems. Perhaps this is not surprising given the predominance of deviance-focused narratives about serious mental health problems. However, during the past 30 years, the voices of people with serious mental health problems have become increasingly more influential and have greater prominence in how competing interests of social control, diversity/deviance and self-determination are balanced (Chamberlin, 1990; Everett, 1994).

Although not universally accepted, many contemporary policy deliberations are strongly influenced by people who have struggled with their own mental health problems and are acting on behalf of themselves and their peers to address their needs. These voices are challenging the predominate narratives of serious mental health problems with stories of their own empowerment and recovery. The narratives document abuses of treatment, the negative effects of social control and the discrimination that results from reliance on deviance-focused narratives. Many of these stories provide a guide for how appropriate treatment can be a component of recovery, but make the distinction that treatment is not necessarily the primary component. The articulation of these alternative narratives about serious mental health problems has given credence to efforts to change community responses that focus narrowly on treatment and rehabilitation to those that focus on empowerment and community integration (Nelson, Lord & Ochocka, 2001b).

Through individuals' articulation of their experience, consumer/survivor movements emerged in many cities around the world in the 1970s, 80s and 90s (Chamberlin, 1978, 1990; Deegan, 1988). These movements have dedicated themselves to bring together people with serious mental health problems for collective action and mutual support. The terms 'consumer', 'survivor', or 'consumer/survivor' are used in North America by people with serious mental health problems to refer to themselves rather than the terms used by mental health professionals: 'patient', 'ex-patient', or 'client'. The use of the term 'consumer' is meant to emphasize the importance of individual choice in using services and the respect given to people who have rights and expectations about the services they use. The term 'survivor' emphasizes the negative consequences that many people with serious mental health problems have experienced as a result of past mental health treatment; it is also a political statement about past mistreatment, individuals' resilience in living and self-determination in current life choices. Some people with serious mental health problems have strong preferences for one term over the other and the identity that the terms represent. The term *consumer/survivor* was coined to include the political and personal perspectives of both terms. Regardless of the terms used, this new paradigm recognizes the value of using 'people-first language' to promote citizenship and personhood over all subsuming client or patient identities (Carling, 1995).

Unlike past reforms, consumer/survivor movements have articulated needs and interests that argue for the priority of transformative approaches to change, those that will promote liberation, as well as ameliorative approaches that promote well-being (Chamberlin, 1978; Nelson, Lord & Ochocka, 2001b). Priorities of the movements have included: the need for affordable housing; employment opportunities; self-determination in treatment and life decisions; developing alternatives to treatment; challenging discrimination based on societal assumptions about people with serious mental health problems; and abolition of abusive practices of social control (Carling, 1995; Chamberlin, 1978, 1990; Deegan, 1988). Because of the articulation of these priorities by people with serious mental health problems, these issues are being addressed in mental health policy and practices. Consumer/survivor movements accomplished these gains through the formation of advocacy groups and initiatives, expansion of mutual assistance organizations, development of informational resources based upon lived experience (for example books, education courses, websites) and the formation of consumer operated services. Many movements partner with interested professionals and citizen groups to promote social change in their communities; see Nelson, Lord & Ochocka (2001b) for a case study.

The success of these consumer–citizen–professional collaborations can be seen in part through the growth of mutual aid and self-help organizations and their growing acceptance in treatment communities (Chinman, Kloos, O'Connell & Davidson, 2002; Kessler et al., 1997); the formation of consumer/survivor advocacy movements with political clout (Davidson, Chinman, Kloos, Weingarten, Stayner & Tebes, 1999; Nelson, Lord & Ochocka, 2001b); representation at governmental agencies charged with policy and funding decisions (for example advisory panels, grant review panels); and the emergence of the recovery metaphor for interventions and accompanying practice (Fisher, 1994; Weingarten, 1994).

From the ecological standpoint presented in Chapter 4, there are many niches where people with serious mental health problems can make contributions 'inside' and 'outside' the formal mental health systems. These include roles as: advocates; community leaders; guides for recovery; service-providers; and advisors. *Advocates* have been successful in pursuing lawsuits to end practices judged to be abusive, in providing more resources to community services, in building collaborations with professionals and civic groups and in protesting negative media portrayals of serious mental health problems. *Community leaders* organize consumer/survivor organizations and serve on policy-making boards of agencies or governments. The role of a *guide* recognizes the value of the lived experience in recovery journeys to well-being and liberation that only people with serious mental health problems can share. Mutual aid and self-help groups are founded on this principle and have grown greatly in the last 30 years. The role of a *service provider* has emerged in the past 15 years as consumer/survivor organizations have created their own services because of dissatisfaction with the services available (for example Salzer & Mental Health Association of Southeastern Pennsylvania Best Practices Team, 2002). New services have included crisis respite services in lieu of emergency rooms, recovery-oriented case management services, housing and, increasingly, treatment (Chamberlin, 1990; Davidson et al., 1999). Finally, people with serious mental health problems act as *advisors* to policy-making bodies by serving on committees and consult with community leaders to develop practices and policies that are more sensitive to the needs of people with serious mental health problems.

Community Psychology's Role in Supporting Consumers

What can CP offer in promoting the well-being and liberation of consumer/ survivors? The framework of CP's values, principles and conceptual tools presented in Chapter 2 is very helpful in organizing an answer to these questions. Using this framework, take a moment to think about how CP can assist in supporting consumer/survivors. Below I provide examples of how the conceptual tools can be applied to address a range of issues raised by people with serious mental health problems. I also highlight a particular concern, that of living in community housing, across all six principles to illustrate how most problems can benefit from consideration of each of these conceptual tools.

Ecology

People with serious mental health problems are often identified as being the source of the problems they experience. Difficulties with housing, workplace problems or lack of adherence to treatment recommendations are too often attributed to a failing of the person, without looking at the broader context to account for contributions to difficulties (for example troublesome neighbours or unsafe housing, co-worker substance abuse at the workplace or treatment programs that are unresponsive to individuals' needs). The traditional treatment system's emphasis on an individual level of analysis misses the positive and negative transactions that a person has in her housing environment, workplace and the treatment system itself (Kelly, 1966). Such a narrow focus is not only inaccurate, it is typically ineffective in addressing the problems of concern. It misses the oppressive effects of discrimination resulting from the stigma of serious mental health problems, inadequate resources and access to resources, and high levels of social isolation.

A commitment to using an ecological approach prompts an analysis of these problems that goes beyond the individual. This approach can help avoid victim-blaming assessments that impede efforts to collaborate with people with serious mental health problems to address issues of concern (Rappaport, Davidson et al., 1975). It can also legitimize the viewpoints and concerns of people with serious mental health problems as relevant stakeholders. The competencies of people with serious mental health problems are often overlooked as resources for addressing their concerns and those of the community. An ecological approach to problem definition also allows for greater consideration of the needs of 'whole person' rather than focusing primarily on the personal deficits of a 'patient'.

Problem conceptualization across levels of analysis underscores the importance of social policy for addressing macro-level phenomena that affect the well-being of people with serious mental health problems that goes far beyond the scope of mental health policy. For example, an ecological approach to assisting a person with serious mental health problems may include an examination of his or her housing. Poor quality of housing, distressed neighbourhoods and lack of affordable apartments contribute to many of the difficulties people with serious mental health problems experience, such as exposure to harmful community environments and a cycle of increased serious mental health problems symptomatology (for example Breakey & Fischer, 1995; Newman, 2001). Most people with serious mental health problems live in inadequate housing conditions (Carling, 1995) and most countries, such as the US and Canada, have failed to provide adequate resources and policies. Even when people have their own apartments, the rising cost of housing and the reduction in affordable housing stock make many residential arrangements tenuous.

Prevention and Promotion

Chronic strains have a significant impact on functioning (Lazarus & Delongis, 1983). Common chronic strains stemming from poverty, discrimination, racism, abusive relationships, exposure to violence, crime and poor housing conditions are associated with higher rates of mental health problems. Prolonged exposure to such *risk factors* may overwhelm a person's *protective factors* (for example coping skills, social support) and make a person more vulnerable to constitutional predispositions for developing mental health problems. Based upon this *stress-diathesis* model of mental health problems, the equation proposed by George Albee (1982) and presented in Chapter 4, is a good heuristic for thinking about where to focus preventive and health promotive interventions. As shown in this equation, the numerator of the equation focuses on reducing exposure to risk factors from organic (for example biological) and environmental stressors. The denominator focuses on increasing stress-buffering factors, such as coping skills, self-esteem and social support. In theory, interventions can focus on any component of this equation to reduce risk for people. However, it is most likely that coordinated interventions are needed to focus on several aspects of risk and protection to be an effective strategy in preventing serious mental health problems.

As a field, the prevention of serious mental health problems is relatively young and predominately concerned with selected or indicated prevention. There has been some promising work with young people who have experienced their first episodes of psychosis (McGlashan, Miller & Woods, 2001). Focusing on organic factors, these strategies seek to identify patterns of abnormal functioning indicative of heightened risk for developing specific disorders (for example schizophrenia). Interventions have primarily administered medications to reduce psychotic symptoms, although there has been some effort to develop accompanying psychosocial interventions (for example support groups, supportive therapy, education). The goal of these programs is to intervene early in the development of problems to prevent full-scale episodes of serious mental illness and the chain of accompanying life disruptions (McGlashan, 1998). Although this approach is similar to those for other long-term health conditions (for example diabetes, heart disease), investigators are still building the scientific base necessary to identify risk factors reliably and to develop effective interventions (Tsuang & Faraone, 2002).

The prevention of depression has a more substantial empirical base and focuses on promoting the development of cognitive skills to lessen the impact of stressors. Ricardo Muñoz and colleagues have developed interventions with primary care patients aimed at changing maladaptive patterns of thinking and promoting problem-solving skills (Muñoz et al., 2002; Muñoz, Ying, Bernal & Perez-Stable, 1995). These interventions also emphasize early identification of symptoms of heightened risk. Similar programs have been developed for schoolchildren who have been identified as living in conditions that place them at higher risk for developing problems (Burns & Hickie, 2002; Cardemil, Reivich & Seligman, 2002).

Unfortunately, primary or universal prevention efforts are virtually non-existent for serious mental health problems. Similarly, there are few interventions to reduce environmental stressors for developing serious mental health problems. While epidemiologic research has documented how the stressors of poverty, racism, exposure to violence and poor housing are associated with higher rates of diagnosis of serious mental illness (c.f. Neighbors & Williams, 2001; Williams & Williams-Morris, 2000), few interventions have been researched. Universal prevention of these conditions probably requires broad advocacy movements and changes in governmental policies; targeted interventions do not have the resources necessary to address these conditions. As discussed below, community psychologists can do more to affect structural changes that prevent exposure to living conditions that exacerbate vulnerabilities for developing serious mental health problems.

Community

Because of the experience of being pushed to the margins of society, people with serious mental health problems often experience alienation, isolation and demoralization in their attempts to live in community settings (Davidson et. al., 1996). Mutual aid and self-help groups can provide a particularly promising opportunity for creating community experiences for people with serious mental health problems (Davidson et. al, 1999). The most rigorous research on mutual aid/self-help groups has been done on GROW, an international mutual aid organization with over 800 groups worldwide, primarily in Australia and the US. Research has shown that people participating actively in the groups had larger social networks (Rappaport, Seidman et al., 1985) and better social adjustment than people who were not active in groups (Roberts et al., 1991). GROW members also had shorter hospital stays than matched comparisons (Rappaport, 1993).

Another example of a community-level approach to the problem of social isolation has been developed by the Canadian Mental Health Association (CMHA). The CMHA's Framework for Support (Trainor, Pomeroy & Pape, 1993) draws upon principles of self-help to ensure that people with serious mental health problems live rich and fulfilling lives, while minimizing the need for professional intervention. (See Box 21.4 for a URL to obtain a version available online). The framework emphasizes utilizing three domains of community support before using formal mental health services: self-help; family/friends/neighbours; and generic community resources. The articulation of the framework is needed because of the tendency in communities to expect that the mental health system will take on all responsibilities for support. 'Instead of being the "back-up" to those domains of support, professional services then become the only support sector with a person becoming increasingly isolated from natural supports' (Carling, 1995, p. 57). This framework envisions mental health systems having a new goal, strengthening other domains of support so that they bolster a person's abilities to address his own problems with the help of his relationships and community resources. The Framework for Support strives to promote *community integration*, which is the integration of a person with serious mental health problems into 'normal' community settings and relationships (Aubry & Myner, 1996). See Box 21.4 for an example of a mental health system working to strengthen community supports.

Box 21.4   **Promoting Connections Between Community Supports and Mental Health Services**

The New Haven Landlord-Service Provider Forum was developed from the efforts of a city-wide housing programme for people with smhp. The Forum seeks to improve communication and promote shared problem solving between landlords, service-providers and tenants, thereby increasing the housing stability of tenants (Kloos, Zimmerman, Scrimenti & Crusto, 2002). The Forum has developed a Welcome Guide with practical information for people moving into housing and a website making local community housing information more widely available (www.housingresourceinfo.org).

Power

As presented at the beginning of the chapter, self-determination of people with serious mental health problems is often restricted by oppression and social control invoked in the name of addressing deviant behaviour. Personal and collective empowerment by people with serious mental health problems are necessary pathways to recovery and liberation. The consumer/survivor social change movements have demonstrated that transformative change is possible (Chamberlin, 1984; Chamberlin, 1990). In the US, consumer/survivor movements and their supporters worked to pass the Americans with Disabilities Act that made it illegal to discriminate on the basis of a history of psychiatric disability (Americans with Disabilities Act, 1991). Their advocacy and collaboration with interested professional partners has increased the number of consumers who work as providers within mental health systems, thereby challenging the strict treatment focus of some of their colleagues and offering role models to people with serious mental health problems newly in recovery (Davidson et al., 1999).

Community psychologists can further aid the consumer/survivor movement by drawing attention to oppressive conditions. For example, researchers have drawn attention to the need for greater choice in affordable housing for people with serious mental health problems (Carling, 1995; Nelson, Walsh-Bowers, et al., 1998). The majority of housing for people with serious mental health problems in North America is custodial in nature and emphasizes high levels of surveilance and social control (Parkinson, Nelson & Horgan, 1999). One way of expanding choice is through housing subsidy programs such as the *supported housing model*, where tenants with serious mental health problems hold their own leases and have the choice of where to live in 'market housing' (Cohen & Sommers, 1990). Research on housing subsidy programs has found that people participating had higher levels of residential tenure (Shern et al., 1997; Tsemberis, 1999), increased supportive contact with family (Wood, Hurlburt, Hough & Hofstetter, 1998) and reduced psychiatric hospitalization compared with people receiving similar mental health services without housing supports (Dickey, Gonzalez, Latimer & Powers, 1996).

Inclusion

Why are serious mental health problems seen within the framework of deviance rather than diversity? By challenging this focus, people with serious mental health problems are no longer subsumed by patient or outcast roles but can become contributing members of their communities. The experience and life examples of advocates with serious mental health problems can be instrumental in promoting community change and greater access to resources for others with serious mental health problems (Rowe, Kloos, Chinman, Davidson & Cross 2001). However, while we celebrate notable accomplishments of consumer/survivor advocates, there is a risk that we implicitly expect that people need to 'accomplish recovery' before they can be included in community life (for example be consulted for decisions, meet for lunch). This is ironic given that participating in community life is an important component in the recovery process. Efforts to promote inclusion must meet people with serious mental health problems 'where they are at', and find ways to make communities more receptive to and accessible for their participation.

Two of the most common social outcomes of serious mental health problems are loneliness and isolation. The Compeer Program was developed in New York and promoted by the US National Mental Health Association to encourage mental health systems to create opportunities for people with serious mental health problems to meet and interact with other citizens in their communities (Skirboll, 1994). Davidson and colleagues adapted this model into a 'supported socialization' program that paired interested people with serious mental health problems with interested community members. Their program did not require people to master social skills to participate, but it provided them with a modest monthly stipend to cover their social expenses, and introduced them to a community member. Even though a prerequisite of study participation was to have serious mental health problems and be withdrawn and isolated, they found that 67% of those offered the opportunity to develop a friendship did so and with minimal structure or support from project staff members (Davidson, Stayner, Nickou, Styron, Rowe & Chinman, 2001; Davidson, Stayner, Rakfeldt, Weingarten & Tebes, in press). Similar interventions have been developed to support people with serious mental health problems in housing (cf. Tsemberis & Eisenberg, 2000) and in employment (cf. Drake & Becker, 1996).

Although receiving less attention, interventions can also be focused on community settings to make them more receptive to, and inclusive of, people with serious mental health problems. Community settings can counter stereotypes that are prevalent about serious mental health problems. Strategies that are most effective in countering stigmatizing stereotypes facilitate interaction between people who have serious mental health problems and fellow citizens where: a joint task defines the interaction; there is institutional support for the contact; high levels of intimacy; and the person with serious mental health problems does not differ greatly from the stereotype and is thus less likely to be discounted as 'not really having serious mental health problems' (Corrigan & Penn, 1999). An increased openness to inclusion can also be institutionalized in the form of laws and statutes, such as the US Americans with Disabilities Act. Interventions that target particular settings or social experiences illustrate how support for inclusion requires sustained effort and institutional support.

Commitment and Depowerment

As outlined in the review of mental health system reforms, people with serious mental health problems have been left out of most efforts to improve their living conditions. These principles require mutual accountability in relationships with people who have serious mental health problems and the creation of structures that allow for such collaboration (for example advisory panels, advocacy offices, co-investigators). Nelson and colleagues (Nelson, Lord & Ochocka, 2001b) describe a multi-year research and social change initiative in Ontario where each aspect of the process involved joint decision making with consumer/survivors – articulation of research questions, decisions about who to recruit, decisions about the foci of research, interpretation of research results and application of findings. They characterized this research as being 'nothing about me without me' – a phrase taught to them by their collaborators.

Community psychologists committed to promoting macro-level interventions need to collaborate with advocates to achieve the social changes necessary to improve the conditions of people with serious mental health problems. Decisions about the allocation of resources (for example housing subsidy programs, supported employment, access to health care) may be informed by research, but they are political decisions that all too often disregard research evidence. After more than 10 years of action, political influence from consumer, family and professional groups have increased US government funding for research and consumer involvement in providing services that promote recovery (Carling, 1995).

Chapter Summary

This chapter reviewed the competing narratives in society's responses to serious mental health problems throughout western history. The emergence of consumer/survivor movements has introduced a new dynamic in how tensions of self-determination, deviance, diversity and social control are balanced; to the greatest extent in history, people with serious mental health problems are actively involved in many personal, communal and societal deliberations about responses to serious mental health problems. Supporting these efforts through research and action is consistent with the practice and principles of CP.

Decades from now we will be able to evaluate whether the changes spurred by the emergence of consumer/survivor movements reflect the balance of tensions at one moment in time, like other mental health reforms, or are evidence of the dawning of a new dimension in how societies respond to mental health problems. I am optimistic that the emergence of organized mutual help and consumer/survivor movements creates an effective lobby and significant precedent for sustaining changes at micro and meso levels of analysis. However, much work needs to be done at a macro-level of analysis to promote structural change that helps prevent serious mental health problems (for example efforts to address discrimination, poverty, unemployment and poor housing conditions).

Community psychologists have an important role to play in promoting broader, multilevel understandings of serious mental health problems and ways that communities can promote well-being and liberation. By standing with people who have experienced serious mental health problems, community psychologists can help to promote empowerment and liberation, which may transform expectations for how well-being is articulated and expressed. The resources listed below can assist efforts to support people with serious mental health problems in their labours to participate fully in our communities and promote their recovery.

COMMENTARY: Forging New Partnerships Between Consumers and Researchers: A Call to Action
Allan Strong

I would like to state a bias I have about research as part of my commentary of the chapter. I am reluctant to give any great weight to research done for purely academic reasons. I believe in research as long as it has a practical application. Too often in the past consumer/survivor groups have been studied for research purposes, but the learning from the research is not shared with the consumer/survivor groups upon completion of the research. I firmly believe that research should be done in active partnership with the groups being studied and that it should not occur in a vacuum. That is, both parties involved in the process are affected. I may have a naive approach to research but I feel that liberation and empowerment come through access to knowledge and information. As Francis Bacon said, 'Knowledge is power' and access to knowledge allows for empowerment, liberation and recovery. Having said that, there needs to be equality in the power relationship that exists between the researcher and consumer/survivors. A truly equal relationship would see the sharing of knowledge and information between the researcher[1] and consumer/survivors. I envision a relationship characterized by equality and shared responsibility for the outcomes of the research process. I argue that the relationship historically has not been equal and reciprocal. The consumer/survivor has often been the subject for research without much concern for the practical supports that research could be providing.

I feel there needs to be a fundamental shift in the way that research is carried out. This shift will also require a new perspective on the role of the consumer/survivor group and its role and function in the research process. The consumer/survivor group will have to be seen as an equal partner in the design, implementation and outcomes of a research project. It is only through an equal sharing of the process that information and knowledge become a joint responsibility of the researcher and the consumer/survivor. This style of research

process will recognize the ability of the consumer/survivor to be an informed commentator on his or her experience and that commentary is as valuable as the researcher's. In this research process the consumer moves from being a passive participant observed by the researcher to being an equal, informed, skilled and valued participant. This style of research values the consumer/survivor's input and sees the consumer as an equal partner to the research. The consumer/survivor also becomes critical to the shaping of the outcomes of the research, which hopefully will reflect the reality of the consumer/survivor's context. I would hope that any recommendations arising from this style of research would be rooted in practicality and applicable to the real-life context of the consumer/survivor. As stated earlier, I do not feel that research done in a vacuum is valid research. The consumer/survivor needs to be involved as a full and active partner. If the style of research described above is accepted, then there will be a model of interaction between professionals and consumer/survivors that can be applied to other professionals and the community.

The chapter does a good job of summarizing the issues facing consumer/survivors and how these issues have acted as impediments to consumer/survivors achieving full citizenship in their respective communities. For too long consumer/survivors have been perceived as not having the insight or awareness to be full participants in their treatment. The history of the community's reaction to those with significant mental health problems has been one of disdain and rejection. Historically those with significant mental health problems have been seen and treated as being deviant. Consumer/survivors often live in poverty and are considered part of the disenfranchised of our society. There also exists a profound stigma about those coping with a serious mental health problem. The role of the professional community has also been twofold, in that profes-

---

1 For the purposes of this discussion, researcher is used to mean community psychologists.

sionals provide treatment, but they also play the role of judge in that they can make decisions about the loss of liberty and rights.

How can these issues be addressed in way that focuses on the strengths and skills of consumer/survivors as opposed to perceived weaknesses and deviance? How can the language of recovery be incorporated into the day-to-day reality of consumer/survivors?

I feel that the answers to these questions can be addressed through the effective use of research and its application. The challenge to researchers is focusing on the issue that will be of most importance to consumer/survivors. That issue is recovery. The recovery model is currently in vogue with professionals, but it is the first time we, as consumers, have been allowed to believe that recovery is possible. This has been a dramatic turn of events and any research that can support a recovery-based orientation will certainly contribute to the legitimizing of the recovery model. Consumers need to be supported in their struggle for recovery, and research highlighting recovery can be of benefit. It goes without saying that the style of research will be similar to that described earlier. For the purposes of the research it is important that consumer/survivors have the opportunity to define what they mean by 'recovery' and how they see recovery occurring in their lives.

The focus on recovery can become a new paradigm for relationships between professionals and consumer/survivors, and researchers can play a critical role in helping to provide a context for that new relationship. As stated earlier, true empowerment can only occur if there is a reciprocal relationship between the researcher and the consumer/survivor. The relationship between these two parties can become a model for relationships between consumers and other professionals. The challenge for both the consumer and the researcher will be making the benefits of the new relationship known to the broader community. That must be the agenda for the future. There have been examples of work done by consumers and researchers that have demonstrated how effective this relationship can be (Nelson et al., 2001b). Work still needs to be carried out to strengthen and enhance the relationship between consumers and researchers, but it will be a worthwhile endeavour and, I think, a mutually beneficial relationship.

Community psychologists can play an important and significant role in supporting consumer/survivors' struggle for wellness and recovery. The community psychologist can lend her or his credibility to the research process while the consumer/survivor brings her or his real life experience to the research process. The two combined make for a credible argument in support of recovery, wellness and liberation.

Chapter glossary

case management support provided to people with serious mental health problems in the community

community integration the integration of people with serious mental health problems into 'normal' community settings and relationships

community mental health centres the creation of community-based mental health services, beginning in the 1960s, in many developed nations as an alternative to state and provincial hospitals

consumers a term used to describe people with serious mental health problems that emphasizes individual choice in using services, and the respect given to people who have rights and expectations about the services they use

consumer/survivors another term used to describe people with serious mental health problems that combines the ideas underlying the two terms

deinstitutionalization a social policy emphasizing the reduction or closure of state/provincial mental hospitals

deviancy narratives stories about people with serious mental health problems that emphasize how they are different (and deviant) and need to be controlled or treated by mental health professionals

empowerment narratives stories that emphasize the role that people with serious mental health problems can play in recovery and the contributions they can make to their communities

Framework for Support a model

for supporting people with serious mental health problems developed by the National Office of the Canadian Mental Health Association. It emphasizes utilizing three domains of community support before using formal mental health services: self-help, family/ friends/ neighbours and generic community resources

medical model the creation of large state and provincial hospitals in the mid to late 1800s, emphasizing medical treatment for people with serious mental health problems, inspired by the advocacy of Dorothea Dix

mental hygiene movement at the turn of the 20th century, Clifford Beers started this movement in the US to improve mental health services

Chapter glossary

moral treatment movement ushered in by Phillipe Pinel in France in the 1790s, this movement emphasized kind and compassionate care of people experiencing serious mental health problems

recovery personal goals of experiencing hope, healing, empowerment and connection with others after life disruptions from serious mental health problems

self-determination the right of individuals, regardless of how their behaviour is judged, to pursue their own life goals and make their own choices

serious mental health problems persistent psychiatric disabilities that can have a profound effect on a person's behaviour, thinking, emotions and relationships, including diagnoses (for example schizophrenia, bipolar disorder and severe major depression) and related social experiences (for example fear, discrimination and prejudice) resulting from community responses to people with these diagnoses

social control societal control over individuals whose behaviour is judged to be deviant (for example involuntary hospitalization, policies that restrict opportunities for people based upon diagnosis)

stigma negative stereotypes about people with serious mental health problems that are not warranted and are overgeneralized

supported housing an approach to housing that is based on the principles of choice and community integration, where tenants with serious mental health problems hold their own leases and have the choice of where to live in 'market housing'. This approach has also been applied to education, employment and socialization, with all applications emphasizing that individuals have the support that they need to 'choose, get and keep' the resources they want

survivor a term that is used to describe people with serious mental health problems that emphasizes the negative consequences that they have experienced as a result of past mental health treatment, individuals' resilience in living and self-determination in current life choices

---

■ RESOURCES ■

Recovery Resources

1. 'Handling Your Psychiatric Disability in Work and School' http://www.bu.edu/cpr/jobschool/ *An interactive site for people with a serious mental health problems with information about issues and reasonable accommodations related to work, school and the Americans with Disabilities Act (ADA).*

2. Emerging into the Light Gallery http://www.cmha.ca/emergingintolight/ *Emerging into the Light Gallery is an interactive site designed to 'celebrate resilience and recovery' as well as 'share sorrows and honour heroes'. It includes personal empowerment narratives, fiction and poetry and encourages people to contribute to the site.*

3. Framework for Support (edited and abridged) Trainor, Pomeroy and Pape (1993) http://www.cmha.ca/english/research/framework/framework_full.htm *A model for promoting community integration and ways that mental health services can collaborate with community resources.*

4. Best Practice Guidelines for Consumer-delivered Services http://www.bhrm.org/guidelines/mhguidelines.htm *A review written as a collaboration by a researcher and a consumer advocacy group on the theory, empirical evidence and practical considerations for implementing effective consumer-delivered services.*

Resources for Providers, Consumer/Survivors and Families

These organizations create networks of resources, undertake advocacy, promote policy initiatives, provide services, sponsor research, sponsor publications and hold meetings.

1. Canadian Mental Health Association http://www.cmha.ca/english/
2. Center for Psychiatric Rehabilitation (US) http://www.bu.edu/cpr/
3. The Clifford Beers Foundation (UK) http://www.charity.demon.co.uk/jmain.htm
4. Mental Health Council Australia http://www.mhca.com.au/
5. Mental Health Ireland http://www.mensana.org/
6. World Federation for Mental Health http://www.wfmh.org/ (This site has links around the world).

Consumer/Survivor Organizations

These organizations collect and provide information about advocacy, technical assistance, human rights perspectives and alternative approaches to mental health services.

1. National Empowerment Center (US) http://www.power2u.org/
2. National Mental Health Consumers' Self-Help Clearinghouse (US) http://www.mhselfhelp.org/
3. The Ontario Council of Alternative Businesses http://www.icomm.ca/ocab/
4. Ontario Peer Development Initiative http://www.opdi.org/about_us.html
5. Support Coalition International http://www.mindfreedom.org.

22
Disadvantaged Children and Families

Leslea Peirson

Warm-up Exercise

Reflecting on your childhood or, if applicable, your current role as a parent, think about the privileges that you enjoyed.

1. What assets have you and/or your family been afforded because of your privileged status in society?
2. Alternatively, what resources or opportunities have you and/or your family been denied due to disadvantage?

Introduction

In this chapter you will learn how community psychology helps us to understand the context of disadvantaged children and families and how we can act on behalf of and with these families to change their conditions of marginalization and oppression. In my discussion I consider how families and their problems have been understood and how society has responded to family needs. I also examine some of the difficulties associated with understanding families in such ways and some of issues that arise from a traditionally reactive and micro-level response. The values that are central to understanding families and their needs from a perspective of liberation and well-being are outlined, and guiding principles and concepts from community psychology (CP) that help us understand or reframe our notions of families and their needs are discussed. Finally, multi-focused, community-driven interventions and social policies for disadvantaged children and families are described.

In Chapter 1, Geoff and Isaac use the metaphor of a journey as a means of explaining the context of CP. The analogy is also appropriate for this chapter which focuses on disadvantaged children and families. Families are not static entities. As they journey through life they experience many developmental and situational transitions. These transitions result in a dynamic context for family life that presents both opportunities and challenges. Disadvantage may also be conceived of as a journey, if it is understood as a process of needs not being met which leads to distress and crisis, the likely outcomes of oppression.

It is important, at the outset, to be clear about the meanings that are associated with the designations 'children and families' and 'disadvantage'. Although there are many family constellations, this chapter is focused on families in which there is at least one infant, preschool or elementary school-aged child and at least one primary caregiving adult all of whom share a biological, adoptive or foster relationship. Why focus on families with children? Unlike most other groups in society, children are wholly dependent on others to meet their needs; they are in essence 'only beneficiaries of values' (Prilleltensky, Laurendeau, et al., 2001, p. 147). Within society, children are relegated to a subordinated position; they possess neither political nor economic power. The actualization of their rights, which are stipulated in the United Nations Convention on the Rights of the Child (1991), is contingent on the ability and willingness of others to provide them with education, health care, protection and adequate resources. Although children's primary context is the family, their well-being is influenced by, and therefore must also be understood in relation to, forces operating at broader levels of analysis.

Elsewhere Isaac, Geoff and I have defined well-being or wellness as 'a favourable state of affairs brought about by the combined presence of cogent values, satisfactory psychological and material resources, effective policies and successful programs' and family well-being as 'a state of affairs in which everybody's needs in the family are met' (Prilleltensky, Peirson, et al., 2001, p. 8). Disadvantage can be considered in contrast to well-being, as a state of affairs in which values, resources, policies and/or programs are not satisfactory to meet the needs of children and families. Disadvantage may be acute, transitory and related to singular constraints or it may be chronic, generational and related to multiple factors. Regardless, the consequence is that the ability of families to function effectively in the ecological system (that is, the personal, relational and collective contexts) is compromised and there is a need for formal or informal interventions to support them and respond to their unmet needs. Although disadvantage may derive from many sources, in this chapter the impact of low-income or poverty and the associated risks of such circumstances are considered to be the primary causes of disadvantage for children and families. Globalization and market expansion have lead to profits for some, but many more children and families have been negatively impacted by this recent economic trend. In the last two decades of the 20th century the number of people living in poverty swelled to over 1.2 billion, approximately 20% of the world's population, about half of whom were children (UNICEF, 2000).

Poverty is an affliction that strikes children and families in developed and developing nations alike, with perilous consequences. A recent UNICEF report on child poverty across the 30 member countries of the Organization for Economic Cooperation and Development (OECD) concluded that 47 million children, or one in six children, live in poverty, despite living in the wealthiest nations in the world (UNICEF Innocenti Research Centre, 2000). For some of these children, physical needs go unmet, resulting in risks to their health and growth. For other children, relative poverty means that while they may have their basic needs met, they are marginalized and denied opportunities available to their non-poor peers. In developing nations, hundreds of millions of poor children and young people, some as young as three and four years old, are forced to work, often in hazardous environments, to support their families (Aristide, 2000; Feuerstein, 1997; UNICEF, 2000). Millions more children suffer or die each year from diseases such as HIV/AIDS, malnutrition and starvation and violence and war, and countless others are orphaned when their parents succumb to such afflictions or are killed in conflicts (Narayan et al., 1999; Narayan, Chambers, et al., 2000; UNICEF, 2000, 2002). Mortality rates and life expectancies also corroborate the disadvantages of poverty. In the year 2000, for infants and children in developing countries, the probability of dying between birth and one year and birth and five years was 63 and 91 per 1,000 live births respectively and in the least developed countries these rates were considerably higher at 161 and 102. In striking comparison, the infant and under-five mortality rates in industrialized nations both stood at six per 1,000 live births in the year 2000 (UNICEF, 2002). Life expectancy is also much lower in the developing and least developed countries at 62 and 51 years respectively, compared to 78 years in developed countries (UNICEF, 2002). However, within industrialized nations there is variability with respect to life expectancy among social classes, with women and men in the lower classes living, on average, several years less than those in the upper classes (Shaw et al., 1999). While these statistics reflect only a fraction of the harm and injustice that is caused by poverty, they expose the grave consequences of not addressing this oppression and the critical need for national and global action.

Box 22.1   **My Journey: Revealing Privilege**

'Do you have any children?' Until recently I was always puzzled by the knowing looks other parents (friends and those with whom I was conducting research) gave one another when I answered 'no' to this question. I have spent many years researching children and families. I thought I had a lot of knowledge about their needs and realities, but as it turns out, what I really had was information, not a practical understanding. In May 2001 my son Reece was born and I have begun to appreciate what it means to have another person entirely dependent upon you to meet their needs and the intensity of emotions, responsibilities and lifestyle changes that come with being a parent. However, my journey as a parent has not been one of disadvantage, but rather one of privilege and the outcomes, so far, are successful. My experience thus suggests that I cannot presume

to know what it is really like to raise a family while being subjected to adverse conditions.

One of the exercises I have given to my community psychology students is based on McIntosh's (1990) insightful article 'White privilege: Unpacking the Invisible Knapsack'. In this article McIntosh reflects on the concept of privilege and how members of dominant groups are afforded, and take for granted, many assets due to their privileged status. She then identifies 26 conditions in her experience that she attributes to her privilege as a white person. I have asked my students to consider their own privileged status and to generate other lists of unearned advantages that rest on social or economic class, religion, sexual or ethnic identity, age, ability and gender. Although this exercise does not manifest the experience of subordination, it does cultivate an awareness of one's own privilege and what others who lack similar privilege may be subjected to or denied. McIntosh suggests that knowledge of unearned advantage and privilege can be used to challenge the status quo and transform oppressive systems of power.

Over the past year and a half I have spent a lot of time unpacking my own invisible knapsack of privilege and considering the advantages that have been available to me in my role as a parent. Reflecting on the values and concepts that will be discussed in this chapter, I have identified many examples of assets and resources that have benefited myself and my family. I am married and was so before becoming pregnant; my pregnancy was also planned. Given these conditions there was no social stigma attached to the birth of our child. We have close connections with both of our extended families and grandparents, uncles, aunts and cousins are interested and involved in our lives. Although I would not say we are wealthy, we are certainly economically privileged. We are able to provide ourselves and our son with not only the basics for living, but additional comforts and incidentals, including setting aside funds for future opportunities such as Reece's post-secondary education. We were able to pay for prenatal classes and through employment benefits had additional health coverage to upgrade hospital accommodation following our son's birth. There is a strong sense of community where we live and our neighbours provide one another with both generalized and specific supports. There is a family down the street that provides us with child care in an exceptionally nurturing environment and for a very reasonable cost which we are also able to pay. Community level resources have also been available to help us meet the needs of our child. Public health nurses connected with us upon our return from the hospital and provided in-home visits. Unlike many families, we have a family physician who has provided continuity of care throughout the prenatal, delivery and postnatal stages. I utilized the services of a breast feeding clinic at a local hospital for eight weeks, a resource which was invaluable in teaching and supporting me to become successful at nursing my son. There are also many programs offered by community organizations such as the library and recreational facilities that provide opportunities for stimulation and social connection. On a macro level we have also benefited from various social policies. Universal health insurance granted us access to free prenatal, delivery and postnatal care and parental leave policies enabled me to take a year off from my doctoral program to spend with my son.

Admittedly my journey as a parent has just begun, but clearly my family has already benefited greatly from the advantages available to us as a result of our privileged status in society. Do other families deserve any less?

Reframing Our Notions of Families and Disadvantage: Towards an Agenda of Well-being

In this section of the chapter I examine traditional or neoliberal approaches to understanding and responding to disadvantaged families. I also consider some of the challenges that arise from such ways of knowing and acting. The values and principles of CP are invoked to help reframe our notions and to better understand and respond to the realities and needs of families experiencing disadvantage. The conceptual framework presented in Chapter 2 is used as an organizing structure for the discussion.

From Individualism and Victim-blaming to a Holistic, Strengths-based Ecological Perspective

Individualism and Victim-blaming

The traditional approach to understanding disadvantaged families is focused on a micro level of analysis and looks either for difficulties within the family unit or within particular family members. The dominant worldview in western cultures is that of individualism. The assumptions of this narrative which include initiative, independence, personal responsibility and freedom of choice can be transferred onto families. Families are expected to be self-sufficient entities and when problems arise they are attributed to poor choices or deficits within the family. Not recognizing the broader forces that influence disadvantage leads to victim-blaming and a doctrine of personal culpability, (Goldenberg, 1978; Ryan, 1971) and encourages social acceptance of the negative consequences for families (for example dislocation to segregated environments such as social housing or the streets, working at menial jobs, living on social assistance). Furthermore, there is evidence suggesting that individualism is associated with negative outcomes, that in turn lead to more problems for disadvantaged families (Lipset, 1996). For example, in conservative times of economic restraint, individualism allows us to blame families on social assistance for their problems and rationalizes cutbacks in social spending. Reductions in benefits and/or withdrawal of employment programs further increase the problems experienced by families and leave little hope for overcoming adversity.

The conventional approach to helping disadvantaged families is equally problematic. The response is often reactive, treating or administrating the family (for example counselling, assistance programs) after problems have occurred. Since individualism views the source of disadvantage within the context of the family, it is at this level that intervention is directed. The influences of community and societal level forces on family functioning are rarely considered. We try to change families, not situations of poverty, unemployment, poor housing, limited or inaccessible resources and lack of social cohesion. We focus on the surface manifestations of disadvantage, not the deep causes (Joffe, 1996). As such, our efforts are ameliorative rather than transformative as we try to teach families how to live with adversity rather than working to change the unjust social conditions that lead to problems in the first place. This approach puts disadvantaged families in a subordinate position to the rest of society and implies that they need to be repaired somehow or that their lives need to be managed by others.

Holistic, Strengths-based Ecological Perspective

Adopting a holistic perspective redirects our attention from a deficit-orientation towards a focus on the strengths of families living in adverse conditions. An empowering or strengths-based focus identifies assets and capacities in families that offers hope and opportunities not only to families but also to service providers. Consider the following scenario. The Smith family includes a single mother and two children aged four and six. Child support payments are non-existent and their only source of income is through social assistance benefits which are usually insufficient to cover expenses for basic needs. They live in a social housing complex that is in poor repair and frequented by local drug dealers and users. The family does not own a car, so many community resources, including grocery stores, the library, parks and doctors' surgeries, which are located several miles away, are not easily accessible. What does this description lead us to believe about the Smiths and the possibilities for improving their situation? The picture looks rather bleak for this family and it would not be unreasonable for a community service worker to feel powerless to assist in a meaningful way, given the complexity of challenges. However, if the assessment was reframed to also consider the strengths of the Smith family and their environment (for example a supportive grandmother who will care for the children while the mother attends an employment retraining program, interest from residents in the housing complex in forming a neighbourhood watch program, a community kitchen and a co-operative day-care centre) the situation and potential opportunities might appear quite different.

The value of holism also draws on the ecological principles, described in Chapter 4, which allow us to contextualize the problems experienced by families over time and across multiple levels of analysis. It reflects the importance of focusing on the whole family in the context of the relationships, settings and environments in which the family is embedded. Within families, members rely on one another for cognitive, emotional, psychosocial and economic needs. Often the analysis stops here; looking at the individual or microsystem, but not beyond. The ecological principles acknowledge that families are impacted by individual members and the family setting, but also by other components of the microsystem (for example extended family, peer networks), the organizations they are connected to, the community environment, social norms and values, social and economic policies, and global and environmental issues. The problems associated with, or leading to, family disadvantage do not always originate within the family or a particular member of the family, rather they often arise due to conditions or changes within broader structures that in turn influence the health and well-being of families. Consistent with this understanding, the focus of interventions targeting disadvantaged families should go beyond educational or skill-building programs offered to parents and children, to efforts aimed at altering or improving social and economic conditions within the meso and macro levels.

From Psychosocial Problems to Prevention and Promotion

Psychosocial Problems

Traditionally, psychological research and action has focused on psychosocial problems within individuals or the family unit (for example addictions, teenage pregnancy, child maltreatment, delinquency and crime). Dysfunctions are conceived as emanating not from adverse economic conditions or individual attempts to cope with inequalities in social and economic power, but rather from inferior genes, poor parenting skills, lack of problem-solving skills, ineffective communication patterns and so on. In essence, our understanding of disadvantage has been reduced to the psychosocial level or to the surface manifestations of the problem. This perspective has led to a treatment orientation that seeks to ameliorate difficulties at the personal or relational (within family) levels. This approach does not challenge the status quo, rather it attempts to reduce maladaptive behaviours or adapt the individual and/or family to enable them to function within established societal structures and norms.

Prevention and Promotion

The principles of prevention and promotion invoke the value of health and are used to resist psychosocial problems and to encourage well-being. In our everyday use of the term, health has two meanings, one negative and one positive. The negative definition of health, the one that is widely accepted in western cultures, refers to the absence of disease or illness. The positive interpretation of health, as defined by the World Health Organization in its 1946 constitution, is 'a state of complete physical, mental and social well-being, not merely the absence of disease or infirmity' (p. 2).

It is the latter definition that is of interest to CP for it recognizes that health is a multidimensional concept that can and should take a positive form. A more recent publication of the World Health Organization, the *Ottawa Charter* (1986), states that 'health is a positive concept emphasizing social and personal resources, as well as physical capacities' and calls for 'coordinated action by all concerned: by governments, by health and other social and economic sectors, by non-governmental and voluntary organizations, by local authorities, by industry and by the media' in meeting the prerequisites for health which include 'peace, shelter, education, food, income, a stable eco-system, sustainable resources, social justice and equity'. These ideas are also of interest to CP as they reflect a competency orientation, the influence of the social context on health and well-being, intersectoral cooperation at multiple ecological levels, as well as social ethics and emancipatory values (refer back to Table 1.1 which outlines the assumptions and practices of CP).

Prevention and promotion aimed at disadvantaged families can reflect personal, collective and relational dimensions. At a person/family-centred level, interventions can focus on: decreasing or dealing effectively with stress created by adverse living conditions; reducing the detrimental effects of physical vulnerabilities which may have contributed to, or resulted from, disadvantage; increasing problem-solving, decision-making, social and coping skills; expanding perceived networks of social support; and developing self-esteem and self-efficacy (Albee, 1982). Such efforts respond to the values of self-determination, caring and compassion and health.

Interventions that foster collective well-being emphasize the role of broader structures in preventing psychosocial problems and promoting health. At an environmental level, efforts can be directed towards: decreasing or removing stressors in socialization settings (for example schools, workplaces, health care); reducing the presence of risk factors in the environment that lead to increased physical vulnerabilities (for example poor prenatal care, exposure to hazardous substances, inadequate heating and ventilation); developing positive socialization practices (for example effectively preparing parents, teachers, employers and others to assume their roles); expanding the strength, availability and accessibility of social support resources; and, increasing opportunities for positive relatedness to others and connections with formal and informal settings (Elias, 1987). At the societal level, through the unified action of all sectors, healthy public policies can be established to '[reduce] differences in current health status and [ensure] equal opportunities and resources to enable all people to achieve their fullest health potential [which] includes a secure foundation in a supportive environment, access to information, life skills and opportunities for making healthy choices' (World Health Organization, 1986). These programs and policies foster the values of support for community structures and social justice and accountability.

Promoting relational well-being requires that interventions, both in the personal and collective domains, respect differences among disadvantaged families, allow families to define their needs, promote acceptance and facilitate meaningful involvement of disadvantaged families in making decisions affecting their lives. In so doing, the values of respect for diversity and participation and collaboration are advanced. Relational well-being may also be supported through interventions that encourage involvement and collective responsibility, such as mutual aid groups, community development initiatives and social and political action.

From Social Isolation to Community

Social Isolation

Physical isolation or geographic separation, can pose significant challenges for disadvantaged families (for example limited interaction with extended family or friends, lack of access to needed resources and services such as physicians, schools and transportation). On the other hand, simply living in close proximity to others does not ensure that disadvantaged families are socially integrated. Families may choose, or be forced, to become insulated from their neighbours and surrounding community for a variety of reasons such as a fear of crime or violence, suspiciousness and the burdens of caring for children or working at multiple jobs.

As one of the structures of oppression, containment serves to intensify the social isolation experienced by disadvantaged families. Goldenberg (1978) describes containment as 'limit[ing] the range of free movement available to a particular group ... increasingly restrict[ing] and narrow[ing] the scope of possibilities that can be entertained ... [and effectively] quarantining ... people from the possibilities of change' (pp. 1 5). Families with limited economic resources are often forced to move into social housing or other lower income neighbourhoods. The quality of life and the prospects for a better future for residents in these areas are hampered by poor conditions, absentee landlords, violence, stigma and distance from important community resources such as quality schools, clinics and grocery stores. Mobility issues also contribute to the social isolation experienced by disadvantaged families. Not having a car or a reliable vehicle or other convenient and affordable means of travel can limit the possibilities available to families. Getting to work, attending appointments, grocery shopping, visiting community resources such as libraries, parks and other facilities and taking family trips can be arduous journeys which may often be avoided, passed up or impossible. Disadvantaged families are excluded from participating in their communities due to their inability to pay for many services and opportunities such as recreational activities, summer camps and training courses. Endowments that might once have been available to support the inclusion of disadvantaged children and families in community activities have diminished or been eliminated in response to government funding cutbacks. Essentially the oppressive social and economic conditions experienced by disadvantaged families trap or 'contain' them in abject environments with limited opportunities for inclusion in the broader community.

Community

The values of caring, compassion and support for community structures involve empathy and concern for the welfare of others and emphasize the importance of networks and settings that facilitate the pursuit of personal and communal goals (Prilleltensky, Laurendeau, et al., 2001). Although there are many caring and compassionate practitioners who have dedicated their working lives to helping disadvantaged families, there is not, nor will there ever be a sufficient number of professionals trained to deal with the needs of the population (Albee, 1959). Nor is the traditional professional–client relationship the only, or best, context for responding to many of the problems associated with adversity. Disadvantaged families need more than therapy or other professional services, they need access to informal supports and strong community structures.

Informal relationships can provide disadvantaged families with ongoing generalized support as well as specific support related to particular stressors (Sarason, Sarason & Pierce, 1990). Although adverse conditions may lead to a sense of containment, most disadvantaged families do not live in complete physical isolation from others. Psychological sense of community and social integration can be facilitated through mechanisms of connecting families to one another, such as block or neighbourhood associations, community cooperatives and religious congregations. The relationships formed within these networks can provide families with a sense of belonging, emotional support, socialization, encouragement, advice, tangible supports such as child care, money, clothing, meals and transportation, as well as opportunities to reciprocate with support when others require assistance. Relational well-being may also be promoted through self-help and mutual-aid groups that deal with problems or issues affecting disadvantaged families and which provide connections to others and various specific supports in egalitarian, respectful and reciprocal contexts.

In addition to social networks, developing the capacity to promote family well-being can occur through building support for the community structures that disadvantaged families interact with in their everyday lives. Ensuring a broad range of accessible, responsive and publically funded institutions is a critical factor in preventing problems associated with disadvantage and for promoting the well-being of all citizens (Prilleltensky, Laurendeau, et al., 2001). Included in this array would be health care services, schools, transportation systems, waste management and water treatment facilities, libraries, cultural and recreational opportunities, police and other justice services, insurance and assistance programs and many other vital resources and agencies. However, these structures that work for the common good are often taken for granted and tend to be noticed more in their absence, in times of shortages, cutbacks or strikes. These institutions are also threatened by neoconservative and neoliberal forces intent on dismantling the welfare state and privatizing many community services (O'Neill, 1994). Withdrawal of such fundamental public resources or initiating fee-for-service policies would further disadvantage many families already living in adversity and might also result in negative consequences for families that are currently coping adequately because of supports they receive from these various institutions. Recognizing, valuing, protecting, maintaining and expanding the welfare state are important steps towards promoting collective responsibility for the well-being of society's most vulnerable families.

From Powerlessness to Power

Powerlessness

Disadvantaged children and families lack both a sense of control and actual control over many aspects of their lives. Despair over the past and present and hopelessness for the future are created and maintained by their oppressive social context. Limited economic resources mean that disadvantaged families are often forced to live in social housing, low-income neighbourhoods or are even homeless. They usually do not own their homes so they are subjected to the conditions imposed by governments and landlords. They usually cannot afford to register in skills-training programs or to send children to college or university. Without post-secondary education they are often relegated to menial, low-paying jobs with little opportunity for advancement or they must rely on social assistance benefits. The initiative of many families receiving social assistance benefits is repressed as income received from other sources is clawed back from support payments or there is a threat that benefits may be cut off entirely. These conditions and restrictions reflect the concept of containment and another structure of oppression, compartmentalization. 'Compartmentalization is the process which encourages partial rewards at many levels but denies fulfilment at any one level' (Goldenberg, 1978, p. 11). Disadvantaged families are powerless because they cannot change their living situations without risking their access to shelter and means of survival. They lack choice and opportunity and are subordinated to others who control, monitor and administrate their lives.

Disadvantaged families also experience powerlessness in the contexts of service provision (for example mental health, physical health, legal, child welfare) and research. The traditional approach views professionals as expert technicians, as specialists who have expertise and are given authority to assess and treat families. Families, on the other hand, are viewed as clients, as passive recipients of services that are under professional control. Unable to pay for private consultation, disadvantaged families are without choice in terms of service options or specific practitioners. They are often in lengthy waiting lists to access services which are deemed appropriate by others and which are provided by agency-appointed staff. Disadvantaged families are also often treated as passive objects of research. Traditional research has circumscribed the role of the family to that of a data source. In a number of qualitative studies I have been involved in, parents and young people have commented that researchers repeatedly come to them for information about the realities of disadvantaged living, but they are never certain what happens to the knowledge they convey because their adverse situations persist.

Power

How can disadvantaged families that experience such an extreme lack of control acquire power and assert authority over their own lives? The principle of power emphasizes the values of participation, self-determination and social justice. It is through the intertwining of these three values that disadvantaged families can gain both voice and choice.

The value of participation refers to respectful collaborative processes wherein all stakeholders have meaningful input into decisions that affect their lives (Prilleltensky, Laurendeau, et al., 2001). The practical experience of families living under adverse conditions must not be dismissed. Disadvantaged families should be involved in identifying their needs and determining appropriate responses. However, their participation must not be based on token strategies of inclusion, for this denotes a subordinated position. Instead, the power to define problems and shape solutions must be shared in value-based relationships of partnership (Nelson, Amio et al., 2000; Nelson, Prilleltensky and MacGillivary, 2001). Responding to the value of accountability, the principles of commitment and depowerment direct researchers, service-providers and policy makers to work with disadvantaged families, not for them. Through its inter-disciplinary ties, community psychologists are learning how to promote the active participation of marginalized populations in decision-making processes. Feminist-oriented participatory action research and the application of traditional native teachings are two examples of approaches to involving the often unheard voices of disadvantaged groups.

To acquire power, disadvantaged families must have more than voice, they must also have choice. The value of self-determination refers to the ability of families to pursue chosen goals and direct their lives without facing formidable obstacles (Prilleltensky, Laurendeau, et al., 2001). Rather than having their lives externally orchestrated or regulated, disadvantaged families need to have control over decisions that affect their present and future well-being. Personal empowerment is enhanced when families maintain a sense of agency and experience autonomy in their everyday lives. Self-efficacy, which develops through having such control, acts as a protective mechanism against various risks associated with disadvantage and helps families cope with the daily stressors of living in adversity (Prilleltensky et al., 2001b). However, self-determination is dependent upon the actualization of the third value connected to power, social justice.

In order for families to be able to make choices, options must exist and opportunities must be accessible. Social justice reflects the fair and equitable distribution of bargaining powers, responsibilities and resources in society (Prilleltensky, Laurendeau, et al., 2001). This value blends the components of voice and choice such that the needs of disadvantaged families are identified by those who live the experience and there are programs and policies in place that respond to these needs. In the current conservative climate which discriminates against disadvantaged families and other marginalized groups, social justice is brought about through social change movements that promote the notion of collective well-being and a vision of a more just and caring society. There are many national, provincial and local organizations that have been formed across Canada and elsewhere to address the issues of disadvantage, fight poverty and advocate for equity in the division and distribution of societal and regional resources.

From Discrimination to Inclusion

Discrimination

What is a family? Each of us, no doubt, has our own opinion as to what constitutes the 'ideal' family which is shaped by personal experience and attitudes, social norms and media influences. The image often conjured up is one similar to the Cleaver family portrayed in the 1950s/60s television series, *Leave it to Beaver*. But is this suburban, two-parent (working father, stay-at-home mother), two well-adjusted (although adventurous) children family 'normal'? This scenario may be true for some families, but in contemporary society there are various family constellations. Families today take many forms and function under diverse circumstances. For instance, there are two-parent married families, single-parent families, blended families, cohabitating families, reconstituted families, grandparent and grandchildren families, teenage-parent families, same-sex families, shared-home families, immigrant families, mixed ethnicity or religion families, dual-earner families, poor families, adoptive or foster families and so on (McCoy, 1996). Although 'recent studies have expanded the data base to many cohorts ... diverse families still tend to be evaluated in comparison to one standard' (Walsh, 1996, p. 268). Ideologically we still romanticize the Cleaver family model popularized in the conservative era of the 1950s. Although contemporary discourse reflects diversity and an acknowledgment of the different types of families, conservative values dominate and non-traditional families continue to be rejected (Leonard, 1997) and discriminated against by policies and social norms (Eichler, 1997; Lindeman Nelson, 1997; Nicholson, 1997). In turn, non-traditional families internalize this discrimination and are made to feel ashamed for their differences and responsible for their oppression (Goldenberg, 1978).

Inclusion

The principle of inclusion calls upon the value of respecting diversity. Families should not be judged against a single standard, they should have the right to be different and they should not be made to suffer because of their differences. The unique social identities of families need to be respected and accepted. Our notions about families guide our assumptions and the allocation of societies' resources. To promote equity, it is important that our policies and programs reflect the different types of families and respond to their varying needs.

Interventions for Children and Families: Ecological and Empowerment Approaches

Community psychology involves both thinking and action. In the previous section I discussed ways in which we understand families and disadvantage. In this next section I focus on the action component, describing some of the programs and policies that benefit disadvantaged children and families. A review of the literature indicates that there are numerous preventive interventions targeting disadvantaged children and families (Nelson, Laurendeau, et al., 2001). Given that these families are already experiencing adversity and may be at risk for additional problems, the types of interventions they encounter tend to be selective or indicated (Institute of Medicine, 1994). Many programs adopt a single focus (for example cognitive problem-solving, social decision-making, stress management, home visitation), are targeted at the micro level (on children, parents or families) and are of a relatively short duration. Numerous programs are also professionally driven or led and are implemented in a single context (for example home, school, workplace). While there is substantial evidence that supports the effectiveness of many of these programs in realizing their goals, they do not respond to the range of values and principles promoted by CP. In order to advance personal, relational and collective well-being for disadvantaged families and to support a transformative social agenda we must look beyond traditional approaches to multi-focused, community-driven and policy level interventions.

Multi-focused, Community-driven Programs

Multi-focused programs acknowledge the value of holism, recognizing that targeting a single contributing factor is unlikely to address the complexity of cumulative and interacting variables leading to and perpetuating disadvantage. Drawing on the ecological principle, multi-focused programs also recognize that factors beyond the microsystem, at the meso and macro levels, significantly influence the incidence and conditions of disadvantage. Although psychosocial problems associated with disadvantage may be addressed within multi-component interventions, this focus may be balanced by long-term efforts to develop social support and community capacity. Community development is a major component of many multi-focused programs often resulting in the creation of neighbourhood organizations. These organizations typically respond to the needs of families of preschool and elementary school-aged children, offering a variety of resources including child care and family support (Zigler, Finn-Stevenson & Stern, 1997). Reciprocal informal support among neighbours is also stimulated by such interventions (Garbarino & Kostelny, 1992; Korbin & Coulton, 1996; US Advisory Board on Child Abuse and Neglect, 1993).

The fact that these programs are community-driven advances several additional values including self-determination, participation, respect for diversity and accountability. While researchers and other professionals may be involved in the process, it is in partnership with disadvantaged community members who have a major voice in identifying their needs and wants as well as choice in determining what types of interventions are necessary and how they will be implemented (Nelson, Amio et al., 2000; Nelson, Prilleltensky et al., 2001; Rothman & Tropman, 1987). Program participants become involved and contribute to the management and delivery of their community projects in various ways including formal and informal opportunities to express views and opinions, volunteering in the delivery of programs, participating on committees that provide advice to the project governing bodies and/or research teams or sitting on governing bodies that make decisions about the projects and their programs.

Although most programs targeting disadvantaged families are more narrowly focused and professionally directed, there is evidence that multi-component, community-driven interventions are becoming more salient. Descriptions of proactive universal applications for disadvantaged families are beginning to emerge in the literature. While these programs are situated in high-risk communities, they fit the description of universal programs because the services and supports are available to all families in the area with children in the targeted age range and thus reduce stigma associated with such assistance.

Where I live, in Canada, there are three notable examples of multi-focused, community-driven universal prevention programs being implemented with children and families living in socioeconomically disadvantaged communities. Better Beginnings, Better Futures is a 25-year longitudinal prevention research demonstration project that started in 1991 and is currently being implemented in eight culturally diverse communities across Ontario (Peters, 1994; Peters et al., 2000). In 1995 the 1,2,3 GO! program began in six high-risk neighbourhoods in greater Montreal (Bouchard, 1997, 1999; Centraide of Greater Montréal, 2001). Developed out of the 1990 World Summit for Children at the United Nations, the Community Action

Program for Children (CAPC) is a national programme with over 400 locality-based projects operating across the provinces and territories (Health Canada, 1999, 2001). A common overriding goal of these programs is to prevent serious social and psychological problems and to promote the health and well-being of at-risk families with young children. The models followed in these programs incorporate a comprehensive, multi-level ecological framework emphasizing community empowerment and collaborative partnerships among parents, practitioners, researchers, decision makers and other citizens. There are many different activities offered across the project sites that are shaped with community input to meet the unique needs of residents. However, there are many similarities in supports and services across the programs including informal and professional home visitation for expectant parents and families with young children, drop-in centres, parent-training classes, social-skills training and literacy enrichment for children, collective kitchens and recreational opportunities. Preliminary outcomes for these three programs are beginning to emerge with mixed results. Sites within some projects report positive impacts on children and families, while other sites show no impacts on children and families but do suggest positive impacts on community collaboration (Health Canada, 1999, 2001; Peters et al., 2000). Given the longitudinal nature of these programs and the fact that evaluative research is ongoing, the full picture of the effectiveness of these interventions has yet to unfold.

Another multi-focused, community-driven, universal prevention program was initiated in 1999 in the UK. Strikingly similar to some of the Canadian initiatives, the Sure Start program is described in Box 22.2.

Box 22.2   Program Profile: Sure Start

Sure Start originated in 1999 as part of a national evidence-based campaign to address child poverty and social exclusion in the United Kingdom. As of 2004 there are more than 500 local Sure Start programs operating in socioeconomically disadvantaged neighbourhoods across the UK. Although it targets high-risk families, Sure Start is an example of universal prevention, since services are available to all local families, regardless of economic status. The primary aim of Sure Start is to work with families with children, prenatally up to age four, to promote the physical, intellectual and social development of infants and young children and to enhance family and community functioning. To advance this goal the Sure Start programs concentrate on four main objectives: improving social and emotional development; improving health; improving children's ability to learn; and strengthening families and communities.

Local programs are sensitive to diversity and are driven by the unique needs identified at the neighbourhood level. However, there are core services that each Sure Start program is expected to provide including: outreach and home visiting; family and parent support; opportunities for quality play, learning and childcare; primary and community health care; and support for children and parents with special needs. In terms of community participation, a key principle of the Sure Start approach is promoting the involvement of all local families in the design and implementation of services. In addition to 260 local evaluations, there is a team of academics and practitioners conducting a national process and impact evaluation of Sure Start. The first phase of the national evaluation began in January 2001 and will continue for six years. (http://www.surestart.gov.uk/home.cfm)

Social Policy Interventions

While multi-focused, community-driven approaches can respond to the needs of disadvantaged children and families for prevention, inclusion, support, sense of community and personal empowerment, they cannot change the macrosocial and political factors that significantly influence conditions of adversity (Febbraro, 1994).

> The patterns of poverty that are passed from one generation to the next can and will be broken when the poor have the means and opportunity to be healthy and well-nourished enough and educated and skilled enough to fully participate in the decisions that affect their lives. (UNICEF, 2000, p. 6)

The means and opportunity to pursue a healthy and satisfying life are bestowed through vehicles of social, economic and health policy. To address socioeconomic inequalities and poverty and to promote the well-being of children and families, social interventions must be mounted to advocate and develop policies that will ensure a more just and equitable distribution of resources among all members of society, nationally and globally.

There is a belief that the absolute wealth of a country produces health, but this perspective does not look at conventions that privilege control over material and human resources and ideology. This philosophy neglects the importance of other structural factors such as race and gender and it fails to point to the need for broader emphasis on social, political and economic activities like affordable housing and full employment policies. The importance of focusing on a transformative social justice agenda through equitable and responsive policies is supported by research on the social determinants of health. Wilkinson (1994, 1996, 1997) and others (Ben Shlomo, White & Marmot, 1996; Kaplan, Pamuk, Lynch, Cohen & Balfour, 1996; Kennedy, Kawachi & Prothrow-Stith, 1996) have argued from an economic perspective that in advanced industrial societies a country's wealth status does produce health to some extent, but there is a point beyond which the relationship between wealth and health disappears becoming instead a function of the relative gap between rich and poor. Furthermore, it should be noted that it is not just the health status of those individuals who exist at the polar extremes of poverty and wealth that is at stake, but rather we are all affected as inequalities of morbidity and mortality have been found to apply across the socioeconomic gradient (Adler et al., 1994). From this perspective the focus of policy should not be relegated to wealth generation strategies in the pursuit of improving health and the reduction of health-related problems, but on developing and instituting fundamental mechanisms for ensuring the equitable distribution of wealth and resources across the population. Social interventions promoting a model of collective responsibility will thus serve not only those children and families who are most vulnerable, but the whole of society.

While there is much more that needs to be done at the macrosociopolitical level to address poverty and its consequences, there are numerous examples of policies that respond to the needs of disadvantaged children and families. Social, economic and health policies can redistribute income to those in lower socioeconomic classes through cash benefits and tax transfers; encourage nurturing caregiving environments for children by supporting parental leaves and early childhood care; protect children and adults from disease and disability through universal health coverage and immunization programs; advance learning and literacy through publically funded education; and safeguard children and families from violent conflicts.

As part of the Family Wellness Project (Prilleltensky, Nelson & Peirson, 2001a), Ray Peters and his colleagues (2001) conducted a comprehensive review of policies to promote the well-being of children and families. In their research they found that some countries, including France, the Netherlands, the UK and Sweden, have implemented universal family allowance policies that effectively reduce economic inequalities through tax and transfers. Other countries such as Canada, Australia and Germany have abolished the universality of such support to families, instead providing means-tested, targeted benefits that are comparatively lower than benefits provided by nations using universal measures. Furthermore, Kamerman (1996) has noted that countries implementing income-tested benefits have been less effective in preventing families with children from falling into poverty, compared to nations that have maintained the universality of these benefits.

At the selective level of intervention, Peters et al. (2001) found that some countries (for example Sweden and France) have instituted advance maintenance child support policies that guarantee payments to custodial parents and thus protect single-parent families which are often vulnerable to poverty and psychosocial problems. If a non-custodial parent defaults on support, the government makes the payment to the custodial parent and then assumes responsibility for collecting from the non-custodial parent. Limited advance maintenance policies, which emphasize the state's role in debt collection and enforcement of non-custodial parental responsibility, are prominent in countries such as the Netherlands, the UK and US. In most Canadian provinces child support payments must be privately enforced and while the paying parents (usually fathers) are provided with tax concessions for their support contributions, the custodial parents (usually mothers) are regressively taxed on the payments they receive.

Universal policies that provide other benefits such as parental and extended child-care leave and early childhood care and education, are also important for promoting family health and well-being during the early stages of parenthood. Compared to Anglo-American countries, European nations provide more weeks of paid leave and a higher rate of pay and many of these countries also offer supplementary benefits to women who are raising children, regardless of their participation in the workforce (Peters et al., 2001). Child-birth related leaves in the European countries range from a minimum of three months in the Netherlands to three years in Austria, Finland, France, Germany and Hungary (Peters et al., 2001). With respect to child care, despite advocacy efforts from various sources, many countries, including Canada and the US, still do not have a national policy to support a public system of early childhood care and education services for their children. This is a significant issue since child care is often the single largest child-related expense a family incurs and, at least in Canada, it can more than double the annual costs of raising younger children (Government of Manitoba, 2001). Public models of child care responsibility that provide well-subsidized, high-quality child care to a large percentage of parents have, once again, been established in a number of European countries such as France and Sweden (Peters et al., 2001).

The importance and power of focusing, not on economic growth, but rather on social policy as a means of alleviating poverty and fighting oppression is demonstrated by the remarkable transformations that have occurred in the State of Kerala in India with respect to social development and population health. Beset by poverty, malnutrition, overcrowding and other health and social problems, Kerala instituted a series of policies reflecting a campaign of social justice focused on ensuring a more equitable distribution of existing resources, goods and services across the population. The approaches and advances in this state are profiled in Box 22.3.

Box 22.3   Social Justice Through Transformative Policy: The Kerala Experience

India's Kerala State provides an excellent example of how engaging in broad structural reforms within a region's political economy, can lead to important gains in the health status of its citizens. Some of the specific structural reforms that were accomplished as a result of various social movements over the course of a century, included amendments to the land tenure system, equalization of income, legislation to provide better social security, pensions and working conditions, free primary and secondary level education, increased production of high-yield crops and access to price-controlled food, enforcement of child labour laws and increases in female participation in the labour force (Ratcliffe, 1978). Recent research indicates that Kerala has successfully improved quality of life for its citizens to levels comparable to conditions in developed nations (Franke & Chasin, 1995, 2000; Kannan, 2000; Parayil, 2000). Adult literacy rates have risen to 94 per cent in Kerala, compared to rates of 65 and 96 per cent in the rest of India and the United States, respectively. Despite gross differences in GNP per capita, the life expectancy for women living in Kerala is 72 and in the United States it is 80. At 13 per 1000 live births, the infant mortality rate in Kerala is still higher than in industrialized countries, but it is significantly lower than in the rest of India (65 per 1000) and other low income countries (80 per 1000). Public health indicies also show Kerala ahead of the rest of India with the lowest rates of diseases such as malaria and cholera, higher rates of immunization for child tuberculosis, polio, diptheria-pertussis-tetanus and measles and greater access to and utilization of health professionals and facilities. Increased understanding of rights by the poor majority has also led to raised political consciousness and persistent grassroots activity to force the government to listen to the poor and respond to their needs. Although still a poor state, even by India's standards, Kerala has managed to significantly improve the quality of life for the broad majority of its citizens through structural changes based on equity considerations, rather than an emphasis on aggregate economic prosperity.

Chapter Summary

In this chapter, through a traditional lense, we see that when disadvantaged families are viewed in terms of deficits, blamed for their misfortunes, measured against single standards, discriminated against and treated as passive recipients of services, they become socially isolated, excluded and powerless. However, viewed through a CP lense we see that disadvantaged families have strengths, are impacted by forces at multiple ecological levels, reflect diversity and have rights to power, inclusion and self-determination. It is also evident that interventions that focus on multiple components, that involve participants as meaningful stakeholders and that promote equity and social justice, can foster hope, social change and enhance opportunities for disadvantaged children and families to become valued members of society and have their health needs met. By focusing on values, principles and interventions that support personal, relational and collective well-being we can work to transform unequal systems of power and privilege thereby improving the lives of disadvantaged children and families.

COMMENTARY: Disadvantaged Children and Families: The Power of a Just Asymmetry

Camil Bouchard

In her chapter, Leslea Peirson sought to describe how traditional individualistic approaches to problems experienced by disadvantaged families may create more problems for these families. She also prescribed a change in our course of action in terms of the values and principles of CP, as well as some of the newest community-based intervention strategies. Her chapter raises some very interesting questions.

As oppression is a central theme of this chapter, it is useful to refer back to definitions of the concept used by some community psychologists.

In Chapter 2, Nelson and Prilleltensky define oppression as 'a state of domination where the oppressed suffer the consequences of deprivation, exclusion, discrimination, exploitation, control of culture and sometimes even violence'. Earlier, Prilleltensky and Gonick (1994) commented more on the process than on the end state of oppression: 'Oppression occurs when an asymmetry or unequal relationship is used unjustly to grant power and resources to one group and withhold them from another' (p. 165).

The word 'unjustly' is important here. It implies that asymmetry could be used in a just and fair manner, as long as it provides an opportunity for the less powerful group to restore or improve its position and permits a better distribution of resources, including power, among people (Rawls, 1987). For example, progressive taxation rates conform to this rule of a just asymmetry as it tilts the burden of taxation in favour of the disadvantaged. The understanding of this counteracting process is, from my point of view, a very important element to be considered as a part of a global strategy, expressed at every layer of the socioecological system, for eliminating or reducing inequalities in health, well-being, social participation and economic integration.

Where oppression exists, there is a privileged group and a subordinated group. The author delivers a very compelling phenomenological illustration of what it is to be a member of the privileged group in describing her own experience as a parent. Elements of all layers of the ecological system are present in the description of her experience. As a member of the privileged group, the author has opted to reject the victim-blaming model. The question then becomes: What are the factors which permit and reinforce such an option? What conceptual elements and strategic assets can we count on to encourage citizens, academics and service-workers to raise their consciousness and take similar stances vis-à-vis their privilege? In *Pedagogy of the Oppressed*, Freire (1972) makes a convincing case that to liberate the oppressed, the 'oppressors' (or members of the privileged group) also have to raise their consciousness as to their role in maintaining systems of oppression. In the context of many western, democratic regimes, the presence of oppression and its transformation is often rendered invisible or at least difficult to detect. As the author makes clear, victim blaming , often disguised under a well or not so well-intentioned approach, is a more dominant narrative than the denunciation of relative privilege; oppression is covert. For those favouring a more critical stance, raising awareness

about oppression and privilege could well be one of the many demanding research and action tasks they will have to face in the next decades.

CP is very much context-oriented in its theoretical approaches and actions. One malaise I felt in reading Peirson's chapter was related to the fact that when she used the term 'government' or 'state,' it was difficult to identify the specific entity to which she was referring. As a citizen of the province of Quebec, I took exception to her claim about the paucity of desirable and just social policies for families. The Quebec government has, during the past two decades, adopted several very progressive family policies which are in sharp contrast with what other Canadian provinces or states in the US offer to families. For example, Quebec has created a universal $5 a day childcare network providing families with a unique set of resources for parents and their children. This was in response to years of claims-making by the Quebec feminist movement and was also consistent with recommendations presented in the 1991 report *Un Québec fou de ses enfants* (Québec crazy about its kids, Bouchard et al., 1991). This report has had a profound impact on the eagerness of family associations and childcare services to sustain pressure on the government for reforming its family policy and for investing in high quality daily environments for all children from birth to five years in Quebec. This is another example of a just asymmetry approach in political action, as taxes are redirected to the less affluent families through systemic changes.

In my reading of the part of the chapter that dealt with interventions, I was puzzled by the apparent gap between framing the problems of disadvantaged families in terms of oppression and the various illustrations of community-based interventions reported by the author. At the community level of intervention there is reference to the fact that community-driven strategies offer opportunities for building community capacity, for creating more neighbourhood organizations and for advancing such values as self-determination, participation, respect for diversity and accountability. Although these could be coherently presented as second-order changes at the local micro- and meso-systemic levels (Dalton et al., 2001), one can argue that solving the problem of oppression demands far more than opportunities for minor local adjustments to social roles. It demands power reversal strategies. For parents, having a major voice in the identification of their needs at the local level does not necessarily change social, economic and political conditions, especially if these parents opt for more psychosocial programs directed at improving individual deficits, which is very often the case. I suggest that there are no significant cultural and political significant changes in such approaches unless there are transformative changes in power relations in favour of the marginalized and disadvantaged. I am not certain that the examples of community-driven initiatives which were selected by the author pretend to make such changes (Bouchard, in press; Peters, 1994).

At the level of social policy intervention, examples are provided by the author as to how some countries try to reduce inequalities though social programming. These illustrations are illuminating as to how political constituencies can use their power to influence the daily quality of life of disadvantaged families. Moreover, the processes that lead some countries to adopt more socially just policies are of interest to community psychologists. As an illustration of such an interest, I briefly comment on a fascinating social experiment that took place in Quebec during the last four years. A Quebec coalition led by a very determined female social activist (trained in psychology and ethnology) has pushed, pressed and inspired the Quebec government to adopt Bill 112, a law to *combat poverty and social exclusion*, ' a framework law unique in North America and which constitutes a significant political innovation, if only because it makes poverty reduction an explicit and central policy priority' (Noël, 2002). The coalition succeeded in influencing the government to adopt that law for various reasons.

The coalition was broad (22 very active lobby groups); it succeeded in engaging the major union confederations and student associations; and it worked on a long time basis and with intensity. As well as several other tactics, including a petition signed by over 215,000 people, it launched a very dynamic process of consciousness-raising under the format of a preliminary law.

This law, written by poor people in collaboration with lawyers and activists, was discussed in over 200 popular parliamentary sessions. The final draft of the bill was the result of over 20,000 suggestions and 5000 comments (see Noël (2002) for a more detailed description and visit the coalition web site: http://www.pauvrete.qc.ca/). But most importantly, the coalition gained access to prepublication discussions of the annual government budget. From now on, its members, including people on welfare, have access to the formulation of the provincial budget and can prepare themselves within the same rules and privileges accorded to business, union organizations and the media. This to me, this is an example of true second-order, transformative change and is directly in line with an approach relevant to fighting oppression. Community psychologists have a lot to learn from such genuine, well planned, transformative experiments which illustrate the principle of a just asymmetry in which the powerful open their eyes and use their power to serve a more equalitarian and just society.

Chapter glossary

community-driven interventions interventions that are guided by a community development philosophy in which local residents have a significant voice

compartmentalization the process which encourages partial rewards at many levels but denies fulfilment at any one level

containment limiting the range of free movement available to a particular group, increasingly restricting and narrowing the scope of possibilities that can be entertained and effectively quarantining people from the possibilities of change

doctrine of personal culpability a synonym for 'blaming the victim'

family well-being a state of affairs in which everybody's needs in the family are met

health a state of complete physical, mental and social well-being, not merely the absence of disease or infirmity

means-tested family benefits financial support policies that are targeted at low-income families, as determined by a 'means test'

multi-focused interventions interventions that have several different program components (for example preschool education for children, home visitation for parents and so on)

universal family allowance policies policies designed for all families that effectively reduce economic inequalities through tax and transfers

Recommended Websites

1. Better Beginnings, Better Futures is major prevention policy research demonstration project that is being implemented and evaluated in Ontario, Canada. To learn about the research on Better Beginnings go to http://bbbf.queensu.ca/.

2. The Community Action Program for Children is a large-scale community-based prevention initiative with over 400 programs operating across Canada. To find out more about these programs and their evaluations go to http://www.hc-sc.gc.ca/hppb/childhood-youth/cbp/capc/ or enter CAPC (search Canadian sites) into your internet browser for links to various community-level programs.

3. 1,2,3 GO! is a multi-neighbourhood community-driven prevention project being implemented and evaluated in Montreal, Canada. To learn more about this initiative go to http://www.centraide-mtl.org/centraide/static/where/go.shtml.

4. Sure Start is large-scale prevention policy initiative that is being implemented and evaluated in the UK. To find out more about Sure Start and its evaluation go to the following websites, http://www.surestart.gov.uk/home.cfm and http://www.ness.bbk.ac.uk/.

5. The website of the United Nation's Children's Fund provides information on children's rights and other issues related to children living in poverty in developing nations, with links to UNICEF publications, speeches, frequently asked questions and statistical information. To find this website go to http://www.unicef.or.

6. Among the links within the website of the World Health Organization is information on child and adolescent rights including the United Nations Convention on the Rights of the Child. To find this website go to http://www.who.int/child-adolescent-health/right.htm.

7. The website of the World Bank Group provides resources for people and organizations working to understand and alleviate poverty. This website is accessible at http://www.worldbank.org/poverty/.

8. The Annie E. Casey Foundation in the U. S. has a good site on disadvantaged children and families, see http://www.aecf.org/ and http://www.kidscount.org.

Recommended Readings

1. Albee, G. W., Bond, L.A. & Monsey, T. (1992). *Improving children's lives: Global perspectives on prevention* (Volume XIV of the *Primary prevention of psychopathology* series). Thousand Oaks, CA: Sage.

2. Cicchetti, D., Rappaport, J., Sandler, I. & Weissberg, R. (eds). (2000). *The promotion of wellness in children and adolescents*. Washington, DC: Child Welfare League of America Press.

3. Mrazek, P. & Haggerty, R. (1994). *Reducing risks for mental disorders: Frontiers for preventive intervention research*. Washington, DC: National Academy Press.

4. Prilleltensky, I. (2003a). Poverty and power: Suffering and wellness in collective, relational and personal domains. In S. Carr & T. Sloan (eds). *Psychology and poverty*, (pp. 19–44), New York: Kluwer/Plenum.

5. Prilleltensky, I. & Laurendeau, M.-C. (eds). (1994). Prevention: Focus on children and youth [Special Issue]. *Canadian Journal of Community Mental Health*, 13(2).

6. Reynolds, A., Walberg, H. & Weissberg, R. (eds). (1999). *Promoting positive outcomes: Issues in children's and families' lives*. Washington, DC: Child Welfare League of America Press.

7. Weissberg, R., Gullotta, T., Hampton, R., Ryan, B. & Adams, G. (eds). (1997a). *Enhancing children's wellness*. Thousand Oaks, CA: Sage.

8. Weissberg, R., Gullotta, T., Hampton, R., Ryan, B. & Adams, G. (eds). (1997b). *Establishing preventive services*. Thousand Oaks, CA: Sage.

9. Weissberg, R. P. & Kumpfer, K. L. (eds). (2003). Prevention that works for children and youth [Special issue]. *American Psychologist*, 58(6/7).

■ RESOURCES ■

23
Environmental Degradation and Ecologically Minded Alternatives

Ed Bennett

I wonder if we wouldn't become more gracefully productive by recognizing that we are all living cells with organisms like cities, bioregions, continents and the earth itself. Could we lessen our stress, become healthier and more whole, if we saw our work as simply helping these organisms realize their living wholeness?

Daniel Kemmis, Mayor of Missoula, Montana (1995)

Warm-up Exercise

What's your share of the global commons (the natural and social ecology of individuals and societies)? Check your 'ecological footprint' on http://www.lead.org/leadnet/footprint/intro.htm

After you respond to the questions, it can be particularly helpful to join with others in your class to discuss the experience.

In this chapter, I begin by presenting the 'big picture' of environmental degradation and sustainable alternatives. I argue that corporate globalization – which is creating massive environmental devastation, poverty and community disintegration – is leading us to an evolutionary dead end. The global economic system has become delinked from place and people and has developed a tendency to extract and degrade environmental resources for short-term monetary gain (Korten, 2001). I argue that the central goals of an ecological revolution towards sustainable alternatives are to create an earth community with economies which are: driven by social needs; linked to place; and biased towards creating small communities, finding long-term solutions, living in balance with nature, conserving resources and living co-operatively with all people. The conceptual framework of this chapter consists of two main components: the issues and problems of environmental degradation; and the values, principles and ideas which lead towards sustainable living and social justice.

Environmental problems are community problems. We all have a responsibility to enhance and protect the planet that we inhabit. The solutions to these problems rest in the hands of individuals and communities of citizens. They will require the actions of informed citizens willing to tread more lightly on the planet and to move their neighbours to make the commitment to do the same. They also will need governments to develop the political will and legislation to stop the senseless destruction of the planet we all share.

Environmental problems are also transdisciplinary problems. Although most of the students reading this book will be taking a community psychology (CP) course, the conceptual framework utilized in this chapter integrates material from multiple disciplines, including ecology, ecological economics, biology, general systems theory, psychology, sociology, planning and popular education.

The solutions to global environmental decline are coming from individual citizens and communities of people who value the resources of the earth and who believe in freedom, justice, democracy and equality for all people who inhabit the planet that we share.

Environmental Degradation and Community Psychology

Kidner (1994) has argued that, as a discipline, psychology has been mute about the environmental crisis because its ideological preconceptions are similar to those of the ideological–economic–technological systems which are largely responsible for the crisis. Even though the health of the natural ecology is fundamental to the well-being of people, the transactions between individuals and the natural world remain largely unconsidered in CP research and practice. While community psychologists have adopted ecological concepts from the field of biology and have postulated ecological principles as a frame of reference for their work (Kelly, 1970; Trickett, 1984; Trickett et al., 1985), the focus has been on social ecology rather than on natural ecology or on the transactions between human systems and the natural world. That is, the transactional analyses legitimate a worldview in which people are seen as separate from the natural environment rather than as interdependent with it. Further, few community psychologists have been actively engaged in 'change of the system' work (Bennett & Foy, 1987, as cited in Bennett, 1987; Prilleltensky & Nelson, 1997). This is particularly problematic in the face of the burgeoning global ecological crisis.

There is evidence, however, that these attitudes may be starting to change. Recent CP textbooks (for example Dalton et al., 2001) have included environmental psychology in their descriptions of conceptual perspectives for describing ecological context and its impact on individuals. Further, there have been some high-profile, intensive and longitudinal community-level studies of the psychological effects of living in close proximity to toxic disasters (Baum, 1987; Baum & Fleming, 1993) and toxic waste sites and of citizen activism in response to these conditions (Levine, 1982; Rich, Edelstein, Hallman & Wandersman, 1995; Stone & Levine, 1985). Excellent work also has been done in researching and popularizing the area of community-based social marketing as a means of fostering sustainable development (McKenzie-Mohr, 2000; McKenzie-Mohr & Oskamp, 1995).

Environmental Degradation: Issues and Problems

The Environmental Crisis, Psychosocial Dysfunctions and Macroeconomics

A significant transformation has been taking place in North American communities and in communities around the world during the past 50 years. Accelerated economic growth has placed extraordinary demands on the ecosystem, demands that exceed what the earth community is capable of sustaining. As a result, we are witnessing a burgeoning of social disintegration and environmental degradation in almost every country in the world. In the past century, people have managed to destroy much of the planet's 'living capital', which took two billion years to create. The evidence is everywhere – ozone-layer depletion, climate change, epidemics of new diseases such as AIDS, an expanding population and the loss of biodiversity, fish stocks, agricultural land, forests and the global water supply. All of this is in addition to the social and economic injustices discussed earlier in this book.

The relentless and insatiable quest for economic growth and the pursuit of profit for its own sake have served as the organizing principles for public policy in North America and countries around the world and are the central threats to the earth community. The requirements of an economic system driven by a growth mentality have been the main causes of the global environmental crisis and the crisis in community. The documentation of the ecological costs of the growth orientation pursued by conventional macroeconomic policies is overwhelming.

Daly and Cobb (1989), two internationally respected economists, foresee current global economic policies leading civilization to a dead end. They argue that contemporary economic growth has meant an exponential increase in the extraction of resources from the environment and the emission of waste products into the environment – all with little regard for the exhaustion of natural resources, pollution or the human community. The bottom line is that 'we are living by an ideology of death and accordingly we are destroying our own humanity and killing the planet' (Daly & Cobb, 1989, p. 21).

Box 23.1 **The East Coast Cod**

The exhaustion of Canada's east coast cod in 1992 because of overfishing is a good example of socioeconomic displacement because of ecological destruction. The east coast cod collapse displaced more than 20,000 fishermen, trawlerworkers and plant workers, most of them Newfoundlanders. Small fishermen, like the ones displaced on the east coast of Canada, make up 90% of those employed in the world's fishing industry.

Roberts, McRae and Stahlbrand (1999) estimate that 10 million small fishermen will lose their livelihood in the next decade. They argue that a billion people who rely on local fish for the main source of their protein will be affected. They observe that the British Columbia salmon fishery and catches in 13 of the world's 17 largest oceans and seas are in jeopardy and identify the industrialized offshore fishing industry as the root cause of the problem. Where the inshore fishing indus- try thought about diversity and worked with nature by harvesting limited volumes of fish and at the appropri- ate times of the spring and summer, the offshore factory ships catch, process and freeze more than 500 tons a day. At that volume of catch, much of the fish is rotten by the time it is processed and ends up as prison food or fast food. Worldwide government subsidies and investment in industrial factory fishing are estimated at US $54 billion annually (Roberts, McRae et al, 1999).

Psychologists and other professionals who have been interested in mental health issues have observed that environmental factors give rise to stress, overpower the coping mechanisms of the individuals they affect and undermine mental health (Cowen, 1977; Epp, 1986, 1988; Horney, 1937; Lalonde, 1974; Lazarus & Folkman, 1984; Rappaport, 1977, 1984b). Among those environmental stressors, Cahill (1983) includes structural characteristics of the macroeconomy. The link between macroeconomic conditions and psychosocial dysfunctions is further substantiated by Seidman and Rapkin's (1983) literature review and Wachtel's (1989) in-depth treatment of the psychological underpinnings of our insatiable desire for growth.

Economics: Chrematistics or Okonomia?

Environmental issues fit Mills's (1959) discussion of 'public issues'. Public issues transcend the local environments of individuals and their inner lives and have to do with the organization and structure of social and historical life. They are connected to an economic paradigm that measures human welfare in relation to the Gross National Product (GNP). Some scholars (Daly & Cobb, 1989; Wachtel, 1989), however, observe that the tendency to treat the GNP as a general index of national well-being is a fallacy of misplaced concreteness that ignores many social, psychological and environmental costs.

According to Daly and Cobb (1989), the GNP is a poor measure not only of national welfare but also of income. True income, they argue, is sustainable – and the GNP subtracts neither the expenditures associated with economic growth (such as degradation of the environment) nor the social costs of development. Further, in the GNP, harmful consumption (for example of unhealthy fast foods and tobacco) is viewed favourably because it appears as an indicator of 'growth'. The income accounting of GNP does not calculate the maximum amount that we can consume without impoverishing ourselves; thus, Daly and Cobb conclude, we are living beyond our means.

Accordingly, Daly and Cobb advocate a paradigm shift from the present-day economics of *chrematistics* – 'the manipulation of property and wealth to maximize the short term monetary exchange value to the owner' – to the economics of *okonomia* – economics for 'the larger community of land, of shared values, biomes, institutions, language and history' (1989, p. 138). The key to economics for a sustainable future, they contend, is to acknowledge the carrying capacity of the ecosystem and to understand that the economy has a proper scale relative to the ecosystem. Only in this way, they argue, can we avoid extinction.

Loss of Biodiversity

The loss of biodiversity serves as evidence of the threat to the earth's structural and functional undergirding systems – its atmosphere, chemical fabric and biological essence. The loss of biodiversity and global climate change introduce a new class of problems to the prototypical complex adaptive system called the *biosphere* (Levin, 1999) – problems which threaten its internal organization and capacity to maintain itself. Few people fully understand the significance of biodiversity to the sustenance of life or the implications of its loss: with the increasing loss of ecological systems, we are speeding up our own extinction.

One of the most serious aspects of the loss of biodiversity is the exponential rate of environmental destruction. An ecosystem may be attacked in hundreds of ways from hundreds of sources, all at once and not always with warning. Because of the interdependent nature of the ecosystem, the extinction of some species can speed up extinction rates overall. Environmentalists label this phenomenon *exponential environmental destruction* (Suzuki, 2002, as cited in Barlow and Clarke, 2002). The net effect is the creation of a *biodiversity deficit*, 'where species and ecosystems will be destroyed faster than nature can create new ones' (Coddington, 2002).

Ehrlich and Holdren (1971) argue that the most significant event in the two-billion-year history of life on earth has been the ascendancy of the *Homo sapiens* species. Only 10,000 years ago, the human population (numbering only about 5 million) was but one of many species of large mammals living on this planet. As a result of the agricultural revolution, the human population had risen to 500 million by 1650 and now exceeds 6 billion. This exponential population growth and its accompanying agricultural, industrial, biomedical, biological and technological revolutions have come with staggering costs to biodiversity at all levels – from large mammals and old-growth trees to the smallest of organisms. Humanity has realized enormous achievements (such as the exploration of space), but we have failed miserably in living in harmony with nature and in eliminating global injustices such as poverty and hunger.

Agriculture, Food and Environmental Degradation

There have been serious consequences to the globalization of the food system. The economic colonization of the global food system has forced many countries in the Third World to stop growing crops necessary for the subsistence of their population and, instead, to sell cash crops for export as a means of paying their foreign debts. Further, it has diminished the capacity of local areas to produce their own food, contaminated the food with herbicide and pesticide residues and reduced the nutritional value of the food itself.

Environmental degradation is one of the most serious elements of the crisis in agriculture. The protection of the biodiversity of farm soils is essential to agriculture, the environment and human and animal health. Yet industrial methods of farming such as monoculture (reliance on a single crop or livestock) have contributed to the loss of hundreds of millions of tons of topsoil each year to erosion, have dramatically reduced essential biodiversity in agricultural soils and threatened the integrity of the soil and our ability to grow healthy food. The industrial paradigm of agriculture, which has been promoted by public policy, relies heavily on the use of farm inputs such as chemical fertilizers, pesticides, herbicides, fungicides, irrigation and large-scale equipment for working the land, planting the seeds and harvesting the crops. Modern farm strategies – along with the lack of regulations for the disposal of toxic animal wastes, the environmental and health risks associated with feed contamination and the problems in the meat packing and food processing industries – have become an ecological disaster.

Closely related to the health and environmental risks posed by our food supply system is the unhealthy nature of our diet. Schlosser (2002) argues that high-sugar, high-fat, fast-food diets have had staggering health impacts on citizens around the world. They increase the risk of heart disease, hypertension, certain cancers and diabetes. In the US, where 25% of the population eat at least one meal a day from a fast-food outlet and where fast food is served in school cafeterias, obesity is the second highest ranking cause of death (approximately 60% of adults and more than 20% of children are overweight). And, as Schlosser notes, the US is exporting its fast food and dietary problems: US beef exports increased to 2417 billion pounds in 1999, up from 40 million pounds in 1970; Coca-Cola is now Africa's largest employer; and Mexico surpasses the US in per capita consumption of Coke (Lappé & Lappé, 2002).

Box 23.2   **Drug-resistant Bugs**

More than half of all antibiotics produced are for live-stock and agriculture. The long-term practice of feeding antibiotics to farm animals contributes to the growing problem of antibiotic resistance by human infections. Resistant bacteria can pass through animal waste to other animals, into the production environment and into waterways and other ecosystems. Untreated manure is spread on the land and may run off into our creeks, rivers and lakes and end up in our water supply. All of this contributes to the creation of super-bugs (antibiotic-resistant bacteria) such as the deadly *E.coli* 01 57:H7 found in the water supply in Walkerton, Ontario, which resulted in the death of seven people and the illness of

2500 in May, 2000. Scientists at the World Health Organization, the US Centers for Disease Control and the Alliance for the Prudent Use of Antibiotics (APUA) have warned that the threat of drug-resistant bugs is so great that the overuse of antibiotics must be curbed immediately. Recently, these organizations advised of the grave danger of reducing the world to a pre-antibiotic age in the next 10 to 20 years. The threat may be closer than anyone has predicted. In June, 2002, the US Centers for Disease Control announced the first confirmed case of staphylococcus aureus that is resistant to vancomycin, which had served as the drug of last resort.

Water

Barlow and Clarke (2002) posit that the degradation and the depletion of the world's water supply is perhaps the greatest threat to the survival of our planet. The world is running out of fresh water: The Third World is already facing a water crisis (which endangers human beings and other species) and, they argue, other areas of the world, including North America, are on the brink of one.

Not only are we polluting our fresh water supply but, in some cases, Barlow and Clarke (2002) argue, we also are using water at a greater rate than ground water reserves can be replenished by precipitation. They assert that unless we change our ways, as much as two thirds of the world's population will experience severe water shortages in the next quarter-century. They observe that global water consumption is doubling every 20 years – more than twice the rate of human population growth:

'Put in economic terms, instead of living on fresh water *income*, we are irreversibly diminishing fresh water *capital*. At some time in the near future, we will be fresh water *bankrupt*' (p. 15).

Box 23.3 The Great Lakes

The future of the Great Lakes, which contain 20% of the world's fresh water, is in jeopardy. Barlow and Clarke (2002) report that high levels of dioxins, polychlorinated biphenyls (PCBs), mercury, lead and furans and many other toxic chemicals have been pouring into the Great Lakes from rural and industrial sources and can be found at every level of depth in every lake. Each year between 50 and 100 million tons of hazardous waste are generated in the surrounding watershed, including 25 million tons of pesticides, and there are serious build-ups of radioactive waste from nuclear power stations. Many of the toxins will never break down and appear in higher concentrations as they move up the food chain. A person eating one fish out of the lakes will be exposed to more PCBs than would be acquired from a lifetime of drinking water from the lakes. The surrounding wetlands, which have acted like the kidneys of the lakes, serving to prevent floods and filter out pollution, have been disappearing to development at a rate of 20,000 acres per year – only 20% of the original wetlands remain. Because of all this, less than 3% of the lakes' shorelines are suitable for swimming.

Environmental Degradation and the Crisis of Governance

It is the responsibility of a government to govern in the interests of its citizens and to protect the commons (the natural and social ecology of individuals and societies). However, influenced by a business-first ideology and by their close relations with the corporations that cause pollution and other environmental problems, government officials often abdicate this responsibility.

On June 13, 2002, the US announced proposals to amend its Clean Air Act to make it easier for utilities to expand coal-burning power plants. Buck Parker, executive director of the environmental law firm Earth Justice, argued that this amendment would result in millions of tons of additional pollution and made a powerful analogy to the recent disclosure of the feared 'terrorist' dirty bomb: 'With the release of this report the Bush administration dropped a dirty bomb and its going to cost thousands of American lives.' David Anderson, Canada's environment minister, believes the proposed changes to the US Clean Air Act could result in more pollution drifting into Canada (*Kitchener-Waterloo Record*, June 14, 2002, p. A–3).

The power of some elite transnational corporations has been consolidated by international trade agreements – such as the North American Free Trade Agreement (NAFTA) – which are backed by the World Bank, the World Trade Organization (WTO) and the International Monetary Fund (IMF). This increased power has resulted in a crisis of governance. Governments around the world seem unable to protect the commons against the ideological and legal–political–technological forces of economic globalization. Increasingly, governments are giving corporations a new set of rights which have no responsibilities to the welfare of individuals or community tied to them. Under NAFTA, virtually any government action (including action to protect the health of the country's citizens) that interferes with a corporation's reasonably expected profits can result in an obligation to pay millions of dollars in damages to the corporation.

Box 23.4   **Politics and Clean Air**

Texas rancher Wayne Brinkley and his family are literally choking in the legacy of George W. Bush's business-first pollution policies. The Brinkley family, who own a 290-acre ranch In Rockdale, Texas and a local group called Neighbors for Neighbors have been in a David-and-Goliath struggle with Alcoa Aluminum over compliance with federal and state clean-air laws. The Alcoa plant, about two miles down the road from the Brinkley ranch, continuously burns high-sulphur lignite coal and releases more than 114,000 tons of pollution each year, including 66,000 tons of sulphur dioxide, a cause of chronic lung disease. The Brinkley family's children have developed severe asthma, attributed to the acrid air released over their ranch home from the Alcoa smokestacks. On January 9, 2002, the Texas Natural Resource Conservation Commission and the federal Environmental Protection Agency notified Alcoa that it was violating both state and federal clean air laws. But Alcoa has friends in high places. Confident that it would be protected by President Bush and his successor as governor of Texas, Rick Perry, Alcoa said that it would lower emissions by 2007. When Bush was governor, he 'grandfathered' Alcoa and many other industrial polluting plants, exempting them from clean-air laws. According to the records of the environmental lobby, grandfathered polluters contributed as much as $10 million over 6 years to Bush, Perry and Texas state legislators. The polluters were also heavy contributors to Bush in his presidential campaign (Walker, 2002).

Box 23.5   **Guadalcazar vs. Metalclad**

In the late 1990s the people of Guadalcazar, Mexico, denied Metalclad Corporation permission to build a toxic-waste landfill in their town because they had concerns that it would pollute their drinking water. There was a realistic basis to their fears. Another company had previously operated a toxic waste facility on the same site and there were concerns that it had polluted their water. When Metalclad Corporation applied for a permit to reopen the landfill site, the community protested. The town council refused to provide Metalclad with a building permit. In the summer of 1999, the government of Mexico appeared before a NAFTA tribunal in a conference room at the World Bank in Washington, DC. The NAFTA tribunal ruled in favour of Metalclad, reasoning that it wasn't up to the town of Guadalcazar to judge the environmental risks as the basis for refusing the permit. Mexico was ordered to pay Metalclad damages of US$16.7 million (McQuaig, 2001).

Summary of the Big Picture

The earth is in serious trouble. Around the globe we see countless examples of life-threatening environmental problems which are the result of unsustainable, large-scale human activity. Indeed, we have become almost inured to the daily reports of ecological devastation. Most of us want to breathe clean air and drink safe water. Yet our environmental problems persist and, as they are multiplied across diverse ecosystems and communities, they increase exponentially with each passing year.

While there is serious cause for concern, there are also thousands of examples, involving millions of citizens, that give us hope that we can save our troubled planet (Barlow & Clarke, 2001; Korten, 2001; Lappé & Lappé, 2002; Roberts & Brandum, 1995; Suzuki & Dressel, 2002). As grim as things may seem, I can't imagine what the world would look like today without civil society fighting for its rights.

Towards Sustainable Living: Values, Principles, Ideas and Strategies

Values and Social Change

When we begin to believe that there is a greater joy in working with and for others than just for ourselves, then our society will truly become a place for celebration.

Jean Vanier

Prilleltensky and Nelson (1997) have identified the values of CP as being: health; caring and compassion; self-determination and participation; human diversity; and social justice. I believe that a shift in emphasis towards these values can make feasible a more harmonious balance with nature. So far, our relationship with nature has been largely absent from CP's conceptual models of ecological context. But I believe that CP's values must, in their definitions of ecology and well-being, explicitly embrace the natural environment (Bennett, 1992; Bennett, 2003).

A main argument of this chapter is that the choices which individuals and society make regarding their relationship with the environment are informed by values. Our economic system and our relationship with nature have gone astray and are out of control because we have lost sight of what is really important. In this chapter, I join an increasing number of critics who argue that the dominant value influencing the escalating global environmental crisis is human greed – an insatiable appetite for economic growth and wealth. This appetite has disrupted the psychological foundations of well-being – for individuals and for society. It is my view that we have choices; we can prevent the eco-catastrophe that is facing our civilization and attain a harmonious ecological balance. To do so, though, we need to make a fundamental shift in values from an economic definition of well-being to a more holistic one.

There are an increasing number of worldwide social movements based on the desire to create a world that works for all – a fight for life, democracy and well-being. Examples include: Ekins (1992), grassroots movements to promote self-reliant and healthy alternatives; Hallman (2000), a global movement to enhance spiritual values for earth community; Korten (2001), the Global Movement For A Living Democracy – seeking transformative justice through non-violent means; Sarkar (1992), the emergence of green alternative politics that began in the 1970s in Germany; Shiva (1988), the growing social movement of women in the Third World fighting for survival and the environment; Mies and Shiva (1993), the ecology and feminist movements and the meaningful advancement of some ecofeminist subsistence alternatives.

Fundamental Principles: Justice and Accountability

> It is the awareness of having faults, I think and the knowledge that this links us to everyone on Earth, that opens us to courage and compassion.
>
> *A. Walker (1999)*

Justice, accountability and appropriate process are important aspects of social change. When there are power imbalances or an abuse of power, it is especially important to name problems and to hold people and governments accountable for their actions and values.

A broad scientific consensus exists, for example, that increased CO_2 emissions and other human-produced greenhouse gases are precipitating warming of the global atmosphere and contributing to disastrous climatic changes. Since 1989, governments have been negotiating to address climate change under the auspices of the United Nations. Scientists and non-governmental organizations (NGOs) have been important contributors to the negotiation process.

In 1992, at the Rio Earth Summit, the first major agreement was adopted. From a justice perspective, there were two significant aspects to the treaty: that the governments of the world acknowledged that they must work together to solve the problem and that some countries have more responsibility for the problem than others; and that there is an urgent need to stabilize greenhouse concentrations in the atmosphere – by reducing the annual emissions of CO_2 by more than 60% – to prevent dangerous anthropogenic interference with the climate system.

By December, 1997, governments had negotiated the Kyoto Accord, a specific protocol for reducing emissions to a level still considerably higher than that called for by the scientific community. An important element of the Kyoto negotiation process was the 'Justice Statement' presented by the delegation of the World Council of Churches, which transcended the legal negotiations and was directed primarily at the lack of moral conduct of the world's rich nations.

Box 23.6   **Summary of World Council of Churches Justice Statement**

Aspects of Justice

1. Justice means being held responsible for one's actions.
2. Justice means being held accountable for promises you make.
3. Justice means being held responsible for the suffering you cause to others.
4. Justice means being held accountable for abuse of power.
5. Justice means an equitable sharing of the earth's resources.
6. Justice demands truth.
7. Justice requires honesty.

Confidence-building Measures

1. The industrial countries of the world must demonstrate significant reductions in greenhouse emissions in the immediate future. Economic studies have demonstrated there would be a sizeable net benefit.
2. Many developing countries which should not be subject to emission limitation requirements continue in their efforts to limit greenhouse gas emissions.
3. The sharing of financial, technical and knowledge resources is important to the development of learning to live in a socially just and ecologically sustainable way.

The Kyoto Accord has major shortcomings – not least of which is that the US withdrew from the Accord in January, 2001. Nonetheless, it is an important step towards finding justice and assigning moral responsibility for a serious world environmental problem. As such, it serves as an important 'small win' in the move towards sustainable living.

The Power of Ideas

Until we have a reasonable idea of where we want to go, we are unlikely to get there.

David Korten (2001)

Why are we facing environmental degradation and death in a world so rich in resources? Fromm (1973) argues that we all have the power to create realities which defy common sense and are destructive to our lives and to future generations. If we follow a map of ideas which are destructive to the environment and the planet, we can be destroyed. But we can also choose to follow a map of ideas that leads us towards a long and healthy future.

Among the many ideas that can contribute to the transformation work which points us to sustainable living, are: schooling for emotional intelligence; understanding health as well-being; developing eco-cities; promoting eco-literacy; reclaiming agriculture; promoting biodiversity; reforming banking practices; and providing tools for living simply.

Schooling for Emotional Intelligence

Goleman (1995) presents well-documented arguments to indicate that modern society lacks emotional literacy and would benefit from the idea of schooling for emotional intelligence. As was discussed in Chapter 9, he argues that emotional intelligence: meaningfully contributes to reducing self-centred focus and impulses; strengthens character, moral conduct, self-discipline and empathy; and is essential to both democracy and a healthy society. In recognition of such arguments community psychologists have developed intervention programs in schools and other settings, for children, young people and adults (for example Caplan, Vinokur & Price 1997; Shure, 1997; Weissberg, Barton & Shriver, 1997). In 1995, health promotion and prevention-oriented action researchers joined to establish the Collaborative to Advance Social and Emotional Intelligence (CASEL). The mission is to advance the social and emotional competencies of children and adolescents (Dalton et al., 2001).

While Goleman and others have argued for schooling the emotions in publicly funded schools, I think that there are also strong arguments to introduce such programs into business schools and for corporate executives and government leaders. Indeed, the evidence provided by the examples in this chapter strongly suggests that the leaders of North America's government and corporations lack the body of skills which emotional intelligence represents – character and moral conduct.

Understanding Health as Well-being

When Marc Lalonde served as Canada's Minister of Health and Welfare, he proposed a policy document which recommended that Canada's health system make a profound shift to incorporate an orientation toward wellness. The document, *New Perspectives for the Health of Canadians* (Lalonde, 1974), argued for a holistic approach to health which highly valued the health of the natural and social environment. The Lalonde report was a significant government document. It represented a 'paradigm shift' in thinking about health because it argued that the major improvements in health would emerge not from changes in health services but primarily from changes in lifestyle and in the environment. The concepts of the Lalonde report have since been added to by others and implementation strategies have been developed. In 1986, the first International Conference on Health Promotion was convened in Ottawa, Canada by the World Health Organization (WHO). An influential and enduring document was produced, the *Ottawa Charter for Health Promotion*. The document focused on the importance of health promotion as a process of enabling citizens to improve their health and defined health promotion as extending beyond healthy lifestyles to well-being. Also in the mid-80s, Healthy Communities projects were initiated in Europe and Canada. In Canada, the initiative has been called the Canadian Healthy Communities project and includes all types of local governments and communities.

Box 23.7   Healthy Communities Projects

The 'healthy communities approach' is one way for communities to achieve a better social, economic and environmental future. Caton and Larsh (2000) describe the healthy communities approach as 'a process whereby people from many sectors – seniors, youth businesses, labour, local governments community groups, environmentalists, educators and faith organizations – work together to create a clean, safe, friendly and vibrant place to live, work and play. In a Healthy Community, residents respect and support each other and are involved in local political decision making' (p.7). The idea that health is influenced by community, environmental and economic factors is fundamental to healthy community initiatives (Hancock, 1993). A healthy communities approach is an idea that exists in many countries around the globe. Norberg-Hodge (1992) observes that it has existed in traditional countries such as Ladakh in Kashmir for many centuries and is fundamental to community well-being. It has also come into prominence when living conditions have been unhealthy. Healthy community initiatives in Europe in the mid-1800s, led to significant transformations in the view of the 'determinants of health'. For example, in 1840s' England, a healthy community initiative promptly led to the passing of the Public Health Act and to dramatic improvements in 'sanitation systems' (Ashton, 1992).

Developing Eco-cities

It is possible to restore cities so that we can enhance various forms of human exchange – goods, money, ideas, different forms of concourse – and improve our quality of life (Engwicht, 1993). In 1975, for example, Richard Register and his colleagues founded Urban Ecology, an organization dedicated to planning and revitalizing cities, based on ecological principles. Among the paradigms and social movements on which Urban Ecology was based were 'healthy communities, appropriate technology, community economic development, social ecology, the green movement, bioregionalism, native world views and sustainable development' (Roseland, 1997, p. 4). It is interesting to note the similarities in values between the principles and concepts of CP and the paradigms for creating ecological cities.

Among the many viable manifestations of these paradigms and concepts in US and Canadian cities, community gardens provide an excellent example. Community gardens are plots, typically situated in urban areas, for people who don't have access to land. They are used for growing food and for connecting people to the land and to one another.

Box 23.8   10 Principles for Creating Ecological Cities

1. Revise land use priorities to create compact, diverse green, safe, pleasant and vital mixed-use communities near transit nodes and other transportation facilities.
2. Revise transportation priorities to favour foot, bicycle, cart and transit over cars and to emphasize access by proximity.
3. Restore damaged urban environments, especially creeks, shore lines, ridgelines and wetlands.
4. Create decent, affordable, safe, convenient and racially and economically mixed housing.
5. Nurture social justice and create improved opportunities for women, people of colour and the disabled.
6. Support local agriculture, urban greening projects and community gardening.
7. Promote recycling, innovative appropriate technology and resource conservation while reducing pollution, waste and the use and production of hazardous materials.
8. Work with businesses to support ecologically sound economic activity while discouraging pollution, waste and the use and production of hazardous materials.
9. Promote voluntary simplicity and discourage excessive consumption of material goods.
10. Increase awareness of the local environment and region through activist and educational projects that increase public awareness of ecological sustainability issues.

From: Urban Ecology (1996).

Promoting Eco-literacy

The resurgence of school gardens has provided children with an option to grow their own food, prepare it, share it with their peers and teachers and preserve it to extend the season. School gardens can help children to re-establish their connection with nature and to food as a social and cultural good. They can also provide a viable alternative to fast foods. Lappé and Lappé (2002) report that one-fifth of Californian schools now have school gardens and thousands more have been sprouting up across the US. With curriculum development assistance for eco-literacy, students start to make connections between seemingly disconnected parts of life (for example the connections between the regular consumption of fast foods and soft drinks and the problems of childhood obesity) and learn to develop an ecological perspective.

Reclaiming Agriculture

Pirages and Ehrlich (1974) introduced the concept of the dominant social paradigm (DSP) to describe a society's frame of reference. The DSP mostly values: a bigger-is-better growth orientation; survival-of-the-fittest social and corporate Darwinism; strong faith in globalization of resources and markets; strong faith in science and technology; and control over nature. Working within the DSP, people have created wastelands and destroyed vast areas of our planet.

Wes Jackson (1997) argues that succession in agriculture is necessary for ecological survival. He further contends that, to achieve sustainable agriculture, we need to give emphasis to two important ecological concepts, redemption and transcendence, both of which are fundamental to the Judeo-Christian worldview. The concept of *redemption* is important because it is hopeful. Nature has shown that it can heal itself in time – particularly if it is aided by tender loving care (although some damage may be irreversible or take thousands of years to repair). The notion of *transcendence* moves us from the reductionist thinking of conventional agriculture, which continues to move us away from the interdependent harmony of nature. Transcendence, at a cultural level, is essential to succession.

At a cultural level, I have witnessed the power of transcendence in my Amish neighbours' relationships to community and human-nature interactions. The Amish farmers live in harmony with the natural world. The Amish worldview stands in sharp contrast to the dominant social paradigm (DSP) of the global industrial society. Baltaz (1998) provides other examples of ecologically minded Ontario farmers who, like the Amish, are transcending the reductionist notions of modern industrial agriculture and the DSP. For these practitioners, farming is a way of life, a way of working with nature. Sick crops and animals are symptoms of imbalances between management practices and nature and these farmers recognize that they must address the source of the problem and the holistic approach to a solution transcends the industrial quick-fix approach.

Box 23.9 **The Amish: Cultural Transcendence**

Amish society practices an ecology-oriented holistic lifestyle that includes valuing human–nature interactions.

The Amish – by farming family-style on a small scale with horses, with few outside inputs, using technology compatible with nature – practice sustainable farming. Most Amish families farm on 100 acres of land or less. I am aware of a few Amish families who earn their living on 15 acres of land or less. Because they have few expenses, after taxes, they get to keep most of what they earn. They 'transcend' modern agricultural economics because they don't value the pursuit of wealth or the consumption of material things. They believe that being good stewards of the land and helping their neighbours are the highest callings ordained by God. Since 1993, I have assisted them with their struggle for the 'right' to farm on a small scale and to continue to live a holistic lifestyle (Bennett, 2003).

Promoting Biodiversity

For the past few years organic agriculture has been the fastest growing sector in North American agriculture. The movement has been driven by consumers who want food that is produced without the use of pesticides, herbicides and antibiotics. However, because it does not fit the DSP, the ecological farm movement has not benefited from the support of either governments or the knowledge sectors of society. Cuba, on the other hand, has made a national commitment to the development of sustainable farm practices. Cuba's accomplishments serve as a positive example of what is possible, when there is the political will to take such action.

To meet its economic challenges, Cuba has been slowly transforming its industrial methods of food and fibre production into a more sustainable, self-reliant, low-input-use and organic-farming style of agriculture. The government has given priority to ensuring that there is food for all and to becoming self-reliant in food production through encouraging: the use of animal power and traditional farming knowledge; the aid of Cuba's network of research laboratories and research stations; and the benefits of education. The research stations and the country's traditional farmers have helped Cuba move successfully towards the goal of total elimination of agrochemicals through the use of agro-ecological methods. In comparison with other Third World nations which have faced food crises, Cuba stands alone as a country that looked primarily to its own resources to solve the problem. As such, Cuba represents a wonderful natural experiment of a nation on a journey to transform its entire food production system to sustainable agricultural methods.

Box 23.10   Cuba: A Positive Exemplar of Resistance and Change

Make human life more rational. Build a just international economic order. Use all science for a more sustainable development that does not contaminate the environment. Pay the ecological debt and not the external debt. Fight hunger, not people.

Fidel Castro (1992) – Speech given at the United Nations conference on Environmental Development, Rio de Janeiro, Brazil

Scientific and educational development for over three decades is cited as the cornerstone of sustainability in Cuba's new agricultural model, which gives priority to 'organic fertilization, soil conservation and recovery, the use of draft animals, alternative energy sources, integrated pest management, crop rotations and intercropping, on-farm integration of crops and livestock, alternative veterinary medicine, urban agriculture, co-operative land use, the adaptation of cropping systems to local conditions, a reduction in the scale of farming with increased community participation and alternative methods of research and education' (Garcia, 2002, p. 91). An ongoing commitment to agro-educational training and ecological pest management have been vital components of Cuba's ability to transform its system of food production.

Reforming Banking Practices

The Grameen Bank (Bangladeshi for 'The Village Bank') has accomplished what many thought to be impossible – building a 'microcredit' system for the poor. The bank, which was founded in Bangladesh in 1976, now has approximately 2.5 million borrowers and more than 10,000 employees. The liberating work of the Grameen Bank includes reclaiming Bangladesh's fishing ponds and reviving traditional crops. Microcredit is expected to be extended to 100 million people, all of whom live on less than $2 a day, by 2005. The model of the Grameen Bank has been so successful that it has been replicated in 56 countries. It has been growing at an exponential rate because people have been empowered to help one another (Lappé & Lappé, 2002).

Box 23.11   **Community-centred, Socially Just Banking**

The founder of the Grameen Bank, Professor Muhammed Yunus, turned the rules of the banking community upside down. He saw microcredit as a means of eliminating poverty and building community. Working with Yunus' vision, bank employees became community-development and social-justice workers. Because borrowers had no collateral, the bank's securities were bonds of trust between the borrowers. In the early years, groups of five borrowers (now it is groups of 30 people) came together and agreed to back each others' loans. They shared responsibility for each loan. In time, bonds of trust evolved between the villagers and the bank workers. Learning from the borrowers, in the mid-1980s the bank evolved to the point where it began to ask each prospective borrower to memorize and commit to 16 pledges (decisions). These pledges were arrived at after long discussions with the borrowers. The pledges have helped to create new social norms and to promote strong health, ecological and social-justice values in the villages (Lappé & Lappé, 2002).

Providing Tools for Living Simply

For more than 20 years, the Working Centre, in Kitchener, Ontario, has been assisting people to acquire tools for living. The centre's spirit is captured in the words of Christian Agaard, a local newspaper columnist, 'A few people with a few tools can do extraordinary things for their neighbourhoods. It is street level democracy that sows community gardens and fixes bikes for people who can't afford main street rates.' The community tools projects of the centre have attempted to respect and enhance a simple way of living that honours people and the environment. Following in the footsteps of E. F. Schumacher (1973) – one of the world's most influential thinkers since World War II (*London Times*, 1995) – the centre practices a form of community and household economics which starts and ends with people and their desire to be self-determining and to live in ways that are harmonious with nature.

The Working Centre does not provide services or formal programs; rather, it provides a setting where citizens can meet formally or informally, around concrete resources, to determine ways in which they can become involved in personal and community development. The centre provides access to tools, support and assistance. Citizens are given the opportunity to discover their own dreams and opportunities for relationship building. The centre is described by its founders, Joe and Stephanie Mancini, as 'an independent instrument of self-help community development'. The Working Centre's diverse projects demonstrate a remarkable intelligence about the necessities of everyday life, about the creation of community and about the need to facilitate a balance between the human needs and the health of the natural world. One illustration is their clean air initiatives.

> **Box 23.12**   **Living Simply: Clean Air Initiatives**
>
> According to the Ontario Medical Association, 'There is no safe level of ozone in the air. Ozone is one of the most harmful elements of smog.' And, they estimate, smog kills approximately 2,000 people a year in the Province of Ontario and costs the economy approximately $10 billion in lost work and production. Given these data, the Working Centre is rightfully alarmed by reports that the Region of Waterloo has Canada's highest levels of ground-level ozone. Among its many initiatives, therefore, it includes participating in the annual Clean Air Festival, creating the People's Car Co-op (a local car sharing organization), establishing the Recycle Cycles project (to restore discarded bicycles and resell them at affordable prices) and co-ordinating the Commuter Challenge (a partnership initiative with the Citizens' Advisory Committee on Air Quality to involve the region's largest employers and the local transport authority in encouraging mass transportation, walking, car-pooling and biking). The Working Centre's 'small wins' (Weick, 1984) Clean Air Initiatives, along with those of other environmental activists, have helped to influence a Waterloo Region proposal to develop an electric light rail transit (LRT) as a way to curb pollution and transform the urban landscape.

Chapter Summary

In this chapter I provided an introduction to the central environmental issues and problems and to some of the values, concepts, ideas, tools and examples of sustainable alternatives that people are pursuing. The chapter represents one community psychologist's way of thinking about the challenges and the alternatives. I hope that you will build on this way of thinking and the examples introduced in the chapter and join with neighbours and friends and the millions of people worldwide who are successfully finding answers to environmental problems.

World history changed on September 11, 2001, when a group of terrorists who had no fear of death demonstrated the vulnerability of the US, the most powerful nation on the planet. I believe that the lesson of September 11 is that we cannot have peace and security without eliminating world poverty, hunger, environmental degradation and global injustices. With First World countries having failed to live up to the Rio Accord of 1992 and with the US having failed even to ratify the Kyoto Accord of 1997, the need for a global ethical framework based on justice for all is clear. The problem of modern government is that it has taken a fragmented approach to world affairs and has uncritically embraced economic globalization, which favours profit over community wellness and environmental stewardship. We all need to ask questions about how we live: Is it just? Is it sustainable? We need to make a commitment to build consensus that terrorism against the environment will be resisted.

What can citizens like you and me do to reduce and prevent the health-threatening environmental pollution that surrounds us? You have already started by measuring the size of your own ecological footprint in the warm-up exercise at the beginning of the chapter. To a greater or lesser extent, we are all participants in the destruction of the planet. We are part of the problem and we can be part of the solution. In closing, I ask you to think about the questions in the Class Exercise which follows the Commentary.

COMMENTARY: 'It Is Almost Always More Complicated Than It Seems'

Adeline Levine and Murray Levine

Ed Bennett wrote an impassioned statement of the 'social disintegration and environmental degrada-

tion' ... 'destroying our own humanity and killing the planet' (Daly & Cobb, 1989, p. 21 – cited by

Bennett). His chapter is a contribution to CP in two ways. First, he shows the causal relationship between the global economic system and local stresses on individuals and communities. He calls our attention to the biosphere (see Levine & Perkins, 1987, 1997), a concept most community psychologists have neglected. He asks community psychologists to pay more attention to local, national and international environmental issues. He also provides a vision of a sustainable world and calls for action to fulfil that vision. In that quest, he is in keeping with a goal of CP, to promote human growth and development. We shall critique his recommendations below, but first consider why community psychologists have not been more involved in environmental issues.

Historically, CP began in the 1960s with the community mental health movement. Community mental health centres were to have an outstretched arm devoted to prevention and community consultation, but it was never strong. Prevention and consultation were not insurance reimbursable; they went by the wayside with the funding crunch. Thus an institutional base for community psychologists to interact with the community was quickly diminished.

In the 1960s, some community psychologists (including Ed Bennett) became involved with the federally sponsored anti-poverty program and social problems associated with that effort (see Sarason, Levine, Goldenberg, Cherlin & Bennett, 1966). Bennett does not consider the social and political world within which community psychologists work. First, the development of the field itself depended more on President John Kennedy's concerns with mental health, mental retardation, poverty and prevention than on Rachel Carson's *Silent Spring* (1962). Second, community psychologists have to make a living and it is not surprising that effort follows the money. Community psychologists worked for independent consulting firms, state or federal agencies or under contract from government agencies doing evaluation research, needs assessment and similar applied work. The subject matter was set by the agencies sponsoring the program. Nonetheless, CP had a profound influence on practice. Programs based on community concepts now reflect the conventional wisdom.

Third, government funded studies and intervention into social problems assumed that problems reflected the deficits of individuals. Our most successful preventive interventions involve teaching social and cognitive mediators to prevent adjustment problems (for example Elias, 1997; Shure, 1997; Weissberg et al., 1997). There is little or no funding for those who point to government or corporate excesses as the source of human problems. Funding has become scarcer with the political ascent of conservatives. A conservative philosophy emphasizes that the social world is the best of all possible social worlds and those who cannot thrive in the best of all possible social worlds are deficient (Levine & Levine, 1970, 1992). An emphasis on biological rather than social determinants of social problems follows naturally from that perspective.

Community psychologists have no institutional base to provide 'standing' to take on problems. Lawyers own the courts and the legal system, physicians the hospitals, educators the schools and social workers social agencies. We are guests in someone else's home and must be invited. Moreover, we may not have the expertise (epidemiology, toxicology, geology, engineering and so on) needed to engage in the discourse defining environmental problems.

Community psychologists do have roles. Some community psychologists work for government agencies and may help them improve their relationships and communications with communities. We can be helpful to some groups as Ed Bennett shows in his work with the Amish (Box 23.9). We can offer research and writing skills and the ability to conceptualize problems. But we can only offer these; the affected people decide whether to use what we offer. Affected people are more interested in arguments that make their case rather than 'objectivity'. The ambiguities and weaknesses of data that lead us to be tentative seem like obstructions to people in crisis seeking relief. Adherents of research ethics may be put off by the tendency of affected people to use only cause-helpful information and to ignore or distort contradictory information.

Let us turn now to the pace of change. Although *Love Canal* (Levine, 1982) is coming up to its 25th anniversary, its full lessons have not yet been learned. Rachel Carson's (1962) seminal work is now over 40 years old and, as Bennett shows, many of its lessons have not been absorbed by government, industry or indeed by consumers who are not deterred by largely invisible environmental threats. Moreover many environmental problems are unintended by-products of the growth of wealth and an abundant life style. Without a level of wealth created by technology, we may not be able to afford to pay attention to environmental problems (Cox & Alm, 2002). Bennett's discussion neglects the positive aspects of our modern world. He mentions the AIDS epidemic, but he ignores advances in medicine that have reduced morbidity and mortality in industrialized societies.

The emergence of an activist movement has resulted in environmental improvements because activism imposes a cost on those who otherwise externalize costs. Since the 1960s, we do have cleaner air and water and better pollution controls. We do have demands to reduce pollution at its source by developing alternative manufacturing methods and better methods of disposing of environmentally dangerous substances. Opposition by organized activists, even if it does not result in immediate victories, is still important.

Deferring present gratification for some future, uncertain reward demands great individual and societal maturity. Nonetheless, some advances occur. Both smoking and deaths from drunk driving have decreased greatly in the US. These changes came about slowly through much effort, research, education, community action and eventually government action. The larger problems lie within the political sphere where corporate dollars and dominant ideologies trump the public interest. Population control could solve a good many of the problems Bennett cites, but population control is being fought effectively by religious extremists who have moved into influential positions in our government.

Bennett's proposals reflect noble sentiment. They are an educational effort that may lead to a social climate that supports change. Bennett is fulfilling one of the roles academics have, that of keeping and transmitting if not forming the culture. He is holding forth a vision not to be underestimated in its potential for influencing attitudes and actions. However, his approach is but one step in creating 'normative change', change in what most people believe is right and proper (Levine, 1998).

It is a first step to point to the dangers, but how many people want to live as the Amish do, devoting all their time and energies to making a bare living? How many of us will refrain from getting a newer, more powerful computer because we are polluting the environment when we dispose of our older, less powerful machines? How many will revert to non-polluting slates and chalk? We need to think more about how normative change is brought about. We need a time perspective, a conception and a strategy that goes beyond simply informing or decrying the immorality of power.

Questions to consider:

1. What can citizens do to influence business-first environmental policies that threaten the planet and the lives of their families?

2. What can you and others do to become more informed, and to express and act on your environmental concerns?

Chapter glossary

chrematistics the manipulation of property and wealth to maximize the short term monetary exchange value to the owner

biodiversity biological diversity in an environment as indicated by the numbers of different plant and animal species

biosphere the earth and its atmosphere that are capable of supporting life

dominant social paradigm (DSP) a bigger-is-better growth orientation, survival-of-the-fittest, social and corporate Darwinism, strong faith in globalization of resources and markets, strong faith in science and technology and control over nature

eco-literacy an understanding of the connections between humans and the natural environment and how to protect and preserve the biosphere

Kyoto Accord an international protocol for reducing emissions to protect the environment

okonomia economics for the larger community of land, of shared values, biomes, institutions, language and history

urban ecology healthy communities, appropriate technology, community economic development, social ecology, the green movement, bioregionalism, native worldviews and sustainable development

Here is a list of some selected names and addresses of settings that can help citizens who wish to become involved in ecologically-minded research and action. The settings listed are valuable resources and can assist you to link to hundreds of other resource settings.

1. Canadian Centre for Policy Alternatives (CCPA): An action research and advocacy organization on diverse public issues. National office: www.policy alternatives.ca.

2. Council of Canadians: A Canadian citizens' watchdog organization involved in a diverse range of social and environmental issues. email: <inquiries@canadians.org>; www.canadians.org.

3. Conservation Ecology www.consecol.org email: questions@consecol.org. Electronic peer-reviewed scientific journal on conservation themes with 10,000 subscribers.

4. Cuba: Sustainable agriculture www.foodfirst.org/cuba;www.cityfarmer.org/cuba. Resource on Cuba's agricultural revolution.

5. Environmental Rights Action (ERA): A Nigerian-based organization which disseminates information on the human and environmental abuses of transnational corporations in the Third World. email: <eluan@infoweb.abs.net> or <obebi@infoweb.abs.net> or <oilwatch@infoweb.abs.net>.

6. Greenpeace Canada www.greenpeacecanada.org tel. 416-597-8408.

7. Greenpeace USA www.greenpeaceusa.org tel. 1-800-326-0959; 202-462-1177; fax. 202-462-4507.

8. Greenpeace International Keizersgracht 176, 1016 DW Amsterdam, the Netherlands tel. 31 20 523 6222; fax. 31 20 523 6200.

Greenpeace has active campaigns on diverse issues. Sometimes the campaigns are listed separately. Start by going to their main site.

9. Institute for Policy Studies in Washington www.seen.org. Good information on big oil corporations and their links to World Bank Funding.

10. International Forum on Globilization www.ifg.org. A San Francisco-based organization of approximately 60 leading activists, scholars and economists engaged in public education work on diverse environmental issues.

11. John Ikerd, 'Sustainable agriculture – A positive alternative' www.ssu.missouri.edu.

12. Rainforest Action Committee www.amazonwatch.org: An active NGO concerned with drilling in ecologically sensitive areas of Central and South America.

13. The Union of Concerned Scientists www.ucsusa.org. Consists of hundreds of prominent scientists who have organized to disseminate research information on diverse global environmental issues.

14. The International Rivers Network www.irn.org. A worldwide network of activists and professionals working for policy changes and community-based river management.

15. The Natural Step: The list of conditions by which to live. Canada: jmacdonald@naturalstep.ca; www.naturalstep.ca. USA: tns@naturalstep.org.

16. The Sierra Club of Canada email: <sierra@web.net>; www.sierraclub.ca/national. A very active and effective environmental organization.

17. The Small Planet Fund www.smallplanetfund.org. Supports groups across the globe who are re-embedding economics in values that sustain land and community.

18. Utne Reader www.utne.com: An outstanding alternative magazine with regular contributions and contacts on sustainable activities.

19. World Wildlife Fund www.panda.org. A global organization with action programs that are particularly effective in the Third World.

20. YES! A Journal of Positive Futures. An excellent resource for people in search of sustainable alternatives. email: <yes@futurenet.org>; www.yesmagazine.org.

RESOURCES

Part VI

Looking Towards the Future

The goal of this part of the book is to answer the question: Where is community psychology (CP) headed? This part consists of one chapter (Chapter 24), written by Maritza Montero and accompanied by a commentary by Bob Newbrough. Montero uses the metaphor of a journey to reflect on the past and present of CP, as well as to look forward to the future. As she states:

> I would like to provide some hints for an itinerary for future voyages, knowing that every time one embarks on an expedition one should be prepared to be surprised; to assume different perspectives; to get lost and to arrive at unexpected destinations. At the same time, one should keep on hand personal and collective maps in order to find the many ways to get to the next port ...

> ... new itineraries continuously open before us and, with them, the need for new tools, cameras and methods. What should we take then in future voyages? What kind of a luggage should we carry? Based on prescriptions from previous chapters, allow me to suggest the following first aid kit:

> - a predisposition to scrutinize established mores and notions of right and wrong;
> - a reluctance to take interpretations and research results for granted;
> - a tendency to keep irregularities in mind, like those odds and ends that do not fit in an otherwise well-arranged framework;
> - a proclivity to watch our likes and dislikes;
> - a propensity to travel light. Do not load yourself with too many prefabricated notions or coloured lenses that may prevent you from being surprised.

Similarly, Newbrough begins his commentary with a quote from John Dewy about how one can make a choice to 'build a building' or 'go on a journey' in life. Like Montero, Newbrough suggests that the journey is a more apt metaphor for human sciences such as CP. In this regard, it is instructive that Montero does not try to 'predict' some end-state in the future of CP as a natural scientist might do. Instead, she poses questions, notes lessons learned and contributors to the journey towards liberation and well-being and suggests that we suspend judgement and pay attention to paradoxes, contradictions and conflicts, all of which can teach us about

CP. Montero notes that these resources will serve to equip community psychologists in future journeys and help us to respond to both old and new challenges that arise in the process of social change. We can't delude ourselves into thinking that some day we will be able to relax when we have finally landed upon *the* solution to a social problem.

There are a number of important themes in the last chapter that are raised by Montero and amplified by Newbrough in his commentary. These themes include the complexity of community phenomena, the interdependence of the local and the global community and the political side of community work. Montero also relates French sociologist Pierre Bourdieu's concept of habitus, as a social process that maintains the status quo. Questioning, problem-posing, reframing and consciousness-raising are the tools that community psychologists and their partners can use to examine and strive to alter habitual ways of social, economic, political and interpersonal relationships that are oppressive.

24

Between Person and Society: Community Psychology's Voyage into Complexity

Maritza Montero

Chapter Organization

Point of Departure: What Discipline, What Objectives?	**From Where to Where? Preparing for the Voyage**
Different Practice, New Aims, New Definitions	**The Liberating Journey of Community Psychology**
Co-presence: The Complex Character of Community Phenomena	
Understanding Power in Community Contexts	**Community and Society: Exchanges and Influences**
The Political Side of Community Work	**The Size and Speed of Community Changes**
Knowledge is Everywhere	**Conclusion**	**Chapter Summary**
COMMENTARY: Reflections on the Journey of Community Psychology	**Glossary**

Warm-up Exercise

Based on what you know about community psychology and the community where you live:

1. What community practices and norms should be changed?
2. What specific modes of relating to people should be the targets of change?
3. What modes of being and doing in the community should be changed?
4. Can you tell how much of your criticism comes from personal experience, prejudice or theoretical notions?
5. What dominant social discourses prevent these changes from occurring?

In this chapter, you will learn to:

- reflect on current and future trends within CP
- describe tensions within the field of CP
- highlight the complexity of community phenomena
- discuss the political character of CP and the possibility of a political CP
- explore the relations between the local and the global and how communities are affected by and may respond to social problems.

This chapter should be read like a brochure for future travels across the sea of CP; a brochure describing exciting sites, daring and stimulating expeditions, unique places and circumstances, provoking dilemmas and wonderful opportunities to meet interesting people. What these contrasting combinations demonstrate is that the subject matter of CP is made up of paradoxes and complexity. In community work one can find both very difficult and very rewarding situations. Community life is dynamic, changing, complex and unexpected. It can be simultaneously predictable and unpredictable, scary and reassuring, stimulating and irritating.

In the preceding chapters we have travelled from ontological, epistemological and methodological issues, to ethics and politics in community affairs. Now, I would like to provide some hints for an itinerary for future voyages, knowing that every time one embarks on an expedition one should be prepared to be surprised; to assume different perspectives; to get lost and to arrive at unexpected destinations. At the same time, one should keep on hand personal and collective maps in order to find the many ways to get to the next port. As happened during the 15th and 16th centuries, we should also be ready to fill the blank spaces in those maps (*pars ignota* – ignored region) with our discoveries.

Point of Departure: What Discipline, What Objectives?

In order to know where we are going, we need to have an idea of where we stand. Previous chapters have provided us with descriptions of the present whereabouts of CP. We have also seen glimpses of future destinations. We should keep in mind that in its 40 years of existence CP has kept some of its intents but it has also changed course. It has been innovative but faithful to its original intents at the same time. Some of its ways, critics might argue, have been paternalistic: observing, classifying, categorizing. Others, however, are quick to point out that participatory methodologies now constitute one of the main research and intervention tools of the field. Faithfulness to its original aims is seen in its steadfast pursuit of inclusion, integration and empowerment of oppressed people. The very definition of community within CP has changed from one based on deficits to one based on strengths, agency and resilience. The field has moved from a concentration on psychological variables to an appreciation of political, social, economic and contextual dynamics.

The objectives and priorities of CP have kept up with the times. They have moved from a concern with 'the right to be different' (Rappaport, 1977), to preoccupation with access to services, to liberation and well-being catalysed by external agents and validated by community members themselves. Theoretical and methodological foundations have also changed. From the initial adoption of social psychological and clinical conceptions, CP has come to produce its own theories, explanations and action-research methods. Changes notwithstanding, within CP and within the community at large, the conviction has remained that we ought to attend to holism in all we do (Newbrough, 1974). This book pays tribute to Newbrough's invocation of holism as a cornerstone of CP.

From Where to Where? Preparing for the Voyage

Community psychologists broker between the community and society at large. Tönnies ([1887]1957) said that what identifies communities is the fact that they are an amalgam of human beings that stay together in spite of all the factors that pull them apart. Tönnies distinguished between community *(gemeinschaft)* and society *(gesselschaft)*. In both of them exist diversity and passions, qualities that unite and separate people at the same time.

CP has had to deal with that psychological space in which people construct their specific identities as a community and a society. In that sense, CP has had to keep pace with social changes, for the dominant forces that create people's identities are dynamic and fluid. As a result, CP is trying to study a moving target, a dynamic culture and a changing society. By the time we calibrate our equipment to take a picture of the present state, new dynamics have arisen that make our picture blurry and imperfect.

That means that new itineraries continuously open before us and, with them, the need for new tools, cameras and methods. What should we take then on future voyages? What kind of a luggage should we carry? Based on prescriptions from previous chapters, allow me to suggest the following first-aid kit:

- a predisposition to scrutinize established mores and notions of right and wrong
- a reluctance to take interpretations and research results for granted
- a tendency to keep irregularities in mind, like those odds and ends that do not fit in an otherwise well-arranged framework
- a proclivity to watch our likes and dislikes
- a propensity to travel light. Do not load yourself with too many prefabricated notions or coloured lenses that may prevent you from being surprised.

Different Practice, New Aims, New Definitions

At the beginning of the 1980s, community psychologists in Latin America embraced the following definition of the field:

> The study of psychosocial factors enabling the development, growth and maintenance of the control and power that people can exert over their individual lives and social environments, in order to solve problems and achieve changes in these environments and social structures. (Montero, 1980)

The definition stressed the need to place control and power within the community, thereby defining the role of psychologists as catalysts for social change. What was being proposed at the time was a shift in the centre of gravity, away from psychologists and towards people in the community. Escovar (1977, 1980) focused this socially sensitive psychology on the notion of social development, which he defined as control over the environment.

Another important aspect was the recognition that change was bidirectional: the individual changed the group while the group changed the individual. What was envisioned was a dialectical interplay of mutual changes. Social change was the goal of that type of CP. However, change and increased control could not be achieved in the absence of power to transform social structures. Reflective practice, expressed in the action–reflection–action model initiated by Brazilian educator, Paulo Freire (1970), was set to become a key tool in the pursuit of popular power.

In Latin America, we quickly became aware that the issue of power could not be addressed in an isolated way. Ideology and its counterpart, de-ideologization, had to be considered, as were processes of problematization and naturalization (Martín-Baró, 1986, 1987–89/1990; Montero, 1992, 1994b, 1998c, 2000b). *Problematization* is a concept introduced by Paulo Freire (1970) to oppose what he called 'banking education', one in which the student is considered an empty vessel, a recipient of knowledge coming from outside. *Problematization*, on the contrary, is a cognitive process by which people critically analyse their living circumstances and their role in shaping their fate. Problematizing helps in challenging naturalizing processes whereby the status quo is regarded as a natural state of affairs, dictated by unseen and untouchable forces; the product of nature (Montero, 2003).

The Liberating Journey of Community Psychology

The idea of liberation was also introduced by Paulo Freire (1970, 1973), who invoked freedom to convert silent acquiescence into vocal discontent. He compared liberation to childbirth, painful but needed in order to have a new person: neither oppressed nor oppressor. Psychologists of various persuasions should be the midwives or obstetricians in that process; collaborating with parents and surrogate parents in delivering liberation. As Freire put it, 'nobody liberates anyone; no one is liberated by her or himself alone' (1970); liberation is a collaborative enterprise. The very definition of liberation implies collective action, always a relational endeavour. Freire advocated a process of action–reflection–action to engage in dialogical processes of collaboration within and across sectors of society.

In 1986, Martín-Baró envisioned what he called a psychology of liberation, which he understood as:

- A psychology less worried by its social and scientific status and more concerned with the urgent problems of people in need
- A psychology mindful of people's virtues and assets in pursuing change
- A systematic study of popular organizations as instruments of liberation
- A new way to understand reality based on the vicissitudes of marginalized populations
- A new psychological praxis contributing to change in Latin American societies
- A recovery of collective memory
- A way to conceive liberation as a historic and collective process (Martín-Baró, 1986, 1987–89/1990, 1994).

During the 1990s, liberation psychology developed as a reflective practice, stressing the values, capacities and actions of oppressed people in fighting their oppression. Liberation struggles led to processes of de-ideologization, by which people renounce hegemonic constructions of fate and inevitability (Montero, 1992). During the past decade, two lines of thought and action emerged within liberation psychology. One is the emancipatory psychology practised by political, social, educational, health and community psychologists in several countries (Montero, 1992, 2001; Pacheco & Jimenez, 1990). The second variant of liberation psychology concentrated more on the psychology of oppression (Prilleltensky & Gonick, 1994,

1996). The two are really opposite sides of the same coin and cannot be regarded as autonomous branches of psychology, for they ought to permeate all aspects of theory and practice.

Change and well-being, the primary and most evident goals of CP, needed the concept of liberation. Well-being on its own is highly commendable, but it can be easily distorted into a welfare orientation which is based on charity and not justice. Change, in turn, can also be highly commendable, but in the absence of liberation, there is no way to confirm that changes will address power differentials.

Co-Presence: The Complex Character of Community Phenomena

An important aspect of psychosocial community phenomena needs to be discussed: their mobile, complex and dynamic character. As quantum theory shows, light can be at the same time particles and waves. In the same vein, it is not possible to talk about foreground without background. If we want to consider community phenomena without fragmenting or reducing them, we cannot define them as just states or processes. Social phenomena can be, simultaneously, states *and* processes. Permanence and change can go together. This is not an untenable state but a paradox. Paradoxes are not errors, mistakes or flaws making our lives unnecessarily difficult, they are part of everyday life. Although we tend to reject them because they make us feel uncomfortable, we should heed their message and try to cope with the tension they create. That very tension reminds us that contradictory forces exist in the community and that we should be attentive to them.

Co-existence or co-presence of phenomena is much more common than we would like, but they are inevitable aspects of community phenomena. We want some people to take more control over their lives, but we also want them to take into consideration other people's need for control while they exercise their newly acquired sense of empowerment. How can we ascertain that people achieve just the right dose of empowerment and don't become over-empowered? How do we promote collaboration without pushing conformity at the expense of diversity? How do we advance an agenda of caring when some of the people who abuse others seem to listen only to the language of power?

What may seem to be the right answer to a social problem today or in this geographical and cultural context, may prove to be wrong for other historical, geographical or cultural contexts. Hence, we are faced with the task of pursuing a clear line of thinking, while at the same time questioning its applicability and validity across situations. In essence, we struggle to pursue clarity without dogmatism and diversity without paralysing relativism.

Understanding Power in Community Contexts

In order to produce power, power is needed. This means the notion of power has to be redefined and reconceptualized. The traditional way to define power considered it the capacity to influence other people; leading, forcing or convincing them to do something in line with the interests of the source of influence. This asymmetrical conception of power has been dominant in social sciences since the beginning of the 20th century when it was formulated by the sociologist Max Weber ([1925]1964). That began to change when Michel Foucault (1975, 1979b) introduced the idea that power is omnipresent; it is not in the exclusive domain of the seemingly powerful. Power is everywhere and its manifestations are present in all realms of society. In CP, Serrano-García and López-Sánchez (1994) proposed a relational definition of power whereby people create or disrupt norms in their interactions. The main point in this immanent and relational conception of power is that every human being has some power.

Empowerment, then, is based on the ability of community members to effectively use the resources they have to acquire new ones and to overcome oppressive conditions while they change their own lives in the process. We cannot disentangle the acquisition of material power from the process of personal empowerment of the soon-to-be-empowered community member. We are talking about a very personal and societal process at the same time. If we forget the former part of the equation we err on the side of sociologism. If we forget the latter part we err on the side of psychologism.

Liberation, change and well-being also illustrate the complexity of community phenomena. These three aspects must operate in concert. In order to carry out changes in the world around us, we must have the necessary consciousness to know where to act, why, when and how. In doing so, well-being may emerge out of people's actions. Consciousness will help define what well-being is, while, at the same time, provide enough dissatisfaction with the status quo as to keep the change process going.

Community and Society: Exchanges and Influences

Issues of globalization, colonization, poverty and all manners of exclusion (such as racism, sexism, marginalization or disability), infrequently discussed in CP textbooks, permeate all social phenomena. Disadvantage is experienced in thousands of communities across the world. This is why liberation and well-being are the main goals of CP. But liberation and well-being, as much as oppression, surpass the scope of community. Locating disadvantage in a global context is consistent with the values of CP.

It is important that we avoid the illusion of communities as cosy and isolated microcosms, unaffected by global dynamics. Consequently, our values must be directed at the local and the global at the same time. We have to think of ways of expressing our values in proximal and distal environments at the same time:

- Holism must apply to the whole person, the whole community and the whole context
- Health must apply to physical and spiritual well-being
- Solidarity must reflect caring, support and compassion not only for those close to us but also for those we may never get to know in far away places
- Self-determination should be about personal decisions while collectively determining what to do about *our* community and *our* world

- Social justice ought to encompass both rights and duties towards those close to us and far away from us
- Diversity should be about the right to be different in equality
- Accountability must be to oppressed groups and to the groups we work with; while
- Participation should reflect the fact that community research and action are not isolated tasks but the joint labour of many people, sometimes across continents.

Does this mean that CP is evolving towards a more comprehensive and holistic discipline ('global community psychology')? Will it abandon the community as it has been hitherto defined within the discipline? Is that the next destination for the journey begun in Chapter 1? We ought not to sacrifice the local for the global or vice versa, neither in research nor in action. Although invisible sometimes to the naked eye, the connections between global trends and local suffering are very powerful. This is why we must develop ways of seeing the part in the whole and the whole in the part. Perhaps holographic principles could help. In 1947 Gabor (Nobel Prize in Physics, 1971) came out with an explanation that challenges conventional wisdom with respect to the relation between the whole and the parts. Each point of a hologram receives light coming from every part of a focused object. Each fragment of the hologram, in turn, contains information about the whole. Thus, if the hologram is broken, each piece allows for the reproduction of the complete image. What physics discovered about holograms is what has always happened in social life: not only are the parts contained within the whole, but the whole is also contained within every part. As Ferrarotti (1981) noted, the life of each person reflects the society in which that person lives. In a similar way, communities reflect the societies in which they are embedded and societies mirror the world around them. All these spheres of life orbit around a centre of gravity: relatedness. People are not islands, no matter how aloof or anti-social they might be. People are relational beings living in a world of relations. No one can be outside of a relationship; even to reject them we need them, for history is like a thread linking the person, the community, the society and the world. History is about life and each individual life can only be told because it is part of a web consisting of multiple histories that weave that life and construct that history. Again, complexity rules the understanding of these relations.

The Political Side of Community Work

An exciting interdisciplinary field seems to be emerging out of this relatedness between micro, meso and macro social levels and out of the social repercussions of community research and action: a political CP. Some chapters in this book give grounds to say so, for who will be in charge of 'linking the global and the local' (Chapter 15)? Who will export to other social sciences and settings the knowledge produced in CP to achieve liberation and well-being? Who will provide social planning and policy-making teams with a community perspective and know-how? It has to be psychologists with community experience; psychologists who have observed and participated in community decision-making processes and who have witnessed first-hand the outcomes of oppressive policies and practices. This new field of political CP would foster bottom-up approaches to balance the current administrative tendency to use top-down methods of planning and intervention.

De-ideologizing, conscientizing and problematizing are political means of advancing liberation and well-being. This way of doing CP fosters its political base and provides an alternative mode of political action (Montero, 1995, 1998c). This is an alternative mode of political behaviour because it does not fit conventional modes such as voting or party militancy.

Conventional political behaviour follows normative lines established by customs. Political campaigns, political rallies, fund raising and advocacy groups are all forms of conventional politics. Protest, networking, alternative and participatory budgets and mass movements present viable alternatives. They are means of exerting citizenry. Sit-ins, land occupation (that is, the *Sem Terra*, the Landless Movement in Brazil), art and crafts (music, dance, theatre, story-telling, caricature) are non-conventional political actions as well (Klandersmans, 1997; Lederer, 1986; Marsh & Kaase, 1979; Montero, 1995, 1998c; Schmidtchen & Uehlinger, 1983).

Struggles, movements and changes happening in the communities are modes of empowering civil society and of constructing the *polis* (the Greek name that gave origin to the word politics). These are ideal sites for community psychologists to intervene in the community. Thus, community action rejuvenates the concept of politics, going to its very foundations: dealing with social issues in the public sphere of civic life. This approach enhances participatory democracy, first enunciated in CP by Heller and Monahan in 1977 and widely practised in Latin American political and CP (Montero, 1996a, 1998c).

Participatory democracy is a notion that goes beyond representation; it draws on the original meaning of the concept: government of the people. As such, it is totally dependent on people's effectiveness to intervene in political events (Sabucedo, 1988). The challenge in enacting participatory democracies is not only in initiating but also in sustaining involvement of people who hitherto have been disenfranchised or alienated by the electoral process.

Some community movements created in Venezuela in the 1970s illustrate this point. First, the Movement for the Integration of the Community (MIC) and CESAP (Centre at the Service of Popular Action), today transformed in a coalition of community-based NGOs, are such an example. In the 1980s, the Neighbours Movement and currently Synergia (synergy, that is, joint action for change), stated that the exercise of politics is a civil right of the citizenry and not the privilege of political parties.

However meritorious these notions and movements are, they are not without risks. Participatory democracies and mass movements can be co-opted and corrupted. Furthermore, they are not always very efficient and occasionally they are plagued with internecine conflict. So, approach with caution and avoid romantic notions. Keep your eyes open, watch where you're walking and keep your scepticism ready at hand.

The Size and Speed of Community Changes

The capacity of organized communities to transform themselves through the process of conscientization can have repercussions for society as a whole. Although this does not mean a revolution with dramatic changes, it is part of social change nevertheless. It is an investment in the future of social change. Change and liberation cannot occur in the absence of psychological and political education. The drama may not be of enormous proportions, but it is change all the same. So, perhaps, it is a homeopathic revolution. Moghaddam (2002) observed that 'the maximum speed of change at the macro level of legal, political and economic systems is faster that the maximum speed of change at the micro level of everyday behavior' (2002, p. 33). In other words, change can happen quite quickly at the institutional level, but it will not be rooted in society for quite some time. Daily interactions do not change for a while after macro changes have taken place. It takes some time for new ways of being to become *habitus*. Bourdieu's (1972) notion of habitus is explained in Box 24.1.

Box 24.1   **Characteristics Defining a *Habitus***

- It is a regular practice associated with a socially structured environment.
- It is a lasting behaviour.
- It is a structured and structuring behaviour, following a stable and established pattern.
- It is carried out without either a consciously chosen direction or explicit mastery of the operations needed to achieve its goals.
- It adjusts to collective regulations without specific instructions.

- It allows people to cope with unexpected situations.
- There is an implicit anticipation of the consequences of such situations.
- It is a socially coded and expected response.
- It tends to reproduce objective social structures of which it is an effect.
- It lacks strategic intention of its own.

From: Montero (2000b, 2001)

Habitus can explain how and why certain practices last despite efforts to alter them. Habitus sustains those acts one does not have to think about. In doing so, habitus keeps action flowing; it becomes a main ingredient in naturalizing social practices and in automating 'what one does'. This is not unconscious behaviour. It is, however, an unprocessed behavioural pattern absorbed through cultural interactions with people, the media and the educational system. Habitus are the guardians of the ways and relations that produced them. They need processes of familiarizing, naturalizing and internalizing to protect the status quo in relationships, organizations and government. To challenge habitus we need problematization and conscientization. They can help us reveal contradictions and ways of disrupting habitus.

We have to keep in mind that most of the changes we may be facing as a society may be unintentional or ill-directed. Changes in habitus may occur, but are these the changes we really want? Technology, globalization and war may change the way we relate to each other and conceive of the 'other'. But are these the changes we want? Will they result in more or less well-being for the oppressed? Will they produce liberation or more oppression? Will they benefit the rich or the poor? Hence, we must not be too jubilant at the pace of change in society. Change is not an aim in itself. Change that promotes values for well-being and liberation is hard to come by.

Knowledge is Everywhere

Relatedness, based on participation, entails exchange of knowledge. Exchanging wisdom is a necessity. Community psychologists bring their own contributions and so do community members. A horizontal, dialogical mode of relating to stakeholders, so often implored by Freire (1973) and Fals Borda (2001), can only be achieved through the full participation of stakeholders (see Chapters 16,19,20,21,22). The co-optation of community leaders or the assignment of pre-determined tasks for stakeholders is not participation (Montero, 2000a). Participation means deciding, acting, reflecting, analysing, interrupting, forming an opinion and being open to learn (and teach) from anyone sharing knowledge. It is not a neat and clean process and it requires consultation and listening skills. Community members don't become adept at sharing or expressing their incipient knowledge overnight. They require an enabling environment that will help them recognize their current strengths and potential contributions.

Hitherto, globalization has been mostly unidirectional, going from the minority world to the majority world. This means that knowledge is flowing mostly from the west to the east and from the north to the south. This is the dominant conception of globalization: what an effective globalization ought to be, some might argue. But there is the possibility and the need to reverse the flow of knowledge. How can we embrace diversity if we keep exporting ethnocentric knowledge? One way to do it is by exchanging ideas and establishing dialogues with communities that may have tried alternative ways of being.

Conclusion

As an epilogue to this chapter I would like to reflect on the idea of being open to accept the unusual, the unknown, the diverse – something very well expressed in the poem *The exception and the rule* by the German playwrite Bertolt Brecht, whose reading I recommend. I have often used his words in introductory classes of CP at Universidad Central de Venezuela, and would like, once more, to make an exhortation to inquire; to look further than the appearances of people and things lead to; to probe deeper, to go under the skin and get to the heart of matters, for that is what CP is about. CP is trying to recognize what is unfair under the mask of daily practices. It is trying to see what is diminishing, impoverishing and oppressing under the semblance of 'proper behaviour'. It denounces and fights exclusion and hypocrisy under the mantle of welfare or self-appointed charity.

That is why CP aims for *change–well-being–liberation*, for what we are dealing with is not only access to material goods. It is also a state of mind, a sense of belonging and fitting and having an impact in society, accepting others and being accepted. Are well-being and liberation a community version of the Holy Grail? Most certainly not. They are the same old goals that humankind has been pursuing for ages. CP is just a contemporary response to that eternal pursuit.

Problematizing, de-naturalizing and conscientizing are the bases for a critical attitude in our pursuit of liberation and well-being. Challenging what Bacon ([1620]1952) defined as unquestioned idols (*idola*) is the preparatory phase of our journey. Bacon's understanding of *idola* referred to notions deeply rooted in human understanding, so much so that they become difficult to access and transform.

These idols are constructed by habitual, familiar and quotidian modes of thinking, and pertain both to scientific and folk ways of understanding the world. They are modes of thinking that can be at the basis of ideology, that ever-present way of giving hegemony to certain ideas, present everywhere so there are no privileged spaces immune to it, neither in the university nor in the community.

But as places once visited often change, so does our knowledge of community and interventions. No knowledge is final, no intervention lasts forever. Our role will remain as co-producer of knowledge and interventions until such time that the community no longer needs us, either because it has solved its problems or because it has learned to do without us.

Chapter Summary

This chapter began as a brochure for a travel agency. But unlike those glossy booklets, this one reminded the traveller that the journey may be bumpy and full of surprises. In talking about the journey it described the sites as paradoxical and dynamic. Hence, do not depart without a critical perspective. CP has not aimed for one single destination but for many, intersecting ones. Well-being, change and liberation feature prominently in the list of ports. Descending in one and forgetting the others will create a partial vision of CP. Visiting them all will complicate your journey but will make it worthwhile. Bon voyage!

COMMENTARY: Reflections on the Journey of Community Psychology
J. R. Newbrough

I

John Dewey is reported to have begun a graduation speech with the observation: 'You can make one of two choices for your life – build a building or go on a journey.' Using the two images to consider the scientific enterprise, I consider the laboratory science (for example experimental psychology) of the modern period to be symbolized by building a building, while the field sciences (for example CP) of the postmodern period are like going on a journey. This new 'human science' (Polkinghorne, 1983) of CP uses critical analysis to identify paths in one's professional journey.

Critical analysis is a way of identifying alternatives for action that might not otherwise be discovered (Held, 1980). It requires a penetrating First Question that goes behind the topic under consideration and situates the discussion in a particular frame of reference. To illustrate, suppose that you as a community psychologist were asked to support legislation licensing the practice of CP. Asking the following First Question, 'How does this legislation promote community at the local level?' puts the issue in the frame of reference of

community development. Another formulation, 'Whose interest is being served ?' puts the issue in the frame of reference of professional interests. The community psychologist may begin with various different First Questions, depending on the frame of reference to be considered.

'Whose interest ...' opens a political discussion. It leads to identification of stakeholders and potential allies. When I was president of the Division of Community Psychology in 1979, a group of clinical psychologists proposed to formalize the practice of all types of psychology by certifying graduate training programmes and licensing individual professionals. At that time, my First Question was, 'Whose interests are being served by certification and licensure?' I wrote a memo raising this question to the presidents of the other Divisions of the American Psychological Association. That started a chain reaction of inquiry and eventually the proposal was withdrawn. My presidential address presented the results of my critical analysis of certification and licensure and the conclusion that this move would benefit the professionals and not the community (Newbrough, 1980).

As I look back over the nearly 50 years since the passage of the Community Mental Health Act in 1963 in the US, the establishment of the profession of CP and the evolution of CP into an interdisciplinary profession of 'community research and action', it appears that three First Questions have predominated in the field: Can clinical psychologists be trained to deliver effective community-based and community-oriented mental health services? Can mental health programming influence systems change (that is second-order, transformative change) sufficiently to alter the production of mental health problems? Can mental health programming influence systems change sufficiently to provide more life choices to the socially disempowered? Each of these questions is a variation on the issue of community vs professional interests. As with all paradoxes, this issue is never fully resolved but is an aspect of daily life. Thus, critical questioning should be part of the professional's everyday life so that their programs and the practices they engage in will be forced to evolve.

II

Maritza Montero, author of the preceding chapter, a social psychologist by training, is very experienced in the use of critical questioning in social action research. She brings to this book a strong interest in futures, that is, in identification of alternative forks in the road in the professional journey of community psychologists. She has done considerable work on theory of community development and she regards my formulation of holism as a cornerstone of the field (Newbrough, 1973, 1997). I take this to mean that it is crucial which First Question begins one's analysis of an issue. For her, the purpose of our work is liberation and that is carried out by collaboration with 'parents and surrogate parents'. Thus, the analytic domain is political and a First Question of 'Whose interest is being served' would always be a productive starting place for it will identify the relevant stakeholders.

Political processes use power as a primary explanatory concept. Montero notes that power has been used to mean '... the capacity to influence other people; leading, forcing or convincing them to do something in line with the interests of the source of influence'. Using Foucault's idea that '... power is omnipresent; it is not in the exclusive domain of the seemingly powerful', she redefines power as 'the ability of community members to effectively use resources that they have to acquire new ones and to overcome oppressive conditions while changing their own lives in the process'. This is a conception that locates power in 'the natural course' of daily experience, which she calls 'habitus'. It is at this person level that empowerment takes place and it is from this level that changes to the community and social levels occur. I am reminded of William James's description of habit as 'the flywheel of society'.

Montero's ideal is for a society that functions as a participatory democracy. It is the job of the community psychologist to help make the community structures more participatory. This is consistent with my notion that we are professionals who work primarily with mediating structures that connect individuals with larger social institutions including the family, the neighbourhood, the church, the workplace or school, local voluntary organizations and government.

Montero reminds us that global networks of influence are rapidly bringing about change that strongly influences local communities. I believe that the two most influential sectors of the community are the economic and political (Newbrough & Christenfeld, 1974) and that both domains should be considered when doing a critical analysis. The following is an example.

In Latin America, where there are severe resource shortages, one sees that there is a colonized relationship to the developed world. Latin American countries are conceived of as 'markets' which are areas to be exploited for natural resources and for money for products. Resources move from these countries to the developed world, with very little re-investment of resources. In the developed world, a similar relationship is found between the urban and rural areas. People and materials move to the city; resources flow to the central urban areas and are not re-invested in small towns and rural communities. Given the capital base for the global process of modernization, economics has to be a central part of the work of the community psychologist and other community developers. We have yet to incorporate economics into our training and functioning as a profession. When we do so, it may be possible to gain real second order influence in society.

III

What is the future of CP? I have concluded that CP is evolving away from the parent discipline of psychology. I expect it to become an interdisciplinary field combining community research and community development (Newbrough, 1997). This is based on my assessment of trends within the general field of psychology (Newbrough, 1992a, 1997).

It is probably also important to take into account social and global changes. I pose two scenarios. In the first, the societal assumption is that the US will continue to be more or less a political democracy and that the United Nations will be an important multilateral organization. In the second scenario, the US will lose its participatory character and the government will become more directive and the United Nations will lose its influence. These two scenarios need to be addressed in conversations at the local and national level. CP has the potential to help to develop and implement conflict management strategies to enable these conversations to occur without destructive polarization.

At present, however, CP as a profession is not ready either to initiate the conversation or to participate effectively in the conversation. I suggest several ways in which CP may better prepare itself. First, there is a need for an articulated theory of the competent community and the common good (Etzioni, 2001). Second, a research methodology must be developed that incorporates both quantitative and qualitative approaches. Third, a more articulated role of the professional could be developed as a reflective, generative practitioner (Dokecki, 1996; Newbrough, 1992b). Priority should be put on identifying effective best-action practices for local community development.

Chapter glossary

conscientization a term imported from the Portuguese *conscientizaçao* (from the Brazilian Paulo Freire), according to which a person or group achieve an illuminating awareness of social forces shaping their destiny and of their ability to transform that reality

de-naturalizing critical examination of notions, beliefs, assumptions and procedures that we usually take for granted and do not question. By de-naturalizing we question the interests and power dynamics that lead to the creation of such assumptions in the first place

de-ideologizing creation of a new understanding of the world around us, relatively free of dominant beliefs and ideologies that distort social phenomena

familiarization process of assimilation and acceptance of what is strange and unusual into something that feels familiar

habitus undisputed, expected and non conscious behaviour, in tune with social norms, which helps the person to cope with unanticipated circumstances in ways that reproduce and support the social structure

naturalization process by which certain phenomena and certain behaviour patterns are considered an essential part of society's nature

participation organized, collective, free and inclusive process whereby citizens who share certain values collaborate to achieve common goals

participatory democracy extension of the traditional concept of representative democracy. In participatory democracy the voice of the under-represented is heard and people assume active roles in decision-making processes

problematization process by which people critically analyse their living circumstances and their role in shaping events, revealing contradictions and challenging naturalizing processes whereby the status quo is regarded as a natural state of affairs, dictated by unseen forces

References

Aboriginal and Torres Strait Islander Commission (1998). *As a matter of fact.* Canberra: Aboriginal and Torres Strait Islander Commission.

Aboud, F. (2001). Health psychology program prepares students for international service. *Psychology International,* **12**(4), 4–5.

Action for Mental Health (1961). Final report of the Joint Commission on Mental Health and Illness. New York: Basic Books.

Addams, J. (1910). *Twenty years at Hull-House.* New York: Signet Classic.

Adler, N., Boyce, T., Chesney, M., Cohen, S., Folkman, S., Kahn, R. & Syme, L. (1994). Socioeconomic status and health: The challenge of the gradient. *American Psychologist,* **49**, 15–24.

Agnitsch, K. & Flora, J. Ryan, V. (2001). *Bridging and bonding social capital and community action.* Paper presented at the 8th Biennial Conference of the Society for Community Research and Action, Atlanta, Georgia.

Ahmed, R. Pretorius-Heuchert, J. (2001). Notions of social change in community psychology: Issues and challenges. In M. Seedat (ed.), N. Duncan & S. Lazarus (consulting eds), *Community psychology: Theory, method and practice – South African and other perspectives* (pp. 67–85). Oxford: Oxford University Press.

Albee, G. W. (1959). *Mental health manpower trends.* New York: Basic Books.

Albee, G. W. (1981). Politics, power, prevention, and social change. In J. M. Joffe & G. W. Albee (eds), *Prevention through political action and social change* (pp. 5–25). Hanover, NH: University Press of New England.

Albee, G. W. (1982). Preventing psychopathology and promoting human potential. *American Psychologist,* **32**, 150–61.

Albee, G. W. (1986). Toward a just society: Lessons from observations on the primary prevention of psychopathology. *American Psychologist,* **41**, 891–8.

Albee, G. W. (1990). The futility of psychotherapy. *Journal of Mind and Behavior,* **11**(3/4), 369–84.

Albee, G. W. (1996a). Introduction to the special issue on Social Darwinism. *Journal of Primary Prevention,* **17**, 3–16.

Albee, G. W. (1996b). The psychological origins of the white male patriarchy. *Journal of Primary Prevention,* **17**, 75–97.

Albee, G. W. (1998). The politics of primary prevention. *Journal of Primary Prevention,* **19**, 117–27.

Albee, G. W. & Perry, M. J. (1998). Economic causes of sexism and the exploitation of women. *Journal of Community and Applied Social Psychology,* **8**, 145–60.

Alcoff, L.M. & Mendieta, E. (eds). (2000). *Thinking from the underside of history: Enrique Dussel's philosophy of liberation.* Lanham, MD: Rowman & Littlefield.

Alinsky, S. (1971). *Rules for radicals.* New York, NY: Vintage Books.

Alvesson, M. & Sköldberg, K. (2000). *Reflexive methodology: New vistas for qualitative research.* London: Sage.

Alvesson, M. & Willmott, H. (eds). (1992). *Critical management studies.* London: Sage.

American Psychiatric Association. (1988). *Diagnostic and statistical manual of mental disorders* (4th edn). Washington DC: Author.

American Psychological Association (2000). *Resolution on poverty and socioeconomic status.* www.apa.org/pi/urban/povres.html.

American Psychological Association (2001). *Publication manual of the American Psychological Association* (5th edn). Washington, DC: Author.

Americans with Disabilities Act (Public Law 101–336). Federal Register. July 26, 1991; 56(144):35,545–35,555.

Amnesty International (2001). *Broken bodies, shattered minds: Torture and ill-treatment of women.* London: Author.

Anderson, B. (2000). *Doing the dirty work? The global politics of domestic labour.* London: Zed Books.

Anderson, S. & Cavanagh, J. (2000). *Field guide to the global economy.* New York: New Press.

Anthony, W. A. (1993). Recovery from mental illness: The guiding vision of the mental health service system in the 1990s. *Psychosocial Rehabilitation Journal,* 16, 11–24.

Anzaldua, G. (1990). "La conciencia de la mestiza: Towards a new consciousness." In. G. Anzaldua (ed.) *Making face/making soul/Hacienda caras: Creative and critical perspectives by women of color* (pp. 377–90). San Francisco: Aunt Lute Press.

Ardila, R. (1986). *La psicología en América Latina. Pasado, presente y futuro* [Psychology in Latin America: Past, present and future]. México, D.F.: Siglo Veintiuno.

Arellano, L. & Ayala-Alcantar, (2002). To be or not to be a feminist: Does feminism have any utility for Latinas/os? *The Community Psychologist,* 35(2), 5–7.

Aristide, J. B. (2000). *Eyes of the heart: Seeking a path for the poor in the age of globalization.* Monroe, ME: Common Courage Press.

Asenso-Okyere, W. (1993). Health financing and social security in Ghana. *Monograph Series,* No. 2. Legon: Institute of Statistical, Social and Economic Research.

Ashton, J. (1992) The origins of healthy cities. In J. Ashton (ed.), *Healthy cities* (pp. 1–11). Buckingham: Open University Press.

Astbury, J. (1996). *Crazy for you: The making of women's madness.* South Melbourne: Oxford University Press Australia.

Asuni, T. (1990). Nigeria: Report on the care, treatment, and rehabilitation of people with mental illness. *Psychosocial Rehabilitation Journal,* 14, 35–44.

Atweh, B., Kemmis, S. & Weeks, P. (1998). *Action research and social justice: Partnerships for social justice in education.* London: Routledge.

Aubry, T. & Myner, J. (1996). Community integration and quality of life: A comparison of persons with psychiatric disabilities in housing programs and community residents who are neighbours. *Canadian Journal of Community Mental Health,* 15(1), 1–16.

Australian Psychological Society. (1997). *Racism and prejudice: Psychological perspectives.* Melbourne: Australian Psychological Society.

Awatere-Huata, D. (1993). Challenges to psychology in Aotearoa. In L. W. Nikora (ed.), *Cultural justice and ethics* (pp. 13–20). Waikato: National Standing Committee on Bicultural Issues, New Zealand Psychological Society.

Babarik, P. (1979). The buried Canadian roots of community psychology. *Journal of Community Psychology,* 7, 362–7.

Bacon, F. (1952/1620). *Novum organum* (pp. 105–98). Chicago: Encyclopedia Britannica, Vol. 30.

Bakan, D. (1966). *The duality of human existence: An essay on psychology and religion.* Chicago: Rand McNally.

Balcazar, F. E. (1990). Behavioral training program to teach advocacy skills to people with disabilities. *The Community Psychologist,* 23, 13–14.

Balcazar, F. E., Keys, C. B., Kaplan, D. L. & Suarez-Balcazar, Y. (1998). Participatory action research and people with disabilities: Principles and challenges. *Canadian Journal of Rehabilitation,* 12, 105–12.

Baltaz D. (1998). *Why we do it: Organic farmers on farming.* Ayr, ON.: Sand Plains Publisher.

Banton, M. (1999). National integration and ethnic violence in Western Europe. *Journal of Ethnic and Migration Studies,* 25, 5–20.

Barbato, A. (1998). Psychiatry in transition: Outcomes of mental health policy shift in Italy. *Australian and New Zealand Journal of Psychiatry,* 32, 673–9.

Baritz, L. (1974). *The servants of power: A history of the use of social science in American industry.* Westport, CT: Greenwood.

Barker, Debi, and Mander, Jerry. (1999). *Invisible government: The World Trade Organization – Global government for the new millennium?* San Francisco: International Forum on Globalization, 'The Banana Case,' http://www.ifg.org/aboutwto.html.

Barker, J. (1999). *Street-level democracy: Political settings at the margins of global power.* West Hartford, CT: Kumarian.

Barker, R. G. (1968). *Ecological psychology.* Stanford: Stanford University Press.

Barker, R. G. & Gump, P. V. (1964). *Big school, small school.* Stanford: Stanford University Press.

Barlow, M. & Campbell, B. (1995). *Straight through the heart: How the Liberals abandoned the just society.* Toronto: HarperCollins Publishers Ltd.

Barlow, M. & Clarke, T. (2001). *Global showdown: How the new activists are fighting global corporate rule.* Toronto: Stoddard.

Barlow, M. & Clarke, T. (2002). *Blue gold: The battle against the theft of the world's water.* Toronto: Stoddart Publishing Co.

Barnes, C. (1998). The social model of disability: A sociological phenomenon ignored by sociologists? In T. Shakespeare (ed.), *The disability reader: Social science perspective* (pp. 65–78). London: Cassell.

Barnes, C., Mercer, G., Shakespeare, T. & Taylor, S. (1999). *Exploring disability: A sociological introduction.* Cambridge: Polity Press.

Barrera, M. (2000). Social support research in community psychology.In J. Rappaport & E. Seidman (eds), *Handbook of community psychology* (pp. 215–45). New York: Kluwer Academic/Plenum Publishers.

Bartky, S. L. (1990). *Femininity and domination: Studies in the phenomenology of domination.* New York: Routledge.

Barton, L. (1998). Sociology, disability studies, and education: Some observations. In T. Shakespeare (ed.). *The disability reader: Social science perspective* (pp. 53–64). London: Cassell.

Baum, A (1987). Toxins, technology, and natural disasters. In G. VandenBos & B. Bryant (eds), *Cataclysms, crises and catastrophes: Psychology in action* (pp. 5–54). Washington, DC: American Psychological Association.

Baum A. & Fleming, I. (1993). Implications of psychological research on stress and technological accidents. *American Psychologist*, **48**, 665–72.

Bayer, R. (1981). *Homosexuality and American psychiatry: the politics of diagnosis.* New York: Basic Books.

Beckwith, J. (ed.) (1999). Power between women. Special feature. *Feminism and Psychology*, **9**, 389–430.

Beckwith, J. & Shopland, J. (2001). Community-friendly counselling – deconstructing therapy. Paper presented at the *Seventh Trans-Tasman Conference in Community Psychology*, Melbourne, Australia.

Beehr, T. & O'Driscoll, P. (2002). Organizationally targeted interventions aimed at reducing workplace stress. In J. Thomas & M. Hersen (eds), *Handbook of mental health in the workplace* (pp. 103–19). London: Sage.

Beers, C. W. (1908). *A mind that found itself.* New York: Doubleday.

Beiser, M., Gill, K. & Edwards, R. G. (1993). Mental health care in Canada: Is it accessible and equal. *Canada's Mental Health*, **41**(2), 2–7.

Belenky, M. F. (1997). Public homeplaces: Nurturing the development of people, families, and communities. In N. Goldberger, J. Tarule, B. Clinchy & M. F. Belenky (eds), *Knowledge, difference, and power* (pp. 393–430). New York: Basic Books.

Belenky, M. F., Bond, L.A., Weinstock, J.S. (1997). *A tradition that has no name: Nurturing the development of people, families, and commuities.* New York: Basic Books.

Belenky, M. F., Clinchy, B., Goldberger, N. & Tarule, J. (1986). *Women's ways of knowing: The development of self, voice, and mind.* New York: Basic Books.

Bellah, R. N., Madsen, W. M., Sullivan, W. M., Swidler, A. & Tipton, S. M. (1985). *Habits of the heart.* Berkley, CA: University of California Press.

Benhabib, S. (1996). From identity politics to social feminism: A plea for the nineties. In D. Trend (ed.), *Radical democracy: Identity, citizenship, and the state* (pp. 27–41). New York: Routledge.

Bennett, C. C., Anderson, L. S., Cooper, S., Hassol, L., Klein, D. C. & Rosenblum, G. (eds). (1966). *Community psychology: A report of the Boston conference on the educaiton of psychologists for community mental health.* Boston: Boston University Press.

Bennett, E. M. (ed.). (1987). *Social intervention: Theory and practice.* Lewiston, NY: The Edwin Mellen Press.

Bennett, E. M. (1992). Community-based economic development: A strategy for primary prevention. *Canadian Journal of Community Mental Health,* 11(2), 11–33.

Bennett, E.M. (2003). Emancipatory responses to oppression: The template of land-use planning and the Old Order Amish of Ontario. *American Journal of Community Psychology,* 31, 157–71.

Bennett, E. M. & Hallman, D. (1987). The centrality of field experiences in training for social intervention. In E. M. Bennett (ed.), *Social intervention: Theory and practice* (pp. 93–123). Lewiston, NY: The Edwin Mellen Press.

Ben Shlomo, Y., White, I. R. & Marmot, M. (1996). Does the variation in the socioeconomic characteristics of an area affect mortality? *British Medical Journal,* 312, 1013–14.

Berkman, L. F. (1995). The role of social relations in health promotion. *Psychosomatic Research,* 57, 245–54.

Bernal, G. (1985). A history of community psychology in Cuba. *Journal of Community Psychology,* 13, 222–35.

Bernal, G., & Enchautegui-de-Jesús, N. (1994). Latinos and Latinas in community psychology: A review of the literature. *American Journal of Community Psychology,* 22, 531–57.

Bernal, G. & Marín, B. (eds). (1985). Community psychology in Cuba [special issue]. *Journal of Community Psychology,* 13(2).

Berry, J. W. (1992). Acculturation and adaptation in a new society. *International Migration Quarterly Review,* 30, 69–87.

Berry, J. W. (1997). Immigration, acculturation, and adaptation. *Applied Psychology: An International Review,* 46, 5–34.

Berry, J. W. (2001). A psychology of immigration. *Journal of Social Issues,* 57, 615–31.

Bess, K., Fisher, A., Sonn, C. & Bishop, B. (2002). Psychological sense of community: theory, research, and applications. In A. Fisher, C. Sonn & B. Bishop (eds), *Psychological sense of community: Research, applications, and implications* (pp. 3–22). New York, NY: Kluwer Academic/Plenum Publishers.

Bhasker, R. (1975). *A realist theory of science.* Bristol, England: The Thetford Press.

Bhatia, S. & Ram, A. (2001). Rethinking 'acculturation' in relation to diasporic cultures and postcolonial identities. *Human Development,* 44, 1–18.

Bicknell, E. (1895). Custodial care of the adult feeble-minded. *Charities Review,* 5, 76–88.

Birman, D. (1994). Acculturation and human diversity in a multicultural society. In E. J. Trickett, R. J. Watts & D. Birman (eds), *Human diversity: Perspectives of people in context* (pp. 261–84). San Francisco: Jossey Bass.

Bishop, B. J., Higgins, D., Casella, F. & Contos, N. (2002). Reflections on practice: Ethics, race, and worldviews. *Journal of Community Psychology,* 30, 611–21.

Black, M. (ed.). (1993). Girls and girlhood: Time we were noticed. *New Internationalist,* 240, 4–28.

Black, R. (1997). *Beyond the pale: An exploration of Pakeha cultural awareness.* Unpublished Master's Thesis, Psychology Department, University of Waikato, Hamilton.

Blakeley, G. (2002). Social capital. In G. Blakeley & V. Bryson, (eds), *Contemporary political concepts: A critical introduction* (pp. 198–213). London: Pluto Press.

Blane, D., Brunner, E. & Wilkinson, R. (eds). (1996). *Health and social organization.* London: Routledge.

Blumenfeld, W. J. (ed.). (1992). *Homophobia: How we all pay the price.* Boston: Beacon Press.

Blumenfeld, W. J. & Raymond, D. (1988). *Looking at gay and lesbian life.* New York: Philosophical Library.

Blumenfeld, W. J. & Raymond, D. (1993). *Looking at gay and lesbian life* (2nd ed.). Boston: Beacon Press.

Bochner, S. (1982), The social psychology of cross-cultural relations. In S. Bochner (ed.) *Cultures in contact: Studies in cross-cultural interactions* (pp. 5–44). Elmsford, NY: Pergamon Press.

Bolam, B. & Chamberlain, K. (2003). Professionalisation and reflexivity in critical health psychology practice. *Journal of Health Psychology*, **8**, 215–18.

Bond, M. A. (1995). Prevention and the ecology of sexual harassment: Creating empowering climates. *Prevention in Human Services*, **12**(2), 147–73.

Bond, M. A. (1999). Gender, race, and class in organizational contexts. *American Journal of Community Psychology*, **27**, 327–55.

Bond, M. A., Hill, J., Mulvey, A. & Terenzio, M. (eds). (2000a). Feminism and community psychology [special issue Part I]. *American Journal of Community Psychology*, **28**(5).

Bond, M. A., Hill, J. & Mulvey, A. & Terenzio, M. (eds). (2000b). Feminism and community psychology [special issue Part II]. *American Journal of Community Psychology*, **28**(6).

Bond, M. A. & Keys, C. B. (1993). Empowerment, diversity and collaboration: Promoting synergy on community boards. *American Journal of Community Psychology*, **21**, 37–57.

Bond, M. A. & Mulvey, A. (2000). A history of women and feminist perspectives in community psychology. *American Journal of Community Psychology*, **28**, 599–630.

Borkman, T. (1999). *Understanding self-help/mutual aid: Experiential learning in the commons.* New Brunswick, NJ: Rutgers University Press.

Bostock, J. (1997). Knowing our place: Understanding women's experiences and causes of distress. *Feminism and Psychology*, **7**, 239–47.

Bouchard, C. (1997). *The community as a participative learning environment: The case of Centraide of Greater Montréal 1,2,3 GO! project.* Conférence prononcée devant l'Institut canadien de recherches avancée (Human Development Program) lors de la 14ième biennale de l'International Society for the Study of Behavioural Development, Québec.

Bouchard, C. (1999). The community as a participative learning environment: The case of Centreaide of Greater Montréal 1, 2, 3 Go! Project. In D. P. Keating & C. Hertzman (eds), *Developmental health and the wealth of nations: Social, biological, and educational dynamics* (pp. 311–21). New York: The Guilford Press.

Bouchard, C. (in press). Searching for impacts – The case of a community-based initiative: 1,2,3 GO!. In J. Scott & H. Ward (eds). *Promoting the wellbeing of children.* London: Jessica Kingsley Publishers.

Bouchard, C. et al. (1991). *Un Québec fou de ses enfants.* Rapport de Groupe de travail pour les jeunes, Québec, Direction des Communications, Ministère de la Santé et des Services Sociaux.

Bourdieu, P. (1972). *Esquisse d'une théorie de la pratique.* Geneva, Switzerland: Droz.

Bourdieu, P. (1986). The forms of capital. In J. Richardson, (ed.), *Handbook of theory and research for the sociology of education* (pp. 241–58). New York, NY: Greenwood Press.

Bourdieu, P. (1990). *In other words: Essays towards a reflexive sociology.* Stanford, CA: Stanford University Press.

Bourdieu, P. (1998). *Acts of resistance: Against the myths of our time.* Cambridge, UK: Polity Press.

Bourdieu, P. & Passeron, J.C. (1977). *Reproduction: In education, society and culture.* London: Sage.

Boyd, A., Geerling, T., Gregory, W., Midgley, G., Murray, P., Walsh, M. & Kagan, C. (2001). *Capacity building for evaluation: A report on the HAZE Project to the Manchester, Salford and Trafford Health Action Zone*. Centre for Systems Studies, University of Hull.

Boyd, N. & Angelique, H. (2002). Rekindling the discourse: Organization studies in community psychology. *Journal of Community Psychology, 30,* 325–48.

Boydell, K. M., Goering, P. & Morrell-Bellai, T. L. (2000). Narratives of identity: Representation of self in people who are homeless. *Qualitative Health Research,* **10,** 26–38.

Braddock, D. L. & Parish, S. L. (2001). An institutional history of disability. In G. L. Albrecht, K. D. Seelman & M. Bury (eds), *Handbook of disability studies* (pp. 11–68). Thousand Oaks: Sage Publications.

Bradshaw, P. (1998). Power as dynamic tension and its implications for radical organizational change. *European Journal of Work and Organizational Psychology,* 7(2), 121–43.

Brazier, C. (1999, January/February). The radical twentieth century. *New Internationalist,* **309,** 7–36.

Breakey, W. R. & Fischer, P. J. (1995). Mental illness and the continuum of residential stability. *Social Psychiatry and Psychiatric Epidemiology,* 30, 147–51.

Brecher, J., Costello, T. & Smith, B. (2000). *Globalization from below: The power of solidarity*. Boston: South End Press.

Brigham, C. C. (1923). *A study of American intelligence*. Princeton, NJ: Princeton University Press.

Brodsky, A. E. (2003). *With all our strengths: The Revolutionary Association of the women of Afghanistan*. Routledge: New York.

Bronfenbrenner, U. (1977). Toward an experimental ecology of human development. *American Psychologist,* **32,** 513–31.

Bronfenbrenner, U. (1979). *The ecology of human development*. Cambridge, MA: Harvard University Press.

Broome, R. (1994). *Aboriginal Australians: Black responses to white dominance, 1788–1994.* St. Leonards, NSW: Allen & Unwin.

Brown, D. (1971). *Bury my heart at Wounded Knee: An Indian history of the American west*. New York: Bantam Books.

Brown, L. D. & Tandon, R. (1983). Ideology and political economy in inquiry: Action research and participatory research. *Journal of Applied Behavioral Science,* **19,** 277–94.

Brydon-Miller, M. (2001). Education, research, and action: Theory and methods of particpatory action research. In D. L. Tolman & M. Brydon-Miller (eds), *From subjects to subjectivities: A handbook of interpretive and participatory methods* (pp. 76–89). New York: New York University Press.

Bryson, L. & Mowbray, M. (1981). 'Community': The spray-on solution. *Australian Journal of Social Issues,* 16, 255–67.

Bulhan, H. A. (1985). *Franz Fanon and the psychology of oppression*. New York: Plenum Press.

Bullough, V. L. (1994). *Science in the bedroom: A history of sex research*. New York: Basic Books.

Bullough, V. L. (2000). Transgenderism and the concept of gender. *International Journal of Transgenderism.* **4**(3), July–Sept. Symposion Publishing, Germany, http://www.symposion.com/ijt/gilbert/bullough.htm .

Burdekin, B. (1995). Human rights and people with disabilities. *International Journal of Disability, Development and Education,* 42, 7–16.

Burman, E. (1997). Developmental psychology and its discontents. In D. Fox & I. Prilleltensky (eds), *Critical psychology: An introduction* (pp. 134–49). London: Sage.

Burns, J. & Hickie, I. (2002). Depression in young people: A national school-based initiative for prevention, early intervention, and pathways to care. *Australasian Psychiatry,* 10, 134–8.

Burton, M. & Kagan, C. (1995). *Social skills and people with learning disabilities: A social capability approach*. London: Chapman and Hall.

Burton, M. & Kagan, C. (1996). Rethinking empowerment: Shared action against powerlessness. In I. Parker & R. Spears (eds), *Psychology and society: Radical theory and practice* (pp. 197–208). London: Pluto Press.

Burton, M. & Kagan, C. (2000, September). *Edge effects, resource utilisation and community psychology*. Paper given at the European Community Psychology Conference, Bergen, Norway.

Busch, R. & Robertson, N. (1993). "What's love got to do with it?" An analysis of an intervention approach to domestic violence. *Waikato Law Review Taumauri*, **1**, 109–40.

Caceres, C. F. & Rosaco, A. M. (1999). The margin has many sides: Diversity among gay and homosexually active men in Lima. *Culture, Health, and Sexuality*, **1**, 261–75.

Cahill, J. (1983). Structural characteristics of the macroeconomy and mental health: Implications for primary prevention research. *American Journal of Community Psychology*, **11**, 553–71.

Cain, C. (1991). Personal stories: Identity acquisition and self-understanding in Alcoholics Anonymous. *Ethos*, **19**, 210–51.

Campbell, B. (2000). Kawanatanga: a Tauiwi perspective. In *Proceedings of Treaty Conference 2000* (pp. 58–61). Tamaki Makaurau/Auckland: Treaty Conference Publications Group.

Campbell, D. T. & Stanley, J. C. (1966). *Experimental and quasi-experimental designs for research*. Chicago: Rand McNally.

Campbell, R., Baker, C. K. & Mazurek, T. L. (1998). Remaining radical? Organizational predictors of rape crisis centers' social change initiatives. *American Journal of Community Psychology*, **26**, 457–83.

Campbell, R. & Salem, D. A. (1999). Concept mapping as a feminist research method: Examining the community responses to rape. *Psychology of Women Quarterly*, **23**, 67–91.

Campbell, R., Sefl, T., Barnes, H. E., Ahrens, C. E., Wasco, S. M. & Zaragoza-Diesfeld, Y. (1999). Community services for rape survivors: Enhancing psychological well-being or increasing trauma? *Journal of Consulting and Clinical Psychology*, **67**, 847–58.

Campbell, R., Sefl, T., Wasco, S. M. & Ahrens, C. E. (2004). Doing community research without a community: Creating safe space for rape survivors. *American Journal of Community Psychology*, **33**, 253–61.

Campbell, R. & Wasco, S. M. (2000). Feminist approaches to social science: Epistemological and methodological tenets. *American Journal of Community Psychology*, **28**, 773–91.

Cannon, L. W., Higginbotham, E. & Leung, M. L. A. (1991). Race and class bias in qualitative research on women. In M. M. Fonow & J. A. Cook (eds), *Beyond methodology: Feminist scholarship as lived research* (pp. 107–18). Bloomington, IN: Indiana University Press.

Caplan, G. (1964). *The principles of preventive psychiatry*. New York: Basic Books.

Caplan, P. (1995). *They say you're crazy: How the world's most powerful psychiatrists decide who's normal*. Massachusetts, Addison Wesley.

Caplan, R., Vinokur, A. & Price, R. (1997). From job loss to reemployment: Field experiments in prevention focused coping. In G. Albee & T. Gullota (eds), *Primary prevention works* (pp. 341–79). Thousand Oaks, CA: Sage.

Capponi, P. (2003). *Beyond the crazy house: Changing the future of madness*. Toronto: Penguin.

Cardemil, E. V., Reivich, K. J. & Seligman, M. E. P. (2002). The prevention of depressive symptoms in low-income minority middle school students. *Prevention and Treatment*, American Psychological Assocation, http://www.apa.org.

Carling, P. J. (1995). *Return to community: Building supports systems for people with psychiatric disabilities*. New York: The Guilford Press.

Carmichael, S. & Hamilton, C. V. (1967). *Black power: The politics of liberation in America*. New York: Vintage Books.

Carrier, J. M. (1989). Gay liberation and coming out in Mexico. *Journal of Homosexuality*, **17**, 225–52.

Carson, R. (1962). *Silent spring*. Boston, MA: Houghton Mifflin.

Carspecken, P. (1996). *Critical ethnography in educational research*. London: Routledge.

Castillo, R. J. (1997). *Culture and mental illness: A client-centered approach*. Pacific Grove, CA: Brooks/Coles Publishing Company.

Caton, L. & Larsh S. (2000). An idea whose time has come: A decade of healthy community activity in Ontario. In K. Dean (ed.), *Inspiring change: Healthy cities and communities in Ontario* (pp. 7–20). Toronto: Ontario Healthy Communities Coalition.

Cauce, A. M., Comer, J. P. & Schwartz, D. (1987). Long term effects of a systems-oriented school prevention program. *American Journal of Orthopsychiatry*, **57**, 127–31.

CEH/Commission for Historical Clarification [Comisión para el Esclarecimiento Histórico]. (February, 1999). *Report of the CEH* [On-line]. Available: http://hrdata.aaas.org/ceh. Guatemala: Author.

Centraide of Greater Montréal. (2001). *Where the money goes? 1,2,3 GO! Let's pull together for our neighbourhood's babies and toddlers*. (Available on-line at http://www.centraide-mtl.org/centraide/static/where/go.shtml).

Cernovsky, Z. Z. (1997). A critical look at intelligence research. In D. Fox & I. Prilleltensky (eds), *Critical psychology: An introduction* (pp. 121–33). London: Sage.

Cerullo, R. & Wiesenfeld, E. (2001). La concientizacion en el trabajo psicosocial comunitario desde la perspective de sus actores [Agents' perspectives on concientization in psychosocial community work]. *Revista de Psicologia*, **10**(*2*), 11–26.

Chamberlin, J. (1978). *On our own: Patient-controlled alternatives to the mental health system*. New York: McGraw-Hill.

Chamberlin, J.(1984). Speaking for ourselves: An overview of the ex-psychiatric inmates movement. *Psychosocial Rehabilitation Journal*, **2**, 56–63.

Chamberlin, J. (1990). The ex-psychiatric patients' movement: Where we've been and where we're going. *Journal of Mind and Behavior*, **11**, 323–36.

Chamberlin, J. (1997). A working definition of empowerment. *Psychiatric Rehabilitation Journal*, **20**, 43–46.

Charlesworth, S. J. (2000). *A phenomenology of working class experience*. Cambridge: Cambridge University Press.

Charlton, J. I. (1998). *Nothing about us without us: Disability, oppression and empowerment*. Berkeley: University of California Press.

Chavis, D. (2000). Community development and the community psychologist. In J. Rappaport & E. Seidman (eds), *Handbook of community psychology* (pp. 767–71). New York: Kluwer/Plenum.

Chavis, D. (2001). The paradoxes and promise of community coalitions. *American Journal of Community Psychology*, **29**, 309–20.

Chavis, D. & Pretty, G. M. H. (eds). (1999). Sense of community II [special issue]. *Journal of Community Psychology*, **27**(6).

Chavis, D., Stucky, P. E. & Wandersman, A. H. (1983). Returning research to the community: A relationship between scientist and citizen. *American Psychologist*, **38**, 424–34.

Cherniss, C. (1993). Pre-entry issues revisited. In R. T. Golembiewski (ed.), *Handbook of organizational consultation* (pp. 113–18). New York: Marcel Dekker.

Cherniss, C. (2002). Emotional intelligence and the good community. *American Journal of Community Psychology*, **30**, 1–12.

Cherniss, C. & Adler, M. (2000). *Promoting emotional intelligence in organizations*. Alexandria, VA: ASTD.

Cherniss, C. & Deegan, G. (2000). The creation of alternative settings. In J. Rappaport & E. Seidman (eds), *Handbook of community psychology* (pp. 359–77). New York: Kluwer Academic/Plenum Publishers.

Chesler, M. A. (1991). Participatory action research with self-help groups: An alternative paradigm for inquiry and action. *American Journal of Community Psychology*, **19**, 757–68.

Chinman, M., Kloos, B, O'Connell, M. & Davidson, L. (2002). Service providers' views of psychiatric mutual support groups. *Journal of Community Psychology*, **30**, 349–66.

Chomsky, N. (2000). *Rogue states: The rule of force in world affairs.* London: Pluto Press.

Chomsky, N. (2002). *Understanding power.* Melbourne: Scribe Publications.

Choudhury, M. & Kagan, C. (2000). Inter-generational understanding in the inner city: 'Edge effects' and sustainable change in community organisations. In C. Kagan (ed.), *Collective action and social change* (pp. 58–70). Manchester: IOD Research Group.

Church, K. (1995). *Forbidden narratives: Critical autobiography as social science.* Luxembourg: Gordon and Breach Publishers.

Churchill, H., Everitt, A. & Greene, J. (1997). Taken away from community: Older people and sheltered housing. In P. Hoggett (ed.), *Contested communities: Experiences, struggles, policies* (pp. 105–21). Bristol: Policy Press.

Cicchetti, D., Rappaport, J., Sandler, I. & Weissberg, R. P. (eds). (2000). *The promotion of wellness in children and adolescents.* Washington, DC: Child Welfare League of America Press.

Clark, K. B. (1965). *Dark ghetto: Dilemmas of social power.* New York: Harper Torchbooks.

Clark, K. B. (1974). *Pathos of power.* New York, NY: Harper & Row.

Clark, R. (1986). *Power and policy in the Third World.* New York: Macmillan.

Coddington, J. (2002). Biodiversity deficit. In M. Barlow & T. Clarke, *Blue gold: The battle against corporate theft of the world's water* (p. 27). Toronto: Stoddart.

Cohen, A. & Gutek, B. (1991). Sex differences in the career experiences of members of two APA divisions. *American Psychologist*, **46**, 1292–8.

Cohen, M. D. & Somers, S. (1990). Supported housing: Insights from the Robert Wood Johnson Foundation Program on Chronic Mental Illness. *Psychosocial Rehabilitation Journal*, **13**, 43–50.

Cohen, S., Underwood, L. G. & Gottlieb, B. H. (eds). (2000). *Social support measurement and intervention: A guide for social and health scientists.* Oxford: Oxford University Press.

Cohen, S. & Wills, T. (1985). Stress, social support, and the buffering hypothesis. *Psychological Bulletin*, **98**, 310–57.

Cole, E. (1998). Immigrant and refugee children: Challenges and opportunities for education and mental health services. *Canadian Journal of School of Psychology*, **14**, 36–50.

Colley, H. & Hodkinson, P. (2001). Problems with Bridging the Gap: The reversal of structure and agency in addressing social exclusion. *Critical Social Policy*, **21**, 335–59.

Collins, P. H. (1990). *Black feminist thought: Knowledge, consciousness, and the politics of empowerment.* New York: Routledge.

Comas-Diaz, L., Lykes, M. B. & Alarcon, R. D. (1998). Ethnic conflict and the psychology of liberation in Guatemala, Peru and Puerto Rico. *American Psychologist*, **53**, 778–92.

Comer, J. P. (1985). The Yale-New Haven primary prevention project: A follow-up study. *Journal of the American Academy of Child Psychiatry*, **24**, 154–60.

Community Mental Health Project. (1998). Companions on a journey: The work of the Dulwich Centre Community Mental Health Project. In C. White & D. Denborough (eds). *Introducing narrative therapy.* Adelaide: Dulwich Centre Publications.

Connors, E. & Maidman, F. (2001). A circle of healing: Family wellness in Aboriginal communities. In I. Prilleltensky, G. Nelson & L. Peirson (eds), *Promoting family wellness and preventing child maltreatment: Fundamentals for thinking and action* (pp. 349–416). Toronto: University of Toronto Press.

Constantino, V. & Nelson, G. (1995). Changing relationships between self-help groups and mental health professionals: Shifting ideology and power. *Canadian Journal of Community Mental Health*, **14**(2), 55–73.

Cook, T. (1985). Postpositivist critical multiplism. In R. L. Shotland & M. M. Mark (eds), *Social science and social policy* (pp. 21–62). Beverly Hills: Sage.

Cooke, B. & Kothari, U. (2001). *Participation: The new tyranny?* London: Zed Books.

Cooke, H. (2002). Empowerment. In G. Blakeley & V. Bryson, (eds), *Contemporary political concepts: A critical introduction* (pp. 162–78). London: Pluto Press.

Cooperrider, D. L. & Srivastva, S. (1987). Appreciative inquiry in organizational life. *Research in Organizational Change and Development*, **1**, 129–69.

Corey, M. & Corey, G. (2003). *Becoming a helper*. Pacific Grove, CA: Brooks/Coles.

Cornell Empowerment Group. (1989). Empowerment and family support. *Networking Bulletin*, **1**, 1–23.

Corrigan, P. W., Faber, D., Rashid, R. & Leary, M. (1999). The construct validity of empowerment among consumers of mental health services. *Schizophrenia Research*, **38**, 77–84.

Corrigan, P. W. & Penn, D. L. (1999). Lessons from social psychology on discrediting psychiatric stigma. *American Psychologist*, **54**, 765–76.

Council for Reconciliation. (1995). *Going forward: Social justice for the first Australians – a submission to the Commonwealth Government*. Canberra: AGPS.

Cowen, E. L. (1977). Baby-steps toward primary prevention. *American Journal of Community Psychology*, **5**, 1–16.

Cowen, E. L. (1980). The wooing of primary prevention. *American Journal of Community Psychology*, **8**, 258–84.

Cowen, E. L. (1982). Help is where you find it: Four informal helping groups. *American Psychologist*, **37**, 385–95.

Cowen, E. L. (1985). Person centered approaches to primary prevention in mental health: Situation focused and competence enhancement. *American Journal of Community Psychology*, **13**, 87–98.

Cowen, E. L. (1994). The enhancement of psychological wellness: Challenges and opportunities. *American Journal of Community Psychology*, **22**, 149–79.

Cowen, E. L. (1996). The ontogenesis of primary prevention: Lengthy strides and stubbed tocs. *American Journal of Community Psychology*, **24**, 235–49.

Cowen, E. L. (2000). Community psychology and routes to psychological wellness. In J. Rappaport & E. Seidman (eds), *Handbook of community psychology* (pp. 79–99). New York: Kluwer Academic/Plenum Publishers.

Cox, D. R. (1989). *Welfare practice in a multicultural society*. Sydney, Australia: Prentice Hall.

Cox, W. M. & Alm, R. (2002). *Off the books: The benefits of free enterprise that economic statistics miss*. Reasononline, August 2002, http://www.reason.com/0208/fe.wc.off.shtml.

Craig, J. & Craig, M. (1979). *Synergic power: Beyond domination, beyond permissiveness*. Berkely, CA: Proactive Press.

Cram, F. (1995). Ethics and cross-cultural research. [A draft paper.] Auckland: University of Auckland.

Croft, S. & Beresford, P. (1992). The politics of participation. *Critical Social Policy*, **12**, 20–44.

Cronbach, L. J. & Meehl, P. E. (1955). Construct validity in psychological tests. *Psychological Bulletin*, **52**, 281–302.

Crowley-Long, K. (1998). Making room for many feminisms: The dominance of the liberal political perspective in the Psychology of Women course. *Psychology of Women Quarterly*, **22**, 113–30.

Cruikshank, M. (1992). *The gay and lesbian liberation movement*. New York: Routledge.

Dalai Lama. (1999). *Ethics for the new millennium*. New York, NY: Riverhead Books.

Dalton, J. H., Elias, M. J. & Wandersman, A. (2001). *Community psychology: Linking individuals and communities*. Belmont, CA: Wadsworth/Thomson Learning.

Daly, H. E. & Cobb, J. B., (1989). *For the common good*. Boston: Beacon Press.

Damon, W. (1995). *Greater expectations: Overcoming the culture of indulgence in America's homes and schools*. New York: The Free Press.

D'Augelli, A. R. (1989). Lesbian's and gay men's experiences of discrimination and harassment in a university community. *American Journal of Community Psychology*, **17**, 317–21.

D'Augelli, A. R. (1993). Lesbian and gay male undergraduates' experiences of harassment and fear on campus. In R. A. Pierce & M. A. Black (eds), *Life-span development: A diversity reader* (pp. 199–208). Dubuque, IA: Kendall/Hunt Publishers.

D'Augelli, A. R. & Hershberger, S. L. (1993). Lesbian, gay, and bisexual youth in community settings: Personal challenges and mental health problems. *American Journal of Community Psychology*, **21**, 421–48.

Davidson, L., Chinman, M., Kloos, B., Weingarten, R., Stayner, D. & Tebes, J. K. (1999). Peer support among individuals with severe mental illness: A review of evidence. *Clinical Psychology: Science and Practice*, **6**, 165–87.

Davidson, L. Hoge, M. A., Godelski, L., Rakfeldt, J. & Griffith, E. E. H., (1996). Hospital or community living? Examining consumer perspectives on deinstitutionalization. *Psychiatric Rehabilitation Journal*, **58**, 122–32.

Davidson, L., Stayner, D., Nickou, C., Styron, T. H., Rowe, M. & Chinman, M. (2001). 'Simply to be let in': Inclusion as a basis for recovery. *Psychiatric Rehabilitation Journal*, **24**, 375–88.

Davidson, L., Stayner, D. A., Rakfeldt, J. Weingarten, R. & Tebes, J. K. (in press). Friendship and the restoration of community life: Supported socialization for people with psychiatric disabilities. In P. Statsny & J. Campbell (eds), *Social supports and psychiatric rehabilitation*. New York: John Wiley & Sons.

Davidson, P. O. (1981). Some cultural, political, and professional antecedents of community psychology in Canada. *Canadian Psychology*, **22**, 315–20.

Davidson, W. S. (1989). Ethical dilemmas in community psychology: Tarnishing the angel's halo. *American Journal of Community Psychology*, **17**, 355–60.

Davis, L. J. (1995). *Enforcing normalcy: Disability, deafness and the body*. London: Verso.

Deegan, P. E. (1988). Recovery: The lived experience of rehabilitation. *Psychosocial Rehabilitation Journal*, **11**(4), 11–19.

Deegan, P. E. (1993). Recovering our sense of value after being labelled mentally ill. *Journal of Psychosocial Nursing*, **31**, 7–11.

DeJong, G. (1979). Independent living: From social movement to analytic paradigm. *Archives of Physical Medicine and Rehabilitation*, **60**, 435–66.

Della Porta, D. & Diani, M. (1999). *Social movements: An introduction*. Oxford, UK: Blackwell.

D'Emilio, J. (1983). Capitalism and gay identity. In A. Snitow, C. Stansell & S. Thompson (eds), *Power of desire: The politics of sexuality* (pp. 100–13). New York: Monthly Review Press.

Denzin, N. K. (2000). The practices and politics of interpretation. In N. K. Denzin & Y. S. Lincoln (eds), *Handbook of qualitative research* (2nd edn, pp. 897–922). Thousand Oaks, CA: Sage.

Denzin, N. K. & Lincoln, Y. S. (eds). (2000). *Handbook of qualitative research* (2nd edn). Thousand Oaks, CA: Sage.

De Souza, S. R. (2001). A psicologia e os movimentos sociais: Um olhar ataves dos tabalhos comunitarios [The psychology of social movements: A view through communit work]. *Revista de Psicologia*, **10**(2), 27–37.

Deutsch, M. (1948). *The shame of the states.* New York: Columbia University Press.

Diaz, R. M. (1998). *Latino gay men and HIV: Culture, sexuality, and risk behavior.* New York, NY: Routledge.

Diaz, R. M. & Ayala, G. (2001). *Social discrimination and health: The case of Latino gay men and HIV risk.* New York, NY: The Policy Institute of the National Gay and Lesbian Task Force.

Diaz, R. M., Ayala, G., Bein, E., Henne, J. & Marin, B. V. (2001). The impact of homophobia, poverty, and racism on the mental health of gay and bisexual Latino men: Findings from 3 U.S. cities. *American Journal of Public Health*, **91**(6), 927–32.

Dickey, B., Gonzalez, O., Latimer, E., Powers, K. (1996). Use of mental health services by formerly homeless adults residing in group and independent housing. *Psychiatric Services*, **47**, 152–58.

Dimock, H. (1987). *Groups: Leadership and group development.* New York: Pfeiffer.

Dimock, H. (1992). *Intervention and empowerment: Helping organizations to change.* North York, ON: Captus Press.

Dion, K. L. (2001). Immigrants' perceptions of housing discrimination in Toronto: The Housing New Canadians Project. *Journal of Social Issues*, **57**, 523–39.

DiTella, R., MacCulloch, R. & Oswald, A. (2001). Preferences over inflation and unemployment: Evidence from surveys on happiness. *American Economic Review*, **91**, 335–41.

Dobash, R E. & Dobash, R P. (1979). *Violence against wives: A case against the patriarchy.* New York: Free Press.

Dobbin, M. (2003). *NAFTA's Big Brother*, retrieved from www.canadians.org, January 25, 2003.

Dohrenwend, B. P. & Dohrenwend, B. S. (1969). *Social status and psychological inquiry: A causal inquiry.* New York: Wiley.

Dohrenwend, B. S. (1978). Social stress and community psychology. *American Journal of Community Psychology*, **6**, 1–14.

Dokecki, P. (1996). *The tragi-comic professional: Basic considerations for ethical reflective-generative practice.* Pittsburgh, PA: Duquesne University Press.

Dokecki, P. R., Newbrough, J. R. & O'Gorman, R. T. (2001). Toward a community-oriented action research framework for spirituality: Community psychological and theological perspectives. *Journal of Community Psychology*, **29**, 497–518.

Donovan, J. M. (1992). Homosexual, gay, and lesbian: Defining the words and sampling the populations. In H. L. Minton (ed.), *Gay and lesbian studies* (pp. 27–47). New York: The Haworth Press, Inc.

Dooley, D. & Catalano, R. (1980). Economic change as a cause of behavioral disorder. *Psychological Bulletin*, **87**, 450–68.

Dooley, D. & Catalano, R. (eds). (2003). Underemployment and its social costs: New research directions [special issue]. *American Journal of Community Psychology*, **32**(1).

Doyal, L. & Gough, I. (1984). A theory of human needs. *Critical Social Policy*, **4**, 6–38.

Doyal, L. & Gough, I. (1991) *A theory of human need.* Basingstoke: Macmillan.

Drake, R. E. & Becker, D. R. (1996). The individual placement and support model of supported employment. *Psychiatric Services*, **47**, 473–75.

DuBois, B. (1983). Passionate scholarship: Notes on values, knowing and method in feminist social science. In G. Bowles & R. Klein (eds). *Theories of women's studies* (pp. 105–16). Boston: Routledge.

DuBois, D. L., Holloway, B. E., Valentine, J. C. & Cooper, H. C. (2002). Effectiveness of mentoring programs for youth: A meta-analytic review. *American Journal of Community Psychology*, **30**, 157–97.

Dudgeon, P., Garvey, D. & Pickett, H. (eds). (2000). *Working with Indigenous Australians: A handbook for psychologists.* Perth, Western Australia: Gunada Press.

Dudgeon, P., Mallard, J., Oxenham, D. & Fielder, J. (2002). Contemporary Aboriginal perceptions of community. In A. Fisher, C. Sonn & B. Bishop (eds), *Psychological sense of community: Research, applications, and implications* (pp. 247–67). New York, NY: Kluwer Academic/Plenum Publishers.

Dudgeon, P. & Pickett, H. (2000). Psychology and reconciliation: Australian perspectives. *Australian Psychologist, 35*, 82–87.

Dudgeon, P. & Williams, R. (2000). Culturally appropriate therapies, models and services. In P. Dudgeon, D. Garvey & H. Pickett (eds), *Working with Indigenous Australians: A handbook for psychologists* (pp. 389–94). Perth: Gunada Press.

Dunn, J. R. & Dyck, I. (2000). Social determinants of health in Canada's immigrant population: Results from the National Population Health Survey. *Social Science and Medicine, 51*, 1573–93.

Durie, M. H. (1996). *Characteristics of Maori health research.* Paper presented at Hui Whakapiripiri, Hongoeka Marae.

Durlak, J. (1995). *School-based prevention programs for children and adolescents.* Thousand Oaks, CA: Sage.

Durlak, J. A. & Wells, A. M. (1997). Primary prevention programs for children and adolescents: A meta-analytic review. *American Journal of Community Psychology, 25*, 115–52.

Dussel, E. (1998). *Ética de la Liberación en la Edad de la Globalización y de la Exclusión.* [Ethics of liberation in an age of globalization and exclusion]. Madrid: Trotta.

Eckersley, R., (2000). The mixed blessing of material progress: Diminishing returns in the pursuit of progress. *Journal of Happiness Studies, 1*, 267–92.

Eckersley, R. (2001). Culture, health, and well-being. In R. Eckersley, R., J. Dixon & B. Douglas (eds), *The social origins of health and well-being* (pp. 51–70). New York, NY: Cambridge University Press.

Edelman, M. (2001). *The politics of misinformation.* New York, NY: Cambridge University Press.

Edgar, D. (1995). New grist for men's old mill. *The Age*, 11/8/95, p.13.

Edwards, M. & Gaventa, J. (eds). (2001). *Global citizen action.* Boulder, CO: Lynne Rienner.

Ehrlich, P. R. & Holdren, J. P. (1971). An inventory of disaster. In C. Fadiman & J. White (eds), *Ecocide and thoughts toward survival* (pp. 23–46). Santa Barbara, CA: Center For The Study of Democratic Institutions.

Eichler, M. (1997). *Family shifts: Families, policies, and gender equality.* Toronto: Oxford University Press.

Eisler, R. (1988). *The chalice and the blade: Our history, our future.* San Francisco: Harper-Collins.

Ekins, P. (1992) *A new world order: Grassroots movements for global change.* London: Routledge.

Eldering, L & Knorth, E. J. (1998). Marginalization of immigrant youth and risk factors in their everyday lives: The European experience. *Child and Youth Care Forum, 27*(3), 153–69.

Eldon, M. & Chisholm, R. F. (1993). Emerging varieties of action research: Introduction to a special issue. *Human Relations, 46*, 121–42.

Elias, M. J. (1987). Establishing enduring prevention programs: Advancing the legacy of Swampscott. *American Journal of Community Psychology, 15*, 539–53.

Elias, M. (1994). Capturing excellence in applied settings: A participant conceptualizer and praxis explicator role for community psychologists. *American Journal of Community Psychology, 22*, 293–318.

Elias, M. J. (1997). Reinterpreting dissemination of prevention programs as widespread implementation with effectiveness and fidelity. In R. P. Weissberg, T. P. Gullotta, R. L. Hampton, B. A. Ryan & G. R. Adams (eds), *Establishing preventive services* (pp. 253–89). Thousand Oaks, CA: Sage.

Elkins, S. R., Jones, M. L. & Ulicny, G. R. (1987). *The media watch campaign manual* (research edition). Lawrence, KS: The Research and Training Center on Independent Living.

Ellerbe, H. (1995). *The dark side of Christian history*. San Rafael, CA: Morningstar Books.

El-Mouelhy, M. (1992). The impact of women's health and status on children's health and lives in the developing world. In G. W. Albee, L. A. Bond & T. V. Cook Monsey (eds), *Improving children's lives: Global perspectives on prevention* (pp. 83–96). London: Sage.

Engwicht, D. (1993). *Reclaiming our cities and towns: Better living with less traffic*. Gabriola Island, BC: New Society Publishers.

Enwemeka, C. S. & Adeghe, N. U. (1982). Some family problems associated with the presence of a child with handicap in Nigeria. *Child Care, Health and Development*, **8**,113–40.

Epp, J. (1986). *Achieving health for all: A framework for health promotion*. Ottawa: Health and Welfare Canada.

Epp, J. (1988). *Mental health for Canadians: Striking a balance*. Ottawa: Minister of Supplies and Services.

Escovar, L. A. (1977). El psicólogo social y el desarrollo [Social psychologists and development]. *Psicología*, **4**(3–4): 367–77.

Escovar, L. A. (1980) Hacia un modelo psicológico-social del desarrollo.[Towards a social-psychological model for social development]. *Boletín AVEPSO*, **3**(1): 1–6.

Esses, V. M., Dovidio, J. F., Jackson, L. M., Armstrong & Tamara, L. (2001). The immigration dilemma: The role of perceived group competition, ethnic prejudice, and national identity. *Journal of Social Issues*, **57**, 389–412.

Etzioni, A. (1960). Two approaches to organizational analysis: A critique and a suggestion. *Administrative Science Quarterly*, **5**, 257–78.

Etzioni, A. (1993). *The spirit of community*. New York: Touchstone.

Etzioni, A. (1996). *The new golden rule*. New York: Basic Books.

Etzioni, A. (ed.). (1998). *The essential communitarian reader*. Boulder, CO: Rowman & Littlefield.

Etzioni, A. (2001). *Next: The road to the good society*. New York: Basic Books.

Everett, B. (1994). Something is happening: The contemporary consumer and psychiatric survivor movement in historical context. *The Journal of Mind and Behavior*, **15**, 55–70.

Fabrega, H. Jr. (1990). Psychiatric stigma in the classical and medieval period: A review of the literature. *Comprehensive Psychiatry*, **31**, 289–306.

Fabrega, H. Jr. (1991). The culture and history of psychiatric stigma in early modern and modern western societies: A review of recent literature. *Comprehensive Psychiatry*, **32**, 97–119.

Fairweather, G. W. (1972). *Social change: The challenge to survival*. Secaucus, NJ: General Learning Press.

Fairweather, G. W. & Davidson, W. S. (1986). *An introduction to community experimentation: Theory, methods, and practice*. New York: McGraw-Hill.

Fals Borda, O. (1988). *Knowledge and people's power: Lessons with peasants in Nicaragua, Mexico and Colombia* (Translation of *Conocimiento y poder popular. Lecciones con campesinos de Nicaragua, Mexico y Colombia* Bogotá, Siglo XXI Editores, 1985). New York: New Horizons Press.

Fals Borda, O. (2001). Participatory (action) research in social theory: Origins and challenges. In P. Reason & H. Bradbury (eds), *Handbook of action research: Participative inquiry and practice* (pp. 27–37). London: Sage.

Fanon, F. (1963). *The wretched of the earth*. New York: Grove Press Inc.

Fanon, F. (1986). *Black skin, white masks*. London: Pluto Press.

Farber, B. A. & Azar, S. T. (1999). Blaming the helpers: The marginalization of teachers and parents of the urban poor. *American Journal of Orthopsychiatry*, **69**, 515–28.

Fattore, G., Percudani, M., Pugnoli, C., Beecham, J. & Contini, A. (2000). Mental health care in Italy: Organisational structure, routine clinical activity and costs of a community psychiatric service in Lombardy region. *International Journal of Social Psychiatry*, **46**, 250–65.

Fawcett, S. B. (1991). Some values guiding community research and action. *Journal of Applied Behavior Analysis*, **24**, 612–36.

Fawcett, S.B., Paine-Andrews, A., Francisco, V.T., Schultz, J.A., Richter, K. P., Lewis, R.K., Williams, E.L., Harris, K.J., Berkley, J.Y., Fisher, J.L. & Lopez , C.M. (1994). *Work group evaluation handbook: Evaluating and supporting community initiatives for health and development.* Lawrence, KS: Work Group on Health Promotion and Community Development, University of Kansas.

Fawcett, S. B., White, G. W., Balcazar, F. E., Suarez-Balcazar, Y., Mathews, R. M., Paine-Andrews, A., Seekins, T. & Smith, J. F. (1994). A contextual-behavioral model of empowerment: Case studies involving people with physical disabilities. *American Journal of Community Psychology*, **22**, 471–96.

Fawzy, F., Fawzy, N., Hyun, C., Elashoff, R., Guthrie, D., Fahey, J. & Morton, D. (1993). Malignant melanoma: Effects of an early structured psychiatric intervention, coping, and affective state on recurrence and survival 6 years later. *Archives of General Psychiatry*, **50**, 681–9.

Febbraro, A. (1994). Single mothers 'at risk' for child maltreatment: An appraisal of person-centred interventions and a call for emancipatory action. *Canadian Journal of Community Mental Health*, **13**(2), 47–60.

Feldblum, C. R., (2000). Moral law, changing morals. *Nation*, **271**(10), 22–4.

Feldblum, C. R., (2001). Gay rights and the Rehnquist court. *The Gay and Lesbian Review*, **8**, 11–14.

Felner, R. & Adan, A. (1988). The School Transition Environment Project: An ecological intervention and evaluation. In R. Price, E. L. Cowen, R. P. Lorion & J. Ramos-McKay (eds), *Fourteen ounces of prevention: A casebook for practitioners* (pp. 111–22). Washington, DC: American Psychological Association.

Fenton, S. (1999). *Ethnicity, racism, class, and culture.* Houndmills, Basingstoke: Macmillan – now Palgrave Macmillan.

Ferrarotti, F. (1981) *Storia e storie di vita* [History and life histories]. Roma: Laterza.

Ferree, M. M. & Martin, P. Y. (1995). Doing the work of the movement: Feminist organizations. In M. Ferree & P. Martin (eds), *Feminist organizations: Harvest of the new women's movement* (pp. 3–23). Philadelphia: Temple University Press.

Fetterman, D., Kaftarian, S. & Wandersman, A. (eds). (1996). *Empowerment evaluation: Knowledge and tools for self-assessment and accountability.* Thousand Oaks, CA: Sage.

Feuerstein, M-T. (1997). *Poverty and health: Reaping a richer harvest.* London: Macmillan – now Palgrave Macmillan.

Final Report (2001). *Health promotion for persons with disabilities and prevention of secondary conditions.* Lawrence, KS: Research and Training Center on Independent Living.

Fine, M. (1992). *Disruptive voices: The possibilities of feminist research.* Ann Arbor, MI: University of Michigan Press.

Fine, M., Weis, L., Powell, L.C., & Mun Wong, L. (eds). (1997). *Off white: Readings on race, power, and society.* New York: Routledge.

Finkelstein, V. (1998). Emancipating disability studies. In T. Shakespeare (ed.). *The disability reader: Social science perspective* (pp. 28–49). London: Cassell.

Fish, W. B. (1892). Custodial care of adult idiots. *Proceedings of the National Conference of Social Work*, **17**: 203–18.

Fisher, A. T., Karnilowicz, W. & Ngo, D. (1994). Researching the provision of intellectual disability services in a Vietnamese community in Australia. *The Community Psychologist*, **27**(3), 13–14.

Fisher, A. T. & Sonn, C. C. (2002). Sense of community in Australia and the challenges of change. *Journal of Community Psychology*, **30**, 579–609.

Fisher, A. T., Sonn, C. C. & Bishop, B. (eds). (2002). *Psychological sense of community: Research, applications, and implications.* New York, NY: Kluwer Academic/Plenum Publishers.

Fisher, D. B. (1994). Health care reform based on an empowerment model of recvoery by people with psychiatric disabilities. *Hospital and Community Psychiatry*, **45**, 913–15.

Flynn, R. J. & Lemay, R. A. (1999). *A quarter-century of normalization and social role valorization: Evolution and impact.* Ottawa: University of Ottawa Press.

Flyvbjerg, B. (2001). *Making social science matter: Why social inquiry fails and how it can succeed again.* New York, NY: Cambridge University Press.

Fong, A. & Wright, E. O. (2004). *Deepening democracy: Institutional innovations in empowered participatory governance.* London: Verso.

Foster-Fishman, P., Berkowitz, S., Lounsbury, D., Jacobson, S. & Allen, N. (2001). Building collaborative capacity in community coalitions: A review and integrative framework. *American Journal of Community Psychology*, **29**, 241–61.

Foster-Fishman, P., Salem, D., Allen, N. & Fahrbach, K, (2001). Facilitating interorganizational collaboration: The contributions of interorganizational alliances. *American Journal of Community Psychology*, **29**, 875–906.

Foucault, M. (1965). *Madness and civilization: A history of insanity in the age of reason.* London: Tavistock.

Foucault, M. (1975). *Surveiller et punir.* Paris: NRF-Gallimard.

Foucault, M. (1979a). *Discipline and punish.* Harmondsworth, England: Penguin.

Foucault, M. (1979b) *Power, truth, strategy.* Sydney, Australia: Feral Publications.

Foucault, M. (1980). *Power/Knowledge: Selected interviews and other writings* (Colin Gordon, ed.). New York: Pantheon.

Fox, D. R. (1985). Psychology, ideology, utopia, and the commons. *American Psychologist*, **40**, 48–58.

Fox, D. R. (1991). Social science's limited role in resolving psycholcgal social problems. *Journal of Offender Rehabilitation*, **17**, 117–24.

Fox, D. R. (1993a). The autonomy–community balance and the equity-law distinction: Anarchy's task for psychological jurisprudence. *Behavioral Sciences and the Law*, **11**, 97–109.

Fox, D. R. (1993b). Psychological jurisprudence and radical social change. *American Psychologist*, **48**, 234–41.

Fox, D. R. (1999). Psycholegal scholarship's contribution to false consciousness about injustice. *Law and Human Behavior*, **23**, 9–30.

Fox, D. & Prilleltensky, I. (eds). (1997). *Critical psychology: An introduction.* London: Sage.

Francescato, D. & Ghirelli, G. (1992). Continuity and creative change: Reflections on 10 years of experience on community psychology training in Italy. *The Community Psychologist*, **25**(2), 15–16.

Francescato, D. & Tomai, M. (2001). Community psychology: Should there be a European perspective? *Journal of Community and Applied Social Psychology*, **11**, 371–80.

Franke, R. & Chasin, B. (1995). Kerala State: A social justice model. *Multinational Monitor*, **16**(7/8). (Available on-line at http://multinationalmonitor.org/hyper/mm0795.08.html).

Franke, R. & Chasin, B. (2000). Is the Kerala model sustainable? Lessons from the past, prospects for the future. In G. Parayil (ed.), *Kerala: The development experience* (pp. 16–39). New York, NY: Zed Books.

Frankenberg, R. (1993). *The social construction of white women, whiteness race matters.* London, UK: Routledge.

Freedman, J. & Combs, G. (1996). *Narrative therapy: The social construction of preferred realities.* New York: W. W. Norton & Co.

Freeman, H. L., Fryers, T. & Henderson, J. H. (1985). *Mental health services in Europe: 10 years on.* Copenhagen, World Health Organisation. Cited In Fattore, G., Percudani, M., Pugnoli, C., Beecham, J. & Contini, A. (2000). Mental health care in Italy: Organisational structure, routine clinical activity and costs of a community psychiatric service in Lombardy region. *International Journal of Social Psychiatry,* **46**, 250–65.

Freeman, J. (1972). The tyranny of structurelessness. *Berkeley Journal of Sociology,* **17**, 151–64.

Freeman, J. (1999). On the origins of social movements. In J. Freeman & V. Johnson (eds), *Cycles of protest: Social movements since the sixties* (pp. 7–24). New York, NY: Rowman & Littlefield.

Freeman, J. & Johnson, V. (eds). (1999). *Waves of protest: Social movements since the sixties.* Boulder, CO: Rowman & Littlefield.

Freire, P. (1970). *Pedagogy of the oppressed.* New York: Seabury Press.

Freire, P. (1972). *Pedagogy of the oppressed.* New York: Herder and Herder.

Freire, P. (1973) *Education for critical consciousness.* New York: Seabury Press.

Freire, P. (1994). *Pedagogy of hope: Reliving pedagogy of the oppressed.* New York: Continuum.

Freire, P. (1997). A response. In P. Freire (ed.), *Mentoring the mentor: A critical dialogue with Paulo Freire* (pp. 303–29). New York: Peter Lang.

Freire, P. & Faundez, A. (1989). *Learning to question: A pedagogy of liberation.* Geneva: World Council of Churches.

Friedman, T. (2000). *The Lexus and the olive tree: Understanding globalization.* New York: Anchor.

Frey, B. & Stutzer, A. (2002). *Happiness and economics.* Princeton, NJ: Princeton University Press.

Froehlich, A.K., Nary, D.E. & White, G.W. (2002). Identifying barriers to participation in physical activity for women with disabilities. *SCI Psychosocial Process,* **15**, 21–9.

Fromm, E. (1965). *Escape from freedom.* New York: Avon Books.

Fromm, E. (1973). *The anatomy of human destructiveness.* New York: Holt, Rinehart and Winston.

Fukuyama, M. A. & Ferguson, A. D. (2000). Lesbian, gay, and bisexual people of color: Understanding cultural complexity and managing multiple oppressions. In R. M. Perez, A. D. Kurt. & J. B. Kathleen (eds), *Handbook of counseling and psychotherapy with lesbian, gay, and bisexual clients* (pp. 81–105). Washington, DC: American Psychological Association.

Gainor, K. A. (2000). Including transgender issues in lesbian, gay, and bisexual psychology: Implications for clinical practice and training. In B. Greene & G. L. Croom (eds), *Education, research, and practice in lesbian, gay, bisexual, and transgendered psychology: A resource manual, Vol. 5* (pp. 131–60). Thousand Oaks: Sage Publications.

Galuzzi, G.-E. (2001). *Racism: Canada's creeping economic apartheid. The economic segregation and social marginalisation of racialised groups.* Toronto, Ontario: Canadian Social Justice Foundation for Research and Education.

Gamble, A. (2001). Political economy. In G. Philo & D. Miller (eds), *Market killing: What the free market does and what social scientists can do about it* (pp. 170–76). London: Pearson Education.

Garbarino, J. & Kostelny, K. (1992). Child maltreatment as a community problem. *Child Abuse and Neglect,* **16**, 455–64.

Garcia, L. (2002). Agroecological education and training. In F. Funes, L. Garcia, N. Perez & P. Rosset (eds), *Sustainable agriculture and resistance: Transforming food production in Cuba* (pp. 90–108). Oakland, CA: Food First Books.

Garland, R. (1995). *The eye of the beholder: Deformity and disability in the Graeco-Roman World.* Ithaca, NY: Cornell University Press.

Garnets, L. D. & D'Augelli, A. R. (1994). Empowering lesbian and gay communities: A call for collaboration with community psychology. *American Journal of Community Psychology.* **22**, 447–70.

Garnets, L., Herek, G. M. & Levy, B. (1990) Violence and victimization of lesbians and gay men: Mental health consequences. *Journal of Interpersonal Violence*, **5**, 366–83.

Gaventa, J. & Cornwall, A. (2001). Power and knowledge. In P. Reason & H. Bradbury (eds), *Handbook of action research: Participative inquiry and practice* (pp. 70–80). London: Sage.

Gavey, N. (1989). Feminist poststructuralism and discourse analysis: Contributions to feminist psychology. *Psychology of Women Quarterly*, **13**, 459–75.

Gavey, N., Lapsley, H. & Cram, F. (eds). (2001). Specal issue on feminist psychology in Aotearoa/New Zealand. *Feminism and Psychology*, **11**(2).

Gay and Lesbian Medical Association and LGBT Health Experts (2001). *Healthy people 2010 companion document for Lesbian, Gay, Bisexual and Transgender (LGBT) health.* San Francisco, CA: Gay and Lesbian Medical Association.

George, R. (2002). *Socioeconomic democracy.* London: Praeger.

Gergen, K. J. (1985). The social constructionist movement in modern psychology. *American Psychologist*, **40**, 266–75.

Gergen, K. J. (2001). Psychological science in a postmodern context. *American Psychologist*, **56**, 803–13.

Gerlach, L. P. (1999). The structure of social movements: Environmental activism and its opponents. In J. Freeman & V. Johnson (eds), *Cycles of protest: Social movements since the sixties* (pp. 85–98). New York, NY: Rowman & Littlefield.

Gershman, J. & Irwin, A. (2000). Getting a grip on the global economy. In J. Yong Kim, J. Millen, A. Irwin & J. Gershman, J. (eds), *Dying for growth: Global inequality and the health of the poor* (pp. 11–43). Monroe, ME: Common Courage Press.

Gibbs, N. (2002, July 22). Season of mistrust. *Time*, 16–21.

Giddens, A. (1994). *Beyond left and right: The future of radical politics.* Stanford, CA: Stanford University Press.

Gilbert, S. W. (Winter, 1996). *Etymologies of humor: Reflections on the humus pile.* Sincronia, http://fuentes.csh.udg.mx/CUCSH/Sincronia/etymolog.htm.

Gilner, J. A. & Sample, P. (1993). *Participatory action research: An approach to evaluate community integration for persons with developmental disabilities.* Paper presented at the Annual Meeting of the American Evaluation Association, Dallas, TX.

Gittell, M., Ortega-Bustamante, I. & Steffy, T. (2000). Social capital and social change: Women's community activism. *Urban Affairs Review*, **36**, 123–48.

Glaser, B. G. & Strauss, A. L. (1967). *Discovery of grounded theory: Strategies for qualitative research.* Chicago: Aldine.

Glidewell, J. C. (1977). Competence and conflict in community psychology. In I. Iscoe, B. Bloom & C. Spielberger (eds), *Community psychology in transition: Proceedings of the national conference on training in community psychology* (pp. 71–6). Washington, DC: Hemisphere/John Wiley.

Glover, M. (1996). *Evidence and health practice Health Research Council consultative conference: A hui report.* [Unpublished report available from the author.]

Glover, M. (2001). *The effectiveness of a Maori noho marae smoking cessation intervention utilising a kaupapa Maori methodology.* Unpublished PhD thesis, University of Auckland.

Glover, M. & Robertson, P. (1997). Facilitating development of Maori Psychology. In. H. Love, H. & W. Whittaker (eds), *Practice issues for clinical and applied psychologists in New Zealand* (pp. 136–46).Wellington: The New Zealand Psychological Society.

Goering, P. N. & Streiner, D. L. (1996). Reconciliable differences: The marriage of qualitative and quantitative methods. *Canadian Journal of Psychiatry*, **41**, 491–7.

Goffman, E. (1963). *Stigma: Notes on the management of spoiled identity.* Englewood Cliffs, NJ: Prentice Hall.

Gokhale, S. D. (1985). Dynamics of attitude change. *International Journal of Social Work*, **28**, 31–9.

Goldenberg, C. & Gallimore, R. (1995). Immigrant Latino parents' values and beliefs about there children's education: Continuities and discontinuities and generations across cultures and generations. *Advances in Motivation and Achievement,* **9,** 183–228.

Goldenberg, I. I. (1971). *Build me a mountain: Youth, poverty, and the creation of new settings.* Cambridge, MA: MIT Press.

Goldenberg, I. I. (1978). *Oppression and social intervention: Essays on the human condition and the problem of change.* Nelson-Hall: Chicago.

Goleman, D. (1995). *Emotional intelligence.* New York: Bantam.

Goleman, D. (1998). *Working with emotional intelligence.* New York: Bantam.

Gonsiorek, J. C. (1993). Threat, stress, and adjustment: Mental health and the workplace for gay and lesbian individuals. In L. Diamant (ed.), *Homosexual issues in the workplace: Series in clinical and community psychology* (pp. 243–64). Washington, DC: Taylor & Francis.

Good, T., Wiley, A., Thomas, R. E., Stewart, E., McCoy, J., Kloos, B., Hunt, G., Moore, T. & Rappaport, J. (1997). Bridging the gap between schools and community: Organizing for family involvement in a low-income neighborhood. *Journal of Educational and Psychological Consultation,* **8,** 277–96.

Goodman, D. (2001). *Promoting diversity and social justice: Educating people from privileged groups.* Thousand Oaks, CA: Sage.

Gottlieb, B. H. (ed.). (1981). *Social networks and social support.* Beverly Hills, CA: Sage.

Gottlieb, B. (2000). Self-help, mutual aid, and support groups among older adults. *Canadian Journal on Aging,* **19**(Suppl. 1), 58–74.

Government of Manitoba. (2001, August). *Family finance: The cost of raising a child:* **2001.** (Available on-line at http://www.gov.mb.ca/agriculture/homeec/cba 28s02.html).

Granovetter, M. (1973). The strength of weak ties. *American Journal of Sociology,* **78,** 1360–80.

Grant, M. (1919). *The passing of the great race* (revised edn). New York: Scribner.

Gray, A. (ed.). (2001). *World health and disease.* Buckingham: Open University Press.

Gray, R. E., Fitch, M., Davis, C. & Phillips, C. (2000). Challenges of particpatory research: Reflections on a study with breast cancer self-help groups. *Health Expectations,* **3,** 243–52.

Green, J. (1999). The spirit of willing: Collective identity and the development of the Christian Right. In J. Freeman & V. Johnson (eds), *Cycles of protest: Social movements since the sixties* (pp. 153–68). New York, NY: Rowman & Littlefield.

Greenberg, M. T., Domitrovich, C. & Bumbarger, B. (2001). The prevention of mental disorders in school-aged children: Current state of the field. *Prevention and Treatment,* **4,** Article 1.

Greene, B. (2000). Beyond heterosexualism and across the cultural divide: Developing an inclusive lesbian, gay, and bisexual psychology: A look to the future. In B. Greene & G. L. Croom (eds), *Education, research, and practice in lesbian, gay, bisexual, and transgendered psychology: A resource manual,* Vol. 5. (pp. 1–45). Thousand Oaks, CA: Sage Publications.

Greene, J. C. (2000). Understanding social programs through evaluation. In N. K. Denzin & Y. S. Lincoln (eds), *Handbook of qualitative research* (2nd edn, pp. 981–99). Thousand Oaks, CA: Sage.

Guba, E. G. & Lincoln, Y. S. (1989). *Fourth generation evaluation.* Newbury Park, CA: Sage.

Guba, E. G. & Lincoln, Y. S. (1994). Competing paradigms in qualitative research. In N. K. Denzin & Y. S. Lincoln (eds), *Handbook of qualitative research* (1st edn, pp. 105–17). Thousand Oaks, CA: Sage.

Gurin, G., Veroff, J. & Feld, S. (1960). *Americans view their mental health.* New York: Basic Books.

Habermas, J. (1971). *Knowledge and human interests.* Boston: Beacon.

Habermas, J. (1975). *Legitimation crisis.* Boston: Beacon.

Hage, G. (1998). *White nation: Fantasies of white supremacy in a multicultural society.* Sydney, Australia: Pluto Press.

Hahn, A. (1994). *The politics of caring: Human services at the local level.* Boulder, CO: Westview Press.

Hahn, H. (1988). The politics of personal differences: Disability and discrimination. *Journal of Social Issues,* **44**, 39–47.

Haley, A. (1977). *Roots: The saga of an American family.* New York: Dell.

Hall, B. (1993). Introduction. In P. Park, M. Brydon-Miller, B. Hall & T. Jackson (eds). *Voices of change: Participatory research in the United States and Canada* (pp. xiv–xii). Westport, CT: Bergen & Garvey.

Hall, M. F. (1995). *Poor people's social movement organizations.* London: Praeger.

Hallman, D. (1987). The Nestlé boycott: The success of a citizen's coalition in social intervention. In E. M. Bennett (ed.), *Social intervention: Theory and practice* (pp. 187–229). Lewiston, NY: The Edwin Mellen Press.

Hallman, D. (2000). *Spiritual values for earth community.* Geneva: WCC Publications.

Han, S. (2001). Gay identity disclosure to parents by Asian American gay men. *Dissertation Abstracts International. 62(1–A),* 329.

Hancock, T. (1993). Health, human development and the community ecosystem: Three ecological models. *Health Promotion International,* **8**(1), 41–7.

Harding, C. M., Zubin, J. & Strauss, J. S. (1987). Chronicity in schizophrenia: Fact, partial fact, or artifact? *Hospital and Community Psychiatry,* **38**, 477–86.

Harding, S. (1987a). Conclusion: Epistemological questions. In S. Harding (ed.), *Feminism and methodology: Social science issues* (pp. 181–90). Bloomington, IN: University of Indiana Press.

Harding, S. (1987b). Introduction: Is there a feminist method? In S. Harding (ed.), *Feminism and methodology: Social science issues* (pp. 1–14). Bloomington, IN: Indiana University Press.

Harding, S. (1991). *Whose science? Whose knowledge? Thinking from women's lives.* Ithaca, NY: Cornell University Press.

Harding, S. (1993). Rethinking standpoint epistemology: What is 'strong objectivity'? In L. Alcoff & E. Potter (eds), *Feminist epistemologies* (pp. 49–82). New York: Routledge.

Hardt, M. & Negri, A. (2000). *Empire.* Cambridge, MA: Harvard University Press.

Hare-Mustin, R. T. & Maracek, J. (1988). The meaning of difference: Gender theory, postmodernism, and psychology. *American Psychologist,* **43**, 455–64.

Hare-Mustin, R. T. & Maracek, J. (1997). Abnormal psychology: The politics of madness. In D. Fox & I. Prilleltensky (eds), *Critical psychology: An introduction* (pp. 104–20). London: Sage.

Harper, G. W. (2001). Contextual factors that perpetuate statutory rape: The influence of gender roles, sexual socialization, and sociocultural factors. *DePaul Law Review,* **50**, 897–918.

Harper, G. W., Bangi, A. K., Contreras, R., Pedraza, A., Tolliver, M. & Vess, L. (2004). Diverse phases of collaboration: Working together to improve community-based HIV interventions for adolescents. *American Journal of Community Psychology. 33,* 193–204.

Harper, G. W. & Schneider, M. (2003). Oppression and discrimination among lesbian, gay, bisexual, and transgendered people and communities: A challenge for community psychology. *American Journal of Community Psychology,* **31**, 243–52.

Haugaard, M. (1997). *The constitution of power: A theoretical analysis of power, knowledge and structure.* New York: Manchester University Press.

Hazel, K. L. & Mohatt, G. V. (2001). Cultural and spiritual coping in sobriety: Informing substance abuse prevention for Alaska Native communities. *Journal of Community Psychology,* **29**, 541–62.

Health Canada. (1999, December). *A look at families participating in CAPC programs*. Community Action Program for Children National Newsletter describing findings from CAPC's national impact evaluation. (Available on-line at http://www.hc-sc.gc.ca/hppb/childhood-youth/cbp/capc/evaluation/Newsletter_dec99.htm).

Health Canada. (2001, August). *Community Action Program for Children: National Program Profile (NPP) Cycle 1: Summary Report*. (Available on-line at http://www.hcsc.gc.ca/hppb/childhoodyouth/cbp/capc/evaluation/pdf/npp.pdf).

Heath, G. W. & Fentem, P. H. (1997). Physical activity among persons with disabilities: A public health perspective. *Exercise and Sports Sciences Reviews, 25*, 195–234.

Heise, L. (1993). Violence against women: The missing agenda. In M. Koblunsky, J. Timyan & J. Gay (eds), *The health of women: A global perspective* (pp. 171–95). Westview Press.

Held, D. (1980). *Introduction to critical theory: Horkheimer to Habermas*. Berkeley, CA: University of California Press.

Heller, K. & Monahan, J. (1977). *Psychology and community change*. Homewood, Ill: The Dorsey Press.

Heller, K. & Swindle, R. W. (1983). Social networks, perceived social support, and coping with stress. In R. D. Felner, L. A. Jason, J. Moritsugu & S. S. Farber , (eds), *Preventive psychology: Theory, research and practice* (pp. 87–103). New York: Pergamon.

Herdt, G. (1998). *Same sex, different cultures: Exploring gay and lesbian lives*. Boulder, CA: Westview Press.

Herek, G. M. (1991) Stigma, prejudice, and violence against lesbians and gay men. In J. C. Gonsiorek & J. D. Weinrich (eds), *Homosexuality: Research implications for public policy* (pp. 60–80). Newbury Park, CA: Sage Publications.

Herek, G. M. (1992). Psychological heterosexism and anti-gay violence: The social psychology of bigotry and bashing. In K. T. Berrill & G. M. Herek (eds), *Hate crimes: Confronting violence against lesbians and gay men* (pp. 149–69). London: Sage Publications.

Herek, G. M. (1995). Psychological heterosexism in the United States. In A. R. D'Augelli & C. J. Patterson (eds), *Lesbian, gay, and bisexual identities over the lifespan: Psychological perspectives*. (pp. 321–46). New York: Oxford University Press.

Herek, G. M., Gillis, J. R. & Cogan, J. C. (1999). Psychological sequelae of hate-crime victimization among lesbian, gay, and bisexual adults. *Journal of Consulting and Clinical Psychology, 67*, 945–51.

Herek, G. M., Kimmel, D. C., Amaro, H. & Melton, G. B. (1991). Avoiding heterosexist bias in psychological research. *American Psychologist, 44*, 957–63.

Hermans, H. J. M. & Kempen, H. J. G. (1998). Moving cultures: The perilous problem of cultural dichotomies in a globalizing society. *American Psychologist, 53*, 1111–20.

Hertzman, C. (1999). Population health and human development. In D. P. Keating & C. Hertzman (eds), *Developmental health and the wealth of nations: Social, biological, and educational dynamics* (pp. 21–40). New York: The Guilford Press.

Hicks, R., Lalonde, R. N. & Pepler, D. (1993). Psychosocial considerations in the mental health of immigrant and refugee children. *Canadian Journal of Community Mental Health, 12*(2): 71–87.

Hill Collins, P. (1991). *Black feminist thought: Knowledge, consciousness, and the politics of empowerment*. New York: Routledge.

Hill Collins, P. (1993). Black feminist thought in the matrix of domination. In C. Lemert (ed.), *Social theory: The multicultural and classic readings* (pp. 615–26). San Francisco: Westview.

Hilliard, A. G. (1998). *SBA: The reawakening of the African mind*. Gainesville, FL: Makare Publishing.

Himmelman, A. (2001). On coalitions and the transformation of power relations: Collaborative betterment and collaborative empowerment. *American Journal of Community Psychology, 29*, 277–84.

Hirsch, E. L. (1999). Sacrifice for the cause: Group processes, recruitment, and commitment in a student social movement. In J. Freeman & V. Johnson (eds), *Cycles of protest: Social movements since the sixties* (pp. 47–64). New York: Rowman & Littlefield.

Hofstede, G. (1980). *Cultures consequences.* Beverly Hills, CA: Sage.

Holland, S. (1988). Defining and experimenting with prevention. In S. Ramon & M.Giannichedda (eds), *Psychiatry in transition: The British and Italian experiences* (pp. 125–37). London: Pluto Press.

Holland, S. (1991). From private symptom to public action. *Feminism and Psychology,* **1**, 58–62.

Holland, S. (1992). From social abuse to social action: A neighbourhood psychotherapy and social action project for women. *Changes: An International Journal of Psychology and Psychotherapy,* **10**, 146–53.

Hollander, N. C. (1997). *Love in a time of hate: Liberation psychology in Latin America.* New Brunswick, NJ: Rutgers University Press.

Hollway, W. (1991). *Work psychology and organizational behaviour.* London: Sage.

Home Office (2002). *Building cohesive communities: A report of the ministerial group on public order and community cohesion.* Retrieved October 6, 2002, from http://www.homeoffice.gov.uk/new_indexs/index_community_cohesion.htm.

hooks, b. (1990). *Yearning: Race, gender, and cultural politics.* Boston: South End Press.

hooks, b. (2000). *All about love: New visions.* New York: Harper Collins.

hooks, b. (2002). *Communion: The female search for love.* New York: Harper Collins.

Horney, K. (1937). *The neurotic personality of our time.* New York: Norton.

Horacek, J. (1994). Unrequited love Nos 31 & 70. *Unrequited love,* Nos. 1–100. Melbourne, McPhee Gribble.

Howitt, D. & Owusu-Bempah, J. (1994). *The racism of psychology: Time for a change.* London: Harvester and Wheatsheaf.

Hughes, D., Seidman, E. & Williams, N. (1993). Cultural phenomena and the research enterprise: Toward a culturally anchored methodology. *American Journal of Community Psychology,* **21**, 687–703.

Hughes, K.P. (1994). *Contemporary Australian feminism.* Melbourne: Longman Cheshire.

Hughey, J. & Speer, P. (2002). Community, sense of community, and networks. In A. Fisher, C. Sonn & B. Bishop (eds), *Psychological sense of community: Research, applications, and implications* (pp. 69–84). New York: Kluwer Academic/Plenum Publishers.

Hulchanski, D. (1998). *Homelessness in Canada:* **1998** *report to the United Nations.* Available from http://www.tdrc.net/.

Hulchanski, D. (2002). *Can Canada afford to help cities, provide social housing, and end homelessness? Why are provincial governments doing so little?* Available from http://www.tdrc.net/.

Humphreys, K. (1997). Individual and social benefits of mutual aid self-help groups. *Social Policy,* **27**, 12–19.

Humphreys, K., Mavis, B. E. & Stoffelmayr, B. E. (1994). Are Twelve Step programs appropriate for disenfranchised groups? Evidence from a study of posttreatment mutual help involvement. *Prevention in Human Services,* **11**, 165–79.

Humphreys, K. & Moos, R. H. (1996). Reduced substance-abuse-related health care costs among voluntary participants in Alcoholics Anonymous. *Psychiatric Services,* **47**, 709–13.

Humphreys, K. & Rappaport, J. (1993). From the community mental health movement to the war on drugs: A study in the definition of social problems. *American Psychologist,* **48**, 892–901.

Humphreys, K. & Rappaport, J. (1994). Researching self-help/mutual aid groups and organizations: Many roads, one journey. *Applied and Preventive Psychology,* **3**, 217–31.

Hunter, E. (1997). *Double talk: Changing and conflicting constructions of indigenous mental health.* Paper presented to the National Conference on Mental Health Services, Policy and Law Reform in the 21st century. University of Newcastle.

Hunter, S., Shannon, C., Knox, J. & Martin, J. I. (1998). *Lesbian, gay, and bisexual youths and adults: Knowledge for human services practice.* Thousand Oaks, CA: Sage.

Hutchison, P. & Pedlar, A. (1999). Independent Living Centres: An innovation with mental health implications? *Canadian Journal of Community Mental Health,* **18**(2): 21–32.

Huygens, I. (1988). *Empowering our natural communities: An alternative to prevention.* Paper presented at the 24th International Congress of Psychology, Sydney, Australia.

Huygens, I. (1995). *Depowering the powerful – beyond empowerment: Community Psychology's avoidance of world empowerment patterns.* Poster presentation to 5th Biennial Conference of the Society for Community Research and Action, Chicago, IL.

Huygens, I. (1996a). *Anti-racism education: Example of a partnership protocol.* Project Waitangi, Aotearoa, New Zealand.

Huygens, I. (1996b). *Gender safety: Example of a partnership protocol.* Men's Action, Hamilton and Women's Refuges, Aotearoa, New Zealand.

Huygens, I. (1997). *Towards social change partnerships: Responding to empowerment of oppressed groups with voluntary depowerment of dominant groups.* Paper presented at the Biennial Conference of the Society for Community Research and Action, Columbia, South Carolina.

Huygens, I. (1999). An accountability model for Pakeha practitioners. In *Proceedings of Maori and Psychology Research seminar,* University of Waikato: Maori and Psychology Research Unit.

Huygens, I. (2001a). *Journeys away from dominance: Dissonance, struggle and right relationships – the journey to accepting indigenous authority.* Paper presented at the 8th Biennial Conference of the Society for Community Research and Action, Atlanta, Georgia, June, 2001.

Huygens, I. (2001b). Feminist attempts at power-sharing in Aotearoa: Embarrassing herstory or significant learning towards Treaty-based structures? *Feminism & Psychology,* **11**, 393–400.

Huygens, I. & Sonn, C. C. (2000). International community psychology: Stories about reflection and self transformation in the pursuit of social justice. *The Community Psychologist,* **33**(2): 24–5.

Ife, J. (2002). *Community development: Community-based alternatives in an age of globalization.* Frenchs Forest, NSW: Pearson Education Australia.

Institute of Medicine. (1994). *Reducing risks for mental disorders: Frontiers for preventive intervention research.* Washington, DC: National Academy Press.

Institute of Medicine. (1999). *Lesbian health: Current assessment and directions for the future.* Washington, DC: National Academy Press.

International Gay and Lesbian Human Rights Commission (1999). *Sexual orientation and the human rights mechanisms of the United Nations: Examples and approaches.* San Francisco, CA: Author.

International Gay and Lesbian Human Rights Commission (2001, June 5). *Historic progress at the United Nations.* Retrieved June 29, 2002, from http://www.iglhrc.org/.

Iscoe, I. (1974). Community psychology and the competent community. *American Psychologist,* **29**, 607–13.

Isenberg, D., Loomis, C., Humphreys, K. & Maton, K. I. (2004). Self-help research: Issues of power sharing. In L. Jason, C. Keys, Y. Suarez-Balcazar, R. Taylor, M. Davis, J. Durlak & D. Isenberg (eds), *Participatory community research: Theories and methods in action,* (pp. 123–37). Washington, DC: American Psychological Association.

Ivey, A. & Ivey, M. (2003). *Intentional interviewing and counselling: Facilitating client development in a multicultural society.* Pacific Grove, CA: Brooks/Cole.

Ivey, A. E., Ivey, M. B. & Simek-Morgan, L. (1993). *Counselling and psychotherapy: A multicultural perspective* (3rd edn). Boston, MA: Allyn & Bacon.

Jackson, H. & Mupedziswa, R. (1988). Disability and rehabilitation. *Journal of Social Development in Africa*, **3**, 21–30.

Jackson, M. (1996). Maori health research and the Treaty of Waitangi. In Te Ropu Rangahau Hauora a Eru Pomare. (ed.), *Hui whakapiripiri: A hui to discuss strategic directions for Maori health research* (pp. 8–10). Wellington, NZ: Wellington School of Medicine.

Jackson, W. (1997). Call for a revolution in agriculture. In H. Hannum (ed.), *People, land and community: Collected E. F. Schumacher Society Lectures* (pp. 250–64). New Haven: Yale University Press.

Jacobs, S. E., Thomas, W. & Lang, S. (1997). *Two-spirit people: Native American gender identity, sexuality, and spirituality.* Urbana, IL: University of Illinois Press.

Jacobson, N. & Greeley, D. (2001). What is recovery? A conceptual model and explication. *Psychiatric Services*, **52**, 482–85.

Jaggar, A. L. (1994). Introduction: Living with contradictions. In A. L. Jaggar (ed.), *Living with contradictions: Controversies in feminist and social ethics* (pp. 1–12). San Francisco: Westview Press.

Jagose, A. (1996). *An introduction to queer theory.* New York: New York University Press.

James, S. & Prilleltensky, I. (2002). Cultural diversity and mental health: Towards integrative practice. *Clinical Psychology Review*, **22**, 1133–54.

Janvry, A. & Sadoulet, E. (2001). Has aggregate income growth been effective in reducing poverty and inequality in Latin America? In N. Lustig (ed.), *Shielding the poor: Social protection in the developing world* (pp. 21–39). Washington, DC: Brookings Institution Press/Inter-American Development Bank.

Jason, L., Keys, C., Suarez-Balcazar, Y., Taylor, R., Davis, M., Durlak, J. & Isenberg, D. (eds). (2004). *Participatory community research: Theories and methods in action.* Washington, DC: American Psychological Association.

Jason, L. A., King, C., Frankenberry, E. L., Jordon, K. M., Tryon, W. W., Rademaker, R. & Huang, C. F. (1999). Chronic fatigue syndrome: Assessing symptoms and activity level. *Journal of Clinical Psychology*, **55**, 411–24.

Jason, L. A., Taylor, R. R. & Kennedy, C. L. (2000). Chronic fatigue syndrome, fibromyalgia, and multiple chemical sensitivities in a community-based sample of persons with chronic fatigue syndrome-like symptoms. *Psychosomatic Medicine*, **62**, 655–63.

Jenkins, J. C. (1999). The transformation of a constituency into a social movement revisited. In J. Freeman & V. Johnson (eds), *Cycles of protest: Social movements since the sixties* (pp. 277–302). New York: Rowman & Littlefield.

Joffe, J. (1996). Looking for the causes of the causes. *Journal of Primary Prevention*, **17**, 201–7.

John, I. D. (1998). The scientist-practitioner model: A critical examination. *Australian Psychologist*, **33**, 24–30.

John, M. (2003). *Children's rights and power.* London: Jessica Kingsley.

Johnson, D. & Johnson, F. (2000). *Joining together: Group theory and group skills.* London: Allyn and Bacon.

Jones, J. (1997). *Prejudice and racism* (2nd edn). New York: McGraw-Hill.

Joppke, C. (1999). How immigration is citizenship: A comparative view. *Ethnic and Racial Studies*, **22**, 629–52.

Jordan, J., Kaplan, A., Miller, J. B., Stiver, I. & Surrey, J. (1991). *Women's growth in connection: Writings from the Stone Center.* New York: Guilford Press.

Julnes, G., Pang, D., Takemoto-Chock, N., Speidel, G. E. & Tharp, R. G. (1987). The process of training in processes. *Journal of Community Psychology*, **15**, 387–96.

Kagan, C. (1995). *Regional development in health and social services in the U.K. 'Edge effects' and sustainable change in welfare organisations.* Manchester: IOD Research Group.

Kagan, C. (1997). *Regional development for inclusion: Community development and learning disabled people in the north west of England.* Manchester: IOD Research Group

Kagan, C. & Burton, M (2000). Prefigurative action research: An alternative basis for critical psychology. *Annual Review of Critical Psychology,* **2**, 73–87.

Kagan, C., Caton, S. & Amin, A. (2001). *The need for witness support: Report of a feasibility study in Heartlands, Northtown.* Manchester: COP Research Group.

Kagan, C., Lawthom, R., Knowles, K. & Burton, M., (2001). *Community activism, participation and social capital on a peripheral housing estate.* Manchester: COP Research Group.

Kagan, C. & Scott-Roberts, S. (2002). *Family based intervention in the slums of Kolkata for children with cerebral palsy and their inclusion in the community: Community psychology and community occupational therapy perspectives.* Manchester: COP Research Group.

Kagitcibasi, C. (1996). *Family and human development across cultures: A view from the other side.* Mahwah, NJ: Lawrence Erlbaum Associates.

Kahn, S. (1982). *Organizing.* Toronto: McGraw Hill.

Kamerman, S. B. (1996). Child and family policies: An international perspective. In E. F. Zigler, S. L. Kagan & N. W. Hall (eds), *Children, families and government: Preparing for the twenty-first century* (pp. 31–48). Cambridge, MA: Cambridge University Press.

Kane, L. (2001). *Popular education and social change in Latin America.* London: Latin America Bureau.

Kane, R. (1994). *Through the moral maze: Searching for absolute values in a pluralistic world.* New York: Paragon.

Kane, R. (1998). Dimensions of value and the aims of social inquiry. *American Behavioral Scientist,* **41**, 578–97.

Kaner, S. (1996). *Facilitator's guide to participatory decision making.* Vancouver: New Society.

Kannan, K. (2000). Poverty alleviation as advancing basic human capabilities: Kerala's achievements compared. In G. Parayil (ed.), *Kerala: The development experience* (pp. 40–65). New York: Zed Books.

Kanungo, R. & Mendonca, M. (1996). *Ethical dimensions of leadership.* London: Sage.

Kaplan, G., Pamuk, E., Lynch, J., Cohen, R. & Balfour, J. (1996). Inequality in income and mortality in the United States: Analysis of mortality and potential pathways. *British Medical Journal,* **312**, 999–1003.

Karlsen, J. I. (1991). Action research as method: Reflections from a program for developing methods and competence. In W. F. Whyte, (ed.) *Participatory action research* (pp. 143–58). Newbury Park, CA: Sage Publications.

Katsiaficas, G. (1997). *The subversion of politics: European autonomous social movements and the decolonisation of everyday life.* Amherst, NY: Humanity Books.

Kawachi, I. & Kennedy, B. (1999). Social capital and self-rated health: A contextual analysis. *American Journal of Public Health,* **89**, 1187–94.

Kawachi, I., Kennedy, B. & Wilkinson, R. (eds). (1999). *The society and population health reader: Income inequality and health.* New York: The New Press.

Kaye, H. S. (1998). Is the status of people with disabilities improving? *Disability Statistics Abstract,* number 21. Washington, DC: National Institute on Disability and Rehabilitation Research.

Kaye, H. S. & Longmore, P. K. (1997). *Disability watch: The status of people with disabilities in the United States.* Volcano, CA: Volcano Press.

Keane, M. (1990). Contemporary beliefs about mental illness among medical students: Implications for education and practice. *Academic Psychiatry,* **14**, 172–7.

Keating, D. P. & Hertzman, C. (eds). (1999a). *Developmental health and the wealth of nations: Social, biological, and educational dynamics.* New York: The Guilford Press.

Keating D. P. & Hertzman, C. (1999b). Modernity's paradox. In D. Keating & C. Hertzman (eds), *Developmental health and the wealth of nations* (pp. 1–17). New York: Guilford.

Keating, P. (1993). International year for the world's indigenous peoples: Launch speech. *Aboriginal Law Bulletin*, 3 (64), 4–6.

Kekes, J. (1993). *The morality of pluralism*. Princeton, NJ: Princeton University Press.

Kelly, J. G. (1966). Ecological constraints on mental health services. *American Psychologist*, 21, 535–9.

Kelly, J. G. (1970). Toward an ecological conception of preventative interventions. In D. Adelson & B. Kalis (eds), *Community psychology and mental health* (pp. 126–45). Scranton, PA: Chandler.

Kelly, J. G. (1971). Qualities for the community psychologist. *American Psychologist*, 26, 897–903.

Kelly, J. G. (1979). 'Tain't what you do, it's the way you do it.' *American Journal of Community Psychology*, 7, 244–58.

Kelly, J. G. (1986). An ecological paradigm: Defining mental health consultation as preventive service. *Prevention in Human Services*, 4(3/4): 1–36.

Kelly, J. G. (1990). Changing contexts and the field of community psychology. *American Journal of Community Psychology*, 14, 581–605.

Kelly, J. G. (2003). Science and community psychology: Social norms for pluralistic inquiry. *American Journal of Community Psychology*, 31, 213–17.

Kelman, H. C. & Warwick, D. P. (1978). The ethics of social intervention: Goals, means, and consequences. In G. Bermant, H. C. Kelman & D. P. Warwick (eds), *The ethics of social intervention* (pp. 3–33). New York: Halstead Press.

Kennedy, B., Kawachi, I. & Prothrow-Stith, D. (1996). Income distribution and mortality: Cross sectional ecological study of the Robin Hood Index in the United States. *British Medical Journal*, 312, 1004–7.

Kessler, R. C., Mickelson, K. D. & Zhao, S. (1997). Patterns and correlates of self-help group membership in the United States. *Social Policy*, 27, 27–46.

Keupp, H. & Stark, W. (1992). Community psychology and the Federal Democratic Republic of Germany. *The Community Psychologist*, 25(2): 21–3.

Keys, C. & Frank, S. (1987). Community psychology and the study of organizations: A reciprocal relationship. *American Journal of Community Psychology*, 15, 239–51.

Kidder, L. H. & Fine, M. (1997). Qualitative inquiry in psychology: A radical tradition. In D. Fox & I. Prilleltensky (eds), *Critical psychology: An introduction* (pp. 34–50). London: Sage.

Kidner, D. W. (1994). Why psychology is mute about the environmental crisis. *Environmental Ethics*, 16, 359–76.

Kieffer, C. (1984). Citizen empowerment: A developmental perspective. *Prevention in Human Services*, 3, 9–35.

Kiesler, C. A. (1992). U.S. mental health policy: Doomed to fail. *American Psychologist*, 47, 1077–82.

Kilgour, R. & Keefe, V. (1992). *Kia piki te ora: The collection of Maori health statistics*. Wellington: Department of Health.

Kim, J. K., Millen, J. V., Irwin, A. & Gersham, J. (eds). (2000). *Dying for growth: Global inequality and the health of the poor*. Monroe, ME: Common Courage Press.

Kingree, J. B. (2000). Predictors and by-products of participation in a mutual help group for adult children of alcoholics. *Alcoholism Treatment Quarterly* 18(2): 83–94.

Kingree, J. B. & Thompson M. (2000). Mutual help groups, perceived status benefits, and well-being: A test with adult children of alcoholics with personal substance abuse problems. *American Journal of Community Psychology*, 28, 325–42.

Kirpatrick, F. G. (1986). *Community: A trinity of models*. Washington, DC: Georgetown University Press.

Kirton, J. D. (1997). *Paakeha/Tauiwi: Seeing the unseen: Critical analysis of links between discourse, identity, 'blindness' and encultured racism*. Kirikiriroa/Hamilton: Waikato Antiracism Coalition.

Kitzinger, C. (1991). Feminism, psychology and the paradox of power. *Feminism and Psychology*, 1, 111–29.

Kitzinger, C. (1996). Speaking of oppression: Psychology, politics, and the language of power. In E. D. Rothblum & L. A. Bond (eds), *Preventing heterosexism and homophobia: Primary prevention of psychopathology, Vol. 17* (pp. 3–19). Thousand Oaks, CA: Sage Publications.

Kitzinger, C. (1997). Lesbian and gay psychology: A critical analysis. In D. Fox & I. Prilleltensky (eds), *Critical psychology: An introduction* (pp. 202–16). Thousand Oaks, CA: Sage Publications.

Klandersmans, B. (1997). *The social psychology of protest*. Oxford, UK: Blackwell.

Klein, K., Ralls, R. S., Smith Major, V. & Douglas, C. (2000). Power and participation in the workplace: Implications for empowerment theory, research, and practice. In J. Rappaport & E. Seidman (eds), *Handbook of community psychology* (pp. 273–95). New York: Klewer Academic/Plenum.

Klein, N. (September 21, 2002). *Globe & Mail*, F3.

Kloos, B., McCoy, J., Stewart, E., Thomas, E., Wiley, A., Good, T., Hunt, G., Moore, T. & Rappaport, J. (1997). Bridging the gap: A community-based, open-systems approach to neighborhood and school consultation. *Journal of Educational and Psychological Consultation*, 8, 175–96.

Kloos, B. & Moore, T. (2000). The prospect and purpose of locating community research and action in religious settings. *Journal of Community Psychology*, 28, 119–37.

Kloos, B., Zimmerman, S. O., Scrimenti, K. & Crusto, C. (2002). Landlords as partners for promoting success in supported housing: 'It takes more than a lease and a key.' *Psychiatric Rehabilitation Journal*, 25, 235–44.

Korbin, J. E. & Coulton, C. J. (1996). The role of neighbors and the government in neighborhood-based child protection. *Journal of Social Issues*, 52, 163–76.

Korten, D. (1995). *When corporations rule the world*. San Francisco: Berrett-Koehler/Kumarian Press.

Korten, D. (1999). *The post corporate world*. San Francisco: Berrett Koehler/Kumarian Press.

Korten, D. (2001). *When corporations rule the world* (2nd edn). Bloomfield, CT: Berrett-Koehler.

Kretzmann, J. P. & McKnight, J. L. (1993) *Building communities from the inside out: A path toward findings and mobilizing a community's assets*. Chicago, IL: ACTA Publications.

Krogh, K. (1998). A conceptual framework of community partnerships: Perspectives of people with disabilities on power, beliefs, and values. *Canadian Journal of Rehabilitation*, 12(2): 123–34.

Kutchins, H. & Kirk, S.A. (1997). *Making us crazy – DSM: The psychiatric bible and the creation of mental disorders*. New York: The Free Press.

Kyrouz, E. & Humphreys, K. (1997). Do health care work places affect treatment environments? *Journal of Community and Applied Social Psychology*, 7, 105–8.

Ladson-Billings, G. (1997). I know why this doesn't feel empowering: A critical *race* analysis of critical pedagogy. In P. Freire (ed.), *Mentoring the mentor: A critical dialogue with Paulo Freire* (pp. 127–41). New York: Peter Lang.

Lafromboise, T., Coleman, H. & Gerton, J. (1993). Psychological impact of biculturalism: Evidence and theory. *Psychological Bulletin*, 114, 395–412.

Lalonde, M. (1974). *A new perspective for the health of Canadians*. Ottawa: Health and Welfare Canada.

Lamb, H. R. (1993). Lessons learned from deinstitutionalization in the U.S. *British Journal of Psychiatry*, 162, 587–92.

Lamb, H. R. & Zusman, J. (1979). Primary prevention in perspective. *American Journal of Psychiatry*, 136, 12–17.

Lambda Legal Defense and Education Fund (2001, April 20). *Nebraska's highest court unanimously holds sheriff accountable for Brandon Teena's death.* Retrieved June 29, 2002, from http://www.lambdalegal.org/cgibin/iowa/documents/record?record=825.

Lambda Legal Defense and Education Fund (2003, October 1). *Anti-discrimination.* Retrieved October 1, 2003 from http://www.lambdalegal.org/cgibin/iowa/issues/record?record=18.

Lappé, F. M. & DuBois, P. M. (1994). *The quickening of America: Rebuilding our nation, remaking our lives.* San Francisco: Jossey-Bass.

Lappé, F. M. & Lappé, A. (2002). *Hope's edge: The next diet for a small planet.* New York: Tarcher/Putnam.

Laue, J. & Cormick, G. (1978). The ethics of intervention in community disputes. In G. Bermant, H. C. Kelman & D. P. Warwick (eds), *The ethics of social intervention* (pp. 205–31). New York: Halstead Press.

Lavalette, M. & Pratt, A. (eds). (1997). *Social policy: A conceptual and theoretical orientation.* London: Sage.

Lavoie, F., Borkman, T. & Gidron, B. (1994a). Self-help and mutual aid groups: International and multicultural perspectives – Part I [special issue]. *Prevention in Human Services,* **11**(1).

Lavoie, F., Borkman, T. & Gidron, B. (1994b). Self-help and mutual aid groups: International and multicultural perspectives – Part II [special issue]. *Prevention in Human Services,* **11**(2).

Lavoie, F., Vézina, L., Piché, C. & Boivin, M. (1995). Evaluation of a prevention program for violence in teen dating relationships. *Journal of Interpersonal Violence,* **10**, 517–25.

Lawthom, R. (1999). Using the 'F' word in organizational psychology: Foundations for critical feminist research. *Annual Review of Critical Psychology,* **1**, 67–82.

Lazarus, R. S. & DeLongis, A. (1983). Psychological stress and coping in aging. *American Psychologist,* **38**, 245–54.

Lazarus, R. & Folkman, S. (1984). *Stress, appraisal and coping.* New York: Springer.

Lederer, G. (1986). Protest movements as a form of political action. In M. Hermann (ed.), *Political psychology* (pp. 355–78). San Francisco, CA: Jossey-Bass.

Ledwith, M. (2001). Community work as critical pedagogy: Re-envisioning Freire and Gramsci. *Community Development Journal,* **36**, 171–86.

Leighton, D. C. (1979). Community integration and mental health: Documenting social change through longitudinal research. In R. F. Muñoz, L. R. Snowdon & J. G. Kelly (eds), *Social and psychological research in community settings* (pp. 275–304). San Francisco: Jossey-Bass.

Leighton, D. C., Harding, J. S., Macklin, D. B., MacMillan, A. M. & Leighton, A. H. (1963). *The character of danger.* New York: Basic Books.

Lemos, G. (2000). *Homelessness and loneliness – the want of conviviality.* London: Crisis.

Leonard, P. (1984). *Personality and ideology: Towards a materialist understanding of the individual.* London: Macmillan.

Leonard, P. (1994). Knowledge/power and postmodernism: Implications for the practice of a critical social work education. *Canadian Social Work Review,* **11**, 11–26.

Leonard, P. (1997). *Postmodern welfare: Reconstructing an emancipatory project.* London: Sage.

Lerner, H. G. (1985). *The dance of anger.* New York: Harper & Row.

Lerner, M. (1996). *The politics of meaning.* New York: Addison-Wesley.

Levin, S. A. (1999). *Fragile dominion: Complexity and the commons.* Reading, MA: Persus Books.

Levine, A. (1982). *Love Canal: Science, politics, and people.* Lexington, MA: Heath.

Levine, M. (1998). Prevention and community. *American Journal of Community Psychology,* **26**, 189–206.

Levine, M. & Levine, A. (1970). *A social history of helping services*. New York: Appleton-Century-Crofts.

Levine, M. & Levine, A. (1992). *Helping children: A social history*. Oxford: Oxford University Press.

Levine, M. & Perkins, D. V. (1987). *Principles of community psychology: Perspectives and applications*. New York: Oxford University Press.

Levine, M. & Perkins, D. V. (1997). *Principles of community psychology: Perspectives and applications* (2nd edn). New York: Oxford University Press.

Levitas, R. (1998). *The inclusive society? Social exclusion and new labour*. Basingstoke: Macmillan.

Levy, C. W. (1988). *A people's history of the independent living movement*. Lawrence, KS: Research and Training Center on Independent Living.

Levy, L. (2000). Self-help groups. In J. Rappaport & E. Seidman (eds), *Handbook of community psychology* (pp. 591–613). New York: Kluwer Academic/Plenum Publishers.

Lewin, K. (1946). Action research and minority problems. *Journal of Social Issues*, **2**, 34–46.

Lewis, J. A., Lewis, D. M., Daniels, J. A. & D'Andrea, M. J. (2003). *Community counseling: Empowerment strategies for a diverse society* (3rd edn). Pacific Grove, CA: Brooks/Cole.

Lewis, R. (2001). *The construction of identity through the dimensions of race, ethnicity and gender: The experience of 'Coloured' South African women in Western Australia*. Unpublished PhD data, Edith Cowan University. Perth, Australia.

LGA (2002). *Draft guidance on community cohesion*. Retrieved October 6 2002 from http://www.homeoffice.gov.uk/cpd/ccu/commcohe.pdf.

Lincoln, Y. S. & Guba, E. G. (1985). *Naturalistic inquiry*. Newbury Park, CA: Sage.

Lincoln, Y. S. & Guba, E. (1986). But is it rigorous? Trustworthiness and authenticity in naturalistic evaluation. In *New directions for program evaluation* (Vol. 30, pp. 73–84). San Francisco, CA: Jossey-Bass.

Lincoln, Y. S. & Guba, E. G. (2000). Paradigmatic controversies, contradictions, and emerging confluences. In N. K. Denzin & Y. S. Lincoln (eds), *Handbook of qualitative research* (2nd edn, pp. 163–88). Thousand Oaks, CA: Sage.

Lindeman Nelson, H. (1997). Introduction. In H. Lindeman Nelson (ed.), *Feminism and families* (pp. 1–12). London: Routledge.

Linney, J. A. (2000). Assessing ecological constructs and community context. In J. Rappaport & E. Seidman (eds), *Handbook of community psychology* (pp. 647–68). New York: Kluwer Academic/Plenum Publishers.

Lipset, S. M. (1996). *American exceptionalism: A double-edged sword*. New York: Norton.

London Times, Literary Supplement (October 6, 1995).

Longmore, P. (Summer, 1985). Screening stereotypes: Images of disabled people. *Social Policy*, 31–7.

Lonner, W. J. & Malpass, R. S. (eds). (1994). *Psychology and culture*. Needham Heights, MA: Allyn & Bacon.

Lord, J. & Church, K. (1998). Beyond 'partnership shock': Getting to 'yes,' living with 'no.' *Canadian Journal of Rehabilitation*, **12**, 113–21.

Lord, J. & Hutchison, P. (1993). The process of empowerment: Implications for theory and practice. *Canadian Journal of Community Mental Health*, **12**(1), 5–22.

Lord, J., Schnarr, A. & Hutchison, P. (1987). The voice of the people: Qualitative research and the needs of consumers. *Canadian Journal of Community Mental Health*, **6**(2), 25–36.

Lorion, R. P., Iscoe, I., DeLeon, P. H. & VandenBos, G. R. (eds). (1996). *Psychology and public policy: Balancing public service and professional need*. Washington, DC: American Psychological Association.

Loughnan, P. (1999). Questioning that 'cycle of violence.' *Domestic Violence and Incest Resource Centre (DVIRC) Newsletter*, Autumn, 16–17.

Louis Harris & Associates. (1998). *Survey of Americans with disabilities.* New York: Author.

Lubinski, D. & Benbow, C. (2000). States of excellence. *American Psychologist,* **55,** 137–50.

Lyall, S. (1999, September 28). European Court Tells British To Let Gay Soldiers Serve. *New York Times,* p. A8.

Lykes, M. B. (1994). Terror, silencing, and children: International multidisciplinary collaboration with Guatemalan Maya communities. *Social Science and Medicine,* **38,** 543–52.

Lykes, M. B. (1996). Meaning making in a context of genocide and silencing. In M. B. Lykes, A. Banuazizi, R. Liem & M. Morris (eds), *Myths about the powerless: Contesting social inequalities* (pp. 159–78). Philadelphia: Temple University Press.

Lykes, M. B. (1997). Activist participatory research among the Maya of Guatemala: Constructing meanings from situated knowledge. *Journal of Social Issues,* **53,** 725–46.

Lykes, M. B. (1999). In collaboration with A. Caba Mateo, J. Chávez Anay, I. A. Laynez Caba. & U. Ruiz. Telling stories – rethreading lives: Community education, women's development and social change among the Maya Ixil. *International Journal of Leadership in Education: Theory and Practice,* **2,** 207–27.

Lykes, M. B. (2001a). Activist participatory research and the arts with rural Mayan women: Interculturality and situated meaning making. In D. L. Tolman & M. Brydon-Miller (eds), *From subjects to subjectivities: A handbook of interpretive and participatory methods* (pp. 183–99). New York: New York University Press.

Lykes, M. B. (2001b). Creative arts and photography in participatory action research in Guatemala. In P. Reason & H. Bradbury (eds), *Handbook of action research* (pp. 363–71). Thousand Oaks, CA.

Lykes, M. B. (2001c) A critical re-reading of PTSD from a cross-cultural/community perspective. In D. Hook & G. Eagle (eds), *Psychopathology and social prejudice* (pp. 92–108). Cape Town, South Africa: UCT Press/JUTA.

Lykes, M. B. & Hellstedt, J. C. (1987). Field training in community-social psychology: A competency-based, self-directed learning model. *Journal of Community Psychology,* **15,** 417–28.

Lykes, M. B. & Qin, D. (2001). Individualism and collectivism. *Encyclopedia of gender* (pp. 625–31). Editor in chief: Judith Worrell. San Diego, CA: Academic Press.

Macaulay, A. C., Delormier, T., McComber, A. M., Cross, E. J., Potvin, L. P., Paradis, G., Kirby, R. L., Saad-Haddad, C. & Desrosiers, S. (1998). Participatory research with native community of Kahnawak creates innovative code of ethics. *Canadian Journal of Public Health,* **89,** 105–8.

MacLeod, J. & Nelson, G. (2000). Programs for the promotion of family wellness and the prevention of child maltreatment: A meta-analytic review. *Child Abuse and Neglect,* **24,** 1127–49.

Macy, J. (1991). *World as lover, world as self.* Berkeley, CA: Parralax Press.

Macy, J. (2000). The great turning. *Yes! A Journal of Positive Futures,* **13,** 34–7.

Madara, E. J. (1990). Maximizing the potential for community self-help through clearinghouse approaches. *Prevention in Human Services,* **7,** 109–38.

Manderscheid, R. W. & Henderson, M. J. (eds). (1998). *Department of Health and Human Services Publication No. (SMA) 99–3285.* Washington, DC: U.S. Government Printing Office.

Mankowski, E. S. & Rappaport, J. (2000). Narrative concepts and analysis in spiritually-based communities. *Journal of Community Psychology,* **28,** 479–93.

Mar'i, S. K. (1988). Challenges to minority counselling: Arabs in Israel. *International Journal of the Advancement of Counselling,* **11,** 5–21.

Marmot, M. (1999). Introduction. In M. Marmot & R. Wilkinson (eds), *Social determinants of health* (pp. 1–16). New York: Oxford University Press.

Marmot, M. & Feeney, A. (1996). Work and health: Implications for individuals and society. In D. Blane, E. Bruner & R. Wilkinson (eds), *Health and social organization* (pp. 235–54). London: Routledge.

Marmot, M. & Wilkinson, R. (eds). (1999). *Social determinants of health*. New York: Oxford University Press.

Marsella, A. J. (1998). Toward a global-community psychology: Meeting the needs of a changing world. *American Psychologist*, 53, 1282–91.

Marsh, A. & Kaase, M. (1979) Measuring political action. In S. H. Branes & M. Kaase (eds), *Political action* (pp. 82–97). Beverly Hills, CA: Sage.

Martin, J. & Sugarman, J. (1999). *The psychology of human possibility and constraint*. Albany, NY: New York University Press.

Martin, J. & Sugarman, J., (2000). Between the modern and the postmodern: The possibility of self and progressive understanding in psychology. *American Psychologist*, 55, 397–406.

Martin, S. F. (2001). *New issues in refugee research: Global migration trends and asylum* (no. 40). UNHCR. Available: http://www.unhcr,ch/refworld/pubs/pubon/htm>. [Accessed: 20 May2001].

Martín-Baró, I. (1986). Hacia una psicología de la liberación [Toward a liberation psychology]. *Boletín de Psicología*. *UCA*. *V* (22) 219–31.

Martín-Baró, I. (1987–89/1990) Retos y perspectivas de la psicología en América Latina [Perspective and challenges of psychology in Latin America]. In S. Pacheco y & B. Jiménez D. (eds), *Ignacio Martín-Baró. Psicología de la liberación para América Latina*. Guadalajara: Univ. de Guadalajara-ITESO.

Martín-Baró, I. (1994). *Writings for a liberation psychology*. Cambridge, MA: Harvard University Press.

Martín-Baró, I. (1996a). The lazy Latino: The ideological nature of Latin American fatalism. In A. Aron & S. Corne, (eds) *Writings for a liberation psychology* (pp. 135–62). New York: Harvard University Press.

Martín-Baró, I. (1996b). The role of the psychologist. In A. Aron & S. Corne (eds), *Writings for a liberation psychology* (pp. 72–82). New York: Harvard University Press.

Martinez, D. G. & Sullivan, S. C. (1998) African American gay men and lesbians: Examining the complexity of gay identity development. *Journal of Human Behavior in the Social Environment*, 1(2–3), 243–64.

Matthews, H. (2001). *Children and community regeneration: Creating better neighbourhoods*. London: Save the Children.

Maton, K. (2000). Making a difference: The social ecology of social transformation. *American Journal of Community Psychology*, 28, 25–58.

Maton, K., Dodgen, D., Sto Domingo, M. & Larsen, D. (2003). *Religion as a meaning system: Policy implications for the new millennium*. Paper presented at the meeting of the American Psychological Association. Toronto, August.

Maton, K. & Salem, D. (1995). Organizational characteristics of empowering community settings: A multiple case study approach. *American Journal of Community Psychology*, 23, 631–56.

Matustik, M. (1998). *Specters of liberation: great refusals in the New World Order*. Albany, NY: State University of New York Press.

Mayer, J. P. & Davidson, W. S. II. (2000). Dissemination of innovation as social change. In J. Rappaport & E. Seidman (eds), *Handbook of community psychology* (pp. 421–38). New York: Kluwer Academic/Plenum Publishers.

Mayo, M. (1997). Partnerships for regeneration and community development: some opportunities, challenges and constraints. *Critical Social Policy*, 17, 3–26.

Mayton, D. M., Ball-Rokeach, S. J. & Loges, W. E. (1994). Human values and social issues: An introduction. *Journal of Social Issues*, 50(4), 1–8.

McAlister, A. (2000). Action-oriented mass communication. In J. Rappaport & E. Seidman (eds), *Handbook of community psychology* (pp. 379–96). New York: Kluwer Academic/Plenum Publishers.

McCartney, T. & Turner, C. (2000). Reconciliation happens every day: Conversations about working alliances between black and white Australia. *Australian Psychologist*, **35**, 173–7.

McCoy, C. W. (1996). Reexamining models of healthy families. *Contemporary Family Therapy*, **18**(2), 243–56.

McCubbin, M. & Dalgard, O. S. (2002, October). *Le pouvoir comme determinant de la santé publique (power as determinant of population health)*. Presentation to Faculty of Nursing Sciences, Laval University.

McCulloch, A. (1997). 'You've fucked up the estate and now you're carrying a brief-case!' In P. Hoggett (ed.), *Contested communities: Experiences, struggles, policies* (pp. 51–67). Bristol: Policy Press.

McFarlane-Nathan, G. H. (1996). *The bicultural therapy project: Developing a psychological model for working with Maori*. Paper presented to the annual conference of the New Zealand Psychological Society, Christchurch.

McGlashan, T. H. (1998). Early detection and intervention with schizophrenia: Rationale and research. *British Journal of Psychiatry*, **172**, 3–6.

McGlashan, T. H., Miller, T. J. & Woods, S. (2001). Pre-onset detection and intervention research in schizophrenia psychoses: Current estimates of benefits and risks. *Schizophrenia Bulletin*, **27**, 563–70.

McGregor, H. (1990). Conceptualising male against female partners: Political implications of therapeutic responses. *Australian and New Zealand Journal of Family Therapy*, **11**, 65–70.

McHugh, M. C., Koeske, R. D. & Frieze, I. H. (1986). Issues to consider in conducting nonsexist psychological research: A guide for researchers. *American Psychologist*, **41**, 879–90.

McIntosh, P. (1990). White privilege: Unpacking the invisible knapsack. *Independent School*, 31–6.

McKenzie-Mohr, D. (2000). Fostering sustainable behavior through community-based social marketing. *American Psychologist*, **55**, 531–55.

McKenzie-Mohr, D. & Oskamp, S. (1995). Psychology and sustainability: An introduction. *Journal of Social Issues*, **51**, 1–14.

McKillip, J. (1998). Need analysis: Process and techniques. In L. Bickman & D. J. Rog (eds), *Handbook of applied social research methods* (pp. 261–84). Thousand Oaks, CA: Sage.

McKnight, J. (1995). *The careless society: Community and its counterfeits*. New York: Basic Books.

McLaren, P. L. & Lankshear, C. (eds). (1994). *Politics of liberation: Paths from Freire*. London: Routledge.

McMillan, D. W. & Chavis, D. M. (1986). Sense of community: Definition and theory. *Journal of Community Psychology*, **14**, 6–23.

McNamara, M. & Moore, P. (2000). Tino Rangatiratanga in the performing arts: The Story of Magdalena Aotearoa. In *Proceedings of Treaty Conference 2000* (pp.116–21). Tamaki Makaurau/Auckland: Treaty Conference Publications Group.

McNeely, J. (1999). Community building. *Journal of Community Psychology*, **27**, 741–50.

McNeil, J. (1993). *Americans with disabilities: 1991–1992*. Washington, DC: U.S. Department of Commerce, Bureau of the Census.

McQuaig, L. (1998). *The cult of impotence: Selling the myth of powerlessness in the global economy*. Toronto: Viking.

McQuaig, L. (2001). *All you can eat: Greed, lust, and the new capitalism*. Toronto: Penguin Books Canada.

McWhirter, E. H. (1994). *Counseling for empowerment*. Alexandrian, VA: American Counseling Association.

Mead, A. T. (1995, July). *The integrity of the human gene, genes and whakapapa*. Paper presented to the New Zealand Health Research Council Consensus Development Workshop 'Whose genes are they anyway? The use and misuse of human genetic information.' Wellington.

Mead, G. H. (1934). *Mind, self, and society from the standpoint of a social behaviorist*. Chicago, IL: University of Chicago Press.

Meara, N. & Day, J. (2000). Epilogue: Feminist visions and virtues of ethical psychological practice. In M. Brabeck (ed.), *Practicing feminist ethics in psychology* (pp. 249–68). Washington, DC: American Psychological Association.

Mednick, M. (1989). On the politics of psychological constructs. Stop the bandwagon, I want to get off. *American Psychologist*, **44**, 1118–23.

Melluish, S. & Bulmer, D. (1999). Rebuilding solidarity: An account of a men's health action project. *Journal of Community and Applied Social Psychology*, **9**, 93–100.

Mclnyk, G. (1985). *The search for community: From utopia to a co-operative society*. New York: Black Rose Books.

Memmi, A. (1968). *Dominated man: Notes towards a portrait*. New York: Orion Press.

Menchú, R. (1984). *I, Rigoberta Menchú: An Indian woman in Guatemala*. London: Verso.

Meyer, I. H. (1995). Minority stress and mental health in gay men. *Journal of Health and Social Behavior*, **36**, 38–56.

Mies, M. & Shiva, V. (1993). *Ecofeminism*. Halifax, Nova Scotia: Fernwood Publications.

Milligan, M. S. & Neufeldt, A. H. (2001). The myth of asexuality: A survey of social and empirical evidence. *Sexuality and Disability*, **19**(2), 91–109.

Mills, C. W. (1959). *The sociological imagination*. New York: Oxford University Press.

Milne, D. (1999). *Social therapy: A guide to social support interventions for mental health practitioners*. New York: Wiley.

Milord, J. T. (1976). Human service needs assessment: Three non-epidemiological approaches. *Canadian Psychological Review*, **17**, 260–9.

Mirabi, M., Weinman, M. L., Magnetti, S. M. & Kepler, K. N. (1985). Professional attitudes toward the chronic mentally ill. *Hospital and Community Psychiatry*, **36**, 404–5.

Mirowsky, J. & Ross, C.E. (1989). *Social causes of psychological distress*. New York: Aldine de Gruyter.

Mitchell, R. E. & Trickett, E. J. (1980). Task force report: Social networks as mediators of social support: An analysis of the effects and determinants of social supports. *Community Mental Health Journal*, **16**, 27–44.

Moane, G. (1999). *Gender and colonialism: A psychological analysis of oppression and liberation*. London: Macmillan – now Palgrave Macmillan.

Moane, G. (2003). Bridging the personal and the political: Practices for a liberation psychology. *American Journal of Community Psychology*, **31**, 91–101.

Mollison, B. (1988). *Permaculture: A designer's manual*. Tyalgum, NSW, Australia: Tagari.

Moghaddam, F. M. (2002). *The individual and society: A cultural integration*. New York: Worth Publishers.

Montero, M. (1980). La psicología social y el desarrollo de comunidades en América Latina [Social psychology and community development in Latin America]. *Revista Latinoamericana de Psicología*, **12**(1), 159–70.

Montero, M. (1991). Perspectiva de la psicología comunitaria en América Latina [Community psychology's perspective in Latin America]. *Psicología*, **XV**(1–2), 91–105.

Montero, M. (1992). Psicología de la liberación: Propuesta para una teoría psicosociológica [Liberation psychology: A proposal for a psychosocial theory]. In H. Riquelme (ed.), *Otras realidades, otras vías de acceso* (pp. 133–50). Caracas, Venezuela: Nueva Sociedad.

Montero, M. (1993). De-ideologization, conversion, and consciousness raising. *Journal of Community Psychology*, **22**, 3–11.

Montero, M. (1994a). Consciousness-raising, conversion and de-ideologization in community psychosocial work. *Journal of Community Psychology*, **22**(1), 3–11.

Montero, M. (ed.). (1994b). *Psicología social comunitaria: Teoría, método y experiencia* [*Social-community psychology*]. Universidad de Guadalajara.

Montero, M. (1995). Modos alternativos de acción política [Alternative modes of political action]. In D'Adamo, O, V. Garcia Beaudoux & M. Montero (eds), *Psicología de la acción política* [Psychology of political action] (pp. 91–110). Buenos Aires, Argentina: Paidos.

Montero, M. (1996a). Crise, politização e construção psicológica da democracia [Crisis, politicisation and psychological construction of democracy]. *Psicología Revista*, **2**, 83–97. PUC, Sao Paulo, Brazil.

Montero, M. (1996b). Parallel lives: Community psychology in Latin America and the United States. *American Journal of Community Psychology*, **24**, 589–605.

Montero, M. (ed.). (1998a). Community psychology in Latin America [special issue]. *Journal of Community Psychology*, **26**(3).

Montero, M. (1998b). Dialectic between active minorities and majorities: A study of social influence in the community. *Journal of Community Psychology*, **26**, 281–9.

Montero, M. (1998c). Psychosocial community work as an alternative mode of political action (the construction and critical transformation of society). *Community, Work and Family*, **1**, 65–78.

Montero, M. (2000a). Participation in participatory action research. *Annual Review of Critical Psychology*, **2**, 131–43.

Montero, M. (2000b). Perspectivas y retos de la psicología de la liberación [Liberation psychology: Perspectives and challenges]. In J. J. Vázques Ortega (ed.), *Psicología social y liberación en América Latina* [Social psychology and liberation in Latin America] (pp. 9–26). Mexico, DF: Universidad Autónoma Metropolitana.

Montero, M. (2001). *Todo corre, mucho fluye, algo permanece: Cambio y estabilidad social* [All is flux, something is stationary: Social change and stability]. Keynote address presented at the XXVIII Interamerican Congress of Psychology, Santiago, Chile.

Montero, M. (2002). On the construction of reality and truth. Towards an epistemology of community social psychology. *American Journal of Community Psychology*, **30**, 571–84.

Montero, M. (2003). *La tensión entre comunidad y sociedad* [The tension between community and society]. Buenos Aires, Argentina: Paidós.

Moos, R. H. (1994). *The social climate scales: A user's guide* (2nd edn). Palo Alto, CA: Consulting Psychologists Press.

Moos, R. H. (2003). Social contexts: Transcending their power and their fragility. *American Journal of Community Psychology*, **31**, 1–13.

Morales, E. S. (1989). Ethnic minority families and minority gays and lesbians. *Marriage and Family Review*, **14**(3–4), 217–39.

Morgan, A. (2000). *What is narrative therapy? An easy-to-read introduction*. Adelaide, South Australia: Dulwich Publications.

Morgan, D. L. & Krueger, R. A. (eds). (1997). *Focus group kit*. Thousand Oaks, CA: Sage.

Morris, A. D. & Mueller, C. (eds). (1992). *Frontiers in social movement theory*. New Haven, CT: Yale University Press.

Morris, J. (1992). Personal and political: A feminist perspective on researching physical disability. *Disability, Handicap and Society*, **7**(2), 157–66.

Morris, J. (2001). Social exclusion and young disabled people with high levels of support needs. *Critical Social Policy*, **21**, 161–83.

Morton, J. W. (2002/1880). Historical note: The ability of mentally ill persons to live in the community, 1880. *Journal of Nervous and Mental Disease*, **190**, 398.

Morton, T. G. (1897). *The history of Pennsylvania Hospital 1751–1895*. Philadelphia: Times Printing House.

Moscovici, S. (1985). *The age of the crowd: A historical treatise on mass psychology.* Cambridge: Cambridge University Press.

Mott, L. (1997). *Epidemic of hate: Violations of the human rights of gay men, lesbians, and transvestites In Brazil.* Salvador, Bahia: Grupo Gay da Bahia.

Mott, L. & Cerqueira, M. (2001). *Cause of death: Homophobia.* Salvador, Bahia: Grupo Gay da Bahia.

Mukherjee, A. (1992). Education and race relations: The education of South Asian youth. In R. Ghosh & R. Kanungo (eds), *South Asian Canadians: Current issues in the politics of culture* (pp. 145–61). Montréal: Shastri Indo-Canadian Institute.

Mulhall, S. & Swift, A. (1996). *Liberals and communitarians* (2nd edn). Oxford: Blackwell.

Mullaly, B. (2002). *Challenging oppression: A critical social work approach.* Toronto: Oxford.

Mulvey, A. (1988). Community psychology and feminism: Tensions and commonalities. *Journal of Community Psychology, 20,* 70–83.

Mulvey, A., Terenzio, M., Hill, J., Bond, M., Huygens, I., Hamerton, H. & Cahill, S. (2000). Stories of relative privilege: Power and social change in feminist community psychology. *American Journal of Community Psychology, 28,* 883–911.

Muñoz, R. F., Le, H. N., Clarke, G. & Jaycox, L. (2002). Preventing the onset of major depression. In I. H. Gotlib & C. L. Hammen (eds), *Handbook of depression* (pp. 343–59). New York: Guilford Press.

Muñoz, R. F., Ying, Y. W., Bernal, G. & Perez-Stable, E.J. (1995). Prevention of depression with primary care patients: A randomized controlled trial. *American Journal of Community Psychology, 23,* 199–222.

Murray, M. (2000a). Levels of narrative analysis in health psychology. *Journal of Health Psychology, 5,* 337–47.

Murray, M. (ed.). (2000b). Reconstructing health psychology [special issue]. *Journal of Health Psychology, 5.*

Murray, M. & Campbell, C. (2003). Living in a material world: Reflecting on some assumptions of health psychology. *Journal of Health Psychology, 8,* 231–6.

Murray, M. & Chamberlin, K. (1999a). Health psychology and qualitative research. In M. Murray & K. Chamberlin (eds), *Qualitative health psychology: Theories and methods* (pp. 3–15). London: Sage.

Murray, M. & Chamberlin, K. (eds). (1999b). *Qualitative health psychology: Theories and methods.* London: Sage.

Murray, M., Nelson, G., Poland, B., Matycka-Tyndale, E., Ferris, L., Lavoie, F., Cameron, R. & Prkachin, K. (2001). *Training in community health psychology.* Report to Canadian Institutes of Health Research.

Murrell, P. C. (1997). Digging again the family wells: A Freirian literacy framework as emancipatory pedagogy for African-American children. In P. Freire (ed.), *Mentoring the mentor: A critical dialogue with Paulo Freire* (pp. 19–55). New York: Peter Lang.

Mustakova-Possardt, E. (2003). *Critical consciousness: A study of morality in global, historical context.* Westport, CT: Praeger.

Mustard, J. F. (1996). Health and social capital. In D. Blane, E. Brunner & R. Wilkinson (eds), *Health and social organization* (pp. 303–13). London: Routledge.

Naidoo, J. & Edwards, R. G. (1991). Combatting racism involving visible minorities: A review of relevant research and policy development. *Canadian Social Work Review, 8,* 211–36.

Nairn, M. (1990). *Understanding colonisation.* Auckland: Workshop material distributed by CCANZ Programme on Racism.

Nairn, M. (2000). *Decolonisation for Pakeha.* Auckland: Workshop material distributed by CCANZ Programme on Racism.

Nairn, M. (2002). *Director's overview of programme to overcome racism.* Presented to Conference of Churches in Aotearoa New Zealand, August, 2002.

Nairn, R. & McCreanor, T. (1991). Race talk and commonsense: Patterns in Pakeha discourse on Maori/Pakeha relation in New Zealand. *Journal of Language and Social Psychology*, **10**, 245–62.

Nairn, R. & The National Standing Committee on Bicultural Issues (NSCBI) (1997). Cultural justice and ethics in psychological practice. In H. Love & W. Whittaker, (eds), *Practice issues for clinical and applied psychologists in New Zealand* (pp. 127–35). Wellington: The New Zealand Psychological Society.

Narayan, D., Chambers, R., Shah, M. & Petesch, P. (1999). *Global synthesis: Consultations with the poor*. Poverty Group, World Bank.

Narayan, D., Chambers, R., Shah, M. & Petesch, P. (2000). *Voices of the poor: Crying out for change*. New York: Oxford University Press.

Narayan, D., Patel, R., Schafft, K., Rademacher, A. & Koch-Schulte, S. (2000). *Voices of the poor: Can anyone hear us?* New York: Oxford University Press.

Nardi, P., Sanders D. & Marmor J. (eds). (1994). *Growing up before Stonewall: Life stories of some gay men*. New York: Routledge.

Nation, M., Crusto, C., Wandersman, A., Kumpfer, K. L., Seybolt, D., Morrissey-Kane, E. & Davino, K. (2003). What works in prevention: Principles of effective prevention programs. *American Psychologist*, **58**, 449–56.

Nation, M., Wandersman, A. & Perkins, D. D. (2002). Promoting healthy communities through community development. In D. Glenwick & L. Jason (eds), *Innovative strategies for preventing psychological problems*, (pp. 324–44) New York: Springer.

National Council on Disability. (1989). *National disability policy: A progress report*. (November 1, 1997–October 31, 1998). Washington, DC: Author.

National Institutes of Health (1995). Physical activity and cardiovascular health. *NIH Consensus Statement*, **13**(3), 1–33.

National Institute on Disability and Rehabilitation Research (NIDRR). (December 7, 1999). *Long-range plan for fiscal years 1999–2003*. Washington, DC: Federal Register, Part V, Vol. 64(234): 68576–614.

Neighbors, H. W. & Williams, D. R. (2001). The epidemiology of mental disorder. In R.L. Braithwaite & S. E. Taylor (eds), *Health issues in the Black community* (pp. 99–128). San Francisco: Jossey-Bass.

Neisen, J. H. (1990). Heterosexism: Redefining homophobia for the 1990s. *Journal of Gay and Lesbian Psychotherapy*, **1**(3), 21–35.

Nelson, G. (1994). The development of a mental health coalition: A case study. *American Journal of Community Psychology*, **22**, 229–55.

Nelson, G., Amio, J., Prilleltensky, I. & Nickels, P. (2000). Partnerships for implementing school and community prevention programs. *Journal of Educational and Psychological Consultation*, **11**, 121–45.

Nelson, G. & Earls, M. (1986). An action-oriented assessment of the housing and social support needs of long-term psychiatric clients. *Canadian Journal of Community Mental Health*, **5**(1), 19–30.

Nelson, G. & Hayday, B. (1995). Advancing prevention in Ontario, Canada: Follow-up to a utilization-focused evaluation. *Prevention in Human Services*, **12**(1), 43–68.

Nelson, G., Laurendeau, M.-C., Chamberland, C. & Peirson, L. (2001). A review and analysis of programs to promote family wellness and prevent the maltreatment of pre-school and elementary school-aged children. In I. Prilleltensky, G. Nelson & L. Peirson (eds), *Promoting family wellness and preventing child maltreatment: Fundamentals for thinking and action* (pp. 220–72). Toronto: University of Toronto Press.

Nelson, G., Lord, J. & Ochocka, J. (2001a). Empowerment and mental health in community: Narratives of psychiatric consumer/survivors. *Journal of Community and Applied Social Psychology*, **11**, 125–42.

Nelson, G., Lord, J. & Ochocka, J. (2001b). *Shifting the paradigm in community mental health: Towards empowerment and community*. Toronto: University of Toronto Press.

Nelson, G., Ochocka, J., Griffin, K. & Lord, J. (1998). 'Nothing about me, without me': Participatory action research with self-help/mutual aid organizations for psychiatric consumer/survivors. *American Journal of Community Psychology*, 26, 881–912.

Nelson, G. & Pancer, S. M. (1990). The Ontario Prevention Clearinghouse: Part II – Program evaluation. *Journal of Primary Prevention*, 10, 251–59.

Nelson, G., Prilleltensky, I. & MacGillivary, H. (2001). Building value-based partnerships: Toward solidarity with oppressed groups. *American Journal of Community Psychology*, 29, 649–77.

Nelson, G., Prilleltensky, I. & Peters, R. DeV. (2003). Prevention and mental health promotion in the community. In W. L. Marshall & P. Firestone, *Abnormal psychology: Perspectives* (2nd edn, pp. 462–79). Scarborough: Prentice Hall, Allyn & Bacon Canada.

Nelson, G., Walsh-Bowers, R. & Hall, G. B. (1998). Housing for psychiatric survivors: Values, policy, and research. *Administration and Policy in Mental Health*, 25, 55–62.

Nelson, G., Westhues, A. & MacLeod, J. (2003). A meta-analysis of longitudinal research on preschool prevention programs for children. *Prevention and Treatment*, 6 (December), available at http://journals.apa.org/prevention/volume6/toc-dec18-03.html.

Newbrough, J. R. (1973). Community psychology: A new holism. *American Journal of Community Psychology*, 1, 201–11.

Newbrough, J. R. (1974). Editorial opinion. Community psychology: Some perspectives. *Journal of Community Psychology*, 2, 204–6.

Newbrough, J. R. (1980). Community psychology and the public interest. *American Journal of Community Psychology*, 8, 1–17.

Newbrough, J. R. (1992a). Community psychology in the post-modern world. *Journal of Community Psychology*, 20, 10–25.

Newbrough, J. R. (1992b). The postmodern professional: Reflective and generative practice. *Interamerican Journal of Psychology*, 27, 1–22.

Newbrough, J. R. (1995). Toward community: A third position. *American Journal of Community Psychology*, 23, 9–37.

Newbrough, J. R. (1997). Community psychology: A new gestalt psychology? In R. Fuller, P. N. Walsh & P. McGinley (eds), *A century of psychology: Progress, paradigms, and prospects for the new millennium* (pp. 139–55). London: Routledge.

Newbrough, J. R. & Christenfeld, R. M. (1974). *Community mental health epidemiology: Nashville. A feasibility study for a program to monitor depressed mood in the local community* (Final report on Grant MH-20681 to the Center for Epidemiological Studies, National Institute of Mental Health), Nashville, TN: John F. Kennedy Center for Research on Education and Human Development, Vanderbilt University.

Newman, S. J. (1994). The housing and neighborhood conditions of persons with severe mental illness. *Hospital and Community Psychiatry*, 45, 338–43.

Newman, S. J. (2001). Housing attributes and serious mental illness: Implications for research and practice. *Psychiatric Services*, 52, 1309–17.

Newton, L., Rosen, A., Tennant, C., Hobbs, C., Lapsley, H. M. & Tribe, K. (2000). Deinstitutionalization for long-term mental illness: An ethnographic study. *Australian and New Zealand Journal of Psychiatry*, 34, 484–90.

Ngawhika, N. (1996). *Te Awa a Te Atua: Traditional and contemporary practices of menstruation in the lives of Ngati Awa women*. [Unpublished Summer Studentship report prepared for the Health Research Council.]

Nicholson, L. (1997). The myth of the traditional family. In H. Lindeman Nelson (ed.), *Feminism and families* (pp. 27–42). London: Routledge.

Nielsen, J. M. (ed.). (1990). *Feminist research methods*. Boulder, CO: Westview.

Nikelly, A. G. (1987). Prevention in Sweden and Cuba: Implications for policy and research. *Journal of Primary Prevention*, 7, 117–31.

Nikora, L. W. & Robertson, N. (1995). *Parallel development: A model for the delivery of culturally safe social services*. Poster presentation to 5th Biennial Conference of the Society for Community Research and Action, Chicago, IL.

NIMH Committee on Prevention Research. (1995). *A plan for prevention research for the National Institute of Mental Health: A report to the National Advisory Mental Health Council.* Washington, DC: Author.

Nisbet, R. (1953). *The quest for community.* New York: Oxford University Press.

Nobles, W. W. (1991). Extended self: Rethinking the so-called Negro self-concept. In R. L. Jones (ed.), *Black psychology* (3rd edn, pp. 295–304). Berkeley, CA: Cobb & Henry.

Noël. A. (2002). *A law against poverty: Quebec's new approach to combating poverty and social exclusion.* Canadian Policy research Network Incorporated, http://www.cprn.com/cprn.html.

Norberg-Hodge, H. (1992) *Ancient futures: Learning from Ladakh.* Toronto: Random House of Canada.

Nosek, M. A., Howland, B. A., Rintala, D. H., Young, M. E. & Chanpong, M. S. (2001). National study of women with physical disabilities: Final report. *Sexuality and Disability,* **19**(1), 5–39.

Nosek, M. A., Young, M. E., Rintala, D. H., Howland, C. H., Foley, C. C. & Bennett, J. L. (1995). Barriers to reproductive health maintenance among women with physical disabilities. *Journal of Women's Health,* **4**(5), 505–15.

Noyoo, N. (2000). From resistance to development: Civil society and democracy in post apartheid South Africa. *Scottish Journal Community Work and Development, Autumn,* 35–44 (special issue in collaboration with IACD 'Citizen Action and Democratic Renewal').

Nukunya, G. K. (1992). *Tradition and change in Ghana: An introduction to sociology.* Accra: Ghana Universities Press.

Nursing Council of New Zealand (1996). *Guidelines for the cultural safety component in nursing education.* Wellington: Ministry of Education.

Nystrom, N. M. & Jones, T. C. (2003). Community building with aging and old lesbians. *American Journal of Community Psychology,* **31**, 293–300.

O'Brien, J. & O'Brien, C. L. (1996). *Members of each other: Building community in company with people with developmental disabilities.* Toronto: Inclusion Press.

Ochocka, J., Janzen, R. & Nelson, G. (2002). Sharing power and knowledge: Professional and mental health consumer/survivor researchers working together in a participatory action research project. *Psychiatric Rehabilitation Journal,* **25**, 379–87.

O'Connor, D. (2002). Toward empowerment: ReVisioning family support groups. *Social Work with Groups,* **25**(4), 37–56.

O'Day, B. (1999). Employment barriers for people with visual impairments. *Journal of Visual Impairment and Blindness,* **93**(10), 627–42.

ODHAG/Oficina de Derechos Humanos del Arzobispado de Guatemala [Office of Human Rights of the Archdiocese of Guatemala]. (1998). *Nunca más: Informe proyecto interdiocesano de recuperación de la memoria histórica [Never again: Report of the inter-diocescan project on the recovery of historic memory]* (Vols. 1–5). Guatemala: Author.

O'Donnell, C. R., Tharp, R. G. & Wilson, K. (1993). Activity settings as the unit of analysis: A theoretical basis for community intervention and development. *American Journal of Community Psychology,* **21**, 501–20.

Offord, D. R., Boyle, M. H., Szatmari, P., Rae-Grant, N. I., Links, P. S., Cadman, D. T., Byles, J. A., Crawford, J. W., Munroe Blum, H., Byrne, C., Thomas, H. & Woodward, C. A. (1987). Ontario Child Health Study: I. Six-month prevalence of disorder and rates of service utilization. *Archives of General Psychiatry,* **44**, 832–36.

Offord, D. R., Boyle, M., Campbell, D., Cochrane, J., Goering, P., Lin, E., Rhodes, A., Wong, M. (1994). *Mental health in Ontario: Selected findings from the Mental Health Supplement to the Ontario Health Survey.* Toronto: Ontario Ministry of Health.

Ofori Atta, L. A. (2001). Who is the identified patient? Any hidden agendas? A behavioural-systems perspective to therapy in Ghana. *Ghana Journal of Psychology,* **1**(1), 17–24.

Ogbu, J. U. (1994). From cultural differences to differences in cultural frame of reference. In P. M. Greenfield & R. R. Cocking (eds), *Crosscultural roots of minority child development* (pp. 365–91). Hillsdale, NJ: Erlbaum.

Okunda, A. D. (1981). Visual, auditory and physical handicaps in Nigerian children. *International Nursing Review*, **28**, 176–7.

Olds, D., Eckenrode, J., Henderson, C. R., Kitzman, H., Powers, J., Cole, R., Sidora, K., Morris, P., Pettitt, L. M. & Luckey, D. (1997). Long-term effects of home visitation on maternal life course and child abuse and neglect: Fifteen-year follow-up of a randomized trial. *Journal of the American Medical Association*, **278**, 637–43.

Olds, D., Henderson, C. R., Chamberlin, R. & Tatelbaum, R. (1986). Preventing child abuse and neglect: A randomized trial of nurse home visitation. *Pediatrics*, **78**, 65–78.

Olds, D., Henderson, C. R., Cole, R., Eckenrode, J., Kitzman, H., Luckey, D., Pettitt, L., Sidora, K., Morris, P. & Powers, J. (1998). Long-term effects of nurse home visitation on children's criminal and antisocial behavior: Fifteen-year follow-up of a randomized controlled trial. *Journal of the American Medical Association*, **280**, 1238–44.

Olesen, V. L. (2000). Feminisms and qualitative research at and into the millenium. In N. K. Denzin & Y. S. Lincoln (eds), *Handbook of qualitative research* (2nd edn) (pp. 215–55). Thousand Oaks, CA: Sage.

Oliver, M. (1990). *The politics of disablement*. Basingstoke: Macmillan – now Palgrave Macmillan.

Oliver, M. (1996). A sociology of disability or a disablist sociology? In L. Barton (ed.) *Disability and society: Emerging issues and insights* (pp. 18–42). London: Longman.

Oliver, M. & Barnes, C. (1998). *Disabled people and social policy: From exclusion to inclusion*. Harlow, England: Longman.

Oliver, P. & Hamerton, H. (1992). Women, peace and community psychology: A common agenda for social change. In D. Thomas & A. Veno (eds), *Psychology and social change: Creating an international agenda* (pp. 55–73). Palmerston North, NZ: Dunmore.

Olkin, R. (1999). *What therapists should know about disability*. New York: The Guilford Press.

O'Neill, J. (1994). *The missing child in liberal theory*. Toronto, Ontario: University of Toronto Press.

O'Neill, P. (1976). Educating divergent thinkers: An ecological investigation. *American Journal of Community Psychology*, **4**, 99–107.

O'Neill, P. (1989). Responsible to whom? Responsible for what? Some ethical issues in community intervention. *American Journal of Community Psychology*, **17**, 323–41.

O'Neill, P. (1998). Communities, collectivities, and the ethics of research. *Canadian Journal of Community Mental Health*, **17**(2)   0, 67–78.

O'Neill, P. (2000). Cognition in social context: Contributions to community psychology. In In J. Rappaport & E. Seidman (eds), *Handbook of community psychology* (pp. 115–32). New York: Kluwer Academic/Plenum.

O'Neill, P. & Trickett, E. J. (1982). *Community consultation*. San Francisco: Jossey-Bass.

Orford, J. (1992). *Community psychology: Theory and practice*. Chichester: John Wiley.

Ornish, D. (1997). *Love and survival: The scientific basis for the healing power of intimacy*. New York: Harper and Collins.

Pacheco, G. & Jimenez, B. (1990). *Ignacio Martín-Baró: Psicología de la liberación para América Latina* [Ignacio Martín-Baró. Psychology of liberation for Latin America]. Guadalajara, Mexico: University of Guadalajara Press.

Pancer, S. M. (1997). Program evaluation. In S. W. Sadawa & D. R. McCreary (eds), *Applied social psychology* (pp. 47–53). Englewood Cliffs, NJ: Prentice Hall.

Pancer, S. M. & Cameron, G. (1994). Resident participation in the Better Beginnings, Better Futures prevention project: I. The impact of involvement. *Canadian Journal of Community Mental Health*, **13**(2), 197–211.

Pancer, S. M. & Nelson, G. (1990). Community-based approaches to health promotion: Guidelines for community mobilization. *International Quarterly of Community Health Education*, **10**, 91–111.

Pancer, S. M., Nelson, G. & Hayday, B. (1990). The Ontario Prevention Clearinghouse: Part I – History and program description. *Journal of Primary Prevention*, **10**, 241–50.

Pancer, S. M. & Pratt, M. (1999). Social and family determinants of community service involvement in Canadian youth. In M. Yates & J. Youniss (eds), *Roots of civic identity: International perspectives on community service and activism in youth* (pp. 32–55). New York: Cambridge University Press.

Papineau, D. & Kiely, M. C. (1996). Participatory evaluation in a community organization: Fostering stakeholder empowerment and utilization. *Evaluation and Program Planning*, **19**, 79–93.

Parayil, G. (ed.). (2000). *Kerala: The development experience*. London: Zed Books.

Pargament, K. I. (1997). *The psychology of religion and coping: Theory, research, and practice*. New York: Guilford Press.

Park, P., Brydon-Miller, M., Hall, B. & Jackson, T. (eds). (1993). *Voices of change: Participatory research in the United States and Canada*. Westport, CT: Bergen & Garvey.

Parker, I. (1997). Discursive psychology. In D. Fox & I. Prilleltensky (eds), *Critical psychology: An introduction* (pp. 284–98). London: Sage.

Parker, R. (1989). Youth, identity, and homosexuality: The changing shape of sexual life in contemporary Brazil. *Journal of Homosexuality*, **17**(3–4), 269–89.

Parkinson, S., Nelson, G. & Horgan, S. (1999). From housing to homes: A review of the literature on housing approaches for psychiatric consumer/survivors. *Canadian Journal of Community Mental Health*, **18**(1), 145–64.

Pate, R. R., Pratt, M., Blair, S. N., Haskell, W. L., Macera, A. A., Bouchard, C., Buchner, D., Ettinger, W., Heath, G. W., King, A. C., Kriska, A., Leon, A. S., Marcus, B. H., Morris, J., Paffenbarger, R. S., Patrick, K., Pollock, M. L., Rippe, J. M., Sallis, J. & Wilmore, J. H. (1995). Physical activity and public health: A recommendation from the Centers for Disease Control and Prevention and the American College of Sports Medicine. *Journal of the American Medical Association*, **273**, 402–7.

Patterson, L. E. & Welfel, E. R. (2000). *The counselling process* (5th edn). Belmont, CA: Brooks/Cole.

Patton, M. Q. (1997). *Utilization-focused evaluation: The new century text* (3rd edn). Thousand Oaks, CA: Sage.

Patton, M. Q. (2002). *Qualitative research and evaluation methods* (3rd edn). Thousand Oaks, CA: Sage.

Peirson, L. Laurendeau, M.-C. & Chamberland, C. (2001). Context, contributing factors, and consequences. In I. Prilleltensky, G. Nelson & L. Peirson (eds), *Promoting family wellness and preventing child maltreatment: Fundamentals for thinking and action* (pp. 41–123). Toronto: University of Toronto Press.

Peirson, L. & Prilleltensky, I. (1994). Understanding school change to facilitate prevention: A study of change in a secondary school. *Canadian Journal of Community Mental Health*, **13**(2), 127–44.

Peirson, L., Prilleltensky, I., Nelson, G. & Gould, J. (1997). Planning mental health services for children and youth: Part II – Results of a value-based community consultation project. *Evaluation and Program Planning*, **20**(2), 173–83.

Pennington, N. & Hastie, R.(1992). Explaining the evidence: Test of the story model for juror decision making. *Journal of Personality and Social Psychology*, **62**, 189–206.

Perez, R. M., DeBord, K. A. & Bieschke, K. J. (2000). *Handbook of counselling and psychotherapy with lesbian, gay, and bisexual clients*. Washington, DC: American Psychological Association.

Perkins, D., Hughey, J. & Speer, P. (2002). Community psychology perspectives on social capital theory and community development practice. *Journal of the Community Development Society*, **33**(1), 33–52.

Perkins, D. & Long, A. (2002). Neighborhood sense of community and social capital: A multi-level analysis. In A. Fisher, C. Sonn & B. Bishop (eds), *Psychological sense of community: Research, applications, and implications* (pp. 291–318). New York: Kluwer Academic/Plenum Publishers.

Perkins, D. D. & Wandersman, A. (1990). 'You'll have to work to overcome our suspicions': The benefits and pitfalls of research with community organizations. *Social Policy*, **20**, 32–41.

Perkins, D. & Zimmerman, M. (1995). Empowerment theory, research, and application. *American Journal of Community Psychology*, **23**, 569–80.

Perkins, R. (1991). Women with long-term mental health problems: Issues of power and powerlessness. *Feminism and Psychology*, **1**, 131–9.

Perry, M. J. (1996). The relationship between social class and mental disorder. *Journal of Primary Prevention*, **17**, 17–30.

Peters, R. DeV. (1994). Better Beginnings, Better Futures: A community-based approach to primary prevention. *Canadian Journal of Community Mental Health*, **13**(2), 183–8.

Peters, R. DeV., Arnold, R., Petrunka, K., Angus, D. E., Brophy, K., Burke, S. O., Cameron, G., Evers, S., Herry, Y., Levesque, D., Pancer, S. M., Roberts-Fiati, G., Towson, S. & Warren, W. K. (2000). *Developing capacity and competence in the Better Beginnings, Better Futures communities: Short term findings report*. Kingston, ON: Better Beginnings, Better Futures Research Coordination Unit technical report.

Peters, R. DeV., Peters, J. E., Laurendeau, M.-C., Chamberland, C. & Peirson, L. (2001). Social policies for promoting the well-being of children. In I. Prilleltensky, G. Nelson & L. Peirson (eds), *Promoting family wellness and preventing child maltreatment: Fundamentals for thinking and action* (pp. 177–219). Toronto: University of Toronto Press.

Peterson, J. L. (ed.). (1998). HIV/AIDS prevention through community psychology [special issue]. *American Journal of Community Psychology*, **26**(1).

Petras, J. & Veltmeyer, H. (2001). *Globalization unmasked: Imperialism in the 21st Century*. London: Zed Books.

Pfaefflin, F. (1997). Sex reassignment, Harry Benjamin, and some European roots. *International Journal of Transgenderism*. **1**(2).

Pheterson, G. (1990). Alliances between women: Overcoming internalized oppression and internalized domination. In L. Albrecht & R. M. Brewer (eds), *Bridges of power: Women's multicultural alliances* (pp. 34–48). New Society Publishers.

Phillips, D. (2000). Social policy and community psychology. In J. Rappaport & E. Seidman (eds), *Handbook of community psychology* (pp. 397–420). New York: Kluwer Academic/Plenum Publishers.

Phinney, J. S., Horenczyk, G., Liebkind, K. & Vedder, P. (2001). Ethnic identity, immigration, and well-being: An interactional perspective. *Journal of Social Issues*, **57**, 493–510.

Phinney, J. S., Ong, A. & Madden, T. (2000). Cultural values and intergenerational value discrepancies in immigrant and non-immigrant families. *Child Development*, **71**, 528–39.

Pierce, D. (2001). Language, violence, and queer people: Social and cultural change strategies. *Journal of Gay and Lesbian Social Services*, **13**, 47–61.

Pihama, L. (1996). Kaupapa Maori health research. In Te Ropu Rangahau Hauora a Eru Pomare (ed.), *Hui whakapiripiri: A hui to discuss strategic directions for Maori health research* (pp. 14–30). Wellington: Wellington School of Medicine.

Pilger, J. (2002). *The new rules of the world*. London: Verso.

Pirages, D. C. & Ehrlich, P. R. (1974). *Ark II: Social response to environmental imperatives*. New York: The Viking Press.

Poindexter, C. C. (1997). Sociopolitical antecedents to Stonewall: Analysis of the origins of the gay rights movement in the United States. *Social Work*, **42**, 607–15.

Poland, B., Coburn, D., Robertson, A. & Eakin, J. (1998). Wealth, equity and health care: A critique of the 'population health' perspective on the determinants of health. *Social Science and Medicine*, **46**, 785–98.

Polkinghorne, D. (1983). *Methodology for human sciences*. Albany, NY: State University of New York.

Pols, H. (2000). Between the laboratory, the school, and the community: The psychology of human development, Toronto, 1916–56. *Canadian Journal of Community Mental Health*, **19**(2): 13–30.

Pomare, E. (1992). Te Manawa Hauora: Background information for HRC site visit, Friday 24 April 1992. Wellington: Wellington School of Medicine.

Porter, A. (1997). Immigration theory for a new century: Some problems and opportunities. *International Migration Review*, **31**, 799–825.

Posavac, E. J. & Carey, R. G. (1997). *Program evaluation: Methods and case studies* (5th edn). Upper Saddle River, NJ: Prentice Hall.

Potter, G. A. (2000). *Deeper than debt: Economic globalisation and the poor*. London: Latin America Bureau.

Potter, J. & Wetherell, M. (1987). *Discourse and social psychology: Beyond attitudes and behaviour*. London: Sage.

Potts, R. (1995). Plenary session comments at the 5th Biennial Conference of the Society for Community Research and Action (SCRA), Chicago, IL.

Potts, R. G. (2003). Emancipatory education versus school-based prevention in African American communities. *American Journal of Community Psychology*, **31**, 173–83.

Power, A. (1996). Area-based poverty and resident empowerment. *Urban Studies*, **33**, 1535–65.

Pretorius-Heuchert, J. W. & Ahmed, R. (2001). Community psychology: Past, present, and future. In M. Seedat (ed.), N. Duncan & S. Lazarus (consulting eds), *Community psychology: Theory, method and practice – South African and other perspectives* (pp. 17–36). Oxford: Oxford University Press.

Price, R. H. & Cherniss, C. (1977). Training for a new profession: Research as social action. *Professional Psychology*, **8**, 222–31.

Price, R. H., Cowen, E. L., Lorion, R. P. & Ramos-McKay, J. (eds). (1988). *Fourteen ounces of prevention: A casebook for practitioners*. Washington, DC: American Psychological Association.

Price, R. H., Van Ryn, M. & Vinokur, A. D. (1992). Impact of a preventive job search intervention on the likelihood of depression among the unemployed. *Journal of Health and Social Behavior*, **33**, 158–67.

Prilleltensky, I. (1994a). Empowerment in mainstream psychology: Legitimacy, obstacles, and possibilities. *Canadian Psychology*, **35**, 358–75.

Prilleltensky, I. (1994b). *The morals and politics of psychology: Psychological discourse and the status quo*. Albany, NY: State University of New York Press.

Prilleltensky, I. (1999). Critical psychology and social justice. In M. Fondacaro (Chair), *Concepts of Social Justice in Community Psychology*. Symposium at the Biennial Meeting of the Society for Community Research and Action, New Haven, CT.

Prilleltensky, I. (2000). Value-based leadership in organizations: Balancing values, interests, and power among citizens, workers, and leaders. *Ethics and Behavior*, **10**, 139–58.

Prilleltensky, I. (2001). Value-based praxis in community psychology: Moving toward social justice and social action. *American Journal of Community Psychology*, **29**, 747–78.

Prilleltensky, I. (in press). The role of power in wellness, oppression, and liberation: The promise of psychopolitical validity. *Journal of Community Psychology*.

Prilleltensky, I. (2003a). Poverty and power: Suffering and wellness in collective, relational, and personal domains. In S. Carr & T. Sloan (eds), *Psychology and poverty*, (pp. 19–44). New York: Kluwer/Plenum.

Prilleltensky, I. (2003b). Understanding, resisting, and overcoming oppression: Towards psychopolitical validity. *American Journal of Community Psychology, 31,* 195–201.

Prilleltensky, I. & Fox, D. (1997). Introducing critical psychology: Values, assumptions, and status quo. In D. Fox & I. Prilleltensky (eds), *Critical psychology: An introduction* (pp. 3–20). London: Sage Publications.

Prilleltensky, I. & Gonick, L. (1994). The discourse of oppression in the social sciences: Past, present, and future. In E. J. Trickett, R. J. Watts & D. Birman (eds), *Human diversity: Perspectives on people in context* (pp. 145–77). San Francisco: Jossey-Bass.

Prilleltensky, I. & Gonick, L. (1996). Polities change, oppression remains: On the psychology and politics of oppression. *Political Psychology, 17,* 127–47.

Prilleltensky, I., Laurendeau, M.-C., Chamberland, C. & Peirson, L. (2001). Vision and values for child and family wellness. In I. Prilleltensky, G. Nelson & L. Peirson (eds), *Promoting family wellness and preventing child maltreatment: Fundamentals for thinking and action* (pp. 124–73). Toronto: University of Toronto Press.

Prilleltensky, I., Martell, E., Valenzuela, E. & Hernandez, P. (2001). A value-based approach to smoking prevention with immigrants from Latin America: Philosophy and program description. *Revista de Psicologia, 10*(2), 81–100.

Prilleltensky, I. & Nelson, G. (1997). Community psychology: Reclaiming social justice. In D. Fox & I. Prilleltensky (eds), *Critical psychology: An introduction* (pp. 166–84). London: Sage.

Prilleltensky, I. & Nelson, G. (2000). Promoting child and family wellness: Priorities for psychological and social interventions. *Journal of Community and Applied Social Psychology, 10,* 85–105.

Prilleltensky, I. & Nelson, G. (2002). *Doing psychology critically: Making a difference in diverse settings.* London: Palgrave Macmillan.

Prilleltensky, I. & Nelson, G. (2004). Research and solidarity: Partnerships for knowing with community members. In D. Pare & G. Larner (eds), *Critical practice in psychology and therapy,* (pp. 243–58). Binghampton, NY: Haworth Press.

Prilleltensky, I. Nelson, G. & Peirson, L. (eds). (2001a). *Promoting family wellness and preventing child maltreatment: Fundamentals for thinking and action.* Toronto: University of Toronto Press.

Prilleltensky, I., Nelson, G. & Peirson, L. (2001b). The role of power and control in children's lives: An ecological analysis of pathways towards wellness, resilience, and problems. *Journal of Community and Applied Social Psychology, 11,* 143–58.

Prilleltensky, I., Nelson, G. & Sanchez Valdes, L. (2000). A value-based approach to smoking prevention with immigrants from Latin America: Program evaluation. *Journal of Ethnic and Cultural Diversity in Social Work, 9*(1–2), 97–117.

Prilleltensky, I., Peirson, L., Gould & Nelson, G. (1997). Planning mental health services for children and youth: Part I – A value-based framework. *Evaluation and Program Planning, 20*(2), 163–72.

Prilleltensky, I., Peirson, L. & Nelson, G. (2001). Mapping the terrain: Framework for promoting family wellness and preventing child maltreatment. In I. Prilleltensky, G. Nelson & L. Peirson (eds), *Promoting family wellness and preventing child maltreatment: Fundamentals for thinking and action* (pp. 3–40). Toronto: University of Toronto Press.

Prilleltensky I. & Prilleltensky O. (2003a). Reconciling the roles of professional helper and critical agent in health psychology. *Journal of Health Psychology, 8,* 243–6.

Prilleltensky, I. & Prilleltensky, O. (2003b). Towards a critical health psychology practice. *Journal of Health Psychology, 8,* 197–10.

Prilleltensky, I., Sanchez Valdes, L., Walsh-Bowers R., & Rossiter, A. (2002). Applied ethics in mental health in Cuba: Dilemmas and resources. *Ethics and Behavior, 13,* 243–60.

Prilleltensky, I., Walsh-Bowers, R. & Rossiter, A. (1999). Clinicians' lived experience of ethics: Values and challenges in helping children. *Journal of Educational and Psychological Consultation, 10,* 315–42.

Prilleltensky, O. (2003). A ramp to motherhood: The experiences of mothers with disabilities. *Sexuality and Disability,* **21**(1), 21–47.

Prilleltensky, O. (2004a). *Motherhood and disability: Children and choices.* New York: Palgrave Macmillan.

Prilleltensky, O. (2004b). My child is not my carer: Mothers with physical disabilities and the well-being of children. *Disability and Society,* **19**(3), 209–23.

Proceedings of Treaty Conference 2000: Tauiwi communities come together to affirm the Treaty of Waitangi and explore the future of Aotearoa (2000). Tamaki Makaurau/ Auckland: Treaty Conference Publications Group.

Prochaska, J., Norcorss, J. & DiClemente, C. (1994). *Changing for good.* New York: Avon Books.

Public Education for Peace Society (1999). *The World Trade Organization and war: Making the connection* (No. 6 in a series of papers on militarism and globalization). Vancouver, BC: Public Education for Peace Society.

Public Education Regarding Sexual Orientation Nationally (1999). *Teen perceived as being gay brutally murdered.* Retrieved June 29, 2002 from http://www.youth.org/ loco/PERSONProject/Alerts/International/list.html.

Putnam, R. (2000). *Bowling alone: The collapse and revival of American community.* New York: Simon & Schuster.

Putnam, R. (2001). Social capital: Measurement and consequences. *Isuma: Canadian Journal of Policy Research,* **2**, 41–51.

Quarter, J. (1992). *Canada's social economy: Co-operatives, non-profits, and other community enterprises.* Toronto: Lorimer.

Quarter, J. & Melnyk, G. (eds). (1989). *Partners in enterprise: The worker ownership phenomenon.* Montreal: Black Rose.

Quick, J. C., Quick, J. D., Nelson, D. & Hurrell, J. (1997). *Preventive stress management in organizations.* Washington, DC: American Psychological Association.

Quintal de Freitas, M. de F. (2000). Voices from the south: The construction of Brazilian community social psychology. *Journal of Community and Applied Social Psychology,* **10**, 315–26.

Rae-Grant, N. I. (1994). Preventive interventions for children and adolescents: Where are we now and how far have we come? *Canadian Journal of Community Mental Health,* **13**(2), 17–36.

Ralston Saul, J. (1995). *The unconscious civilization.* Concord, ON: Anansi.

Ralston Saul, J. (2001). *On equilibrium.* New York: Penguin.

Ramsden, I. (1991). *Kawa Whakaruruhau: Cultural safety in nursing education in Aotearoa.* Wellington: Ministry of Education.

Randall, S. (1995). City Pride – from 'municipal socialism' to 'municipal capitalism'? *Critical Social Policy,* **14**, 40–59.

Rappaport, J. (1977). *Community psychology: Values, research, and action.* New York: Holt, Rinehart & Winston.

Rappaport, J. (1981). In praise of paradox: A social policy of empowerment over prevention. *American Journal of Community Psychology,* **9**, 1–25.

Rappaport, J. (1984). Studies in empowerment: Introduction to the issue. *Prevention in Human Services,* **5**, 1–7.

Rappaport, J. (1987). Terms of empowerment/exemplars of prevention: Toward a theory for community psychology. *American Journal of Community Psychology,* **15**, 121–48.

Rappaport, J. (1990). Research methods and the empowerment social agenda. In P. Tolan, C. Keys, F. Chertok & L. Jason (eds), *Researching community psychology: Issues of theory and methods* (pp. 51–63). Washington, DC: American Psychological Association.

Rappaport, J. (1993). Narrative studies: Personal stories and identity transformation in the mutual help context. *Journal of Applied Behavioral Science,* **29**, 239–56.

Rappaport, J. (1998). The art of social change: Community narratives as resources for individual and collective identity. In X. B. Arriaga & S. Oskamp (eds), *Addressing community problems: Psychosocial research and intervention* (pp. 225–46). Thousand Oaks, CA: Sage.

Rappaport, J. (2000). Community narratives: Tales of terror and joy. *American Journal of Community Psychology,* **28,** 1–24.

Rappaport, J., Chinsky, J. M. & Cowen, E. L. (1971). *Innovations in helping chronic patients: College students in a mental institution.* New York: Academic Press.

Rappaport, J., Davidson, W. S., Wilson, M. N. & Mitchell, A. (1975). Alternatives to blaming the victim or the environment. *American Psychologist,* **30,** 525–8.

Rappaport, J. & Seidman, E. (eds). (2000). *Handbook of community psychology.* New York: Kluwer Academic/Plenum Publishers.

Rappaport, J., Seidman, E. & Davidson, W. S. (1979). Demonstration research and manifest versus true adoption: The natural history of a research project to divert adolescents from the legal system. In R. F. Munoz, L. R. Snowden & J. G. Kelly (eds), *Social and psychological research in community settings* (pp. 101–44). San Francisco: Jossey-Bass.

Rappaport, J., Seidman, E., Toro, P. A., McFadden, L. S., Reischl, T. M., Roberts, L. J., Salem, D. A., Stein, C. H. & Zimmerman, M. A. (1985). Collaborative research with a mutual help organization. *Social Policy,* **15,** 12–24.

Rappaport, J. & Stewart, E. (1997). A critical look at critical psychology: Elaborating the questions. In D. Fox & I. Prilleltensky (eds), *Critical psychology: An introduction* (pp. 301–17). London: Sage.

Ratcliffe, J. (1978). Social justice and the demographic transition: Lessons from India's Kerala State. *International Journal of Health Services,* **8**(1), 123–44.

Ratima, K. H., Durie, M. H., Potaka, U. & Ratima, M. M. (1993). *Cervical screening in Maori women: Knowledge and service factors.* Palmerston North: Massey University, Te Pumanawa Hauora.

Rawls, J. (1987). *Theorie de la justice.* Paris: Éditions du Seuil. (French translation by Catherine Audard of a 1975, altered version of *A Theory of Justice,* originally published in 1971).

Reason, P. & Bradbury, H. (eds). (2001). *Handbook of action research: Participative inquiry and practice.* London: Sage.

Redfield, R., Linton, R. & Herskovits, M. L. (1936). Memorandum for the study of acculturation. *American Anthropologist,* **38,** 149–52.

Reinharz, S. (1979). *On becoming a social scientist.* San Francisco: Jossey-Bass.

Reinharz, S. (1984). Alternative settings and social change. In K. Heller, R. H. Price, S. Reinharz, S. Riger & A. Wandersman, *Psychology and community change: Challenges of the future* (2nd edn, pp. 286–336). Homewood, IL: The Dorsey Press.

Reinharz, S. (1992). *Feminist methods in social research.* New York: Oxford University Press.

Reinharz, S. (1994). Toward an ethnography of 'voice' and 'silence.' In E. J. Trickett, R. Watts & D. Birman (eds), *Human diversity: Perspectives on people in context* (pp. 178–200). San Francisco: Jossey-Bass.

Reppucci, N. D., Woolard, J. L. & Fried, C. S. (1999). Social, community, and preventive interventions. *Annual Review of Psychology,* **50,** 387–418.

Research and Training Center on Independent Living (2001). *Guidelines for reporting and writing about people with disabilities* (6th edn) [Brochure]. Lawrence, KS: Author.

Reuters Press Wire (Dec 23, 2002). Protesting may be good for your health. Retrieved January 5, 2003. from <http://story.news.yahoo.com/news?tmpl=story2&u=/nm/20021223/hl_nm/protests_demonstrations_dc>.

Rhodes, J. E. & Bogat, G. A. (eds). (2002). Youth mentoring [special issue]. *American Journal of Community Psychology,* **30**(2).

Rich, R. C., Edelstein, M., Hallman, W. & Wandersman, A. (1995). Citizen participation and empowerment: The case of local environmental hazards. *American Journal of Community Psychology*, **23**, 657–76.

Richardson, F. C. & Fowers, B. J. (1997). Critical theory, postmodernism, and hermeneutics: Insights for critical psychology. In D. Fox & I. Prilleltensky (eds), *Critical psychology: An introduction* (pp. 265–83). London: Sage.

Richardson, J., Shelton, D., Krailo, M. & Levine, A. (1990). The effect of compliance with treatment on survival among patients with hematologic malignancies. *Journal of Clinical Oncology*, **18**, 356–64.

Riger, S. (1990). Ways of knowing and organizational approaches to community research. In P. H. Tolan, C. Keys, F. Chertok & L. Jason (eds), *Researching community psychology: The integration of theories and methods* (pp. 23–31). Washington, DC: American Psychological Association.

Riger, S. (1992). Epistemological debates, feminist voices: Science, social values, and the study of women. *American Psychologist*, **47**, 730–40.

Riger, S. (1993). What's wrong with empowerment. *American Journal of Community Psychology*, **21**, 279–92.

Riger, S. (2000). *Transforming psychology*. New York: Oxford University Press.

Ristock, J. L. (2002). *No more secrets: Violence in lesbian relationships*. New York: Routledge.

Ristock, J. L. & Pennell, J. (1996). *Community research as empowerment: Feminist links, postmodern interruptions*. Toronto: Oxford University Press.

Rivers, I. & D'Augelli, A. R. (2001). The victimization of lesbians, gay, and bisexual youths. In A. R. D'Augelli & C. J. Patterson (eds), *Lesbian, gay, and bisexual identities and youth: Psychological perspectives* (pp. 199–223). New York: Oxford University Press.

Roberts, F. K. (1986). Education of the visually handicapped: A social and educational history. In G. T. Scholl (ed.), *Foundations of education for blind and visually handicapped children and youth: Theory and practice* (pp. 1–18). New York City: American Foundation for the Blind.

Roberts, L. J., Luke, D. A., Rappaport, J., Seidman, E., Toro, P. & Reischl, T. (1991). Charting uncharted terrain: A behavioral observation system for mutual help groups. *American Journal of Community Psychology*, **19**, 715–37.

Roberts, L. J., Salem, D, Rappaport, J., Toro, P., Luke, D. & Seidman E. (1999). Giving and receiving help: Interpersonal transactions in mutual-help meetings and psychosocial adjustment of members. *American Journal of Community Psychology*, **27**, 841–68.

Roberts, M., Norman, W., Minhinnick, N., Wihongi, D. & Kirkwood, C. (1995). Kaitiakitanga: Maori perspectives on conservation. *Pacific Conservation Biology*, **2**, 7–20.

Roberts, W. & Brandum, S. (1995). *Get a life*. Toronto: Get a Life Publishing House.

Roberts, W., McRae, R. & Stahlbrand, L. (1999). *Real food for a change*. Toronto: Random House of Canada.

Robertson, N. R., Thomas, D. R., Dehar, M-A. B. & Blaxall, M. (1989). Development of community psychology in New Zealand: A Waikato perspective. *New Zealand Journal of Psychology*, **18**, 13–24.

Rochefort, D. A. (1993). *From poorhouses to homelessness: Policy analysis and mental health care*. Westport, CT: Auburn House.

Roger, M. & White, B. (1997). *Pakeha process in the Bicultural Therapy Project*. Paper presented at Psychological Services Annual Conference, Department of Corrections, Rotorua.

Rogers, E. S., Chamberlin, J., Ellison, M. L. & Crean, T. (1997). A consumer-constructed scale to measure empowerment among users of mental health services. *Psychiatric Services*, **48**, 1042–7.

Rogers, E. S. & Palmer-Erbs, V. (1994). Participatory action research: Implications for research and evaluation in psychiatric rehabilitation. *Psychosocial Rehabilitation Journal*, **18**(2), 3–12.

Romo-Carmona, M. (1995). Lesbian Latinas: Organizational efforts to end oppression. *Journal of Gay and Lesbian Social Services*, **3**(2), 85–93.

Rosa, A. (1997). *The courage to change: Salvadoran stories of personal and social transformation*. Unpublished MA thesis: Wilfrid Laurier University, Ontario.

Rosario, M., Hunter, J., Maguen, S., Gwadz, M. & Smith, R. (2001). The coming-out process and its adaptational and health-related associations among gay, lesbian, and bisexual youths: Stipulation and exploration of a model. *American Journal of Community Psychology*. **29**, 113–60.

Rosario, M., Rotheram-Borus, M. J. & Reid, H. (1996). Gay-related stress and its correlates among gay and bisexual male adolescents of predominantly Black and Hispanic background. *Journal of Community Psychology*. **24**(2), 136–59.

Rose, N. (1996). *Inventing our selves: Psychology, power, and personhood*. New York: Cambridge University Press.

Rose, N. (1999). *Powers of freedom: Reframing political thought*. New York: Cambridge University Press.

Roseland, M. (1997). Dimensions of the future: An Eco-city overview. In M. Roseland (ed.), *Eco-city dimensions: Healthy communities, healthy planet* (pp. 1–12). Gabriola Island, BC: New Society Publishers.

Rosen, M. (1996). *On voluntary servitude: False consciousness and the theory of ideology*. Cambridge, MA: Harvard University Press.

Rossi, P. H., Freeman, H. E. & Lipsey, M. W. (1998). *Evaluation: A systematic approach* (6th edn). Thousand Oaks, CA: Sage.

Rossiter, A., Prilleltensky, I. & Walsh-Bowers, R. (2000). Postmodern professional ethics. In B. Fawcett, B. Featherstone, J. Fook & A. Rossiter (eds), *Postmodern and feminist perspectives in social work practice* (pp. 83–103). London: Routledge.

Rossiter, A., Walsh-Bowers, R. & Prilleltensky, I. (2002). Ethics as a located story: A comparison of North American and Cuban professional ethics. *Theory and Psychology*, **12**, 533–56.

Rothman, J. (2000). Collaborative self-help community development. When is the strategy warranted? *Journal of Community Practice*, **7**(2), 89–105.

Rothman, J. & Tropman, J. E. (1987). Models of community organization and macro practice perspectives: Their mixing and phasing. In F. M. Cox, J. L. Erlich, J. Rothman & J. E. Tropman (eds), *Strategies of community organization* (4th edn, pp. 3–26). Itasca, IL: Peacock Publishers.

Roussos, S. T. & Fawcett, S. B. (2000). A review of collaborative partnerships as a strategy for improving community health. *Annual Review of Public Health*, **21**, 369–402.

Rowe, M., Kloos, B., Chinman, M., Davidson, L. & Cross, A. B. (2001). Homelessness, mental illness, and citizenship. *Social Policy and Administration*, **35**, 14–31.

Rudner, W. A. & Butkowsky, R. (1981). Signs used in the deaf gay community. *Sign Language Studies*, **30**, 36–48.

Ruffner, R. H. (1984). The invisible issue: Disability in the media. *Rehabilitation Digest*, **15**(4). Reprinted in M. Nagler (ed.). (1990). *Perspectives on disability* (pp. 143–6). Palo Alto, CA: Health Markets Research.

Rumbaut, R. (1997). Assimilation and its discontent: Between rhetoric and reality. *International Migration Review*, **31**, 923–60.

Rush, B. (1812). *Medical inquiries and observations, upon the diseases of the mind*. Philadelphia: Kimber & Richardson.

Rush, B. & Ogborne, A. (1991). Program logic models: Expanding their role and structure for program planning and evaluation. *Canadian Journal of Program Evaluation*, **6**, 93–105.

Russell, G. M. & Richards, J. A. (2003). Stressor and resilience factors for lesbians, gay men, and bisexuals confronting antigay politics. *American Journal of Community Psychology*, **31**, 313–28.

Rutman, L. (1980). *Planning useful evaluations: Evaluability assessment*. Beverly Hills, CA: Sage.

Rutter, M. (1979). Protective factors in children's responses to stress and disadvantage. In M. W. Kent & J. E. Rolf (eds), *Primary prevention of psychopathology, Volume III: Social competence in children* (pp. 49–74). Hanover, NH: The University Press of New England.

Rutter, M., Maughan, B., Mortimore, P. & Ouston, J. (1979). *Fifteen thousand hours: Secondary schools and their effects on children.* Cambridge, MA: Harvard University Press.

Ryan, C. & Futterman, D. (1998). *Lesbian and gay youth: Care and counseling.* New York: Columbia University Press.

Ryan, W. (1971). *Blaming the victim.* New York: Random House.

Ryan, W. (1994). Many cooks, brave men, apples and oranges: How people think about equality. *American Journal of Community Psychology,* **22**, 25–35.

Saegert, S. & Winkel, G. (1996). Paths to community empowerment: Organizing at home. *American Journal of Community Psychology,* **24**, 517–50.

Salazar, L. & Cook, S. (2001). *Violence against women in the nineties: The psychological community uncovered.* Paper presentation to the 7th Biennial Conference of the Society for Community Research and Action (SCRA), Atlanta, Georgia.

Salem, D., Foster-Fishman, P. & Goodkind, J. (2002). The adoption of innovation in collective action organizations. *American Journal of Community Psychology,* **30**, 681–710.

Salzer, M. S. & Mental Health Association of Southeastern Pennsylvania Best Practices Team (2002). *Best practices guidelines for consumer delivered services.* http://www.bhrm.org/guidelines/mhguidelincs.htm.

Sampson, E. (1993.) Identity politics: Challenges to psychology's understanding. *American Psychologist,* **48**, 1219–30.

Sanborne, E. L. (2001). Personal communication.

Sánchez, E. (1999). Todos para todos: La continuidad de participación comunitaria [Everybody for everybody: The continuity of community participation]. *Psykhe,* **8**, 135–44.

Sánchez, E. & Wiesenfeld, E. (1991). Special issue: Community social psychology in Latin America. *Applied Psychology: An International Review,* **40**, 111–236.

Sánchez Valdés, L., Prilleltensky, I., Walsh-Bowers, R. & Rossiter, A. (2002). Applied ethics in mental health in Cuba: Guiding concepts and values. *Ethics and Behavior,* **13**, 223–42.

Sánchez Vidal, A. (1999). *Ética de la intervención social* [Ethics of social intervention]. Barcelona: Paidos.

Sanchez Vidal, A. (2002). *Psicologia Social Aplicada: Teoria, metodo y practica.* [Applied social psychology: Theory, method, and practice]. Madrid: Prentice Hall.

Sandel, M. (1996). *Democracy's discontent.* Cambridge, MA: Harvard University Press.

Sandler, I. (2001). Quality and ecology of adversity as common mechanisms of risk and resilience. *American Journal of Community Psychology,* **29**, 19–55.

Santelli, B., Singer, G. H. S., DiVenere, N., Ginsberg, C. & Powers, L. E. (1998). Participatory action research: Reflections on critical incidents in a PAR project. *The Journal of the Association for Persons with Severe Handicaps,* **23**(3), 211–22.

Sarason, B. R., Sarason, I. G. & Pierce, G. (eds). (1990). *Social support: An interactional view.* New York: Wiley.

Sarason, S. B. (1972). *The creation of settings and the future societies.* San Francisco: Jossey Bass.

Sarason, S. B. (1974). *The psychological sense of community: Prospects for a community psychology.* San Francisco: Jossey-Bass.

Sarason, S. B. (1976). Community psychology and the anarchist insight. *American Journal of Community Psychology,* **4**, 243–61.

Sarason, S. B. (1978). The nature of problem solving in social action. *American Psychologist,* **33**, 370–81.

Sarason, S. B. (1988). *The psychological sense of community: Prospects for a community psychology* (2nd edn). Cambridge, MA: Brookline Books.

Sarason, S. B. (2003). The obligations of the moral-scientific stance. *American Journal of Community Psychology*, 31, 209–11.

Sarason, S. B., Levine, M., Goldenberg, I. I., Cherlin, D. L. & Bennett, E. M. (1966). *Psychology in community settings*. New York: Wiley.

Sarkar, S. (1992). *Green alternative politics in West Germany*. New Delhi: Promilla.

Savin-Williams, R. C. (1996). Self-labeling and disclosure among gay, lesbian, and bisexual youths. In J. Laird & R. J. Green (eds), *Lesbians and gays in couples and families: A handbook for therapists* (pp. 153–82). San Francisco, CA: Jossey-Bass.

Sawaia, B. B. (1995). Comunidade: A apropiacao de um conceito tao antigo quanto a humanidade [Community: Appropriation of a concept as old as humankind]. In R. H. Freitas (ed.), *Psicologia Social Comunitaria* [Community social psychology] (pp. 35–53). Petropolis, Brazil: Vozes.

Schank, R. C. (1990). *Tell me a story: A new look at real and artificial memory*. New York: Scribner.

Schlosser, E. (2002) *Fast food nation: The dark side of the all-american meal*. New York: HarperCollins.

Schmidtchen, G. & Uehlinger, H. (1983) Jugend und Staat. In U. Mtaz & G. Schmidtchen (eds), *Gewalt und legitimität*. Oplade, Germany: Westdeutsches Verlag.

Schneider, M. (1991). Developing services for lesbian and gay adolescents. *Canadian Journal of Community Mental Health*, 10(1), 133–51.

Schofield, W. (1964). *Psychotherapy: The purchase of friendship*. Englewood Cliffs, NJ: Prentice Hall.

Schorr, L. (1997). *Common purpose: Strengthening families and neighborhoods to rebuild America*. New York: Doubleday.

Schriner, K. (2001). A disability studies perspective on employment issues and policies for disabled people: An international view. In G. L. Albrecht, K. D. Seelman & M. Bury (eds), *Handbook of disability studies* (pp. 642–62). Thousand Oaks: Sage.

Schuller, T. (2001). The complementary roles of human and social capital. *Isuma: Canadian Journal of Policy Research*, 2, 18–24.

Schumacher, E. F. (1973). *Small is beautiful: Economics as if people mattered*. New York: Harper & Row.

Schwab, M. (1997). Sharing power: Participatory public health research with California teens. *Social Justice*, 24, 11–29.

Schwandt, T. A. (2000). Three epistemological stances for qualitative inquiry: Interpretivism, hermeneutics, and social constructionism. In In N. K. Denzin & Y. S. Lincoln (eds), *Handbook of qualitative research* (2nd edn) (pp. 189–213). Thousand Oaks, CA: Sage.

Schwartz, D. (1997). *Who cares: Rediscovering community*. Boulder, CO: Westview Press.

Schwartz, S. H. (1994). Are there universal aspects in the structure and contents of human values? *Journal of Social Issues*, 50(4), 19–46.

Schweinhart, L. J. & Weikart, D. P. (1989). The High/Scope Perry Preschool study: Implications for early childhood care and education. *Prevention in Human Services*, 7(1), 109–32.

Scott, Eryn. (1995–96). Differences and intersections between feminism in Africa and feminism in the United States. *Sister*. [On-line]. Available: http://www.columbia.edu/cu/sister/Differences.html.

SCRA (Society for Community Research and Action) (2002). Mission and goals. [On-line]. Available: http://www.apa.org/divisions/div27/goals.html.

Scull, A. T. (1977). *Decarceration: community treatment and the deviant – a radical view*. Englewood Cliffs, N. J.: Prentice Hall.

Seedat, M. (ed.), Duncan, N. & Lazarus, S. (consulting eds) (2001). *Community psychology: Theory, method, and practice – South African and other perspectives*. Oxford: Oxford University Press.

Seekins, T. & Fawcett, S. B. (1982). *Guide for personal testimony*. Lawrence, KS: Research and Training Center on Independent Living, University of Kansas.

Seekins, T. & Fawcett, S. B. (1984a). *Guide to writing letters to public officials.* Lawrence, KS: Research and Training Center on Independent Living, University of Kansas.

Seekins, T. & Fawcett, S. B. (1984b). *Guide to writing letters to the editor.* Lawrence, KS: Research and Training Center on Independent Living, University of Kansas.

Segal, S., Silverman, C. & Baumohl, J. (1989). Seeking person-environment fit in community care placement. *Journal of Social Issues*, **45**, 49–64.

Segall, M. H., Dasen, P. R., Berry, J. W. & Poortinga, Y. H. (1999). *Human behavior in global perspective: An introduction to cross-cultural psychology* (2nd edn). Needham Heights, MA: Allyn & Bacon.

Sehl, M. (1987). *The creation of a multi-ethnic housing cooperative: A social intervention.* Unpublished Master's Thesis, Wilfrid Laurier University, Waterloo, ON.

Seidman, E. (ed.). (1983a). *Handbook of social intervention.* Beverly Hills, CA: Sage.

Seidman, E. (1983b). Unexamined premises of social problem solving. In E. Seidman (ed.), *Handbook of social intervention* (pp. 48–67). Beverly Hills, CA: Sage.

Seidman, E. & Rapkin, B. (1983). Economics and psychosocial dysfunction: Toward a conceptual framework and prevention strategies. In R. D. Felner, L. A. Jason, J. N. Moritsugu & S. Farber (eds), *Preventive psychology: Theory, research and practice* (pp. 175–98). New York: Pergamon Press.

Seidman, E. & Rappaport, J. (eds). (1986). *Redefining social problems.* New York: Plenum Press.

Seligman, M. E. P. (1995). The effectiveness of psychotherapy: The *Consumer Reports* study. *American Psychologist*, **50**, 965–74.

Seligman, M. E. P. (2002). *Authentic happiness.* New York: The Free Press.

Sen, A. (1999a). *Beyond the crisis: Development strategies in Asia.* Singapore: Institute of Southeast Asian Studies.

Sen, A. (1999b). *Development as freedom.* New York: Anchor Books.

Sen, A. (2001). *Culture and development.* Paper presented at the World Bank Tokyo Meeting, 13 December. www.worldbank.org/wbi/B-SPAN/sen_tokyo.pdf.

Senge, P. (1990). *The fifth discipline: The art and the practice of the learning organization.* New York: Doubleday.

Senge, P. & Scharmer, O. (2001). Community action research: Learning as a community of practitioners, consultants and researchers. In P. Reason & H. Bradbury (eds), *Handbook of action research: Participative inquiry and practice* (pp. 238–49). London: Sage.

Serrano-García, I. (1984). The illusion of empowerment: Community development within a colonial context. *Prevention in Human Services*, **3**(2/3), 173–200.

Serrano-García, I. (1990). Implementing research: Putting our values to work. In P. Tolan, C. Keys, F. Chertok & L. Jason (eds), *Researching community psychology: Issues of theory and methods* (pp. 171–82). Washington, DC: American Psychological Association.

Serrano–García, I. (1994). The ethics of the powerful and the power of ethics. *American Journal of Community Psychology*, **22**, 1–20.

Serrano-García, I. & Bond, M. (eds). (1994). Empowering the silent ranks [special issue]. *American Journal of Community Psychology*, **22**(4).

Serrano-García, I. & López-Sánchez, G. (1994). Una perspectiva diferente del poder y el cambio social para la psicología social comunitaria. [A different perspective of power and social change for social community psychology]. In M. Montero (ed.), *Psicología social comunitaria* (pp. 167–209). Guadalajara, Mexico: Universidad de Guadalajara.

Serrano-García, I. & Vargas, R. (1992). La Psicologia Comunitaria en America Latin. Estado actual, controversias y nuevos derroteros [Community psychology in Latin America. Present state, disputes and new trends]. *Proceedings of the Iberoamerican Congress of Psychology* (pp. 114–28). Madrid: Colegio Oficial de Psicologos.

SEU (2001a). *A new commitment to neighbourhood renewal: National strategy action plan.* London: Cabinet Office, Social Exclusion Unit.

SEU (2001b). *National strategy for neighbourhood renewal: Policy action team audit.* Social London: Cabinet Office, Social Exclusion Unit.

SEU (2001c). *Preventing social exclusion.* London: Cabinet Office, Social Exclusion Unit.

SEU (2002). *Making the connections: Transport and social exclusion.* Retrieved from the Social Exclusion Unit website October 6, 2002. http://www.socialexclusionunit. gov.uk/publications/.

Sève, L. (1975). *Marxism and the theory of human personality* (D. Paveti, trans.). London: Lawrence & Wishart.

Shakespeare, T. (1999). Coming out and coming home. *Journal of Gay, Lesbian, and Bisexual Identity,* **4**, 39–51.

Shakespeare, T. & Watson, N. (1997). Defending the social model. In L. Barton (ed.). *Disability studies: Past, present and future* (pp. 263–73). Leeds: Disability Press.

Shaoul, J. (2001). Privatization: Claims, outcomes and explanations. In G. Philo & D. Miller (eds), *Market killing: What the free market does and what social scientists can do about it* (pp. 203–15). London: Pearson Education.

Shapscott, M. (2001). *Housing, homelessness, poverty – and free trade in Canada.* Available from http://www.tdrc.net/.

Shaw, M., Dorling, D. & Smith, G. D. (1999). Poverty, social exclusion, and minorities. In M. Marmot & R. Wilkinson (eds). *Social determinants of health* (pp. 211–39). New York: Oxford University Press.

Shelter (2002). *Where's home?* London: Shelter.

Sherif, M. (1966). *In common predicament: Social psychology of intergroup conflict and cooperation.* Boston, MA: Houghton Mifflin.

Shern, D. L., Felton, C. J., Hough, R. L., Lehman, A. F., Goldfinger, S., Valencia, E., Dennis, D., Straw, R. & Wood, P. A. (1997). Housing outcomes for homeless adults with mental illness: Results from the Second-Round McKinney Program. *Psychiatric Services,* **48**, 239–41.

Shinn, M. (2000). Homelessness. In J. Rappaport & E. Seidman (eds). *Handbook of community psychology* (pp. 976–9). New York: Kluwer/Plenum.

Shinn, M. & Rapkin, B. D. (2000). Cross-level research without cross-ups in community psychology. In J. Rappaport & E. Seidman (eds), *Handbook of community psychology* (pp. 669–95). New York: Kluwer Academic/Plenum.

Shinn, M. & Perkins, D. N. (2000). Contributions from organizational psychology. In J. Rappaport & E. Seidman (eds), *Handbook of community psychology* (pp. 615–42). New York: Kluwer Academic/Plenum.

Shinn, M. & Toohey, S. M. (2003). Community contexts of human welfare. *Annual Review of Psychology,* **54**, 427–59.

Shiva, V. (1988). *Staying alive: Women, ecology and survival.* London: New Delhi and Zed Books.

Shonkhoff, J. & Phillips, D. (eds). (2000). *From neurons to neighbourhoods: The science of early childhood development.* Washington, DC: National Academy Press.

Shure, M. B. (1997). Interpersonal cognitive problem-solving: Primary prevention of early high risk behaviors in the preschool and primary years. In G. W. Albee & T. Gullota (eds), *Primary prevention works* (pp. 167–88). Thousand Oaks, CA: Sage.

Sidanius, J. (1993). The psychology of group conflict and the dynamics of oppression: A social dominance perspective. In S. Iyengar & W. J. McGuire (eds), *Explorations in political psychology* (pp. 183–219). London: Duke University Press.

Singh, K. (2001). Handing over the stick: The global spread of participatory approaches to development. In M. Edwards & J. Gaventa (eds), *Global citizen action* (pp. 175–87). Boulder, CO: Lynne Rienner.

Sixsmith, J. (1999). Working in the hidden economy: The experience of unemployed men in the UK. *Community, Work and Family,* **2**, 257–78.

Skirboll, B.W. (1994). The Compeer model: Client rehabilitation and economic benefits. *Psychosocial Rehabilitation Journal,* **18**, 89–94.

Sloan, T. (1997). *Damaged life: The crisis of the modern psyche.* London: Routledge.

Sloan, T. (ed.). (2000a). *Critical psychology: Voices for change*. London: Palgrave Macmillan.

Sloan, T. (2000b). Ideology criticism in theory and practice. *International Journal of Critical Psychology*, **1**(2), 163–8.

Smedley, B. D. & Syme, S. L. (eds). (2000). *Promoting health: Intervention strategies from social and behavioural research*. Washington, DC: National Academy Press.

Smith, D. E. (1990). *The conceptual practices of power: A feminist sociology of knowledge*. Toronto: University of Toronto Press.

Smith, L. T. (1995). *Toward kaupapa Maori research*. Paper presented at Matawhanui Conference (Maori University Teachers Conference), Massey University.

Smith, L. T. (1996). Kaupapa Maori health research. In Te Ropu Rangahau Hauora a Eru Pomare (ed.), *Hui whakapiripiri: A hui to discuss strategic directions for Maori health research* (pp. 14–30). Wellington: Wellington School of Medicine.

Smith, L. T. (1999). *Decolonizing methodologies: Research and indigenous peoples*. London: Zed Books and Dunedin: University of Otago Press.

Snow, L. (1995). Economic development breaks the mold: Community-building, place-targeting, and empowerment zones. *Economic Development Quarterly*, **9**, 185–97.

Solarz, A. (2001). Investing in children, families, and communities: Challenges for an interdivisional public policy collaboration. *American Journal of Community Psychology*, **29**, 1–14.

Sonn, C. C. (2002). Immigrant adaptation: Understanding the process through sense of community. In A. T. Fisher, C. C. Sonn & B. J. Bishop (eds), *Psychological sense of community: Research, applications, and implications* (pp. 205–22). New York: Kluwer Academic/Plenum Publishers.

Sonn, C. C., Bustello, S. & Fisher, A. T. (1998). *Sense of community: A different look at migrant adaptation*. Paper presented at the 6th National Australia-New Zealand/Aotearoa Community Psychology conference held at Hamilton/Kirikiriroa, 2–5 July.

Sonn C. C. & Fisher, A. T. (1996). Sense of community in a politically constructed group. *Journal of Community Psychology*, **24**, 417–30.

Sonn, C. C. & Fisher, A. T. (1998). Sense of community: Community resilient responses to oppression and change. *Journal of Community Psychology*, **26**, 457–72.

Sonn, C. C. & Fisher, A. T. (2003). Identity and oppression: Differential responses to an in-between status. *American Journal of Community Psychology*, **31**, 117–28.

Speer, P. (2002). Social power and forms of change: Implications for empowerment theory. Manuscript submitted for publication.

Speer, P., Dey, A., Griggs, P., Gibson, C., Lubin, B. & Houghey, J. (1992). In search of community: An analysis of community psychology research from 1984–88. *American Journal of Community Psychology*, **20**, 195–209.

Speer, P. & Hughey, J. (1995). Community organizing: An ecological route to empowerment and power. *American Journal of Community Psychology*, **23**, 729–48.

Speer, P., Hughey, J., Gensheimer, L. & Adams-Leavitt, W. (1995). Organizing for power: A comparative case study. *Journal of Community Psychology*, **23**, 57–73.

Spiegel, D., Bloom, J., Kraemer, H. & Gottheil, E. (1989). Effect of psychosocial treatment of survival of patients with metastatic breast cancer. *Lancet*, **14**, 888–91.

Staggenborg, S. (1999). The consequences of professionalization and formalization in the Pro-Choice movement. In J. Freeman & V. Johnson (eds), *Cycles of protest: Social movements since the sixties* (pp. 99–134). New York: Rowman & Littlefield.

Stanley, D. S. (2003). *Finding her voice*. Community fieldwork paper, Pacifica Graduate Institute, Carpenteria, CA.

Stansfeld, S. (1999). Social support and social cohesion. In M. Marmot & R. Wilkinson (eds), *Social determinants of health* (pp. 155–78). New York: Oxford University Press.

Stevens, J. (1975). *Women's liberation broadsheet*. Women's Electoral Lobby, Sydney, Australia.

Stewart, A. (2000). Unpaid work in the community: An account of becoming a community activist. *Community, Work and Family*, **3**, 111–14.

Stewart, E. (2000). Thinking through others: Qualitative research and community psychology. In J. Rappaport & E. Seidman (eds), *Handbook of community psychology* (pp. 725–36). New York: Kluwer Academic/Plenum Publishers.

Stiglitz, J. (2002). *Globalization and its discontents.* London: Penguin.

Stiker, H. (1997). *A history of disability.* Translated by W. Sayers. Ann Arbor: University of Michigan Press.

Stoecker, R. (1999). Are academics irrelevant? Roles for scholars in participatory research. *American Behavioral Scientist,* **42**, 840–54.

Stokols, D. (2003). The ecology of human strengths. In L. Aspinwall & U. Staudinger (eds), *A psychology of human strengths: Fundamental questions and future directions for a positive psychology* (pp. 331–43). Washington, DC: American Psychological Association.

Stone, R. A. & Levine, A. G. (1985). Reactions to collective stress: Correlates of active citizen participation at Love Canal. *Prevention in Human Services,* **4**, 153–77.

Stone, W. & Hughes, J. (2002). *Social capital: Empirical meaning and measurement validity.* Research paper No. 27. Melbourne: Australian Institute of Family Studies.

Stout, L. (1996). *Bridging the class divide and other lessons for grassroots organizing.* Boston, MA: Beacon Press.

Strauss, A. L. & Corbin, J. (1998). *Basics of qualitative research: Grounded theory procedures and techniques* (2nd edn). Thousand Oaks, CA: Sage.

Strauss, J. S. & Carpenter, W. T. (1974a). Characteristic symptoms and outcomes in schizophrenia. *Archives of General Psychiatry,* **30**, 429–34.

Strauss, J. S. & Carpenter, W. T. (1974b). The prediction of outcome in schizophrenia II: Relationships between predictor and outcome variables. *Archives of General Psychiatry,* **31**, 37–42.

Stringer, E. T. (1996). *Action research: A handbook for practitioners.* Thousand Oaks, CA: Sage.

Suarez de Balcazar, Y., Fawcett, S. B. & Balcazar, F. E. (1988). Effects of environmental design and police enforcement on violation of a handicapped parking ordinance. *Journal of Applied Behavior Analysis,* **21**, 291–8.

Suarez de Balcazar, Y., Seekins, T., Paine, A., Fawcett, S. B. & Mathews, R. M. (1989). Self-help and social support groups for people with disabilities: A descriptive report. *Rehabilitation Counseling Bulletin,* **33**, 151–8.

Sue, D. W. & Sue, D. (1990). *Counselling the culturally different: Theory and practice.* New York: John Wiley & Sons.

Sullivan, E. V. (1984). *A critical psychology.* New York: Plenum Press.

Suzuki, D. & Dressel, H. (2002). *Good news for a change: Hope for a troubled planet.* Toronto: Stoddart.

Svyantek, D. & Brown, L. (2002). Dysfunctioinal behavior in the workplace and organizational design, climate, and culture. In J. Thomas & M. Hersen (eds), *Handbook of mental health in the workplace* (pp. 477–500). London: Sage.

Swan, W. K. (1997). The agenda for justice. In W. K. Swan (ed.), *Gay/lesbian/bisexual/transgender public policy issues: A citizen's and administrator's guide to the new cultural struggle.* New York: Harrington Park Press.

Swan, P. & Raphael, B. (1995). *'Ways forward': National consultancy report on Aboriginal and Torres Strait Islander mental health.* Canberra: Australian Government Publishing Service.

Swartz, D. (1997). *Culture and power: The sociology of Pierre Bourdieu.* Chicago: The University of Chicago Press.

Swift, C. & Levin, G. (1987). Empowerment: An emerging mental health technology. *Journal of Primary Prevention,* **8**(1–2), 71–94.

Swindle, R., Heller, K., Pescosolido, B. & Kikuzawa, S. (2000). Responses to nervous breakdowns in America over a 40-year time period. *American Psychologist,* **55**, 740–9.

Tamasese, K. (1993). Interface of gender and culture. In L. W. Nikora (ed.), *Cultural justice and ethics.* Waikato: National Standing Committee on Bicultural Issues, New Zealand Psychological Society.

Tajfel, H. (1981). *Human groups and social categories.* Cambridge, UK: Cambridge University Press.

Tarrow, S. (1998). *Power in movement: Social movements and contentious politics.* New York: Cambridge University Press.

Tavris, C. (1992). *The mismeasure of woman.* New York: Touchstone/Simon & Schuster.

Taylor, A. R. & Botschner, J. V. (1998). *The evaluation handbook.* Kitchener, ON: Center for Research and Education in Human Services.

Taylor, C. (1992). *Multiculturalism and 'the politics of recognition'.* Princeton, NJ: Princeton University Press.

Taylor, C. (2002). Building community through anti-homophobia education. In D. Sutherland & L. Sokal (eds), *Resilience and capacity building in inner-city learning communities* (pp. 127–47). Winnipeg: Portage and Main Press.

Taylor, D. (ed.). (1996). *Critical social policy.* London: Sage.

Taylor, J. M., Gilligan, C. & Sullivan, A. (1995). *Between voice and silence: Women and girls, race and relationship.* Cambridge, MA: Harvard University Press.

Taywaditep, K. J. (2001). Marginalization among the marginalized: Gay men's anti-effeminancy attitudes. *Journal of Homosexuality,* **42**, 1–28.

Te Awekotuku, N. (1991). *He tikanga whakaaro: Research ethics in the Māori community.* Wellington: Manatu Maori.

Te Awekotuku, N., Neich, R., Pendergrast, M., Davidson, J., Hakiwai, A. & Starzecka, D.C. (eds). (1996). *Maori art and culture.* Auckland: David Bateman.

Tebes, J. & Irish, J., (2000). Promoting resilience among children of sandwiched generation caregiving women through caregiver mutual help. *Journal of Prevention and Intervention in the Community,* **20**(1–2), 139–58.

Tefft, B. M. (ed.). (1982). Community psychology in Canada. *Canadian Journal of Community Mental Health* [special issue], **1**(2).

Temm, P. (1990). *The Waitangi Tribunal: The conscience of the nation.* Auckland: Random Century.

Teo, T. (1999). Methodologies of critical psychology: Illustrations from the field of racism. *Annual Review of Critical Psychology,* **1**, 119–34.

Te Pumanawa Hauora ki Te Whanganui-A-Tara (1993). *Report to the Te Runanga O Toa Rangatira on the Whanau Wellbeing Project of the Ora Toa Health Unit: First evaluation report.* Wellington: School of Medicine.

Ter Wal, J., Verdun, A. & Westerbeek, K. (1995). The Netherlands: Full or at the limits of tolerance. In B. Baumgartl & A. Favell (eds), *New xenophobia in Europe* (pp. 33–48). The Hague: Kluwer.

Thekaekara, S. & Thekaekara, M. (1995). *Across the geographical divide.* London: Directory of Social Change and Centre for Innovation in Voluntary Action.

Thomas, D. R., Neill, B. & Robertson, N. (1997). Developing a graduate program in community psychology: Experiences at the University of Waikato, New Zealand. *Journal of Prevention and Intervention in the Community,* **15**(1), 83–96.

Thomas, J. & Hite, J. (2002). Mental health in the workplace: Toward an integration of organizational and clinical theory, research, and practice. In J. Thomas & M. Hersen (eds), *Handbook of mental health in the workplace* (pp. 3–14). London: Sage.

Thompson, J. (1984). *Studies in the theory of ideology.* Berkeley, CA: University of California Press.

Thompson, S. A., Bryson, M. & de Castell, S. (2001). Prospects for identity formation for lesbian, gay, or bisexual persons with developmental disabilities. *International Journal of Disability, Development and Education,* **48**(1), 53–65.

Thompson, S. K. & Seber, G. A. F. (1996). *Adaptive sampling.* New York: Wiley.

Tolan, P. Keys, C., Chertok, F. & Jason, L. (eds). (1990). *Researching community psychology: Issues of theory and methods.* Washington, DC: APA.

Tolman, D. L. & Brydon Miller, M. (eds). (2001). *From subjects to subjectivities: A handbook of interpretive and participatory methods.* New York: New York University Press.

Tong, R. (1998). *Feminist thought: A more comprehensive introduction* (2nd edn). London: Allen & Unwin.

Tönnies, F. ([1887]1957). *Community and society.* Chicago, IL: Michigan State University Press.

Toro, P. A., Rabideau, J. M. P., Bellavia, C. W., Daeschler, C. V., Wall, D. D., Thomas, D. M. & Smith, S. J. (1997). Evaluating an intervention for homeless persons: Results of a field experiment. *Journal of Consulting and Clinical Psychology,* **65**, 476–84.

Torre, C. & Calviño, M. (1996). Logros, problemas y retos de la psicologia en Cuba [Accomplishments, problems and challenges of Cuban psychology]. *Revista Cubana de Psicologia,* **13** (2–3), 113–22.

Torrey, E. F., Erdman, K., Wolfe, S. M. & Flynn, L. M. (1990). *Care of the seriously mentally ill: A rating of state programs,* (3rd edn). Washington, DC: Public Citizen Health Research Group and National Alliance for the Mentally Ill.

Trainor, J., Pomeroy, E. & Pape, B. (1993). *A new framework for support for people with serious mental health problems.* Toronto: Canadian Mental Health Association.

Traub-Werner, M. (2002). Sustaining the student anti-sweatshop movement: Living workers' struggles. In M. Prokosch & L. Raymond (eds), *The global activist's manual* (pp. 191–8). New York: Thunder's Mouth Press.

Tremble, B., Schneider, M. & Appathurai, C. (1989). Growing up gay or lesbian in a multicultural context. *Journal of Homosexuality,* **17**(3–4), 253–67.

Triandis, H. C. (1995). *Individualism and collectivism.* Boulder, CO: Westview Press.

Triandis, H. C. (1996a). The psychological measurement of cultural syndromes. *American Psychologist,* **51**, 407–15.

Triandis, H. C. (1996b). Culture and social behavior. In W. J. Lonner & R. S. Malpass (eds), *Psychology and culture* (pp. 169–73). Needham Heights, MA: Allyn & Bacon.

Triantafillou, P. & Nielsen, M. R. (2001). Policing empowerment: The making of capable subjects. *History of the Human Sciences,* **14**(2), 63–86.

Trickett, E. J. (1984). Toward a distinctive community psychology: An ecological metaphor for the conduct of research and the nature of training. *American Journal of Community Psychology,* **12**, 261–75.

Trickett, E. J. (1986). Consultation as a preventive intervention: Comments on ecologically based case studies. *Prevention in Human Services,* **4**(3/4), 187–204.

Trickett, E. J. (1994). Human diversity and community psychology: Where ecology and empowerment meet. *American Journal of Community Psychology,* **22**, 583–92.

Trickett, E. J. (1996). A future for community psychology: The contexts of diversity and the diversity of contexts. *American Journal of Community Psychology,* **24**, 209–29.

Trickett, E. J. & Birman, D. (1987). Taking ecology seriously: A community development approach to individually based preventive interventions in schools. In L. Bond & B. Compas (eds), *Primary prevention and promotion in the schools* (pp. 361–90). Beverly Hills, CA: Sage.

Trickett, E. J., Kelly, J. G. & Todd, D. M. (1972). The social environment of the high school: Guidelines for individual change and organizational redevelopment. In S. E. Golann & C. Eisdorfer (eds), *Handbook of community mental health* (pp. 331–406). New York: Appleton-Century-Crofts.

Trickett, E. J., Kelly, J. G. & Vincent, T. A. (1985). The spirit of ecological inquiry in community research. In D. Klein & E. Susskind (eds), *Knowledge building in community psychology* (pp. 283–333). New York: Praeger.

Trickett, E. J., Watts, R. & Birman, D. (1993). Human diversity and community psychology: Still hazy after all these years. *Journal of Community Psychology,* **21**, 264–78.

Trickett, E. J., Watts, R. J. & Birman, D. (eds). (1994). *Human diversity: Perspectives on people in context.* San Francisco, CA: Jossey-Bass.

Tsemberis, S. (1999). From streets to homes: An innovative approach to supported housing for homeless adults with psychiatric disabilities. *Journal of Community Psychology*, **27**, 225–41.

Tsemberis, S. & Eisenberg, R.F. (2000). Pathways to Housing: Supported housing for street-dwelling individuals with psychiatric disabilities. *Psychiatric Services*, **51**, 487–93.

Tseng, V., Chesir-Teran, D., Becker-Klein, R., Chan, M., Duran, V., Robers, A. & Bardoliwalla, N. (2002). Promotion of social change: A conceptual framework. *American Journal of Community Psychology*, **30**, 401–28.

Tsuang, M.T. & Faraone, S.V. (2002). Diagnostic concepts and the prevention of schizophrenia. *Canadian Journal of Psychiatry*, **47**, 515–17.

Turnbull, A. P., Friesen, B. J. & Ramirez, C. (1998). Participatory action research as a model for conducting family research. *The Journal of the Association for Persons with Severe Handicaps*, **23**(3), 178–88.

Tyler, F. (2001). *Cultures, communities, competence, and change.* Boston, MA: Kluwer/Plenum.

UNICEF. (2000). *The state of the world's children 2000. Summary – A vision for the 21st century.* (Available on-line at http://www.unicef.org/sowc00/summary.htm).

UNICEF (2001). *The State of the world's children 2002.* New York: Author.

UNICEF Innocenti Research Centre. (2000, June). *A league table of child poverty in rich nations. Report card No. 1.* Florence, Italy: Author.

UNICEF. (2002). *Official summary: The state of the world's children 2002.* (Available on-line at http://www.unicef.org/sowc02summary).

United Nations. (1991). *United Nations Convention on the Rights of the Child.* (Minister of Supply and Services Canada, Catalogue No. S2-210/1991E). Hull, Québec: Communications Branch, Human Rights Directorate, Department of Canadian Heritage.

United Nations. (1993). *Disability statistics: Percentage of persons with disability by age and sex*; Australia, 1993 survey. Retrieved July 11, 2002, from http://unstats.un.org/unsd/disability/disform.asp?studyid=180.

United Nations (1996). *The United Nations and the advancement of women, 1945–96.* New York: UN Department of Public Information.

United Nations Development Programme (2000). *Human development report 2000.* New York: Oxford University Press.

United Nations Population Fund (2000). *Lives together, worlds apart: Men and women in a time of change. The State of World Population Report 2000.* New York: United Nations Publications.

UPIAS (1976). *Fundamental principles of disability.* London: Union of Physically Impaired Against Segregation.

Urban Ecology (1996). *Ten principles for ecological cities.* Retrieved on December 17, 2002, from http://www.ecoleader.org/partners/.

US Advisory Board on Child Abuse and Neglect (1993). *Neighbors helping neighbors: A new national strategy for the protection of children.* Washington, DC: Department of Health and Human Services, Administration for Children and Families.

US Department of Health and Human Services (1996). *Physical activity and health: A report of the surgeon general.* Atlanta: US Department of Health and Human Services, Centers for Disease Control and Prevention, National Center for Chronic Disease Prevention and Health Promotions.

Van der Gaag, N. (ed.). (1995). Women: Still something to shout about. *New Internationalist*, **270**, 7–30.

Van Genugten, W. & Perez-Bustillo, C. (eds). (2001). *The poverty of rights: Human rights and the eradication of poverty.* London: Zed Books.

van Uchelen, C. (2000). Individualism, collectivism and community psychology. In J. Rappaport & E. Seidman (eds), *Handbook of community psychology* (pp. 65–78). New York: Kluwer Academic/Plenum Publishers.

Veenstra, G. (2001). Social capital and health. *Isuma: Canadian Journal of Policy Research*, **2**, 71–81.

Vera, E. & Speight, S. L. (2003). Multicultural competence, social justice and counseling psychology: Expanding our roles. *The Counseling Psychologist*, **31**, 249–52.

Vitz, P. C. (1990). The use of stories and moral development: New psychological reasons for an old educational method. *American Psychologist*, **45**, 709–20.

Wachtel, P. L. (1989). *The poverty of affluence: A psychological portrait of the American way of life*. Philadelphia: New Society Publishers.

Wadell, D., Cummings, T. & Worley, C. (2000). *Organisation development and change*. Melbourne: Nelson Thomson Learning.

Waldo, C. R. (1998). Out on campus: Sexual orientation and academic climate in a university context. *American Journal of Community Psychology*, **26**, 745–74.

Waldo, C. R., Hesson-McInnis, M. S. & D'Augelli, A. R. (1998). Antecedents and consequences of victimization of lesbian, gay, and bisexual young people: A structural model comparing rural university and urban samples. *American Journal of Community Psychology*, **26**, 307–34.

Walker, A. (1999). The power of one: A daring compassion. *Yes! A Journal of Positive Futures*, 12–14.

Walker, R. (1990) *Ka whawhai tonu matou: stuggle without end*. Auckland: Penguin.

Walker, W. *Out of breath in America*. Toronto Star, June 16, 2002 (pp. B1 & B3).

Walkerdine, V. (1996). Working-class women: Psychological and social aspects of survival. In S. Wilkinson (ed.), *Feminist social psychologies* (pp. 145–62). Philadelphia: Open University Press.

Walkerdine, V. (1997). *Daddy's girl: Young girls in popular culture*. London: Macmillan – now Palgrave Macmillan.

Walsh, F. (1996). The concept of family resilience: Crisis and challenge. *Family Process*, **35**(3): 261–81.

Walsh, R. T. (1987). The evolution of the research relationship in community psychology. *American Journal of Community Psychology*, **15**, 773–88.

Walsh, R. T. (1988). Current developments in community psychology in Canada. *Journal of Community Psychology*, **16**, 296–305.

Walsh-Bowers, R. (1998). Community psychology in the Canadian psychological family. *Canadian Psychology*, **37**, 281–7.

Walter, L. J., Nosek, M. A. & Langdon, K. (2001). Understanding of sexuality and reproductive health among women with and without physical disabilities. *Sexuality and Disability*, **19**, 167–76.

Walters, K. L., Simoni, J. M. & Horwath, P. E. (2001). Sexual orientation bias experiences and service needs of gay, lesbian, bisexual, transgendered, and two-spirited American Indians. In M. E. Swigonski & R. S. Mama (eds), *From hate crimes to human rights: A tribute to Matthew Shepard* (pp. 133–49). New York: Haworth Social Work Practice Press.

Wandersman, A. (2003). Community science: Bridging the gap between science and practice with community-centered models. *American Journal of Community Psychology*, **31**, 227–42.

Wandersman, A. & Florin, P. (2000). Citizen participation and community organizations. In J. Rappaport & E. Seidman (eds), *Handbook of community psychology* (pp. 247–72). New York: Kluwer Academic/Plenum Publishers.

Wang, C. (1999). Photovoice: A participatory action research strategy applied to women's health. *Journal of Women's Health*, **8**, 185–92. See also http://www.photovoice.com/.

Wang, C. & Burris, M. (1994). Empowerment through photo novella: Portraits of participation. *Health Education Quarterly*, **21**, 171–86.

Washington, P. (2001). Who gets to drink from the fountain of freedom? Homophobia in communities of color. *Journal of Gay and Lesbian Social Services*, **13**(1–2), 117–31.

Watene-Haydon, N., Keefe-Ormsby, V., Reid P. & Robson, B. (n.d.). *Issues of research and evaluation by indigenous peoples.* Paper presented at the Australasian Evaluation Society Conference on Evaluation: Are you being served? Sydney.

Watts, R. J. (1992). Elements of a psychology of human diversity. *Journal of Community Psychology,* **20**, 116–31.

Watts, R. J. (1994a). Oppression and sociopolitical development. *The Community Psychologist,* **12**(2), 24–6.

Watts, R. J. (1994b). Paradigms of diversity. In E. J. Trickett, R. J. Watts & D. Birman (eds), *Human diversity: Perspectives on people in context* (pp. 49–80). San Francisco, CA: Jossey-Bass.

Watts, R. J., Griffith, D. M. & Abdul-Adil, J. (1999). Sociopolitical development as an antidote for oppression – Theory and action. *American Journal of Community Psychology,* **27**, 255–72.

Watts, R. & Serrano-García, I. (2003). The quest for a liberating community psychology: An overview. *American Journal of Community Psychology,* **31**, 73–8.

Watts, R. J., Williams, N. C. & Jagers, R. J. (2003). Sociopolitical development. *American Journal of Community Psychology,* **31**, 185–94.

Watzlawick, P., Weakland, J. & Fish, R. (1974). *Change: Principles of problem formation and problem resolution.* New York: Norton.

Weber, M. ([1925]1964). *Economía y sociedad* [Economy and society]. México, FCE.

Weick, K. L. (1984). Small wins: Redefining the scale of social problems. *American Psychologist,* **39**, 40–9.

Weick, K. & Quinn, R. (1999). Organizational change and development. *Annual Review of Psychology,* **50**, 361–86.

Weinberg, R. (2001). *Incorporating mental health policy research and advocacy in clinical training: The Florida Mental Health Institute predoctoral psychology internship.* Tampa, Florida: University of South Florida and Florida Mental Health Institute, Unpublished paper.

Weingarten, R. (1994). The on-going process of recovery. *Psychiatry,* **57**, 369–75.

Weinstein, R. (2002). Overcoming inequality in schooling: A call to action for community psychology. *American Journal of Community Psychology,* **30**, 21–42.

Weisbrod, B. A., Test, M. A. & Stein, L. (1980). Alternative to mental hospital treatment: II. Economic benefit-cost analysis. *Archives of General Psychiatry,* **37**, 400–5.

Weisbrot, M. (1999). *Globalization: A primer.* Washington, DC: Center for Economic and Policy Research. Available from http://www.cepr.net/GlobalPrimer.htm.

Weiss, C. H. (1972). *Evaluation research: Methods of assessing program effectiveness.* Englewood Cliffs, NJ: Prentice Hall.

Weissberg, R. P. Barton, H. A. & Shriver, T. P. (1997). The social-competence promotion program for young adolescents. In G. Albee & T. Gullota (eds), *Primary prevention works* (pp. 268–89). Thousand Oaks, CA: Sage.

Weissberg, R. P. & Greenberg, M. T. (1998). School and community competence-enhancement and prevention programs. In W. Damon (editor-in-chief), I. E. Sigel & K. A. Renninger (vol. eds), *Handbook of child psychology (Volume 4: Child psychology in practice)* (pp. 877–954). New York: John Wiley.

Weissberg, R. P. & Kumpfer, K. L. (eds). (2003). Prevention that works for children and youth [special issue]. *American Psychologist,* **58**(6/7).

Weisstein, N. (1993). Psychology constructs the female, *or* the fantasy life of the male psychologist (with some attention to the fantasies of his friends, the male biologist and the male anthropologist). *Feminism and Psychology,* **3**, 195–210.

Wenzel, S. L., Koegel, P. & Gelberg, L. (2000). Antecedents of physical and sexual victimization among homeless women: A comparison to homeless men. *American Journal of Community Psychology,* **28**, 367–90.

Werner, D. (1987). *Nothing about us without us: Developing innovative technologies for, by, and with disabled persons.* Palo Alto: Health Wrights.

Wetzel, J. W. (2001). Human rights in the 20th century: Weren't gays and lesbians human? *Journal of Gay and Lesbian Social Services,* **13**(1–2), 15–31.

Whang, P., Fawcett, S. B., Suarez de Balcazar, Y. & Seekins, T. (1982). *Systematic method for disabled citizens to set agendas for community development*. Lawrence, KS: Research and Training Center on Independent Living, University of Kansas.

Whitaker, R. (2002). *Mad in America: Bad science, bad medicine, and the enduring mistreatment of the mentally ill*. Cambridge, MA: Perseus Books.

White, G. W. (2002). Disability outcomes research: The golden rule as a guide for ethical practice. *Rehabilitation Psychology*, **47**, 438–46.

White, G. W., Chapman, V., Jay, A., Branstetter, A., Mayo, L. & Isola, J. (2000) *Using the Consumer Concerns Report Method to identify key issues for Perúvians with disabilities*. Presented at the 128th Annual Meeting of the American Public Health Association, Disability Forum, Boston, MA.

White, G. W., Jones, M. L., Ulicny, G. Powell, L. K. & Mathews, R. M. (1988). Deterring unauthorized use of handicapped parking spaces. *Rehabilitation Psychology*, **33**, 207–12.

White, G. W., Nary, D. E. & Froehlich, A. K. (2001). Consumers as collaborators in research and action. *Journal of Prevention and Intervention in the Community*, **21**, 15–21.

White, G. W., Nary, D. E. & Gutierrez, R. G. (1997). *Tools for empowerment for persons with disabilities using individual, group and community engagement*. Paper presented at the 6th Biennial Conference on Community Research and Action, Columbia, SC.

White, G. W., Thomson, R. & Nary, D. E. (1997). An empirical analysis of the effects of a self-administered advocacy letter training program. *Rehabilitation Counseling Bulletin*, **41**(2), 74–87.

White, G. W., Thomson, R., Nary, D. E. (eds). (1999). *The Action Letter Portfolio*. Lawrence, KS: Research and Training Center on Independent Living, University of Kansas.

White, M. (1988/9). The externalizing of the problem and the re-authoring of lives and relationships. *Dulwich Centre Newsletter*, Summer, 3–20.

White, M. (2000). *Narrative therapy*. Melbourne: University of Melbourne.

White, M. & Epston, D. (1990). *Narrative means to therapeutic ends*. New York: Norton.

Whitmore, E. (1991). Evaluation and empowerment: It's the process that counts. *Networking Bulletin: Empowerment and Family Support*, **2**(2), 1–7.

Whyte, W. F. (ed.). (1991). *Participatory action research*. Newbury Park, CA: Sage.

Whyte, W. F., Greenwood, D. J. & Lazes, P. (1989). Participatory action research: Through practice to science in social research. *American Behavioral Scientist*, **32**(5), 513–51.

Wiesenfeld, E. (1998). Paradigms of community social psychology in six Latin American nations. *Journal of Community Psychology*, **26**, 229–42.

Wilbur, C. T. (1888). Institutions for the feebleminded. *Proceedings of the Fifteenth National Conference of Charities and Correction*, **17**, 106–13.

Wilkes, N. (2000). The last word. In P. Dudgeon, D. Garvey & H. Pickett (eds), *Working with Indigenous Australians: A handbook for psychologists* (pp. 519–22). Perth: Gunada Press.

Wilkinson, R. G. (1994). The epidemiological transition: From material scarcity to social disadvantage? *Daedalus*, **123**(4), 61–77.

Wilkinson, R. G. (1996). *Unhealthy societies: The afflictions of inequality*. London: Routledge.

Wilkinson, R. G. (1997). Socioeconomic determinants of health: Health inequalities: Relative or absolute material standards? *British Medical Journal*, **314**(22), 591–4.

Wilkinson, S. (1988). The role of reflexivity in feminist psychology. *Women's Studies International*, **11**, 493–502.

Williams, C. (2002). Social exclusion in a consumer society: A study of five rural communities. *Social Policy and Society*, **1**, 203–11.

Williams, C. L. & Berry, J. W. (1991). Primary prevention of acculturative stress among refugees: Application of psychological theory and practice. *American Psychologist*, **46**, 632–41.

Williams, D. R. & Williams-Morris, R. (2000). Racism and mental health: The African American experience. *Ethnicity and Health*, **5**, 243–68.

Williams, M. (2001). Towards more democracy or more bureaucracy? Civil society, NGOs and the global justice movement. *Social Anarchism*, (30), 5–26.

Williams, P. N. (1978). Comments on 'The ethics of intervention in community disputes.' In G. Bermant, H. C. Kelman & D. P. Warwick (eds), *The ethics of social intervention* (pp. 233–42). New York: Halstead Press.

Willig, C. (2001). *Introducing qualitative research in psychology: Adventures in theory and method*. Buckingham, UK: Open University Press.

Winefield, H. (2001). *Emotion workers – Trained and untrained*. Keynote address to the 36th Annual Conference of the Australian Psychological Society, Adelaide, Australia.

Wingenfeld, S. & Newbrough, J. R. (2000). Community psychology in international perspective. In J. Rappaport & E. Seidman (eds), *Handbook of community psychology* (pp. 779–810). New York: Kluwer Academic/Plenum Publishers.

Wolf, N. (2001). *Misconceptions: Truth, lies and the unexpected on the journey to motherhood*. London: Chatto & Windus.

Wolfensberger, W. (1972). *The principle of normalization in human services*. Toronto: National Institute on Mental Retardation.

Wolfensberger, W. & Tullman, S. (1982). A brief outline of the principle of normalization. *Rehabilitation Psychology*, **27**, 131–45.

Wolff, T. (2000). Applied community psychology: On the road to social change. In J. Rappaport & E. Seidman (eds), *Handbook of community psychology* (pp. 771–8). New York: Kluwer/Plenum.

Wolff, T. (ed.). (2001). Community coalition building – Contemporary practice and research [Special section]. *American Journal of Community Psychology*, **29**(2).

Wollman, N., Lobenstine, M., Foderaro, M. & Stose, S. (undated). *Principles for promoting social change: Effective strategies for influencing attitudes and behaviors*. Washington, DC: Society for the Psychological Study of Social Issues [available online: http://www.spssi.org/ppsc.html].

Women of PhotoVoice/ADMI & Lykes, M. B. (2000). *Voces e imágenes: Mujeres Mayas Ixiles de Chajul/Voices and images: Mayan Ixil women of Chajul*. Guatemala: Magna Terra. Texts in Spanish and English, with a methodology chapter by Lykes.

Wood, P. A., Hurlburt, M. S., Hough, R. L. & Hofsetter, C. R. (1998). Longitudinal assessment of family support among homeless mentally ill participants in a supported housing program. *Journal of Community Psychology*, **26**, 327–44.

World Bank (2000). *World development report 2000/2001: Attacking poverty*. http://www.worldbank.org/poverty/wdrpoverty/report/index/htm.

World Health Organization (1946). *Constitution of the World Health Organization*. (Available on-line at http://whqlibdoc.who.int/hist/official_records/constitution.pdf).

World Health Organization (1986). *Ottawa Charter for Health Promotion: An international conference on health promotion*. (Available on-line at http://www.hc-sc.gc.ca/hppb/phdd/docs/charter/).

Yates, B. T. (1998). Formative evaluation of costs, cost-effectiveness, and cost-benefit: Toward cost–procedure–process–outcome analysis. In L. Bickman & D. J. Rog (eds), *Handbook of applied social research methods* (pp. 285–314). Thousand Oaks, CA: Sage.

Yin, R. K. (1994). *Case study research: Design and methods* (Rev. edn). London, CA: Sage.

Yip, K. (2002). Strengths and weaknesses of self-help groups in mental health: The case of Grow. *Groupwork*, **13**(2): 93–113.

Zea, M. C., Reisen, C. A. & Diaz, R. M. (2003). Methodological issues in research on sexual behavior with Latino gay and bisexual men. *American Journal of Community Psychology*, **31**, 281–91.

Zigler, E. F., Finn-Stevenson, M. & Stern, B. M. (1997). Supporting children and families in the schools: The school of the 21st Century. *American Journal of Orthopsychiatry*, **67**, 396–407.

Zigler, E. F. & Valentine, J. (1997). *Project Head Start: A legacy of the War on Poverty* (2nd edn). Alexandria, VA: National Head Start Association.

Zimmerman, M. A. (2000). Empowerment theory: Psychological, organizational, and community levels of analysis. In J. Rappaport & E. Seidman (eds) (2000). *Handbook of community psychology* (pp. 43–63). New York: Kluwer Academic/Plenum.

Zimmerman, M. A. & Perkins, D. D. (eds). (1995). Empowerment theory, research, and application [special issue]. *American Journal of Community Psychology*, **23**(5).

Author Index

Subject Index